# POST-COLONIAL SOUTHEAST ASIA

LUZON

REPUBLIC

Manila

MINDORO SAMAR

OF THE LEYTE

PANAY

PALAWAN NEGROS MINDANAO

PHILIPPINES

Zamboanga Davao

NORTH BORNEO

BRUNEI

OIL OIL

TION

NEW GUINEA or IRIAN

Ternate HALMAHERA

Menado

RAWAK

CERAM

SULAWESI BURU AMBOINA

BORNEO

Banjermasin

Macassar

ESIAN REPUBLIC

TIMOR (Portuguese)

FLORES

ang Surabaya

A BALI

Jogjakarta

1353

*Southeast Asia*

ITS HISTORICAL DEVELOPMENT

**John F. Cady**

*Professor of History*
*Ohio University*

# *Southeast Asia:*
## ITS HISTORICAL DEVELOPMENT

**McGraw-Hill Book Company**   *New York   San Francisco   Toronto   London*

III

SOUTHEAST ASIA: ITS HISTORICAL DEVELOPMENT

# *Preface*

This volume endeavors to reflect the current stage of research in a fast-growing field of history. It affords little information that is new, but it seeks nevertheless to contribute a fresh interpretation. The author is convinced that both the general reader interested in the area and the college student can profit from a thoughtful and documented account which undertakes to define major trends. The main stream of historical development can be placed in perspective and context without exploring all the minor tributaries. An attempt has been made, as far as sources permit, to mirror the life of the people of the various countries, to picture them facing concrete situations and alternative choices, and to appraise the motivations for their actions. Such an approach calls for an examination of many kinds of relevant historical literature, including studies of social and governmental organization, religion, and artistic standards. While it is manifestly impossible at this stage to undertake a definitive work, this introductory effort to put the available pieces of the puzzle in place may help uncover the many areas where additional detailed research is urgently needed.

That the widely distributed area currently designated as Southeast Asia has experienced a cohesive history is not clearly obvious from surface appearances. Perhaps the region's most characteristic peculiarities are its differences between island and mainland, its diversity of soils and terrain, its varied ethnic groups, and its contrasting religions and levels of cultural development.

Three or four factors can nevertheless be identified which have bound the region together historically. One involves internal regional relationships operating in a kind of chain reaction. Thus, on the mainland, early Mon inhabitants of Lower Burma and Siam influenced culturally their ancient Pyu neighbors on the west, their Khmer cousins to the east, and subsequently the Burmans to the north. Similiarly, Cham and Vietnamese neighbors along the Annamese shore of the South China Sea reacted reciprocally for more than a millennium, while both sustained contacts, friendly and otherwise, with the Khmers. The late-entering Thai, or Shan, peoples copied from the more highly civilized Mons, Burmans, and Khmers, whom they partly conquered. Toward the end of the thirteenth century, the Thai state of Siam extended its political influence far down the Malay Peninsula. For five centuries the Shans and Thai were the inveterate rivals of the Burmans. Similarly, the Malays of the peninsula long maintained intimate contact with kindred peoples in Sumatra and western Borneo. The more sharply differentiated Javanese, Buginese, Malaccan, and south Borneo traders were closely associated in

*v*

the commerce of the calm waters of the shallow Java Sea and the Malacca Straits. North Borneo, the Spice Islands, and the Philippine archipelago were eventually integrated into the history of Southeast Asia after the arrival of Islam and the Europeans. The many peoples of Southeast Asia also shared characteristics of their indigenous cultural heritage—similarities of technical development, cultivation methods, religions, and social and political institutions.

Supplementing these interrelationships between parts of Southeast Asia were the widely shared economic and cultural influences exerted by Indian, Chinese, and Arab and Persian visitors to the area. The alien traders were concerned partly with establishing through contacts by water between the ports of South China and the shores of the Bay of Bengal. The Malay Peninsula and adjacent islands lay athwart this essential avenue of contact between two mature commercial and cultural centers, India and China. The several regions of Southeast Asia experienced this foreign impact in unequal measure, but few of them apart from the peripheral Philippine Islands escaped its substantial influence. Indian cultural patterns in particular became widely disseminated during the early centuries A.D.; while Chinese influence, although culturally less contagious, virtually dominated from Sung times (960 and later) the trade and politics of the eastern seas.

The modern period brought divisive influences. The massive intrusion of Islam after 1400 created a new cultural element which became widely influential along the principal routes of the spice-and-pepper trade. The nature of the subsequent effects of Western powers in their trading activities and as colonial rulers varied widely. Especially after the intensive colonization of the mid-nineteenth century the Western presence tended to cancel out traditional intraregional contacts, whether cooperative or hostile, and to relate both the cultural orientation and the commerce of the colonies to selected worldwide contexts. But in the end, the contact with the West became itself a common experience of all the leading peoples of Southeast Asia.

The withdrawal of Western control since World War II has afforded opportunity for Southeast Asian peoples to reestablish regional associations, but always in the broader world context introduced by the period of colonial rule. All the emerging states of Southeast Asia today face similar problems of governmental instability, economic underdevelopment, and the need to establish helpful relations with powerful Asian neighbors such as India, China, and Japan. Such similarities of experience, interest, and outlook require that their individual histories, despite admitted political, cultural, and economic disparities, be regarded as segments in an interrelated story of development if they are to become intelligible and meaningful.

The author's interest in Southeast Asia dates from a short-term teaching assignment at a mission college in Burma prior to World War II.

He saw service in the area as a member of the State Department in the 1940s. Since 1949, he has been teaching an advanced college course in Southeast Asian history. This book represents, therefore, the fruits of more than a quarter century of study of the region. It describes in a general way the significant developments among the peoples of Southeast Asia throughout their long history. The author's debts are many. The general pattern of the political and cultural history of early Southeast Asia was first summarized by Georges Coedès in his pioneering *Les États Hindouisés d'Indochine et d'Indonésie,* written at Hanoi during the war while he was held as a prisoner of the Japanese. It covered only the pre-European phases of the story. Brian Harrison contributed the first short general history in 1954. These works were amplified by D. G. E. Hall, who added many political details in his basic *History of South-East Asia,* published in 1955. Between and since the appearance of these general summary studies, an increasing number of valuable monographs on particular aspects of the story have been made available, and much of this material is reflected in the present work.

The author is happy to acknowledge his special indebtedness to the Social Science Research Council for a grant-in-aid affording opportunity for a summer's reading at the Library of Congress. Very substantial assistance was also accorded by Ohio University through a special award which was made possible by the munificence of Mr. Edwin L. Kennedy of New York, an alumnus of Ohio University. The John Simon Guggenheim Foundation contributed a fellowship to facilitate a seven-month association with the University of London during the course of the preparation of the manuscript. Special appreciation is due to Prof. D. G. E. Hall and to Mr. O. W. Wolters of the staff of the School of Oriental and African Studies of the University of London for their constructive criticism of early chapters, and to the generous hospitality of the director and the librarians of the same institution. Acknowledgment is here made to the University of California Press and the University of Malaya Press for permission to draw upon copyrighted materials. Apart from standard French spellings, the use of diacritical marks has been limited to the bare essentials, for example, the Ś in Sanskrit which is pronounced as "sh."

*John F. Cady*

# Table of Contents

PREFACE  *v*
LIST OF MAPS  *xv*
PERIODICAL ABBREVIATIONS  *xvii*

## Part One, Setting

1. GEOGRAPHICAL SETTING AND LEADING PEOPLES  3
Topographical Characteristics, 3. Rainfall Patterns, Monsoon Winds, and Soil Utilization, 7. Agricultural Centers and Methods of Cultivation, 8. Characteristics of Major Peoples: Malays and Javanese, 12. Leading Austroasiatic-speaking Peoples: Mons and Khmers, 14. The Vietnamese, 16. The Pyu and Burmans, 17. The Shans, or Thai, 19.

2. TRADE PATTERNS AND THE PROCESS OF INDIANIZATION  21
China's Meager Role in Early Southeast Asian History, 22. Indian Trading Patterns, 25. Early Trade Patterns from India to China, 27. Fa-Hsien's Voyage from Ceylon to China, 31. The Historic Sources of Indianization, 33. Hinduism as It Affected Southeast Asia, 36. Indian Buddhism in Its Variant Forms, 38. The Process of Indianization, 41. Southeast Asian Appropriation of Indian Culture, 44.

## Part Two, Early Empires

3. FUNAN AND ITS NEIGHBORS  51
Early History of Funan, 51. Funan: High Tide and Decline, 53. Vassal and Succession States in the Isthmus, 56. Mon Dvaravati and Thaton, 58. Champa and Borneo, 59.

4. JAVA AND ŚRIVIJAYA TO 1025  62
Java and Sumatra Prior to the Seventh Century, 62. Revival of Southeast Asian Trade, Persia to China, 65. The Rise of Indianized Śrivijaya and Java, 68. I-Ching's Report on Śrivijaya, 70. Śailendra Rule in Java: Borobudur, 74. Java after Śailendra Times, 78. Śailendra Rule at Śrivijaya, 80.

5. CAMBODIA AND ITS NEIGHBORS  84
The Pre-Angkor, or Chenla, Period, 85. Establishment of the Cambodian Empire in the Ninth Century, 88. The Great Rulers of Cambodia, 92. The Principal Monuments of Angkor, 96. Cultural and Social Aspects of Angkor, 100. Cambodia's Neighbors: The Rise of Nam Viet, 103. Cambodia's Cham Neighbors, 106. The Mons, 108. The Decline of Cambodia, 109.

6. PAGAN BURMA: DEVELOPMENT AND DECLINE  111
The Mons and the Ancient Pyu, 112. The Advent of the Burman State, 114. Burman Cultural Characteristics, 115. The Foundation of the Pagan Empire, 1044–1084, 116. Characteristics of the Pagan Burmans, 119. Pagan during the Burman Period, 123. Five Temple Monuments of Pagan, 125. The Col-

lapse of the Pagan Dynasty, 128. The Advent of Shan Rule in Upper Burma, 128.

## Part Three, Transition to Modern Times

7.  MONGOL INTERVENTION, THAI HEGEMONY, AND MAJAPAHIT JAVA  133
The Mongol Intervention, 133. Java and the Straits from Airlangga to Kertanagara, 135. Mongol Naval Expeditions, 1292–1293, 138. Majapahit Java, 141. Establishment of Thai Hegemony, 143. Later Development of Siam, 145. Areas Peripheral to Siam: Cambodia, Laos, Burma, 147. The Feud between Ava and Pegu, 149.

8.  MUSLIM MALACCA: HISTORY, TRADE, ISLAMIZATION PROCESS  152
The Advent of Islam in Southeast Asia, 152. The Founding of Malacca, 154. Government and Politics in Malacca, 157. Malacca's Population and Trading Attractions, 159. The Javanese-Gujerati Trade, 161. The China Trade to Malacca, 163. Malacca's Trade with the Bay of Bengal, 164. The Chronology of Islamization, 166. Islamization: Commercial and Political Factors, 168. Islam's Social and Religious Appeal, 170.

9.  THE SIXTEENTH-CENTURY PORTUGUESE INTRUSION, TOUNGOO BURMA, AND SIAM  172
The Coming of the Portuguese, 173. Albuquerque's Conquest of Malacca, 174. The Development of Portuguese Malacca, 176. Contradictions in Portuguese Policies, 179. Malacca's Warfare with Malay Neighbors, 181. Malacca: Trading System and People, 183. Portuguese Access to the Spice Islands, 184. Portuguese Relations with China, 186. Portuguese Influence in the Bay of Bengal, 188. Toungoo-dynasty Burma: Bayinnaung's Empire, 190. Siam's Recovery of Independence, 192. The Twilight of Portuguese Influence, 194. The Decline of Portuguese Power, 197.

## Part Four, European Commercial Dominance

10.  THE DUTCH COMMERCIAL EMPIRE  203
The European Context, 204. Dutch Victory in the Indies, 205. Southeast Asia Setting: The Java Sea, 208. Sumatra and Malaya under the Dutch, 210. Siam, Burma, and Vietnam: Relations with Europeans, 213. Establishment of Dutch Trading Supremacy, 215. The Conquest of Ceylon, 217. Dutch Control over Major Indonesian Islands, 219. The Dutch Commercial Empire, 221. Particular Items in the Dutch Trading System, 225. Dutch Rule in Java: Seeds of Decay, 227.

11.  SPANISH RULE IN THE PHILIPPINES  232
The Pre-Spanish Philippines, 233. The Spirit and Purpose of the Spanish Undertaking, 234. Spanish Conquest and Government, 235. The Chinese at Manila, 238. Manila's Relations with China and Japan, 240. Spanish Intervention in Cambodia, 1596–1599, 241. Manila's Relations with the Macao and the Moluccas, 244. The Manila Galleon Trade, 245. The Clergy and Missionary Operations to 1610, 249. Missionary Methods and Accomplishments, 251. The Filipinization of Christianity, 253. Rebellions and the British Occupation of Manila, 254. Reforming Efforts, 256. The First Half of the Nineteenth Century, 257.

12. SIAM AND VIETNAM IN THE SEVENTEENTH AND EIGHTEENTH CENTURIES 260
Siam from 1605 to 1670, 261. Vietnam in the Seventeenth Century, 264. Alexander of Rhodes and the French Vicars Apostolic, 267. The French Intrusion, 1662–1682, 268. English Fortune Hunters and Constantine Phaulkon, 271. The Phaulkon-Tachard Conspiracy, 274. Siam after 1688, 277. Continuance of French Interest in Southeast Asia, 279. The Unification of Vietnam: Pigneau de Behaine, 281.

13. BURMA'S KONBAUNG DYNASTY 285
Burma from 1635 to 1740, 286. The Mon Rising and the Emergence of Alaungpaya, 288. Capture of Ayuthia and the Chinese Invasions, 291. The Reign of Bodawpaya, 292. Burma-Bengal Relations, 295. Konbaung Burma: Government, 296. Konbaung Burma: Economy and Society, 298.

14. ESTABLISHMENT OF BRITISH COMMERCIAL HEGEMONY 303
"Country" Vessels, Opium, and British Commercial Supremacy, 304. Strategic Factors: British-French Rivalry, 308. Suggestions for a Pattern of Free Trade, 310. Problems of the British Company Trade, 313. The Status of British Trade in the Orient to 1820, 313. Daendels and Raffles in Java, 1808–1816, 316. Raffles at Benkulen and Singapore, 320. The Results of the First Anglo-Burman War, 1824–1826, 322.

15. NINETEENTH-CENTURY SIAM: RAMA III AND MONGKUT 324
The Early Reigns of the Chakri Dynasty, 325. Kingship and Government in Nineteenth-century Siam, 326. Social and Religious Characteristics, 328. Siam's Foreign Trade in 1820, 331. The Crawfurd Mission to Bangkok, 332. Rama III and the Burney Mission, 334. The Post–Burma War Period, 336. The Missionary Impact on Siam, 339. King Mongkut and the Vogue of Westernization, 341. Siam's New Treaty System, 344. Siam's Modernization Program, 348. The Accession of Chulalongkorn, 351.

## Part Five, Intensive Economic Development

16. JAVA: THE DEVELOPMENT OF DUTCH RULE, 1830 to 1920 355
The Netherlands and the Indies, 1816–1830, 356. Status and Authority in Java, 359. The Cultivation System in Operation, 362. From Government Monopoly to Private Enterprise, 364. Dutch Control of the Outer Islands, 368. Ameliorative Efforts and the Ethical System, 369. Economic Expansion, 373. Rise of Sarekat Islam, 374. Collapse of the Reform Program, 376. An Appraisal of Dutch Rule to 1920, 378.

17. BURMA UNDER BRITISH-INDIAN RULE TO 1914 380
Burma under Kings Bagyidaw, Tharrawaddy, and Pagan, 381. British Tenasserim and Arakan, 383. British Rule in Lower Burma, 384. The Reign of Mindon Min, 1852–1878, 387. British Absorption of the Burma Kingdom, 390. Annexation and Pacification of Upper Burma, 392. The New British Administrative System in Burma, 395. Circumstances and Incentives to Agricultural Expansion, 398. Cultural and Religious Decline, 400. The Problem of Growing Lawlessness, 401. Renaissance of Burmese Cultural Traditions, 403.

18. VIETNAM AND FRENCH INDOCHINA 460
Vietnam under Gia Long and Minh Mang, 407. Revival of French Contacts,

409. The Missionary Feud with Minh Mang, 411. The Basilan Episode, 413. Increased Tension in Indochina, 413. Louis Napoleon's Decision to Intervene, 415. The Tourane-Saigon Expedition, 416. The Making of Peace, 418. The Expansion of French Holdings, 419. Naval Monopoly of Imperialistic Concern in Indochina, 421. French Acquisition of Annam and Tongking, 423. The Rule of the Admirals, 424. French Control of Laos, 1893, 425. The French Administrative System for Indochina, 428. The French Cultural and Political Impact, 432.

19.  **THE STRAITS SETTLEMENTS AND BRITISH MALAYA  435**
The Straits Settlements Trade, 436. Piracy and Its Suppression, 437. British-Dutch Relations: Borneo, 438. Origins of British Chartered-Company Rule in North Borneo, 441. The Role of the Chinese Immigrants, 442. British Intervention in Peninsular Malaya after 1874, 443. Effects of Closer Contacts with Europe, 446. Increased Tin and Rubber Production, 447. Depression and the End of the Kangany System, 450. Malays and Chinese, 451. Conclusions on British Malaya, 454.

## Part Six, Political Reform and Nationalist Revival

20.  **THE PHILIPPINES: FROM SPANISH TO AMERICAN RULE  459**
Spain's Faltering Effort to Revive the Philippines, 460. Development of Nationalist Resistance, 461. The Influence of José Rizal, 463. American Annexation of the Philippines, 466. Beginnings of Self-government and Land Reform, 468. Social-improvement Efforts, 470. Problems of Economic Development, 472. The Process of Filipinization, 474. The Regime of General Wood, 478. Sequel to the Wood Era, 479. The Attainment of Philippine Self-rule, 481. Application of the Tydings-McDuffie Act, 483. The Assessment of American Rule, 484.

21.  **SIAM FROM CHULALONGKORN TO WORLD WAR II  487**
King Chulalongkorn as Liberal Reformer, 488. Problems of Administrative Adjustment, 489. The Reforming Program of Prince Damrong, 491. Aspects of Siam's Economic Development, 493. The Successors of Chulalongkorn, 496. Revision of the Unequal Treaties, 498. The Revolution of 1932, 501. The Course of the Revolution, 503. Pibun Songgram and Siam's Fascist Orientation, 504.

22.  **BURMESE NATIONALISM BETWEEN THE WARS  506**
Emergence of Burmese Nationalism in World War I, 507. Postwar Reform Proposals, 508. The Operation of the Dyarchy Constitution, 511. The Simon Commission Investigation, 513. Xenophobia and Rebellion, 1930–1931, 515. The Problem of Burma's New Constitution, 516. Burma's Separation from India, 518. Burma's Constitution of 1935, 519. The Student Movement and the Thakins, 520. Burma under the 1935 Constitution, 522. From Ba Maw to U Pu, 524. The Ministry of U Saw, 1940–1941, 527.

23.  **THE NETHERLANDS INDIES BETWEEN THE WARS  528**
Postwar Administrative-reform Proposals, 529. The Volksraad, 530. Administrative Reform at Lower Levels, 532. Economic and Social Developments during the Twenties, 533. The Impact of Modernization, 534. Political Fragmentation, 538. Sarekat Islam, Communism, and Nationalist Parties, 540.

Economic Collapse and Remedial Measures, 542. Official Rejection of Reform Proposals, 543.

24. FRENCH INDOCHINA FROM 1920 TO 1941   546
    Development of the Mercantilist Program, 546. The Dominant Role of Alien Residents, 548. General Characteristics of French Rule, 549. Postwar French Gestures at Reform, 552. Postwar Economic Development, 554. Effects of French Rule on the People, 555. Beginnings of Nationalist Agitation in Vietnam, 557. Emergence of Communist Leadership, 560.

25. THE JAPANESE CONQUEST AND OCCUPATION   563
    Steps in the Development of Japan's War Commitment, 564. Japanese Objectives and Plans, 565. The Japanese Conquest of Southeast Asia, 566. Japanese Policies in General, 568. Japanese Tactics in Indonesia, 569. Japanese Policy in Malaya, 572. Burma under the Japanese, 574. British Defeat of the Japanese in Burma, 577. Thailand and the Japanese Occupation, 579. The Rise of Communist-led Nationalism in Indochina, 581. Filipinos and Japanese, 582. Summary of the Effects of the Japanese Occupation, 584.

26. RELEVANCE OF THE HISTORY   586
    Characteristics of Social Changes, 587. The Scope of the Western Influence, 590. Persistence of the Traditional, 592. Historic Rivalries and Relationships, 594. The Problem of Chinese Relations, 596. The Potency of Traditional Symbols of Authority, 597. Waning Symbols of Authority: Burma and Vietnam, 598. Postwar Government in Indonesia, 599. The Political Future of Southeast Asia, 601. Epilogue, 602.

CHRONOLOGY OF HISTORICAL DEVELOPMENTS BY REGIONS AND COUNTRIES   *605*
SELECTED BIBLIOGRAPHY   *617*
INDEX   *631*

# List of Maps

EARLY SOUTHEAST ASIA  29

FUNAN AND ITS NEIGHBORS  55

ŚRIVIJAYAN EMPIRE  69

JAVA FROM ŚAILENDRA TO MAJAPAHIT TIMES  79

MAINLAND SOUTHEAST ASIA: SEVENTH TO
      TWELFTH CENTURIES  102

MONGOL INTRUSIONS (1253–1293)  136

MUSLIM MALACCA (TO 1511)  160

EARLY MODERN TIMES  185

SOUTHEAST ASIA IN THE MID-SEVENTEENTH CENTURY  223

THE PHILIPPINES  247

THE NETHERLANDS EAST INDIES  357

BRITISH BURMA  394

MAINLAND SOUTHEAST ASIA: NINETEENTH TO
      TWENTIETH CENTURIES  429

TWENTIETH-CENTURY SIAM AND FRENCH INDOCHINA  495

POST-COLONIAL SOUTHEAST ASIA  589

# *Periodical Abbreviations*

The following abbreviations of major periodicals have been used in the chapter footnotes and the bibliography:

BEFEO    BULLETIN DE L'ECOLE FRANÇAISE D'EXTRÊME ORIENT (HANOI)

BSOAS    BULLETIN OF THE SCHOOL OF ORIENTAL AND AFRICAN STUDIES (LONDON)

FEQ    FAR EASTERN QUARTERLY (ITHACA, N.Y.)

FES    FAR EASTERN SURVEY (NEW YORK)

JAOS    JOURNAL OF THE AMERICAN ORIENTAL SOCIETY (NEW HAVEN, CONN.)

JBRS    JOURNAL OF THE BURMA RESEARCH SOCIETY (RANGOON)

JRAS    JOURNAL OF THE ROYAL ASIATIC SOCIETY (LONDON)

JRASMB    JOURNAL OF THE ROYAL ASIATIC SOCIETY, MALAYAN BRANCH (SINGAPORE)

JSEAH    JOURNAL OF SOUTHEAST ASIAN HISTORY (KUALA LUMPUR)

JSS    JOURNAL OF THE SIAM SOCIETY (BANGKOK)

NBW    NEW BURMA WEEKLY (RANGOON)

PHR    PACIFIC HISTORICAL REVIEW (BERKELEY, CALIF.)

PART 1

*Setting*

# CHAPTER I

# Geographical Setting
# and Leading Peoples

$\mathcal{T}$his introductory chapter does not purport to be a systematic treatise on the geography and ethnology of Southeast Asia. It will confine itself instead to a description of a number of constant factors in both fields which have conditioned the historical development of the region. It will describe the principal topographical features, such as mountain ranges, river systems, coastlines, and islands and their distribution, which affected population movements, commercial intercourse, and cultural and political developments. Also important are climate variations, the incidence of rainfall, and soil characteristics, as well as the influence of the pattern of the seasonal monsoon winds, which determined the rhythm of seaborne trade. The location and identification of the leading population groups that have contributed to historical development will be followed by descriptions of cultural characteristics and achievements prevailing at the beginning of the historical period. Finally, the outlines of historical chronology will be indicated.

## Topographical Characteristics

The mountain ranges of continental Southeast Asia run for the most part parallel in a north-south direction. This circumstance discouraged transverse communication between adjacent river valleys and oriented virtually all avenues of commercial and population movement in a north-south direction. An exception to this rule may be found in the narrower portions of the Malay isthmus. Here alternative portage routes, the most important of which were located south of the Kra area, were widely used down to fairly recent times. Commercial contact by land between the two oceans was long preferred to the usually pirate-infested Malacca and Sunda Straits passages to the north and east of Sumatra.

Three series of hills separating Burma from India constituted a formidable barrier. The connected Arakan, Chin, and Naga frontier ranges attain an altitude of up to 12,000 feet in the northern regions. The meager trickle of westward migration from early times across this mountain barrier by Mongoloid peoples into Manipur, Assam, and other Indian provinces was reversed only in fairly modern times by Indian movement into the Akyab area from nearby Chittagong. Hill peoples inhabiting this India-Burma watershed were politically retarded, and the most feasible mountain passes connecting Manipur with Burma's Chindwin Valley were not suitable for extensive commercial use. The Chindwin River paralleling the frontier escarpment on the Burma side was only partly navigable as a tributary of the Irrawaddy River.

The Irrawaddy provided the principal artery of travel and trade from Upper Burma to the Bay of Bengal. Caravan routes reaching into China started from the headwaters of river navigation above Bhamo. Separated from the lower Irrawaddy Valley by the Pegu Yoma hills to the east runs the parallel but smaller Sittang River debouching in the Gulf of Martaban. The early Burman inhabitants of the two valleys entered the upper Irrawaddy from eastern Tibet presumably via the longer Salween River gorge. The northernmost mountainous reaches of Burma have been inhabited throughout historic times by groups of kindred Tibetan peoples known collectively as the Kachin tribes. *Kachin* is the Burmese word for savage. Parts of the Arakan coastal region as well as the lower Irrawaddy Valley were previously occupied by another people akin to the Burmans, known as the Pyu. The Arakan region was separated from Burma proper by the not too formidable Arakan Yoma mountains.

To the east of the central valley areas of Burma rises the abrupt escarpment of the broad Shan plateau, a largely mountainous area bisected by the mighty but nonnavigable Salween River. The plateau extends eastward into the upper regions of modern Thailand and across the middle Mekong Valley into the Lao country of Indochina. Among the earliest peoples migrating southward from the upper reaches of the Mekong and Salween Rivers were the Austroasiatic Mons, who were apparently well established at the dawn of history in the delta coastal region of Lower Burma and along the Tenasserim coast. Another group of Mons settled along the eastern side of the Salween-Tenasserim watershed extending to the shores of the Gulf of Siam. Mountainous areas between the two centers of Mon occupancy were inhabited by hill-cultivating tribesmen including several kinds of Karens. The broad valley of the Menam was the cradle of both the Mon and Siamese civilizations.

Another Austroasiatic people, the Khmers, presumed to be cousins of the Mons, moved into the middle reaches of the Mekong Valley probably somewhat after the Mon migration. They halted for a time in the low Korat plateau area of northeast Siam, unable, until the early seventh century, to reach the seacoast. They eventually overran a Malayo-Polynesian state known to the Chinese as Funan. It centered on the delta of the Mekong and around the Tonle Sap–Great Lake area above and to the west of the delta. The valley of the Great Lake was cut off on the south from the Gulf of Siam by the fairly formidable Cardoman Mountains, which reached at several places elevations of 6,000 feet.

The longer cordillera originating in Laos and running east of the Mekong River and parallel to the Annamese coast constituted a formidable barrier to both trade and population movement. The southern portion of the narrow Annam littoral was inhabited in early historic times by the Chams, another Malayo-Polynesian people. The Vietnamese occupied the Red River delta to the north and also the upper reaches of the Annamese coast. The mountain mass of Indochina's hinterland, like the upland and plateau areas of Burma, was inhabited by a variety of culturally retarded peoples, who played no important role in the history of the region. The mountains constituted both a climatic and an ethnic frontier.[1]

The Vietnamese, although pretty thoroughly Sinicized by a millennium of Chinese rule (100 B.C. to A.D. 900), were composed of a mingling of peoples ethnically akin to the Mons and Khmers and to other peoples living south of Han China proper. The population substratum was apparently a mixture of Indonesian, Melanesian, Negrito, and Thai. The Chams, like the Funanese, were for the most part a Malay people, intermingled with primitive indigenous groups and more recent Khmer arrivals. The habitable portions of the coastal region shared by the Vietnamese and the Chams consisted mainly of numerous small delta enclaves. The region was dangerous for coastal navigation and was subject to periodic tidal waves and to violent typhoon storms in the late summer and early autumn.[2]

The watershed dividing the lower Salween and Menam River Valleys in the north continues southward down the length of the Malay Peninsula. It could be penetrated with some difficulty behind Moulmein, Tavoy, and Mergui from the Tenasserim coast side and somewhat more easily further south, where harbors were readily available on both sides of the isthmus. The principal portage routes traversing the narrower portions of the isthmus south of Kra served for many centuries to connect substantial trading centers on both shores, one side serviced by Indian ships, the other largely by the Funanese. From Kedah state southward the mountains paralleling the western coast of Malaya became more formidable in character. To the east lay the swamp-covered, heavily forested interior two-thirds of Malaya. Rich tin deposits found along the western slopes of the isthmus and the Malay mountains and extending also across the Malacca Straits to Banka and Billiton Islands attracted attention of miners from early times. Pahang state in east central Malaya was, for a time, a source of gold. Otherwise Malaya was attractive commercially only as a source of perfumed woods.

The volcanic island chain which forms the outermost rim of the Indonesian arc is a southward and eastward extension of Burma's Arakan Yoma. It emerges above the sea in the barren Andaman and Nicobar Islands, inhabited by pre-Malay Negritic savages. Appearing again at the

---

[1] André Masson, *Histoire du Vietnam* (1960), chap. I.
[2] Pierre Gourou, *The Peasants of the Tonkin Delta* (1955), 140–143.

northern tip of Sumatra and paralleling the western shores of the island, the range attains considerable proportions, inhibiting cross-island intercourse. Sumatra drains for the most part toward the shallow Malacca Straits. The larger island is bordered on the west by a maze of low-lying islands which served as hideouts for pirate-fisherman folk from early times. Although cut briefly at the Sunda Straits, the Sumatran range reemerges along the southern shores of Java. To the east of Java it turns northward along western Borneo and thence to the Philippines. On the borders of this extensive mountainous arc have been found oil deposits, first in Burma's Chauk-Yenangyaung area, again behind the Sumatran port of Palembang, and finally in northeastern Borneo.

The shallow and usually calm sea which extends from the Gulf of Siam across to Borneo and Java and up the Straits of Malacca constitutes, along with adjacent peninsular and island areas, what is known as the Sunda platform. Its limited depth (120 to 150 feet) and the identity of plant and animal forms throughout the platform suggest that it was probably connected with the continent in glacial times, when the sea level was substantially lower than today. To the east of the shelf and south of Java, the sea drops off to great depths. The mountains of the Celebes and the easternmost islands of the Flores Sea are heavily saline and coral-infested and constitute a distinctly different geologic region.

Except for Buginese and other trading peoples living along the northern shores of the Java Sea, the inhabitants of the mountainous jungles of Borneo, the Celebes, and Mindanao were and are backward culturally and commercially. Early centers of Indianization were located in southern Indochina, around the shores of the Gulf of Siam, among the Mons, in the Malacca Straits, and in Java. Indian culture affected the Philippines and the Spice Islands very meagerly.

Three general conclusions emerge concerning the historical importance of these geographical facts. Agricultural resources were obviously basic. In the upper peninsula most of the peoples who were important historically occupied delta areas (the Irrawaddy, Sittang, Menam, Mekong, and Red Rivers). Burman power from the Pagan period centered on three inland irrigated areas of Upper Burma, while the Khmers developed the agricultural potentialities of the Great Lake basin of Cambodia. Java alone among the islands afforded a broad basis for agricultural development. Secondly, throughout much of the region seaborne commerce was as important as agriculture. The isthmian portage routes served mainly to supplement ocean-going transportation. Even for peoples unable to develop any substantial agricultural base, such as the Chams of the lower Annam littoral, the Buginese of the Macassar Strait, and the Achehnese of northern Sumatra, opportunity to participate in the principal currents of commerce afforded a substantial basis for political power. Patterns of trade as well as the possession of food and commercial resources conditioned in large measure the development of historically important states.

Bearing directly on agricultural resources and trade were climatic factors, such as patterns of rainfall, the direction of seasonal winds, and the quality and utilization of soil resources.

## Rainfall Patterns, Monsoon Winds, and Soil Utilization

Except for several rain-shadow areas isolated from moisture-bearing clouds by mountains on the windward side, as in central Burma, Southeast Asia enjoys a surfeit of annual rainfall. To most regions situated north of 8 to 10°N latitude from the Bay of Bengal inland toward southern China, the summer monsoon winds bring torrential rain, continuing from late May to early October. Rangoon receives well over 100 inches of rain in four months, and Moulmein around twice that amount. The west coasts of Borneo and the Philippines also experience similarly heavy summer rainfall. With the onset of cooler weather, the low-pressure center which prevails over the Asian land mass during the hot summer months changes into a chronic high-pressure zone, which persists during the autumn, winter, and early spring. Prevailing northerly winds during these seasons are arid in Burma, Laos, Cambodia, and Siam. But the winter monsoon brings heavy rains to the eastern coasts of Borneo and the Philippines and also along the eastern coastlines of Indochina and Malaya.

The monsoon winds affect less the rainfall patterns of areas located near the equator and south of it. The southern tip of Malaya enjoys a rain shower almost every day of the year, and winds in the Malacca Straits region are notoriously unpredictable, especially during the summer season. The mountainous southern coasts of Sumatra and Java absorb much but not all of the northward-moving summer precipitation. Java's principal rains come from the north and east during the winter season. Rainfall in the central and eastern two-thirds of Java and adjacent islands is affected by the arid summer winds which cross the wastes of Australia en route. This area of Java experiences, therefore, a prolonged dry season during the summer period.[3] In the Moluccas area and the southern reaches of the Philippines, eastward-moving moisture-laden winds blow the year round, so that there is no seasonal pattern of precipitation here.

Generally abundant rainfall would seem to offer to Southeast Asia almost unlimited agricultural possibilities. Several factors nevertheless combine to make large areas generally unsuited for intensified agriculture. The first is the heavy erosion suffered by drenched land along choked river systems and in uplands partly denuded of vegetation by shifting hillside cultivation. This process of erosion has produced from prehistoric times the enormous deltas found at the mouths of such rivers as the Red in Tongking, the Mekong in Cochin-China, the Menam in Siam, and the Irrawaddy in Burma.

[3] J. J. Van Klavern, *The Dutch Colonial System in the East Indies* (1953), 9–10; George Cressey, *Asia's Lands and Peoples* (1951), chap. 33.

Much silt is also deposited inland where rivers in spate back up into valleys less full. Examples are the Tonle Sap in Cambodia connecting the upper Mekong delta with the Great Lake, and Inlé Lake in Burma's Shan plateau.[4]

A second factor affecting adversely the agricultural potential of the region is the widespread tendency for nonvolcanic water-impregnated soils subject to downward drainage to become either laterized or leached because certain soluble minerals are drained away. Where soil temperatures remain steadily above 75° Fahrenheit, a temperature facilitating the breakdown of organic matter by microorganisms, the silica (sandstone and granite) content is dissolved and sinks to lower levels. This leaves a porous surface soil of heavy clay and iron content called laterite (Latin *later*, or brick). When exposed to the sun, laterite becomes hard enough to use for building purposes and roads; when unexposed it is spongy and unstable and also notoriously lacking in essential plant nutrients.

Conversely, where the land temperature is habitually below the 75° mean, downward-draining groundwater with heavy organic matter in solution frequently dissolves the clay and iron, leaching the surface soil of iron oxides needed by plants. Thus the heavy rains have tended to ruin much of the soil except for deep-rooted forest and plantation crops capable of tapping water tables far below the surface.[5] The third problem develops where groundwater evaporation exceeds downward drainage, as is the case throughout the Korat plateau of northeastern Siam and in much of Indochina. Here the abundance of plant nutrients deposited near the surface encourages the growth of rank grasses characteristic of savanna soils. The grasses choke out all competing vegetation and in time render such areas largely useless for agriculture.

## Agricultural Centers and Methods of Cultivation

Geography and soil deterioration apparently dictated the wide dispersion of centers of population and political power throughout much of Southeast Asia. Silt-rich delta areas of the major river systems were capable of indefinite development as sources of food, depending on the skill and sustained industry of the occupants. Where successfully mobilized, the population of delta regions demonstrated advanced patterns of political and social organization. The disciplined character and the economic vitality characteristic of the Vietnamese people, for example, were derived in large measure from their successful age-long struggle to curb the turbulent Tongking delta of the flooding Red River. Similar circumstances contributed to the early economic and political preeminence of the Funanese and Khmer states located around the Mekong delta and the adjacent Great

[4] E. H. G. Dobby, *Southeast Asia* (1954), 47 ff. Dobby estimates that the Irrawaddy in modern times deposits annually more than a quarter-billion tons of silt at the delta.

[5] *Ibid.*, 74–84; Cressey, 494–500.

Lake area. The lower reaches of the Menam River afforded a similar setting for early Mon development. On the Burma side, the Mons created food-surplus areas in the lower Sittang Valley and along the borders of the steadily advancing Irrawaddy delta. The Mons also contributed to the development of inland irrigation systems both in the upper valleys of Siam and in central Burma. The traditional center of political power in central Burma was adjacent to the aforementioned granary areas of Kyaukse, Shwebo, and Minbu, where the royal service lands were concentrated.

Smaller districts on both shores of the historic portage routes across northern Malaya (modern Perlis on the west and the regions adjacent to the Bay of Bandon and Ligor on the east) were capable of substantial agricultural development. Separate states of Lankasuka and Tambralinga, the former located to the south of the latter, appeared successively in this area in early times, although they were normally vassal states to the more powerful Funanese and Khmers or to Sumatran Śrivijaya. As already explained, most of Malaya proper was of meager value agriculturally, the soil being laterized along the western slopes of the watershed and waterlogged throughout the central and eastern reaches of the peninsula.

Much the same incapacity for surplus-food production obtained for most of Sumatra. The potentially fertile topsoil of volcanic ash in the uplands eroded away, and extensive laterization occurred. Inadequate drainage facilities hampered development of many eastern shore areas. The gifted Minangkabau Malays inhabiting the central highlands of western Sumatra developed extensive systems of wet-rice cultivation, although never to the point of supporting a dense population. The peoples of central Luzon in the Philippines similarly created extensive irrigation facilities with terraces extending far up the hillsides. But they, like the Minangkabau, never generated sufficient political power and cohesion to become determiners of regional historical developments.

The island of Java was a special case. The western third of the island was subject to the heavy year-round rainfall and consequent soil deterioration characteristic of neighboring Sumatra. Prior to the arrival of the Dutch this area never advanced agriculturally much beyond the stage of subsistence hillside cultivation. But in other parts of Java where the summer rainfall drops off because of arid winds from Australia, opportunity was afforded for water control and soil conservation. Java's topsoil, volcanic in origin, possessed valuable mineral elements contributing to perennial fertility. The gifted Javanese learned to trap mountain rivulets at upper levels and to direct the water through an amphitheater of terraced fields capable of producing rice and other crops year after year. Thus they controlled the water supply and prevented the dissipation of valuable topsoil.

Wet-rice cultivation (called *sawah*) produced in Java the integrated social structure needed to provide communal labor for construction of dams and canals. Thus an assured food supply was afforded for a large sedentary population capable of being organized into sizable political units. Organized cultivation and consequent political integration were similarly possible along the principal river valleys leading mainly to the north coast of Java. The climate and soil of eastern Java also permitted the growth of forests of teakwood (otherwise available only in Burma and Siam) capable of providing valuable timber resources for shipbuilding and other construction. The economically and politically disciplined Javanese peoples generated in time an indigenous civilization of substantial vitality and depth, which added to their advantages of food supply and superior political cohesion. The emerging feudal society and government made slavery almost nonexistent in sawah-cultivated Java. The tradition of collective responsibility for welfare and order, especially in evidence in the *desa* system of Java, subjected private rights in land to the superior authority of the local community.[6]

An alternative to sawah cultivation was the widely practiced method of migrant hillside culture, extending over enormous stretches of elevated terrain throughout Southeast Asia. The name for it is *caiñgin* in the Philippines, *ray* in Indochina, *tam rai* in Thailand, *taungya* in Burma, *ladang* in Indonesia. The preparation of fields for dry-rice and vegetable cultivation by cutting down and burning the forest cover of hillsides afforded a feasible method of utilizing for food production vast stretches of mountain terrain. In western Java and in areas of northern Sumatra, ladang cultivation was associated with pepper production. In the larger Outer Islands of Indonesia, hillside cultivators sometimes operated from relatively permanent homesites, extending their operations over a wide radius of land accessible by river transportation. Only during the ripening season was it necessary in such situations to live near the fenced-in crop to protect it from possible theft and from the depredations of wild pigs.

Elsewhere in Southeast Asia, hillside cultivators usually shifted village sites every year or two, since a given clearing could produce only one or two acceptable crops. The ashes deposited by the burning helped provide needed minerals and also sweetened the accumulated humus of the forest floor. An abandoned clearing often required from fifteen to twenty-five years for full renewal of fertility, but the utilizing communities were usually unable to wait that long before the migration cycle brought them back. Where tree roots were killed by fire, the hillside fields often reverted to tall grass. In remote mountainous areas the village community units were quite small (thirty to fifty persons), the size varying with soil resources and ease of transportation. Strife between rival claimants to the soil often led to enslavement of defeated groups. Sanitation facilities were rudimentary, so that malaria and cholera took a deadly toll.

Hillside cultivation, however primitive and inadequate, demonstrated survival inertia as a way of life. This was true even in agricultural situations capable of sawah, or irrigated, cultivation. Under the ladang system, every family enjoyed access to as much land as it could clear, and

[6] Van Klavern, 9–13; B. H. M. Vlekke, *Nusantara* (1960), 13.

the work was distributed throughout the year. Little weeding was necessary during the first season, so that a new location could be prepared while the crop matured. Selection and occupation of sites for cultivation called for spirit consultations and were associated with other religious taboos, tenacious in character. Transfer to a more sedentary kind of existence required a greater measure of organization and discipline than primitive communities were usually capable of achieving. Thus ladang cultivation prevailed throughout western Java into the nineteenth century, and it still survives in the westernmost Bantam province and along the southern Java coast.[7] Contraction of accessible cultivable areas due to grass take-over, to excessive damage from forest fires, and to topsoil erosion sooner or later forced the overfrequent use of hillside fields. When occupants returned after intervals of eight to ten years, the operation reached the point of diminishing returns. Such problems forced cultivation groups to range widely, their very mobility defying efforts at achieving wider political organization. For this reason unorganized hill folk usually posed no formidable threat to sawah cultivators, who were socially and politically integrated.

The Melanesian peoples of the eastern archipelago were predominantly fishermen and sago collectors. They obtained a kind of flour from the core of the mature sago palm which they consumed along with yams in lieu of rice or other cereal food. The smallness of the island units which produced the marketable clove, nutmeg, and mace spices usually precluded the development of political organization capable of exercising centralized power. Exchange of spices for Javan rice eventually improved the menu for the occupants of the more prosperous islands.[8]

The hazards which plagued hillside cultivators with meager security, health liabilities, and livelihood deficiencies contributed to the uniform lack of interest in hill areas which was displayed historically by more advanced peoples. The Vietnamese, Mons, Khmers, Burmans, Minangkabau and Javanese were little concerned, as a rule, with lateral expansion of their rule over less crowded hill areas adjacent to their centers of agriculture and of political power.[9] A notable exception to this general rule was the Thai, or Shan, peoples, who achieved a high level of political organization in the Nan Chao and kindred states in Chinese Yunnan before they entered Southeast Asia. Following their dispersal southward during the twelfth and thirteenth centuries, their political control extended from the upper Irrawaddy Valley across Burma's Shan states area into Laos, and eventually as far southward as the upper provinces of Malaya. Even so, effective Thai control in plateau regions was limited, for the most part, to the small valleys capable of wet-rice cultivation. They usually left primitive taungya and tam rai culti-

[7] Van Klavern, 11–12, 14–15; Karl J. Pelzer, *Pioneer Settlement in the Asian Tropics* (1945), 16–20.

[8] Van Klavern, 13, 28–29.

[9] Gourou, 236–239.

vators in undisturbed possession of watersheds separating the narrow valleys.

The presence of culturally retarded peoples between centers of civilization and political power was historically important mainly as a negative factor. Primitive food-gathering folk, Negrito and Veddoid, survived into the twentieth century not only in the Andaman and Nicobar Islands, as previously mentioned, but also along the eastern lowlands of Sumatra and in the remote interiors of Cambodia, Malaya, Borneo, and the Philippines.[10] Even after backward peoples developed sedentary types of agriculture in areas of advancing development, they long continued their gathering of fruit, yams, berries, sago, and edible barks as important sources of food. They killed game with blowguns and poisoned darts, wore clothing (if at all) made from barks, rattan, and palm fiber, and slept on raised platforms shielded by windbreaks in lieu of houses. In time, some of the wavy-haired Sakai of Malaya borrowed vocabulary from their neighbors and became house dwellers and hillside cultivators.[11] When the Portuguese attacked Malacca in 1511, for example, many of the defenders made effective use of poisoned darts from blowguns. But such primitive folk could seldom exert important historical influence.

## *Characteristics of Major Peoples: Malays and Javanese*

The more advanced Malay peoples can be differentiated into two groups. The "older," or Proto-Malay, group resided in the interior regions and contributed to the ethnic composition of such important peoples as the Minangkabau in central Sumatra. The Proto-Malays also predominated in the population of the Greater and Lesser Sunda Islands to the east. The "younger," or Deutero-Malay, group was apparently more Mongoloid in character. The Deutero-Malays tended to settle in coastal areas and became more mobile, especially after traders arrived from the outside. This group established coastal enclaves at attractive points along the eastern shores of Sumatra and contributed the bulk of the Javanese population. Sea-gypsy fishermen-pirates who long infested the Malacca Straits and the northern coasts of the Java Sea, along with the Buginese traders of the Celebes north of Macassar, were of this group.[12]

Basic cultural accomplishments of the Malays generally included the preparation of stone adzes, the use of outrigger canoes, wet-rice cultivation,

[10] Pelzer, 3–15. Primitive peoples included the Semang Negritos and Sakai of Malaya, the Veddoid Kuba of Sumatra, the Taola of the Celebes, the Punan of Borneo, the Aeta of the Philippines.

[11] Ivor H. N. Evans, *Papers on Ethnology and Archeology of the Malay Peninsula* (1927), 2–3, 5–8, 11–17.

[12] See Raymond Kennedy, "A Survey of Indonesian Society," in G. P. Murdock, *Studies in the Science of Society* (1937), 267–279. Kennedy classified sixty-one basic ethnic divisions among Indonesian peoples, plus fifty-two subdivisions.

domestication of cattle and buffaloes, weaving, and pottery making. Particularly gifted among them were the Javanese, who apparently profited from contact with the Chams and Vietnamese living along the narrow coastal corridor of Annam and northward into the Tongking delta. This region was a center of the so-called Dongs'on culture with its advanced work in iron and bronze weapons, utensils, and drums and its improved types of pottery.

At some time B.C., Deutero-Malay seamen carried their products and their language far into the southern ocean areas beyond India to the coasts of East Africa and Madagascar. They may have introduced yams, bananas, and sugar cane into Africa. The Hova inhabitants of central Madagascar still speak an Austronesian dialect.[13] The basic Malay language also spread to the Pacific islanders east of the Moluccas. On the southern shores of the Gulf of Siam the Malay inhabitants in later times borrowed the use of the Mon numerals from one to ten. The semipiratical Malayo-Polynesian Chams of the south Annam coast also borrowed culturally from northern neighbors, the Vietnamese.[14]

Thanks in part to advantages of rainfall and soil and in part to fruitful outside stimuli, indigenous Malay culture reached its peak in Java. Characteristic of Javanese religion was belief in the presence in both man and rice of a life force, or soul substance, impersonal in character and capable of existing in restricted and concentrated forms. Thus the symbolic use of rice knives for harvesting the first stalks of rice was required to conserve the life force of the grain, since the loud swish of the sickle might frighten it away. A priestess associated with a fertility cult functioned expertly for the entire community and served as custodian of traditional taboos and portents associated wtih the all-important rice cultivation. In the absence of such preparations, the community of cultivators would simply not settle down to perform the necessary work. The earth also could have a concentrated soul, as could the sky. Elaborate ancestor-cult practices in Java found expression in puppet plays and in complicated mortuary ceremonies, usually involving entire villages. Cremations, often long postponed, could include the burning of the actual remains of the deceased or simply a puppet representing his spirit. Special attention was given to the propitiation of ancestral ghosts as well as those evil-intentioned spirits of persons who had suffered violent death from murder, suicide, childbirth, or cholera. The thirty-six identifiable *nat* spirits of the Burmese pantheon were similarly conceived as vagrant spirits.

Highly important nature spirits among the eastern Javanese were father sky and mother earth; lesser spirits represented waterfalls, rivers, beaches, tides, the sun, and the moon. Sacrificial offerings (originally a slave

[13] As early as 1820 John Crawfurd attested the dispersion of Malay contacts in the Indian Ocean. See his *History of the Indian Archipelago* (1820), I, 24–29.
[14] Richard Winstedt, *The Malays: A Cultural History* (1947), 3–5.

and, latterly, a fowl, a goat, or buffalo) contributed a localized spirit dedicated to the protection of a particular house foundation or gateway or rice field. In Burma this practice was called *Myosade*. The magical powers of the shaman (spirit priest) afforded means of communication with the world of spirits. Upright stone fetishes and sacred mountains, both associated with ancestral cults, had a direct relevance to the exercise of political authority in eastern Java, where lordship carried religious and priestly connotations. Among the Buginese of the Celebes, rulers allegedly were generated from marital union between the son of heaven and the daughter of the netherworld goddess—a symbolism widely shared in Southeast Asia.

Although sometimes symbolized in less elaborate forms, such characteristic Javanese beliefs and practices were tenaciously treasured by many Southeast Asian peoples, even after they gave formal affiliation to Hindu, Buddhist, or Islamic faiths.[15] Indigenous concepts of animism, more or less sophisticated, afforded a fertile matrix for the eventual assimilation of important aspects of Indian civilization, as will be indicated in Chapter 2.

## Leading Austroasiatic-speaking Peoples: Mons and Khmers

The ethnic maze prevailing in peninsular Southeast Asia is even more complicated than that on the islands. Frizzy-haired, black-skinned Melanesoid peoples were observed in the Mekong delta by Chinese visitors during periods as far removed as the third century and the thirteenth, and by French observers in the twentieth century.[16] Hillside-cultivating nomads speaking hundreds of distinct dialects occupied the watersheds between the Mekong River and the Annam coast, and were dispersed throughout much of Laos and northern Thailand and the Shan plateau of Burma, was well as in the hills peripheral to the Sittang, Chindwin, and Irrawaddy Valleys. They include the Moi, Mau, and Meo east of the Mekong, the Lahu, Wa, and Kachin tribes on the Yunnan borders, and various types of Karens in Lower Burma. The peoples who were important historically were relatively few and more easily identified.

The first Austroasiatic-speaking people to penetrate deeply into the northern peninsula area was the Mons. They probably entered from South China via the upper bend of the Mekong River in B.C. times, or in any case before making any contact with Chinese civilization, Chou or Han. They entered Lower Burma via the Salween and Sittang River corridors, establishing centers near the coast, first at Thaton and later at Kosma and Pegu.

[15] *Ibid.*, 12–19; Murdock, 292–297; Willen Henri Helsdingen, *Cultural Treasures of the East Indies* (1946), 28–36.

[16] See R. Baradot, "Les Samre ou Pear: Population primitive de l'ouest du Cambodge," *BEFEO*, tome XLI (1941), 1–30.

From the upper Sittang Valley they also moved northward along the Shan plateau escarpment to develop the Kyaukse granary area below modern Ava. The Mons of Lower Burma were closely associated geographically with the Pwo Karens, probably in a master-and-slave relationship. Both the Pwo and the Sgaw Karens borrowed many Mon words. At an early time the Mons became skilled cultivators and also merchants, shipbuilders, and seamen. Their seaborne contacts extended to the northern Coromandel Coast of India and to inland Telingana. Another and larger group of Mons early had control extending virtually through the entire Menam Valley and southward into the isthmus. That they arrived in northern Malaya before their Khmer cousins who advanced southward via the Mekong Valley is attested by the Malay adoption of basic Mon numerals.

The first Mon state located on the eastern side of the Tenasserim divide came to be known by the Indian name Dvaravati. The Chinese called it Tun-sun. It eventually centered at Lavo, or Lopburi. The early and apparently continuous commercial and cultural intercourse of the Mons with India contributed both character and distinction to their civilization. They acted as the teachers successively of the Khmers, the Burmans, and the Thai in matters of art, writing forms, and government. But they were otherwise not particularly creative culturally, save in the realm of poetry. They were seldom politically dominant, and succumbed repeatedly to the superior strength of rival neighbors.

The Khmers probably followed the Mons down the upper Mekong route but turned eastward to settle first in the region of modern Laos and in the Korat Plateau. They occupied both sides of the Mekong Valley north of the Malayo-Polynesian state of Funan in the delta and in the basin of the Great Lake. It was in the second half of the sixth century A.D. that Khmer Chenla began the destruction of the Funan Empire, a process continuing for almost a century. The reunification of the country began around 800, with control eventually centering above the Great Lake. Cambodia proper was fully assimilated by the Khmers near the end of the 800s, after which the Mon territory along the shores of the Gulf of Siam was also brought under Khmer control, including much of the portage area. The superior talents of the Khmers in governmental organization and hydraulic agriculture, as also in architecture, art, and literature, have been explained in various ways. Their close associations at numerous times with the gifted Javanese ruling families were probably a contributing factor. The Khmers also occupied a region rich in agricultural resources and strategically placed commercially, and their cultural contacts with the Mons were fruitful. The history of Cambodia will be considered in a later chapter.

The economic system developed by Mons and Khmers was similar to that of the sawah-cultivating Javanese. It included domestication of the buffalo, the use of bronze and iron tools, artistic craftsmanship in stone and wood, and skill in navigation. Villages were usually located on higher ground adjacent to river lowlands or deltas. Labor needed for production of food was mobilized by conquests and by enslavement of hill folk. Centralized political authority developed in the vicinity of irrigation works. It was the chief's responsibility to commune with the divine powers and ancestral spirits in order to ensure prosperity. Royal shrines were usually situated on real or artificial mountains. An important social peculiarity was the role occupied by the Khmer women; familial affiliation and also inheritance followed the female line. Animistic cults proliferated, with special emphasis, as in Java, on spirits of the soil and the water, and other sources of fertility. A pantheon of identifiable vagrant spirits, victims of tragedy or violence, was common here, as also in Java and Burma. This Austroasiatic civilization apparently penetrated in some unexplained fashion in pre-Aryan times to north India. This circumstance may have contributed a similarity of cultural traditions which afforded a basis for appropriation in historic times by Mon-Khmer peoples of many aspects of a mature Hindu civilization.[17]

## The Vietnamese

The Vietnamese, who constituted the third historically important ethnic group in peninsular Southeast Asia, probably originated in what is now southern China. They settled in the Tongking area, moving from north to south and finding the Red River delta at the outset a morass of swamps and pools. Dikes and drainage channels were constructed at the cost of great labor. The Vietnamese were an Indonesian, non-Chinese people, with linguistic and cultural affinities with the Thai and the Mon-Khmers. During the second century B.C. Tongking and Annam constituted a peripheral southern portion of the kingdom of Nam Viet, which included also the two Kwang provinces of South China. Conquest of this kingdom by Emperor Wu Ti, completed in 111 B.C., brought the Tongking area under Chinese control. It was a century and a half later before Chinese administration was fully imposed. Incidental to the inclusion of Nam Viet within the Han Empire was the Chinese discovery that other parts of Southeast Asia and India lay beyond the southern seas.[18]

Vietnam constituted for a thousand years (to 939 A.D.) the southern frontier province of the Chinese Empire, subjected to the full impact of Chinese culture. The people generally retained their own spoken language, but appropriated Chinese loanwords in such areas as philosophy, business, and formal education. At the outset, Confucian rationalism and sophisti-

---

[17] D. G. E. Hall, *A History of South-East Asia* (1955), 3–8. Dr. Heine-Geldern reports the prevalence of common Austric words for pepper, cloves, onion, and betel in use from India to the Pacific islands. See also G. Coedès, *Les États Hindouisés d'Indochine et d'Indonésie* (1948), 27–30.

[18] Lê Thanh Khôi, *Le Viet Nam* (1955), 92–96.

cated Tao mysticism held out little attraction to the peoples of the southern province. Not until A.D. 187 were Vietnamese mandarins included in the governmental service. Around 200, after the fall of the Han dynasty, Vietnam became a haven of refuge for many Chinese mandarin scholars, a circumstance which intensified the cultivation of Chinese learning. Eventually the Vietnamese appropriated the Confucian classics and the Mahayana form of Buddhism directly from China. This development did not exclude contacts with Indian Buddhism and the persistence of indigenous religious practices. The Vietnamese peasant was strongly attached to his native village with its protective patron spirit, or genie, a fact which greatly reduced population mobility. Many communities of ancient occupancy displayed a limited number of family names, such as Nguyen or Dinh, with seldom more than twelve to sixteen names in one locality.[19]

Early Vietnamese contacts with India were in part commercial and in part religious, because of Buddhist pilgrims' journeys in both directions. Seaborne missions from India stopped in Vietnam en route to China proper, and Vietnamese pilgrims subsequently obtained copies of the sacred Buddhist texts from cultural centers in south Sumatra. But for various reasons Chinese culture took precedence over Indian in Vietnam. For one thing, the Chams immediately to the south, whose Indianized state dated from 192, were inveterately hostile, especially after the mid-eighth century. Furthermore, the Hindu cult of the god-king held out little or no appeal to a Confucianized mandarinate.[20]

Vietnam's eventual separation from China occurred in connection with the decline of the power of the T'ang dynasty, which began in the late 800s. The T'angs were unable to protect Hanoi from a destructive attack of the Nan Chao Thai from Yunnan, who raided down to Red River Valley in 862–863. Complete Vietnamese independence came in 939, following the collapse of T'ang control. Chinese rule nevertheless left an indelible stamp on the governmental institutions, architecture, and art of Vietnam. Vietnam's people, along with the early Javanese, shared in the Dongs'on bronze culture. The Vietnamese resembled other leading peoples of Southeast Asia in practicing animist symbolism and ancestor worship.[21] At the upper levels of society and government the Vietnamese culture became Chinese.

## The Pyu and Burmans

The ancient Pyu probably constituted the first politically important inhabitants of the central Irrawaddy Valley of Burma. They migrated southward from eastern Tibet not later than the third century A.D. presumably down the Salween and Mekong River gorges of western Yunnan and west-

[19] Gourou, 122–123, 134–135.
[20] *Ibid.*, 105–109.
[21] Hall, 169–171.

ward into the Irrawaddy basin. The Pyu capital of Śrikshetra (city of splendor) on the lower Irrawaddy was known by reputation to the seventh-century Chinese traveler I-Ching. The accepted date of its founding is 638, but inscriptions on the site go back to the sixth century. Early Chinese reports dating from the third and fourth centuries refer to commercial relations with a civilized people, possibly the Pyu, located some 3,000 li south of Yunnan, who constituted the westernmost anchor of the Chinese overland trade route to India. The Mons occupied the eastern borders of the Irrawaddy delta ahead of the Tibetan Pyu, but the latter controlled the river itself. The extensive Indian-type ruins at Śrikshetra bear eloquent testimony to the political importance of the Pyu and to their intimate commercial and cultural relations with India. Śrikshetra itself was not a seaport. Some Pyu trading contacts with India extended laterally across the Arakan Yoma to the port of Akyab. Surviving peculiarities of the Arakanese dialect show some affinity to the Pyu language as recorded on the Myazedi inscription of 1133 (Burma's Rosetta stone).

Pyu political influence disappeared from Lower Burma during the course of the eighth century, leaving the Mons in uncontested control. Pyu power in the delta areas was apparently cut off by a lateral westward intrusion of Palaung and Karen peoples into the Minbu-Magwe region. When the Thai chief of Nan Chao, Kolofeng, reopened trade with India in the late 700s, the route proceeded not down the Irrawaddy Valley but via the Chindwin Valley and Manipur or to Arakan and Akyab via the northern An Pass. The Thai rulers of Nan Chao reduced the surviving Pyu state of Upper Burma to vassal status around 800. Pyu musicians were sent by Nan Chao to the T'ang Court at Ch'ang-an, China, in 800–802, and Pyu soldiers participated in the Nan Chao attack on Hanoi in 863. Destruction of the late Pyu capital of Halingyi (near Shwebo) in north Burma in 832–835 by the Thai marked the political extinction of the Pyu state.

Shortly after the collapse of the Pyu state, a second wave of Tibeto-Burmans abruptly entered the valley via the Shan states at a point below modern Ava. Some of them were probably escaped captives from Nan Chao, then at war with Tibetan peoples in the narrow corridor between the upper Yangtse and Mekong Rivers. The entering Burmans had experienced only meager contacts with China, but they had learned from the Thai-Shans the arts of war and horsemanship, rice cultivation, and slope terracing. Their political traditions were rudimentary. Burmans copied the Shan practice of repeating the last syllable of the name of a previous ruler as the first syllable of his successor (called patronymic linkage).

The first home of the Burmans was the central Burma irrigated area of Kyaukse, previously developed by the Mons. They then moved southward to Minbu-Magwe, another irrigated area, which they conquered from the Karens and Palaungs. They finally moved westward up the Chindwin Valley and northward to the Shwebo region, where they quickly assimilated their Tibetan kinsmen, the surviving remnants of the Pyu. The Mons kept control of the Sittang and lower Irrawaddy Valleys.[22] The Burmans eventually founded their capital city of Pagan on a bluff overlooking a bend of the Irrawaddy below the confluence of the Chindwin.

## The Shans, or Thai

The Shan, or Thai, peoples long occupied the watersheds between the headwaters of the Red River on the east, the upper Mekong Valley on the west, and the Yangtse River on the north. Much of the area was brought under Han China's control by Emperor Wu Ti in A.D. 109. A well-defined overland trade route to India via the Mekong, Salween, and Irrawaddy River gorges was opened in 120. When Chinese control declined in the following century, locally established princely families (barbarian Thai) obtained control of the important Lake of Tali area just east of the Mekong gorge. The trade route was closed completely in 342. Western Yunnan Thai chiefs continued to defy Chinese authority even after its revival in southwest China under the T'angs in 624. The T'angs failed to reopen the caravan trade to India via the Mekong despite a major military effort in 648. Eventually (after 670), the rising power of a unified Tibetan state threatened both Chinese Szechuan and the Thai. By the early 700s the Thai chiefs and the now defensively minded T'ang Court, facing a common Tibetan danger, revived cordial relations on a traditional vassal-suzerain pattern.[23]

It was as the loyal vassal of T'ang China against the Tibetan enemy that Pi-lo-ko (730–748), the leader of Nan Chao (south princedom), one of six tiny Thai states in western Yunnan, began to extend his control over his neighbors. He established a center of power in the Tali Lake plain just east of the Mekong, which was protected by precipitous mountains on the east and west and by easily defended gorge entrances on the north and south. From this impregnable position, the Nan Chao prince withstood the attacks of two Chinese armies (751 and 754), blunted the aggressive designs of the Tibetans, and dominated the reopened trade routes leading southward into Burma. Nan Chao conquered the north Burma Pyu state in 832, as previously indicated, and attacked as far away as Hanoi in Tongking in 862–863.

Hostile Tibetan forces long remained in occupation of the region between the parallel Salween, Mekong, and Yangtse basins to the north of Nan Chao. It may have been from marauding bands or from captives gathered by the Thai in this area that Tibeto-Burman immigrants to the Irrawaddy Valley were drawn during the ninth century. Decline of the state of Nan Chao began long before its final liquidation by Mongol armies in

[22] Than Tun, "A History of Burma down to the End of the Thirteenth Century," *NBW*, Aug. 23, 1958, 15–24; Hall, 22, 35, 120.

[23] M. Blackmore, "The Rise of Nan-Chao in Yunnan," *JSEAH*, I (1960), 47–61.

1253.[24] During the intervening centuries, Thai peoples migrated southward over a wide area extending from India's Assam (a variant of Shan) province across northern Burma into the Shan and Laotian plateaus, to the very borders of Tongking and the Khmer Empire of Cambodia.

Such, then, were the principal geographical and ethnic factors which provided the context for the historical development of Southeast Asia. Attention must now be turned to the patterns of trade and cultural infiltration which importantly influenced the character of its early civilization.

[24] *Ibid.*

# CHAPTER 2

# Trade Patterns

## and the Process of Indianization

Trade was a perennial influence in the historical development of Southeast Asia. In association with agricultural and human resources, commercial currents influenced the rise and fall of political units, institutional changes, and the appropriation of alien religious and art forms.[1] Seaborne commerce traditionally followed the rhythm fixed by arrival and ending of the semiannual monsoon seasons on both sides of the peninsula. The principal commodities included perfumed woods and resins, gold and precious stones, and spices and other condiments from Southeast Asia itself; silken yarns and fabrics, tea, and porcelains from China; high-quality cotton textiles from India; glass items, rugs, and tapestries from the Near East; and objects of art from all areas.[2] The volume of the trade varied with market demands, the perils of piracy and shipwreck, the availability of convenient entrepôt centers, and the degrees of political stability prevailing throughout the trading arc extending from India to China. It can nevertheless be assumed that the character of the trade itself, intended as it was for princely and patrician consumption, changed but little from century to century. The transient peddlers, the temporary beach and market bazaars, the more permanent shops and warehouses, the eternal haggling of merchants with each other and with peasant producers, plus the activities of wandering adventurers were the universal and timeless characteristics of port centers. The commercial impact of neither India nor China became historically significant until the second century A.D.

This chapter will concern three problems connected with external commercial and cultural influences on the early history of Southeast Asia. One relates to the evolution of the trading patterns; a second concerns the reasons for the cultural fecundity of Indian contacts as compared with the relative sterility of influences emanating from China; a third covers the

[1] J. C. Van Leur, *Indonesian Trade and Society* (1955), 87–88.
[2] See Cyril Northcote Parkinson, *Trade in the Eastern Seas, 1713–1813* (1937).

nature and impact of the Indianizing process itself. The sources are fragmentary, so the answers must be tentative. But without some attempt to re-
construct the early situation the later story can hardly became intelligible.
The essential fact to be explained is that the cultural influence of India
attained overwhelming predominance during the early centuries of Southeast Asian history. Both the timing of the Indian impact and its intrinsic
qualities appear to have contributed to the outcome.

## China's Meager Role in Early Southeast Asian History

Despite Han China's annexation of its Vietnamese province near the
end of the second century B.C., which brought the Middle Kingdom into
close geographical proximity to Southeast Asia, China's role in the development of the early seaborne trade of the area was relatively unimportant.
This fact was attributable in some measure to the failure of Chinese authorities to maintain the naval power needed for suppressing the pirates who
infested the Fukien and Kwangtung coastal areas. The policing of the south
coast was regarded, apparently, as being not worth the effort required. The
Middle Kingdom's cultural and political center was located in the Yellow
River Valley, so that the distant coasts constituted only a little-used back
door leading to the barbarian world of the southern seas. In general, China
evinced no urge to civilize its southern neighbors, even though at a later
date it set no geographical bounds to the exercise of its political suzerainty
in the area.[3]

China's traditional outlet to the civilized world of India and the
Middle East long remained the overland silk road across Central Asia. It
was by this route that Buddhism reached China from India in the first
century A.D. In the late fourth century it was in reverse along the same route,
dotted at the time with monastic way stations, that the Chinese pilgrim Fa-
Hsien and others found their way back to India for the purpose of visiting
Buddhist shrines and assembling the Pali scriptures.[4] When the Han Chinese
undertook in the first century to develop shorter trade connections with
India, they selected the previously mentioned route from the upper Yangtse
basin through the gorges of the Mekong and Salween Rivers in western
Yunnan to the Irrawaddy Valley of Burma and thence to the coasts of the
Bay of Bengal. Proceeding westward in the winter winds, they made for
the Telingana and Kalinga areas of the eastern coast of India, where the
Mons also maintained their most persistent contacts. The special Chinese

[3] Lê Thanh Khôi, *Le Viet-Nam* (1955), 76–82. The beautifully decorated
bronze drums characterizing the Dongs'on culture of Vietnam were regarded by
the Chinese as barbaric.

[4] Van Leur, 80–87; Lê Thanh Khôi, 108–109. The Roman embassy of 166
reached China at Chiao-chi, or Cattigara, in Tongking. See Pierre Gourou, *The
Peasants of Tonkin Delta* (1955), 146–150.

prefecture of Yung ch'ang, covering the area of western Yunnan, was established in A.D. 69. This route continued to be used until after the collapse of the Han dynasty in the early third century; the Yung ch'ang prefecture was not abandoned until 342.[5]

Official Chinese use of the sea route to Southeast Asia for diplomatic contact with India also occurred during the first century A.D. The Chinese envoys destined for India proceeded cautiously around the shoreline from Kwangtung past Hainan Island to Vietnam and along the coasts of Annam and Cochin-China around to a point at the northwest corner of the Gulf of Siam. Debarking here in the civilized Mon state called Tun-sun by the Chinese, the envoys proceeded overland via the Meklong Valley and the Three Pagodas Pass to the estuary of Burma's Salween River at Martaban. From here they proceeded past the delta of the Irrawaddy and on up the coast of Arakan, whence they traversed a route to India much the same as the final stage of the commercial overland route. It was this same Tun-sun portage route from Martaban to the Gulf of Siam shore which was presumably used in 120 by a China-bound mission from the Roman Empire, which included musicians and jugglers. There is no clear indication, however, that the water route to India via Tun-sun, clearly known to the Chinese, was ever seriously exploited by them for commercial purposes. Occasional private Chinese junks, no doubt, braved the dangers of the southern seas down to various points on the northern and eastern Malay coasts. Fragments of Han porcelains are widely scattered. Patani was an early port of call, and the Emperor Wang Mang reportedly sent to Sumatra for rhinoceros horns. A few Chinese may have proceeded around the peninsula to the port of Takkola (Trang), but official Chinese initiative and participation in the early Southeast Asian trade were very meager.[6]

The reasons for the lack of Chinese interest in the south ocean trade can be surmised. In the first place the navigational hazards were great, and the inferior Chinese ships were obliged to sail close to shore long after Indonesian, Indian, and Arab ships had learned enough about seasonal winds and navigation to strike out across the open sea. The officials at South China ports, furthermore, did not encourage the uncontrolled activity of private traders—a policy which did characterize the urban port-centered kingdoms of India. Even after the attractive commercial possibilities of the south ocean trade became apparent in the second century, the officially acceptable trade from that area was confined for the most part to the Vietnamese port of Chiao-chi. Canton began to be widely used only in the sixth century. It was easier, and no doubt just as profitable, for port officials to control a segregated community of resident Southeast Asian traders operating on a seasonal rhythm than to encourage an expansion of Chinese ship-

[5] D. G. E. Hall, *A History of South-East Asia* (1955), 22, 35; M. Blackmore, "The Rise of Nan-Chao in Yunnan," *JSEAH,* I (1960), 47–48.

[6] Paul Wheatley, "The Historical Geography of the Malay Peninsula before A.D. 1500" (1958), 18–20.

ping. The so-called resident Po-ssŭ trading community at Chinese ports to which Chinese accounts of the early centuries make reference was probably composed of Sumatran or isthmian merchants trading in Persian-type perfumes, scented woods, resins, and pearls produced in and collected from tropical forests and coastal waters of Southeast Asia.[7]

In any case the initiative in the shuttle trade between China on the north and the Malay Peninsula and Sumatra on the south came at first almost entirely from the Malays. If Chinese traders penetrated the south ocean areas, they did so as passengers on Po-ssŭ ships operated by Malays or Indonesians. Even during rapid expansion of Chinese overseas trade in T'ang times (seventh to ninth century), with both Canton and Amoy serving as focal points, Chinese ships continued to be decidedly in the minority. Not until the widespread use of the compass (south-pointing needle) in Sung times (tenth and eleventh centuries) did Chinese shipping attain dominance of the sea routes along the southward monsoon channel to Southeast Asia.[8]

Regular trading contacts between Chinese and Southeast Asian ports were developed by the late second century on the initiative of a dozen or so partly Indianized city-states located on the shores of the Gulf of Siam. These port cities were grouped together into an empire or federation by Funan probably around the middle of the third century. Such trading operations were associated after 240 with the periodic dispatch of official tributary missions to Chinese courts with gifts advertising local wares. Commercial exchanges were made at southern Chinese ports of entry while the successive missions completed their leisurely journey to and from various Chinese courts. Tributary missions also afforded an opportunity for a new Southeast Asian ruler to seek Chinese authentication of his title, a move which could be especially useful in cases of rebellion or disputed succession. Chinese dynastic histories from the fourth to the seventh century (the advent of the T'ang) reported extensive trade by sea in the products of Southeast Asia, Ceylon, India, and the Near East, most of which continued to arrive in non-Chinese vessels.[9]

The advantage in cultural prestige gained for India by the prior impact on Southeast Asia of Indian traders was enhanced by the vogue which Indian Buddhism came to enjoy within China itself in post-Han times. The confusion prevailing during the course of four interim centuries from the Han to the T'ang dynasties cast discredit on Confucianism. Chinese scholars studied Sanskrit and Pali and made repeated pilgrimages to India.

[7] O. W. Wolters, "The 'Po-ssu Pine Trees'," *BSOAS,* XXIII (1960), 324–350; B. H. M. Vlekke, *Nusantara* (1960), 17.

[8] R. Braddell, "Notes on Ancient Times in Malaya," *JRASMB,* XXIII (February, 1950), 5–9.

[9] Between 243 and 287, Funan sent five missions to China; others followed at irregular intervals. See Hall, 23–31; F. Hirth and W. W. Rockhill, *Chau Ju-Kua* (1911), 5–8.

There was no corresponding study in India or Southeast Asia of the Confucian classics, and no missionary zeal emanating from Confucianist or Taoist sources in China emerged to match that of Indian Buddhism. Except in Vietnam, the transmission to Southeast Asian peoples of the knowledge of Chinese literature, law, and governmental institutions was, accordingly, virtually nil. It was during the fourth and fifth centuries, furthermore, when Chinese prestige was at low ebb, that India's Gupta Empire attained an all-time peak for Indian civilization. One characteristic effect was the decision of the independent Thai state of Nan Chao at the time to adapt for its method of writing the Sanskrit and Pali script rather than the Chinese character system.[10]

The Chinese impact on Southeast Asian affairs increased greatly after the seventh century with the reunification of the Middle Kingdom under the T'ang dynasty. But the T'ang rulers found it more convenient to authenticate the accession of friendly tributary rulers in Southeast Asia than to undertake to extend China's political control by outright conquest. Their repeated efforts to conquer the Thai state of Nan Chao in western Yunnan as a means of reopening the trade to Burma failed in the seventh and eighth centuries. The periodic sending of Southeast Asian tributary missions to China required the acknowledgment by visiting missions of inferior status, which itself virtually precluded Southeast Asian appropriation of Confucianist governmental forms. The Sinic world view was a closed system. The Chinese concept of the Emperor's exercise of the ruling mandate of heaven as the effective mediator between sky and earth was present in Southeast Asia, if at all, in the crude form of the assumed need for the ruler's placation of nature spirits. But much more dogmatic and compelling was the Indian affirmation of the ruler's actual divinity as an avatar of Śiva, Indra, or Vishnu. The Confucianist mandarinate system was far too sophisticated for appropriation by Southeast Asian peoples, who lacked any knowledge of Chinese cultural patterns and were already steeped in Indian lore. China eventually earned respect and deference from leading Southeast Asian peoples, but it was not accorded the compliment of cultural imitation, which they gave freely to Indian religious and governmental forms.

## Indian Trading Patterns

It can be assumed that fairly intimate trading connections existed from B.C. times between Indian ports of the Bay of Bengal and leading peoples like the Mons living on the opposite shores. But the primary direction of India's trade until near the end of the first century A.D. was westward rather than toward Southeast Asia or China. Trade between the Mediterranean world and India's western Malabar Coast was developed originally by traders from the lower Red Sea area and by the Hellenistic Seleucids. Roman trade from Egypt to India later attained substantial pro-

[10] Nguyen Khac Kham, *Characteristics of Vietnamese Culture* (1960), 1.

portions around 90 B.C., only to decline sharply during the ensuing sixty years of Roman civil strife. It was revived under Augustus around 30 B.C.[11] Until the first century A.D., when both Red Sea and Roman ships began to use the monsoon passage direct from Aden to India, the shipping routes had cautiously paralleled the Arabian, Persian, and Indian coasts.

This trade between the Roman Empire and India reached very substantial proportions during the century from Augustus to Vespasian (30 B.C. to A.D. 79). The goods were carried for the most part in non-Indian vessels, but India profited greatly. A commercial entrepôt developed at a port located on the southern coast of the island of Ceylon. Here the wares of the Roman world, India, Southeast Asia, and China were exchanged by South Asian merchants, paying little deference at first to the native Sinhalese authorities or population. Roman ships engaged annually in the India trade in A.D. 20 are estimated to have numbered around 120. Commercial activity by Indian coastal ships also increased through the channel between India and Ceylon and up the eastern Coromandel Coast of India. Contact was here made with Anuradapura in northern Ceylon, a large inland city adjacent to extensive irrigation works, which continued operating in northern Ceylon as late as the fifth century.[12]

The insistent demand for Oriental imports at Alexandria and Antioch had the effect of stimulating Indian and Southeast Asian traders to develop their contacts with the Malay Peninsula and beyond. Commodities desired by the Mediterranean world could be obtained either by direct seaborne passage to the South China coast or by moving in stages, shuttle-fashion, on both sides of the isthmus. Thus the more adventurous Indian traders already familiar with the opposite shores of the Bay of Bengal began collaborating with north Sumatran and east coast Malays to bring to the ports of Ceylon spices, forest resins, and scented woods from Southeast Asia and choice Chinese silks and porcelains, all of which were marketable in India and the Near East. Greek and Arab vessels seldom if ever proceeded further eastward than Ceylon, although several score families of Persian traders were allegedly resident at the Malay isthmus in the third century.

Near Eastern cargoes penetrating to the China market were of necessity luxury goods such as frankincense and myrrh, medicinal drugs, jewels, fine textiles and carpets, and glassware. From Southeast Asian sources, China also began to accept, as early as the second century, forest products such as pine resins, benzoin, camphor, scented woods, ebony, ivory, and condiments. The forest items in particular may have first gained entry into China as cheaper substitutes for the rare "Persian" drugs and perfumes of the Near East. This Po-ssŭ trade from Sumatra and the Malay Peninsula

---

[11] G. F. Hourani, *Arab Seafaring in the Indian Ocean in Ancient and Early Medieval Times* (1951), 23–25. Hourani identifies the Red Sea traders as Sabeans; others call them Uxumites or Ethiopians.

[12] F. Hirth, *China and the Roman Orient* (1885), 279–283; Humphrey William Codrington, *A Short History of Ceylon* (1929), 30–31.

eventually (by the third or fourth century) gained Chinese acceptance on its own merits.[13]

The bonanza of expanding commerce between India and Rome faded somewhat after the Emperor Vespasian (A.D. 69–79), alarmed by the rapid depletion of Rome's gold supply to pay for expensive Oriental products, prohibited the further export of bullion. Roman exports did not approximate in value the import demand in the Mediterranean for such bizarre Asian items as rare perfumes, pepper, spices, gems, ivory goods, and strange animals and exotic birds, and for more useful food commodities like India's sugar, rice, and ghee. Many Roman coins in gold and copper, extending in date from the first to the fourth century, have been found amid the ruins of the ancient ports of Ceylon and along India's Malabar Coast. Oriental trade with the Roman world continued to prosper moderately through the second century. Early in the second century the Emperor Trajan cleared the channel of the old canal connecting the Red Sea with the Nile River to facilitate passage. Rome sent successive missions to Cathay via the isthmus. An official one arrived in 120, and another in 166 was sponsored by Alexandrian and Antioch merchants. Similar missions followed in the third century.[14]

Rome's contacts with India declined sharply during the course of the third and fourth centuries. After 225, the Sassanid Persians took over commercially in a rather desultory fashion where the Greeks and Romans left off.[15] Indian attention shifted meanwhile to the Malay Peninsula as a source of gold, following discontinuance of the supply from Central Asia as well as from Rome. After the Sassanids conquered the lower Red Sea area in the fifth century, Persian and Red Sea trade was merged for a time. The Mediterranean and Persian markets for Oriental products revived during the eighth and ninth centuries, when Muslim Arab and Persian ships penetrated to Southeast Asia for the first time, and probably to Chinese ports as well. The trade played out in the tenth century, only to be revived again after the Crusades restored European contacts with the Near East.

## Early Trade Patterns from India to China

It was during the early second century that Indian shippers gained sufficient experience and confidence to abandon early habits of sailing close to the shore. From the Bengal port of Tamralipti at the western

[13] Hirth and Rockhill, 5–8; Wolters, 323–350.

[14] A. L. Basham, *The Wonder That Was India* (1954), 226–231; Hirth and Rockhill, 5–8. Indian loanwords borrowed by the Greeks were usually items of trade, including words for sugar and the spices. Arabian horses were eventually included in Red Sea exports to India.

[15] Hourani, 34–42. The Emperor Justinian tried in vain in the early sixth century to obtain Chinese silks via the Abyssinians; silk worms were eventually brought to Constantinople (by 550).

end of the Ganges delta, sailing ships could proceed southward during the winter season, passing either to the east of the Andaman Islands or via the 10° latitude channel south of them, en route to alternative ports on the isthmus. Bengal ships might also worry their way through the becalmed Malacca Straits to points of rendezvous in lower Sumatra or on the eastern Borneo coast beyond the peninsula. Access to the same isthmian ports and to the upper reaches of the Malacca Straits might be had during the entire period of the summer monsoon by south Indian ships sailing directly across the bay. They could pass either through the 10° channel between the Andamans and Nicobars or between the Nicobars and the northern tip of Sumatra. In October seasonal winds could also carry vessels to the southwest of Sumatra and down to the Sunda Straits, thus avoiding the pirates and the doldrums of the Malacca passage. The lack of ports of call and the perils of the open sea obviously discouraged the use of this route.

At the lower end of Sumatra, on the east coast of Borneo, and possibly at the western end of Java as well, safe havens were developed where China-bound ships from the ports of India, northern Sumatra, and Ceylon could await the north-blowing monsoon winds. From such points, it was fairly easy to proceed up the Malay coast past Patani, Singora, and Ligor across the Siam Gulf to Funan's port of Go Oc Eo near the mouth of the Mekong River. The journey then ran up the coast past Champa to Chiao-chi port in Vietnam or on to Canton. Ships sailing northward from eastern Borneo would probably make a landfall at Champa, which emerged as a thoroughly Indianized state at the end of the second century. The return trip by sea was equally time-consuming. It was particularly dangerous in the Malacca Straits, subject during the summer months to occasional stormy squalls ("Sumatrans") interspersed with extended periods of paralyzing calms which left stranded ships at the mercy of swarms of pirates.[16]

However many of the Sumatran and Indian ships may have undertaken during the early centuries to negotiate the seasonally awkward all-sea journey to the ports of China, the more feasible tactic was to synchronize the shuttle traffic to the isthmian portage terminals from the two directions. This was accomplished for the most part on the initiative of the Indian traders operating on both sides of the peninsula. The three most widely used portage routes ran between Takuapa (above the Junk Ceylon promontory) and Chaiya on the Bay of Bandon, between Trang (Takkola) and Ligor, and between Kedah and Patani (Lankasuka). The older route through the Mon state of Tun-sun (or Dvaravati) to Tavoy or Martaban on the western side was less used for the China trade than were the more convenient newly developed passageways below the Isthmus of Kra. Mergui port apparently was used very little.

At a dozen or more points on both sides of the isthmus, Indianized

---

[16] A. Grimes, "Journey of Fa-Hsien from Ceylon to Canton," *JRASMB*, XIX (1941), 76–92.

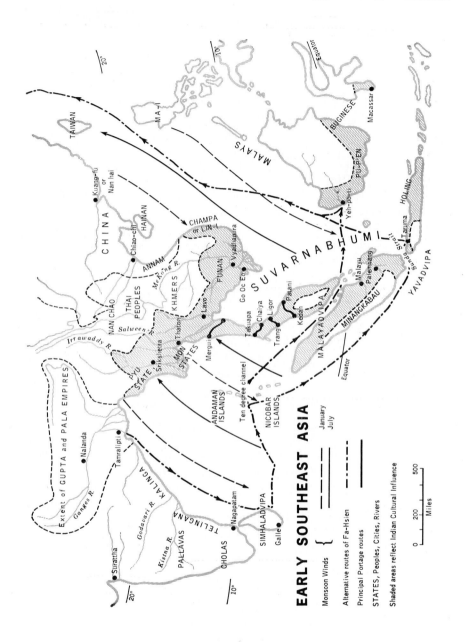

# EARLY SOUTHEAST ASIA

Monsoon Winds { January
               { July

Alternative routes of Fa-Hsien

Principal Portage routes

STATES, Peoples, Cities, Rivers

Shaded areas reflect Indian Cultural Influence

0    200    500
|————|————|
     Miles

city-states developed. They were apparently ruled by native chiefs allied with Indian merchant groups. The development of such states was conditioned not only on port locations and portage facilities, but also on the availability nearby of paddy land for food supplies. Except for the Perlis area around Trang, the best locations for food purposes and for political development were on the eastern shores, especially around Ligor and on the Bay of Bandon. None of these city-state enclaves was strong enough to conquer the rest of them, although several of them were grouped from time to time under single governments.[17]

Special reference must be made to the role of the port of Kedah, which was used for both portage purposes and as a point of rendezvous in connection with the passage through the Malacca Straits. It was most easily approached from the west via the passage between Sumatra and the Nicobar Islands during the summer monsoon. The silhouette of Mount Kedah afforded a landfall to guide approaching ships. The original port of Kedah was located up the then broad estuary of the Kuala Merbok, now swamp-filled, entering the sea some distance above Penang Island. Ruins in the vicinity have been explored on the higher ground to the north, adjacent to the foothills of the peak. In the course of time the centers of settlement moved seaward. Kedah was widely used by Indian traders from the early centuries of the Christian era and probably from the eighth century by Muslim Arabs and Persians. Products available locally, besides food and water supplies, included camphor, perfumed woods, tin, and gold. The port of Patani at the eastern end of the Kedah portage route was also used by Indian traders in the early second century. Kedah may have been used by ships making the northward trip through the straits en route to Bengal, the south Indian ports, or Ceylon.[18]

The Mons ports of Thaton, Martaban, and Tavoy were widely used for direct trade with Ceylon and the Coromandel Coast of India, but less so in connection with the transit trade with China. It was difficult to proceed from Bengal to the Mon ports during either monsoon period partly because of treacherous tidal currents found to the east of the Irrawaddy delta. Four routes of trade and communication led inland from the Tenasserim ports of the Mons. The northernmost ran eastward to the upper Menam Valley and thence to the Mun and Mekong Rivers, coming to a dead end in the Korat plateau at Bassac, early center of power of the Chenla Khmers. Another, used early by India-bound Chinese envoys, started at modern Moulmein, proceeded by the Three Pagodas Pass southeastward

[17] Braddell identifies Takkola with Trang; Majumdar identifies it with Takuapa. See also Wheatley, 263–264, 416–417.

[18] Wheatley, 353; Braddell, 33; H. G. Quaritch Wales, "Archeological Researches on Ancient Colonization in Malaya," *JRASMB*, XVIII (1940), 1–45. It is a bit surprising that Marco Polo's account of his passage through the straits in 1292 made no mention of Kedah, since the port continued in use by both Arabs and Chinese to the fourteenth century.

into the Meklong Valley and the Tun-sun (Dvaravati) country to the west
of the lower Menam. The other two ran eastward from Tavoy and Mergui
to the Gulf of Siam.[19] Neither of the latter two rivaled the importance of
the Takuapa and Trang portages.

## Fa-Hsien's Voyage from Ceylon to China

The perils attending the early attempts to negotiate the trip from
Ceylon to China were portrayed in some detail in the account by the famous
Chinese Buddhist pilgrim, Fa-Hsien, covering from 413 to 415. Instead of
retracing his arduous outward journey from China via the Khyber Pass
and Central Asia, Fa-Hsien decided to take a ship from Tamralipti port
in Bengal to Ceylon and to proceed thence to China by sea. From Bengal,
he reached Ceylon in fourteen days, sailing in late 411 or early 412. He
described a great Sinhalese trading entrepôt and also praised Ceylon as
an important center of Hinayana Buddhist scholarship. He referred to
two Buddhist temples in particular, one developed around an alleged
footprint of the Buddha and the other housing a sacred tooth. Fa-Hsien
remained in Ceylon for two years completing his collection of manuscripts
of the Pali scriptures. He eventually departed for the Malay coast, probably in mid-September and presumably on an Indian vessel. Apparently
the navigator was attempting at the very end of the summer monsoon to
pass between the Nicobar Islands and Sumatra, hoping to take advantage
of the easterly October winds blowing down the Sumatran coasts. The main
ship had two hundred persons aboard, mainly merchants, and it had a
smaller vessel in tow for safety purposes. After two days of favorable
winds, the vessels encountered a thirteen-day storm which drove them off
course and caused the larger ship to leak dangerously near the water line.
The crew of the smaller ship cut it loose when the panicked merchants attempted to transfer to it. The damaged ship managed to remain afloat only
because all heavy cargo was thrown overboard.

The actual course which the ship followed has become a matter of dispute. It was beached for repairs on the shore of some pirate-infested island located either near the north point of Sumatra or in the Nicobar-
Andaman group. The traditional view has been that the interrupted eastward voyage, which lasted for a total of ninety additional days, was resumed
via the open sea to the southwest of Sumatra and that the vessel eventually
passed through the Sunda Straits to a landing in late December of 414 or
January of 415 on the western end of Java. This view is supported by
the ship's obvious need to avoid encounter with pirates and by the lack
of any mention by Fa-Hsien of landfalls encountered en route. If to the
fifteen days of initial sailing is added several additional days for repairs,
the seasonal October wind pattern down the west Sumatran coast would

[19] H. G. Q. Wales, *Towards Angkor in the Footsteps of the Indian Invaders*
(1937), 163.

probably have been adequate for the passage. On the other hand, if the storm was a typical September cyclone blowing from the southwest, the halt for repairs could have been made as far north as the Andaman Islands. In this case, passage to the south and eastward below Sumatra would have been difficult if not impossible. Fa-Hsien's failure to mention any pirate encounters during the sailing and his frightening description of a voyage over a sea "without bottom and with no place to anchor" which continued for more than ninety days suggests something other than a journey down the island-bordered and pirate-infested Malacca Straits.[20] But whether the eventual landing at the port called Yeh-po-ti was made in western Java or on the western coast of Borneo, the trip was obviously a harrowing one, and especially so to a Chinese unaccustomed to ocean travel.

The pilgrim's trials were far from over when he reached the safety of Yeh-po-ti. After five or six months of delay, Fa-Hsien and his party embarked on another Indian or Southeast Asian ship of similar size destined for China. Storms again struck the ship. It was driven for sixty to eighty days before the wind until both food and water were exhausted. On the assumption that the Chinese Buddhist party was an ill-fated omen, Hindu partisans threatened to throw Fa-Hsien overboard. They were prevented, allegedly, only by fear of probable vengeance from the pro-Buddhist Chinese ruler. A landfall was finally made on the coast of Shantung province in northern China, where Fa-Hsien served helpfully as interpreter for Indian merchant passengers. Almost a full year had elapsed since his leaving Ceylon.[21]

It cannot be assumed, of course, that all vessels attempting the all-water trip from India to China encountered the same dismal fortunes of those transporting Fa-Hsien, but the account is nevertheless highly instructive. The passage was by no means a novel enterprise. But the Indian navigator's attempt to cut corners by making the passage to Malaya and down the straits from south India in the early autumn season was demonstrably dangerous. As previously mentioned, the feat was probably more easily feasible during the winter monsoon from the ports of Bengal. Until such time as experience could be gained and better facilities developed for traversing the sea route, Indian traders preferred to remain in the Bay of Bengal. They therefore utilized alternative routes for commercial intercourse with China via Mon Dvaravati or, more frequently, across the various portage routes developed south of the Kra isthmus.

Most vessels proceeding to China from Ceylon or south India probably used the late-summer winds for the eastward passage to a landfall at Takkola (Trang) or Mount Kedah on the Malay coast. At a trading center there they waited for favorable northerly winds to proceed southward through the straits. The slowness of the straits passage and the

20 Herbert A. Giles (trans.), *The Travels of Fa-hsien,* or *Record of Buddhist Kingdoms* (1923 and 1956), 108–110; Grimes, 76–92.

21 Giles, 90–110.

danger from pirates suggest the advantage of their sailing in convoy groups. This tactic then entailed another delay at some additional point of rendezvous, perhaps on the eastern Borneo or south Sumatran coast, before a second summer monsoon season arrived to take them northward on the last portion of the China voyage. The interim periods could be used for local trading. Similar delays were encountered on the return journey. The round trip from India to China thus usually consumed the better part of a year and a half, but the trip was safer than Fa-Hsien's harrowing voyage, and it afforded opportunity for trading along the way.

A final significant statement in the account of Fa-Hsien's voyage is his report that orthodox Buddhism (presumably the Hinayana type) was not present at all in Yeh-po-ti, whether it was located in western Borneo or at the Sunda Straits. "Heretics and Brahmans," he reported, "are numerous there, [but] the law of Foe [Buddhism] is in no wise entertained."[22] The crews of the ships on which he took passage, and the merchant passengers as well, were apparently partisan Hindus rather than Buddhists. The conclusion that the early Indian traders penetrating the South China Sea were predominantly Hindu receives a measure of confirmation from the Hindu character of the early archaeological remains found not only at Kedah and at the Sunda Straits but also at other possible way stations located on the western coast of Borneo and in mainland Champa. Buddhism, by contrast, was apparently much stronger than Hinduism in territories ruled by the Mons, who had long enjoyed intimate contact with India and Ceylon; and the same was true for the portage cities of the isthmus.

## The Historic Sources of Indianization

The India from whose culture Southeast Asian peoples borrowed so extensively was partly united for the first time politically in the third century B.C. The Mauryan Empire (330 to 180 B.C.) included the north Indian valleys westward to Greek Bactria and southward along the eastern Indian coast to the mouths of the Kistna and Godavari Rivers. Mauryan power centering at Patna in the lower Ganges Valley reached its peak in the mid-third century B.C. under the leadership of the great Asoka, who was a political exemplar of Buddhist ideals and humanitarian principles of government. Asoka unified and promoted the Buddhist faith without persecuting dissident elements; he built India's first shrines of cut stone and burned brick; he sponsored missionary efforts within India and beyond. Mauryan rule declined rapidly after his death in 237 B.C.

The successor Pallavan, or Andhra, state of the Telegus (230 B.C. to A.D. 225), centering in the Kistna and Godavari Valleys of the Deccan, was the contemporary of Han China. It was strongly but not exclusively Hindu. It contributed substantially to the early phases of India's cultural influence on Southeast Asia, which came largely from south India. The

22 *Ibid.*, 111–112.

characteristic art forms of Amaravati (the Pallavan capital), both Buddhist and Hindu, have been found at widely dispersed points in Southeast Asia.

A century after the decline of Pallavan Telegu leadership, the Gupta Empire (320 to 500) revived the traditional supremacy of north India, centering again at Patna in the Ganges basin. It was only a little smaller geographically than the Mauryan had been, including at one time the region extending from Assam to the Punjab and down the eastern coast into the Telegu country. Culturally the Gupta period provided an unexcelled expression of Hindu civilization. It reflected the humanitarian influence of the Buddhist faith but also represented a creative and tolerant Hinduism. Buddhism continued strong in Bengal, in the Punjab, and in Ceylon, but the variant Mahayana (greater vehicle) form was gaining vogue in north India.[23] The empire reached its peak under Chandra Gupta II (375–415). His rule was glowingly praised by the Chinese pilgrim Fa-Hsien as mildly administered, prosperous, and peaceful; travelers could proceed unmolested everywhere within the state without passports or special protection. Hospitals were available for the sick, and vegetarianism was widely practiced. Sculptured figures in the Gupta style were characterized by robes resembling transparent garments through which body and limbs were clearly visible. In its day, Gupta India was alleged to be the "happiest and most civilized country in the world."[24]

Although the influence of Vishnu and Śiva cults was by no means absent, Buddhist missionary influences during Gupta times were directed southward toward Ceylon and eastward toward the Pyu, the Mons, and the portage section of the Malay isthmus. Ceylon became a fountainhead of the Hinayana faith. As previously indicated, Fa-Hsien reported a large Hinayana Buddhist community in Ceylon, but found no orthodox Buddhists along the sea route to China.[25] The exodus from India during Gupta times and under the Buddhist Emperor Harsha (605–646) probably included also a large number of emigrants of the Kshatriya (warrior or princely) caste from both the Ganges and the Coromandel Coast areas. Pallavan emigrants from Kanchi played a major role during the fifth century in the Hindu revival in the isthmian state of P'an P'an and in the lower Mekong Valley.[26]

The Gupta Court in particular patronized the best artistic and literary talent, working generally to adjust indigenous pre-Aryan forms to Hindu themes. It produced the epic Sanskrit poetry of Kalidesa and the collation of Indian historical traditions known as the *Puranas,* a kind of popular scripture and a source of moral principles, monotheist in tendency, which gained wide favor in Southeast Asia. Gupta Empire con-

[23] Pierre Dupont, "Les Buddhas dits d'Amaravati en Asie du Sud-Est," *BEFEO,* XLIX (1959), 631–636; Basham, 117, 213.

[24] Basham, 65–66.

[25] Wales, *Towards Angkor,* 29–35.

[26] G. Coedès, *Les États Hindouisés* (1948), 413–414.

tributions to Southeast Asian culture also included the transference of the older legal Code of Manu, along with the classic political treatises, art forms in architecture, sculpture, painting, music, and dancing, and the religious sanctions buttressing governmental authority.[27]

The basic political classics of Hindu literature transmitted to Southeast Asia, including the Code of Manu, the *Santiparvan* from the *Mahabharata* epic, and the Arthasastra, were masterpieces of political realism. The king must protect his people from injustice and violence, refrain from evil, and eschew caprice, malice, and brute force. But in times of distress and crisis, he must be prepared to employ deception, simulate tearful trust when facing disaster, and be at heart as sharp as a razor toward his foe.[28] All servants of the ruler had to be tested for their loyalty and spied upon, under the assumption that none was completely trustworthy. In foreign policy an inferior prince made peace; a superior made war; neutrality was more appropriate in a stalemate while a double policy of peace and war was sometimes advantageous. Treachery, murder, intrigue, pretense of friendship were praised as effective weapons.[29] One Hindu symbol of monarchial power widely used in Southeast Asia was the white umbrella. It represented the protective sheltering *Dharma,* or firmament of the law, and the ultimate sovereign power, whose instrument the king became when he received the umbrella during the coronation ritual. But the theoretical obligation which it imposed, according to the Code of Manu, to place public welfare above personal desires, was largely lost in the cynical realism of the political treatises.[30]

By 500, Indian access to Central Asia was cut off by the White Huns and other invaders from the northwest. When the later-famous Chinese pilgrim-scholar I-Ching came to India in the 670s, he was obliged to travel by sea. By this time, order had disappeared within north India. The pilgrim was repeatedly robbed in his journeys between Tamralipti port and the Buddhist University of Nalanda located in the Ganges Valley. The same I-Ching discovered that the lower Sumatran port center of Śrivijaya (modern Palembang) was in that day a thriving center of Buddhist studies little inferior to Nalanda itself. During the period from around 650 to 670, the Malacca Straits had apparently come into general use by traders en route to China.

Pallavan dominance along the Coromandel Coast from 500 to 700 was eventually eclipsed (after 900) by the rising Chola Empire of the

[27] W. Norman Brown, *The United States and India* (1953), 21–22.

[28] D. W. Brown, *The White Umbrella* (1953), 35–48. For example: "A king should be farsighted as a vulture, patient like a crane, vigilant like a dog, valiant like a lion, fearful like a crow. . . . The king who does not crush a foe reduced to subjection by military force, provides for his own death."

[29] *Ibid.,* 49–52.

[30] *Ibid.,* 157–161. The white-umbrella symbol was used at Southeast Asian courts down to the nineteenth and twentieth centuries.

Tamils.[31] South Indian states and Bengal profited from their remoteness from the repeated Central Asia invasions of northwest India and the Ganges Valley and doubtless also from their growing participation in overseas trade with Southeast Asia and China.

Sinhalese Buddhism continued vigorous not only because of the close trade relations Ceylon had with Buddhist Bengal but also because of the exodus of Buddhist exiles from the neighboring Chola state, especially during the 900s. The Cholas eventually extended their conquest to Ceylon, in 1017. It was from Ceylon that the Hinayana Buddhism of Burmans, Mons, Khmers, Laotians, and Thai drew inspiration following its disappearance in India.[32]

## Hinduism as It Affected Southeast Asia

Hinduism as a cultural system was far too complex and deeply rooted in the context of India itself to be capable of transfer to Southeast Asia in any complete way. It included many sects and many philosophical systems; its religious values were relative to time and place, to a person's social level, and also to his intellectual and spiritual capacity to discern. Its cohesion in India derived from tenacity of social custom and from the organized caste structure in particular. Hinduism was thus a religious accumulation derived from all periods of India's history; primitive cults of fertility, hero reverence, and sun worship were combined with Aryan governmental practices and overlaid with an elaborate system of philosophical speculation. Hinduism countenanced almost every level of religious belief from crude animism to metaphysical monism.

Hinduism could be transferred, therefore, only in a selective way. Sophisticated Indians affirmed the mystical principle that the phenomenal world was illusion (*maya*) and that the ultimate reality of all life was Brahma, the indestructible soul of the universe. Failure to realize the soul's potential identity with the absolute essence (through mystical and ascetic exercises) bound an individual to phenomenal existence in a physical body through an endless series of rebirths. Persons of inferior spiritual capacities conceived their relative levels of truth in more tangible symbols. Moral and social duties in India thus varied according to caste status, itself determined by karma, or the law of deeds, which derived its character from previous existences. Neither the full philosophical implications of Brahmanism nor the full scope of the caste system proved capable of transference to Southeast Asian peoples. Southeast Asia's matrilineal tradition also rejected for the most part the severe restraints imposed by Hinduism upon women, such as seclusion, suttee, and child marriage.)

For persons unable to grasp the truth of Brahma, the Hindu pan-

[31] W. H. Moreland and A. C. Chatterjee, *A Short History of India* (1953), 83–85, 102–103, 118–119.

[32] Coedès, 413–414.

theon provided two rival gods, each capable of theoretical embodiment in many variant forms. Śiva, the destroyer, personified the principle of attrition, the malevolent or destructive aspects of time which devours all, neither compassionate nor forgiving. His wives, especially Parvati and Kali, assumed the role of the universal mother. The *linga,* or phallic symbol, was widely employed. During the development of Hinduism in India, Śiva worship absorbed a large number of pre-Aryan spirit cults. It did the same in Southeast Asia, where an easy accommodation was made to indigenous animistic worship of the godlings of forest, rivers, and mountains and of the earth goddess of fertility and to various expressions of supernatural malevolence.

The second god, Vishnu, and his favorite wife, Lakshmi, represented the more optimistic principles of restoration and prosperity. Krishna and Rama, the heroes of the *Bhagavad-Gita (Song of the Blessed One)* and of the *Ramayana* epic respectively, were conceived as incarnations of Vishnu. Rama represented ideal kingship, and his wife, Sita, represented the highest pattern of motherhood.[33] For various reasons, Vishnu found less wide acceptance than Śiva among the peoples of Southeast Asia. Cult practices appropriate to both gods were nevertheless widely copied. Images of Śiva and Vishnu, whether used in India or in Southeast Asia, could be symbolic intellectual principles to the sophisticated and at the same time crude idols to the simpler folk. In the Hinduized states, the divine rulers were frequently represented as *avatars* (reincarnations) of either Śiva or Vishnu.

Three other religio-political principles borrowed from Hindu culture were widely appropriated in Southeast Asia, often in combination. The first of these was derived from the idea that magical astrological forces emanating from the cardinal points of the compass and from heavenly bodies determined the destiny of individuals and states. Indian cosmology identified Mount Meru, the abode of the gods, as the cosmic center of the universe (Jambudvipa), around which the sun, moon, and stars revolved. Mount Meru was allegedly protected by eight guardian gods and surrounded by seven concentric rings of mountains and eight ocean belts separating it from the four man-inhabited islands located at the cardinal points of the compass. The city of the gods occupied the mountain's central summit. Buddhist as well as Hindu countries in Southeast Asia demanded as an important requirement for stable governmental authority the location of the royal palace at the exact center of the universe, magically determined by learned astrologers. The divine authority of Southeast Asian rulers was thus derived not only from their status as divine reincarnations but also in large measure from their occupancy of a palace conceived as a mundane Mount Meru.

Buddhist rulers as well as Hindu princes frequently identified themselves as agents or reincarnations of the ancient storm god Indra (derived from Rudra, the Aryan god of sky and storm), representing kingly

[33] W. Norman Brown, 28–33.

authority and power. Thus the Pyu capital at Old Prome (Śrikshetra) was allegedly built by Indra. Its gates, each protected by a sacrificed guardian spirit, numbered thirty-two, a multiple of eight and four, and the thirty-two provinces of the Pyu state plus the capital corresponded to the thirty-three gods, including Indra, who were supposed to reside on Mount Meru. Preoccupation with the numbers four, eight, sixteen, and thirty-two as attributes of the famous Mount Meru was a persistent legacy of all Southeast Asian courts. The same symbolism for kingly authority has been identified in the fourteenth-century Pegu state of the Mons. Burma's coronation building at Pagan was designated "Indra's palace," and around the enthroned Burmese king eight Brahman priests served as specialists in cosmologic magic and acted as counterparts of the eight guardian gods of Mount Meru. The royal regalia—crown, sword, and white umbrella—also symbolized magical authority under the Indian tradition of royalty. Kings of Burma and Thailand normally had a palace of four walls, with gates in multiples of fours, plus four major queens, four chief ministers, and four assistant ministers.[34]

A third symbol of royalty was the multiple-headed Naga snake, traditional god of the soil. The fabulous role of the Naga spirit was to combine the magical resources of soil fertility with the royal principle of ownership and sovereignty over the land. In peninsular Southeast Asia it was widely applied and identified immediately with the indigenous fertility god of the soil. Kings often attributed their credentials as rulers to the alleged marriage of an ancestor with the beauteous daughter of the Naga snake. The royal symbol of the Naga's head has been long used in Thailand and Cambodia, and somewhat less frequently in Burma.

## Indian Buddhism in Its Variant Forms

Buddhism appeared in India during the sixth century B.C. as part of a protest against the presumptuous claims of Brahman priestly superiority and the degrading implications of caste. It was associated with the teachings and personality of Gautama, a Kshatriya-caste prince of the minor Indian state of Oudh. In revulsion against the brutality of warfare and suppression, Gautama left his throne and his family and became an ascetic and mendicant. His Buddhahood, or enlightenment, provided a new interpretation of life and destiny. It was based on characteristic Hindu premises of maya and karma, but the new faith emphasized moral principles of conduct as affording an escape from the otherwise endless and burdensome gyrations of the wheel of existence.

Gautama's message was for ordinary men. It afforded a practical moral approach to life, not dependent on spells or priestly magic. Life's

[34] Robert Heine-Geldern, "Conceptions of State and Kingship in Southeast Asia" (1956), 1–8.

suffering, he affirmed, stemmed from desire, which could be conquered by following the meritful eightfold path of right belief, aspiration, speech, action, honest livelihood, sustained mental exertion, alertness, and serenity. Buddhist teachings provided the inspiration for the splended reign of Emperor Asoka in the third century B.C., and they became the basis of much of the ethical appeal which India's culture later held out to leading peoples of Southeast Asia.

In its original interpretations, Buddhism placed everyone on his own, with no possibility of borrowed merit. It condemned outright as sinful or criminal such deeds as stealing, deceit, adultery, murder, and drinking of intoxicants. Buddhism accepted much Hindu legend, mythology, and folk-lore. It affirmed the principle of the sacredness of all life with its corollary obligation of *ahimsa,* noninjury to men and animals. The Buddhist goal of Nirvana, a merging with the absolute essence, thus ending life's cycle of suffering existences, corresponded to the Hindu principle of Brahma, except that the Buddhist path to the goal was one of righteous living, serenity, and peace, theoretically available to all men. By implication, Buddhism rejected priestly magic and the elaborate Hindu pantheon of the gods, but it was not dogmatic and was therefore subject to reinterpretation. It was missionary in spirit, not because it presumed to set forth any final or exclusive statement of truth, but rather because its message was broadly humanitarian and its appeal intended for all stations and races of men.[35]

Some indication of the spirit and teachings of orthodox Indian Buddhism as it developed at the famous Nalanda monastery in the Ganges Valley can be gleaned from the writings of the Chinese pilgrim I-Ching, who visited the place during the last quarter of the 600s. The monastery at the time housed three thousand monks and had two hundred villages assigned to its support. The recluse-scholars were free of administrative responsibilities and of concern for providing food and clothing needs. According to I-Ching, Buddhism favored forest contemplation over the "noisy pursuit of fame and profit" and also deprecated land cultivation, which carried the hazards of taking the lives of creatures living in the soil. Drinking water must be strained, not to purify it for human consumption, but to avoid the possible sin of swallowing live organisms present in the water. The monks were nevertheless permitted to accept pieces of silken cloth presented to them, since, in I'Ching's view, there was really no point in being over-meticulous about the sin of taking the life of the silkworm. The Buddhist view was lugubrious but not hopeless:

*Life here below . . . is but a dungeon for beings who have gone astray but look eagerly for the shore of Nirvana, which is the open gate of enlightenment and quietude. The ship of the Law should be manned ready for the sea of suffering, and the lamp of wisdom should be held up during the long*

[35] Moreland and Chatterjee, 40–43.

*period of darkness. . . . Each individual must himself be responsible for the*
*results of his own practices, whether good or bad.*[36]

The variant form of Buddhism called Mahayana (greater vehicle)
developed to its full expression in the middle Ganges area during Gupta
times. It succeeded by the mid-seventh century in entirely supplanting in
India the simpler Hinayana, or Theravada (teacher's), sect, only to succumb
itself to Hinduism in time.[37] The Mahayana system included three innovations which were important in strengthening its impact on Southeast Asia.
In the first place, it posited the not unreasonable proposition that Gautama
was only the most recent of a long series of Enlightened Ones and that other
Buddhas would doubtless follow him. It also affirmed the possibility of the
transference of merit of Buddhist saints about to enter into Nirvana, who
generously elected to endure life's suffering a little longer in order to help
struggling brethren along the path. They drew aid, as it were, from a kind
of Buddhist treasury of grace. A third idea closely associated with the other
two established the Bodhisattva status of near divinity for a meritful ruler
who could be presumed to qualify as an emergent Buddha. This idea was
perennially popular with the rulers of Buddhist countries of Southeast Asia,
who frequently aspired to the pretensions of Bodhisattva status as a kind
of substitute for royal divinity denied to them as a reincarnation (avatar)
of Śiva, Vishnu, or Indra. Mahayana Buddhism in Southeast Asia frequently
degenerated into corrupted and magical forms. In Java and Cambodia in
particular, Buddhist courts found the transition fairly easy back to Śiva or
Vishnu worship as providing a more effective religious sanction to the
authority of the divine ruler.[38]

In its acceptability to the peoples of Southeast Asia Buddhism was
strong where Hinduism was weak, and vice versa. As a revealed faith re-
pudiating caste and race, Buddhism could be transmitted by Indian missionary devotees and also by Southeast Asian converts and pilgrims. It was
also a trader's religion. Hinduism, on the other hand, could be transmitted
only by high-caste immigrants, Kshatriya or Brahman. Hinduism buttressed
royal authority through the system of divine kingship, synthetically achieved
by priestly intervention. Apart from the indispensable services of Brahman
advisers at coronations, they assisted the rulers as clerks and scribes, as
astrologers and numerologists, and also in the development of larger-scale
systems of administration, revenue, and military operation. Buddhism, by
contrast, could contribute little to political authority or government, except
insofar as kings might choose to exploit the Bodhisattva principle. On the
other hand, Hinduism was unable to attract the degree of popular accept-

[36] J. Takakusu (trans.), *I-Ching: A Record of the Buddhist Religion as Prac-*
*ticed in India and the Malay Archipelago* (1896), I, 53–61, 65–66, 72.

[37] King Harsha's Council excluded the Hinayana sect in 643.

[38] See L. P. Briggs, "The Syncretism of Religions in Southeast Asia,"
*JAOS,* LXXI (1951), 239–247.

ance so widely accorded to the more democratic Buddhist faith. Caste was not transferable in its full sense to the peoples of Southeast Asia. Lacking popular roots, the Hindu cult was dependent on royal favor and therefore on the vagaries of rulership, such as war, economic disaster, or governmental decay. Although remnants of the Hindu cultural impact long survived in many areas of Southeast Asia, the vitality of Śiva and Vishnu worship ebbed away not long after direct cultural contact was lost with sources in India.[39]

## *The Process of Indianization*

The several attempted explanations of the process of Indianization in the various regions of Southeast Asia vary rather widely. They agree only in the conclusions that it was accomplished by peaceful and nonpolitical means, that Indian culture was ingratiating and assimilable in terms of indigenous traditions, and that it proved particularly attractive to local ruling princes.[40]

One leading south Indian historian argues that substantial colonies of resident Indian merchants, intermarrying locally, became the basic transmitters of India's culture. Political and social leaders in such communities enlisted the services of Brahman priests from India capable of magical intervention with higher powers. Indian liaison was also enhanced, he suggests, by the presence of adventurous Kshatriya plunderers, who married into the local ruling families and subsequently procured Brahmans to buttress their political authority. The earliest inscriptions, he points out, were invariably written by literate Brahmans in good Sanskrit, linguistic adulterations from the local tongues appearing in them at later stages. Indian residents included clever imposters who themselves posed impressively as possessors of magical healing powers, as exorcisers of spirits, as numerologists, and as astrologers. The logic of this explanation suggests that coastal ports would be the most thoroughly Hinduized and that Indianization would be roughly proportional to the strength and persistence of the trading-adventurer relationship.[41] Buddhism eventually gained recognition by its own intrinsic appeal and also as a response to the inevitable protest against divine kingship and incipient caste discriminations.[42]

Georges Coedès, in his pioneering study of the early Hinduized states, agreed in many particulars with the picture presented by the Indian historians. He characterized the local populations as passive recipients, awed by the impressive demonstration of the expansive power of Indian culture, the dynamic nature of which the Indians themselves only dimly perceived. The

[39] *Ibid.*

[40] Richard Winstedt, *Malaya and Its History* (1957), 24–27.

[41] K. A. Nilakanta Sastri, *South Indian Influences in the Far East* (1949), 122–130.

[42] R. C. Majumdar, *Ancient Indian Colonies in the Far East: II, Suvarnadvipa* (1955), 91–111.

cultural role of the merchant colonies, involving intermarriages at increasingly higher social levels, was described as effective in spite of ritual obstacles to Brahman departures from India and the presumed anti-Indian racial prejudices of the Southeast Asians themselves.[43] Coedès attributed the acceptability of Hindu religious symbols among peoples of Southeast Asia to the assumed remarkable similarities of the indigenous cultures within the two areas. Hinduism thus accomplished in areas of its major impact in Southeast Asia essentially the same process of assimilation of spirit cults which it had just completed in south India. Śiva worship provided in both regions the most adaptable agency for such amalgamation. This theory made of the Hinduizing process far less an exclusively aristocratic movement than others have assumed it to be. Brahman priests functioned to complete the merger with local cults, to make rulers avatars of Hindu gods, to concoct impressive royal genealogies, and eventually to transmit Hindu literature, legal codes, and governmental forms.[44]

Although serious objections have been leveled against the "Indian merchant colonies" explanation of the Indianizing process, it probably contains elements of historical truth. This explanation could well apply in certain areas lacking vigorous indigenous political and cultural development and in ports which became especially important to Indian colonist-traders as commercial entrepôt centers. In such categories would be the western terminal points of the important portage regions, Trang and Takuapa and probably Kedah also in its beginnings. But Buddhism was stronger among merchant groups than Hinduism. The earliest Sanskrit inscriptions found at Kedah, dating from the fourth century, are Buddhist.[45] Early Palembang probably developed its original importance in the sixth and seventh centuries as an entrepôt containing an influential Indian merchant colony. The same could be true for Indianized ports on the west coast of Borneo and also in some measure for the ports of Champa. Nevertheless, such places developed as Indianized societies rather than as colonies of Indians.

The "Indian merchant colonies" explanation is clearly inadequate for many regions. Some of the strongest centers of Indian influence, such as central Java, Mon Dvaravati, Cambodian Angkor, and Pagan Burma, were not centers of seaborne commercial intercourse at all, but rather advanced political entities in their own right. The Dutch scholar Van Leur has argued, furthermore, that peddlers, who made up the preponderance of the merchant community at all trading posts, could not become the effective transmitters of sophisticated Hindu, or even Buddhist, culture. Most port cities were controlled by a local oligarchy or aristocracy, which enforced trading regulations, monopolized political power, asserted ownership of

---

[43] Coedès, 419–424.

[44] *Ibid.*, 33–36, 45–52; see also J. C. Van Leur, *Indonesian Trade and Society* (1955), 96–98.

[45] Winstedt, 128.

adjacent land, and also conducted trading operations in its own right. The social and political distance was very great between this patriciate and the mass of resident peddler traders drawn from many countries. The latter lived, as a rule, in their own several quarters of the city as self-contained communities. The status of such traders probably changed but little over the centuries, according to Van Leur. They were shrewd bargainers who knew market possibilities and prices over the vast extent of the trading arc from India to China. But they probably possessed neither the inclination nor the capacity to concern themselves with the transmission of cultural forms.[46]

It was therefore, according to Van Leur's theory, the local port patricians and princes themselves who usually took the initiative in appropriating Indian culture. To facilitate the enhancement of governmental authority and extension of their princely domains, the local rulers enlisted the services of learned Brahmans from India to perform useful functions at their emerging courts. These were used to legitimize dynastic authority, to exploit their mastery of astrology and numerology, and to assist in expanding governmental operations generally. Van Leur's point of view is supported by the complete lack of evidence of any substantial amalgamation of Hindu-native offspring at the higher levels of Indonesian or Mon society and the similar absence of widespread local adoption of the caste system or of Indian vernacular languages. Consecration formulas, royal edicts, and charters were invariably couched in the sacral language of the learned Brahman priests. In the advanced political communities of Southeast Asia, Indian cultural influence probably emanated from the court or the royally endowed temples, monasteries, and hermitages, rather than from the trading community.[47] Another Dutch scholar has summarized this view as follows:

> *The so-called "Hindu-colonization process" is reduced, in the modern conception, to the presence at the Javanese courts of a comparatively small number of very influential Indian Brahmins, lending political support to Javanese rulers by providing them with a kind of investiture and with a genealogic confirmation of membership in a high caste, and acting at the same time as advisers in affairs of government and things sacral.*[48]

Whereas Hinduization was mainly an aristocratic process, Buddhism involved cultural transfer at popular levels. Pilgrimages of Southeast Asian monks and scholars to Indian mainland monasteries and, in the case of the Hinayana sect, to Ceylon were commonplace. Endowed hostelries were established periodically at convenient points in India such as Negapatam and Nalanda for the care and entertainment of such pilgrims. Southeast Asian Buddhist scholars trained in India or Ceylon could be called back

[46] Van Leur, 66–68, 100–105.
[47] *Ibid.*, 96–105.
[48] W. F. Wertheim, *Indonesian Society in Transition* (1956), part I, 274.

home to fill prominent posts at court or in monasteries. The vogue of
Buddhism in early Southeast Asia coincided with the visits of large numbers
of such pilgrims to India in Gupta and post-Gupta times. It is more than
likely that the vast majority of the hundreds of Buddhist scholars whom the
Chinese pilgrim I-Ching found studying at Śrivijaya during his visits from
671 to 695 were indigenous Malays or Javanese.[49] It is also highly probable
that some Southeast Asian students visiting India may have advanced
Brahman pretensions when they returned.

## Southeast Asian Appropriation of Indian Culture

Several final questions concern the thoroughness of the Indianizing
process. Did Hinduism and Buddhism overwhelm the indigenous culture
patterns, or were they merely an accretion added as a veneer to the traditional systems? Did contributions from India provide Southeast Asia with a
cultural base from which further progress was possible?

The broad cultural gaps between cosmopolitan port cities dependent
for food on imported grain, the court-oriented capitals with their Indianized atmosphere and their highly articulate symbolization of political authority, and the rural villages producing food and forest products under
traditional social and religious patterns were never completely closed. The
history of the region, in fact, drew its dynamics from just such contrasting
situations. The alien trader vied with the local potentate; rulers who were
bent on personal glorification and monument construction were forced in
time to come to terms with a people wincing under heavy tax and *corvée*
exactions and the burdens of warfare. Even so, the impact of Indian culture
was massively impressive down to the time of its diminution in the late
thirteenth century. It demonstrated its genius for incorporating local deities
and religious practices, reinterpreting them as variants of the great Vedic
tradition. Thus, indigenous traditions concerned with worship of the lord of
the mountain became part of the Devaraja cult, with Śiva as lord of the
mountain and the ruler as an emanation of Śiva. The process generated in
time a measure of cultural homogeneity, a kind of synthesis developed from
a profusion of crude animistic practices reinterpreted on a higher level.

While the transmitters of Indian culture (priests, poets, philosophers,
scholars) were careful to preserve the traditional law ritual (*kuladharma*),
they also encouraged accretions to it (*sheeladharma*) on the part of local
scholars and rulers.[50] The results were occasionally impressive. The Sanskrit
classics—*Ramayana, Mahabharata,* and the *Puranas*—provided the basic
inspiration for the development of local literature, art, and architecture.

[49] Coedès, 63–66; Wertheim, 274–276. Hall's interpretation (*A History
of South-East Asia,* 12–18) borrows from Indian sources and from Coedès.

[50] O. V. Raghavan, "Variety and Integration in the Pattern of Indian
Culture," *FEQ,* XV (1956), 497–503; Harry Benda, "The Structure of Southeast
Asia History," *JSEAH,* III (1962), 112–114.

The writing systems of every literate Southeast Asian people except the Muslim Malays and the Vietnamese were adapted from the Indian alphabet. The Code of Manu and the Dharmashastras (legal treatises) were widely revered, as was the Arthasastra, which set forth realistic standards of royal administration. The terminologies for medicine, law, and government were usually borrowed directly from the Sanskrit. Kings took Sanskrit names, adopted Vedic sacrifices, and usually claimed association with some Hindu god or hero. Even where the Indian governmental system was not fully introduced, as among the Buginese and the eastern Indonesian islanders, Hindu influences were reflected at the higher levels of social stratification. Not all accretions from India were equally commendable; suttee and Tantric-cult practices were examples. But the total impact was clearly impressive.[51]

It is obvious, nevertheless, that Indianized court civilization never completely dominated centers where indigenous cultural vitality was strong, as in Java or Cambodia. Southeast Asian peoples appear to have oscillated between their appropriation of Indian forms and the resurgence of pre-Indian standards of civilization. Old customs were often preserved under a veneer of Indianization. Much was rejected in the absence of any affirmative response—caste, and subordination of women, for example. In times of social crisis traditional behavior and symbolism often displayed what Wales terms a kind of "activated inertia." Always operative as selective factor was "local genius," which determined preferences for congenial aspects of the new culture pattern. Hence came the preference for Śiva over Vishnu in the eastern zone (eastern Java, Cambodia, Champa), where fertility and ancestral rites, combined with deification of the life-giving power of the soil, constituted compatible elements of indigenous culture. The upright stone symbolizing the fertility god of the earth was readily identified with the linga of the Śiva cult, and came, under the Devaraja system, to represent the very magical essence of royalty. The ashes of the ancestral chief were mingled with the soil in another fertility rite. Pyramidal or terraced structures simulating the sacred mountain of the gods became also the bearer of the Śiva linga and the royal tomb. In Buddhist countries the palace itself became a replica in miniature of cosmic Mount Meru.[52] In many instances the resulting system was as much indigenous as it was Indian.

The Hinduized Javanese court system, in particular, developed in a distinctive local context which colored the entire response. In rural regions of sawah (irrigated) cultivation, the traditional *adat* law remained unimpaired in its definition of social organization.[53] The eighth-century Borobudur Buddhist monument in central Java reflected the characteristic sym-

[51] Raymond Kennedy, "A Survey of Indonesian Society," in G. P. Murdock, *Studies in the Science of Society* (1937), 272–276, 292; Coedès, 422–424.

[52] H. G. Q. Wales, *The Making of Greater India* (1951), 7–13, 17–19, 47–65.

[53] Wertheim, 276–277.

metry and the cosmologic standards of Indian architecture, but the conception of items included within the carved relief panels was Javanese, as was their artistic execution. East Javanese architecture and sculpture after Borobudur (Hindu in its inspiration) also saw the reemergence of animistic motifs, including ancestor worship and shadow plays, which owed little or nothing to India.[54]

Selectivity in the appropriation of Indian culture was also marked in Khmer Angkor. Here the mass of the population continued honoring traditional animistic and ancestral cults, little affected by alien cultural accretions at court, except insofar as the people had to sustain the burden of temple building. But the Angkor monuments themselves were creative achievements, going beyond any mere adaptation of Indian artistic patterns. The Khmers were also capable of creative contributions to Sanskrit literature, as will be indicated in a later chapter. The Chams demonstrated a similar quality of local genius, albeit on a less impressive scale than at Angkor.[55]

The absence of evidence of impressive artistic or literary achievements by the Malays on both Sumatra and the peninsula and also by the Mons of Lower Burma and the Menam Valley seems to suggest that the massive cultural impact of India was here virtually overwhelming. More intensive Indian acculturation combined with a relative lack of local cultural vitality probably contributed to this. The Mons were a highly civilized people, but their role as teachers was probably more important than their original contributions to art and literature. They were the original recipients and the perennial custodians of Hinayana Buddhism, a faith which they in turn transmitted to the Khmers, the Burmans, and the Thai.[56]

Pagan Burma, from the eleventh to the thirteenth century, borrowed heavily from both the Mons and India. The nonindigenous character of the most impressive monuments built during the middle Pagan period is rather conclusively attested by the fact that the last of them, the Mingalazedi of the late thirteenth century, reverted to the same simple stupa pattern of solid masonry used at the outset in the eleventh-century Shwezigon pagoda. Pagan also demonstrated that the Burman religion of the day was a confused and syncretic mingling of both forms of Buddhism, plus Tantrism and other Hindu elements, all of it constituting a veneer for an animistic substratum. The Burmans demonstrated capacity for creative expression in their vernacular literature, but the higher levels of their civilization seem to have been largely borrowed.

The limitations of the Indianization process are related to the sterility of the institution of divine kingship—to its lack of developmental

[54] Justus M. van der Kroef, "The Hinduization of Indonesia Reconsidered," *FEQ*, XI (1951), 17–30.

[55] Briggs, 231.

[56] Wales, *Greater India*, 17–19. Pyu Śrikshetra was Indian in its plan and execution.

capacities. The deification of the king, whether as the occupant of Mount Meru, as the avatar of Śiva, Vishnu, or Indra, or as a descendant of the daughter of the Naga-snake earth god, gave him such exalted status that he was completely unapproachable by his people. He was the sole owner of the soil of his country; the people were legally and theoretically his abject slaves at all levels below that of deified royalty. The belief that the ruler's own karma contributed to his elevated state afforded further authentication of his authority, if any were needed. The system of divine kingship provided no orderly way by which a ruler could be held accountable for his actions and no method by which royal succession could be easily determined. The element of cosmic magic was everywhere amazingly potent. The mere recall of ancient sayings or prophecies sometimes exerted a determining influence on the fortunes of government. A usurper or murderer often seized control of the sacred palace precincts by open use of force, destroyed the magic linga of his rivals, and then authenticated his assumed role by additional religious sanctions. The only assurance against the risk that similar action would be attempted by a ruler's numerous half brothers, the products of the harem, was simply to eliminate all possible rivals.[57]

In the Indian tradition, the world was a setting for a spiritual drama involving the pilgrimage of souls through many experiences and existences in search of fusion with deity. Indians themselves were organized not politically as citizens, but socially as castes. Family and caste provided the basis of moral obligation, and public morals were usually enforceable only in tightly knit village units. Therefore, the Code of Manu and the Dharmashastras were concerned primarily with buttressing royal authority and not with establishing the concept of the role of law in promoting justice and protecting the rights of the people.[58] In such a context, government and political events were of little consequence in comparison to karma, which determined everyone's personal destiny. Historical sensitivity to events as part of an on-moving development, so strongly present in China, was simply lacking in India. Time to the Indian mind moved in familiar cycles, dawn to dusk, season to season, year to year, youth to age, existence to existence, era to era on the ever-spinning wheel of life.

In a situation where the context was cosmic rather than mundane, as in India, the inspiration for creative governmental development eventually atrophied. The historical promise of an Asoka or a Chandra Gupta II was never realized. India's history in the post-Gupta period has been described by Pandit Nehru as a "sluggish stream moving slowly through an accumulation of dead centuries" as if in a coma. This history portrayed the "slow banking of national fires," a "beauty of enervation," in which rough and creatively contradictory elements were dissolved. Buddhism thus died in the land of its birth. India's heavy price for its one-sided otherworldliness and lack of interest in political progress has been called the perceptible deteriora-

[57] Heine-Geldern, 7–10.
[58] Guy Wint, *The British in Asia* (1947), 34–35, 41–44.

tion and the eventual death of its free and self-reliant spirit.[59] The political elements of the Hindu heritage of Southeast Asian peoples were at best
subject to serious limitations.

The one promising political idea derived by Southeast Asia from
India which might have served as a basis for responsible kingship was perhaps the Bodhisattva principle. Here an aspiring ruler, seeking to attain
righteousness in terms of the Buddhist eightfold path, could aspire to saint-
hood more or less in the Asoka tradition. But aspiring Bodhisattvas usually
exhausted their people by building costly temple monuments as contributions to their personal merit. Such situations frequently reverted to Śiva or
Vishnu cults or repudiated Mahayana Buddhist forms. The only Buddhism
which survived, that of the Theravada sect, flatly rejected the Bodhisattva
principle, no doubt for reasons based on experience. Even in the Buddhist
states, the people usually classified government with such standard calamities
as fire, flood, and evildoers, all of which simply had to be endured.

[59] *Ibid.,* 35–40.

PART 2

*Early Empires*

# CHAPTER 3

# Funan and

## Its Neighbors

$T$he first important state in Southeast Asia in historic times was known as Funan, this name being derived from Chinese records. Funan proper, which dated from the late second century A.D., was centered on the delta of the Mekong River and in the basin of the Tonle Sap, or Great Lake. As a naval power, it lay astride the main trading route connecting the isthmian harbors with the ports of South China. It developed imperial dimensions in the early third century and reached its peak sometime after 400, when the portage traffic assumed near-monopoly proportions as compared with the straits trade.

The Funan Empire began to disintegrate around 550 as a result of sustained southward pressure from Chenla, the Khmer state centering at Bassac, which was located some distance up the Mekong River. Former vassal states of Funan situated in northern Malaya and to the west of the Menam River fell away and assumed, during the course of the two succeeding centuries (550 to 750), varying degrees of independence. Funan's cultural borrowings from India, both Hindu and Buddhist, were extensive, but they appear to have constituted at the early stage a kind of secondhand adaptation of Indian contributions transplanted in the Malay portage states and in the Mon state of Tun-sun. The history of Chenla and the partial reestablishment of the former Empire of Funan by the Khmers in the ninth and tenth centuries will be treated in a later chapter.

## Early History of Funan

The earliest information concerning the state of Funan comes from a record preserved in the Chinese dynastic annals originating in the mid-third century, when an imperial Chinese mission visited the state. The Chinese name for the ruler at the time was Fan Hsun. The founder of the Funan Empire, called Fan Shih-man by the Chinese, had died during the first quarter of the third century while preparing to engage in military operations to the west, presumably in the region of peninsular Burma. His nephew and successor, a usurper named Fan Chan (225 to 245), sent a diplomatic mission to a state called Murunda in the Ganges Valley of India around 240 and a similar mission to China in 243. The return missions from both China and Murunda met at the Court of Fan Hsun around 250, providing a setting for the account surviving in the Chinese annals.

The origin of the Funan dynasty was explained at the time and perennially thereafter by reference to a borrowed version of an ancient Pallavan legend. It affirmed that the mythical founder, a conquering Brahman foreigner named Kaundinya, had won local acceptance after an initial clash with the local queen, who later became his bride. The queen was identified as the daughter of the Naga snake, god of the soil and waters. Thence was derived the dynasty's claim to lordship over the land. Later rulers invariably took great pains to establish relationship with Kaundinya's line. The nine-headed-cobra representation of the Naga symbol persisted down to modern times as a characteristic symbol of Khmer and Thai iconography.[1] The dynasty's title, Funan, meant "king of the mountain," probably referring to Mount Meru of the Indian cosmologic tradition. The local word for mountain was *Phnom*, a frequently used name for the seat of government.[2] The capital city, identified later by the Indian name Vyadhapura (city of the hunters), was located near the top of the Mekong delta on the left bank of the river, below the confluence of the Tonle Sap River and some 120 miles from the river-mouth port of Go Oc Eo. The sea power of Funan dominated the shore of the shallow Gulf of Siam, including the northern Malay coasts, and also controlled ports and shipping up the Annamese coast as far as Camranh Bay, abutting neighboring Champa.

Traffic and communication within Funan were waterborne, utilizing the river channels and the delta. Native boats 80 to 90 feet long were used. The Tonle Sap connection and the Great Lake itself seem not at first to have been an integral part of Funan,[3] but the interior valley afforded the natural region of expansion for needed agricultural resources and for an abundant supply of fish. During the latter portion of the rainy season, July to October, the river connecting the Great Lake and the lower Mekong flowed in reverse, raising the level of the lake by some 40 feet and making its area some $3\frac{1}{2}$ times as great. Alluvial deposits from the floodwaters contributed great fertility to valley soil. The retreat of the waters was the occasion for a water festival, and the extreme recession of the lake during the dry season brought the annual fish harvest.[4]

[1] M. Ghosh, *A History of Cambodia* (1960), 29–36. Entrances of Thailand's Chulalongkorn University are today flanked by the nine-headed-snake symbol, just as were the approaches to Angkor Wat.

[2] K. A. Nilakanta Sastri, *South Indian Influences in the Far East* (1949), 28–33.

[3] D. G. E. Hall, *A History of South-East Asia* (1955), 23–25; R. C. Majumdar, *Kambuja-Desa* (1944), 36–42, and *Ancient Indian Colonies in the Far East* (1955), I, 22–24.

[4] Ghosh, 21–23.

The Chinese description of third-century Funan suggested the prevalence of wide variations in wealth and status. The principal buildings at the capital city were constructed of brick covered with lime plaster, and the capitol itself was protected by brick walls. The ruler at the time of the Chinese visit was probably a patron of Buddhism; court records were kept in Sanskrit script. Taxes were paid in pearls and perfumed woods; sculptors worked in gold and silver as well as in cheaper materials. Cities located in the isthmus area were described as less pretentious, being protected only by wooden palisades. Outlying settlements were ruled by their own tribal chiefs. The population as a whole lived mainly in bamboo houses resting on pilings lining the waterways. Surrounding fields grew rice, cotton, and sugar cane. Where the facts concerning crime could not be ascertained, ordeals by hot water, by immersion in water, and by hot iron were used in reaching judicial decisions. Such practices persisted into modern times in Burma and Thailand. The literate elite was apparently Indonesian, the language modulating in time in the direction of Old Khmer. The population as a whole was Indonesian and Negrito or Melanesoid. The people, described by the Chinese visitor around 250, were ugly and black, their hair frizzy, their bodies naked above the waist, their feet bare. They used stone ornaments and utensils and were fond of such sports as cock and pig fighting.[5] Chinese accounts of tributary missions sent by Funan between 267 and 287 added little to the 250 story. Friendly relations with China were broken temporarily in 270 when Funan joined Champa in attacking Chinese Tongking.[6] Tributary missions were later renewed, in 357.

## Funan: High Tide and Decline

A sharp advance in the degree of Indianization of Funan occurred during the late fourth and fifth centuries. Both Pallavan and Gupta influences were much in evidence, the former probably transmitted by immigrants and the latter borrowed directly from the dominant Gupta cultural sources in north India. The full Indianization of Funan traditionally owed much to a ruler of the early fifth century (d. 434) called Kaundinya II. He apparently came from the isthmian portion of the Funan Empire, and may have represented a projection of Indian immigration. Kaundinya II occupied the throne under Indian supernatural sanctions including the state cult of the Śiva linga. Buddhism persisted from the previous period.[7] The second Kaundinya curried favor with China by refusing to aid the neighboring state of Lin-i (Champa) in a war with China and by dispatching two

[5] G. Coedès, *Les États Hindouisés* (1948), 68–76. The Chinese mission, an essentially commercial one, was sent by the first Wu Emperor (222–252).

[6] Hall, 28–31; Majumdar, *Kambuja-Desa,* 36–42.

[7] F. J. Moorhead, *A History of Malaya and Her Neighbors* (1957), 52–53; G. Coedès, *Pour Mieux Comprendre Angkor* (1947), I, 96–100. Ghosh affirms that both Kaundinyas came directly from India, but evidence is lacking on this point.

tributary missions (431 and 434) to the Chinese capital. His successors followed a similar policy.[8]

The next important ruler, King Jayavarman I (478–514), also sent a tribute mission to China in 484. Its members praised in successive breaths the advantages of the Śaivite cult in reducing the population to submission and the Buddhist propagation of mercy and compassion to all. Śiva was the patron deity of the realm, worshipped in the form of a linga.[9] Sanskrit words were in wide use by Jayavarman's time, especially in the areas of government, law, and medicine. *Varman* (protégé of, or protected by), a term used by the princely Kshatriya caste in India, became henceforth the established suffix for royal names.

Hindu practices were much in evidence in Funan. Widows and widowers did not remarry, and the ashes of the dead, encased in costly containers varying with the status of the deceased, were thrown as offerings into the river or sea. Royal processions attended by musicians and guards were described, with the ruler sitting atop a caparisoned elephant under the canopy of a white umbrella. The Sanskrit term *esvara* (god) appeared prominently in both the Śaivite cult of Mahesvara and the Mahayana Buddhist cult of Lokesvara.[10] The close association of Mahayana Buddhism and Śiva worship persisted up to the very end of the Funan Empire, but not to the exclusion of the Vishnu cult. The widowed queen of Jayavarman I left an invocation to Vishnu written in perfect Sanskrit. Gupta-style images survived, but no architectural monuments.[11]

Funan's commercial and political relations with China, as reflected in the sending of periodic tribute missions, were particularly close during the first four decades of the sixth century. Jayavarman I traded actively with Canton, solicited Chinese aid against a rebel son who had seized control of Champa, and in 503 was accorded the grandiose title of General of the Pacified South by the new Liang Court of China.[12] The last important King of Funan—Rudravarman, a usurper who faced serious internal troubles—sent no fewer than six embassies to China from 514 to 539. He succumbed after 540 to the southward pressure of the Khmer state of Chenla.

A new era dawned in 540, when a prince pretender named Bhavavarman, married to a Khmer princess, seized power for Chenla, thus displacing the Kaundinya line. The immediate change was probably little more than a shift of dynasty, but the long-term implications were important. The Funan Empire quickly fell apart, leaving in its wake a number of succession states. The Indianization process slowed down. Funan proper was com-

[8] Ghosh, 37–38.

[9] L. P. Briggs, "The Syncretism of Religions in Southeast Asia," *JAOS*, LXXI (1951), 239–247. The wife and son of Jayavarman I were Vishnu devotees.

[10] L. P. Briggs, *The Ancient Khmer Empire* (1951), 24–27.

[11] Nilakanta Sastri, 28–33; Ghosh, 39–42.

[12] Ghosh, 39–42.

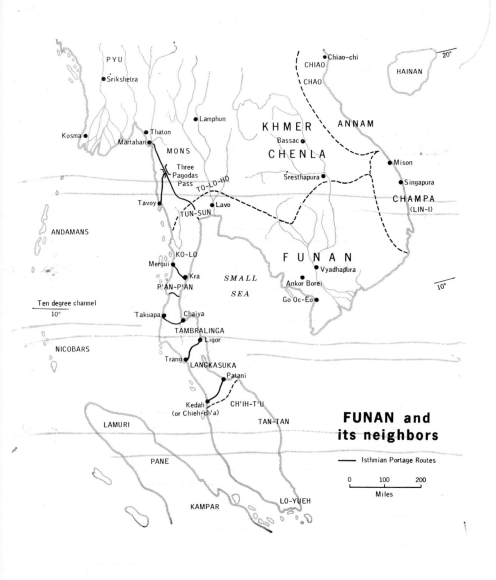

PYU

Srikshetra

Kosma

Lamphun

Thaton
Martaban

MONS

Three
Pagodas
Pass

TO-LO-HO

Tavoy

TUN-SUN

Lavo

ANDAMANS

KO-LO

Mergui

Kra

P'AN-P'AN

Takuapa

Chaiya

TAMBRALINGA

Trang

Ligor

LANGKASUKA

Patani

Kedah
(or Chieh-ch'a)

CH'IH-T'U

TAN-TAN

LAMURI

PANE

KAMPAR

LO-YUEH

Chiao-chi

CHIAO

CHAO

HAINAN

20°

KHMER

ANNAM

Bassac

CHENLA

Mison

Sresthapura

Singapura

CHAMPA
(LIN-I)

10°

SMALL

SEA

FUNAN

Vyadhapura

Ankor Borei

Go Oc-Eo

Ten degree channel

10°

NICOBARS

**FUNAN and
its neighbors**

Isthmian Portage Routes

0      100      200

Miles

pletely overrun by the invading Khmers during the ensuing century.[13] Surviving the political debacle in Funan was the persisting use of Indian-type alphabets and the Sanskrit language as a kind of lingua franca. Also permanent were the organized governmental system, the practices of establishing charitable foundations to support Sanskrit scholarship and the official status of the Śiva cult, and the active presence of Vishnu worship and Buddhism.[14]

## Vassal and Succession States in the Isthmus

Although the earliest Sanskrit inscriptions in Funan, dating perhaps from the late fourth century, preceded by a number of years those found in northern Malaya, the latter area was subject to the same Gupta and Pallavan cultural impacts which struck Funan.[15] In fact the vassal centers along the isthmian trade route probably constituted the principal avenues of cultural transmission. The upper isthmian state of P'an P'an, as described in 515 by a Chinese visitor, had many Brahmans at court, plus ten Buddhist monasteries and a single Taoist convent.[16] The earliest inscriptions at Kedah, both Hindu and Buddhist, were made in the Pallavan script. They are intermingled with art objects in the Gupta style. Pallavan influence extended northward along the western coast to Takuapa but was less evident in Mon Burma and Dvaravati. One Kedah inscription contained a prayer for the safety of a junk crossing the Gulf of Siam.[17] The states centering along the northern coasts of eastern Malaya were similarly affected by heavy Pallavan influence from Deccan India, but little trace of early Indianization has been found south of Patani on the eastern coast. Following the Gupta period, during the late sixth and seventh centuries, the Pallavan Śaivite cultural influence revived, especially along the west coast ports of Malaya (Kedah and Klang) and in the southeast in the direction of Java.[18]

The most important successor state in northern Malaya following the disintegration of the Funan Empire was Lankasuka, which dated from the second century. Lankasuka centered either at Ligor or Patani. It encompassed the eastern ends of two important portage crossings of the isthmus

[13] Hall, 28–31; Moorhead, 53–55; Briggs, *Khmer Empire*, 10, 24–27.

[14] Ghosh, 46–58. Under one fifth-century Mahayana Buddhist system, Gautama became one of the ten incarnations of Vishnu.

[15] Coedès, *Les États*, 86–87; Hall, 28–31. Hall points out that one Funan ruler in the mid-fourth century (357) carried the title of an Iranian-Scythian ruler who had been driven from north India by Samudragupta around 350.

[16] Coedès, *Les États*, 88–91.

[17] Hall, 33; Richard Winstedt, *The Malays: A Cultural History* (1950), 19–21; H. G. Q. Wales, *The Making of Greater India* (1951), 32–34.

[18] R. Braddell, "Notes on Ancient Times in Malaya," *JRASMB*, XXXIII (1950), 17–19; H. G. Q. Wales, *Towards Angkor* (1937), 148–150, 155. The later Pallavan impact, by comparison, had little noticeable effect in Chenla or along the shores of the Gulf of Siam.

and extended westward to the shores of the Bay of Bengal, including both Takuapa and Trang. It probably did not include Kedah. Even as a vassal of the Funan Empire, Lankasuka had maintained its separate Indianized court. The Chinese Liang annals of the fifth century describe a Malay ruler of the country wearing a sleeveless cotton garment, riding an elephant, accompanied by a bodyguard carrying drums and flags. The state of Lankasuka was itself a source of perfumed woods and essences, but its principal importance, which outlasted by some two centuries the collapse of Funan's power, lay in its control of the frequently used transisthmian routes of trade between China and India.[19]

Power in the state of Lankasuka centered on the eastern coast because of the superior agricultural resources adjacent to Ligor and the excellent harbor facilities on the Bay of Bandon. From the end of the 400s to the last third of the 600s these isthmian routes apparently carried most of the interocean trade. Takuapa at the western terminus of the corridor was located at the end of the 10° channel running between the Andaman and Nicobar Islands. It was connected with Chaiya harbor on the Bay of Bandon by a short 5-mile portage joining the heads of river navigation to the east and west. Fragments of glazed Chinese pottery have been found at Takuapa—a yellow type from third-to-sixth-century China and green items from the T'ang period (seventh to ninth). The heavy Indianization of Lankasuka from early times is reflected in the ruins of Hindu temples, in the reportedly Indian-featured people still living around Bandon, in local traditions of the dance, and in the Indian name currently applied to the eastward-flowing river.[20]

The narrower Kra isthmus to the north was probably used also, but it lacked both agricultural resources and harbor facilities on the eastern coast. Much the same could be said of the less used routes running eastward behind Mergui. The longer Tavoy route linked up with the Meklong Valley. The Chinese annals from Funan times described the kingdom of P'an P'an, apparently located between Kra and Mergui, which may have been an Indian trading colony. It was reported to include some five hundred resident merchants from India, many of them married to daughters of the local people, plus an estimated one thousand Brahman priests. P'an P'an was heavily Indianized. Suttee was practiced by widows; bodies of important persons were cremated and thrown into the sea. The main city was reported to be located inland up a river, about 10 li from the shores of the Bay of Bengal. It was one of the vassal states of Funan from the third century to the sixth.[21]

Lankasuka continued to be an important avenue of trade after

[19] Hall, 33–34; Coedès, *Les États,* 72–73; Moorhead, 43–52; Braddell, 9–21.

[20] Wales, *Towards Angkor,* 46–47, 51–76; Majumdar, *Ancient Indian Colonies,* 83–87.

[21] Paul Wheatley, "The Malay Peninsula as Known to the Chinese of the Third Century," *JRASMB,* XXVII (1955), 1–23.

Funan's decline. During the 670s, when mentioned by the Chinese traveler
I-Ching, it was described as an independent state. It was subject during
the ensuing century to pressure from Mon invaders pushing southward via
the Kra isthmus. An inscription dating from 775 indicated that Ligor was
the part of the Srivijayan Empire, ruled at the time by a vigorous Sumatran
dynasty. The northern part of the old Lankasuka state eventually reemerged
as independent in the tenth century under the name Tambralinga. The new
state apparently maintained a primary affinity to the Mon-Khmers, even
though the Sanskrit scribes at the court continued to follow characteristic
Javanese and Srivijayan writing patterns. During the Tambralinga period
the port of Trang on the western coast assumed increased importance.
Tambralinga was definitely allied with Srivijaya against Javan Mataram in
the 990s and subsequently against the Chola Tamil state in south India.
Both Mataram and the Cholas were apparently trying to obtain a greater
share in the growing India-to-China trade. On the other hand, a Tambralinga prince during the same decade intervened decisively in the strife between the rival Mon states of Dvaravati (Lavo) and Haripunjaya
(Lamph'un). Lavo merged with the Khmer Empire during the ensuing
century.[22]

## Mon Dvaravati and Thaton

During the long interim between the collapse of the Funan Empire
and the creation, some three centuries later, of an equally extensive
Cambodian domain as its successor, the Mon states of Dvaravati and
Thaton enjoyed a considerable measure of importance. Dvaravati was located on the right bank of the lower Menam River extending westward to
the Tenasserim range and southward into the isthmus. It sent an independent embassy to China in the seventh century.[23] Mon power at Thaton
on the Burma side was enhanced in the eighth century by the fall of the
Pyu city of Srikshetra (Old Prome) on the lower Irrawaddy River.[24] Both
Mon areas maintained intimate contacts with Ceylon as a source of
Hinayana Buddhism, and also with the Telingana section of Telegu India
(from which the Burman epithet Talaing for the Mons was derived)[25] and
with the Gupta Empire. Although at Thaton and Lavo, as in Funan, only
the foundations of brick structures have survived and virtually no inscriptions antedate 500, the important role of the Mons as the transmitters
of Indian culture is well attested. Their areas of influence lay somewhat
north of the main stream of commerce via the portage route and Funan. But

---

[22] O. W. Wolters, "Tambralinga," *BSOAS*, XXI (1958), 587–600; Briggs,
*Khmer Empire*, 16.

[23] L. P. Briggs, "Dvaravati, Most Ancient Kingdom of Siam," *JAOS*, LXV
(1945), 102.

[24] Nilakanta Sastri, 72–73.

[25] Hall, 36.

they taught the Chenla Khmers, fellow Mons of Haripunjaya residing in northern Siam, and the later-entering Burmans and Thai the principles of Vishnu worship and of Hinayana Buddhism especially.[26] Long-established Mon contacts with Ceylon were particularly important after the Hinayana cult of the Buddhist faith was excluded from India in 643.[27]

The Dvaravati state, centering at Lavo, was hemmed in both geographically and politically. It appears never to have been able to develop close political ties across the mountain barrier with fellow Mons in Thaton, Burma, or up the Menam Valley with the rival Mon state of Haripunjaya at Lamph'un. The Thaton Mons by contrast were at times fairly closely associated with Lamph'un politically. Dvaravati control of some of the Malay portages to the south prior to and during the Tambralinga period was apparently tenuous and short-lived. Tambralinga actually conquered Lavo in the 990s. During the eleventh century the Mons on both sides of the Tenasserim watershed were completely overshadowed respectively by the emergence of the Cambodian and Burman Empires, and similarly in the thirteenth century by the Thai. They were never displaced as residents, however. It was a Dvaravati Mon leader, one Uthong, who later founded the Thai capital of Ayuthia, in 1350.[28] The Mons of Burma contested with the Burmans control of the Irrawaddy Valley from the sixteenth to the eighteenth centuries. No people of Southeast Asia was more receptive of Indian art and literature than the Mons. Hindu images and symbols abound in Dvaravati, along with fragmentary accounts of Buddha's miracles and sermons. India's symbolic wheel of the law has been found only there.[29]

## Champa and Borneo

The state of Champa (Lin-i to the Chinese) profited from the disintegration of Funan after 540 by the acquisition of the coastal strip of Annam extending from Camranh Bay southward to the northern edge of the Mekong delta. As an Indonesian-ruled state dating from 192, Champa apparently developed importance through efforts to establish coastal points of contact, independent of Funan and perhaps of the portage routes also, with the seaborne trade with China. The weakening of Han authority in Vietnam in the late second century also afforded the opportunity to consolidate Cham control at Quang-nam, located just south of modern Hué. The Chams had control along the western slopes of the Mekong watershed, but the population of the interior was more closely akin to the Funanese and the Khmers. The full Indianization of Champa under King Bhadravar-

---

[26] As one example of Mon cultural dispersion, Wales (*Towards Angkor*, 93–94) cited ruins, at Śri Deva in the Korat area, of a Vishnu temple in the Gupta style dating from late Funan times.

[27] Hall, 36.

[28] Briggs, "Dvaravati, Most Ancient Kingdom of Siam," 102.

[29] Nilakanta Sastri, 63–73.

man developed, as in the case of Funan, during the Gupta period of the late 300s and the 400s. The earliest Indian inscriptions in the area date from around 400.[30] Indian Buddhism apparently entered Tongking in a very limited fashion in the third century.[31]

The Chams were the Barbary pirates of the Annamese coast. As the inveterate enemies of the Vietnamese, they captured and lost the harbor of Port d'Annam in 336–339, and twice in the succeeding century (405–414 and 431–432) attacked China's Tongking region. These and later attacks failed because of the superior cohesion and continuity of the Chinese administrative system in Annam.[32] Although predominantly Indian, Cham architecture and sculpture also reflected the country's propinquity to China.[33] But the Chams also looked southward. As previously indicated, Jayavarman I (478–514) of Funan won from China his proud recognition as General of the Pacified South by successful military measures taken against the Chams. After Funan began to decline in the sixth century, the Cham rulers turned their interests definitely southward and persistently sought investiture and moral support in this endeavor from the Chinese authorities. They took over the lower Annamese coast after 540.[34] The Chams were skilled fighters, and their strong sea power and their virtually unassailable land position also contributed to Champa's longevity as an independent state.

The discouraging perils of the sea journey from India to the straits and thence to China were responsible for the establishment of a number of additional ports of call, where seasonal shifts of the wind could be awaited. One was located in lower Sumatra (probably Palembang or Jambi) and another at the Sunda Straits (called Taruma).[35] Several other Indianized centers appeared in the fourth century, along the southern coasts of Borneo within easy access of vessels traversing the Malacca Straits or Java Sea and also up the Mahakam River in eastern Borneo. The Borneo ports, like Champa, were basically Indonesian in rulership; the courts, again similarly, were Indianized. A late-fourth-century or early-fifth-century inscription in correct Sanskrit with no Indonesian intrusions, found at the mouth of the Mahakam River in Borneo, tells of a ruler named Mulavarman, who was the grandson of the Indonesian founder of the same state. The dynasty was being Hinduized. Sandstone statues of Śiva, the ruins of a wooden Hindu temple, a four-armed Vishnu image of gold, and various inscriptions have also been found at Sepauk and at Batu Pahat in Borneo. Little evidence

---

[30] Moorhead, 52; Coedès, *Les États,* 99.

[31] Pierre Gourou, *The Peasants of the Tonkin Delta* (1955), 146–147.

[32] *Ibid.,* 144–146.

[33] Wales, *Greater India,* 150–158.

[34] Moorhead, 43–52; Coedès, *Les États,* 98–99, 120–121; Hall, 27–28. Chams sent missions to China in 530 and 534 and also in 568 and 572. They later developed close relations with the new T'ang dynasty by missions in 623, 625, and 628.

[35] Moorhead, 52.

of Buddhism was present.[36] These Indianized commercial centers in Borneo apparently lost direct contact with India during the fifth century, presum-ably because of the temporary abandonment by Indian traders of the use of Borneo in the difficult all-sea route to China. Similarly, in the 500s and into the 600s, the previously evident process of Indianization of Java, east-ern Borneo, and the Celebes virtually ceased.[37]

[36] Nilakanta Sastri, 137–143; Majumdar, *Ancient Indian Colonies, II Suvarnadvipa* (1936), 127–131; Hall, 33–36; Moorhead, 43–52.

[37] Nilakanta Sastri, 143; Wales, *Towards Angkor,* 51–74; B. H. M. Vlekke, *Nusantara* (1960), 19–20.

# CHAPTER 4

# Java and

# Srivijaya to 1025

During the course of the century which saw the breakup of the Funan Empire, the commercial leadership of Southeast Asia shifted to lower Sumatra. The shift was produced in large measure by the increase of seaborne trade via the Malacca Straits consequent on improved navigational facilities and the commercial stimulation afforded by the Persian Empire to the west and a reunited China in the east. The T'ang dynasty established full control of the South China coast by 628. The commercial entrepôt of Śrivijaya rose thereafter from its early status as a port of call on the Palembang River estuary in southern Sumatra. By the 670s it had become an important center of Buddhist learning. Increased use of the straits by north Indian ships in particular also greatly intensified previous cultural contacts between India and the port cities of central and eastern Java. Control of central Java during the eighth century fell to the Buddhist Śailendra dynasty, which seems to have exerted a measure of external control extending into northern Malaya and Cambodia. The Śailendras created the Buddhist Borobudur and other monuments in central Java, thereby establishing a high artistic standard which successor Hindu rulers emulated. After being expelled from their original Javan base in the mid-ninth century, the Śailendras gained control over the Śrivijayan government. This chapter will trace the development of Southeast Asian trade and the history of Śrivijaya, Śailendra Java, and its successor Mataram state, to the Chola wars of the 1020s.

## Java and Sumatra prior to the Seventh Century

Indian cultural influence in Sumatra, Borneo, and Java prior to 500 was both scattered and meager. Three way stations for ships en route to China were in operation around 400—one on the favored coast (facing China) of lower Sumatra dating from the previous century, another in southwestern Borneo,[1] and another at the western end of Java. The port of Taruma (Yeh-po-ti?) where Fa-Hsien's ship found haven was probably located in western Java. Ports on the eastern coast of Borneo seem to have been more directly affected by Indian cultural contacts during the 400s than were those in eastern and central Java, but the Javanese traders developed connections with Indianized mainland regions of Funan and Lin-i (Champa). Around 400 both Indian and Chinese traders entertained the erroneous impression that Indonesian Java (Sanskrit Yavadvipa and Chinese San-fo-ch'i) was composed of a single large island mass.[2] The local ruler of the state of Taruma in the late fifth century carried the Hindu title of Purnavarman, but little else is known of him except that he was reportedly the third of his line. At the same time one Śri Varnarendra was allegedly ruling over a south Sumatran port located at or near Palembang, which was probably becoming a favorite rendezvous for vessels trading with China.

The impact of Indian contacts in Sumatra and Java increased sharply during the second half of the sixth century, concurrently with the beginning of the disintegration of the Funan Empire. The relaxation of Funan's commercial domination was also contemporaneous with the rise of the political and commercial influence of the new Śrivijayan Empire centering at Palembang on the lower Sumatran coast. The other factor contributing to the increase of seaborne traffic to and from lower Sumatra was the reemergence after 618 of a united and orderly China under the vigorous T'ang dynasty, which became actively concerned with stimulating seaborne trade. The ensuing increase of traffic via the Straits of Malacca during the late seventh century was mainly Indian and Sumatran in character, with Indian Buddhism constituting the principal outside source of cultural inspiration.[3]

The process of Śrivijayan conquest, during the final decades of the seventh century, of numerous rival trading centers located along the shores of the straits and in northern Sumatra was difficult and prolonged. The operation included crushing both foreign and domestic enemies; princes, military leaders, local shippers and alien merchants, palace servants and slaves were all involved. The inscriptions of the period disclose, for example, numerous recordings of magical curses directed against the ruler's enemies and any who dared betray the royal cause. The loyalty of distant chiefs was buttressed by the exaction of awesome ritual oaths. High officials had to drink "imprecation water" allegedly saturated with the curse, which would take effect if they committed any of the catalogue of crimes

---

[1] L. P. Briggs, *The Ancient Khmer Empire* (1951), 23.

[2] K. A. Nilakanta Sastri, *South Indian Influences in the Far East* (1949), 100–113; G. Coedès, *Les États Hindouisés d'Indochine et d'Indonésie* (1948), 53–62. Fa-Hsien's possible visit to Taruma in western Java runs contrary to Coedès's opinion that the Sunda Straits were not used at the time.

[3] D. G. E. Hall, *A History of South-East Asia* (1955), 35–36.

cited during the ceremony. Some curses could make men go insane; others bewitched the victim; all of them carried dire threats of misfortune. Such imprecations constitute more than half of the contents of the available epigraphic remains of early Śrivijaya.[4]

Meanwhile, in the sawah-cultivated sections of central and eastern Java, a well-integrated political and social system developed on a semi-feudal basis quite independent of any Indian cultural inspiration. A Javan state apparently sent tribute and trading embassies to China on three occasions between 430 and 473. This was followed by a second round of missions from 502 to 523. The strength of the central Javan state lay in the interior, where the ruler could exact forced labor from his subjects plus additional rental payments for land tenure. The regimented rural populations of central Java produced a surplus of food and labor available for use in monument building. Food exports became the basis for Javanese trade with the eastern islands, where spices were obtained for exchange at points of Javanese interception of the trading arc between India and China. Local landlord chiefs in Java were obliged to accord vassal allegiance to the central Javan ruler, to reside part time at his court, and to send their daughters to the royal harem as semihostages. The government of interior Java also was suzerain over the more or less autonomous port cities of the north coast, places which provided avenues for trade and entry points for Indian cultural influence.

Indian influence was somewhat stronger in eastern Java than in the center, and it generally developed little importance in the ladang-cultivated western third of the island. The Javan economy as a whole was essentially agricultural rather than commercial. The feudal political structure coupled with the harem system often gave rise to disputes over royal succession, but the frequent changes of dynastic control apparently left the established social and economic order unimpaired. The indigenous order demonstrated abundant vitality, so that recovery from recurring periods of political confusion was usually prompt.[5]

The innate strength of the indigenous culture of central and eastern Java underneath subsequent Hindu, Buddhist, and Islamic contributions was probably responsible for the characteristically dynamic response of the area to stimuli from the outside. Much of the traditional pattern survived in the adaptation of Javanese art forms to Indian themes. Shadow plays associated with the cult of ancestor worship persisted down to modern times. From the outset, the Javanese placed exaggerated dependence on the magical and religious aspects of warfare, such as the ceremonial preparation of

[4] J. G. de Casparis, *Selected Inscriptions from the 7th to the 9th Century A.D.* (1956), 6–7, 16, 20–21, 29–32.

[5] J. C. Van Leur, *Indonesian Trade and Society* (1955), 92–96, 105–107; J. J. Van Klavern, *The Dutch Colonial System in the East Indies* (1953), 19–25; Hall, 34–36.

the *kris* daggers, rites of invulnerability, and the habit of fighters to work themselves into a frenzied mood and become oblivious to danger, by the use of gongs and drums.[6] While the early literature of Cambodia and Champa was largely Sanskrit (and only occasionally original and creative), writers in Java habitually used the indigenous languages as their principal vehicle of literary expression, utilizing the Sanskrit influence without being dominated by it.[7]

## Revival of Southeast Asia Trade: Persia to China

As previously indicated, trade via the Straits of Malacca became increasingly important during the late seventh century. This development contributed much to the rise of Śrivijayan power, centered at the Sumatran ports of Palembang and Malayu. Extensive use of the seaborne route had to await the construction of more seaworthy ships in both India and China and the establishment of unified control over access corridors to the South China and Java Seas by Śrivijaya.[8] Once safe passage was assured, even at a cost of payment of substantial port fees, the all-sea passage quickly demonstrated its advantages over the portage routes in the handling of the increased volume of trade. Commerce converged from all parts of Southern Asia and China. Even with the improvement of ships and navigational skills, however, the passage through the Malacca Straits from Kedah to Palembang often required a full month's time and had its traditional perils of doldrums and pirates.[9]

The revival of Southeast Asian trade from the China end of the trading arc was a fairly slow process. China's seaborne imports in the sixth century had been limited very largely to Buddhist relics and emblems, such as Bo-tree leaves, carved images, miniature stupas, and ceremonial perfumes. The restoration of order along the South China coast by the successive Sui and T'ang dynasties during the early decades of the 600s was an indispensable condition of expanding commercial activity. The new policy began tentatively in 607, when an official Chinese mission undertook to open trade with the north Malay port of Ch'ih T'u. Progress was slow. The first T'ang-dynasty Chinese pilgrim to visit the Buddhist shrines in India made the round trip between 629 and 645 via the traditional Central Asian route. Seaborne communication began to improve during the third quarter of the century. By the 670s another Chinese Buddhist pilgrim, I-

[6] H. G. Q. Wales, *The Making of Greater India* (1951), 83, and *Ancient South-east Asian Warfare* (1952), 46, 84–89, 95–97.

[7] R. C. Majumdar, *Ancient Indian Colonies in the Far East: II, Suvarnadvipa* (1955), 67–69.

[8] Richard O. Winstedt, *Malaya and Its History* (1948, 1956), 7–8.

[9] R. Braddell, "Notes on Ancient Times in Malaya," *JRASMB*, XXIII (1950), 26.

Ching, proceeded southward on a Po-ssŭ (probably Sumatran) ship to
Śrivijaya, and thence to India. Trade revival was in full swing by the end
of the century, with Arab and Persian traders becoming increasingly in
evidence at Chinese ports. The T'ang government welcomed trade because
a much-needed source of revenue was provided from ship taxes, duties on
goods, and monopolistic handling of selected items which were in great demand. By 713, an official inspector of customs at Canton began registering
the captains of all visiting ships and subjecting them to prescribed regulations.[10]

Commercial encouragement from the Persian-Arab end of the arc
was also vigorous. The Sassanid Persian conquest of Yemen near the end
of the sixth century and the consequent Persian absorption of much of the
Arab trade to the east made Ctesiphon, in Persia, the focal point of expanding commercial activity. The Arab-Mohammedan conquest of Yemen in
635 brought added stimulation to the entire Red Sea area, leading to increased activity in warfare, travel, and commerce. Evidences of increasing
Persian trade in the eighth century are numerous. In 717, for example, an
Indian vessel sailed from Ceylon to Śrivijaya to Canton in the company
of a Persian convoy numbering some thirty-five ships. By 748, a large West
Asian colony was reported living on Hainan Island, with similar groups
resident at more northerly Chinese ports. In 750, the seat of the Muslim
caliphate shifted from Damascus to Baghdad, which functioned for a full
century thereafter as the center of a vast Islamic Empire actively interested in the China trade.[11]

Arab maritime accounts dating from the late ninth century indicate
that regular sailings were made for China via India's Malabar Coast,
Malaya's Kalah-bar (probably Kedah), down the straits, and thence via
Cochin-China and Champa. At the port of Tiyuma, located about six days'
sailing south of Kalah-bar, an Arab account stated that slaves and fugi-
tives were allegedly occupying a nearby mountain jungle area. Some Arab
knowledge of Oriental ports as far north as Korea was indicated. The total
round trip from Arabia to China required eighteen months of sailing, with
a two-year cycle required for making repairs and collecting new cargo.[12]

Evidences from the Chinese side include detailed eighth-century sail-
ing directions which described the successive landfalls for the voyage to
Śrivijaya and Kedah. They included Hainan Island, the Annamese and
Champa coasts, Cochin-China, Poulo Condore Island, the Singapore passage,

[10] F. Hirth and W. W. Rockhill, *Chau Ju-Kua* (1911), 8–18; Paul Wheatley,
"Geographical Notes on Some Commodities Involved in Sung Maritime Trade,"
*JRASMB,* part 2 (June, 1959), 20–21.

[11] Wheatley, 25–29; G. F. Hourani, *Arab Seafaring in the Indian Ocean*
(1951), 52–53.

[12] Gabriel Ferrand, *Abu Zaid Hasan: Voyage du Marchand Arabe Sulyaman
en Inde et en Chine* (1922), 38–45; Hourani, 66–75; Paul Wheatley, *The Golden
Khersonese* (1961), 216–224. Wheatley unconvincingly places Kalah at Mergui.

and the east Sumatran shore. This route suggests that Malayu was an alternative point of Śrivijayan control. The cruel pirates infesting the central straits were still much feared. The contemporaneous Chinese description of the route beyond Kedah (to India, Ceylon, and Persia) was by comparison vague and secondhand, a circumstance suggesting that Kedah or northern Sumatran ports probably marked the limit of regular Chinese trading contact. An important alternative center in China for Persian and Arab traders developed during the ninth century at Amoy, where contact was also made with traders from Japan (Okinawa) and Korea. Trading activity at Chinese ports increased enormously during the second quarter of the eighth century. The T'ang government cleared harbors and shipping lanes of rock and silt and accorded special honors to officials successful in promoting the south ocean trade. Persian-Arab trading communities at the principal ports were entrusted to the control of responsible headmen of their own selection who exercised a large measure of extraterritorial control under Muslim law.[13]

The Near Eastern trade with China eventually ran into serious difficulties. Violence erupted in 758 at Canton when a powerful alien Muslim force sacked and burned the city. For a generation thereafter Tongking ports became the termini for the Arab-Persian trade; Canton was reopened to them in 792. At the Persian end of the trading arc, a naval force from Basra in 825 punished Bahrayn pirates guilty of raiding ships returning from India and China.[14] Losses suffered by Persian ships from storms, from pirate plunder, and from forced disposal of valuable Chinese wares en route home took a heavy toll. Many more Chinese goods were taken from Canton than ever arrived in al-Uballah port at the top of the Persian Gulf. Virtually all the Chinese silks were sold in Southeast Asia. The charges levied at China ports were also very heavy, amounting at times to 30 per cent of the value of the import cargo, to which were added export duties and freight-handling costs. Arab accounts also indicate costly losses by fire at Canton warehouses and from looting Chinese rebel bands during the declining years of T'ang rule in the late 800s. Canton, for example, was sacked in 878 by the rebel Huang Ch'ao, who murdered and oppressed resident foreigners. Also contributing to the decline of trade between Persia and China in the late ninth century was the breakup of the Abbassid Empire after 850 and the sack of al-Uballah in 870.

During most of the tenth century, direct voyages from Persia to China were apparently abandoned in favor of meetings of Arab and Chinese traders at Kedah or in Sumatra or Java. The Arab trade was concerned mainly with India's Malabar ports, especially Surat, Goa, and Calicut. The Muslim cloth merchants of Indian Gujerati came subsequently (thirteenth and fourteenth centuries) to dominate the procurement of spices

---

[13] Hourani, 61–62, 64–67.

[14] F. J. Moorhead, *A History of Malaya and Her Neighbors* (1957), 55–56.

for the medieval Mediterranean trade.[15] One of the permanent relics of the Persian trade with Southeast Asian ports from the late seventh to the tenth century and in its later revivals was the generally used Persian term *Shahbandar* (ruler of the port) for the harbor master, an official who down to modern times was usually a resident foreigner.

## The Rise of Indianized Śrivijaya and Java

It seems unlikely that seaborne Indian trade with China ever matched in volume that of the Persians at its peak period. In any case no Indian colonies at Canton and other Chinese ports ever attained the importance of the Arab-Persian colonies. But the Indians clearly made very extensive use of the opened straits in their massive contact with Śrivijayan ports and Java. Indian ports along both the Malabar and Coromandel Coasts and up to Bengal participated actively in the trade through the straits.[16]

The early Indian Buddhist impact on Śrivijaya during the mid-600s may well have been stimulated by the exclusion of the Hinayana sect from India by King Harsha in 643. Similarly the vogue of Buddhism in Śailendra central Java a century later clearly reflected the Mahayana revival by the Pala dynasty (730 and later) centering in the lower Ganges Valley but extending also into coastal Kalinga. The initiative in the spread of Buddhism was by no means all on the Indian side. Śrivijayan and Javanese authorities provided students of Buddhism with hostel accommodations at the Pala University center of Nalanda and later at the south Indian port of Negapatam. During the period of rapid assimilation of Indian culture by Java and Śrivijaya, both Gupta and Pallavan art patterns were much in evidence, coupled with the use of an improved level of Sanskrit in the royal inscriptions.[17]

The creation of the Śrivijayan Empire during the last quarter of the seventh century was the product of the greatly enhanced volume of trade but also contributed to it. When the Chinese pilgrim I-Ching traversed the straits in 671–672, he found safe haven at three independent ports, Śrivijaya (Palembang River), Malayu on the Sumatran shore nearer the entrance of the straits, and at Chieh-ch'a, generally identified with Kedah. By 685, or shortly thereafter, Malayu was incorporated into the budding empire, and a Śrivijayan expedition was in preparation against port cities located in western Java adjacent to the Sunda Straits. The strategic advantage of Śrivijaya lay in its location on the favored coast from which trade could be resumed with the summer monsoon in the direction of China. Easy

---

[15] Hourani, 72–79; Ferrand, 40–45.

[16] Hall, 37–39; Coedès, 93–94.

[17] L. P. Briggs, "The Syncretism of Religions in Southeast Asia," *JOAS*, LXXI (1951), 239–247; Nilakanta Sastri, 112, 121. The Ligor stele of 775 was an example of pure Sanskrit.

access could also be had to the Java Sea and the Moluccas.[18] From Malayu, Śrivijayan control was extended northward to include Kedah and several other more northerly isthmian ports along the Bay of Bengal. The exact dates of this imperial expansion are not known. While the centers at Palembang and Malayu maintained naval dominance throughout both straits areas, effective Śrivijayan control apparently did not extend over the entire stretch of the Sumatran coastline. Pirate lairs in island areas along the straits were never entirely eliminated. By 775, Śrivijaya controlled Ligor and the newly emerging Tambralinga state, extending up Malaya's eastern coast as far as the Bay of Bandon. Divided Chenla was unable at the time to challenge Śrivijaya's control of the north Malay Peninsula. Sumatran ships traded actively with India and apparently somewhat less with China.[19]

The entrepôt center of Śrivijaya was presumably a city of rafts assembled along the banks of the Palembang River, flanked on the banks by pile-supported houses. Iron chains protected its harbor limits, and the city itself was fortified. The river bordered a ladang-cultivated countryside, sparsely populated, hilly and infertile, meagerly administered. Śrivijaya's market place was undoubtedly crowded with scores of money-changers and several thousand peddlers, largely itinerant, drawn from many lands, each

[18] Nilakanta Sastri, "Śri Vijaya," *BEFEO*, XL (1941), 247–249. In 644–645, Malayu had sent its own separate embassy to China. Malayu was perhaps a Mahayana Buddhist center, while Śrivijaya was more Hinayana.

[19] Coedès, 146–148; Majumdar, *Ancient Indian Colonies: II*, 120–123.

competing with the others. Craftsmen were distinctly in the minority. The government realized substantial income from services rendered in refitting ships, providing supplies, and affording a safe haven where the shift of the monsoon winds could be awaited. State authorities devoted their energies and resources to classifying merchandise, dominating trade, making war, and amassing personal wealth, much of which they spent in the early days patronizing Buddhist monasteries on a lavish scale. Hindu symbols of kingship were long used in the area and were generally accepted as valid. The indigenous language and the population were Malay.[20]

Śrivijaya's role was characteristic of the political and economic development to be found around a trading emporium located adjacent to a ladang-cultivated area productive of no food surpluses. Although the port afforded a market for such local products as pepper, aromatic oils and woods, drugs, areca nuts (*pinang*), and possibly gold, Śrivijaya operated mainly as a source of nonagricultural employment and wealth. The chieftains at all port centers of the empire not only controlled trade but participated actively in it; the less favorably situated and less enterprising straits rulers, acting sometimes as semipirates, exacted similar dues from passing ships and from resident merchant colonies. Officials acted vigorously to enforce Śrivijayan authority and to curb the activities of rival trade centers, while maintaining only limited governmental connections with neighboring noncommercial ladang cultivators. Śrivijaya, as a city, had to import rice from Java to feed the workers in the royal pepper gardens.

The remarkable thing about Śrivijaya was that it persisted as a major power for six centuries even though it produced very little locally other than forest products. Its long-continued power, like that of the Chams of Annam or the Buginese of the Java Sea, provides irrefutable testimony to the historical importance of Southeast Asian trade. Śrivijaya was not the first or the last state to appreciate the opportunities afforded a militarized community to draw sustenance in parasitic fashion from the perennial stream of commerce passing by its front door. But despite Śrivijaya's longevity and wealth and its promising beginning as a center of Buddhist scholarship, it made few durable contributions to civilization. It lacked the essential economic base, the disciplined labor supply, and the broad cultural integration required for creative achievement in literature, art, and, especially, architecture.[21]

## I-Ching's Report on Śrivijaya

By far the most revealing description of seventh-century Śrivijaya and the prevalence of Buddhist scholarship comes from the reports of the thirty-seven-year-old Chinese Buddhist pilgrim I-Ching, who first visited

[20] Van Leur, 105–107.
[21] Van Klavern, 16–19.

the city in 671.[22] His itinerary was instructive, although some details are in dispute. I-Ching's passage from Canton to lower Sumatra aboard a Po-ssŭ ship in late 671 required twenty days. The novel character of the ocean journey for a Chinese was reflected in the careful preparations made for it and the solicitous concern of relatives and friends. Finding at Śrivijaya a community of some one thousand Buddhist monks devoted to religious scholarship, the pilgrim remained there for six months studying Sanskrit grammar. He spent another two months at Malayu before proceeding northward on a Śrivijayan vessel to Chieh-ch'a (Kedah) and thence past the Nicobar and Andaman Islands to the Bengal harbor of Tamralipti.[23]

Traveling in India, I-Ching found the mountainous road between Tamralipti and the Buddhist center of Nalanda in the Ganges Valley infested with robber bands. After spending more than a decade at Nalanda studying and collecting the sacred texts of the Buddhist Tripitaka (some 500,000 phrases in all), he returned to Śrivijaya in leisurely fashion via Ceylon, Kedah, and Malayu, where he arrived in 685. He found in Ceylon another thriving center of Buddhism where he made additional scholarly notations while awaiting the southern monsoon passage to Kedah. His voyage from Kedah to Malayu required a full month's time. By 685 Malayu had become an integral part of the Śrivijayan Empire, which it had not been in 671. As a distinguished Buddhist scholar from T'ang China, I-Ching was accorded special consideration by the authorities of Buddhist Śrivijaya. He remained at the capital some three or four additional years, learning the Malay language and progressing in his translation of his Buddhist documents from Sanskrit into Chinese.[24]

I-Ching returned to China unintentionally in mid-689. He boarded a China-bound ship lying at anchor near the mouth of the Palembang River while endeavoring to arrange for the delivery of a letter to friends at Canton. He was asking for a supply of paper and cakes of ink plus additional money to be used to employ scribes. The ship's captain sailed abruptly when a favorable wind developed, affording no opportunity for the Chinese visitor to debark. I-Ching's entire Tripitaka manuscript collection was thus left behind. The ship, probably Indian, stopped at a Champa port en route to Canton. The accidental trip turned out well, however, for his friends in Kwangtung province provided for his needs, and he was able to return to Śrivijaya later in the same year with a scholar companion. Four Chinese assistants arrived later. After spending an additional five years in Sumatra, the group returned to China in 695 in possession of some four

[22] J. Takakusu (ed. and trans.), *I-Ching: A Record of the Buddhist Religion as Practiced in India and the Malay Archipelago* (1896). A French translation of I-Ching by Chavennes in 1894, covered different materials from Takakusu's. Chinese references to Po-ssŭ trade were associated generally with all southern ocean trade in perfumes and drugs.

[23] Takakusu, xxviii–xxxi.

[24] *Ibid.*, xxxiii–xxxiv.

hundred translated Buddhist texts. Before his death in China in 713, I-Ching translated and published no less than fifty-six Buddhist works in an impressive total of 230 volumes.[25] His account advised any Chinese pilgrim en route to India to stop at Śrivijaya for at least one or two years to study Sanskrit and the Buddhist faith.[26]

Although the Mahayana form of Buddhism may have predominated at Śrivijaya in I-Ching's time, both forms were present and the distinctions between them were not sharply drawn. I-Ching deplored making too much of the differences between the two forms, pointing out that both would conquer passion and lead to salvation. Rather than to indulge in endless speculation regarding the illusory nature of existence, involving much labor and little gain, it would be well, he argued, to go directly to the Vinaya scriptural sources for understanding. I-Ching's description of southern Buddhism as practiced in Sumatra and India was highly detailed, covering forty-odd major topics. They included worship forms, priestly property, ordination standards, ablutions, bathings, sitting and sleeping exercises, illness and medicines, food, water, and raiment.[27]

The rules regulating conduct were many and sometimes rather inconsequential. Sandals must be removed in the presence of teachers and sacred images. Unclean food must be left (as counseled in the *Sutras*) for the consumption of departed spirits and birds. The mouth must be rinsed and the hands washed after every meal (no eating utensils were used), for otherwise prayers and charms would have no efficacy. Insects must be strained from drinking water, not to purify the water, but rather to protect the insects from injury. I-Ching described elaborate celebrations of certain offering and fast days in the southern islands. They called for sermons and hymns, for ceremonial bathing of both images and guests in perfumed water, and for the extensive placing of flowers and incense before images of the Buddha. The preparation of betel nut mixed with oils was an essential preliminary activity. Kings often turned servants on festival occasions to gain merit by feeding the monks. Priestly prayers for rewarding the participants included within their scope appeals to the Naga-snake earth god and also to vagrant spirits and the ancestral dead.[28]

The essential emphasis of Buddhist teaching, according to I-Ching, was the importance of freeing one's self from worldly attachments. The goal was to obliterate the differences between subject and object. Reverence of students for elder monks and teachers must be balanced by the responsibility of the latter for careful instruction of all candidates to be ordained. Such Hindu practices as self-immolation, the cutting of one's flesh, and throwing one's body on a funeral pyre or into the waters of the sacred

25 *Ibid.*, xxxiv–xxxviii; see also Gabriel Ferrand, *L'Empire Sumatranais de Çrivijaya* (1922), 3–6.

26 Nilakanta Sastri, "Śri Vijaya," 250–251.

27 Takakusu, 15–16, 19–21.

28 *Ibid.*, 22–50.

Ganges were denounced as heresies explicitly forbidden by the Buddha. Kindly charity was extolled. Greet all visitors with "Welcome" and visiting strangers with "Most welcome."[29] I-Ching praised the trading profession as a faultless occupation because it did not involve the imperiling of insect life as in farming, the slaughter of animals as in husbandry, or the killing of silkworms as in cloth manufacture. He expressed the belief, nevertheless, that rigid rules forbidding monks to accept pieces of silk as merit offerings were overmeticulous.

I-Ching's account also cast some light on the perennial importance of perfumed woods and forest products (sandalwood, aloeswood, camphor) as staple items of Southeast Asian commerce. He pictured at Buddhist temples rows of jars of perfumed water used for the ceremonial washing of both venerable monks and images. Larger images were anointed twice a month, smaller ones more frequently, with the muddy residue of ground sandalwood and then were rinsed with perfumed water and dried with scented cloths.[30] He reported also that scented artificial flowers of silk were used in temples when fresh flowers were not available. Generally speaking, he preferred fragrant herbs to animal excretions as medicines, although the pilgrim conceded that the use of offal from cows and calves was permissible under some circumstances.[31] The aesthetic aspects of Buddhist piety were obviously not inconsiderable.

How long the Śrivijayan Court continued its lavish support of Buddhism as described by I-Ching it is impossible to calculate. Presumably the state became too preoccupied in the late eighth century with maintaining its precarious political and military position to sustain its ruler's initial dedication to Buddhism. In any case, no durable monuments appeared.[32] Eighth-century Bodhisattva images found at Palembang were derived mainly from Bengal and from the same University of Nalanda sources in Magahda state in north India which I-Ching had visited.

The sending of Śrivijayan embassies to China came to a halt after 742, and it was apparently not resumed until the tenth century. From 767 to 873, central Java enjoyed preferred T'ang recognition politically and commercially, if it may be assumed that the reception of tribute missions afforded evidence of such status. During the late 700s the Mahayana form of Buddhism found its most enthusiastic reception in the state of Mataram in central Java. When the Śailendra rulers eventually lost out in Java between 832 and 856, the last representative of the line took over as ruler at Śrivijaya itself (by 860). Tribute missions to China from Śailendra-ruled Śrivijaya were revived during the latter half of the tenth century on a continuing basis. Śrivijayan relations with China became especially close after 960, when the new commercially minded Sung dynasty reestablished naval

[29] *Ibid.*, 118–125, 189–198.
[30] *Ibid.*, 147–150.
[31] *Ibid.*, 118–125.
[32] Coedès, 221–223.

control of the South China coast.[33] It is on the rise of the Śailendra dynasty of Mataram in central Java that attention must next be centered.

## Śailendra Rule in Java: Borobudur

The first important Śailendra ruler of the state of Mataram in central Java, Sanjaya by name, came to power in 732. He was Śaivite by faith. Because the dynastic title Śailendra and Funan both meant king of the mountain, some have assumed that Sanjaya was descended from exiled princes of Funan. This conclusion is unproved, but it is supported by the fact that the collapse of Funan in the early 600s apparently coincided with the starting of Śailendra rule in Java.[34] Sanjaya was supposed to have been the ninth of his line, but he was the first to attain substantial power. The names of his immediate successors, Indra (750), Vishnu (775), and a second Indra (782), provide clear evidence that Hindu ideas of royal reincarnation prevailed. Events in early Javanese history were chronicled in cycles, connected with Indian divination patterns.

After 750, Javan Mataram experienced the full impact of a Mahayana cultural inundation emanating from the Pala state and also from Bengal in north India. Pala art and Pala script continued much in evidence in Mataram during the golden age of the ninth century. Mataram shared control of central and eastern Java with a minor Hindu vassal state, also ruled by a descendant of Sanjaya. It seems probable that the Śailendra King Vishnu (775–782), otherwise known as Pañcapana, started the Borobudur monument. Although intended as a dynastic tomb, it developed into an impressive expression of Buddhist fervor. Buddhism and the Śailendras lost out after 832, when the only adult successor to the line, a woman, married the ruler of the rival vassal state. The queen's younger brother, named Balaputra, a mere boy in 832, made an abortive effort some twenty years later to recover control for the Śailendras. After he failed, in 856, he fled to Śrivijaya, where he became the ruler,[35] as indicated above.

The Śailendras continued traditional connections with the Indianized states located on the Southeast Asian mainland, a policy which reflected their desire to maintain the right to use the sea lanes to China. Plundering raids from Java were allegedly directed after 760 against Ligor, Champa, and Tongking, extending over a fifteen-year period. In 802, a Khmer prince who may previously have been exiled to Java, one Jayavar-

---

[33] Nilakanta Sastri, "Śri Vijaya," 251–276; Ferrand, *L'Empire Sumatranais,* 6–22; Casparis, 256–264, 294–299. Śrivijayan tribute missions to China were recorded for 670, 695, 716, 724, 728, and 742. They were renewed after the Sung accession, with seven recorded from 960 to 988, four during the war crises of 1003 to 1028, and five from 1067 to 1083.

[34] Coedès, 244–250; Casparis, 204.

[35] Coedès, 152–160, 165–166; Casparis, 200–203.

man II, with Śailendra help seized Lower Chenla from a dynastic rival and
unified the new kingdom of Cambodia.[36] During the course of the ninth
century, Javanese cultural patterns made a substantial contribution to
both Cambodia and Champa. Nalanda-type Buddhism was for a time vigorously present in Ligor. The Chams preferred the Chinese-dragon symbol to
that of the Naga snake for decorating palace balustrades, but they accorded
a high place to elegantly graceful scrolls and art patterns which they apparently borrowed from Java.[37]

The dynastic and religious monuments constructed in central Java's
Kedu plain in the eighth and ninth centuries, of which Borobudur was the
outstanding example, marked a high point in Java's culture. The assembled
monuments reflect a superior level of social and economic development as
well as the remarkable maturity of the Javanese people in the field of
artistic conception and execution. As temple burial shrines, they presented
in relief sculpture and in symbolic illustrations all aspects of the Indian
Mahayana texts, obviously inspired by patterns adapted from Nalanda and
Bengal. The Indian themes were combined with traditional Javanese patterns of ancestor worship, which called for royal tombs enshrined on a sacred
mountain. The ashes of nine Śailendra rulers previous to Pañcapana were
deposited at Borobudur. A nearby Chandi funeral temple, called the
Mendut, housed nine sculptured figures representing the same ancestral
line. Preparations for deposit of the ashes of the tenth ruler of the dynasty
were, for some unknown reason, never carried through.[38]

The cosmic mountain of Borobudur, developed in square pyramidal
form, was Indian in concept and convention but Javanese in choice of pattern and decorative detail. Its hundreds of scenes in relief depict local
plants and animals as well as characteristic activities of the people. They
also suggest the religious and intellectual standards characteristic of the
time and place. The aesthetic and moral appeal of Buddhism was compromised here as elsewhere under the Mahayana system by the persistence
of Hindu cult forms. Both found expression in the refinement and delicacy
of the Javanese tradition.[39]

The foundation of Borobudur was a steep-sided but round-topped

[36] The Śailendra Java ruler Pañcapana seized Ligor temporarily in 775,
when it was part of the Śrivijayan Empire; he later attacked and burned the Cham
capital in 782. See Coedès, 165–166; Moorhead, 62–68; Briggs, *Khmer Empire*,
65–69. Legend tells of the Chenla ruler's contemptuous demand for the head of
his rival, which provoked the Javanese attack.

[37] Wales, 150–156.

[38] J. G. Casparis, *Inscripties Uit de Cailendra-Tijd* (1950), 200–203. Coedès,
152–161.

[39] Wales, 101–114. The ancestral-spirit cult of Java, as celebrated by the
shadow play, found expression on Borobudur in the distortion of certain images
as if they were shadows projected on a screen. See Kenneth P. Landon, *Southeast
Asia: Crossroads of Religion* (1947), 80–83.

hill of virgin rock. It was ornamented on its slopes by bas-reliefs arranged in concentric series. It included eight terraces, five of them square-cornered and three circular, crowned on the leveled top by a domed stupa more than 100 feet high. The masonry façade covered the entire surface of the hill. It contained almost 3 miles of terraced walks lined at the back by sculptured friezes. Wall niches for images of the Buddha numbered well over four hundred. Some seventy bell-shaped stupas, lacking ornaments or decorations, occupied the three circular terraces located on the crest of the hill.[40] From the extensive monastery quarters at the base of the hill, a broad road led eastward to the numerous smaller monuments of similar aesthetic quality located in the Mendut area. One can envisage the sacred precincts as a busy place, inhabited by many monks and pilgrims with attendant slaves or servants assigned to care for the buildings and living needs.[41]

In the construction of Borobudur, the superstructure was apparently put in place before the lower-gallery reliefs were completed. Sockets holding the retaining wall to the living rock of the hill may have proved inadequate to withstand the ever-growing stress of the successive upper terraces. This problem probably required that a broad earthen embankment be thrown up to buttress the base. In any case, an additional series of unfinished reliefs was covered by earth. Observers have noted also that several alterations of plans were made during the course of construction, which must have consumed a number of decades.[42]

The images and reliefs found in the successive levels and galleries of Borobudur portray the entire life of the Buddha, starting with his previous existence as a white elephant; to these were added imaginative Mahayana projections of future Buddhas. The buried base included a sensational representation of criminal violence, attacks, hangings, and the torments of hell, adding up to a hopeless and disgusting cycle of painful human existences. Here the cruder folk were armed with poisoned blowpipe, bow and arrow, sword and dagger. This representation of a savage kind of existence was apparently intended to be outside the sanctuary proper and to contrast with its depicting of the Buddhist tradition.[43]

In the relief sculptures of the four square-cornered terraces above the base, the atmosphere was one of labored peace and serenity. All suggestions of violence were taboo, even to the extent of omitting dramatic scenes from the life of Gautama himself. The earthly life and teachings of the Buddha were elaborately depicted, accompanied by scenes from numer-

[40] Landon, 74–79; R. Grousset, *The Civilizations of the East*, vol. II, *India* (1931), 278–292.

[41] N. J. Krom, *Barabudur: Archaeological Description* (1927), I, 2–3, 6–9, 14.

[42] *Ibid.*, I, 23–29. Major changes at Borobudur included an enlargement of the central stupa and elaborations of texts for the first gallery.

[43] *Ibid.*, II, 175–178, 198; Casparis, *Selected Inscriptions*, 203. Casparis suggests that the buried lower stage was supposed to be the abode of King Indra as a Bodhisattva but that it was not to be uncovered until he attained such status.

ous edifying tales, some of them unidentifiable. The theme moved quickly beyond the historic Gautama, the Sakyamuni, to the several more significant Buddhas-elect who were presumed to follow him. Thus Gautama's Nirvana was treated in the upper galleries as being of little importance compared with the ultimate blessings achieved by the final Dhyani Buddha. The Bodhisattva ideal, placing happiness of fellow creatures above one's own, became here the expression of the highest wisdom and enlightenment, a role accessible to all believers.

This significant emphasis on the Mahayana creed, as demonstrated in the monument of Borobudur, developed during the latter half of the eighth century, apparently as the result of direct cultural contact with Pala India. The same period probably marked the eclipse of the somewhat simpler form in Śrivijaya.[44] In eastern Java, where the Pala impact was obviously much less strong, the Mahayana trend merged quickly with kindred Śaivite Tantric elements and Yoga practices in a syncretic association of contradictory ideals. Śiva dominance was even more markedly present in the island of Bali, located off the eastern end of Java. After the Śailendras had been expelled by eastern Javan princes in the middle of the ninth century, Mahayana Buddhism was smothered in Java, as in India, in the inclusive Hindu embrace.[45]

As important historically as the religious and cultural reflections of Borobudur were the representations it afforded of the life and activities of the people of the time. Large retinues of followers, unimportant to the Buddhist story, filled up the spaces in the panel reliefs. Participants were usually presented as types, lacking individuality. The gods and Bodhisattva kings, for example, were everywhere similarly represented; the Brahman priests were bearded, mustachioed foreigners; the monks and hermits were conventionally robed and shaven Javanese. Evidences of repetition and lack of uniformity indicate that the carvings were done piecemeal by large numbers of craftsmen; varied patterns of hairdress and clothing appeared.

The details were of great variety. A coronation scene depicted the royal umbrella, the jewelry bearers (necklaces, earrings, bracelets), the Brahman sprinklers of holy water with their bowls and brushes, the palanquins and elephants of state, and horse-mounted attendants and horse-drawn carriages. Palace and temple scenes were richly decorated, including eating and drinking sequences, reception halls furnished with costly couches, thrones, and armchairs, down to simple stools and benches. Other scenes pictured storage boxes and chests, dishes, bowls and utensils, lamps, vases, and incense burners. Games and dancing girls, accompanied by instrumental music, enlivened the scenes of homage paying and religious observances. Nursemaids wore a distinctive dress and ornamentation. Many

---

[44] Krom, II, 281–294.

[45] *Ibid.,* II 293–325. Krom concludes that the seeds of corruption of the Buddhist faith, including both Yoga and Tantric elements, were actively present in the Borobudur form as well.

trades and occupations were represented, such as bridge builders working with bamboo, pottery makers, farmers, merchants, vendors with wooden carrying yokes, hunters and fishermen, scholars and artists. Transportation facilities included four-wheeled carts, sailing junks, five types of outrigger ships, and dugout canoes.[46]

The ninth-century shift from Buddhist to Śaivite rule in Mataram Java was dynastic rather than revolutionary in character, although the new rulers were apparently less commercially minded than the Śailendras had been. The ensuing Śaivite religious revival, following Pallavan patterns, evidenced no impairment of cultural vitality, either local or Indian. Eight additional major galleried temples which were constructed in the Kedu plain between 898 and 928 took as their theme the *Ramayana* rather than the Buddhist tradition. They were executed in the same dynamic Javanese fashion demonstrated at Borobudur. Among the impressive new temples were mausoleum monuments including a three-terraced court near Prambanan surrounded by two concentric protecting walls and including no fewer than 156 separate buildings.[47] Central Java in particular assimilated the full Indian cultural impact, absorbed much of its spirit, and came up with a creative synthesis which was far more than a mere combination of borrowings. Under leadership of the progressive King Sindok, after 929, the center of power shifted to eastern Java, where swamps were drained and trade was expanded. Here Javanese scholars translated the entire *Mahabharata* into their own tongue. Buddhism in Java gave place thereafter to a hyphenated Śiva-Buddha cult, which still survives in Bali.[48]

## Java after Śailendra Times

A description of Java by a thirteenth-century Chinese superintendent of maritime customs, Chao Ju-Kua, afforded additional details. He described the government as bureaucratic and equipped with official granaries and an army. Subjects squatted beside the road as the turbaned King, carried on elephant or chair and under a white umbrella, passed by escorted by hundreds of armed retainers. The Javanese wore clothing from chest to the knees. Copper and silver coins were in use; urban folk lived in fine houses and enjoyed good food and instrumental music; countryfolk, as in old Funan, enjoyed pig- and cockfighting. Traders were reported to be treated more generously in central Java than in the eastern regions. The contrasting unsavory reputation of the less civilized inhabitants of eastern Java and the semisavages of the nearby islands doubtless mirrored traditional views, but it may also have reflected lack of acquaintance. Chao Ju-Kua commented: "The foreign head-men of Eastern Java are brave and fierce. They take wives from pirate states of the eastern borders. The people

[46] *Ibid.,* II, 175–185, 210–244.
[47] Hall, 58–63; Van Klavern, 24–25; Casparis, 260.
[48] Hirth and Rockhill, 186–198; Wales, 194–199.

of the latter, under pretext of visiting relatives . . . on board ships, frequently plundered ships in this way. . . . Kidnapping for sale as slaves became so bad that trade was broken off."[49]

None of Mataram's Indonesian neighbors matched its highly civilized performance. The Balinese, who were also heavily Indianized, came closest to the standard of the central Javanese; the ladang cultivators of Sundanese western Java, by contrast, enjoyed meager contact with Hindu culture, and appear to have been on the whole less courteous, less tolerant religiously, and less developed intellectually than their neighbors to the east. The cattle-raising and navigating Madurese islanders, also rather meagerly affected by Hindu influences, earned a modern reputation for impulsive violence, suspicion, and vindictiveness, although demonstrating withal a high level of integrity. The sawah-cultivating Javanese have usually been adjudged by modern observers as more intelligent and polite, more calm and self-controlled, more reverent of authority, and more creative in literature and art than their neighbors. They have also frequently been called kind, hospitable, industrious but not thrifty, tenacious of adat custom and ancestral home ties, and religiously tolerant.[50]

The strong cultural influence of India on Java may also have contributed to the prevalence of what a modern Javanese has described as the nonhistorical view of life prevailing among his countrymen. The causation and direction of events were conceived in Java, as in India, as being rooted outside the temporal order, reflecting cosmic influences beyond the reach of human responsibility. Official Javan history was not descriptive of events as such, but partook of the character of verbal magic. Human effort exerted in the face of trial could achieve spiritual adjustment and a distinctive quality of personality, in comparison with which the external happenings themselves were transient and unimportant. Events generally did not add up to any meaningful experience except as they might be crystallized in tales and traditions clarifying cosmic relationships and assisting human adjustment to fateful developments beyond mundane control. Thus the re-

[49] Wales, 70–86.
[50] E. S. de Klerck, *History of the Netherland East Indies* (1938), I, 118–122.

finements associated with the long-experienced Indian acculturation of the Javanese were balanced by the negative factors of political and social enervation. In Java occurred an eventual "banking of the cultural fires," as was the case in India itself.[51]

## Śailendra Rule at Śrivijaya

The accession of the Śailendra Prince Balaputra at Śrivijaya, following his abortive effort to recover control in central Java in 856, is probably attributable in part to his mother's having been a Śrivijayan princess. Shortly after his accession, Balaputra revived the traditional Śailendra alliance with the Pala state of north India, the fountainhead of Mahayana Buddhism, by founding a temple monastery at Nalanda for the use of visiting Śrivijayan pilgrims. A charter was established around 860, which assigned five Bengal villages for the support of the foundation. The pro-Buddhist Śailendra dynasty thus ruled for a time at Palembang following its withdrawal from Java.[52]

Although Śrivijaya continued to control most of the commerce through the straits and via the portage routes of northern Malaya as well, its trade and income began to decline sharply during the later ninth and early tenth centuries. This decline was mainly the result of disorders developing along the China coast with the collapse of T'ang rule. It was also associated with the abandonment of the seaborne trade to China by Persian and Arab traders. A Śrivijayan trade mission, sent to China in 904, was probably intended to demonstrate that Persian and Indian goods as well as those of Southeast Asia were still obtainable at Palembang despite the discontinuance of the seaborne contact with the Middle East. But the financial difficulties of the fading authority of the T'ang dynasty resulted in the prohibition of the export of rare and precious items from Chinese ports. By 925 came the virtual exclusion of all foreign merchant communities from China. Disorder and piracy prevailed for several decades thereafter along China's southern coasts. Vietnam took advantage of the situation to bring to an end a millennium of Chinese rule, in 939. Contacts between the Chinese ports and those of Southeast Asia, including those on the Bay of Bengal side, were partly revived after 943. The new Sung dynasty established effective general control around 960 and over the Canton area by 971. Under vigorous Sung encouragement, Chinese shipping subsequently took over much of the eastern trade as far as the straits port of Kedah.

The revival of profitable China trade in the late 900s created for Śrivijaya new and serious rivalries. Tambralinga took over control of the isthmian traffic after 971, but maintained fairly cooperative relations with

[51] Soedjatmoko, *An Approach to Indonesian History: Towards an Open Future* (1960), 3–6.

[52] Casparis, *Selected Inscriptions,* 297; Hall, 47–50.

Śrivijaya. Serious trouble developed for Śrivijaya around the turn of the century with eastern Java's Mataram state and also with the Chola Tamil state of south India. The controversies involved dynastic rivalry and probably resentment over Palembang's vexatious monopoly policy under which the two outside powers were being denied a fair share in the use of the straits and in the reviving China trade. The Cholas were also angered by the difficulties imposed by Tambralinga-Lavo, supported after 1001 by the power of Cambodia, in connection with the Indian use of the portage routes. Competition for the China market was underscored by Śrivijaya's sending of seven tributary missions to China between 1003 and 1018, advertising the availability of South Asian products as well as perfumed woods, spices, and pepper. Eastern Java was also trying at the time to cultivate direct trade relations with Sung China, and the Cholas themselves got a mission through to China in 1015. Such commercial tensions reached major proportions between 990 and 1025.[53]

Skillful diplomacy on the part of Śrivijaya apparently prevented its two rivals from getting together. In 992 King Dharmavamsa of Mataram launched a powerful naval attack which threatened Palembang for a time. It was beaten off by 995 with the aid of Malay vassals of Śrivijaya. Good relations were maintained meanwhile between Śrivijaya and the Chola Tamil state, which was preoccupied at the time with expanding its control in south India at the expense of the neighboring Pallavan state and Ceylon.[54] Śrivijaya took murderous revenge on Mataram in 1006 and 1007, reducing the east Javan region to near chaos. Mataram's capital was burned, and its ports and shipping were destroyed. For some two decades thereafter eastern Java remained prostrate.[55]

Chola relations with Śrivijaya began to deteriorate again after 1011, when a new Tamil ruler instituted changes in the Negapatam hostelry agreement and claimed status as a descendant of previous rulers of the straits area. The Chola mission sent to China in 1015 constituted an open bid for a share in the China trade. In 1017, the Chola Empire incorporated Ceylon, capturing its ruler.[56] Rivalry with Śrivijaya finally erupted into an open break in 1025, when Chola forces attacked both sides of the straits down as far as Palembang. The Chola navy raided the entire Sumatran coast from northernmost Acheh to Palembang and captured Kedah and Takuapa on the west Malay coast and Ligor (Tambralinga) on the east. Much treasure was seized, and the Śrivijayan ruler himself was captured.

[53] O. W. Wolters, "Tambralinga," *SOAS*, XXI, 601–605. Moorhead (*A History of Malaya*, 77–82) cites twelve missions to China sent by Śrivijaya from 960 to 1003. See also Van Klavern, 24–25.

[54] Hall, 52–54. As part of the 1005 alliance with Śrivijaya, the Cholas endowed a Buddhist temple at Negapatam, where visiting merchants and pilgrims could find quarters.

[55] *Ibid.*, 52–53; Wolters, 601–605.

[56] H. W. Codrington, *A Short History of Ceylon* (1929), 40–42.

But these seemingly disastrous raids were not followed up by effective Chola occupation. A new Śrivijayan King appeared in 1028 and arranged a matrimonial alliance with King Airlangga of the erstwhile east Javan enemy state in 1030. They apparently agreed to cooperate against the common Chola threat. The confused history of Java from Airlangga's times will be considered later.

Continuing participation in expanding Chinese trading operations through the straits area stimulated general economic recovery.[57] Śrivijaya never quite regained its onetime commercial and naval dominance, but by clever diplomacy and by virtue of its strategic location, it did manage to survive for another $2\frac{1}{2}$ centuries as a trading empire.[58]

The predominant characteristic of the later Śrivijayan state, as described by a Chinese observer of the thirteenth century, was its unbridled belligerency and its concentration of vast wealth in the ruler's hands. All foreign ships were forced to pay toll on pain of outright destruction by native craft, which were ever ready to launch a concerted attack. "This is the reason," wrote Chau Ju-Kua, "why the country is a great shipping center." The local population lived on rafts or on stilt-supported homes, paid no taxes, and overflowed the protecting brick walls of the capital into the countryside. The once-broken harbor chain had not been replaced. No coinage was in use, but chopped silver pieces of varying sizes were employed in business. The enormously wealthy ruler sometimes distributed his weight in silver for relief of the poor. On a Buddhist hill of gold and silver, the King's (Bodhisattva) images were cased in gold. Writing was in Sanskrit characters; the King walked under a silken umbrella; loyal courtiers threw themselves on his funeral pyre as an act of devotion; intoxicating wines were much in use. Of scholarly activity and cultural promise at this late date there was, at Palembang, no suggestion. The actual center of the empire apparently had shifted to Malayu (Jambi) prior to 1225.[59]

The active solicitation of trade with the south seas on the part of Sung China, theoretically under a system of a government monopoly, was a major factor in Śrivijaya's economic revival in the eleventh century. Under the Chinese customs' inspectorate system operating at Canton, Foochow, Hangchow, and at a half-dozen other ports, licensed articles had to be bought and sold at official prices, rigidly enforced. During the course of the twelfth century (by 1178), Arab shipping succeeded in reentering the direct China trade for a time. Eastern Javanese and Palembang vessels also made frequent appearances at Chinese ports. But the bulk of the widely diversified trade of the South China ports in Sung times was carried in Chinese vessels, whether by authorized merchants or by smugglers. They ranged beyond Palembang to Java and the Spice Islands to the east, to Kedah, Cey-

[57] Moorhead, 79–82; Coedès, 238–243; Hall, 52–54.

[58] Coedès, 250–251; Nilakanta Sastri, "Śri Vijaya," 287–289. Palembang later allied with Chola, in 1068.

[59] Hirth and Rockhill, 60–67; Paul Wheatley, *Golden Khersonese,* 12.

lon, and India's Malabar Coast on the west. Southeast Asian countries were primary producers for the trade, with Palembang and Malayu acting as gigantic entrepôt centers collecting items for the seemingly insatiable Chinese market.[60] The principal items of commerce continued to be aromatic woods, drugs (including the rhinoceros-horn panacea), spices, luxury items such as porcelains and silks, ivory, coral, amber, and rock crystal, and hundreds of items of minor importance.

Serious difficulties developed in China during the last quarter of the eleventh century (by 1074) because smuggling activities began to get completely out of hand. The South Asian trade, although much needed as a source of revenue by the Sungs, began to occasion an intolerable drain on the cash and precious metals of China. Because of official corruption at ports of call, the drain of metals consequent on the unfavorable trade balance could not be halted.[61] For a time following the disastrous loss of North China in 1127, involving the devastation of the central Yangtse Valley, the Sungs tried to halt overseas trade entirely. But the government was so dependent on revenues available from south ocean commerce that the policy was abandoned a decade later. The drain on copper cash continued; the Chinese smugglers continued to thrive; but the potentialities of the China market eroded away in time. During the 1200s, in part because of the increasing importance of the spice trade, east Javanese ports began to rival Śrivijaya, and the principal center of Śrivijayan control shifted from the Palembang area to Malayu.[62]

[60] Wheatley, *Golden Khersonese,* 40.

[61] *Ibid.,* 18–24. Only the larger Arab ships made the journey from Malabar ports to China in Sung times.

[62] *Ibid.,* 21, 30, 37–38; Hirth and Rockhill, 18–24.

# CHAPTER 5

# Cambodia

## and Its Neighbors

$\mathcal{T}$he story of the rise and decline of the Cambodian Empire can be conveniently divided into four chronological periods. The pre-Angkor or Chanla era, about which little is known, extends from the Khmer conquest of Funan during the latter half of the sixth century and continues through the better part of $2\frac{1}{2}$ centuries. The revitalization of Cambodia began in a preliminary way under Jaya-varman II (802–850) and continued through the 900s. Real unification came during the last quarter of the ninth century under Indravarman (877–889) and his son Yasovarman (889–900). The seat of Khmer power was transferred during this second period from the middle Mekong Valley to a site above the Great Lake, where the impressive monuments of Angkor were later to be developed. A third period began around the year 1000, with the temporary usurpation of power by a Tambralinga prince from north Malaya. It lasted some three centuries and witnessed the maximum extension of Khmer control westward to upper segments of the Menam and Mekong Valleys, to the isthmian shores of the Bay of Bengal, and thence northward to the boundaries of Pagan Burma in Tenasserim. At this time Cambodia achieved its most impressive artistic and cultural performance. A fourth and final period, beginning in the middle 1200s, was one of territorial contraction and cultural decline. It may be considered as ending with the eventual destruction of Angkor by the Thai in the fifteenth century, although a short-lived revival was staged in the late 1500s.

The sources for study of the history of Cambodia, although ample as compared with those of contemporary kingdoms in Śrivijaya, are far from complete. Chinese dynastic histories provide a basis for chronology in the recording of reign names and the dates of the reception of successive tribute missions. A vivid firsthand description of thirteenth-century Angkor was provided by one Chou Ta-kuan, a member of a visiting Mongol Chinese commercial mission.[1] This informative description was apparently based

[1] Chou Ta-kuan, "Mémoires sur les Coutumes du Cambodge de Tcheou Ta-Kouan," *BEFEO*, XI (1902), 141–176. Translated by Paul Pelliot.

on secondhand data drawn from resident Chinese interpreters in Cambodia, who were not always fully informed. A third principal source of historical information is derived from some nine hundred Sanskrit and Khmer inscriptions found on surviving stone monuments, many of which have been deciphered and translated by French and Indian scholars.[2] Bas-relief details found on the more impressive monuments of Angkor also provide pictorial information concerning the population and its varied activities. These are supplemented by sculptured figures, Buddhist and Hindu, which reflect the art patterns and the influence of successive phases of Indian cultural contributions. The fragmentary and inconclusive character of the sources leaves much of the story conjectural, but one can nevertheless make a fairly accurate assessment of the social structure of the Cambodian people themselves and of the achievements of the more important rulers of the kingdom. This chapter will also include a description of neighboring states, especially Champa and Nam Viet, which became independent of China after 929.

## The Pre-Angkor, or Chenla, Period

The overthrow of the power of Funan by the Chenla Khmers during the latter half of the sixth and the early seventh century inaugurated a period of political and economic decline for the lower Mekong River and Great Lake basins. The Khmer conquerors were not frontier barbarians unappreciative of the civilization of Funan, for they had long lived as contiguous vassal subjects. Khmers had infiltrated southward into the lower Mekong Valley at all the social levels extending from the peasant cultivators to the elite of the royal court. The Khmers had also been recipients of cultural influence both Buddhist and Hindu, coming from the Mons via the Menam Valley and the Korat plateau.[3] The fact that Chenla rulers invariably claimed descent from the ancient Kaundinya line affords eloquent testimony to the continuing prestige of Funan. But the early Chenla rulers were simply unable to hold the Funan Empire together.

Political fragmentation in early Chenla times stemmed from the dissipation of both the symbols and the reality of Funan's traditional authority in areas distant from the Mekong River Valley and delta. The portage states of north Malaya and the Mon states of the upper isthmus assumed independent status, while the lower Annamese coast below Camranh Bay fell away to the Chams, as previously explained. The authority of the Chenla rulers was tardily applied to the Great Lake region and to the more distant interior. Efforts to extend Khmer control into the Lao territory above the

[2] The best history of Cambodia, by L. P. Briggs, based on translations of inscriptions, is *The Ancient Khmer Empire* (1951). More important for the inscriptions themselves are G. Coedès, *Pour Mieux Comprendre Angkor* (1947), and R. C. Majumdar. *Ancient Indian Colonies in South-East Asia: II* (1955).

[3] Several such sites have been identified in the Mun Valley, northwest of Angkor.

bend of the Mekong River and to the frontier territories of Thai chieftains ruling over the borderlands of China also diverted attention from the gulf region.[4] Some fourscore years were therefore required for the Khmer subjugation of Funan. A much longer period elapsed before imperial authority was reestablished on the traditional pattern of the Funan rulers.

Economic decline within Khmer-ruled areas accompanied the political fragmentation. The interior state of Upper Chenla had no direct interest in protecting and promoting seaborne commerce. The emerging states of Mataram Java and Śrivijaya, previously described, and city-states located along the portage routes of the isthmus generally were far better able at the outset than Lower Chenla to take advantage of the expanding seventh-and-eighth-century trade with T'ang China. The political situation in the portage area as of 675 included a number of small states, none of which was able to overcome its neighbors. In the upper isthmus, Dvaravati (Tun-sun) was located above Ko-lo (Tavoy) and P'an P'an (Mergui to Kra). Further south lay the Takuapa-Bandon portage route, the commercial corridor from Takkola (Trang) to Ligor in the revived state of Lankasuka (Patani). Kelantan (Ch'ih-t'u) and Trengganu (Tan-tan) were further down the lower eastern Malaya coast, and Kedah was on the western side. The port cities from Ligor southward were later absorbed for a considerable period of time into the Śrivijayan Empire, while Tambralinga appears to have absorbed several of the north isthmian states around 1000.[5]

The early political history of Chenla can be summarized briefly. The founding of the state was the cooperative achievement of two warrior brothers who took the Śaivite reign names of Bhavavarman (550–600) and Mahendravarman (600–611); they were protégés of Śiva and Indra. They were related in a collateral way to the old Funan Court through the female line, either by parentage or by marriage. The younger of the two long served the older King Bhavavarman as the military leader of the realm. Both maintained a measure of continuity with the old Court of Funan by accepting as chief ministers on a hereditary basis the nephews of the former physicians of Rudravarman, the last of the Funan kings.[6]

The conquest of Funan proper was completed by Isanavarman (611–635), a son of Mahendravarman, who ousted rival claimants, but retained the services of the same line of hereditary ministers. He erased the last remnants of Funan control and also pushed his authority westward to the lower Menam River and northward to the borders of the Lao country. He shifted

[4] Pierre Dupont, "Études sur l'Indochine Ancienne: I. La Dislocation de Tchen-la et la Formation du Cambodge Angkorien, VIIe–IXe Siècles," *BEFEO,* XLIII (1943–1946), 17–55.

[5] Paul Wheatley, "The Historical Geography of the Malay Peninsula before A.D. 1500" (1958), 98–99, 383.

[6] D. G. E. Hall, *A History of South-East Asia* (1955), 85–87; M. Ghosh, *A History of Cambodia* (1960), 64–81. The nephews were named Dharmadeva and Simhadeva.

the Chenla capital from its early site along the lower Mekong River above the delta to the city of Isanapura, located above Tonle Sap near the Great Lake. Brick remains, associated with remnants of Hindu statuary and decorative sculpture, mark the locale of Isanapura. Isanapura was located near the center of Khmer power, at a point more easily defensible from coastal attack than were former capitals and also adjacent to a source of abundant food.[7]

The third quarter of the seventh century witnessed the conquest by a descendant of the old Bhavavarman line, King Jayavarman I (657–681), of all of Laos up to the borders of Thai Nan Chao, which was at the time also under attack by T'ang China.[8] Numerous contemporaneous inscriptions attest the military achievements of Jayavarman's reign. They also reflect a revival of the study of the basic Hindu classics (the *Ramayana* and *Mahabharata,* and the newer *Puranas* of Gupta times), plus the increasing use of the written Khmer language itself. Contact with south Indian Pallavan culture during the seventh century is indicated by evident improvement in standards of Sanskrit verse and grammar.[9] The Hindu tradition prevailed concerning the impurity of the left hand, the arranging of weddings on auspicious days, and in the requirement of triple prostrations in the presence of the king. Mourning practices required fasting and shaven heads of the children of the deceased.[10]

For more than a century following Jayavarman's death (he died in 681 without a recognized heir), confusion and rebellion prevailed. This resulted after 706 in a sharp division between Upper Chenla (of the Land) and Lower Chenla (of the Water).[11] Upper Chenla was politically the more united and vigorous of the two; it also sent repeated missions to China. It was a centralized rather than a federated state, with administrative centers located at some thirty fortified provincial capitals. An artificial combination of Śiva and Vishnu worship known as the Harihara cult was practiced for a time, but Śiva worship eventually predominated. The government functioned along Indian lines, with a divine ruler presiding over a grand court, but it lacked the full pretensions of the imperial Devaraja cult of Funan times.[12] Buildings were of brick, and few of them survived. Sculpture was crude; music and dance forms were developed in connection with the religious cults.

During the course of the eighth century Lower Cambodia split into

[7] Hall, 86–87; Ghosh, 72–75.

[8] Upper Chenla also allied briefly with China in 753–754 against the common Thai enemy of Nan Chao.

[9] G. Coedès, *Les États Hindouisés d'Indochine et d'Indonésie* (1948), 115.

[10] Ghosh, 90–106.

[11] Hall, 87–89. Khmer history from 635 to 657 and from 681 to 717 is virtually empty of information. Bhavavarman II ruled after 635. Jayavarman's widow attempted in vain to keep the peace.

[12] Briggs, 47–57; R. C. Majumdar, *Kambuja-Desa* (1944), 59–66.

at least five dynastic units, only one of which, Water Chenla, was under Khmer control. Water Chenla was confined to the western portion of the delta and extended up the Mekong Valley to the old Khmer center at Bassac. It appears to have become, during the later decades of the 700s, more or less tributary to Java.[13] Destructive Indonesian naval raids, presumably Javanese, were directed against Tongking, Champa, and Chenla from 767 to 799. The last of the Lower Chenla rulers, a rash person named Mahipativarman whose capital was at Angkor (Borei), was allegedly assassinated around 790 at the instigation of a Śrivijayan ruler whom he had offended. The eventual victor in the ensuing civil war, attaining power in 795, presumably as a vassal of Java, took the reign name of Jayavarman II in 802.

Jayavarman II was a prince from the minor Khmer state of Sambhupura (above the delta), who had been temporarily domiciled in Java as an exile or hostage. He had apparently been nominated by the Javanese King as a puppet vassal ruler of Chenla.[14] Starting from Indrapura on the lower Mekong in 802, Jayavarman conquered Lower Chenla in six stages, using a new frontier capital as a base each time. As soon as he had established a firm footing near the protected site of Angkor, around 819, he threw off Javan-Śrivijayan suzerainty and declared Cambodia's independence by reviving the Devaraja cult. His reign marked the partial reunification of Cambodia and the beginning of the Angkor period of Cambodian history. Although no contemporary records survived from his reign, or possibly because of that fact, Jayavarman's reputation grew over a period of some two centuries to one of exaggerated importance, unsurpassed in Cambodian historical annals.[15]

## Establishment of the Cambodian Empire in the Ninth Century

Jayavarman II's accomplishments were substantial even though his traditional reputation as an empire builder has been subjected to considerable qualification by modern historians. He employed the king's prerogative to dispose of the land by fief grants carved out of newly conquered areas. His kingdom in the end was therefore essentially feudal rather than unitary in character. Hariharalaya, the third of his six acquisitions, located in the Angkor area above the Great Lake, had been an important independent political center since the end of the Funan period. His later conquests carried him to the west and northwest, after which he returned to make Hariharalaya his permanent capital. He died around 850. His control apparently never extended beyond the limits of Cambodia proper. Land Chenla, with its capital at Bhavapura, was united peacefully with the rest of

[13] Dupont, 27, 39–43, 54–55.

[14] Pierre Dupont, "Études sur l'Indochine Ancienne: II," *BEFEO*, XLVI (1952), 152–157.

[15] Briggs, 47–57; Majumdar, *Kambuja-Desa,* 72–83; Hall, 91–92.

Cambodia during the reign of Rajendravarman II (944–948), who inherited the crowns of both segments of Khmer control.[16]

Jayavarman II's revival of the ancient Devaraja symbolism of universal kingship occurred after his occupation of Hariharalaya (819 or 820). The impressive ceremony was performed at Mount Mahendra (Phnom Kulen), where a religious center of long standing was located in a rocky concave profile at the edge of a plateau. With the solicited aid of a learned Brahman teacher, trained in India, he was subjected to mystical rituals calculated to accomplish his transformation into an independent manifestation of Śiva. The office of the high priest, or Purohita, thereafter became responsible for perpetuating the proper ritual exercises. Custody of the sacred-sword symbol was likewise entrusted to responsible Brahman hands. The ruler thus became a Chakravartin, or universal ruler, allegedly the living embodiment of the Devaraja, or the divine essence of kingship. The latter centered symbolically in the royal linga housed in a temple located at the center of the capital. This ceremony presumably marked the final repudiation of Jayavarman's previous vassalage to Java.

The Devaraja cult of Cambodia also assimilated the older naga-serpent tradition, according to which the royal consort in the form of a female transfiguration of the god of the soil had nightly intercourse with the divine king at the top of a sacred pyramidal tower. The mountain temple was located, in the Mount Meru tradition, at the magically determined center of the axis of the universe. The linga temple of the Devaraja frequently became later the tomb of the divine ruler.[17]

The new Cambodian state was thus strongly Śaivite in its religious orientation. Also present were the surviving remnants of the combined Śiva-Vishnu-Harihara cult, as reflected in the name of the capital, and also traces of earlier Hinayana Buddhist traditions. The Devaraja symbolism later proved capable of adaptation under the Mahayana Buddhist faith, with the god-king conceived as an emergent Buddha or Bodhisattva. The Khmer concept of kingship included finally an element of ancestor worship indigenous to Cambodia and Java and not derived at all from India. Royal incarnations in Cambodia were also conceived in personal rather than generalized terms, contrary to the practice of the Indian tradition.[18]

The actual authentication in political terms of the pretensions of Devaraja status was the work of Indravarman I (877–889) and his son, Yasovarman I (889–900). Indravarman, a cousin of the nonentity Jayavarman III, inherited several states lying outside the bounds of the older domain of Jayavarman II, and he also subjected the allocation of royal fiefs to thoroughgoing reexamination. By 900, Cambodia extended from Chantaban on the west coast to Cochin-China on the east and northward to Bassac

[16] Dupont, "Études: I," 50–55, and "Études: II," 152–163.

[17] Briggs, 90; Coedès, *Pour Mieux Comprendre Angkor,* II, 62–64; Chou Ta-kuan, 145; Ghosh, 109–113.

[18] H. G. Q. Wales, *The Mountain of God* (1953), 150–151.

and the southern Lao country. In the heart of the domain was concentrated an imposing array of water-control devices—dikes, irrigation channels, tanks and reservoirs, and elevated roadways. Heavy rainfall from the four months of the summer monsoon was conserved in laterite catchment basins for judicious use during the seven months of the dry season, making possible irrigated-rice production throughout the year in favored areas. Canals were used for transportation of both commodities and building stone. This system was destined to be further elaborated by the great Cambodian rulers of the eleventh century.[19] Indravarman I was a pro-Vishnu ruler, who also constructed a number of temple shrines of stone, several hermitages for charitable purposes, and was something of an artist-designer in his own right.[20]

The Devaraja cult helped bridge political rifts and the always-troublesome episodes connected with the shift of rulers. Symbols of authority were impressively maintained, and the priestly offices at court were transmitted by hereditary succession. The difficult problem of determining royal succession, in a situation where the many sons of multiple queens could with a mother's intriguing aid raise conflicting claims, was entrusted to a Great Council. This body was customarily convened by the chief minister following the death of a king. It included four or five of the ministers, the hereditary custodian (*Bako*) of the sacred sword, and other high officials present at the capital. Since all royal descendants of queens as remote as five generations back were theoretically eligible,[21] the rivalry between claimants both at court and outside the palace could become very tense. The claims of the designated heir apparent (*Yuvaraja*) were carefully reviewed by the Council in making its final selection. Kings, once chosen, had to be extremely cautious, frequently feeling obliged to kill off all rival brothers. Only female servants and guards were customarily permitted within the palace area, and the ruler left the palace precincts only under heavy guard protection. Enforced prostration by all people along his route of travel was required, probably for security as well as prestige.[22]

The hereditary character of the high priestly offices and their important role in matters of succession made of the Cambodian government something of a theocracy. All royal monuments were religious in character, as were all inscriptions. The king was the protector of religion, the patron of piety, the guardian of the established sacred law, and the performer of ritual sacrifices and ceremonies calculated to enlist divine favor. His moated

[19] Dupont, "Études: II," 169–171; Bernard Philippe Groslier, *Angkor et le Cambodge au XVIe Siècle* (1958), 109–112.

[20] Ghosh, 115–125.

[21] A princely family lost one status grade during each of five successive generations, after which the descendants were reduced to commoner rank. A nearly identical tradition survives in twentieth-century Thailand.

[22] Briggs, 25, 81–82; Chou Ta-kuan, 176.

capital was a miniature Mount Meru, the center of the universe, the abode of the gods. He was also, by his inherited ancestry from the naga-serpent spirit, the proprietor of the soil, the "owner" of his people, and the "eater" of his kingdom. He was finally the governing judge of last resort. The chief religious officials of the Cambodian Court, including the royal astrologer and the high priest (Purohita) of the Devaraja cult, were invariably recruited from the Brahman *hotar* chaplaincy. The same was true of the custodian (Bako) of the sacred sword.[23] Important civilian and military posts were usually occupied by members of the royal family. Both royal and priestly inheritance was usually transmitted through the female line. Marriages between Brahman families and court Kshatriyas occurred frequently, so that after a time the Hindu intellectual elite differed little racially from the rest of the Khmer population. New Brahman scholarly recruits probably arrived periodically from India.

The chief ministers of state of Cambodia were entrusted with the supervision of provincial administration, armies and royal arsenals, *corvée* labor, courts and police control.[24] All officials of the realm who were royal appointees (some four thousand all told) were bound by exacting feudal oaths of loyalty to the ruling monarch. These ties were buttressed in many cases by diplomatic family alliances through the provision of daughters for the royal harem. Apart from the thirty or so districts ruled directly by royally appointed provincial governors, vassal states enjoyed varying degrees of autonomy under subkings. In the 1000s some ninety subordinate administrative units of all types were operative, each one ruling from a palisaded center. The king's judicial authority was delegated to high-level officials. Trial by ordeal was practiced where contradictory evidence of guilt was otherwise unresolved. In the absence of prisons, criminal punishment was inflicted by mutilation (fingers, toes, limbs) or by burial alive. Minor civil offenses were presumably left to local arbitral adjudication.

The royal palace itself was constructed of wood rather than stone, but it was richly ornamented with paintings, mirrors of burnished metal, and various items of furniture decorated in gold. The windows of the Great Council chamber were allegedly framed with gold. The king wore costly crowns and garlands of flowers; the court ladies displayed pearl necklaces, ornamented belts, gold rings, bracelets, and anklets. The palace was inhabited largely by women, beginning with the five main queens (one for the center and one for each cardinal point of the compass). Proceeding down the status scale were the royal concubines, musical and dancing entertainers, chess players, gladiators, servants, and Amazon guards.[25] A royal procession of palanquins, horse and elephant mounts, and troop escort, as described

[23] Coedès, *Les États,* 202–204; Briggs, 41, 82, 151, 167–168, 249; Majumdar, *Kambuja-Desa,* 60; Chou Ta-kuan, 161, 249.

[24] Coedès, *Les États,* 204–206.

[25] Chou Ta-kuan, 145, 152, 176.

by a Chinese visitor in 1225, included also several hundred women carrying lighted tapers, along with bearers of banners, the royal white umbrella, and a sampling of gold and silver utensils of the palace.[26]

## The Great Rulers of Cambodia

Four or five additional Cambodian kings, selected from the twenty-five identifiable rulers down to the end of the thirteenth century, are probably worthy of historical reference. The first was Yasovarman I (889–900), who founded the first extensive capital city, Yasoharapura, on the Angkor site. Although the extremely laudatory inscriptions referring to his reign have been discounted by some scholars,[27] he was a tolerant and progressive ruler, a builder of scores of temple hermitages (four great ones in honor of Śiva, Vishnu, Brahma, and Buddha respectively), and also a scholar and artist in his own right. During his short reign the use of the Nagari alphabet of north India suggests close connections with Nalanda University of the Pala dynasty. The use of the south Indian Pallavan script revived after 900. Yasovarman I established Cambodian suzerainty over the Mon peoples of the Menam Valley extending over to the Burma border and as far north as the Shan-Thai state of Kengtung.[28]

Of the six rulers of tenth-century Cambodia, the most important was Rajendravarman II (944–968). He intervened from Upper Chenla to oust a usurper ruler and to restore the capital of the empire to Yasoharapura, the site of Angkor. This action united in his person the Crowns of Chenla and Cambodia proper. The capital was rebuilt and the construction of a number of outstanding monuments and temples, such as the Phnom Bakeng and Banteay Srei, was begun. He also staged a successful invasion of Champa in 945–946. His son, Jayavarman V (968–1001), completed the monuments previously named and started some new ones. Jayavarman V's reign was marred by political unrest, which erupted into civil strife following his death in 1001. The controversy apparently centered on widespread resentment against the extensive power wielded at court by hereditary priestly families of the Śiva cult.[29]

The decade following Jayavarman V's death witnessed the seizure of power in Cambodia by a collateral relative of the old Khmer dynasty, the son of the vassal ruler of the Tambralinga state centering at Ligor in northern Malaya. Between 775, when the port of Ligor was definitely part of the Śrivijayan Empire, and the tenth century, Tambralinga had emerged as

---

[26] Coedès, *Les États,* 360–361.

[27] Briggs, 103–105. For the full list of thirty-five kings of Angkor down to 1432, see Hall, 738–739.

[28] Briggs, 103–105; Ghosh, 125–236. Yasoharapura was temporarily abandoned by Jayavarman IV (928–942), but was rebuilt by his successor Rajendravarman II.

[29] Hall, 99–100; Briggs, 144–149.

an independent state. It was nominally subordinate to Śrivijaya and generally antagonistic to any presumption of rival Cambodian or Javan overlord-ship.[30] During the period of the 990s, when eastern Java went to war with Śrivijaya (see Chapter 4), a Tambralinga ruler named Sujita embarked on an independent adventure to the north. He intervened in the strife then raging between the Mon state of Lavo (including Mon Dvaravati) and its upper Menam colony of Haripunjaya (at Lamph'un). Sujita attacked Lavo by sea and land and, after establishing his control, made an abortive expedi-tion, in 995, against Haripunjaya also. Sujita's son and heir, Suryavarman I, a moderately tolerant Buddhist partisan, intervened in Cambodian affairs after 1001, operating from his new base of power in Mon Lavo.

The ensuing contest apparently assumed something of an inter-national character. The pro-Śaivite candidate in Cambodia, Jayaviravarman, sought aid in vain from the friendly eastern Javan state, which was then at odds with Śrivijaya. In turn, Suryavarman I seems to have solicited support from both Śrivijaya and Sung China.[31] In any case, some ten years of fighting ensued, with the invading pro-Buddhist Lavo forces enlisting local support from an anti-Śaivite faction within Cambodia. Suryavarman's conclusive victory of 1011 inaugurated a long and fruitful rule extending to the mid-century. Tambralinga's political alliance with Śrivijaya during this decade and after was doubtless responsible for their sharing in common the ire of the Tamil Cholas of South India in a series of hostile raids from 1017 to 1026. Punitive Chola raids may have affected adversely the Ligor area on the eastern coast, but the south Indian attacks were certainly registered against the Tambralinga ports located on the Bay of Bengal side. Suryavarman's Cambodian state was apparently not directly involved in the Chola attacks.[32] Except for a short period of interrupted relations following 1065, Tambra-linga nevertheless remained generally associated with the Cambodian Empire whenever Angkor was strong. Tambralinga continued to be rather strongly Theravada Buddhist until the advent of Thai power in the middle 1200s.[33]

Suryavarman I (1011–1050) must be ranked among the greatest of the kings of Cambodia. His firm control of the shores of the Gulf of Siam put an end to the Buddhist Mon Confederacy of Ramanyadesa. This in-cluded Dvaravati-Lavo, Mon Thaton in Burma, and Haripunjaya, which were all united in a kind of loose defensive alliance.[34] By pursuing a tolerant

[30] Mon political influence was apparently exerted from time to time in Tambralinga, but not to the point of full domination.

[31] Tambralinga sent diplomatic missions to China in 1001, presumably seeking recognition and aid.

[32] O. W. Wolters, "Tambralinga," *BSOAS*, XXI (1958), 591–597.

[33] Briggs, 146–149; Coedès, *Les États*, 228–235. Inscriptions in Tambralinga dating from 1183 and 1230 were in the Khmer language.

[34] The Pagan Burmans' capture of Thaton in 1054–1057 was expedited by the disruption of the Mon Confederacy; the larger Cambodian threat from the south probably enlisted the local Mons to seek help from the Pagan forces.

religious policy which left the official Devaraja cult undisturbed in Cambodia proper (yet broke the power monopoly of sacerdotal families) and which permitted at the same time both forms of Buddhism to function freely, he established internal security and strengthened his governmental organization. He completed the Phimeanakas palace and also the five-towered, stone-vaulted Takeo structure, foreshadowing the pattern of Angkor Wat.[35]

The fourth great Cambodian ruler was Suryavarman II (1113–1150). His reign was a busy one. It witnessed efforts to halt the first serious Thai infiltrations into the upper Menam Valley and Laos. Available inscriptions indicate that he spent much of his time in the north. Professional Thai soldiers were enrolled in his armies. He also renewed tributary and trading relations with China early in his reign. The old Mon state of Lavo-Lopburi (possibly Chen-li-fu to the Chinese) made several abortive efforts to regain independent status, involving the sending of diplomatic envoys to China in 1115 and 1155.[36] Cambodia's Cham neighbors in Annam, preoccupied heretofore with resisting the southward pressure from the now-independent Vietnam state, also began to cause serious trouble. Suryavarman II waged a series of three wars, not wholly successfully, against the Chams (1123–1124, 1138, and 1145–1149). He also found the time and the resources to build the splendid Vishnu temple of Angkor Wat, to be described later. Śaivism and the Devaraja cult persisted in a perfunctory way as the official state religion, but Vishnuism became the supreme faith in Suryavarman's realm. It was often found in syncretic combination with Śiva worship (in the Harihara tradition) and associated with Mahayana Buddhism. Suryavarman II was also responsible for creating an extensive road system and a vast complex of reservoirs and irrigation works.[37]

Following Suryavarman's death in 1150, the Chams repeatedly staged savage attacks on Cambodia. These culminated in the expedition of a Cham fleet up the Mekong River and into the Great Lake itself in 1177, when Yasoharapura was captured and destroyed and its ruler slain. The ensuing period of disorder and travail was aggravated by an abortive effort of Mon Haripunjaya to invade Lavo, which also again made a bid for independence in 1180.[38] Jayavarman VII (1181–1219) emerged to redeem this discouraging situation. He was to become famous as the builder of Angkor Thom and the impressive Buddhist monument of the Bayon, but he was first of all a statesman. His initial accomplishment was to drive out the Cham invaders and to restore stable rule. Using dissident Cham refugees in Cambodia and also some enlisted Thai forces to assist him, Jayavarman VII won a great naval victory over Champa in 1181, and later successfully brought Lavo

[35] Briggs, 152–167.

[36] O. W. Wolters, "Chên-Li-fu, a State on the Gulf of Siam at the Beginning of the 13th Century," *JSS*, XLVIII (November, 1960), 17–18.

[37] Briggs, 189–192; Coedès, *Les États*, 269–277; Groslier, 110–112.

[38] Briggs, 207–210.

under control. He invaded Champa again in 1190. His final victory over the Chams in 1203 witnessed the installation of a puppet Cham prince as ruler, backed by Khmer troops. For some twenty years Champa was virtually a province of Cambodia. During the 1203 campaign against Champa, the Mons of Lavo rose once more, seeking in vain to obtain Sung China's recognition. Faced by the rising Mongol threat, the Sungs received no Southeast Asian embassies after 1205. In spite of Jayavarman's vigorous efforts, the Cambodian state continued to disintegrate. Sukhotai in the upper Menam Valley gained its independence in 1219.[39]

At its largest, Jayavarman VII's domain stretched from the lower Annamese coast westward to the borders of Pagan Burma and from near Vientiane in Laos southward to include most of the Malay Peninsula. He personally was an ardent adherent of the Buddhist faith. A Khmer prince (possibly the ruler's own son), journeyed to Ceylon in 1190 in the company of a Mon monk-scholar named Chapata on a mission intended to restore to unadulterated Theravada standards the prevailing corrupted Buddhist cult. This renewed Sinhalese version of the faith penetrated the Menam Valley during the middle 1200s.[40] In addition to building the major edifices mentioned above, Jayavarman VII constructed elevated military roads dotted with resthouses at 10-mile intervals. He also established many hospitals for the sick and infirm.

The cumulative costs in terms of treasure and forced labor incurred by Jayavarman VII's exhausting wars combined with his many charitable and building ventures were apparently more than the economy of Cambodia could sustain. An estimated 300,000 priests and temple servants of some twenty thousand shrines reportedly consumed 38,000 tons of rice per year and also absorbed vast riches in gems and precious metals. His illustrious reign proved, therefore, to be a prelude to Cambodia's eventual decline. Trade from Sung China, which had been particularly strong between 1050 and 1175, declined thereafter, partly because of Sung embarrassment over the heavy drain of bullion which it entailed and partly because of civil war in China and the rising Mongol threat after 1200.[41] When Cambodia's trade with China subsequently revived in Mongol times, it was virtually monopolized by the Chinese themselves. Meanwhile, Indian trading activity to the east of Malaya also decreased sharply. More ominous for Cambodia's future hegemony was the increasing southward movement of Thai peoples from the borderlands of China during the early thirteenth century.

But Cambodia was destined, better than most of its neighbors, to

[39] Wolters, 19.

[40] Coedès, *Les États*, 286–292; Hall, 106–111. Jayavarman VII had himself been an exile in Champa prior to his advent as ruler of Cambodia.

[41] Briggs, 167–168, 236; Coedès, *Pour Mieux Comprendre Angkor*, II, 188–196; Majumdar, *Kambuja-Desa*, 129–131. The last recorded missions to Sung China were sent by Cambodia in 1147, by Champa in 1168, by Java in 1170, and by Śrivijaya in 1178; an abortive diplomatic effort was made by Lavo in 1205.

survive the immediate impact of the Mongol-Thai intrusion. Pagan Burma, the Mon lands west of the Menam, Vietnam, and Champa suffered from the Mongols far sooner and more disastrously than did Cambodia. As described by Chou Ta-kuan in 1225, Angkor still exhibited abundant economic vitality as the meeting place of east and west. Its busy market places were crowded with thousands of merchants, trading by barter or using silver bars for major transactions. The stall spaces, rented from officials of the market, exhibited wares on low tables or on mats, often protected by umbrellas. The perennial bargaining was animated. Chinese apparently handled virtually all foreign imports from whatever source; precious metals, silks, lacquer ware, paper, umbrellas, copper ware, cotton textiles, porcelains, saltpeter, musk, needles, wheat, and beans were mentioned. Native women shopkeepers sold most of the local produce—ivory, medicinal rhinoceros horns, bird feathers, beeswax, cardamon, vegetable oils, parrots, perfumes, and pearls.[42] Cambodia's day of greatness was fading, but its collapse was long deferred.

## The Principal Monuments of Angkor

The artistic and cultural achievements of Cambodia excelled those of its Southeast Asian neighbors in several important particulars. The Dvaravati Mons, for example, produced no imposing buildings and never quite emancipated themselves from the pre-Angkor standards of sculpture borrowed from Gupta India. The Chams also reflected strong Gupta dominance in their sculpture, although some specific examples, such as the famous 15-inch bust of Parvati and a relief panel of some exotic jewel-bedecked nude dancers, apparently surpassed the best Indian standards. But Cham architecture was in brick, not stone, a limitation which handicapped progress in both decorative design and in technical construction. Cham buildings included no extensive bas-reliefs and no vaulted galleries. After Indian influence began to wane, the degenerating standards of Cham art became crudely local in character, cold, barbarous, sometimes grotesque.[43]

Khmer superiority in architecture during the Angkor period is seen in its advance from brick to stone, which was capable of bolder feats of construction and development in elaborate bas-relief designs. The Khmers improved on the closed vaulted gallery supported by two walls by having one side rest on pillars so as to admit light for viewing the relief sculpture placed on the one interior wall. Khmer art also eventually emancipated itself from rigid Indian standards, such as conventionalized eyebrows, lips, and beards, to achieve an approximation of the humanistic sensitivity of Borobudur. Indian standards can be seen in the symbolic contentment suggested in the bland smile and half-closed eyes, but some of the nude figures

[42] Chou Ta-kuan, 167, 175, 247; B. P. Groslier, *Recherches sur les Cambodgiens* (1921), 22–26.

[43] R. Grousset, *The Civilizations of the East,* vol. II, *India* (1931), 316–336.

in the relief scenes were fashioned in the native, not the Hindu style. If a Hindu heaven was represented in the bas-reliefs, the landscape and the people were emphatically earthy and Khmer. Representations of the queens at court, the royal barges and palanquins, the elephant hunt, the army marching through the forest, battles and market places, festive occasions, the grotesquely humorous dwarf images holding the body of the ponderous naga serpent on their laps—all of this and more was creatively Khmer.[44]

Some of the best-executed figures and decorative detail were developed on the minor Angkor monuments, such as the Banteay Srei, a temple dedicated in 968. It marked the advent of the stone vault, the escape from the ponderous pyramidal mass, and the development of deep-relief sculpture and beautifully proportioned frontals and façades, elaborately decorated.[45] The Banteay Srei, along with other early Khmer masterpieces, may have reflected a measure of Javanese influence, for example, in the smaller figures with their softened facial contours, their rounding eyebrows, and deep plump lips. Javanese influence was not notably in evidence, however, in the larger Khmer monuments of a later period.[46] Banteay Srei was preceded by the imposing Phnom Bakeng located at the center of Yasoharapura; it was followed by the Takeo, the Phimeanakas, and numerous minor structures. The Khmers thus had long practice in preparing stone materials in accordance with elaborate plans, all to be fitted together without the aid of mortar. The conclusion is at least arguable that no other nation in premodern times built so many first-rate architectural monuments as did the Khmers within any comparable period of time.[47]

The most splendid of the Khmer architectural monuments and also the most instructive for historical purposes was Angkor Wat, a Vishnu temple built during the reign of Suryavarman II (1113–1150). The temple area was rectangular in shape and enclosed by a colonnaded wall measuring 850 meters in width and 1,000 meters in depth. It was surrounded by a water-filled moat 200 meters across. The western frontal approach was via an earth-and-stone causeway leading to the central gateway, flanked at some distance on either side by two larger entryways for elephants. Three towers guarded the elaborately colonnaded entrance areas. The outer gallery contained relief friezes measuring in total length more than 500 meters. A kind of continuous embroidery decoration, minute in design, covered much of the interior surface of the wall.

The first division of the slightly elevated interior was traversed by a raised pavement some 450 meters long, flanked on both sides by stone balustrades in the form of an elongated naga serpent. The balustrades culminated at the end of the avenue in the customary nine-headed-snake

[44] *Ibid.*

[45] Briggs, 135–137.

[46] H. G. Q. Wales, *The Making of Greater India* (1951), 182–193.

[47] K. P. Landon, *Southeast Asia: Crossroads of Religion* (1949), 80–89; Ghosh, 222–224.

symbols, which also appeared prominently elsewhere in the design. Priestly quarters, including a library, flanked the long approach. The temple proper was designed as a series of three concentric rectangular galleries enclosing successive stages of the temple pyramid. Symmetrical towers shaped like the lotus bud were raised at the four corners of both of the two inner galleries, topped by a crowning tower at the center about 210 feet high. The five central towers were symbolic of peaks of Mount Meru, the mountain of the gods; the lotus-bud pattern suggested vitality, as well as beauty and fragrance. All nine central towers were originally gilded in gold. Even in its ruined condition, the effect of the temple today is highly impressive. An elaborate frieze relief carving portrayed at multiple levels the entire Vishnu tradition, including adventures of the god's most famous avatars, Rama and Khrishna. It was placed against the interior wall of the vaulted corridor surrounding the temple area proper. Pillars supported the outer edge of the roof.

In addition to details of the Hindu legend (including some aspects of the Śiva story) all portrayed with great narrative skill, the relief carvings reflected many phases of the life of the local people, as had Borobudur. Here were soldiers in battle array marching to war, royal parades, people preparing food, handicraft workers, agriculturalists, and local plants and animals, all presented with vitality and obvious enthusiasm. The royal builder was deified as a Vishnu incarnation, and the Wat was his tomb. But the temple constituted a far more meaningful monument to the artistic genius of the people who contributed so much to its perfection. Several panels of the frieze relief at the rear of the Wat remained only partly finished, and others were laid out only in drafted outlines.[48]

From the topmost passageway near the central tower of Angkor Wat, the guide can point to the distant hills, visible above the treetops of the encircling jungle, where the stone for construction work was quarried. A specially constructed canal was utilized for transporting stone in enormous quantities to the building area. The quarried stone had to be cut into units of usable size and roughly dressed by thousands of stonecutters before being turned over to the skilled masons and sculptors entrusted with its final preparation. Behind the stonecutters were the construction foremen, the master architects, and draftsmen. Still further removed were the Hindu scholars fully acquainted with the Sanskrit sources from which the Vishnu legend was drawn, some of them presumably brought over from India on invitation by the sophisticated Cambodian King. A building operation of the magnitude of Angkor Wat required also a high degree of economic and social integration, plus a government strong enough to command the labor and talents of vast numbers of trained participants. It reflected also the presence of an abundant food supply, a prosperous commerce, and a

[48] Briggs, 189–196, 201–204; Majumdar, *Kambuja-Desa,* 136–138; Hall, 105–106.

widely shared sensitivity to aesthetic values. Such considerations suggest the historical significance of Angkor Wat.

The neighboring Bayon temple was an integral part of the city of Angkor Thom, the creation of the Mahayana Buddhist ruler, Jayavarman VII (1181–1219). The city was enclosed by a stone wall, square in form and about 2 miles long on each side. At the mid-point of each side, causeways across the encircling moat leading to the major gateways were flanked by dwarf figures of giant proportions supporting the naga serpent on their laps. A fifth gateway leading directly into the palace area was cut near the north-east corner. The gateways were narrow vaulted structures flanked by two square towers on the three exposed faces of which the impassive Buddha-like physiognomy of Jayavarman himself looked out in all directions. The four principal entryways into the city converged on the Bayon temple, which occupied the very center of Angkor Thom.

The pattern of the Bayon was more intricate than that of Angkor Wat and in its ruined condition is much less easy to comprehend. Its base was rectangular and longer east to west like Angkor Wat, but smaller and more highly concentrated. It was hardly pyramidal in design, although the structure rises at irregular stages to a central tower of impressive dimensions. Every one of its fifty or more gilded towers presented on all four faces in high relief the same image of the ruler-builder to be seen on the five gateways. Jayavarman VII was an aspiring Bodhisattva in the Mahayana tradition, an emergent Buddha. In whatever direction an observer of Bayon might turn, he encountered the haunting multiple presence of the ruler's face, frontally or in silhouette. Staircases connected the successive levels of the structure, the walls of which were decorated by religious images cut in shallow relief. These were mainly Buddhist in character, but occasionally they were altered by later rulers to conform to Śaivite standards. The Bayon has appeared to some as a labored effort, lacking in essential reverence, an egoistic performance intended to exalt an over-ambitious ruler rather than to give expression to religious aspiration.[49] But its impressiveness was surpassed only by that of Angkor Wat.

Little of Jayavarman VII's palace at Angkor Thom has survived except the bases of several of the entry staircases and the impressive elephant-frieze foundation façade. The structure itself was of perishable timber construction. Opposite the palace entrance was a row of elaborately built brick-and-stone hostelries erected presumably for the entertainment of vassal emissaries or for important visiting governmental personages. Only the massive pyramidal foundations of the Phimeanakas palace, its original base lying some 20 feet below the present ground level, survive to suggest the splendor of the Cambodian capital as described by the thirteenth century Chinese visitor Chou Ta-kuan. Attention must now be turned to the Cambodian Court as a cultural center.

[49] Wales, *Greater India,* 171–177.

## Cultural and Social Aspects of Angkor

The fountainhead of cultural as well as political influence in Cambodia was the royal court. The political importance attached to the Devaraja cult guaranteed the continued influence at court of the Śaivite Brahman caste, or hotars. From this hereditary group were selected the *acharya* instructors at court, the *guru* teachers of the royal princes, the coronation officials, the court physicians, and the royal advisers on cosmological architecture. As previously explained, these officials were led by the chief priest (Purohita) of the Devaraja cult and the caretaker (Bako) of the sacred sword. Such Brahmans were identified in the relief carvings by their conical caps, their flowing hair, and their ceremonial gowns.[50]

The political power of the great sacerdotal families was curbed from time to time (by Suryavarman I, Suryavarman II, and Jayavarman VII), but it was never destroyed. Even the atmosphere of the Mahayana temple of Bayon represented the all-seeing deity of the Devaraja pattern quite as much as it represented Buddhist contemplation.[51] When Vishnu was temporarily popular, Devaraja symbolism shifted from the Śaivite linga to the statues of Vishnu; it took on the features of the King himself in the Mahayana Bayon temple. Angkor Thom's representation of the Hindu idea of the cosmic mountain in the symbolic churning of the earth's sea of milk by the Naga-serpent lever was apparently a traditionalist gesture not taken very seriously. At any rate, the sculptors of the huge dwarfs with their grimacing faces on the causeways displayed a lively sense of humor.[52]

In support of the entrenched Śaivite tradition was the important role which Sanskrit grammar and vocabulary played as an indispensable lingua franca for all of the important governmental units of Southeast Asia. Inscriptions from virtually all periods of Cambodian history attest the prevalence of a high degree of competence in Sanskrit. The study of the Hindu classics was directly patronized by the kings; princes and queens were well trained in the language. Cambodia was uniquely productive in examples of original contributions to Sanskrit literature, especially in poetry.[53] Some of the poetic inscriptions ran up to ninety or one hundred verses and a few to two or three hundred verses. The writers demonstrated full knowledge of the Hindu epics as well as the differing philosophies and mythologies of various Indian sects. They mastered the rhetorical and literary conventions (puns, alliterations, similes) and employed virtually all of the varied meters of Sanskrit poetry.[54]

[50] Nilakanta Sastri, *South Indian Influences in the Far East* (1949), 75–80.

[51] H. G. Q. Wales, *Prehistory and Religion in South-east Asia* (1957), 166–174.

[52] Wales, *Greater India*, 171–177.

[53] Ghosh, 208–225.

[54] Majumdar, *Kambuja-Desa*, 105–109.

Literary accomplishment and learning in religion and science contested with military prowess as criteria for court preferment.[55] Intermarriage between Brahmans and the Kshatriya (warrior) caste was allowed, but a tenth-century attempt, by Jayavarman V, to establish by decree the rights and prohibitions of the two lower-caste groups was only partly effective, and this not for long. Since by custom hereditary rank, even that of princely descendants, was dissipated completely after five generations if unrenewed, the maintenance of social rank was actually dependent on royal preferment. Upper social levels were thus closed to many on racial as well as cultural grounds.

The lower levels of society were divided into three main groups. First came the run-of-the-mill commoners, who were liable for both forced labor (*corvée*) and periodic military service. Marching conscript troops, variously armed, were frequently portrayed in bas-reliefs accompanied by crowds of servants and by musical bands. Below the commoners came the slave population, including debtors, war prisoners, and descendants of leaders of rebellion. Official grants of foreign war-prisoner slaves to monasteries and temples were considered laudatory acts of piety. Finally came the still-numerous hill savages—crude, black, frizzy-haired—who clung to their primitive ways (poisoned darts, lean-to shelters, meager cotton clothing). Some of them also were enslaved. Some bas-reliefs show construction slaves wincing under the whip of exacting taskmasters.[56]

Rigid rules prohibited relations of commoners with the upper classes. For the latter, symbols of rank included the type and size of house, possession of a tile rather than a thatched roof, the quality of clothing materials, the use of a gold or a silver palanquin, the number of accompanying parasol bearers, and the color of the parasols and their decoration with gold or silver handles.[57] Personal adornment of the upper classes included a variety of hair styles, and a profusion of jewelry, perfumes, rouge, rings, and bracelets. Eating utensils of gold and burnished metal mirrors were used at the highest levels. Here was no democratic society even if Hindu caste principles did not strictly apply. It was not until the privileged groups had begun to lose power during the period of Cambodia's decline that the leveling influence of Hinayana Buddhism began to achieve increased popular and official acceptance. In 1225 Chou Ta-kuan described pious Buddhist monks reciting Pali texts to monastic novices from palmleaf books, living simply, drinking no wine, possessing neither cymbals, drums, nor silk pennants.[58] Women played a prominent role in Cambodia. They ran the local market stalls and staffed the palace establishment. Some were guards and servants; others were skilled entertainers and royal concubines. At higher social levels they attained recognized status in

[55] Briggs, 147, 179; Groslier, *Rechérches*, 335.

[56] Majumdar, *Kambuja-Desa*, 64; Briggs, 142, 160, 169, 179, 243.

[57] Chou Ta-kuan, 145–148.

[58] *Ibid.*, 148–149; Groslier, *Recherches*, 130–133.

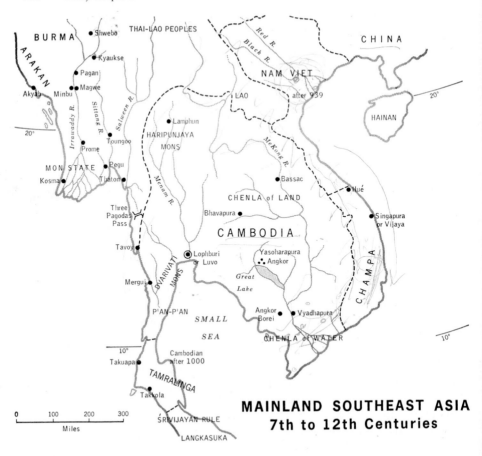

**MAINLAND SOUTHEAST ASIA**
**7th to 12th Centuries**

many areas of learning and occasionally held such high government positions as judges or secretaries to the king.[59]

For purposes of communication and calculation, the Khmers developed their own written script and used a counting system based on units of five, not dissimilar to the decimal system. The calendar delineated a thirteen-month year and a seven-day week. Long boats with ornamental prows, usually rower-propelled, were used for water transportation. Rafts carried the quarried stone along the canals. Carts and chariots, pulled by oxen, horses, or elephants, were well constructed. Important or wealthy persons traveled by slaveborne litter; private wealth was often measured in slaves. Weaving and pottery making were meagerly developed. Chinese weights and measures were in general use in the markets by the thirteenth century. Apart from their recognized prowess as workers in stone, the Cambodians were skilled as carpenters, as fashioners of wood and metals, as fishermen, and as agriculturalists. They sometimes raised three crops of

[59] Groslier, *Recherches*, 335; Briggs, 135, 179, 247; Chou Ta-kuan, 160.

rice yearly, plus fruits, onions, mustard, sugar cane, grapes and other sources of wine. Their animal husbandry, besides the larger draft animals, included pigs, sheep, goats, chickens, and geese.[60]

## Cambodia's Neighbors: The Rise of Nam Viet

The emancipation of Nam Viet (or Vietnam) from its thousand-year incorporation in China began during the last decade of the ninth century, when much of South China broke away from T'ang control. In 906 the fading T'ang dynasty acknowledged the right of the Vietnamese to select a local notable as mandarin-governor to replace the expelled Chinese incumbent. The first selectee was succeeded in turn by two sons who assumed powers to nominate all officials, although still seeking investiture from China as semivassal rulers. After 923, Nam Viet had to repel the powerful attacks of the ruler of the separate Chinese state of Canton. Canton was finally forced to withdraw in 939 following eight years of determined Vietnamese rebellion.[61] Nam Viet at long last was free.

Tongking province in the tenth century was, nevertheless, an impoverished and ravaged land, in no sense a center of prosperity and culture. It had constructed no buildings of note; it could manufacture neither the brushes nor paper required by Confucianist scholars. The Vietnamese King was described in 990 by a contemptuous Chinese observer as a barefoot fisherman fashioning rice balls in his fingers and snapping them into his mouth. Tongking's cultural attainments were, at the time, far below the high standards exhibited by regular Chinese provinces under the T'ang.[62]

The new state was destined to encounter trouble, not only periodically with China to the north but chronically with its southern neighbors, Champa, and Cambodia. The first round (982–997) of what proved to be a five-hundred-year Vietnamese feud with the Chams ended in a virtual draw. It was not until the original Dinh dynasty was replaced by the Lê in 1009 that Nam Viet assumed a vigorous and aggressive role in Southeast Asian affairs. Even so, political progress was slow.[63]

At the outset it appeared that Vietnamese enthusiasm for Buddhism might accomplish the new state's incorporation in the general cultural milieu of Southeast Asia. Confucianist scholars were at first suspected of being pro-Chinese, and Buddhism correspondingly took on new vitality. Buddhist monks were widely used as officials, court advisers, and as diplomatists, as was the case in the reception of the first visiting Sung envoy from China in 987. Indian Buddhism was, of course, known to the Vietnamese from pilgrimages to shrines in India and from the occasional visits of Buddhist monks en route to China in late Funan and early Chenla

[60] Groslier, *Recherches,* 95–114, 123, 128–133; Chou Ta-kuan, 157–162, 174, 176.

[61] Lê Thanh Khôi, *Le Viet-Nam* (1955), 133–134; Hall, 169–171.

[62] Pierre Gourou, *The Peasants of the Tonkin Delta* (1955), 146–150.

[63] Coedès, *Les États,* 209–213.

times. Vietnamese Buddhism cherished such Hinayana emphases as contemplation, the direct perception of Buddhist truth, and the ideals of indifference to mundane concerns and achievement of peace and tranquility. On the list of illustrious Buddhist scholars prepared by I-Ching in the late seventh century had appeared no fewer than twelve Vietnamese names. But Vietnamese Buddhism had developed in the context of the Confucianist and Taoist patterns rather than in association with the Brahmanic court system of Southeast Asia. Nam Viet witnessed no hyphenated Siva-Buddhism, such as appeared in Java and Cambodia, and the Buddhist monkhood in Nam Viet was fairly sharply divorced, as in China, from the official politico-religious elite. Monks were closely associated with the common people and not infrequently led them in rebellions. There was in Nam Viet no possible tradition comparable to the Hindu acceptance of the Buddha as a reincarnation of Vishnu.

The inevitable trend under the pro-Confucianist eleventh-century Lê dynasty was to revert to Chinese standards. This was associated with the eventual Buddhist acceptance (1068) of indigenous or Taoist adulterations involving sorcery, magical cures, apparitions, and the search for an elixir of immortality. Study of the Confucian classics was revived vigorously under Trinh rule (1225 and later), and mandarin examinations were re-inaugurated in 1246. A triumphant Confucianism thus came in the end to dominate Vietnamese literary concern, coupled with scholarly aspiration to qualify for governmental posts. Hinduism and Indian concepts of kingship never gained any acceptance in Nam Viet.[64]

The Lê dynasty (1009–1225) inaugurated the long-continuing southward expansion against Cham neighbors. The movement was backed by Vietnamese population pressure and superior social and economic organization. The first victory over the Chams came in 1044, when the Vietnamese took advantage of an internal Cham rebellion to capture Vijaya, the capital. This exploit was repeated in 1068–1069, after a Cham counterattack was repelled. Vijaya was burned, and three Cham border districts were eventually annexed, in 1074, as ransom for the captured Rudravarman III.

But expansion for Nam Viet thereafter was slow. Sung China staged a major effort to reconquer the southern region in 1075–1079, acting in alliance with Champa and the Khmers. The Lê rulers had to surrender five border provinces to China temporarily as the price of Sung withdrawal. These territories were recovered and the northern frontier clearly delimited by treaty in 1084. During the twelfth century the Khmers loomed as the principal stumbling block to Vietnamese expansion. Suryavarman II attacked Nam Viet on four occasions (1128, 1132, 1138, and 1150) with inconclusive results.[65]

[64] Lê Thanh Khôi, 142–143, 152–154, 174–177; Harry Benda, "Structure of Southeast Asian History," *JSEAH*, III (1962), 114–117.

[65] Lê Thanh Khôi, 158–168; Coedès, *Les États*, 235.

The Chams demonstrated remarkable stubbornness in their slow retirement before relentless Vietnamese pressure, especially so in view of the fact that they faced hostility from the Khmers as well. Jayavarman VII, as previously indicated, virtually ruled Champa for a score of years, installing a puppet prince on its throne in 1202. The Vietnamese took full advantage of the situation. By the end of the Lê dynasty (1225), the boundary had been pushed southward halfway between the old Vijaya frontier and the Col de Nuages.[66] Wastefulness, heavy taxes, *corvée* burdens, and brigandage eventually caused Lê decline, however, affording respite to the Chams.

Political developments along the coast of Annam were dominated during the latter half of the thirteenth century by successive interventions of Mongol Chinese forces. The Mongols, moving down the Red River Valley from the interior, sacked Hanoi in 1257, and after 1260 Kublai Khan attempted to force the rulers of all former tributary states to pay homage to him in person. When the issue came to a head in 1281–1285, the Chams and Annamese cooperated to repel and defeat the Mongol sea and land invasions. Champa's subsequent offer to send an envoy with the required tribute was accepted by Kublai Khan, who made no further effort to intervene in so difficult an area. But both countries suffered heavy damage during the trying period.[67]

A break in the cordial relations between Nam Viet and Champa again occurred in 1312, an event which inaugurated a half century of Vietnamese hegemony. Champa revived after 1360 under a vigorous leader who captured Hanoi in 1371 and kept Tongking cowed until his death in 1390. When the Vietnamese attacks were renewed in the early fifteenth century, the Chams were again saved, in 1407, by the intervention of the Ming Chinese fleet, which dispersed the attacking Annamese naval forces and then reimposed Chinese control on Annam briefly, from 1409 to 1428. During this period of respite Champa preyed on the enfeebled Cambodia state.

The ravages resulting from the Ming Chinese occupation of Annam were eventually repaired by a second Lê dynasty which gained control after 1428. Land was redistributed and reclamation projects were pushed by royal initiative. Canals were dug, and improvements were made in the law code and in administration. When the contest for control of the Annam littoral was reopened in 1446, the outcome was no longer in doubt. Champa's appeals for Chinese assistance were carefully pondered but not acceded to by Peking, for the Mings had lost interest in Southeast Asia. Champa was finally extinguished as a viable state in 1471, only a tiny remnant surviving in the far south.[68] Later advances were to carry the domi-

[66] Lê Thanh Khôi, 516–527.

[67] F. Hirth and W. W. Rockhill, *Chau Ju-kua* (1911), 45.

[68] Hall. 165–174; Gourou. 148–150.

nant Vietnamese across the Mekong delta and into Cambodia itself in modern times.

The indigenous religion of the Vietnamese, like that of other peoples of Southeast Asia, centered around a belief in spirits and in the necessity of placating them. This was usually accomplished without the aid of a priestly intermediary, although Taoist magicians could provide specialized services for a price. The problem was to find out the particular spirit offended, the reason for its vindictive mood, and what to do about it. The unseen world was thus often more important than the seen. It was particularly important to keep ancestral spirits happy. Offerings of food and wine were placed at regular intervals before ancestral tablets representing the vital essence of the departed. Additional attention must be given to the great mass of the uncared-for spirits of thieves, childless women, and victims of violent deaths; all these were capable of doing great mischief.

Deference was paid to the presence of ancestral spirits at all important events involving the family or clan. Responsibility toward them devolved on all living members, with the eldest exercising executive leadership. Particularly elaborate feasts and ceremonies marked the annual offerings to the ancestors of the ruling dynasty, as well as to the heaven and earth spirits. The Chinese dragon here replaced the naga-serpent symbol. Offerings to the spirits were accompanied by chanting routines, choral singing, and rhythmic dancing. The essential function of the ruler, following the Confucianist pattern, was to mediate between heaven and earth for the welfare of all. His authority and responsibility differed only in degree, not in kind, from that of other members of the highly integrated Confucianist familial system of ancestor and spirit worship.[69] Herein lay the essential differences between the governmental and cultural systems of the Vietnamese and the Indian god-king system appropriated by other leading Southeast Asian peoples.

## Cambodia's Cham Neighbors

In many respects the state of Champa was a carbon copy of neighboring Cambodia. The Chams had the same system of divine kingship minus the extreme pretentiousness of the Devaraja cult. Control was exercised by the same kind of effective collaboration between the court Brahmans and the princely caste of Kshatriyas, so that religious and governmental administrations were amalgamated. Kings in both countries vied with each other in erecting and endowing temples.

But the claims for parallelism must not be pressed too far. The Chams, unlike the Khmers, were a Malayo-Polynesian people[70] devoted to

[69] Landon, 32–62.

[70] A distinguishing custom of the Chams was their suspension of large pendants in pierced and extended ear lobes, as is done by Borneo tribes in modern times.

maritime endeavor. This difference was enforced by the narrowness of the Annam littoral inhabited by the Chams. It was composed of a dozen or so narrow basins bordered by rocky islands and deep inlets, which afforded little geographical continuity. Ports on the river estuaries were often uncertain of access, and the coastal waters were subjected periodically to violent storms. The meagerness of Champa's agricultural resources also imposed inescapable limitations on its population. It forced the Chams to exploit their mineral and forest resources, and to emphasize seaborne mercantile and other naval pursuits. Cham products for export included camphor and sandalwood, porcelain and lacquer ware, sugar, and lead and tin.

But the greater portion of the maritime income of the Chams probably derived from semipiracy. They traded actively in captured slaves. They imposed at times exactions of some 20 per cent of the cargo value on those passing commercial vessels that were too timid to navigate beyond the reach of the shore line. The Cham navy was usually commanded by a royal prince, and it numbered at times up to one hundred turreted vessels. Cham armies, although unavoidably small, were well disciplined and included contingents of both horse and elephant mounts. Cities were well fortified, and army camps were palisaded.[71] The Chams were not noted for their hospitality or their generosity to strangers. This may or may not have had some relationship to their chronic belligerency and to the fact that Buddhism gained only a meager following among them.[72]

Indianization was probably more exclusively Hindu in Champa than among any other Southeast Asian people. Cham temples included images of the Brahma, which were seldom found elsewhere. The pantheon also included minor Hindu gods, such as the elephant Śri Vinayaka, the war god Skanda riding his peacock mount, the bull Nandin, and the Garuda bird, which served as bearers for Śiva and Vishnu. Kautilya's famous specifications for the perfect prince were copied almost verbatim in a famous inscription found at Mision.[73] Widows did not remarry, and beloved queens followed deceased rulers in suttee death. The cow was held sacred; beef was not eaten. The Hindu calendar fixed the dates of annual feasts, which were conducted according to the proper Indian pattern. Yoga exercises were practiced. All branches of Sanskrit literature were studied, but with little or no evidence

[71] R. C. Majumdar, *Ancient Indian Colonies in the Far East: I, Champa* (1927), 152–154. The ranking Cham army commander was called the Mahasenapati, while ordinary generals were only Senapatis.

[72] *Ibid.*, 224–225; Georges Maspero, *The Kingdom of Champa* (1949), 1–10, 26–27, 42–46. Translated by John Embree. See also the description by Hirth and Rockhill, 42–49, taken from the account of Chau Ju-kua.

[73] Maspero, 10–14, 20–25; R. C. Majumdar, *Ancient Indian Colonies: I, Champa*, 149–154. According to Kautilya's treatise, a king must be a man of grace, ability, and courage, a leader and a warrior, knowledgeable in the laws, capable of self-control, given to spiritual exercises, and astute in diplomacy.

of creative literary endeavor in either Sanskrit or the vernacular.[74] Champa thus represented in many respects the boldest and most literal projection of Indian civilization among the indigenous peoples of Southeast Asia.

Hindu culture was apparently maintained in Champa almost entirely by direct maritime connections. Overland cultural infiltration via the Burmans, the Mons, the Cambodians, or the Thai failed to penetrate to any substantial degree as far east as Champa. The very security and prosperity of the state depended on maintaining naval predominance off its shore line, and Champa's vulnerability to outside attack afforded little leeway for political or religious experimentation. Champa remained steadfastly in the Śaivite tradition.

Champa exhibited a number of other political and social peculiarities. The state government was organized unitarily rather than federally. Three main provinces were broken down into thirty-eight districts. Officials received no salaries but enjoyed assigned incomes either from taxes and trade or from fief-type *jagir* estates assigned to them. The produce of both the land and the forest was taxed at rates varying from 10 to 17 per cent. Crime was severely curbed. An Assembly of Notables, corresponding in character and function with the Great Council of Cambodia, undertook to facilitate ruler succession. Royal descent followed mainly the matriarchal pattern. Kings adopted varman-suffixed names at the time of their coronations. Royal harems absorbed selected girls from prominent families, and these girls sometimes numbered up to two hundred. Wealthy merchants enjoyed superior standing, but caste gradations lacked clear definition at lower levels of society. Little is known about the common people except that many were slaves. Carved-relief scenes are lacking, as are detailed firsthand descriptions.

Overseas Cham traders operated as far away as China and Java. Cham craftsmen were expert in the making of elaborate woven cloth, both cotton and silk, and in the fashioning of weapons and other metal objects. Their brick buildings lacked the beauty and majesty displayed by Cambodia's monuments of stone, partly because Cham resources and manpower were too limited to undertake such large projects.[75] The most remarkable thing about Champa was simply that it managed to survive as a political entity through approximately twelve centuries, from 192 to 1471.

## The Mons

A final, brief statement is needed concerning Cambodia's Mon neighbors to the west. Until the early eleventh century when Suryavarman I took over Cambodia's Crown from his Lavo base in the lower Menam Valley, the loose Mon Confederacy of Ramanyadesa had maintained a kind of defensive Theravada Buddhist alliance against outside threats from the

[74] Maspero, 42–54; Majumdar, I, 149–163, 215–221, 234.
[75] Majumdar, I, 149–163, 167–173; Maspero, 26, 54.

Khmers, Burmans, and Thai. Two of the Confederacy members, Thaton and Haripunjaya, remained permanently outside the Khmer Empire, Sujita's conquest of Lavo in the 990s broke up the Mon Confederacy. Lavo was directly incorporated into Cambodia after 1011, and the Thaton Mons, facing a similar threat from Cambodia, were conquered by the Pagan Burmans instead in 1054–1057, as will be described below. Haripunjaya continued to enjoy independent status for a time longer, while maintaining close cultural ties with the Mons of Burma. It was finally overrun by Thai invaders in the mid-thirteenth century.[76] As custodians of Hinayana Buddhism and scholarship in the Pali Tripitaka scriptures, the Mons acted as the teachers of both the Pagan Burmans and of the later-arriving Thai. They also contributed much to the increasing vogue of Buddhism among the Cambodians from the time of Jayavarman VII.

## The Decline of Cambodia

Political developments of the thirteenth and fourteenth centuries contributed materially to the eventual disintegration of the Cambodian Empire. The temporary control which Jayavarman VII established over Champa was abandoned around 1219, partly because of difficulties faced by Cambodia elsewhere. Lavo, Tambralinga, and additional segments of the vassal area of the north Malay isthmus fell away during the ensuing decade. On the occasion of Jayavarman's death in 1219, a Cambodian military leader of Thai ancestry, married to a Khmer princess, usurped power as governor of a central Menam Valley Khmer province known as Sukhothai. The second son of the Thai chieftain, Rama Khamheng by name, established himself after 1270 as an independent ruler. He eventually extended his control southward through the isthmus and into northern Malaya. The Thai inundation of the Menam Valley and of Upper Burma as well was accelerated by the Mongol conquests of Nan Chao in 1253 and of Pagan Burma in 1287, historical developments which will be discussed in a subsequent chapter. These territorial losses were accompanied by a revival of factional feuding within late-thirteenth-century Cambodia.

The Śaivite party recovered its ascendancy under Jayavarman VIII (1243–1295), the last ruler to make any important building contribution to Angkor. Near the end of his reign, the aged Jayavarman VIII was virtually a prisoner in his own palace, while much of his domain was being ravaged by Sukhothai armies. He was finally assassinated in 1295 by a soldier son-in-law, who usurped the throne in the following year under the reign name of Indravarman III. The sands of time were running out. For more than half a millennium the Khmer government had spent its resources, both material and spiritual, with lavish abandon. Its inevitable collapse was delayed only by the fact that its enemy, the Thai, also experienced internal troubles.

[76] Briggs, 159–160, 169.

Even in decline, Angkor Thom was sufficiently magnificent in 1296 to impress the Chinese visitor Chau Ju-Kua. He described the gilded towers of the Bayon monument, the gateway faces, the gold-framed windows of the Great Council hall, the long veranda and corridors of the palace with its scores of metallic mirrors and its thousands of female attendants and concubines, and the splendid accoutrements of the royal processions. The Chinese visitor was also shocked by the general prevalence of sexual promiscuity not only among the womenfolk but also among gangs of wandering homosexual perverts. Chinese merchants found the country attractive; rice was abundant, women easy to find, houses easy to manage, commerce easy to control. The observer also indicated that Hinayana Buddhist monks, living simply and devoting their efforts to the education of youth in the Pali scriptures, enjoyed wide respect. Buddhism's higher moral standards and its more democratic social approach eventually provided a rallying standard for a people weary of forced labor, warfare, and aristocratic domination.

In terms of popular regard, Theravada Buddhism gained the ascendancy in Cambodia after 1300. The new Cambodian King himself turned Buddhist in 1308, abdicating his throne to devote himself to religious concerns. Brahmanism held on at court for a while longer, assisted by a helpful decade of confusion in the Sukhothai state following Rama Khamheng's death in 1317. The last Sanskrit inscription, a poem of 103 stanzas presented in flawless grammar and reflecting a thoroughgoing knowledge of Hindu literature, was dated in 1327. Hinayana Buddhism was clearly in the ascendancy after 1350.

The founding of the new Thai capital of Ayuthia in 1350 was the prelude to a revival of Siamese attacks on Angkor. The contest nevertheless persisted for another eighty years before Angkor was finally captured and sacked by the Thai forces in 1430–1431. The Cambodian domain shrank thereafter to a tiny area located below the Great Lake and to the west of the Mekong River, the delta of which already was being heavily infiltrated by marauding Chams and by the ultimately victorious Vietnamese.[77] A brief return to Angkor occurred after 1560. Popular religious disaffection, decline of material resources including slave labor, and outside political pressures took their inexorable toll.

[77] *Ibid.*, 251–258; Ghosh, 199–204.

# CHAPTER 6

# Pagan Burma:

## Development and Decline

Although the Tibeto-Burman tribesmen who erupted into the central Irrawaddy Valley in the mid-ninth century were distant cousins of the Pyu, whose north Burma state had been eliminated approximately a score of years previously, it was the Mons and not the Pyu who became their teachers. The basic reason stemmed, in all probability, from the maturity and stability of Mon culture, as compared with that of the thoroughly beaten and demoralized Pyu. There was also the accident that the Kyaukse granary area, first to be seized by the Burmans, was a traditional stronghold of Mon settlement and influence. But the early Burmans were better conquerors than scholars. Two centuries later (1050s), when Aniruddha created the Pagan Empire, the writing of the Burmese language was still only in a rudimentary state of development. The King's name was signed at the time in Sanskrit, and for approximately a century and a quarter thereafter the Mon tongue and script constituted the official means of written communication. The Burmans also borrowed heavily from the religion and the architectural patterns of the Mons. The cultural autonomy of Pagan Burma was not fully achieved until the final quarter of the twelfth century. By that time the empire had only a little more than a century left before its course was run.

In the relatively short period of $2\frac{1}{3}$ centuries, half of it Mon and half Burman in character, the Pagan dynasty accomplished impressive results in the military and political spheres and very noteworthy achievements in religious architecture. In this latter area, the dynasty's work rivaled Borobudur and Angkor. The dynasty came to an abrupt end after 1287 when an invading Mongol Chinese army captured the capital. The heirs of the Pagan Empire were Thai chieftains in the north and the revived Mon state of Pegu in the south. For some $2\frac{1}{2}$ centuries following the fall of Pagan, Burma was in a state of confusion. The Burmans eventually emerged again as a unifying political factor in the 1540s under the leadership of the princes of Toungoo.

The early phase of Burmese history can be divided into five periods of unequal length: (1) to 1077, the origins and founding of the empire, (2) to 1113, the period of Mon cultural supremacy, (3) to 1174, the transition to Burman cultural autonomy, (4) to 1287, the purely Burman period, and (5) the subsequent eclipse of the Burman power. The history of the empire rests very largely on inscriptional sources collected from architectural monuments found mainly at Pagan. Their transcription and decipherment owe much to a number of British scholars long connected with the University of Rangoon.[1] The royal chronicles of the kings are of qualified value historically because they were usually laudatory in purpose and frequently prepared long after the event.

## The Mons and the Ancient Pyu

The ruling occupants of Lower Burma during most of the pre-Pagan period were the Mons. Their three principal centers of power were Thaton, Pegu, and Kosma, all located on or near the coast. They also occupied the entire Sittang Valley and extended their control thence northward into the Kyaukse irrigated area (below modern Ava) which they developed into the most important granary of central Burma. Their control extended also southward from Martaban at the mouth of the Salween River part way down the Tenasserim coast.

Mon control of the lower Irrawaddy basin and the western portion of the delta was interrupted temporarily by the intrusion of the Tibeto-Burman people known as the Pyu, who probably arrived several centuries after the Mons. The large Pyu capital of Śrikshetra (city of splendor), above the delta and adjacent to the Irrawaddy but not a seaport, was founded by a new (Vikrama) dynasty in 638, only to be abandoned about a century and a half later.[2] From the late eighth century to the mid-eleventh, the Mons were in undisputed possession of Lower Burma, except insofar as they feuded among themselves.

The cultural aspects of Mon society and that represented by Pyu Śrikshetra were in many respects similar. Gupta cultural influence was much in evidence in both of them. The ashes of the dead were buried in urns, the costliness of the containers corresponding with the social status of the deceased. Both peoples were interested in trade, the Mons as a maritime people in their own right and the Pyus as controllers of the Irrawaddy River artery which constituted the southern end of the overland trading route from western China. A substantial Indian trading colony resided at the ports of the delta and also in coastal Akyab, which was accessible overland across the Arakan Yoma from Śrikshetra and via the An Pass further north. The early predominance of Sanskrit writing and the

[1] The five-volume *Epigraphia Burmanica* (1919–1936) was prepared by C. Duroiselle and C. O. Blagden.

[2] Than Tun, "A History of Burma down to the End of the Thirteenth Century," *NBW*, Aug. 23, 1958, 15–18.

cult of Vishnu gave way in time to the vogue of Pali scriptures and the Hinayana Buddhist religion in both states. Mahayana Buddhism was present in a minor way, but the Śiva cult, except in Arakan, was surprisingly absent from Burma. The Mon vernacular script was based on Pali; that of the Pyu was based on a different Indian pattern.[3] Early Mon commercial and cultural contacts with India centered in the Orissa and Telingana districts of the eastern Deccan. The Mons later developed religious contacts with Ceylon.[4] Few architectural remains survive from early Mon times, but Pyu Śrikshetra displays three 150-foot stupas, hollow and tapering at the top, with circular terraces at the base. The hollow-vaulted-temple pattern developed by the Pyu was later copied and developed by the builders of Pagan.

The elimination of the Pyu from Lower Burma in the eighth century was probably the work of a Karen-Palaung group, which cut off Śrikshetra from Pyu connections to the north. Moving laterally westward across central Burma above the Pegu Yoma, the intruders captured an important irrigation center in the Minbu-Magwe area. Presumably, they then pressed southward down the Irrawaddy Valley against Śrikshetra. In any case, the Pyu were obliged to detour and withdraw northward, shifting their capital far upcountry to Halingyi near modern Shwebo. Here they were able to continue to participate in the revived overland commerce with T'ang China, a trade partially under Nan Chao's control. At Halingyi a large number of silver coins and at least one of copper have been found.[5] It is noteworthy in this eighth-century revival that China-India trade found its way to India not via the Irrawaddy River route, now blocked by the Karens and Mons, but mainly across the An Pass (behind Minbu) to Arakan. Mon control quickly returned to Kyaukse and to other areas of central Burma to fill the political vacuum created by the northward withdrawal of the Pyu.

It was at this juncture in the 790s that a T'ang Chinese historian described the society of the Piaó (Pyu), whether of Śrikshetra or Halingyi is not clear. Buddhism prevailed; novice monks from ages seven to twenty shaved their heads. A sacred-white-elephant image near the walled palace allegedly served as a kind of oracle for purposes of justice. Women ornamented their top-knotted hair with flowers, pearls, and precious stones; they were also trained in music and dancing, and used candles of perfumed beeswax.[6] A troop of Pyu dancer-musicians accompanied a Nan Chao mis-

[3] N. Ray, *Brahmanical Gods in Burma* (1932), 3–12, 21, 50–51, 66–67. Vishnu was traditionally regarded by both the Mons and the Burmans as a sage contemporary with Buddha but of inferior rank. The modern dialect of the Arakanese reportedly contains peculiarities similar to the Pyu not present in Burmese.

[4] G. H. Luce, *Mons of the Pagan Dynasty* (1950), 1–2. The Burman word for the Mons, *Talaing,* is presumed to refer opprobriously to their traditional Telingana connections.

[5] Than Tun, 18–19.

[6] G. Coedès, *Les États Hindouisés* (1948), 179.

sion to China's capital around 800, when Halingyi was obliged to accept vassalage status under Nan Chao.

Events moved fast after 800. Halingyi, along with several Mon cities, was captured and destroyed by Nan Chao, from 832 to 835. Some three thousand Pyu captives were carried away as slaves, along with an unknown number of Mons. After the overextended Nan Chao armies withdrew from central Burma, the area was reoccupied temporarily by the Mons. But the Pyu were entirely finished politically. Pyu soldiers accompanied the Nan Chao armies as vassal or slave troops when Thai forces captured Hanoi in 863.

## The Advent of the Burman State[7]

Some two or three decades after the cessation of the Nan Chao raids into the Irrawaddy Valley, a body of half-barbarian Tibeto-Burman tribesmen, escaping southward via the Shan plateau from relaxed Nan Chao or Thai control, captured the eleven villages of Kyaukse from the Mons.[8] They later moved southwards to Minbu (six villages), which they took from the Karen-Palaungs. They then fanned out over a wide area to the west and north, overrunning both sides of the lower Chindwin River and the region between that river and the Irrawaddy. They forced the Mon power to retire southward, although many Mon residents remained behind. The Burmans absorbed the remnants of the debilitated Pyu population, which by this time had little to offer them culturally or politically.

Toward the end of the ninth century, the Burmans founded a capital city at Pagan.[9] It was located on a strategic site in a half-desert area on a bluff overlooking a bend of the Irrawaddy river approximately halfway between the Kyaukse and Minbu granaries. Alien peoples were conquered or absorbed,[10] and a fairly closely knit state was developed on a pattern borrowed from the Mons, but with local adaptations. The semidesert area of central Burma ("parched lands" to the Mons) proved incapable of supporting a large population, and Pagan remained a minor half-barbarian inland state, enjoying no close contact with India or the sea, until after the Burman conquest of the Nan Chao borders and the Lower Burma Mon land under Aniruddha in the 1050s.

Cultural and political collaboration between Burman rulers and older Mon residents was doubtless stimulated by their facing a common enemy in the Thai from the north. But the belligerent, untutored conquerors apparently learned rather slowly. They eventually adapted from

[7] The term "Burman" is here used to refer to the majority ethnic group, "Burmese" to refer to the indigenous inhabitants generally, including minority ethnic groups. The language of the Burmans is nevertheless called Burmese.

[8] Than Tun, 19.

[9] Than Tun, 23.

[10] These peoples included the Sak, Saw, Cakraw (Karens), and the Kantu.

the Mons a writing system and numerals, administrative institutions and symbols of government, architecture and art forms, and the basic ethical principles and practices of the Buddhist and Vishnu faiths.[11] The process was clearly one of adaptation and assimilation, for indigenous aspects of Burman tradition survived, such as spirit worship, the role of the hereditary township chief, later called the *myothugyi,* and traditional aspects of a semifeudal political and social structure.

## Burman Cultural Characteristics

A closer look at traditional Burman religious institutions may properly precede the story of the conquest. The primitive animistic practices of the pre-Pagan Burmans include two categories of nat spirits. One was associated with natural objects—sky, earth, lakes, jungle, trees, and villages. The other category included spirits of people of former days, some ancestral, some vagrant and anchorless. A person must pay special deference to the spirit of his home village, even though temporarily removed, and must also keep on good terms with the nat of his immediate vicinity; the first was a personal, the second a regional deity. Keeping the nats propitiated was a kind of insurance against evil fortune or disease; if neglected, they would allegedly become vindictive and troublesome. Harvest spirits required attention at certain periods of the year, as did those of one's family or clan.

By the eleventh century, the Burmans had developed a special nat pantheon of thirty-six identifiable vagrant spirits, which had little in common except that all had met with violent death. Some were brother and sister. They were headed by the sky god of Mount Popa, a volcanic peak located to the south and east of Pagan where worship ceremonies were performed annually. Eventually a thirty-seventh spirit was added for the Buddha. Such spiritism had no relevance to morality, for as a rule the nats were evil and lecherous.

Spiritism blended with various forms of magic. A protective spirit, for example, was frequently planted at a particularly strategic spot (a palace foundation, a city wall or gateway) by crushing to death some unfortunate victim.[12] Magical talismans and omens were also considered enormously potent, as were astrological signs. The separate days of the week were associated with the eight identified planets, Wednesdays being split in two to fit the total into a seven-day week. A ninth astrological element was eventually added for the Buddha. An infant was always named with

[11] G. H. Luce, *Mons of the Pagan Dynasty,* 2–4, and "Economic Life of the Early Burmans," *JBRS,* XXX (1940), 238–240.

[12] G. E. Harvey, *History of Burma from the Earliest Times to 10 March, 1824* (1925), 320–321. Harvey cites specific instances of Myosade from 1287 to 1860 and also points out that the mortar for the keep of the Norman Tower of London was similarly tempered in 1078 by the blood of slain beasts.

reference to the day of the week of his birth. Astrological factors were also important in selecting propitious times and locations.[13] Before a military campaign, the appropriate spirits were approached with offerings and fare-well visits by participating soldiers. It was considered highly advantageous to enlist in this fashion the aid of friendly spirits against the hostile spirit forces of the enemy. Invulnerability could allegedly be achieved by drink-ing magical concoctions or by tattooing.[14] The Burmans possessed no hero epics until they borrowed from India legends or manufactured them in their own court chronicles.

The Burman newcomers also had to adjust to a new type of eco-nomic livelihood in the plains. They had already learned terraced-rice cultivation in the Nan Chao area, along with the breeding of the horse, the ox, and the buffalo. They eventually substituted for their original barter unit a quantity of salt equal to the Mon value unit of the *tical* (the Burmese *klyap*, or *Kyat*), or one-hundredth of a vis of silver or copper. They learned in time to detest the dairy products which they probably cherished at an earlier day in Tibet.[15] They also learned to appreciate the advantages of trade not only down the Irrawaddy with the rice-surplus areas of the delta but also with Nan Chao in Yunnan, Assam, and Bengal. The first direct Burman contact with Indian culture, especially with certain Tantric ele-ments of Mahayana Buddhism, apparently came via Manipur, prior to the Burmans' eleventh-century era of expansion.[16]

## *The Foundation of the Pagan Empire, 1044–1084*

Accounts of the founding of the Pagan Empire based on the later-devised Burmese chronicles of the kings are not supported by contempo-rary evidence. They tell how a pious Burman ruler, Aniruddha (Anawrahta), impressed by the representations of a Buddhist hermit-missionary, decided that he must procure copies of the correct Tripitaka scriptures available at Mon Thaton. When his request was refused, he attacked and captured Thaton, carrying to Pagan not only the Tripitaka but also King Makuta (Manuha) and the elite of his court. The chronicles also included among

[13] Htin Aung, *Pre-Buddhist Religions of Burma* (unpublished).

[14] H. G. Q. Wales, *Ancient South-east Asian Warfare* (1952), 128–139. Propitiousness sometimes depended on the direction of the wind, on storm clouds, on the location of fallen trees or of cemeteries. Burma's Saya San rebellion of 1931 was an instance of applied magic.

[15] Luce, "Economic Life of the Early Burmans," 283–298. Only in Arakan were coins used in Pagan Burma.

[16] The alleged presence of Tantric forms of Buddhism, corrupted by Śaivite practices, has been challenged by Than Tun ("A History of Burma," *NBW*, Aug. 23, 1958). But Than Tun's identification of the heretical forest-dweller monks of the late Pagan period with the Ari priests mentioned in the royal chronicles does not cancel out pictorial evidences of the practice of traditional Tantric sex orgies from the early period.

Aniruddha's conquests the borders of Nan Chao, the Arakan and Tenasserim coast districts, and the area over to the Menam River, none of which he appears ever to have controlled. They also describe him, quite erroneously, as the founder of the Kyaukse irrigation area.[17]

The actual circumstances of Aniruddha's remarkable conquests relate to a broader political context. They go back to the destruction of the Mon Confederacy of Ramanyadesa in the time of Sujita and Suryavarman I, through their absorption of the Dvaravati-Lavo district into Cambodia in 1010. In the succeeding decades, Haripunjaya, a second member of the old Confederacy, was barely able to protect its independence in the face of alternate Thai and Cambodian attacks. Haripunjaya also experienced at this time a scourge of cholera which led many of its people to seek asylum and assistance in Mon Lower Burma.

In the face of a developing Cambodian military threat to the Mons of Burma, presumably after the death (1050) of the pro-Buddhist Suryavarman I and with the revival of Śaivite supremacy at Angkor, the Mons at Thaton and Pegu were divided as to what policy to pursue. King Makuta of Thaton elected to stand alone and defend his well-fortified capital against the impending Cambodian attack, refusing to heed pleas for help transmitted by Lavo and Haripunjaya refugees. Mon Pegu on the other hand took up the cause of the beleaguered Mons to the east and requested assistance from the vigorous young ruler of Pagan. It was the combined Pagan and Pegu forces which eventually repelled the Cambodian attack via Tenasserim in 1057–1059. The war apparently took on religious overtones as a struggle of Mon Buddhist forces against the Śaivite armies of Angkor. At its successful conclusion, Pegu accepted a subordinate position to Pagan in the alliance, while the noncooperating Makuta and his Thaton capital became the victims of the hostility of both Pagan and Pegu. The victorious Aniruddha had himself transformed into a Chakravartin (universal monarch), Devaraja style, just as Jayavarman II of Cambodia had done in 802.[18]

It appears that Aniruddha's empire was from the outset a cooperative alliance, albeit between unequal and highly disparate partners. The influential Mon faction at Pegu provided scholarship and literacy, trading facilities, religious nomenclature, and art forms; the stronger Burman element provided political and military power. The widely distributed terracotta plaques describing the conquests of Aniruddha, for example, included the King's name inscribed in Sanskrit and recorded the body of the inscriptions in Pali. The plaques were clearly the work, not of the illiterate Burmans, but of Mon scholars. They constitute virtually the only contemporary records from Aniruddha's reign.

When a hard-pressed ruler of Ceylon in 1060 appealed for assistance

[17] Coedès, 251–255. Aniruddha allegedly emerged from a monastery to take over the kingship in 1044, setting a familiar historical precedent.

[18] Than Tun, Sept. 27, 1958, 187.

in his desperate struggle to oust the Tamil Cholas, the Pagan ruler allegedly sent the military supplies which helped turn the tide in favor of Ceylon. The Sinhalese King sent Aniruddha a replica of the Buddha tooth of Kandy in appreciation. But a decade later (1071), when monks were sent from Burma to Ceylon in response to a further request for aid in revising and restoring Buddhist forms and standards in Ceylon, the learned monks who responded were Mons, led by Shin Arahan, the friend of the Burman King. King Aniruddha duly enshrined the Buddha-tooth relic in his pretentious new Shwezigon pagoda near Pagan.[19] It was apparently not the respectfully treated but captive entourage of King Makuta of Thaton which provided the major portion of Mon assistance to the Pagan Court in governmental and religious enterprises, but rather the leadership of Aniruddha's Mon allies at Pegu.

This situation was apparently reversed following the death of King Aniruddha in 1077. At that time, the rebellious governor of Pegu, acting with strong Mon backing, challenged the authority of the great King's weakly son and successor, Man Lulan (Sawlu). The rebel army stormed up the valley, laid siege to Pagan, and raided northward as far as Ava. In this dire emergency, the new King recalled to his service an able general of his father, who was living at the time in exile as prince of the tiny principality of Hiliang near Kyaukse, Thiluin Man (Kyanzittha) by name. After Thiluin Man had driven away and defeated the rebel army of Pegu, he himself took over the Crown in 1084. He then decided to make peace with the rival Thaton faction of the Mons, led at the time by the grandson of the deceased King Makuta. This group had refused to aid the Pegu rebels but had withdrawn from Pagan and was plotting a rebellion of its own. Thiluin Man sealed the alliance by giving his daughter in marriage to the heir of the Thaton line and by agreeing that her son (not the king's own) would become the recognized royal heir and successor.[20] This statesmanlike decision was loyally carried out, and it paid off handsomely in the restoration of peace and prosperity. Thiluin Man was vigorously Burman in governmental matters, but he accorded full scope in such areas as diplomacy, scholarship, religion, and art to the capacities of his gifted Mon allies. The Mon scholar Shin Arahan became his personal confidant. Throughout the course of his reign (1084–1113), the Mon language exclusively was used for inscriptions. Mon standards also governed temple decorations and architecture.

The legendary story of King Thiluin Man's greatness no doubt grew with the telling of it. He completed the Shwezigon pagoda, started by Aniruddha; he constructed the magnificent Ananda temple; he visited the Bodgaya Buddhist shrine in India and contributed repairs. He was also concerned with alleviating the distress of his people; he allegedly organized festivals and folk dances to ease the burden of the monthly payment of

[19] *Ibid.*, 118–189.
[20] *Ibid.*, Oct. 25, 1958, 312–314.

royal dues. The famous Myazedi inscription of 1113 (written at the time of his death in Pali, Pyu, Mon, and Burmese) tells of the King's reconciliation with his estranged son who had been denied the throne by the pact of 1084. The long reign of Thiluin Man's grandson and Makuta's great-grandson, Cansu I (Alaungsithu, 1113–1167) saw the gradual transition from Pali and Mon to the Burmese language, which was eventually reaching maturity as a medium of literary expression, using the Mon script.[21] It is appropriate at this mid-point in the narrative to attempt to characterize the nature of the religion, the government, and the society of Pagan Burma.

## Characteristics of the Pagan Burmans

Although the evidence is convincing that Theravada Buddhism on the pattern of the Mons and the Sinhalese was the official religious system in Pagan Burma, its character was by no means pure nor was its position exclusive. Thiluin Man himself was not fanatically Buddhist in religion. He was proclaimed an avatar of Vishnu after his death. The coronation rites and the court ceremonies at Pagan were carried out, as at Angkor, by Brahman priests, the principal difference being that the Śiva cult was not in evidence in Burma and that Vishnu was subordinate to Buddha.

The Burman ruler's divine authority derived primarily from his Chakravartin transformation in the Vishnu-type Devaraja ceremony. His authority also owed much to his popular prestige as a supporter of the Buddhist faith. The latter consideration became, in time, the very *raison d'être* of the Burman state. Brahmans occupied the posts of court astrologers and cosmologic architects. Court offerings were also made to Indra and to the Naga-serpent god. For the Burmans, an albino (white) elephant was an incomparable royal treasure, regarded as a powerful omen of good things to come and a fit gift to exchange between friendly kings. Gautama's existence previous to Buddhahood had allegedly been as a white elephant, and the appearance of such a beast was a portent of another comparable emanation.

The vogue of Buddhism had its practical applications, which were especially evident near the end of the Pagan period. The law courts, for example, exploited religious beliefs by invoking terrifying sanctions and oaths as security against perjury. In the field of education, Buddhist monks provided instruction for the youth in elementary school subjects and in the Buddhist scriptures. Nearly every village developed its monastic quarters, or *pongyi kyaung,* where the virtues of personal restraint, respect for wisdom and age, and charity and compassion were inculcated educationally and through monastery sermons delivered on successive sabbath days. Monastic dormitory facilities were provided by the wealthy, along with libraries to house the expensive scriptural texts to be studied and reproduced. Contribu-

[21] Luce, *Mons of the Pagan Dynasty,* 11–16; Than Tun, Aug. 23, 1958, 12–13.

tions of grants of land plus entire slave villages were frequently made by princes and high officials for the support of religious institutions.

Aberrations from orthodox Buddhist standards persisted and inevitably ramified in various directions. The Buddha was sometimes treated as a kind of anthropomorphized creator-god, personally in need of gifts. Occasionally a king or a wealthy donor might aspire to actual Buddhahood in the heretical Mahayana tradition. Animistic compromises were made by providing at pagoda entrances guardian griffins which were supposed to frighten away evil spirits. A striking demonstration of deference to spirit worship was made by the inclusion of thirty-seven nat shrines, one for each of the thirty-six identifiable vagrant spirits and the extra one for the Buddha, in the compound quarters of the famous Shwezigon pagoda of Pagan.

Extravagant enthusiasm for Buddhism also had its negative side. The allocation of excessive amounts of wealth in land, slaves, and treasure for religious purposes tended in time to rob the government of tax income which was much needed in the later years of the dynasty. Royal commissions were accordingly instituted to authenticate all land alienation and ownership for religious purposes. The thousands of ruined pagodas of all sizes which clutter the Pagan landscape provide eloquent testimony that this form of merit seeking reached the point of diminishing returns, economically and socially speaking.

Toward the end of the Pagan period an influential group of heretical monks, called the *Arana,* or forest dwellers, won royal favor and some popular acclaim. They strayed from the strict requirements of the Vinaya discipline by adopting an aggressively acquisitive land policy and by the habit of celebrating their land annexations by elaborate feasts involving the consumption of quantities of meat and alcoholic beverages. Minor irregularities included violation of rules prohibiting eating after noon. This sect remained vigorously active long after the Pagan period.[22] For example, an eighteenth-century account of Burma by Turpin, based on missionary observation, described monks of Lower Burma living "far from the haunts of men, in the depths of the forest in a sort of cage built in the upper parts of trees."[23]

The *Sangha,* or collective assembly of monks, was very important socially, enjoying high respect and honor in Pagan Burma. Especially honored were the senior *theras* (teachers). The court chaplains at Pagan, called *Mancharya* or *Rajaguru* (teachers of the king), were learned in Pali rather than in Sanskrit. Except for the Mons, who exhibited some flair for poetic expression, Burman Pali scholarship demonstrated little evidence of

[22] Than Tun, *Mahakasappa and His Tradition,* 4–10. Some inscriptions record that forest-dweller feasts consumed as many as fifteen oxen and thirty pots of liquor.

[23] M. Turpin, *History of the Kingdom of Siam* (1908), 12. Translated by B. O. Cartwright from the original Paris edition of 1771.

creative imagination or wide acquaintance with Indian literature. Monastic discipline was largely self-administered, although disputes between monks sometimes came before the kings' courts for adjudication. Important monasteries utilized specialy trained servants, sometimes gift slaves capable of representing the institution in courts of law. Other slave categories in the monasteries included caretakers, carpenters, repairmen, cooks, agents for buying and selling, and even musicians.[24]

A large proportion of the slave population in Burma was apparently assigned to religious institutions. Persons so assigned, whether caretakers, cowherds, cooks, craftsmen, or musicians, kept their traditional vocational status. They frequently lived in their own separate villages, whose productive output belonged to the monastery. In fact the many listings of donations of pagoda slaves appearing in the inscriptions afford a cross-sectional view of Burman society. The craftsmen, for example, included masons and stonecutters, spinners and weavers, furniture and image makers, wood carvers, painters and decorators, blacksmiths and goldsmiths, and makers of pots, jugs, and trays. Vocational groups included midwives, launderers, water carriers and canal diggers, boatmen, cartmen and harness makers, salt makers, barbers, manicurists, locksmiths, and armorers. The fact that slave status was acquired by large groups of debtors, captured rebels, and war prisoners and even by its voluntary acceptance, and the practice of keeping slaves together as functioning social units, suggest that life as a monastery slave carried no serious stigma and was perhaps superior in some respects to alternatives available for free members of the population. An estimated 10 per cent of Burma's slave population was literate. In any case, slavery was mildly imposed at Pagan; manumission could be purchased for the moderate sum of 5 vis of copper.[25]

Comparable information is not available for Burma's nonslave population, for it was not the topic of inscriptions concerning meritful deeds, as were the slave assignments to the monasteries. But important aspects of the social system can be described. A basic indigenous institution of early Burmese government and society with possible origins in the Pagan period was the myothugyi, or hereditary township headman. He functioned as a local police officer, the arbiter of civil disputes, and a judge in minor criminal cases. He also came to act in time as the census officer and tax collector, as well as the army recruiter and unit commander. The credentials of all who claimed myothugyi rank were authenticated at the king's court. The several kinds of myothugyis ruled over peoples of differing status, with the free population divided into two distinct segments. A purely Burman group made up what was later to be called the *ahmudan* segment, which owed to the royal government, in lieu of direct taxes, periodic services of a personal character.

[24] Than Tun, "A History," *NBW*, Feb. 28, 1959, 305–307.
[25] Than Tun, "Social Life in Burma, A.D. 1044–1287," *JBRS*, XLI (1959), 37–47.

The ahmudan population came in time to occupy the irrigated royal lands, at first located at Kyaukse and Minbu and developed later near Shwebo. The group was divided into hereditary service orders or clans, called *asu* or *athin,* each of which was assigned particular obligations with reference to the royal court. Some served in the army, the river navy, or the elephant corps. Others worked at the palace as guards, masons, or carpenters or simply as general functionaries. The minor fraction of each local asu unit which was on duty at the palace or the capital at any given time was supported by the larger elements of the same unit remaining at home. Members took turns. A person's asu status tended to be hereditary and permanent, a condition made doubly sure by tattooing the distinguishing symbols of the asu on the backs of the necks of all members when they assumed their adult responsibilities within the service order. A myothugyi was assigned to administer each ahmudan unit, designating duty periods and acting as its military commander in case of war.

The second segment of the free population, later known as *athi,* did not inhabit the royal lands and was frequently probably nonBurman in origin. The athi owed various kinds of dues payable through the local myothugyi, who functioned here on a territorial rather than a personal basis. These dues included the payment of a direct household tax, as well as military service in an emergency war situation but not on a routine basis. Control within the villages was autonomously maintained. Ownership of land newly cleared and reduced to cultivation could be freely claimed by the occupant in the "parched lands" of central Burma, but ownership was invariably a community or family rather than an individual affair. An essential element of security, therefore, was the retention of a person's affiliation in a family group and within a village community. Overt expulsion of a troublemaker from the village or township unit came to be a serious disciplinary sanction wielded by the myothugyi or the community elders as a whole. It was on top of this developing indigenous system of control through the myothugyi township system of the Burmans that the Indianized structure of central governmental administration was superimposed.[26]

Little is known concerning the upper levels of the social order of Pagan Burma, except that maintenance of high social status here as elsewhere depended on royal preferment. Even the chief ministers proudly described themselves as "slaves" of the ruler. The royal princes, half brothers of the king, who managed to survive the often-gruesome events of accession to power, where dangerous rivals were regularly eliminated, were usually assigned as *Myosas* (eaters of the town) over athi districts distant from the capital. Here they maintained themselves by absorbing the available local

[26] For a more complete description of the eighteenth-century myothugyi system see John F. Cady, *A History of Modern Burma* (1958), 27–34. The Burman headman system appears to be different in many respects from the *duwa* authority found among the twentieth-century Kachins. See E. R. Leach, *Political Systems of Highland Burma* (1954).

tax income. Villagers in areas subjected to the Myosas' rapacity were probably little better off than the pagoda slaves, even though legally free.

The chief ministers of the king numbered four or five men, usually
not of inherited princely rank, whose duties were variously assigned according to their interests and competence. They subsequently acquired the title
of *Wungyis* (big burden bearers). As at Angkor, important men of the
kingdom contributed daughters to the royal harem. The organization of
the Wungyis into a corporate body known as the *Hlutdaw,* named from the
hall in which meetings were held, apparently developed after the Pagan
period. Royally appointed governors, or *Wuns,* administered provincial
affairs, such as tax collection and transmission, army and police duties, and
criminal jurisdiction, all done in the king's name and at his pleasure. The
Myosa areas and the pagoda lands were all outside the direct control of the
court Wuns and contributed little in revenues to the court.

## Pagan during the Burman Period

The transition from Mon to Burman cultural dominance at Pagan
occurred during the long reign of Cansu I (Alaungsithu, 1113–1167), the
grandson of Thiluin Man and great-grandson of Thaton's Makuta. He was
probably the first of the Pagan kings fully trained in Pali; an important
inscription attributed to him is couched in Pali verse of exceptional quality.[27] He obviously preferred the Mon language to Burmese, a preference
probably derived from his upbringing and no doubt justified by the poetic
quality of Mon and its general superiority to the still-developing Burmese
language.[28]

Cansu I is represented in the chronicles as a saintly King, and ideal
Buddhist ruler caring for his people's needs and performing many works of
merit. He completed the imposing Thatpinnyu temple in 1144, a strikingly
Burmese variant of the Mon-type Ananda built by his grandfather. The final
years of his reign were marred by revolts in distant Arakan and Tenasserim
and by a general relaxation of authority.[29] Disaffection on the part of Burman partisans apparently focused on the continuing preference given to
Mon political and economic interests. Trouble was also brewing with
Ceylon over Burmese interference (possibly Mon-inspired) with the portage
trade of north Malaya. These problems came to a head in the troubled
decade following Cansu's death.

The quarrel with Ceylon apparently began with punitive operations
of Burmese naval units, possibly Mons, along the isthmian coasts of north
Malaya. The issue was Ceylon's freedom to use the portage routes leading
to Cambodia. In controlling a segment of the Malay isthmus Burma took
advantage of Angkor's serious preoccupation with Champa at the time. The

[27] Than Tun, "A History," *NBW*, Oct. 25, 1958, 314.

[28] Luce, *Mons of the Pagan Dynasty*, 16.

[29] D. G. E. Hall, *A History of South-East Asia* (1955), 129–130.

latter state staged repeated attacks on Cambodia following the death of Suryavarman II (1150), culminating finally in the Cham destruction of Angkor in 1177. Cansu's incompetent son and successor, Intaw Syan (Narathu) precipitated the isthmian quarrel in 1165 by refusing to make a requested treaty settlement with Ceylon. Instead he cut off Ceylon's trade relations with Burma (including the isthmus as well), imprisoning Sinhalese envoys found in Malay ports, and actually seizing a Sinhalese princess en route to Cambodia.

The infuriated ruler of Ceylon thereupon went to war with Burma. He prepared an extensive naval expedition allegedly consisting of one hundred ships. The success realized by the Sinhalese was no doubt greatly exaggerated in the Sinhalese accounts, for many ships failed to reach their destinations, some running aground on the Andaman Islands. But the Burman port of Bassein was apparently captured and looted, and other damage was inflicted. King Intaw Syan was captured and killed around 1165 allegedly by "Indians," perhaps by enemies within Burma who were pro-Ceylon in their sympathies and seeking an end of Mon influence at court.[30]

A troubled nine-year interregnum ensued before royal authority was reestablished in Burma and a settlement arranged with Ceylon. The good offices of respected Buddhist monks were used in the peace negotiations. The new Burman King Cansu II (Narapatsithu, 1174–1211) was selected from a descendant of the older Aniruddha line. His accession in 1174 marked the abrupt end of Mon influence at the Pagan Court. No royal inscriptions were made thereafter in Mon, even though the first Burmese ones were of necessity rather simple and short.[31] Close political relations between Burma and Ceylon were restored to their customary status dating from Aniruddha's time, which meant among other things an end to Burman friendship with the Tamil Cholas. The treaty settlement included a Burman pledge of noninterference with Ceylon's trade in the isthmian portage area. For the third time (1057, 1065, and 1165), international considerations were a determining factor in a basic policy orientation for Burma.

The accession of Cansu II in 1174 also signalized for Burma a victory for the Sinhalese type of Buddhism over the partially Vishnuized version long favored by the Thaton faction of the Sangha. Burmese pilgrimages to Ceylon's Hinayana Buddhist shrines, initiated during the interregnum of the 1160s, undertook to restore the purity of the faith at Pagan. A series of visits to Ceylon were made by court-appointed primates (*Thathanabaings*) of the Sangha. The most famous pilgrim was Chapata, himself a Mon, who was reportedly accompanied to Ceylon in 1180 by one of the sons of the Mahayana Buddhist King Jayavarman VII of Cambodia. Chapata remained

---

[30] Than Tun, "A History," *NBW*, Nov. 29, 1958, 83–84. Than Tun's reconstruction of the episode, as here given, is based on both Burmese and Sinhalese records. He discounts extravagant Sinhalese claims that they themselves captured Pagan and killed the King. The entire story needs to be reexamined.

[31] *Ibid.*

in Ceylon for a full decade. The Theravada Buddhist reform inaugurated by Burma became contagious, spreading in time to the Thai, the Laotians, and the Cambodians.[32] Hinayana Buddhism in Southeast Asia, with its roots in the Ceylon tradition, survived the disappearance of the faith from India, whereas the Mahayana form failed to do so.

King Cansu II also undertook an extensive building program at Pagan which must have monopolized much of his time and attention. His two principal monuments were the Gawdawpawlin and the Sulamani temples.[33] The end of his reign witnessed a slight rift with Ceylon. One of his six principal queens was a princess from Ceylon, but she was outranked by others. Consequently her two princely sons were passed over in the succession of Natonmya (Nandaungmya) in 1211. One Sinhalese prince rebelled and was executed.

Natonmya (1211–1231) was Pagan's last great ruler. He was able for the first time to render the northern borders secure by ousting Nan Chao control and by conquering the border Kantu peoples. He established an administrative post located across the Irrawaddy River opposite modern Bhamo and another guardian fort to the north of Bhamo near the upper limit of Irrawaddy navigation. He selected as ministers able men, who helped him curb rebellion and were responsible for particular tasks, one to be registrar, one the army commander (Mahasenapati), and another the chief judge. Here was probably the traditional origin of the subsequent Hlutdaw system, although a fixed meeting place for the group was not maintained. He gave strong support to the Sinhalese Buddhist reform effort to enforce the Vinaya rules of monkhood, a movement which lost ground to the heretical forest-dweller monks after his death. The inordinate acquisitiveness of the forest-dweller group, particularly in land, occasioned in Natonmya's time heavy losses to royal revenue. His usurper son Klacwa (Kyazwa), who ruled from 1235 to 1249, undertook to correct the problem by confiscating monastic lands, but most of them were later returned following examination of various claims by special royal commissions. The growing prevalence of lawlessness was advertised by Klacwa's widespread proclamation of royal edicts threatening dire punishment to thieves and other malefactors.[34]

## Five Temple Monuments of Pagan

The historical evolution of Pagan Burma can be usefully illustrated by reference to five characteristic temples, the Shwezigon, the Ananda, the Thatpinnyu, the Gawdawpawlin, and the Mingalazedi. The first and the

[32] Hall, 130.

[33] The impressive Mahabodi and Htilominlo temples were also built by Cansu II.

[34] Than Tun, "A History," *NBW*, Jan. 3, 1959, 23–25. Endemic lawlessness appears not to have been peculiar to modern Burma. Some 450 village inscriptions were posted by Klacwa containing dire threats against criminals.

fifth of the series are strikingly similar in character, representing perhaps a kind of stolid uninspired pattern with which the Pagan Burmans began and to which they eventually returned. The middle three are representative of a large group of buildings of the middle period far superior both as architectural achievements and as art.

The Shwezigon pagoda, near Pagan, as previously indicated, was started by King Aniruddha and completed by Thiluin Man. It was an especially sacred shrine, noted for its incorporation of the thirty-seven nat shrines and for its housing of the replica of the Buddha tooth from Ceylon. The Shwezigon was in some respects similar to Borobudur, although on a smaller scale and constructed on flat terrain. It was a pyramidal structure, the four lower stages being square in shape and the upper levels circular, culminating in a massive stupa spire in the shape of a pointed bell. As in the case of Borobudur, the successive stages were reached by a series of frontal staircases, the first entrance being gained through an elaborately fashioned gateway. Passageways running to the right and left along each of the successive stages were lined with niches numbering in the hundreds for displaying Buddha figures and plaques. Smaller pointed spires decorated the four corners of successive stages of the pyramid, increasing in size at the higher levels. The whole was covered with gold leaf and the central spire capped by a *hti* umbrella set with precious stones. The monument is still massively vigorous and impressive but very unromantic and matter-of-fact— a symbol of power and of piety.

King Thiluin Man's masterpiece, the Ananda temple, borrowed heavily from traditional Mon standards of temple construction, many smaller examples of which can be found at Pagan. The latter were usually one-story affairs, a semblance of artificial caves. A massive masonry core at the center usually bore the sheer weight of the central spire and also supported one side of the vaulted ceiling of the encircling central passageway. The temple's center was approached traditionally via a darkened corridor flanked by small windows, the interior walls and ceiling of the entranceway being covered with decorative paintings often imaginatively designed. At the end of the darkened tunnel, one encountered the presence of a towering Buddha lighted mysteriously from concealed apertures in the vaulted ceiling above.[35]

This Mon temple pattern was duplicated on a grand scale in the Ananda. It quadrupled the effect by constructing entrances from all four directions. The base was greatly expanded and covered by a tiered roof, varying in height and highly decorated. Narrower passageways were constructed on either side and parallel to the four main entrances, each of which ended in a niche containing a small image of the Buddha. An outer corridor paralleled and encircled the taller inner one which passed in front of the standing images. The huge structure was thus honeycombed with

[35] Luce, *Mons of the Pagan Dynasty,* 16–17.

vaulted corridors. The four gilded Buddhas, about 20 feet tall and standing opposite the main entrances with their backs against the central core of the structure, were impressively lighted from above. The disciples sitting beside one of them represented Thiluin Man himself and his Mon scholar friend, Arahan.

The foundations and inner walls of the Ananda temple were elaborately decorated. They portrayed in terra-cotta plaques some fifteen hundred scenes from the life of the Buddha. Each was described by a legend in the Mon language. Four sculptured porticoes portrayed the end of his life. The upper terraces contained forty bas-reliefs in stone. Four smaller lotus-bud towers located at the corners of the structure, all of them gilded, set off the main tower at the center. Each side of the central tower contained a niche sheltering a Buddha figure. All approaches and extensions were elaborately decorated on the exteriors with conventional and figure designs. It was a masterpiece of temple architecture and is still movingly beautiful, the inspired work of a ruler and a people completely absorbed in their task.[36]

The other two temple masterpieces, Thatpinnyu and the Gawdaw-pawlin, built by Cansu I and Cansu II respectively, are characteristically Burman although borrowing heavily from the Ananda style. The entrances were opened more widely to admit both light and air. A conscious effort was made in the flame-decorated lintels and the structural design to elevate the central mass. The principal Buddha figures in the larger Thatpinnyu are situated on an elevated interior platform approached by long staircases. The similar Gawdawpawlin is perhaps better proportioned but not so large or elaborately constructed. Burman Pagan has been described as lacking the poetic and romantic characteristics of the Mons, but its religious symbolism is considered superior and its inscriptions, although unpretentious as literature, were brief and simple and full of vigor.[37] Pagan's inspiration was, of course, predominantly Buddhist. The type of pagoda did not change abruptly. The last Mon-style structure, modeled on the Ananda, was dated 1165, whereas the Gawdawpawlin was not completed until 1160.[38]

Burman-Mon inspiration faded following the reign of Natonmya (d. 1231), who was the last builder in the grand style. Declining royal resources, to which the heavy absorption of wealth in land and slaves by monasteries contributed, were certainly a factor in this. A disastrous fire swept the capital city in 1225. In any case, the building of the final Mingalazedi pyramidal pagoda by Cansu IV exhausted his people. It reverted to the original Shwezigon pattern of exterior staircases and square passageways lined with terra-cotta plaques. The vigorous genius of Pagan Burma had spent itself by 1280.

[36] Than Tun, *Religion in Burma, 1000–1300* (1958), 7; N. Ray, *An Introduction to the Study of Theravada Buddhism in Burma* (1946), 99–105.

[37] Luce, "Burma's Debt to Pagan," *JBRS*, XXII (1932), 120–127.

[38] Luce, *Mons of the Pagan Dynasty*, 16.

## *The Collapse of the Pagan Dynasty*

The collapse of the Pagan Empire came under the boastful and despotic Cansu IV (Narathihapate, 1252–1287). He abused his people, exhausted the country, and, beginning in 1271, ran afoul of the Mongol authority of China. He flatly rejected the first demand of Kublai Khan, sent via the governor of Yunnan, for Burma's submission as a tributary state. He summarily executed a second mission led by an imperial Chinese envoy sent to reemphasize the demand. Cansu IV then attacked gratuitously two border states which had accepted Mongol suzerainty. His courage failed when he had to face successive Mongol invasion efforts.

The Burmans were first defeated in Yunnan in 1277. Marco Polo's secondhand account of this conflict between the Burman and the Tartar armies in Yunnan told how the dismounted Mongol archers stung the Burmese elephants with arrows until they panicked. The Mongols then used Burmese prisoners to recapture some two hundred of the beasts and to incorporate them into the army of the Great Khan, as its first elephant battalion.[39] The Burmese border fortress above Bhamo fell to the Mongols in 1283, and the country was thereafter open to Chinese invasion. At this critical juncture, the cowardly Burman King ran away southward to Bassein, only to be forced in the face of spreading rebellion by the Mons, Arakanese, and Shans to come to terms with the Mongols in the end. As he was attempting to return to Pagan as a puppet Mongol ruler in 1287, he was murdered by a son. The Mongols thereupon occupied Pagan, from which they witnessed a subsequent fratricidal princely bloodbath taking place in Lower Burma. The survivor of the gruesome ordeal, Rhuynansyan (or Kyawza), was installed as puppet Mongol ruler at Pagan in 1289.[40]

## *The Advent of Shan Rule in Upper Burma*

It was the original intention of the Mongol conquerors of Pagan to organize the acquired territories into two provinces to be integrated with the Chinese Empire. The southernmost of the projected provinces (Meinchung), extending below the Mandalay area and including Pagan itself, was quickly abandoned in 1291 under the revised arrangement under which Kyawza would function as puppet ruler. But without direct Mongol support, Kyawza was unable to maintain control. Three Shan brothers, all Burmanized Buddhists and each in charge (as myothugyi) of a military principality in the Kyaukse district, forced the pretended ruler to recognize their *de facto* control of the key granary area in 1293. From this vantage point they proceeded to apply further pressure. By 1297 the harried King Kyawza

[39] See Henry Yule (ed.), *The Book of Ser Marco Polo* (1929), II, 101–106. Polo's secondhand description of the gold-covered pagodas at Pagan follows on 106–114.

[40] Hall, 131–132.

resorted to the desperate expedient of appealing for Mongol support in his own behalf. Peking obliged by appointing him officially King of Pagan. Meanwhile the Shan brothers had deposed the hapless Kyawza. When it became apparent in 1299 that China intended again to interfere, they proceeded to kill the ex-ruler, to burn Pagan, and to execute all Chinese residents there. The Mongols replied in 1300 by explicitly acknowledging Kyawza's son as the rightful heir at Pagan and by preparing a final invasion, which reached Burma in early 1301.

Again the Mongol plans miscarried. The Chinese invasion was far from popular, and spirited resistance led by the three Shan brothers from a fortified post in the vicinity of Kyaukse (still largely Burman-inhabited) turned back the invaders. The thwarted Mongol commander finally accepted a bribe to withdraw his forces,[41] a deed for which he was later to be executed in Yunnan. The youngest of the three Shan brothers, who survived the others as Burma's ruler from 1312 to 1324, boasted perennially that he was the King who turned back the Chinese army, which deed was without doubt his greatest claim to prestige.

After 1303, Peking abandoned the attempt to maintain control over the north Burma provinces, although the Mongols still endeavored to keep the turbulent Shan tribes along the Yunnan border under control. Central Burma remained Burman ethnically and culturally, but Shan princes were for a long time politically and militarily supreme. They eventually shifted their center of control to the mouth of the Myitngé River (near the Ava site), which was the strategically important water-route outlet from the Kyaukse granary. Significantly, the Shan rulers still claimed descent from the dynasty of Pagan.[42]

Following the collapse of Pagan's control over Lower Burma in 1283, Mon areas fell under the control of an untutored military adventurer named Wareru, who had formerly seen service under Rama Khamheng in Sukhothai. Wareru seized control of Martaban in 1281, collaborated in expelling the Burmans from all Lower Burma, and then, in 1287, murdered his Peguan rival and took over the kingship. Although nominally a vassal of Sukhothai, Wareru also sought and obtained recognition of his control from China. From his new capital at Martaban he extended his rule southward to Mergui and northward as far as Prome and Toungoo.

Under the uninspired leadership of Wareru (d. 1296) and his successors, the Mons of Lower Burma failed to restore the cultural and literary standards of the Thaton period. When the Mon written language eventually reappeared, it was much corrupted by Burmese.[43] Wareru did supervise the preparation by learned monks of Burma's lawbook, a digest of the Indian Code of Manu. Mon Martaban was torn with internal feuding for

[41] Coedès, 350–352.

[42] Hall, 133–134; Than Tun, *History of Burma,* A.D. *1300–1400* (1959), pp. 2–6.

[43] Luce, *Mons of the Pagan Dynasty,* 17.

more than a half century after Wareru's death.[44] Some Burmans from the Pagan, Minbu, and Kyaukse-Ava areas who escaped from the tyranny of Shan misrule retreated southward into the upper reaches of the narrow Sittang Valley. Here they eventually (by the mid-fourteenth century) developed a precarious claim to independence between Shan Ava and Mon Martaban. The Sittang Valley center of Toungoo became the rallying point for a revival of Burman control in the mid-1500s.

[44] Hall, 140–141.

PART 3

*Transition to Modern Times*

# Mongol Intervention, Thai Hegemony, and Majapahit Java

The final decades of the thirteenth century constituted a kind of watershed between the early and the middle period of Southeast Asian history. To the decline of Cambodia and the collapse of Pagan Burma, already described, were added the complete disintegration of the Śrivijayan Empire, the rise of a rejuvenated Majapahit state in Java, and domination from the borders of China southward into Malaya by a new Siamese Empire. What was largely responsible for these simultaneous developments, partly as a catalytic agent and partly as a directly causal factor, was the intervention of the Mongol forces of China's Kublai Khan. The two important positive results of the Mongol intervention were the achievement of Thai supremacy in virtually all the interior and central portions of peninsular Southeast Asia and the emergence of central and eastern Java as the successor to Śrivijaya in the leadership of Indonesia.

## The Mongol Intervention

The creation of the Mongol Empire in the early 1200s, extending from northern China across Central Asia to the Middle East and Europe, exerted at the outset only an indirect effect on Southeast Asian peoples. After capturing Peking and the northern tier of Chinese provinces (1211–1215), Jenghiz Khan's armies turned westward, overrunning Persia by 1222 and moving thence northward into Eastern Europe. The same policy was continued by his successor, the Khan Ogotai (1227–1241). Under the leadership of the sons of Ogotai, the Islamic Near East from Baghdad to Syria was overrun (by Hulegu), as was the Baltic area and Poland (by the oldest brother, Batu). After 1241 the main seat of empire continued to be in Mongolia under Khan Mangu; the youngest brother, Kublai, was made the viceroy of China. Kublai differed markedly from his brothers by becoming enamored of Chinese civilization.

Perhaps the principal effect of westward Mongol expansion on Southeast Asian affairs was to divert a substantial portion of the seaborne commerce of the Persians and Arabs from the Malaya portage and straits passages to the overland caravan routes of Central Asia. The seaborne trade was also adversely affected by Sung China's growing concern over an unfavorable balance of payments. Preoccupation with the Mongol threat was also connected with increasing disorders along the South China coast. The continued existence of the Southern Sung state nevertheless insulated Southeast Asia from the direct Mongol impact for nearly a half century.

The first important change produced by the Mongols along the southern borders of China followed Kublai's conquest of the Thai state of Nan Chao in 1253. This action occurred as an incidental by-product of the effort of the Mongol viceroy to turn the left flank of the revived Sung armies, in order to get behind their Yangtse River defenses. The Mongols overran Nan Chao, seized the Tali plain, and sent the captive Thai ruler to do homage to Khan Mangu in Mongolia. He was eventually returned to his domain as an abject vassal. Meanwhile, large numbers of Thai immigrant refugees, many of them ambitious militarily, moved southward into north Burma, the Shan plateau region, and the upper reaches of the Mekong and Menan Valleys.[1] The three Shan brothers who gained entry to Kyaukse and eventually dominated Pagan were originally leaders of such mercenary bands. Thai recruits also swelled the army ranks of Sukhothai.

The enormous encircling operation performed by Kublai's army ended with its capture of Hanoi in 1257. The Mongol forces by that time were reduced by attrition and disease to a bare one-fifth of their original strength. Kublai therefore proposed to call a temporary halt to permit the reconstitution of his exhausted forces through replacements from conquered peoples. A breathing spell would also afford opportunity for conquered Chinese areas to establish a civilian administration and to recover from material losses previously sustained. An open rift was narrowly averted between Kublai and his senior Sinophobe brother, Khan Mangu, who feared that the young prince was losing his conquering spirit.

The final all-out assault on the Southern Sungs was initiated by the combined Mongol armies in 1260. A delay was occasioned when Mangu died of dysentery during the early course of the renewed campaign and Kublai was obliged to establish his succession rights. When Kublai finally took over supreme Mongol leadership in his own right, he did it more as Emperor of China than as leader of the Mongol horde. As China's new ruler, he was concerned not only with reunifying the Middle Kingdom but also with reestablishing its traditional suzerainty over all states of Southeast Asia which had previously sent tribute missions to the Middle Kingdom. His first demands for submission brought negative responses. As soon as he had completed the elimination of Sung resistance (by 1267), he undertook to enforce by arms his insistence that Southeast Asian rulers come in person

[1] Michael Prawdin, *The Mongol Empire: Its Rise and Legacy* (1953).

to the Court of the Khan to renew their tributary status. The new policy would require real subservience, as in the case of the Nan Chao prince, rather than the customary nominal payment of deference. When Kublai's demands were refused, he inaugurated a momentous twenty-year program of armed intervention by Mongol-Chinese forces in Southeast Asia.[2]

Some aspects of the Mongol invasions have already been described. The Pagan Empire of Burma was destroyed, thereby exposing most of the harassed country to about two centuries of Shan misrule. Confronted by a common danger, Vietnam and Champa adjourned their chronic feuding and united to repel Mongol attacks sent against them by land and sea. The invaders were therefore unable to achieve a decisive military victory in Annam, where they also suffered heavy losses from disease. They left the entire coastal area devastated and famine-ridden but still unconquered. Cambodia was spared invasion largely by the stubborn resistance offered by Champa and Vietnam. All three governments eventually renewed their traditional tributary allegiance to China on a purely nominal basis, not by personal subjection on the part of the rulers.[3] Vietnam returned Chinese war prisoners in 1289 as a gesture of conciliation. China's demands became much less exacting after Timur Khan succeeded Kublai in 1294.[4]

Two of the newly emerging rulers of Southeast Asia, Rama Khamheng of Sukhothai and Wareru of Mon Martaban, established cordial relations with the Mongol regime during the 1280s promptly and without difficulty. Rama visited Peking in person and was accorded support from Kublai for Sukhothai's expanding authority at the expense of his stiff-necked "barbarian" neighbors. The story of Mongol intervention in the Malacca Straits and in Java in the 1290s calls for a review of what had happened in these areas since the early eleventh century.[5]

## Java and the Straits from Airlangga to Kertanagara

Conditions in central and eastern Java were decidedly discouraging in the early eleventh century. Following the abortive Javanese attack on Śrivijaya in the 990s came the devastating retaliatory raid suffered by Java a decade later. Complete confusion prevailed. The first ray of hope was the accession in 1019 of Airlangga, a young Balinese prince with an east Javan bride, who emerged from hiding and took over as ruler of a small principality near Surabaya. He accomplished relatively little until after 1025 when

[2] *Ibid.,* 316–340. The Sung capital fell to Kublai in 1261, but it was some years later before the Kwangtung coastal areas were pacified.

[3] G. Coedès, *Les États Hindouisés* (1948), 321–325.

[4] Lê Thanh Khôi, *Le Viet-Nam* (1955), 179–189; L. P. Briggs, *The Ancient Khmer Empire* (1950), 241–242.

[5] Likhit Hoontrakul, *The History of Siamese-Chinese Relations* (1953), 101–102.

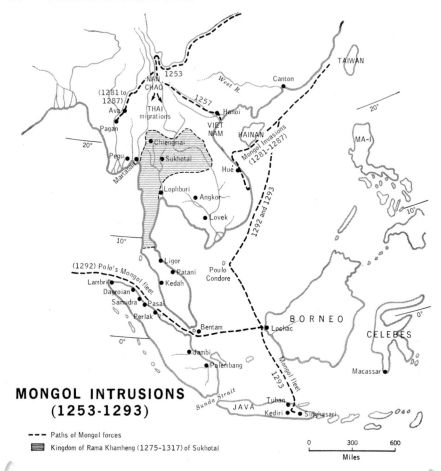

**MONGOL INTRUSIONS**
**(1253-1293)**

- - -   Paths of Mongol forces

▨   Kingdom of Rama Khamheng (1275-1317) of Sukhotai

0        300        600

Miles

the Chola attacks weakened Śrivijaya and afforded him a measure of leeway. From 1028 to 1035, eastern Java staged a full-scale recovery under Airlangga's able leadership. He concluded a diplomatic marriage alliance with Śrivijaya in 1030 and built a new Javanese capital in 1037. Airlangga reverted periodically to forest retreats as a worshipper of Vishnu; he was accordingly enshrined as a revered Vishnu reincarnation after his death. He was tolerant of Buddhism, and Śiva worship was also present in his kingdom. No architectural monuments survived his reign, but it did witness the beginning of an unparalleled flowering of Indo-Javanese literature, a development which continued unabated under his successors. Javanese writers prepared vernacular adaptations of the principal Hindu epics and wrote original poetry. Airlangga's own life story was later fitted into the Hindu allegory of the saint Arjuna, a literary tour de force which has long contributed its share of historical confusion. The alleged legendary division of Airlangga's kingdom into three segments at the time of his death in 1049 cannot be reconciled with the fairly conclusive evidence that central Java's

Kediri state actually took over full control. Airlangga was nonetheless an important political figure.[6]

The Kediri state profited greatly in time from the Mediterranean area's growing demand for spices, which Javanese merchants procured in the Spice Islands in exchange for rice and other products. Kediri in time extended its rule over Bali to the east, parts of south Borneo, and into the Moluccas. The spices collected at north Javan ports were picked up for the most part by Indian cloth merchants for eventual transportation to European markets. Closer commercial and cultural ties between Kediri and southern India permitted the revival in 1089 of the charter for the hostelry at the Negapatam shrine on the Tamil Chola coast, a facility reserved for the use of Javanese visitors. During the following century the Molucca trade began to assume real importance commercially.

The leadership of the Kediri dynasty was apparently replaced around 1222 by a lowborn adventurer named Angrok, who founded the rival east Javanese capital of Senghasari in the valley of the Brantas River. Angrok was alleged to be a drunken rake. He took over control following a rift between the last Kediri ruler and the Brahman priests of his court. Angrok and his successors quickly assumed the role of leadership in the rich spice trade and began to expand their territorial claims. By the mid-thirteenth century, east Javan forces seized control of Banka Island which lay athwart the entrance of Palembang harbor. Reduction of the key Spice Island of Ternate to vassalage status at the other end of the trading arc gave Senghasari a virtual monopoly of the spice trade in the Java Sea. Using Javan rice and India-manufactured cotton cloth, which became the staples of the Moluccan trade, Senghasari controlled the easternmost stage of the fabulously profitable commerce in spices and pepper destined for the growing European market.[7]

Javanese power developed rapidly after the able and aggressive Kertanagara took over Senghasari in 1268. He first extended his control in the eastern islands of Madura and Bali. Taking advantage of the faltering power of Śrivijaya, he then occupied the Sunda Straits, parts of coastal Borneo, and southern portions of Malaya, while also contesting Śrivijayan control over the Malacca Straits themselves. It was this ambitious policy of Senghasari Java, fashioned in part to counter prospective Mongol threats, which attracted the hostile attention of the Chinese authorities. Kublai Khan was interested in general in reviving seaborne trade and especially commerce between China and the Persian Gulf area, ruled over by another prince of the Mongol clan. He was also not inclined to brook political defiance. The break with Kertanagara came in 1292, after three abortive efforts had been

[6] D. G. E. Hall, *A History of South-East Asia* (1955), 63–64. The Dutch scholar Berg casts serious doubt on the authenticity of the standard account of Airlangga's reign.

[7] Coedès, 245–250; F. J. Morehead, *A History of Malaya* (1957), 82–84; Hall, 64; B. H. M. Vlekke, *Nusantara* (1960), 44–52.

made by Peking (1280–1289) to persuade him to send a member of the royal family as a hostage to China. The last Chinese envoy was roughly handled by the Javanese.[8]

Deteriorating conditions in the Malacca Straits also attracted Kublai's attention. The trading entrepôt of Śrivijaya, which had recovered its prosperity quickly following the war with the Cholas (1017–1025), in 1225 still controlled the Sunda and Malacca Straits, a part of western Java, and several ports along the straits coast of Sumatra, with some influence surviving as far north as Tambralinga and the Bay of Bandon in northern Malaya. During the ensuing sixty years it lost out generally. The commercial opportunities in Sung China eroded away. Malayu (Jambi) gained its virtual independence in the very middle of the straits,[9] as did Ligor in northern Malaya. Rama Khamheng's aggressive Thai conquerors overran the northern part of Malaya in the 1280s, while Kertanagara made inroads on the side of the Java Sea. Activities of Palembang designed to force all ships to call at Śrivijayan ports degenerated into semipiracy. Malayu began sending its own tributary missions to China by 1275 in an open bid for Peking's support in the contest for the control of the straits. When Marco Polo passed through the straits in 1292, Śrivijaya was gone. He touched in eastern Borneo but omitted to call at Palembang. He described a number of separate Sumatran city-kingdoms which were remnants of the once-great empire.[10]

## Mongol Naval Expeditions, 1292–1293

The first of two naval expeditions which the Great Khan dispatched to the south seas in 1292 was diplomatic and exploratory in character. It was charged with examining conditions affecting the navigation of the Malacca Straits en route to Ceylon. The fleet of fourteen ships was also charged with the task of escorting to Persia a Mongol princess who was espoused to a nephew of the Great Khan, Argun the Ilkhan of Persia. Its most celebrated passenger was Marco Polo, en route back to Venice after thirty years spent in Eastern Asia.[11]

The Chinese expedition passed by Champa. Polo referred to it as a wealthy country much frequented by traders, paying annual tribute to the Great Khan and famous for its fine blackwood for the manufacture of chessmen. The Cham navy was, in fact, fully mobilized on this occasion to prevent any possible repetition of the invasions of the previous decade. The first stop was at Lochac in eastern Borneo, described by Polo as a Hindu state rich in scented woods and gold. The fleet proceeded thence to Bintang Island off Singapore, bypassing the lower Sumatran coast (Palembang and Malayu), to the port of Samara (Samudra) on the north Sumatran coast.

[8] Coedès, 332–334; Hall, 63–70; Vlekke, 51–57.
[9] Hall, 54–57.
[10] Coedès, 300–316.
[11] *Ibid.*, 308–316, 337–341. An early Muslim mission visited Peking in 1281.

Here it was obliged to halt for five months to await the change of the monsoon winds. The company went ashore and built for itself stockaded and moated defenses, living mainly on fish and rice, coconuts, and toddy-palm wine.

Polo's secondhand decription of Java, based on Arab or Gujerati Indian information, affords some indication of the exaggerated reputation which the island had acquired under Senghasari leadership. Java, he wrote, was "the greatest island in the world," 3,000 miles around, wealthy in pepper, nutmeg, cloves, cubeb, and other kinds of spices. It was visited by a vast number of merchant ships, which reaped fabulous profits from its trade. It lay outside the range of the power of the Great Khan and was tributary to no one.[12]

Polo's description of the half-dozen petty states along the west Sumatran coast illustrated the fragmentation of control and the complete absence of any policing authority capable of restoring order and safe passage. Ferlec (Perlak) was described as an Islamic state frequented by Saracen merchants. Basma (Pasai) claimed to be subject to the Khan and was associated with the bizarre stories about unicorns with boarlike heads and prickly tongues, along with pigmy-cannibal inhabitants. Hindu Samara (Samudra) was described as rich and powerful, but the hinterland was reported also to be cannibal-infested. Lambri and Fansur, both located near the northern point of Sumatra and both idolators (Hindu), were described as sources of excellent camphorwood, brazil nuts, and spices. Fansur ate rice, while Lambri used bread made from tree pulp (sago). Both claimed to be tributary to the Great Khan. Some twelve states all told were listed on the eastern coast of Sumatra. Sumatra was referred to as "little Java" and was regarded as being only one-half as large.[13]

The passage of the Mongol fleet through the straits in 1292 apparently did nothing to improve the political situation, for the action was not followed up in any systematic way. The eventual outcome was that the former Śrivijayan port of Palembang became infested by a band of pirates led by a nucleus of Chinese brigands. They retained control of the place for more than a century.[14]

The Chinese naval expedition to Java in 1292–1293 was equally ineffective and ended disastrously. Despite Javanese efforts to thwart the Chinese invasion at sea, it succeeded in landing at the port of Tuban on the eastern end of Java in early 1293. The Chinese invaders learned that their enemy Kertanagara had been assassinated in late 1292 by a Kediri viceroy, one Jayakatwang. The latter had seized control of the capital during the course of a magical religious orgy. His authority was being contested in 1293 by Prince Vijaya, the legitimate heir and son-in-law of Kertanagara,

[12] Henry Yule (ed.), *The Book of Ser Marco Polo* (1903), II, book III, 266–273.

[13] *Ibid.*, 284–291.

[14] R. O. Winstedt, *Malaya and Its History* (1956), 18.

who left no son to succeed him. The prince had taken temporary refuge in Madura. After the Mongol force captured the Javan fleet of Jayakatwang at Surabaya and penetrated inland, the wily Vijaya decided to feign acceptance of China's tributary demands and to enlist the assistance of the invading army to put down his Javanese rival. The Chinese cooperated by capturing Jayakatwang in his Kediri castle, with Vijaya's own forces acting as a rear guard. While returning under Chinese escort to his own stronghold at Majapahit, ostensibly to arrange tributary payments, Vijaya's own band murdered his Mongol-Chinese escort, rallied Javanese resistance to the invaders, and drove the Mongols back to their ships.

The discouraged invaders eventually departed, taking with them family hostages of the defeated Jayakatwang. The net result of the costly effort was to restore to power the heirs of the very regime of Kertanagara that China had tried to subdue. The victorious Prince Vijaya established a new capital at Majapahit and changed his name to Kertarajasa. He claimed the throne on the basis of victory over his rivals and his alleged marriage to four daughters of Kertanagara. Sometime later he sent to China an innocuous tributary mission. Java remained permanently outside the circle of the close vassal states of China, which included both Champa and Siam.[15]

The enormous expenditure of effort and treasure on the part of Mongol China in Southeast Asia produced few positive accomplishments. Five military expeditions into Burma had destroyed the Pagan dynasty but had left most of the country under the control of Shan or Thai chieftains, whose proudest boast was that they had repelled the Chinese invaders. The Mongol destruction of Nan Chao had accelerated the expansion of Thai power into the Menam Valley and northern Malaya at the expense of Cambodia and the Mons. China's relations with the new state of Siam were friendly, but the gain for Peking was hardly capable of balancing losses sustained elsewhere. Improvement of shipping conditions in the Malacca Straits had to await the arrival of the Ming expeditions in the early fifteenth century. The costly Java expedition had been a total loss, although Kertanagara's attempt to unite Indonesia was thwarted. Friendly Champa was doomed to succumb in time to renewed Vietnamese pressure, for after the dire experiences of Chinese armies in Annam during the 1280s, Peking would ponder long before risking another intervention in the difficult and fever-infested area. After 1293 Javan Majapahit launched on a career of empire in the Kertanagara tradition, quite outside the orbit of China's control.

Possibly the most important direct result of the Mongol intervention was to stimulate the national spirit among the Thai, the Vietnamese, and the Javanese. Meanwhile, to the west of Malaya, Islam was moving in slowly to constitute a rallying standard looking toward the eventual polic-

[15] Coedès, 332–337; Hall, 73–74. Some Dutch scholars regard the alleged marriages as merely symbolic political unions between sections of Kertanagara's empire.

ing of the Malacca Straits under Muslim control and toward the conversion of Indonesia.

## Majapahit Java

It was almost forty years after 1293 before Majapahit Java was able to produce a leader capable of resuming the expansionist program of Kertanagara. King Vijaya, or Kertarajasa (1293–1309), was more concerned with improving his diplomatic relations through marriage alliances than with increasing the substance of his power. He married princesses from Bali, Borneo, Champa, and Malayu. Trouble developed in eastern Java in 1295, when he passed over one or more wives, who in the alternative version of the story were described as daughters of Kertanagara. He made his Sumatran consort his first queen and named her young son, Jayanagara, his heir. His reign was thereafter torn with rebellion, as was that of his son. There were nine uprisings in all from 1295 to 1328. Jayanagara's rule was challenged especially in eastern Java. He was finally killed at the instigation of a military aide of the royal household, Gaja Mada, who had saved the King on a previous occasion but whose wife the King had meanwhile taken away. The new ruler, Queen Tribhuvana, daughter of the old Cham queen, made Gaja Mada her chief minister, or *Mapatih*, in 1330. As Mapatih and later as regent for Tribhuvana's son and heir, Hayam Wuruk, Gaja Mada was the actual ruler of Majapahit from 1330 until his death in 1364.[16]

The era of Gaja Mada was characterized by a policy of overt expansion of Javanese power with the objective of dominating all of Nusantara, or Indonesia. He eschewed the Hinduized symbolism of universal kingship in vogue since the reign of Kertanagara in favor of characteristic Javanese rationalizations of his expanded control. One can recognize a measure of exaggeration in his boasted conquests and still concede that they were probably considerable. He claimed control over Bali, Macassar, parts of Borneo, Tumasik (Singapore), Pahang, all of lower Sumatra, and the Sunda area in western Java, but much of this control probably amounted to little more than receipt of vassal tribute. Actually his conquest of Bali took more than ten years, and the island was never fully Javanized. One of his generals, the son of the King of Malayu and a Javanese princess, became prince of Malayu for a time. The same prince later had to withdraw into the Minangkabau hill-country interior, cut off from the coast by the rising tide of Islam. Gaja Mada's exhausting and inconclusive war with Sunda began in 1351 when he disdainfully rejected a proposed marriage alliance between King Hayam Wuruk and a Sundanese princess. He demanded instead that the princess be regarded as a mere tributary contribution to the Majapahit harem. When the assembled Sundanese notables objected, a gruesome slaughter ensued, during which Majapahit forces killed both the Sunda

[16] Hall, 72–76.

ruler and his retinue. The stubborn and rebellious Sundanese never did submit to Gaja Mada's authority.[17]

Even when the boastful chronicles of the Gaja Mada era of Majapahit are properly discounted, it survived as one of the distinguished periods of Javanese history. The poet Prapanca left an impressive description of the populous palace-capital, surrounded by high walls of red brick. The great western gateway opened into a spacious plaza lined with tall trees and carpeted with flowers, with a pool of water in the center. A second gateway with doors of ornamented iron led from the plaza to the precincts of the place proper. Here were the tournament fields and the royal pavilion. Nearby were the King's audience chambers, the Council halls, the quarters of the ranking Śiva Buddhist priesthood, and the sumptuous residence of Gaja Mada himself. Huge cages of exotic birds decorated the grounds. Visitors carrying tributary gifts approached the royal presence along paths lined with uniformed soldier guards. Formal palace dinners included entertainment by professional buffoons and musicians, masquerades, and the occasional musical participation by the inebriated King and Queen themselves before their enthusiastic guests.

In the area of court religion and ceremonial, the Gaja Mada period witnessed an apparent further modulation from Hindu-Buddhist standards in the direction of indigenous Javanese symbolism. Official Śiva Buddhist rites of the court were sufficiently flexible to condone gluttony in both meat and drink. In general, Indian names and symbols persisted, but their interpretations were Javanese. For example, rituals associated with the worship of the Javanese sun god, identified with Śiva, were conducted by a priesthood skilled in magical access to supernatural powers. Heroes of Indian legends were similarly identified with ancestral deities; temples became spirit homes where ancestors could be approached. Garuda, the Vishnu carrier bird and Hanuman, king of the monkeys, became effective agencies for chasing evil spirits away. The ashes of the deceased King were buried beneath the sanctuary *chandi,* but his spirit, now reunited as in Śiva worship with the sun god, could continue to care for his people. Javanese shadow plays reverted to their traditional relevance to the ancestor cult.[18]

A similar accommodation to indigenous standards occurred in Bali, except that cults of the Javanese type were not so strongly entrenched in Bali, and the smaller island escaped Islamization at a later period. In Bali Śiva took on the status of first ancestor, and a realm temple was maintained for him at the capital city. Bali also retained a liberal degree of Tantric ritual for combating demons and also for the honoring of ruler images in the temples and mountain shrines.[19]

[17] *Ibid.,* 76–81; Vlekke, 71.

[18] Vlekke, 74–75; H. G. Q. Wales, *The Making of Greater India* (1951), 91–100, 123–140. Several writers have challenged Wales's interpretation, but the emphasis is defensible.

[19] H. G. Q. Wales, *The Mountain of God* (1953), 120–130.

The Nusantara imperialist ideal tended to fade after the death of Gaja Mada in 1364. Nevertheless, for perhaps a century thereafter Majapahit maintained widespread connections and influence, extending as far north as Siam and Vietnam. Majapahit was able in 1377 to intercept a Ming Chinese mission sent to certify the ruler of Malayu (or Palembang) as a vassal of China instead of Java, but Majapahit was never able to control the Malacca Straits in its own right. The records cease after Hayam Wuruk's death in 1389, and the history becomes obscure. Majapahit's power began to decline sharply in the late 1400s when Islamized leadership acquired a foothold in the busy Javanese seaports and adjacent coastal plains, forcing the older government to withdraw into the interior of central Java. Many upper-class Javanese migrated to Bali to escape the pressure of Islam. The central Javan state finally disintegrated around 1520.[20]

## Establishment of Thai Hegemony

One of the important consequences of the shock of Mongol intervention in Southeast Asia was to hasten the expansion of Thai power into the peninsula. The southward movement of the Thai peoples represented the last of a long series of such trends, which had begun in prehistoric times with the Mons, Khmers, Pyu, and Vietnamese. Close association of the Thai tribes with the South Chinese over many centuries was reflected in similarities of race, language, dress, craftsmanship, and customs. Identities of Siamese vocabulary with that of the Cantonese, Hainanese, and other South China dialects reinforce assumptions concerning a common geographical origin for peoples living south of the middle Yangtse River.[21]

The infiltration of Thai peoples into Laos, northern Siam, and the Shan plateau of Burma long preceded the fall of Nan Chao in 1253. Their belonging to China's outer fringe of "barbarians" and their attitude of enmity toward the Chinese government may account for the failure of the Thai to appropriate the Chinese system of writing and governmental forms. Those who moved south did so to escape Chinese control and to seek more freedom. The word Thai means free. Nan Chao alone among the states in Yunnan had been able since the eighth century to withstand Chinese pressure and to extend its own domain. This was possible in large measure by reason of its remote location and the strategic advantages of its terrain. It will be recalled that Nan Chao conquered the northern Pyu capital in 832 and also attacked Hanoi in the early ninth century. Thai mercenary troops were portrayed in the reliefs of Angkor Wat, and they were listed among war captives by Champa.

A stronger push of the Thai tribesmen to the south began after 1215, at the very beginning of the Mongol conquest of North China. This was a

---

[20] Wales, *The Making of Greater India*, 141–145; Hall, 80.

[21] Hoontrakul, 61–64, 105–122. Two-thirds of a list of 180 selected Thai words are duplicated in Cantonese, and more than half in Hainanese.

period of weakening Khmer control along the northern frontier following the death of Jayavarman VII. The Thai founded Mogaung in north Burma in 1215 and Muong Nai on the Salween River in 1223. Some of them also moved into Assam around 1229, apparently simultaneously with a sizable migration down the middle Mekong Valley past Luang Prabang. A group calling themselves the Small Thai achieved a signal victory in 1219 (or 1238) by capturing the Cambodian outpost of Sukhothai in the upper Menam Valley. This accomplishment probably occurred thirty-odd years before the fall of Nan Chao to the Mongols. The opportunities for further conquest at the expense of Cambodia attracted adventurers and refugees to Sukhothai from Nan Chao after 1253, greatly strengthening the military power of the new state. Other Thai adventurers found service with Pagan or became minor *sawbwa* or *chao* princelings in their own right. But by far the most promising avenue for immediate gain led into the lower Menam Valley.[22]

During the course of the third quarter of the 1200s, marauding Thai bands raided far to the south, presumably inspired by Mongol exploits. Their military organization and morale were borrowed from the Mongols. They penetrated the Mon country and entered the isthmus, where they attacked Junk Ceylon in 1256. They apparently encountered little resistance save at Lopburi, where the Mons of old Lavo state had recently asserted their independence of Cambodia. The Mongols raised no objection to this piecemeal dismemberment by the Thai of the stiff-necked Cambodian Empire. Tambralinga in the isthmus region also assumed its independence from Angkor.

The actual founding of the Siamese Empire was the work of King Rama Khamheng, or Rama the Brave (1275–1317). He was the second son of the conqueror of Sukhothai, Sri Indradit (d. 1259), and had been preceded on the throne by his elder brother. He spent the first five years of his reign conquering most of the lower Menam Valley, continuing thence down the isthmus and into northern Malaya. Lopburi was not taken until later. Rama captured Ligor and Patani on the eastern coast and ranged southward on the west perhaps as far as Penang Island. Meanwhile Rama Khamheng required King Wareru of Martaban, the Mon adventurer who seized control of Mon Burma during the 1280s, to become a vassal of Sukhothai. Wareru had seen previous military service at Sukhothai and had allegedly eloped with Rama Khamheng's daughter. The last northern Mon state to surrender to the Thai inundation was Haripunjaya, or Lamph'un, in the Chiengmai area. It fell in 1292, not to Rama Khamheng, who was busy elsewhere, but to his ally King Mangrai of Chiengrai. Following the Mongol naval expeditions against Java and the straits in 1292–1293, the Siamese ambitiously laid claim to all of Malaya. Rama also consolidated his control northward, to Luang Prabang in Laos. The elimination of Pagan Burma by the Mongols and by the Shan chiefs of Upper Burma canceled any possibility of challenge to Siam from that quarter. Rama Khamheng's vast domain was far from unified and was to be

[22] Coedès, 317–321; Hall, 145–146.

subjected to disruptive tendencies after his able leadership had passed. But it faced no serious rival in his day.[23]

The stability of the new Siamese Empire was strengthened by the ruler's calculated decision, made at the outset, to accept without protest the full measure of vassalage demanded by Peking. Rama allegedly made two trips in person to the Mongol capital (1294 and 1300) and dispatched five regular tribute embassies during the 1290s. He entered no objection, furthermore, when his own nominal vassal, Wareru, offered unsolicited tribute to the Mongol Court as a means of asserting Mon independence. Such a policy of deference to the Chinese was in sharp contrast to the generally negative Southeast Asian reaction to Mongol demands and doubtless won for Rama useful Chinese support. The Mongols appear to have stopped short only in refusing to encourage Siam's exaggerated claim of dominion over the straits coasts of Malaya. In connection with his friendly negotiations with China, Rama also arranged for the immigration of Chinese artisans to Siam, especially some skilled in the manufacture of pottery.[24]

Rama Khamheng has been properly acclaimed as a ruler of wisdom and learning. He was a patron of justice, a promoter of peace, and a skilled diplomatist. He constructed at Sukhothai a formidable fortress with triple walls, four fortified gates, palaces, and lakes. He reduced the Siamese language to writing for the first time, using Mon letters and an adaptation of the Khmer script. From his Mon subjects and neighbors he also appropriated Hinayana Buddhism, which became the official religion of state.[25] At the same time, he continued to perform at a hilltop temple shrine the traditional rituals propitiating ancestral spirits and those of the earth and sky, on the proper observance of which the prosperity of the realm allegedly depended. From Khmer patterns came Siam's governmental system as well as its art forms and symbols. Rama adopted some aspects of the military organization of the Mongols and also their threefold division of society into the warrior freemen (the Thai), the civilian commoners, and the serfs. This system was roughly analogous to ahmudan and athi in Burma. The Siamese on the whole proved to be better borrowers than creators.

## Later Development of Siam

Siamese history after Rama Khamheng was plagued by periodic confusion, weak rulers, and problems of succession such as were encountered elsewhere in Southeast Asia. The son and grandson of the great Rama, for example, took their Buddhism so seriously that they neglected affairs of

[23] Coedès, 342–355; L. P. Briggs, *The Ancient Khmer Empire* (1951), 240–241; Hall, 146–149.

[24] Coedès, 342–346; Hoontrakul, 102–103; Hall, 149–150.

[25] Siamese Buddhism appears to have differed from Hinayana standards in Burma with respect to the presumed transference of merit from the monastic novitiate to those who contributed to his preparation for monkhood.

state. Under their weak rule, Mon Burma repudiated its vassal relationship, and other sections of the Siamese patrimony began to assume a like degree of independence. Part of the problem was that the Sukhothai capital was far removed from important areas to the south. What was needed was a strong leader operating from a centrally located capital surrounded by a considerable population cultivating an extensive agricultural base.

The necessary requirements for the new state of Siam were eventually provided around 1350 by King Ramadhipati. He was an ambitious prince of the Chiengmai line who got control of Mon Lavo, persuaded the monkish Sukhothai ruler, Lu T'ai, to accept vassalage status, and then established, in 1350, a new capital at Ayuthia south of historic Lopburi. The new city was located on a highly defensible island in the lower Menam River at the center of a prosperous agricultural region. It was within fairly easy reach of Angkor, close to the Gulf of Siam, and accessible to the isthmian passage into Malaya and to Burma's Tenasserim coast.

During the two decades of his reign, Ramadhipati accomplished much to establish on an unassailable basis the power and influence of Siam. He recovered control of the Tenasserim coast up to Martaban and extended his power throughout most of Malaya. Sukhothai was kept under vassal status. He also began to exert relentless pressure against Cambodia, which gradually weakened Khmer resources and forced the eventual abandonment of Angkor in 1432. The Khmer capital was saved in the 1360s, as on subsequent occasions, only because rebellions to the north, involving Sukhothai and Chiengmai, claimed Ramadhipati's attention and concern. Ramadhipati was also famous for his promulgation of the Siamese law code, combining traditional Thai customary principles with adaptations from the Indian Code of Manu.[26] When Siam's second great ruler died in 1369, the country was in the position of unchallenged leadership, although many problems remain unsolved.

For a period of almost seventy years, the most pressing problem of Ayuthia concerned the perennial efforts of Sukhothai to recover its independence, so cheaply surrendered in 1349. A northern campaign directed from Ayuthia was almost an annual occurrence. Sukhothai usually found support from neighboring Chiengmai, which managed to maintain the Haripunjaya tradition going back to Suryavarman I's time of successful resistance to all attacks against its highly defensible terrain coming via the lower Menam Valley. Sukhothai was finally incorporated into Siam in 1438, only to become thereafter the objective of aggressive attacks from its former

[26] Coedès, 363–370. One aspect of the Code of Manu, which found expression both in Wareru's Martaban law code of the 1290s and in Siam's of 1356, concerned the use of trials by ordeal with fire and water in cases where conflicting evidence was given in court. These practices survived into the nineteenth century, and in some cases into the twentieth, in Siam, Burma, Laos, and Cambodia. See G. E. Gerini, "Trial by Ordeal in Siam," *Asiatic Quarterly Review* (April and July, 1895), 1–27.

ally Chiengmai. Ayuthia's conflict with Chiengmai persisted, with a few breathing periods, throughout the fifteenth century, defying the best military leadership which Siam could command. The conflict finally merged in the 1540s with the circumstances attending the revival of Burman power by the state of Toungoo.[27]

The one great ruler of fifteenth-century Siam was King Trailok (1448–1488). He organized the central administration on a departmental basis, putting ranking officers in charge. These administered departments for interior affairs, the capital area itself, the royal household, finances, and agriculture. Officials were allotted lands according to their status and were required to live on the revenues of the estates so assigned. Trailok also promulgated, in 1450, a definitive Code of Palace Law which had been developed in the previous century. This described the obligations of tributaries to the Siamese Court and defined the rankings of court personnel and princely descendants.[28] The code borrowed from Cambodia the principle that princely status was subject to progressive reduction in rank, one grade per generation through five levels, until it degenerated to mere freedom status in the end. King Trailok also undertook with limited success to reduce the difficulties of succession by designating a second or vice-king, called the *Uparat,* as the heir apparent. This precedent persisted for Siam into the nineteenth century, affording some apparent political advantages. The great King's efforts to cope with Chiengmai, whether by military means or by stratagem, were nevertheless unavailing. Other accomplishments of Trailok concern the affairs of the Malacca Straits, which belong to the next chapter.

## *Areas Peripheral to Siam: Cambodia, Laos, Burma*

The preeminence of Angkor ceased with the founding of Ayuthia in 1350, but it continued as the Cambodian capital for more than eighty years thereafter. It was abandoned in favor of the more easily defensible sites of Phnom Penh and Lovek, below the Great Lake, after the devastation of the Angkor area by Siam's King Boromoraja II in 1431–1432. The Siamese destruction of that city itself and, more importantly, of the extensive facilities for irrigation and water conservation in its vicinity left the Khmers with neither the will nor the resources to revive and fortify the once-great center of their power. A worn-out and discouraged people had already found consolation in the milder Theravada form of Buddhism of the Thai, which advocated compassion rather than exploitation and made a virtue of poverty. Even as a minor state, Cambodia managed to resist repeated

[27] For details of this endless feud, see Hall, 150–158, and W. A. R. Wood, *A History of Siam* (1933).

[28] See T. Fitzsimmons, *Thailand* (1957), 29–30. Trailok's code specified that gold fetters must be used for princely culprits and that they should be beaten to death only with perfumed sandalwood clubs.

efforts of Ayuthia to install puppet rulers at Angkor. The struggle was reopened briefly in 1473–1476, when Siamese authority was temporarily expelled.

The greatest of the Cambodian rulers of the sixteenth century, King Ang Chan (1516–1566), attained control at Lovek after having been a refugee in Siam. During trouble which developed in the early 1530s, the Siamese attacked Lovek repeatedly by land and sea and were barely beaten off. Cambodia eventually found relief, in the 1540s, as a result of successive attacks on Ayuthia by Burma's Toungoo dynasty. King Ang Chan managed to reoccupy the Angkor site by 1550, and was able during the ensuing decade to start attacking Siam on his own, from 1559 to 1564.

At the time of the death of this last great statesman of Cambodia in 1566, the Siamese were actually soliciting aid from Lovek against the aggressive Burmans. The Burmans captured Ayuthia in 1569, an event which opened the way for the Khmers to shift the Cambodian Court back to Angkor in 1570 and to begin the restoration of the region's hydraulic-irrigation system. During the ensuing twenty years, the Cambodians maintained their position at Angkor and at times even carried their aggressive operations into Siam's Korat territory to the north. King Satha, who came to power in 1576, began the repair of Angkor Wat as a Buddhist shrine, and of the Bayon as well. The nine central towers of the Wat were regilded in 1577; the Bayon was restored a decade later. These events were elaborately celebrated, as recorded by visiting Portuguese missionaries. The fading of Cambodia's glory following the renewal of pressure from the Siamese in 1583 will be covered in a subsequent chapter in connection with the story of the intervention of Portuguese and Spanish military and missionary adventurers in the kingdom's affairs.[29]

In the upper Mekong Valley, a region long under Khmer control, an independent Laotian kingdom appeared in 1353 called Lan Ch'ang. Its founder was one Fa Ngum, who took advantage of the weakening of Sukhothai power after 1349 and Ayuthia's preoccupation with other problems. Lan Ch'ang included both the Luang Prabang and Vientiane areas. The Laotians appropriated the Pali scriptures from the Khmers and established a stanchly Buddhist state. Its language was the same as Siamese, and many customs, such as the scalp-lock haircut, were identical to those practiced in Siam. The Laotians were described as a gentle, courteous people, lackadaisical, and lovers of pagoda festivals. The country boasted of itself as a source of sandalwood, as the land of elephants and the white parasol. In fact the modern flag of Laos displays a white elephant, standing under a seven-tiered white parasol. The cult of the naga snake also survived in Laos with undiminished vitality.[30]

[29] Briggs, 258–260; Hall, 154; Bernard Phillipe Groslier, *Angkor et Cambodge au XVIᵉ Siècle* (1958), 7–23.

[30] Coedès, 371–375; Oden Meeker, *The Little World of Laos* (1939), 29–34, 47, 75.

During the first eighty years following the death of King Wareru in 1296, the history of the Burma Mons was oriented toward events in Sukhothai and Ayuthia. Relations were punctuated by a brief war with Sukhothai in 1296 following Wareru's assassination. Mon Martaban's first strong ruler, Binnya U (1353–1385) had to cope with formidable attacks beginning in 1356 against the entire Tenasserim coast and his capital, which were levied by King Ramadhipati, the founder of Ayuthia. Both Tenasserim and Martaban were lost to Siam by 1363, and the Mon capital was shifted back to Pegu in 1369, where it long remained. Binnya U's state was a tiny one, consisting of three delta provinces of Pegu, Myaungmya, and Bassein. It was destined during the 1380s to face challenge from the Shan rulers of the Upper Burma state of Ava, to which attention must now be directed.

By 1324, the time of the death of King Thihatthura, the youngest and last of the three Shan brothers who had seized control of Pagan Burma around 1300, the dynasty was becoming Burmanized. Successor rulers at Sagaing and Pinya all claimed descent from the Pagan dynasty; they also accepted the Burman type of Buddhism and patronized religion by erecting large pagodas at a new palace center at Sagaing. (They later became concerned with checking the excessive alienation of lands for religious purposes.) But general economic decline and political confusion prevailed. A destructive flood came in 1331; quarreling over succession to the throne was incessant; reigns were short and fitful (four from 1340 to 1360). Disaster struck Upper Burma in 1359, with the first of a long series of raids by savage Shan (Syam) tribesmen from Mohnyin to the north. A second followed in 1362 when the area around Sagaing was devastated, and local disturbances raged unchecked until 1368. A new capital at Ava was built in 1364, but King Swasawke, who was installed at the new Ava capital in 1368, controlled a very limited area of land.[31]

It was during the troubled 1360s that large numbers of Burman refugees began to flee southward into the upper Sittang Valley, where a new Burman state of Toungoo had been proclaimed in 1347. In that year King Thinhkaba had erected a palace at Toungoo and assumed the attributes of royalty, but under precariously tenuous circumstances. It nevertheless marked the beginning of what would eventually result in a revival of the Burman kingdom. The first Toungoo ruler was succeeded by his able son, Pyanchi, in 1358.

## The Feud between Ava and Pegu

The policy pursued by Mingyi (great prince) Swasawke of Ava (1368–1401) was a daring and imaginative one. His primary objective was to reestablish central Burma control over the rice-surplus areas of Lower Burma on the pattern of Pagan rule. He himself took pains to claim descent from the Pagan dynasty. His sources of manpower were nevertheless limited, and

[31] Than Tun, *A History of Burma*, A.D. *1300–1400* (1959), 6–12.

the restoration of destroyed paddy lands to production within the Ava domain, especially under circumstances of continuing Shan raids, was painfully slow. Some gains were registered at the outset of his reign, including a temporary revival of literature and learning after 1373, but two years later starvation was again widespread throughout his domain. The disorderly situation along the Yunnan borders grew steadily worse during the late 1370s by reason of the diversion of Chinese attention from disorderly border tribes to the task of Ming liquidation of the surviving remnants of Mongol resistance in that area.

The achievement of the final Ming victory in 1381 in Yunnan and China's favorable response two years later to Swasawke's plea for assistance against the Shans brought temporary relief from northern raids. This break afforded an opportunity for the Ava ruler's long-contemplated move to the south. Swasawke had begun his campaign in 1377 by arranging the assassination of the pro-Mon King Pyanchi of Toungoo. His military move was made in 1385 in an effort to contest the succession of Binnya U's son, Razadarit (1385–1423), to the throne of Pegu. Razadarit resisted repeated attacks of the Ava forces (largely Burman in character) and countered by stirring up trouble for his Ava enemy in Arakan and in the far north. Swasawke's time ran out before he could accomplish his political objectives.

The dismal story of strife between Ava and Pegu was repeated during the second decade of the following century. This time Ava created its own opportunity by treacherously eliminating the power of the Mohnyin Shans in 1406, killing the sawbwa prince and despoiling the countryside. By the time Ava was free to renew the war against the Mons, however, King Razadarit of Pegu was able to find other Shan chiefs willing to make a diversionary attack on vulnerable Ava. Pegu was saved in the nick of time in 1415, when only the capital and Martaban were holding out against the Ava forces. A final Burman Ava effort to conquer the Mons two years later ended disastrously with the death of the Ava ruler, King Minhkaung. For more than two decades thereafter, Upper Burma endured confusion and disorder. The Mon state was thus afforded a long-deferred opportunity to recover its prosperity.

The four decades from 1441 to 1481 witnessed a partially successful effort on the part of the Ming Chinese to restore order on the Yunnan-Burma frontier. The effort was made in connection with the attempted reopening of the ancient overland trade route between China and the Irrawaddy Valley, starting in 1438. This was some five years after Cheng-ho's final sea expedition to Malacca, which will be described later. In 1441 the Chinese conquered the troublesome Maw Shans in the old Nan Chao area, and they followed this achievement a few years later with a victory over the Mohnyin state, whence the Maws had fled. When Ava refused to cooperate, a Chinese force invested that city also in 1446, forcing its ruler to accept tributary status. Ava realized in the end some expansion of domain from the episode, and a measure of peace was established along the trade route. But China subsequently refused to administer the Mohnyin area in any effective way and was at the same time too jealous of its own predominant position to allow Ava to take it over. Beginning in 1482, therefore, disorders resumed in Upper Burma on a more extravagant scale than ever. The Mohnyin Shans forced Ava to resort to humiliating appeasement in 1507, defied a subsequent threat of renewed Chinese intervention in 1520, and ended by capturing the Burman city outright in 1527. An orgy of pillage, arson, and massacre ensued. The savage Shans remained in possession of Ava until 1555. The never-ending feud between the rival Shan rulers of Mohnyin and Ava, like the one between Ayuthia and Chiengmai, was finally overtaken by historic events of larger import.[32]

The economic recovery of Mon Pegu following the cessation of the Ava invasions in 1417 was rapid. Expanding agricultural production was balanced by a vigorous extension of Pegu's seaborne trade. The reopening of the straits under Malacca-Muslim control during the fifteenth century was a boon to all mercantile peoples. The principal Mon ports were Bassein, Syriam (near Dagon), and Martaban. Peguan traders were widely known and respected. The period after 1450 also witnessed a vigorous revival of Theravada Buddhist enthusiasm and learning. Important in this were successive missions to Ceylon and a massive renewal in 1476 of Peguan ordination standards comparable to Pegu's contribution to Sinhalese Buddhism in 1171. The Shwe Dagon pagoda was raised in 1453 to an elevation of more than 300 feet, and its monastic quarters were greatly expanded. Exploiting its traditional claim to cover several hairs of the Buddha, the pagoda became increasingly famous as a pilgrimage center. Gigantic Buddhist images appeared near both Dagon and Pegu. The most striking was the enormous reclining Buddha located several miles outside of Pegu. The most important personality in this period of Mon history was King Dammazedi (1472–1492), an ex-monk who was a wise lawgiver, a patron of religion and learning, and a sainted Buddhist ruler of the ideal kind. His contribution to Burmese Buddhism was decisively important. The pattern of his distinguished career found later imitators. The cultured and prosperous civilization of Pegu was not at all prepared for the devastating blow which came in 1539 from the lowly regarded Burman state of Toungoo.[33] The story of the rise of the new Burman dynasty and state of Toungoo will be told in a later chapter.

[32] Hall, 133–143; Than Tun, 14–16; N. Ray, *Theravada Buddhism in Burma* (1946), 182–188.

[33] Hall, 142–143.

# CHAPTER 8

# Muslim Malacca: History, Trade, Islamization Process

The reopening of the Straits of Malacca for commercial traffic during the early decades of the 1400s was accomplished by a combination of local circumstances and outside intervention. The determining factor was the coincidence of urgent desire of the government of Ming China and of the leading trading communities from India, which happened to be Muslim, to suppress the nuisance of piracy which had paralyzed trading operations via the straits throughout virtually the entire fourteenth century. Ming China found in the Malay ruler of the newly founded city-state of Malacca a loyal vassal, who himself turned to Islam in his old age in order to strengthen his standing with the Muslim traders. Malacca was not a particularly good harbor, nor was it situated in a productive agricultural region, but it was located at the narrowest part of the straits and was conveniently situated to receive ships from both directions. Because of the rapidly expanding volume of trade, Malacca developed during the fifteenth century into a fabulously wealthy entrepôt, where virtually every type of merchandise was available. Its commercial preeminence and the aggressively Muslim character of its leadership gave remarkable impetus to the expansion of Islam throughout Indonesia at a time when the stream of traditional Hindu culture had dried up.

## The Advent of Islam in Southeast Asia

The conquest of north India by the Turkish Muslims during the eleventh and twelfth centuries introduced an alien political and cultural element which Hinduism was powerless to absorb. The conquerors established a new elite ruling class in the occupied areas, but they gave a liberal interpretation of Koranic public law by not requiring the people generally or even Hindu vassal princes to accept Islam. In private law, however, the rift was sharp and unbridgeable. Monotheist Muslims abominated the idolatry of the Hindus and regarded it as something of a religious duty to desecrate public shrines. They flouted Hindu sensitivities by eating beef;

they refused to mingle socially or to intermarry except on Muslim terms; their own women were kept in seclusion. The aggressively egalitarian aspects of the new faith also appealed to many Indians, some of them ex-Buddhists as in Bengal, who wished to escape the handicaps of low caste. This group included many artisans and tradesmen in conquered areas like Bengal and Gujerat, areas having long-established connections with Southeast Asian trade. It also included important commercial groups in Hindu majority areas on both coasts of the subcontinent, especially among the Tamils of south India.

A Sufi-type mysticism, a syncretic faith overlaid with Koranic teachings, was transmitted to the Indies during the fourteenth and fifteenth centuries. It was organized into a number of stable and disciplined Islamic foundations. These bridged across national divisions of the faith and challenged traditional Śiva-Buddhist mystics on their own terms. Sufi trader-guildsmen from India in particular reflected the high morale characteristic of new converts. Each Sufi group possessed its own *shaikh,* who functioned as magician-healer and as converting agent. The new attitude contrasted sharply with that of Muslim Arab and Persian traders, who had visited the region for centuries without evincing any concern for converting the inhabitants. Behind Indian Muslims was also the long precedent of Hindu and Buddhist acculturation in the area, the sources of which were now desiccated. They also possessed the inestimable advantage that they came from regions of India leading in the production of cotton cloth, an item of commerce much in demand. The propagation of Islam required no Brahman priests, no scholars learned in Pali, and, in many instances, no professional clergy at all.[1] It stressed brotherhood within the faith; it was minimal in its creedal and social demands. The initial political impulse arose under the annoying circumstances of disorder and piracy in the crucial area of the Malacca Straits following the collapse of Śrivijaya, a situation crying loudly for the establishment of safe havens under commercial control.

The crucial role of the Gujerati traders derived from their middle-man position in the lucrative spice-and-pepper trade to the Mediterranean Sea via Egypt and the Red Sea. To products obtainable from Europe, they added their own contribution of high-quality cotton cloth for the Indies trade. Long before they became Muslims (Gujerat was conquered by Delhi in 1298, and the conversion of its traders is dated at 1325),[2] they were in

[1] D. G. E. Hall (ed.), *Historians of South-East Asia* (1961), 38–49; G. E. Marrison, "Persian Influences in Malay Life," *JRASMB,* XXVIII, part 1 (1955), 52–68; W. H. Moreland and A. C. Chatterjee, *A Short History of India* (1953), 143–147, 185–195; A. H. Johns, "Sufism as a Category in Indonesian Literature and History," *JSEAH,* II (1961), 10–23. Persian influence in Southeast Asia was also reflected in the universal use of such terms as *Shahbandar, laskar* (for army personnel), and words for trader and ship captain.

[2] G. E. Marrison, "The Coming of Islam to the East Indies," *JRASMB,* XXIV (1951), 28–37.

contact via the Sunda Straits with the ports of Senghasari Java, where spices could be obtained. The relevant statement of Tomé Pires, the Portuguese scribe, was as follows: "The Gujaratees used to come [via the Sunda Straits] to Java and to Grisee . . . to take in cargoes of cloves, nutmeg, mace, and white sandalwood . . . before Malacca collected their merchandise. . . . Then the Gujeratees ceased making this voyage, although navigation with the monsoon was good."[3] Even after the Malacca Straits were opened for direct access to the Java Sea, the Gujeratis and other Indian cloth merchants continued to maintain trading contact with island ports off the west coast of Sumatra, where the produce of the prosperous interior Minangkabau state could be tapped.[4]

It appears that the rulers of the first Muslim city-states in northern Sumatra—Perlak and Pasai—were Sumatrans enjoying connections with India's Malabar Coast and the southern Tamil areas, not with Gujerat or Bengal.[5] Pasai, prior to 1400, was certainly a north Sumatran way station in the Malabar and Tamil trade, with northern projections to Pegu and Siam. Muslim political support was lacking, however, to those traders coming from south India. In most south Indian ports, the control of credit sources both for handicraft production and for trade remained under aristocratic Hindu control.[6] Such was not the case in the Gujerati state.

## The Founding of Malacca

The founding of Malacca around 1401 was allegedly accomplished by a Palembang-born Sumatran nobleman named Parameswara, at the time a rebel refugee from Majapahit Java and also at enmity with Siam. He had previously been accorded temporary asylum in Tumasik (Singapore), alternately a vassal of Siam and Majapahit.[7] From this place he was expelled by the Siamese, but not until after he and his several score turbulent Bugis followers had killed the ruler, who was a father-in-law of the Siamese King. The adventurous band then selected the minor port of Malacca, located at the narrowest middle portion of the straits, as their new headquarters. Malacca had long been an obscure fishing village and pirate lair owing nominal vassalage to Siam. Its agricultural resources were meager, as was its population. Minangkabau immigrant cultivators and tradesmen constituted one of its more substantial elements. If the fledgling state was to stand any

[3] Tomé Pires, *Suma Oriental* (1944), I, 159.

[4] *Ibid.*, 162–165. Pires mentions west Sumatran ports of Priaman, Panchur, and Baros, along with Minangkabau ports, as sources of silk, benzoin, camphor, wax, and honey.

[5] Marrison ("The Coming of Islam," 28–37) probably overstates the claim that Indian rulers controlled the early Muslim states of north Sumatra.

[6] J. C. Van Leur, *Indonesian Trade and Society* (1955), 76–77.

[7] R. O. Winstedt, *Malaya and Its History* (1956), 32–35. Siam ousted Majapahit from Tumasik in 1365.

chance of survival in the face of overt hostility of two powerful neighbors, Siam and Majapahit, it would have to find some influential friends.[8]

Parameswara's first windfall came in 1403 with the visit of a Ming Chinese fleet charged with responsibility to reopen seaborne trade with India, Ceylon, and the Middle East. This was the first of seven such Chinese expeditions extending over a thirty-year period. Its objective was urgent because the Central Asian Emperor Tamerlane (Timur) had closed off the land caravan route to China and had invaded north India in 1398. The Chinese naval operations were under the general direction of Cheng-ho, a high eunuch official at the Ming Court. The first expedition was commanded by Admiral Yin Ching, who made it clear to China's long-time loyal vassal Siam that a new political arrangement capable of policing the straits was necessary. Parameswara and Malacca were selected as the most promising agency available to accomplish Chinese ends. Cheng-ho also developed Chinese commercial contacts with Majapahit Java.[9]

In response to Cheng-ho's invitation, Parameswara sent personal envoys to China in 1405. They returned the following year with a commission of appointment for Parameswara as King along with a seal of recognition and protection from his Chinese suzerain. In 1407 Cheng-ho's enlarged fleet, allegedly numbering sixty-six vessels and thirty-seven thousand men, cleaned out the thieving Chinese pirates at Palembang. Malacca was visited again by the Chinese in 1409, when the ruler was explicitly relieved of all vassal obligations to Siam. Cheng-ho's fleet thereafter proceeded to Ceylon and to the shores of the Arabian Sea. Parameswara and a large entourage accompanied the expedition back to China in 1411. This was the first of four personal visits of Malaccan rulers as vassals to the Chinese Court, the others being in 1414, 1419, and 1433. In view of the powerful protection afforded Malacca by China over a period of more than three decades, disgruntled Siam did not undertake to reestablish its assumed control. The trade of the reopened straits was in definite competition with the isthmian portage traffic, which had long been under exclusive Siamese control. By the time Chinese interest waned in the middle 1430s, the new Malaccan state was sufficiently wealthy and powerful to fend for itself. Muzaffar Shah of Malacca (1446–1456) explicitly repudiated vassal subservience to Siam and was able to repel subsequent Siamese attacks both overland via Pahang and by sea in 1445 and 1456.[10] Malacca sent tributary missions to China every three years, and its relations with China continued to be very close until 1511.

But China was not the only support which Malacca successfully solicited. The other came from the active Indian trading communities already firmly established at the north Sumatran ports of Pasai, Perlak, and Pedir. The Indians were quite as interested as the Chinese in recovering

[8] F. J. Moorhead, *A History of Malaya* (1957), 116–120.
[9] D. G. E. Hall, *A History of South-East Asia* (1955), 81–84.
[10] Moorhead, 118–124. He here summarizes the accepted account.

transit rights through the straits, and on its part Malacca needed at the time to import Sumatran rice in the absence of any other convenient supply.

Exactly when and how Parameswara made his opportunist bid for Muslim cooperation is not known. The visiting Chinese mission in 1409 described the Malacca ruler as already an adherent of Islam. The generally accepted date for his conversion is 1414, when he reportedly changed his name to Megat Iskander Shah. A plausible explanation is that the aged ruler (allegedly seventy-two by 1414) cemented a commercial alliance by 1409 with the Indian trading community in Sumatra on terms which included sweeping concessions to Islam if not his formal acceptance of it. He may have been succeeded at his death in 1414 by his son under the Moorish name of Iskander Shah (1414–1424). The alliance may have been sealed by the marriage of the younger Iskander to a princess of Muslim Pasai. The point is in dispute.[11] The account of Tomé Pires indicates that Pasai continued to be the major straits port for Muslim traders until an agreement of friendship with Malacca was worked out under which Parameswara agreed to turn Muslim. Thereupon the rich Tamil, Gujerati, Bengali, Persian, and Arab Muslims shifted their trading headquarters from north Sumatra to the more accessible port of Malacca. They brought their mullah teachers of Islam with them, and Pasai thereupon declined to minor importance.[12]

The fact that the initial acceptance of Islam was for the most part a political and commercial expedient was underscored by the reversion of Iskander's successor, Sri Maharaja, to the Hindu faith. He revived the Hindu symbols of kingship and claimed to be a successor of Śrivijayan rulers of Palembang. This move did not, however, disturb Muslim privileges and trading operations, for the ruler still had a Muslim queen. The political and commercial influence of the Muslim traders was apparently too strong to be long ignored, for Gujerat had been functioning as an independent Muslim state since 1401. Following Sri Maharaja's death in 1446, Malacca returned permanently to its Islamic affiliation under Muzaffar Shah.[13]

Javanese hostility to Malacca's rising importance was dissipated in the course of time by the fact that the island's commercial interests were allied with those of the Indian spice traders, who used the straits. Javanese spice merchants themselves eventually established a headquarters in Malacca in order to participate in the advantages of the entrepôt aspects of the trade. Differences developing between the port cities of Java and interior Majapahit over trade and political policies sharpened in time. Traditionally Hinduphile Majapahit was apparently unable to forget its Nusantara ambitions, while the interests of the coastal merchant communities were allied to those of the Indian Muslim traders. It was under these circumstances that

[11] Hall, *A History of South-East Asia,* 176–180. The accepted version of the story has the aged Parameswara marrying the princess.

[12] Pires, II, 238–243.

[13] Moorhead, 123–124.

the political and cultural influence of Majapahit began to decline and the Islamization of Java began.

## Government and Politics in Malacca

Kingship in Muslim Malacca departed in only minor particulars from the standard model for Southeast Asia based on Indian standards. Much of the traditional Hindu ritual survived, such as the white umbrella, the reservation of the color of gold as exclusively for royalty, the sacredness of the elephant mounts, the Sanskrit word *Bendahara* for chief minister. The sultans were not reincarnations of Hindu gods, but they ruled under the religious sanction of the Koran and enjoyed the same power as before to elevate or to degrade. They could command the services of their subjects on royal works and could enslave war captives and oblige vassals to pay tribute in tin (for Malays) and in gold (for Sumatrans).[14] The principal income of the Malaccan sultan was derived from a basic 6 per cent duty on foreign trade, augmented by an additional 1 per cent in "presents." He was also active personally in both shipbuilding and trade. The tax on domestic trade was 3 per cent, plus an additional levy on food sales in the local markets. Hawkers also paid license fees. The sultan collected dues on sales of land and ships and claimed half of the property of deceased persons, and all of the estate if no will was provided.[15]

Aside from the Bendahara, who was chief minister-treasurer, the sultan's chief ministers were the *Temenggong* as head of the police and courts, the *Laksamana,* or commander of the fleet, and four harbor masters, the Shahbandars, who were selected from the foreign trading communities. One Shahbandar took care of the trade with the Chinese, Liuchiuan, Cham, eastern Borneo, and Siamese ships. A second handled ships coming from Palembang, Java, and other Indonesian islands. A third took care of traders from the Bay of Bengal area, including north Sumatran ports, plus the Malabar Coast of India. A final one was allocated to the Gujeratis alone, who developed much the largest commercial community doing business at the city. The Shahbandars presented arriving merchants to the Bendahara, allotted necessary harborage and warehouse facilities, and supervised both the receipt of presents for the officials and the handling of regular merchandise. The acceptance of presents and bribes was commonplace with judges and police as with other officials of Malacca. The Shahbandars and high officials lived on princely estates located outside the city under circumstances of extreme luxury.[16]

From the accession of Muzaffar Shah (1445–1459) until near the end of the century, real power at Malacca centered in the hands of the Bendahara. For approximately a decade, the office was in the hands of a Tamil

[14] *Ibid.,* 125–127, 145.
[15] *Ibid.,* 140–146; Pires, II, 274–278.
[16] Pires, II, 264–265.

expatriot from Pasai named Tun Ali. He engineered the coup which brought the elevation of Muzaffar, who happened to be Ali's nephew. Tun Ali was unpopular with the rival Malay party, which found a leader in Tun Perak, the victor over the Thai forces in the important naval engagement of 1456.[17] A compromise arrangement was worked out in the form of a marriage liaison with Tun Ali's family, and Tun Perak took over the post of Bendahara. Until his death in 1498, he was the real ruler of Malacca. He maintained his control, as did the shoguns in Japan, by providing from his family the mothers and consorts of future sultans.[18] But because of close marriage connections between leaders of the two factions (each married a sister of the other), Tun Ali was never far removed from influence and power.

Following his defeat of the Siamese, Tun Perak revived Malacca's allegiance to China and solicited its continuing protection. Another of his successful naval ventures in 1459 made a vassal state of gold-rich Pahang, which thereafter contributed a substantial 4 catties of gold per year to the Malacca treasury. Near the end of the century Tun Perak provoked a renewal of war with Siam by aggressions in northern Malaya. He also conquered important trading communities on the Sumatran side of the straits, notably Siak, Kampar, Compocam, and Indragiri, the last being the chief port of the Minangkabau in south Sumatra. He lost Pasai and Perlak to rival Acheh (at the northern tip of Sumatra) and failed repeatedly to conquer the marshy and almost unpenetrable Sumatran domain of the Uru and Bata pirates, neighboring to Perlak, who continued to live by plunder and blackmail.

Malacca declined in influence following Tun Perak's death in 1498. His brother ruled as Bendahara for two years after his death, to be succeeded by Tun Ali's son by Tun Perak's sister, one Tun Mutahir (1500–1511). During the final two decades under Moorish rule, the city managed to survive repeated attacks from Siam and its Ligor vassal. These were made more intense after 1500 by Tun Mutahir's occupation of tin-producing Kedah and his interference with the portage trade at Patani.[19]

The successive sultans were apparently an inferior lot, even when allowances are made for the prejudices of Portuguese reporters. Muzaffar Shah (1445–1459) was virtually a cipher dominated by Tun Ali. Mansur Shah (1459–1477) was a builder of mosques and a diplomatist; but he had a mania for gambling, and his diplomacy found expression in marriages to an assortment of queens, Parsee, Kling (west Deccan), Pahang, and Siamese. Sultan Ala'u'ddin (1477–1488) became an opium addict, the drug being imported at the time in large quantities from the Red Sea area. Banda and

---

[17] Hall, *A History of South-East Asia,* 181–183.
[18] *Ibid.,* 183–185.
[19] Moorhead, 129–137.

Lingga Islands were captured in his time, but he left a host of problems unsolved. The last Sultan, Mahmud (1488–1511), earned the unsavory reputation of being opium-intoxicated, gluttonous, arrogant, presumptuous, and fickle. He was guilty of the crowning folly of provoking conflict with the Portuguese in 1509–1511, in the face of contrary advice from the Bendahara and other relatives, who thereby became victims of the Sultan's wrath. This was done at a time of hostile relations with Siam and when Malacca had no reasonable expectation of receipt of any protective assistance from China.[20] While it lasted, the Malacca sultanate enjoyed a luxuriously parasitic existence, in which all port officials shared handsomely.

## Malacca's Population and Trading Attractions

Malacca was unique in the fact that its population was preponderantly alien to the immediate area of its location. The most substantial element of the Malaccan army and navy was Javanese, bolstered by Bugis mercenaries and by ex-pirates recruited from the straits region. Wealthy Javanese traders at Malacca, princes of the spice trade, directed the work of thousands of slaves and other Javanese laborers, including skilled shipwrights, whom the Portuguese themselves later used. The Javanese were thrifty, well mannered, and respectful of authority. The Minangkabau settlers were also good citizens as small traders, craftsmen, and fruit growers. But the remainder of the Malay population was a lawless lot. The restive element was led by the spirited, quick-tempered Bugis, the turbulent Cellates (straits sea gypsies), and the equally violent Achehnese. Malacca was a dangerous place at night; most foreign visitors slept on their ships.[21]

The indigenous Malay population was small, apathetic, and backward. Agricultural development was neglected; the sultan held title to all the land and yet contributed virtually nothing to its improvement. Malacca faced a chronic food deficit as a consequence. Living costs were inordinately high, and this situation was made worse by special taxes on food. At a level substantially above the Malay subsistence farmers and fishermen and the immigrant laborers and soldiers lived the foreign artisan-craftsmen and the trading community. These included cloth merchants, spice handlers, moneylender Chettyars from Madras, and wealthy shipowners. At the top of the ladder were the Shahbandars and the governmental hierarchy. There existed no Malay middle class, and few persons in positions of authority had any rootage in the area. Even the sultans were part Indonesian and Tamil.

At the outset Islam apparently affected only the government and the trading community, which constituted the important element in the city. The shift to Arabic numerals, alphabet, and script from earlier but little-

[20] Pires, II, 243–256.
[21] Hall, *A History of South-East Asia,* 192–194.

**MUSLIM MALACCA
(to 1511)**

used Sanskrit adaptations was probably less an arbitrary decision of the ruling sultans than a recognition of the predominant position of the Muslim trading community.[22] As of 1510 this group numbered about four thousand merchants all told, some of them being wealthy permanent residents of the city. An estimated one-fourth of the Indian group were Gujeratis, a diligent, quick-witted group, expert in trade. Some four to five thousand Gujerati transient seamen could also be present at one time. The remainder of the foreigners included Parsees, Bengalis, Kalingas (Klings), Persians, and Arabs. The Chinese traders were also important but less numerous at the end than either the Javanese or Indians. This was partly because Chinese commercial operations were widely dispersed via Siam, Acheh, and Java.[23]

Pires estimated that more than threescore countries were represented at Malacca and that some fourscore dialects were spoken. Arising from the necessity of communication between such diverse groups came the imperative adoption of a simplified Malay lingua franca. It included many terms borrowed from Javanese, Buginese, Indian, and Arab sources. It gradually spread to all parts of Southeast Asia, and came to be used later by both the

[22] N. Ginsburg and C. Roberts, *Malaya* (1958), 24–26; A. B. Ramsay, "Indonesians in Malaya," *JRASMB*, XXIX, part I (1956), 119ff.

[23] Pires, I, 45, 103–110, and II, 250–256.

Portuguese and the Dutch, who added their own contributions.[24] The existence of the Malay lingua franca contributed much to Malacca's effectiveness
as a disseminator of Islamic indoctrination.

The attractions of Malacca to foreign traders were many. It provided a safe, quiet anchorage at the place where the monsoons met. The
main channel near the Malay shore was well policed and also serviced by
strongly manned rowboats capable of towing becalmed vessels into port.
The toll and customs charges were low. Traders dealt with Shahbandars of
their own or kindred nationalities. Government revenues were completely
dependent on trade, and concessions were frequently made to soften the
requirement that all ships using the straits must call at Malacca. Chinese
pepper ships apparently did not stop at Malacca but traded directly with
Pedir. Malacca was a center of shipbuilding and repair and a market for
ships constructed elsewhere, coming from south Borneo, Pegu, and Tenasserim.[25] Even more than Śrivijaya had been, Malacca became the crossroads
of the commerce of Asia. At one single entrepôt, virtually all types of marketable seaborne products of the vast Asian continent and the East Indies
islands were available for exchange.

## The Javanese-Gujerati Trade

A principal component of Malacca's expanding volume of trade during the course of the fifteenth century was the exchange of Indian (mainly
Gujerati) cotton cloth for East Indies spices destined for the European
market. But the pattern was more varied than has sometimes been assumed.
Merchants from Middle Eastern ports of the Red Sea and the Persian Gulf,
including Persians, Turks, Sabean Arabs, Armenians, and Parsees, used the
ports of Gujerat on the Bay of Cambay (mainly Surat) as their assembly
points. They brought a great variety of middle Eastern goods, some items
for the Indian market and other items destined for Malacca. These included
Venetian goods, such as arms, colored woolen cloth, vermilion dyes, coral,
copper, quicksilver, silver, nails, hats, and glassware. Goods from Arab and
Persian sources included enormous quantities of opium from Aden and
Mecca, along with horses, incense, rosewater, indigo, tapestries, pearls, saltpeter and sulfur, amber, musk, dried fruits, and an astringent vegetable
extract called catechu. Near Eastern merchants interested in the East Asian
trade usually shifted their goods at Cambay ports to Gujerati ships which
were destined for Malacca. Single Gujerati ship consignments were sent to
selected ports in the Bay of Bengal. The latter included Pasai, Pedir, and
Acheh in north Sumatra, Kedah, Junk Ceylon, Trang, and Tenasserim in
Siam, Dagon in Pegu Burma, and Bengal itself. Four especially heavily

[24] Pires, II, 268–270; E. S. de Klerck, *History of the Netherlands East Indies*
(1938), I, 114–115.
[25] Pires, II, 243–250.

laden Gujerati ships, with cargoes valued at 15,000 to 30,000 cruzados each, sailed directly to Malacca with scarcely a stop en route. One additional larger Cambay ship per year arrived at Malacca with a cargo estimated at 70,000 to 80,000 cruzados. The ships carried opium and other Near Eastern items, Indian products such as cotton, soap, leather goods, grain, honey, wax, butter, and meat, but principally large quantities of high-quality cotton cloth. It must be assumed that valuable Gujerati cargoes were heavily convoyed. They seldom penetrated beyond Malacca, leaving the other leg of the spice trade to the Javanese.

At Malacca, the Gujerati imports were consigned to the several hundred merchants of the same nationality, headed by their own Shahbandar. They paid 6 per cent customs duties, plus one piece of cloth for every hundred imported as presents to the officials. Malacca was essential to the Gujeratis mainly as a source of spices and as an outlet for Cambay cloth. Pires was convinced that neither trade could well exist without the other.[26] The Gujerati ships returned directly to Surat with a largely spice cargo, some of which they themselves took to Ormuz and Aden. The remainder they consigned to Middle Eastern traders represented by agents at Surat for eventual transshipment in their own vessels. Pires stated explicitly that the Gujeratis were better navigators and had more ships at their disposal than any other traders active in the Southeast Asian region.[27]

The complementary spice trade on the East Indies side of Malacca was carried largely by the Javanese. They disposed of Cambay cloth in Java and transported rice and cash to the Spice Islands, where they procured cargoes of cloves, mace, and nutmeg at buyers' prices. They then returned to Malacca for more cloth. Some of the spices were sold at Javan ports to Chinese traders and also at the south Sumatran ports of Palembang and Jambi, which operated in some respects independently of Malacca. Palembang sent rice cargoes to Malacca to the extent of ten to twelve ships per year. The Javanese kept the trade with the Spice Islands to themselves, but otherwise made no attempt to interfere with mercantile operations of the Bugis of Macassar or of port merchants from south Borneo. Both of the latter groups were active slave traders and distributors of cheap Bengali cotton cloth, also obtained at Malacca. South Borneo built ships for sale in Java. The Bugis "gypsies," who lived as families at sea, were adept with their kris daggers and poisoned darts and were therefore greatly feared. They combined legitimate trade, extending over a wide area, with piracy, frequently attacking smaller ships and living in part off the sale of plunder and slaves.[28] The Javanese Shahbandar at Malacca handled the business of all traders of the Java Sea, and Javanese merchant shippers had a tremendous stake in the successful operation of the entrepôt.

[26] *Ibid.*, I, 19–21, 41–47, and II, 268–270.
[27] *Ibid.*, I, 46–47.
[28] *Ibid.*, I, 103, 110, 205–212, 223–227.

## *The China Trade to Malacca*

The trade from China to Malacca was inferior in quantity and value to that of the Javanese and Gujeratis but was far more varied and interesting. The ships had apparently improved but little since Polo's day, most of them being junks. They carried from two to three hundred passengers, each with a store of goods in his custody to be disposed of at the destination. The vessels were rendered seaworthy by watertight compartments designed to contain leaks. They were propelled by sails and oar sweeps,[29] but were clearly inferior navigationwise to those of Gujerat. The Chinese enjoyed a distinct advantage at Malacca over the Indians, probably dating from their protective role in the early 1400s, in that they were required to pay no port dues beyond the customary presents (5 per cent) to the officials in charge. This same exemption from port dues applied to the Javanese, Sumatrans, and other islander traders. Chinese trade was mainly in porcelains and silks of many varieties and high value, including satins, brocades, sashes, damasks, and taffetas. But the Chinese also brought copperware and ironware (vases, kettles, bowls), alum, sulfur and saltpeter, seed pearls, musk, and camphor. The Chinese trade was more individualistic, more varied, less regimented than that of the Indians.

Associated with the Chinese traders and sharing the same Shahbandar were the Liuchiu islanders; one to three of their ships reached Malacca each year. They brought some Chinese wares but also food items such as onions, vegetables, meat, and fish, plus swords and armor, copper and gold objects, paper, and a celebrated kind of green porcelain ware. Unlike the more prosperous Chinese, who bought in return high-quality Cambay cloth, pepper, and spices, the Liuchiu traders purchased cheaper Bengali cotton cloth and also cheap Malacca wine. The Liuchiuans earned a remarkable reputation for integrity at Malacca and at Ayuthia as well. They were described as responsible, dignified, and well dressed.[30] Only the Peguan visitors at Malacca enjoyed as enviable a reputation.

One reason why the Chinese trade at Malacca was less extensive than the Indian was that Chinese merchants also took charge of most of the commerce of Siam. This included the trade of the portage routes, which were still in operation despite Malacca's drawing power. In Siam as at Malacca, the Chinese enjoyed a favored position, paying only a one-sixth duty while others paid 20 and 22 per cent. The Chinese were obviously in a fairly strong bargaining position. Malacca's waiver of duties for the Chinese was apparently an effort, albeit an unsuccessful one, to monopolize the China trade. Aside from the trade with Siam proper, amounting to an

[29] H. Yule (ed.), *Marco Polo* (1929), II, 249–252.

[30] Pires, I, 106–110, 125–131, and II, 294; George H. Kerr, *Okinawa* (1958), 190–191. Pires also mentions a 5 per cent dues levy, without indicating the time of its imposition.

estimated six to seven junks per year, Chinese vessels visiting Ligor, the Bay of Bandon, and Patani picked up the Gujerati wares and Sumatran pepper brought annually to such Bay of Bengal ports as Kedah, Trang, Junk Ceylon, and Tenasserim. As previously indicated, Malacca intruded on the Kedah-to-Patani trade late in the 1400s. The portage operation in itself required only three to four days. Siam's own trade with Malacca in rice, salt, fish, vegetables, and arrack liquor, which was active prior to their break in trade relations in the 1490s, had amounted to some thirty junks per year. Siam's imports from Malacca had been in pepper and spices, opium and quicksilver, Cambay cloth, brocades, and carpets. Its exports westward via the portage routes were mainly in metals (lead, tin, silver, gold) and forest products and rice. Siam also traded directly with Borneo and Palembang.[31]

Traders from the eastern coast of Borneo also visited Malacca and participated in a limited amount of trade with Ma-i (Luzon) in the Philippines. The items exchanged were gold and camphor, wax and honey, and rice and sago in return for Indian cloth, Chinese brassware, and glass and beads from the Mediterranean. A few Ma-i junks reached Malacca via east Borneo. As traders the Filipinos had a poor reputation in Malacca, but they made good workers. Borneo and Filipino Malays were indistinguishable in appearance. Trade on the Annam coast was, by contrast, practically dead. Champa's harbors were silted up, and its merchant marine was gone. Vietnam also had no sea power and carried on little or no trade with Malacca. It did produce raw and manufactured silk and porcelain for the China market. Vietnamese traders came to Malacca, if at all, in Chinese junks. All of these eastern seaboard ships reported at Singapore to the Chinese Shahbandar.[32]

## Malacca's Trade with the Bay of Bengal

The pepper-growing region of northern Sumatra managed to market its products for the most part without using the Malacca entrepôt. Pepper for the China trade from Pasai and Pedir, the ports of Acheh, was marketed via the portage passages and also by direct contact on the part of Chinese ships. A European visitor to Pedir in 1505 told of eighteen to twenty pepper ships per year coming from China. On one street alone in the Pedir market place were hundreds of money-changers, handling coins of tin, silver, and gold. Chinese influence was probably also reflected in Pedir's celebrated fireworks display. It was also a thriving shipbuilding center.[33]

The two most active trading areas in eastern India during the time of Muslim Malacca were the Bengal and Kalinga coasts, the latter being

---

[31] Pires, I, 103–110.

[32] *Ibid.,* I, 110–115, 132–134.

[33] Hall, *A History of South-East Asia,* 192–194. The visitor, di Varthema, published his account at Rome in 1510.

located along the upper section of the western coast, with Pulicat and Nagore as its principal ports. Both were prodigious producers of cotton cloth, most of it inferior to that from the Bay of Cambay. At the main port of Bengal, located some two days' sail up the Ganges River, foreign trader colonies including Parsees, Turks, Arabs, and Malabar Indians were in residence. Despite the fact that port dues at Bengal were an exorbitant 37½ per cent, merchants dealing in cheap Bengali cotton cloth could make the annual trip to Malacca and back, or to north Sumatra and back, and realize a profit of 2½ to 3 times their investment. Bengali ships visiting Malacca numbered up to twenty per year. Many Bengalis were resident in Malacca not only as merchants but also as fishermen, tailors, and laborers. Some were wealthy; all, according to Pires, were reputed to be sharp-witted and treacherous. They also dealt in a variety of textiles, bed canopies, embroidered cloth, and tapestry wall hangings, along with scented earthenware, fruits and vegetables, and steel. They returned to Bengal with the usual variety of China goods, plus spices, pepper and camphor, sandalwood, metals, Javanese krises and swords, and gold. Gold was more highly valued in Bengal than in Malacca.

The Kalinga trade from Pulicat and Nagore represented an assembly of goods from some eleven Coromandel ports and consisted primarily of rich cargoes of cloth, up to three to four shiploads per year. Some Malacca-based junks also visited Pulicat. Its harbor dues were low (6 per cent plus 1 per cent in presents as at Malacca). Pulicat traders lacked the resident sales force which others enjoyed at Malacca; they usually sold their goods in wholesale lots to various local bidders. Being Hindu rather than Muslim, the Kalinga traders suffered less loss than other cloth-producing competitors after the collapse of Muslim Malacca. They became, at least for a time after 1511, the leading Indian traders at the entrepôt under the Portuguese.[34]

The only other substantial participants in the Bay of Bengal trade were the Malabar Coast ports of India and those of Mon Pegu. A small fraction of the Malabar Coast trade skirted the southern shores of Ceylon and made its way to Bengal, Pegu, and the ports of Siam. It competed little in the Malacca market. Ceylon's exports of cinnamon, ivory, and precious stones entered into international commerce fairly actively, but the highly respected island state maintained very little shipping of its own. The Peguans, on the other hand, traded in their own vessels and were very popular at Malacca. They were orderly, good-tempered, and responsible. As food importers and as producers of ships for sale at Malacca, they paid only token duties. Some sixteen to twenty cargo ships per year left Peguan ports of Dagon, Bassein, and Martaban in February or March, bound for Malacca, Pedir, and Pasai. They carried rice, vegetables, and lac, and also musk, rubies, and benzoin from Ava whenever political relations permitted

[34] Pires, I, 18–20, and II, 271–274.

Mon trade with Upper Burma. They returned with the next monsoon carrying Sumatran pepper, silks and porcelains from China, and tin, copper, spices, and gold. Pegu obtained its cloth directly from Gujerati ships visiting its own ports. The Peguans could easily be identified by their characteristic haircut, shared by the Siamese, the Cambodians, and Laotians; their hair was shorn around the edges and left tufted and long on top.[35]

The central coast of eastern Sumatra between Pasai on the north and Jambi on the south was, with some exceptions, under the control of Malacca. The pirates of the marshy, impenetrable Aru and Bata Islands near Pasai, as indicated earlier, defied Tun Perak's efforts to conquer them. They lived by plunder, blackmail, and slave trade, taking advantage of every opportunity which presented itself. The communities of Rohan, Rupot, and Purim were somewhat less disreputable, combining some legitimate fishing with plunder. The other areas were under Malaccan control; Siak was a source of non-grain foodstuffs; Campocam produced gold, aromatic lignaloes wood, pitch, and rattan; Indragiri, the port of the Minangkabau where treatment of visitors was the best of all, was a source of gold.

Such was the picture of the trading empire of which Malacca was the center. This first close look at the peoples and commerce of Southeast Asia is available thanks to the detailed reporting of Tomé Pires, who was the authorized confidential reporter to the King of Portugal. He arrived shortly after the fall of Malacca. He did not describe, beyond giving a rough chronology, the process of Islamization, which had been proceeding apace during the century of Malacca's leadership.

## The Chronology of Islamization

The first and for a long time the only entrenched position which Islam claimed in Southeast Asia was at the northern point of Sumatra. Perlak, as described by Marco Polo in 1292, was the first Muslim port, but it was soon overshadowed by its more powerful neighbor states Pasai, Pedir, and Acheh. It was presumably more than a century later that Malacca's rulers accepted Islam (1408 to 1414), apparently in collaboration with north Sumatran Muslim port merchants. Pasai at first lost heavily to the Malacca trade. Later in the century the city successfully resisted Tun Perak's efforts at conquest, allying itself with Acheh. The Malaccan conquest of the middle portion of the west Sumatran coast from 1450 to 1480 brought that area into the Muslim fold, with the possible exception of the Minangkabau port of Indragiri. The Minangkabau highlanders and several Sumatran states of the western coast resisted Islam for a century longer. Jambi and Palembang fell in line during the late 1400s.[36] As an important pepper port, Pedir developed into a minor commercial rival of Malacca by the early 1500s. Acheh remained inveterately hostile to the Malacca sultanate, displaying a

[35] *Ibid.,* I, 84–87, 95–103, 110.
[36] *Ibid.,* I, 135–145.

fanatic zeal which no religious affinity could curb, and which survived into Portuguese times.[37]

The spread of Islam into Malaya proper, beyond the immediate perimeter of Malacca itself, apparently began with the defeat of the Siamese in Pahang province in 1445.[38] Pahang became part of the Malaccan Empire in 1456. Kedah's conversion to Islam dated from 1460 and that of Trengganu and Patani from around 1474. In most of the Malay states Islam became a local rallying standard against the continued imposition of rule by Buddhist Siam, so that political and religious considerations were closely intertwined.[39]

The island of Java represented a special case. Gujerati and Persian merchant colonists were resident at the coastal ports of eastern Java and at Bantam on the Sunda Straits for a century or more before the Malacca Straits were opened. However much they may have prepared the situation for Islam, the actual acceptance of the new faith by merchant leaders of east Javan ports appears to have awaited a full generation or more of direct Javan contact at the Malaccan entrepôt. The coastal ports of Java were pretty thoroughly Islamized in a political way between 1456 and 1490. The visit of an ardent Muslim Champa prince refugee, the nephew of a queen consort of the Majapahit ruler, made following Champa's collapse in 1471, may have contributed to the trend.[40] But interior areas of central and eastern Java remained stubbornly loyal to the Hindu-Javan heritage for a long time thereafter.[41]

The Majapahit kingdom disintegrated around 1520 with the rising resistance of coastal vassal states. This was followed by the eventual re-emergence of central Javan Mataram. Disorder prevailed in the interior of the island for more than a half century thereafter, until Mataram allied with the Muslim-oriented ports and gradually got the upper hand. Order was finally restored near the end of the sixteenth century.[42] In the western Javan Sunda area, Bantam accepted Islam around 1525, but infiltration of the faith into the hinterland was slow.

Other areas of the Indies outside of Java were affected by Islam with a timing and thoroughness in almost direct proportion to the closeness of their commercial connections with Malacca. Islam reached the Moluccas around 1480, western Borneo and Brunei around 1500, and the ports of southern and eastern Borneo sometime after 1515.[43] The faith also accomplished an entry in the southernmost of the Philippine Islands, Min-

[37] Hall, *A History of South-East Asia,* 285–286.

[38] Pires, II, 243–256.

[39] Van Leur, 110–116.

[40] Klerck, 147–152.

[41] Pires, I, 198–205.

[42] J. J. Van Klavern, *Dutch Colonial System* (1953), 25–26; Harry Benda, *The Crescent and the Rising Sun* (1958), 9–10.

[43] Pires, I, 205, 223–229.

danao, during the middle 1500s, but Luzon's tenuous trade connections with Malacca via Brunei were apparently not close enough to make much of a religious impression.

Champa was something of a special case. Muslim merchants had been resident at Champa since the eleventh century, and the Islamic germ seems to have survived in a limited way among their offspring into the fifteenth. Islam in Champa may even have come from China. No Gujerati or other Muslim Indians are known to have visited the place, and its commercial contacts with Malacca were virtually nil.[44] Islam apparently gained political ascendency in the very final stages of Champa's struggle with the Vietnamese in 1470–1471. The reasons were probably political, considering the facts that contacts with Hindu India had long since been cut, that Ming China, Champa's suzerain, declined to give an affirmative answer to repeated Cham pleas for aid, and that traditional relations with Buddhist Cambodia and Siam were emphatically negative. The leadership of the doomed state shifted to Muslim affiliations locally and grasped at the last possible source of aid, which happened to be Muslim Malacca or Java. It is noteworthy that ranking Cham refugees fled to Malacca, Sumatra, and coastal Java after 1471. Other Cham refugees who moved into Cambodia were also Muslim, whereas the two-thirds of the Chams who remained at their ancestral homes retained their traditional Hindu forms of worship.[45]

The Cham episode affords clear evidence of the political prestige enjoyed by Malacca and Islam generally, which was everywhere a potent factor in the spread of the new faith. Although many of the religious gains for Islam were realized after Malacca's fall, there was ample reason for the city's widespread acclaim, from Aden and Ormuz, from Cambay and Bengal, as a champion of the faith.

## Islamization: Commercial and Political Factors

Some explanation is obviously in order for the political and cultural reorientation of the Indonesian half of Southeast Asia which occurred during the century of Muslim Malacca and continued for several decades after its collapse. The commercial leadership and the religious enthusiasm of the Indian Muslim traders obviously contributed, as did the strongly partisan Islamic leadership exercised by Malacca itself after 1445. But political considerations appear to have been equally important in the spread of Islam. At the very outset, in early 1400, Malacca itself turned to Islam for political support in the straits in order to withstand Hindu-Javanese Majapahit and Buddhist Siam. The conversion of the states of the Malay Peninsula, as previously indicated, was due primarily to a generally shared desire to throw off alien Siamese control.

The case of the Peguan Mons is especially instructive. They traded

[44] *Ibid.,* I, 110–114.

[45] G. Maspero, *Kingdom of Champa* (1949), 14–18; Klerck, 149–152.

regularly with Gujerati ships at their home ports, especially Dagon, and were also active and popular traders at Malacca, and yet came through the experience without a trace of Islamization. The same is true of Siamese ports on the Bay of Bengal side of the portage region, although the outcome is somewhat less remarkable. The vitality of Buddhism no doubt constituted a protective shield, but there was also absent in both instances any political reasons for accepting the new faith. On the other hand, Champa's political leadership plumped for Islam for purely political reasons without having any trade with Malacca worth mentioning and without direct contact with Indian Muslim traders.

The trading operations of Minangkabau Sumatrans with neighboring Islamic ports, including Malacca, and also with Muslim Gujerati shipping were reciprocally cordial and profitable. Yet in the absence of compelling political considerations the Minangkabau state remained for several centuries anti-Islamic and loyal to its traditional and partly Hindu heritage. The same could be said of Bantam and the Sunda province of western Java. In the end, these states found it convenient and profitable to go along with the Muslim tide, but not until after Muslim Malacca had long disappeared. A new politico-religious factor after 1511 was the role of Islam as a weapon against the Christian Portuguese.

In the conversion of Java to Islam, commercial and political factors were closely allied. Friction between the port cities of the north coast of central and eastern Java and the agricultural interior long antedated the appearance of Islam at Malacca. The enormous stake which the Javanese merchants developed in the spice trade from the time of Kediri and Senghasari down to the development of the Malacca entrepôt provided not only an important issue of difference but also the resources for contesting the power of the traditionalist rulers of Majapahit. When the central Javan state fell apart after 1520, the Islamized port-city leadership provided the balance of power in favor of Mataram and also a new religious and cultural orientation. Wealthy port merchants built mosques and brought in the mullah teachers, although the latter usually did not see eye to eye with Java's rulers. Local Javanese *Patihs* (sultans) who preserved their governmental prerogatives under traditional Hindu-Javanese symbolism, usually accepted Islam only in a formal way. They resisted pressure from fanatic Muslim scribes or mullahs who objected to the survival of heretical practices. The same Patihs were perfectly willing to aid the Dutch later against their common mullah enemies.[46] Once Islam started and was accorded control of temples and monastery sites and supporting village communities traditionally allocated to them, the Islamic teachers took over education and thus strengthened their influence. In Bali, on the other hand, where neither economic nor political considerations commended the new faith, Islam made no progress at all.

[46] W. F. Wertheim, *Indonesian Society* (1956), 193–200.

## *Islam's Social and Religious Appeal*

Islam also exerted a direct religious appeal. Port-city artisans and traders welcomed the boon of equality with all true believers in *ummat Islam,* with its corollary of superiority over nonbelievers. The egalitarian appeal of Islam differed from that of Buddhism in its aggressively partisan spirit. It offered a dogmatic monotheistic faith, capable of bridging over many of the disorderly aspects of life which an apparently too precise and intricate Indian philosophy had attempted to rationalize.[47] Islamic teachers usually did not attack the Hindu system directly; they preferred generally to redefine traditional religious practices and symbols under the covering canopy of endless recitations of the Islamic confession of faith in Allah and his Prophet. Arab fairies took over for older spirits, and the heroes of the Hindu epics took on Sassinid Persian names. A Sufi pantheistic sect gained wide acceptance for a time in both Malacca and Java under presuppositions not very different from Brahmanism. Adaptable Malay spirit mediums (shamans) managed to find the same stimulation for their magical capacities under the Islamic regimen of austerity, fastings, and abstinence which the older Hindu rituals had previously provided.

In Java, particularly, the older culture retained its social vitality, including adat law.[48] It absorbed elements of Islam, just as it had previously taken over Hindu and Buddhist accretions. Javanese standards survived the Islamic impact in the higher status of women, in village cohesion and wizardry, in music and puppet shadow plays, in the magical control of evil spirits and the calculations of lucky days, and even in the veneration of ancestral saints, including their embodiment in Hindu and Buddhist statuary. The Islamic confession of faith became for many a new kind of incantation. Islam was sterile artistically, smothering the previously demonstrated Indonesian genius in areas of sculpture and architecture.[49] As late as the early nineteenth century, the Muslim faith in Java was lightly held. Most of the Javanese paid little attention to prayer and fasting regulations, ignored the prohibition of the use of intoxicants and opium, and participated openly in usury. They generally refused to eat pork, but many also observed the Hindu taboo on beef.[50]

Malaya was, in many respects, more thoroughly Islamized than Java, partly because the indigenous culture exhibited less vitality. Even so, the general practice in Malaya was to add an Islamic confession to a familiar Hindu ritual. Allah's aid was invoked under a great variety of names; love charms from the Hindu Vedas were legitimized by simply appending a con-

[47] C. A. O. Van Nieuwenhuijze, *Aspects of Islam in Post-Colonial Indonesia* (1958), 32–40.

[48] R. O. Winstedt, *The Malays: A Cultural History* (1950), 19–26, 34–43.

[49] Kenneth P. Landon, *Southeast Asia: Crossroads of Religion* (1947), 134–164.

[50] John Crawfurd, *History of the Indian Archipelago* (1820), II, 266–271.

fession of faith in Allah. Arab texts properly inscribed in perfumed ink at the right astrological moment afforded protection from evil spirits. The Malay words for religion, fasting, teachers, heaven, and hell were all drawn from Sanskrit roots. Symbols of royal power and enthronement rites, including the twelve steps of purification, followed Brahman standards in Muslim Malaya as in neighboring Theravada Buddhist countries.[51] Indra's thunderbolt symbol continued to appear on the armlets worn by the sultans; Brahman heralds functioned at their courts; capitals in Pahang were still called Indrapura; Mount Meru astrological and numerological considerations influenced the organization of the palace area and choice of the royal regalia. Hindu practices in cremation and in payment of bride dowries also continued in Muslim Malacca after 1511.[52]

The small city-kingdom of Acheh at the topmost point of Sumatra set a pattern all its own. Its extreme spirit of political and commercial partisanship was such that it refused to cooperate with the Malaccans either before or after the displacement of the sultans by the Portuguese. After Malacca's fall, Acheh set itself up as the new center of Islamic studies for Southeast Asia. It even tried to imitate the standards of the rising Mogul Emperors of India, whose court titles, architecture, gardens, and dress Acheh copied. It also cultivated relations with the Arab Middle East, and became the recognized point of departure for pilgrims to Mecca.[53] The Achehnese were a mixed people ethnically, lacking the easygoing qualities of the average Malay. They were often the enemies of their Islamic neighbors, later a thorn in the side of the Portuguese and a nuisance to the Dutch. Islamic partisanship apparently added to their natural belligerency. The cultural transformation accomplished by the advent of Islam in Indonesia during the century of the leadership of Muslim Malacca was obviously far from homogeneous and revolutionary in its effects. Much of Hinduized Indonesian culture survived, along with pre-Hindu practices as well. In the course of time Islam was to become better integrated culturally, but this development had to await firsthand contacts with the sources of the faith in Arabia and Egypt.

[51] Winstedt, *Cultural History*, 19–35.

[52] *Ibid.*, 63–69, 74, 79; F. J. Moorhead, *A History of Malaya* (1957), 145–146.

[53] Hall, *A History of South-East Asia*, 285–286.

# CHAPTER 9

# The Sixteenth-century Portuguese Intrusion, Toungoo Burma, and Siam

In 1511, at the very peak of Malacca's commercial prosperity, the city was captured by a small band of daring Portuguese. They were engaged at the time in a challenging program of worldwide exploration, coupled with a crusade against Islam and a determined effort to take over the enormously profitable spice trade to Europe. All four stages of the spice trade—Javanese, Gujerati Indian, Arab, and Venetian—could be intercepted at Malacca, from which direct control over the Spice Islands themselves might also be achieved. Under Portuguese control, Malacca managed to cooperate with most of the trading groups that had previously been visiting the city, but Portugal's policy of monopoly was ruinous to the spice merchants of central and eastern Java and, in a lesser degree, to the Gujerati cloth merchants of India. Portuguese Malacca also encountered persistent if uncoordinated hostility from Sumatran neighbors. The Siamese were generally cooperative, although they would have been unable to oppose the Europeans in any case after the mid-century because of the renewal of warfare with the Toungoo Burmans.

Growing hatred of the Portuguese because of their abuse of power and their complete disregard for the interests of the people of the Indies islands in particular actually contributed to the rate of acceptance of Islam, despite the contrary efforts of Christian missionary agencies. Inefficient administration, the heavy drain of military expenditures, and frequent interruptions of trade by enemy attack on Malacca eventually bankrupted the potentially profitable operation. The resources of the Portuguese proved, in the end, too meager to maintain their policy objectives, and they yielded their position after 1610 to stronger Dutch opponents who were not bothered by crusading concerns. Malacca itself held out until 1641. Nevertheless, during a short century, a handful of Portuguese traders, fighting men, and adventurers, spending their energies in profligate fashion, had a noteworthy and in some respects a lasting effect on the history and peoples of Southeast Asia.

## The Coming of the Portuguese

Vasco da Gama's feat of 1498 in turning the southern point of Africa en route to the Orient was the outcome of more than two generations of navigational development which owed much of its inspiration to Prince Henry the Navigator. If Prince Henry himself had made the trip in his earlier days, he would have encountered in the Arabian Sea the powerful Chinese fleet of Cheng-ho, who had also been concerned with opening the waterborne trade in the direction of Europe. As it was, da Gama had little trouble finding an Arab-Indian navigator pilot in the Mozambique Channel who pushed aside the Portuguese-developed astrolabe as superfluous and guided the Portuguese fleet safely to Calicut. At the time, Calicut was one of three important ports on India's Malabar Coast (the others were Goa and Cambay) which were centers of Arabian trade.

But even in unfamiliar waters, the Portuguese ships enjoyed very substantial advantages over their Arab-Indian rivals. The European craft could sail closer to the wind and were more sturdily constructed, using nails where the Arabs sewed their hulls together. Portuguese guns had longer range, were more accurate and better manned, and Portuguese ship crews were experienced in navigation outside the easy seasonal rhythm of the monsoon winds. The Portuguese were also fervent nationalists; their natural belligerency and violence were bolstered by a sense of crusading mission against the Moors and by a boundless cupidity born of hardship and poverty in their homeland. Left to their own limited resources in a strange and friendless world, the Portuguese had to triumph if they wished to survive, no matter how great the odds might be against them.[1]

But if the policy of the first Portuguese viceroy, Francisco de Almeida (1505–1509), had been followed, the Portuguese might never have influenced the history of Southeast Asia at all. His policy was to establish unquestioned naval superiority in the Arabian Sea and especially along India's Malabar Coast for the purpose of interrupting only the Arab phase of the spice trade to the Middle East. A single naval base in the Cochin area would have afforded an essential point of naval contact with servicing facilities ashore, and the pepper and spices for transshipment to Europe could be obtained from friendly Indian ports which might welcome an alternative market for their wares. He argued that if Portugal's resources were spread too thin by capturing and fortifying numerous and distant points of land on an imperial pattern, the result would be to weaken its power in the crucial naval sector.

With such a cautious program, the viceroy's lieutenant, Alfonso de Albuquerque, violently disagreed. He insisted that cooperation with

[1] Nicholas Downton wrote of them after the grueling battle of Swalley Hole in 1614: "I never see men fight with greater resolution than the Portugales." See William Foster (ed.), *The Voyage of Nicholas Downton to the East Indies in 1614–1615* (1939), 185.

Indian ports and princes could be obtained only by a resolute show of force and that a number of strongly fortified points, strategically located, were indispensable for control of the spice trade. Such a program, he confidently affirmed, would make King Manoel the richest prince in the world. After a violent quarrel, during which Albuquerque was imprisoned for a time, Almeida was recalled to Portugal in 1509 and affairs were put into the hands of the new viceroy. Almeida's last important action, from which Albuquerque profited greatly, was his defeat of the combined Egyptian and Gujerati fleet off India's Diu in February, 1509.

## Albuquerque's Conquest of Malacca

Albuquerque's first actions as viceroy were to establish a strong base at Goa, to destroy resistance at Calicut, and to persuade Gujerat to cede Diu as a site for a fortress at the western entrance of the Bay of Cambay. He also laid siege to Ormuz (it was finally captured in 1512) and defeated the Arab navy near Aden at the entrance of the Red Sea.[2] Meanwhile he dispatched to Malacca in 1509 a small naval force under Diogo Lopez de Sequeira to obtain information and possibly to create a *casus belli*.

Albuquerque had to capture Goa for a second time in November, 1510, from its tenacious Turkish-Persian ruler, Yusuf Adil Shah. On this occasion, he slaughtered all of its remaining Islamic inhabitants. He repopulated the city by forcing passing ships to call at Goa and by encouraging his followers to marry Hindu wives, selected at the outset from well-to-do families and trained as Christians. Some 450 such marriages were arranged at first, and many more followed. The readiness of the Portuguese to marry locally provided one basis for the rapport which they developed in most places of their permanent occupancy. By the end of 1512, virtually all of the Arab shipping agents had departed from the Malabar Coast of India. When Albuquerque left for Malacca in 1511, his force included three-fourths as many Malabaris as Portuguese.[3]

Goa became the capital of the Portuguese Empire in the Orient, and, after 1558, the seat of an archbishopric of the Catholic Church. It was also a ship repair and building center, using teakwood timber available near at hand. It was a place for the care of the ill and the wounded, a storage depot for military supplies, and a depository for weapons manufactured locally by skilled gunsmiths and armorers. Goa also became important as a trading center. Married Portuguese took up trades, chewed betel nut, wore native clothes, and used slaves as laborers.[4] Malacca by comparison was a mere

[2] F. J. Moorhead, *A History of Malaya* (1957), 137–139, 151.

[3] F. C. Danvers, *The Portuguese in India* (1894), I, 217. Goa's own production for export was limited to betel, areca, rice, and salt.

[4] Jayne Kingsley Garland, *Vasco da Gama and His Successors* (1910), 103–104.

trading station, frequently beleaguered and insecure, populated largely by an alien trader community.

The hostile reception encountered at Malacca by de Sequeira's fleet in 1509 was not surprising in view of the influential position occupied at the metropole by Muslim Gujerati merchants, bitter enemies of the Portuguese. The Bendahara, Tun Mutahir, attempted unsuccessfully to seize de Sequeira's fleet but did manage to kidnap twenty of his men. Two of the Portuguese ships were destroyed. Provocation was apparently afforded for Malaccan attacks by de Sequeira's gratuitous undertaking to build a fort of his own nearby. Malaccan disaffection played into the hands of the Europeans. Instead of making every effort to mobilize a united front in preparation for the inevitable Portuguese rejoinder, Sultan Mahmud fomented internal dissension by executing Tun Mutahir for failing to provide a daughter for his harem. He selected as the new Bendahara the aged son of Tun Perak, who had been Bendahara until 1498, thus reviving the traditional local Malay-Tamil feud. Some of the merchant community, especially the Chinese and some Javanese, were subjected to unfair treatment, so that the Asian trading community was by no means unanimously in favor of the cause of the Sultan.

Preparations for defense were ineffectual. Mahmud failed to take the precaution of entering an early plea for assistance from Peking, although it is very doubtful, in view of China's failure to assist vassal Champa in 1471, that any effective assistance would have been forthcoming. Ming China had lost interest in Southeast Asia. Many of the defensive measures seem to have been initiated by the Gujerati party, which brought in a reported six hundred Turkish mercenary soldiers and provided a large number of matchlocks and cannon. Most of the estimated twenty thousand defenders of the city were contingents sent by Malay vassals, whose most effective weapons were blowguns and poisoned darts.

Albuquerque departed Goa for Malacca in April, 1511, with eighteen vessels and an estimated fourteen hundred men, six hundred of whom were Malabaris. He lost one vessel en route but captured five Gujerati ships. He entered Malacca harbor in mid-June with all guns firing, flags flying, and trumpets blaring. He proceeded to demand restoration of captives and property and the negotiation of peace on his own terms. While the Sultan hedged for time by blaming the executed Bendahara, Tun Mutahir, for the harsh treatment accorded to de Sequeira, the Portuguese destroyed all Muslim shipping in the harbor. Otherwise Albuquerque dealt generously with the trader community. A number of Chinese junk owners offered their assistance to the Europeans. One Chinese later provided the high-decked ship used in the second capture of the bridge spanning the creek which separated the two parts of the town. Another Chinese merchant cooperated by transporting a Portuguese emissary, Duarte Fernandes, to Ayuthia.

Despite the fact that the attackers were outnumbered some 15 to 1 and that some dissension appeared among them following the first abortive attempt to enter the city in late July, the port fell in August, 1511. Most of the city, including the palace, was burned during the initial July attack. The serious European casualties came largely from poisoned-dart wounds, against which sail canvas was used as protection during the final assault. The defending artillery was ineffectively used, and blowguns proved no match for Portuguese arms despite the spirited character of the defense. The place was thoroughly looted by the victors; some three thousand pieces of artillery were captured. A systematic slaughter of Muslim enemies ensued, although the defecting Javanese mercenary troops were spared. Peguans, Hindus, and Chinese came over quickly to the victor's side and were generously treated.[5] The Sultan Mahmud escaped to neighboring Pahang.

## The Development of Portuguese Malacca

The most pressing task faced by the Portuguese victors was to build an impregnable fortress to ensure the defense of the city. The problem of labor was complicated by the expulsion of all Muslim Malays and by widespread illness from fever and dysentery among the Europeans. With the help of cooperating Javanese mercenaries, some fifteen hundred slaves of the ex-Sultan were rounded up. Stone was obtained by razing a mosque located on the site selected for the main fortress tower and also from nearby tombs of former sultans. The enclosing wall of stone, 8 feet thick, paralleled the left bank of the stream bisecting the city and ran along the Straits shore. The main keep, a tall four-story tower named A Famosa (the famous), was located at the mouth of the stream and was therefore easily accessible to relief supplies entering from the straits side in time of siege. Its height enabled defenders to counter any attack from a nearby hill situated beyond the east wall. The Portuguese lived within the walls. The native part of the city extending along the right bank and to the north of the bisecting stream was surrounded by a wood-and-earth palisade, too long to be defended by a limited garrison. The fort tower and wall were completed within a month by dint of strenuous exertion.

Albuquerque departed in early 1512, leaving six hundred men, aided by a fleet of eight vessels, to defend the place. His own flagship, en route to Goa loaded with loot from the city, ran aground and broke up on the Sumatran coast. An accompanying junkload of Javanese shipwrights seized the occasion to mutiny and make their escape. Albuquerque's two surviving vessels limped into Cochin only to learn that Goa was again under siege. Following the relief of Goa, he proceeded again to Aden to chastise the Arab navy. The redoubtable empire builder died in 1515, with much still remaining to be done.[6]

---

[5] Moorhead, 160–170; Danvers, 222–228. Some fatal casualties were suffered at Malacca from poisoned darts.

[6] Moorhead, 169–176; Danvers, 229.

At Malacca as at Goa, the Portuguese residents were encouraged to take native wives, although with considerably less success. Residence for many was transient, and daughters of high-caste Indians were unavailable. The Portuguese garrison seldom numbered as many as six hundred men, and frequently as few as two hundred.[7] All Portuguese descendants, whether legitimate or not, were reared as Christians, and the total nominally Christian population, divided into two parishes, numbered eventually some seventy-four hundred inhabitants. Five churches were constructed within or near the city. Missionary activity outside the limit of Portuguese descendants was virtually nil, in part because of the chronically demoralized state of the inhabitants and in part because of resistance to indoctrination by Muslims and the general apathy characteristic of the Malays.

Considerable efforts were made by the Portuguese to encourage the revival of normal trading operations at Malacca. Kampar and Minangkabau merchants resumed trading almost immediately. Duarte Fernandes' mission to Ayuthia was received by the Siamese Court in friendly spirit; gifts were exchanged between the two parties and a commercial treaty was eventually concluded in 1518. Contacts made with the Peguan Mons were equally friendly, resulting in a treaty negotiated in 1519 by Anthony Correa at Martaban. Antonio de Abreu's first good-will mission to the Moluccas failed to reach the Spice Islands because of the wreck of two of his three ships, but a subsequent effort in 1512 was more successful. Francisco Serrao resided at Ternate for a number of years[8] and concluded an alliance with the Sultan of this important clove island. The early Portuguese trade for spices involved the exchange of Cambay cloth and gold.

Portuguese relations with Asians at Malacca varied with the group and the time. Albuquerque's generous treatment of Chinese traders at Malacca paid off in his securing initial acquiescence by China in Portuguese control. The Peking authorities refused the belated assistance plea of Sultan Mahmud, alleging as an excuse troubles of their own with the Tartars. The Malaccan Sultan's emissary to China, Mudaliar, died on the return trip.[9] But good relations between the Portuguese and China were not destined to continue. The most enthusiastic commercial response came from the non-Muslim Indian traders, especially the Kalingas (Klings) of the Coromandel Coast. The Bengalis and Parsees resumed trading with considerable caution, while the Gujeratis, curbed on the Malabar Coast and forbidden access to spices at Malacca, remained hostile and returned very slowly. The Portuguese permitted all major trading groups to operate under Shahbandars of their own nationality and selection, but with increasingly ill success.

The Javanese traders were among the earliest to indicate their cooperation with the new rulers of Malacca. Javanese troops assisted in the

[7] Ian A. Macgregor, "Notes on the Portuguese in Malaya," *JRASMB*, XXVIII, part 2 (May, 1955), 5–6.

[8] Moorhead, 170–176.

[9] Danvers, 229–234; Tomé Pires, *The Suma Oriental* (1944), I, 205–212.

restoration of order and in the recovery of royal slaves and other properties. An early break came when the Javanese Shahbandar, one Utemutraja, took offense at the obvious preference being given to the Indian Hindus and entered into clandestine relations with the court of the exiled Sultan. Just prior to Albuquerque's departure, the offending official was convicted of treason and publicly executed, to the distress of the resident Javanese, who tended to blame their tattletale Hindu rivals.[10] Portuguese relations with the Javan ports reached the point of open strife as soon as the rivalry for control of the spice monopoly became apparent. In 1513 the Javanese traders, acting in cooperation with Palembang, sent a powerful naval force numbering allegedly one hundred ships to blockade Malacca and recapture it from the redoubtable Portuguese artillerymen. Only seven or eight of the hundred ships survived the attack. Unable promptly to rebuild from local resources or to purchase Pegu-made ships at Malacca, as had previously been done, the Javan ports suffered heavily. Grisee died almost completely. Japara and Surabaya were reduced to a small fraction of their former trade in food supplies, Indian cloth, and spices. Demak alone survived commercially at the time. It eventually suffered decline after 1540 and was conquered by Mataram in 1588. Japara thereafter took the lead in resisting the Portuguese.[11]

At the time of the completion of Tomé Pires' report in 1515, Malacca's trade was far from being restored to its 1511 status. Gujerati ships refused to accept the trading conditions of the Portuguese and sought other outlets for their valuable cloth. Much of the Muslim trade immediately after 1511 came to center at Pasai in Sumatra, including Bengali, Gujerati, Arab, Turk, and Persian vessels. Bengalis were especially prominent at Pasai. Malacca, declared Pires, must make Pasai a vassal or else destroy its trade.[12] Javanese hostility long persisted. The island ports were suffering from hurt pride as well as from destruction of shipping facilities. Malacca's trade with Pegu, Pasai, Uru, Brunei, and Pahang was reported improving by 1515. The Klings among the Indian traders were coming in large numbers, constituting at the time the most important Indian commercial element. Chinese trade had not yet revived sufficiently to warrant the appointment of a Shahbandar. The task of finding responsible Shahbandars who could command confidence was a most urgent consideration. Pires' account closed with an impassioned plea for the sending of more Portuguese help to Malacca and for capital to finance Portuguese voyages to Pegu, the Sunda Straits, and Java. The potentials of the Malacca trade were far from being realized by 1515. Pires' report concluded as follows: "Malacca is a city that was made for merchandise, fitter than any other in the world. . . . The . . . commerce between the different nations for a thousand leagues on every hand must come to

[10] Danvers, 232.
[11] Pires, I, 186–196; B. H. M. Vlekke, *Nusantara* (1960), 94.
[12] Pires, I, 135–145.

Malacca . . . if it were moderately governed . . . and not neglected. . . . Whoever is lord of Malacca has his hand on the throat of Venice."[13]

Shortly after the completion of Pires' report, he himself was designated to proceed to Peking in order to establish a basis for the renewal of trading relations. The story of this ill-starred venture will be considered later.

## Contradictions in Portuguese Policies

In a number of respects, the policies of the Portuguese were contradictory. Malacca was a going concern as a trading entrepôt when they took it over in 1511, and they clearly wanted to keep it so. Its patterns of administration and of trading contacts were well established. The captain of the fort could simply assume the authority of the old sultan-Bendahara government, select a new set of responsible Shahbandars, and, once the physical damage of the conquest was restored, resume where the Malay government had left off. But this promising prospect was destined to be long delayed in its realization. Where the sultans had developed a trading entrepôt at Malacca, the Portuguese tried to make it an outpost of empire. As early as the 1520s informed Portuguese like the historian Barros were concerned lest grandiose military projects should overextend Portuguese resources.[14]

The principal difficulties developed in connection with the Portuguese effort to corner the spice trade. When denied access to spices at Malacca, the merchants of the Bay of Cambay tried to dispose of their valued cotton cloth elsewhere than at the entrepôt. This was done mainly on the Bay of Bengal side. Occasionally large Indian convoys en route through the straits defied Portuguese orders to stop at Malacca. They conspired from time to time with the ports of Acheh (Pasai and Pedir) to capture the Portuguese position, going so far on several instances as to bring in Turkish arms and reinforcements for the task. The Gujeratis were free to trade at Malacca without discrimination so long as they accepted Portuguese terms, and some of them did so. But their lucrative trade with the Near East was disrupted without spice cargoes, and these could be obtained as a rule only by bribing Portuguese officials.

The merchants of Java were in an even more difficult predicament after being denied access to Malacca with their spice cargoes. It was not possible for the Portuguese to close off the entire supply, of course, so that Asian outlets for the China spice trade were developed after 1520 at Brunei and at Patani. But Javanese shipping was in short supply after the disastrous defeat of the Javanese in 1513, and it proved impossible for them to make good the constant attrition suffered from superior Portuguese guns. The sending of occasional cargoes of rice to Malacca was a poor substitute for the

---

[13] Pires, II, 282–289.
[14] D. G. E. Hall (ed.), *Historians of South-East Asia* (1961), 172–173.

once-thriving Javanese spice trade with the entrepôt. By the 1620s, the impoverished Javanese coastal states of Madura, Tuban, Surabaya, and Demak
had all lost their independence, gained from Majapahit about 1520, to a
resurgent Mataram state centered in interior central Java.[15]

The problems of maintaining Malacca's entrepôt status tended to become cumulative. The Chinese, for example, became unhappy over the disruption of the convenient pre-1511 system under which they could obtain
from Malacca virtually any kind of goods they desired and in unlimited
quantities.[16] Peking never developed cordial relations with the stiff-necked
Portuguese barbarians, who refused to accept the customary tributary status
of Malacca to the Celestial Empire.[17] The east Javan coastal state of Demak,
with alternative ports at Japara and Grisee, afforded a second example of
policies operating at cross-purposes. Demak played an active role in the
Islamization of Bantam in western Java and of south Borneo port cities
as a means of denying the Portuguese access to any stopping points on the
way to the Moluccas. East Borneo mariners and the Buginese of the Celebes
took to active piracy. So difficult did the passage through the Java Sea become for the Europeans, that the Portuguese eventually found it safer to
reach the Spice Islands via north Borneo and the dangerous tidal straits of
the Sulu Sea.[18]

Contradictions in Portugal's religious policy were equally apparent.
The crusade against the Gujeratis and Arab Moors fitted neatly into the
primary Portuguese objective to corner the spice trade, but the missionary
program languished in Southeast Asia. Portuguese abuse of Muslim populations among both the Malays and the Banda islanders hopelessly damaged
their reputation for fair dealing and hurt trade as well. Malacca never
became the missionizing center for Christianity that it had occupied for
the Muslim faith. The Catholic Church in Malacca contributed much to
building operations within the city, especially following the establishment of
the bishopric in 1558. The bishop's palace and a cathedral were the principal items.[19] Elaborate pomp and ceremonies marked the veneration of
sacred relics, and Christian schools were promoted. But not even the presence of the Jesuit leader Francis Xavier during the 1540s seems to have made
any difference in the dismal outlook. The Church exercised no influence
outside the Portuguese-integrated population and seemingly little moral
influence on its own members either. Xavier denounced as religiously
poisonous the wicked city with its rapacious and dishonest government. He
shook the dust of the place off his feet when he departed for Japan in 1549.
The famous missionary also worked for a time during the late forties in the
Moluccas where several islands, including Amboina and northern Halma-

---

[15] *Ibid.*, 204; Moorhead, 196–200.
[16] Danvers, 338–339.
[17] Moorhead, 205–210.
[18] *Ibid.*, 204–210.
[19] Macgregor, 5–41. An archbishopric was set up at Goa in 1560.

hera, were not yet Islamized and therefore provided points receptive to Christianity, if adequate material inducements were provided. He found the situation in the Moluccas completely demoralized by the irresponsible spoliation of the area by visiting Portuguese sea captains.[20]

The Portuguese missionary effort was equally ineffective in other countries of Southeast Asia as far as the indigenous population was concerned. Numbers of Portuguese military adventurers found their way, either as captives or as mercenaries, into the military service of Burma, Arakan, or Siam. In most instances they were permitted to have a Christian chaplain resident among them and to rear their offspring as Catholics, but no proselytizing was permitted or attempted. Portuguese conduct and policy in Southeast Asia generally canceled out any possibility of successful prosecution of their missionary objective, however sincerely entertained at Lisbon. The net result of their impact religiously was to stimulate the spread of the hostile Muslim faith as a weapon of alignment against them.

The early Portuguese leaders based their legal claims to the eastern seas on the papal decree of demarcation and conceived their enterprise in moral and religious terms as an expression of Christian zeal. This mood and accompanying activities reached a peak during the decade from 1515 to 1525 following Albuquerque's death. Historical records from the 1520s reflected, nevertheless, an awareness that both Goa and Malacca were over-reaching themselves in their grandiose undertakings, that costs were outrunning profits, and that greed was stultifying missionary concern. The changing point of view is reflected in Mendes Pinto's famous *Peregrinations,* covering the years 1538 to 1557, when he journeyed from Burma to Japan. Although fanciful in many of his details, Pinto cast serious doubts on the capacities of his countrymen in Asia to serve the cause of religion through their murderous greed. The faith of the Portuguese in their own enterprise faded after 1550. A century later it had entirely disappeared.[21]

## Malacca's Warfare with Malay Neighbors

Throughout much of the first sixty-five years of Portuguese control at Malacca, the city was at war with its Malay neighbors. The initial resistance came from ex-Sultan Mahmud. He established himself at Bintang Island in the Riau group of the Singapore channel in an effort to deny the Portuguese exit to the eastern seas. From 1517 to 1521, he also maintained a fortified stockade on the Muar River near Malacca. After he was ousted from Bintang in 1526, he and his heirs shifted their headquarters to Johore, thereafter to play a secondary role.[22] Acheh then assumed the position of

[20] See Danvers (538–540) for examples of offenses committed.

[21] Hall, 171–174, 183–185, 194. In contrast to his Southeast Asian problems, Xavier enjoyed considerable missionary success in Japan, while substantial Christian communities developed at Goa and in Ceylon.

[22] Hall, 198–199; Moorhead, 196–200.

chief Muslim state and enemy of the Portuguese. The feud lasted for many years. Acheh defeated the efforts of the Portuguese in 1529 to take over rival Sumatran ports of Pasai and Pedir. It subsequently staged major attacks on Malacca itself, in 1537, 1548, 1568, and 1574–1575.

Generally speaking, Acheh's megalomania proved her undoing; excessive ambition prevented her sharing the attempted dominance with other opponents of the Europeans. Acheh clearly overreached itself in 1539–1540, when it suffered a defeat at the hands of a Malay coalition led by Johore. The Portuguese seized the opportunity to make separate treaties with the pepper port of Bantam in western Java and also with the Sultan of Brunei in Borneo. The latter broke off his previous relations with Java and gave consent to Portuguese use of the north Borneo channel en route to the Spice Islands.[23] Preliminary to a 1547 attack on Malacca, Acheh seized the important Perlis region (Trang port) in northern Malaya, from which it attempted to interdict the Malacca-bound trade of Bengal, Siam, and Pegu. For a time in the late forties, Goan shipping dared not pass near Acheh's Sumatran ports en route to the straits. Portuguese recapture of Perlis in 1550 was followed by Portuguese defeat of the combined Johore and Japara (Javanese) fleets in 1551. A period of relatively peaceful development after 1551 was again broken in 1568, when Acheh attacked Malacca for the third time, on this occasion reinforced with Gujerati and Turkish guns. Several hundred ships and some twenty thousand men attacked the fort but without success. Malacca experienced the closest call of all from a combined Javan and Achehnese attack in 1574–1575, which came at the same time that the Spanish from Manila were threatening Portugal's position in the Spice Islands.

Acheh finally abandoned the futile effort to achieve hegemony in the straits in 1587. It then made peace with the Portuguese and proceeded to take vengeance on its long-time rival Johore. Therefore, except for two limited periods of relative freedom from hostilities, during the early 1540s and between 1551 and 1568, the Portuguese were involved almost constantly until 1587 in defending Malacca. By that time the Portuguese homeland had fallen under the rule of the Spanish King, Philip II, who did virtually nothing to promote the Portuguese half of his tremendous empire, while his role as King attracted attacks against the Portuguese bases from powerful enemies of Spain, such as the Dutch and the English.

It was a tribute to the remarkable fighting qualities of the Portuguese both at the Malacca fort and on the sea that the garrison survived its many trials. At two periods during every year, it was always shorthanded. One was following the departure of the spice fleet for the Moluccas between November and January,[24] and the second was between April and July after the fleet had left for Europe and before the next monsoon could bring

[23] N. Ginsburg and C. F. Roberts, *Malaya* (1958), 27–28.

[24] This timing of the trip to the Moluccas indicates that passage to Amboina was made during the winter monsoon.

fresh reinforcements from Goa. Even after the Dutch gained naval dominance, however, the Malacca fort held out for decades against them.

## Malacca: Trading System and People

The atmosphere among the European population at Malacca was
generally demoralized. The trading system was conditioned by the fact that
it was a government monopoly in which the Portuguese king was the chief
merchant. Port officials were paid salaries and ration allowances and were
not supposed to traffic on the side. The official system thus afforded no
legitimate way by which the average person could augment his income. The
situation became particularly demoralizing after 1527, when payment of
salaries fell chronically in arrears. Chettyar moneylenders from the Coromandel Coast bought up salary claims at a discount from the impecunious
Portuguese. Furthermore, most Europeans at Malacca preferred mistresses
to wives; spot checks revealed no more than 38 married settlers in 1525 and
114 in 1626. Attrition among the Europeans owed much to the deadly nature
of the climate. Arrivals often died within the first week of residence. During
the Dutch siege of 1629, only 120 fit Portuguese soldiers were available.[25]
Living costs, especially for food, were very high, despite the fact that such
imports were permitted free entry. The surrounding countryside produced
no food surplus. When, during the last third of the sixteenth century, the
Burmese source of rice dried up because of the ravaging of the Irrawaddy
delta by rival armies, Burman and Siamese, a small Javanese merchant
community dealing profitably in rice established itself within the city.[26]

It is difficult to arrive at any valid estimate of the fluctuation of the
volume of Malacca's trade. Inability to honor salary obligations by 1527
affords clear indication of the lack of adequate port receipts to cover military costs during the first fifteen years, a situation which persisted for an indefinite period. Until 1544, when the customs rates were moderated, the
dues were probably assessed at whatever the traffic would bear in an effort
to meet the exorbitant costs of warfare. This policy had the inevitable
result of diverting trade and encouraging piracy. In 1544, the basic duty was
set at 6 per cent of the value of the cargo, but the Chinese were charged 10
per cent and the Bengalis 8 per cent.[27] This modified rate compared un-
favorably with the duty-free status of Chinese and other eastern traders (not
counting "presents") under previous Muslim control. The Portuguese put
little faith in conciliation or good will based on mutual advantage as a
means of encouraging trade. Nor was any attempt made to organize local
production to meet trading or food needs. In the Moluccas, the Portuguese

[25] Macgregor, 5–41.

[26] *Ibid.* In 1512–1513 Martaban rice was worth ten times as much when
shipped to Sumatra.

[27] Moorhead, 205–217.

picked up what spices they wanted, being careful not to glut the European market, and destroyed all the rest, including surplus trees.[28]

A considerable degree of nepotism prevailed at Malacca, and favors were customarily granted in the free allocation of cargo space for private use. But not all port officials were dishonest, and some of the port captains were men of marked ability. The advantages of the location were such that granted a period of sustained peace, such as occurred after 1587, the volume of trade was very substantial.[29]

## *Portuguese Access to the Spice Islands*

The contest for access to the source of cloves in particular centered around the control of two tiny islands, Tidore and Ternate, located near Halmahera. The first was the larger of the two (10 leagues around as compared with 6), but it lacked a suitable anchorage.[30] For the most part the Portuguese preferred to deal with Ternate. The two sultans were related by marriage but were bitter rivals nonetheless.

Spain's claim to the Spice Islands was advanced in 1522 following the return of the one surviving vessel of the ill-fated Magellan's expedition around the world from east to west. One of Magellan's ships visited Tidore. A subsequent conference between the two Iberian states failed to agree as to the exact location of the disputed islands in relation to the previously agreed demarcation line. Spain managed to get a second ship through in 1526. In 1525 Portugal was secretly prepared to withdraw from the Moluccas if the Spaniards should appear there in force, for clove profits were not keeping up with costs. But the expected naval support for Spain's claim from New Spain was not forthcoming, and Madrid relinquished its claim temporarily in 1530. A later Spanish intrusion, in 1542–1545, established by local agreement Spain's prior and exclusive rights in Tidore, subject to later negative review in Europe. Spain's claims were again revived following the founding of Manila in 1570. The Portuguese maintained a fort on Ternate until 1574, when they were driven out by besieging islanders angry over the governor's wanton killing of their Sultan.[31] The Spanish gained a foothold for a time in Ternate as a result.

Portugal's need for a controlled point of contact in the Moluccas following its exclusion from Javanese and Borneo ports led to the occupation of Amboina and the attempted conversion of its population to Christianity. The missionizing effort was largely a failure, as already indicated, despite Francis Xavier's spending several years personally at the task (1546–

---

[28] D. W. van Welderen Rengers, *The Failure of a Liberal Colonial Policy: Netherlands East Indies, 1813–1830* (1947), 2–3.

[29] Macgregor, 5–41.

[30] Pires, I, 217.

[31] D. G. E. Hall, *A History of South-East Asia* (1955), 198–203, and *Historians of South-East Asia*, 183–185; Danvers, 462–465.

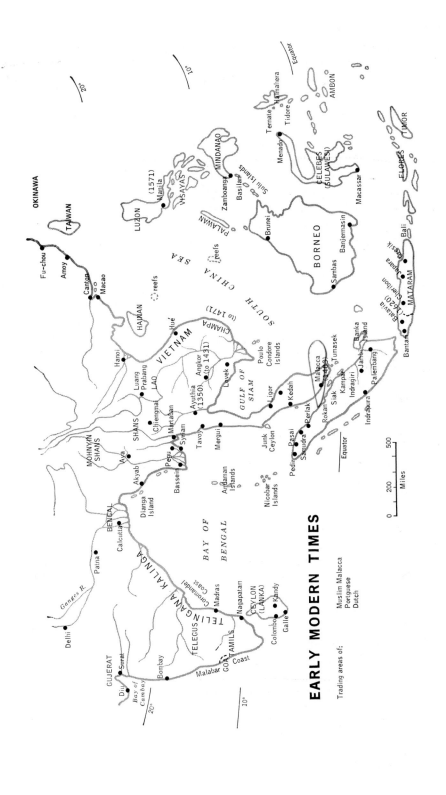

# EARLY MODERN TIMES

Trading areas of:

Muslim Malacca
Portuguese
Dutch

1548). The evil reputation of Portuguese mariners and the ease with which the backward natives could be intimidated by aggressive Javanese and Buginese Muslims were largely responsible. The need for maintaining friendly relations with the anti-Christian Sultan of Ternate counseled Portuguese abandonment of their missionary, but not their colonizing, effort on Amboina. The Portuguese established their spice headquarters at Tidore in 1578, shortly before Francis Drake's famous visit to Ternate.[32]

Aside from the Portuguese policy of limiting the total output of spices, especially on islands not under treaty relations, the European control entailed other handicaps for the population of the Moluccas. Malaccan traders were unable to match the rice exports which had previously reached the islanders from Java, so that the diet lapsed back to the unpalatable sago flour. Portuguese gold and cotton cloth brought in payment for spices went mainly to the ruler, whereas the previously imported rice had been eaten by the people. The great advantage of having direct access to the spice sources lay not only in the control of output, but also in the lower costs, which in 1515 were around one-third of the price for spices payable at Malacca.[33] The Portuguese hold on the islands after 1580 was spared a test with the Spanish at Manila by the direct veto of Philip II, then ruler of both kingdoms. But Portuguese authority in the Moluccas was slipping long before the Dutch arrived around 1600, by reason of increasing hatred on the part of abused peoples of the islands whose interests were being wholly disregarded.[34]

## Portuguese Relations with China

Aside from their virtual monopoly in spices, the efforts of the Portuguese to develop the trade of Malacca by commercial ventures of their own initiation produced minimal results. A principal difficulty derived from the perennial shortage of ships and manpower in the straits area. The tactics employed were also a deterrent. The Portuguese mission to China in 1517 was a case in point. Pires' account of China in his *Suma Oriental,* written in 1515, provided an accurate description of the extensive Chinese vassalage system and of the trading procedures to be encountered at Canton. But he was contemptuous of Chinese naval power, predicting that ten Portuguese vessels could conquer the entire China coast.[35]

A Portuguese expedition of 1517 carried a valuable cargo to Canton under the command of Fernando de Andrade, with Pires himself going along as the chief negotiator. Relations at first were friendly and fruitful.

[32] Hall, *A History of South-East Asia,* 198–203.

[33] Pires, I, 205–212, 216. A favorite import item at Ternate and Tidore, according to Pires, was the tails of white cows and oxen obtained in Bengal. The islands also exported parrots and feathers of birds of paradise.

[34] Moorhead, 200–203.

[35] Pires, I, 116–125.

Fernando apologized for having inadvertently violated Canton's rules by firing a salute before the city, and promised thereafter to observe local regulations. The Portuguese were given permission to build a factory where goods could be assembled. Pires was sent on to Peking, and Fernando returned to Malacca with part of his fleet in September, 1518. The remaining Portuguese vessels, accompanied by junks belonging to Okinawans, proceeded to Ningpo, where they again obtained local permission to establish a factory, for trade with adjacent China provinces and with Japan.[36]

Meanwhile the luckless Pires encountered serious difficulties. Because he was not authorized to concede Malacca's traditional vassalage relationship to China, both his embassy and his presents were rejected. His relations at Peking were further embarrassed by letters received from the ex-Sultan of Malacca denouncing the conduct of the Portuguese sea robbers who had wantonly seized his kingdom. Pires was therefore returned to Canton in 1519 to be held there under police custody until Malacca was properly returned to the Emperor's Malay vassal. Serious difficulties developed in 1521 when the other Andrade brother, Simon, arrived at Canton. Without asking permission, he erected a factory and a fort adjacent to the city, ostensibly as protection against the pirates, and otherwise aroused the ire of the Chinese authorities. A Chinese squadron attacked the Portuguese position, and Simon was lucky to escape with three of his vessels. A second naval force sent from Malacca was repulsed at Canton in 1522.

Pires was pressed by Peking to write a letter to the King of Portugal advising him to return Malacca to its rightful owner. This demand was subsequently transmitted to Patani in 1523 via a Malay-Chinese junk, but the order lacked Chinese naval support. Some twenty-three Portuguese captives held at Canton were executed in 1523 "as petty sea robbers sent by the great robber . . . to spy out our country." Pires himself remained in China until his death, which Pinto placed as late as 1540.[37]

Although Chinese accounts from the sixteenth century indicate that Portuguese Malacca was regarded as a political and commercial nuisance, it was clearly not an intolerable one for the Chinese. Having failed to prevent the establishment of the impregnable A Famosa fort and lacking the naval strength to reassert its suzerainty over the straits, the Peking government had to make the best of an unsatisfactory situation. This did not mean that Chinese junk owners and their pack-tending passengers did not resume making the trip to Malacca as soon as they found it advantageous to do so, regardless of the official policy at Canton. But the Chinese obtained much of their pepper and spices at other ports than Malacca. Portuguese relations with their Chinese visitors were very friendly on the whole. Official relations improved somewhat in 1557, when China acquiesced in Portuguese occupation of the island of Macao just south of the Canton estuary, following joint

[36] Danvers, 337–338.

[37] Armando Cortesão, *The Suma Oriental of Tomé Pires* (1944), xxxvii–xlix, lii–liv.

action against pirate gangs.[38] Macao was never important commercially. It served as a convenient stopover for traders at Canton and a staging point and headquarters for missionary work in China. In the seventeenth century it became an important outlet for the sale of firearms, including artillery, to Vietnam and adjacent areas.

The Liuchiu islanders, who resumed trading operations with Malacca, proved to be as popular and responsible with the Portuguese as they had been with the previous Malay government. The Portuguese often employed them as bodyguards. Portuguese mariner-explorers also made contact with the main Japanese islands, which became a successful center for missionary activity. Francis Xavier spent several years there after 1550.

## Portuguese Influence in the Bay of Bengal

The established Portuguese routine of developing warehouse factories and protecting forts side by side was nowhere carried out more effectively than at various points on the eastern coast of India. Nor were Malacca's commercial relations with any other group more profitable than with the Chettyars of Madras and the merchants of Kalinga. Portuguese military prowess was at first widely respected, and the European community enjoyed full extraterritorial status in the vicinity of the fortified posts. This situation gradually degenerated as the century wore on, for fort captains became increasingly arbitrary, and Goa was unable to police the eastern coast with the same thoroughness exercised along the Malabar side of India. Irresponsible conduct frequently degenerated into open piracy, especially in areas bordering the Bengal delta.

The Goan authorities themselves set a pattern for arbitrary dealings in the island of Ceylon. Almeida was accorded suzerain status by the island authorities as early as 1510, and the first Portuguese fort was built at Colombo in 1518. The viceroy himself took advantage of a disputed succession in 1550 to despoil the Court at Colombo of its valuables, which he never returned despite orders to that effect from Lisbon. In 1560, a second opportunity for intervention was afforded in behalf of the ousted ruler of Jaffna, who fled to Goa and accepted Christianity as the price of aid. The Portuguese sacrificed the claims of their protégé in the final settlement, by which the Europeans were accorded a large sum of money and were permitted to fortify the neighboring island of Manar.[39] It was on this occasion that the famous Buddha tooth was taken from Jaffna to Goa, ground to powder and burned, spurning the offer of Pegu to pay an alleged 300,000 ducats for its

[38] Danvers, 337–339; Moorhead, 205–210; Cortesão, xxxvii–xl; Macgregor, 5–41.

[39] K. W. Goonewardena, *The Foundation of Dutch Power in Ceylon, 1638–1658* (1958), 2–5; Danvers, 518–519; H. W. Codrington, *A Short History of Ceylon* (1929), 94, 101–103.

surrender. Two other teeth immediately took the place of the one destroyed, partisans of each insisting that theirs was really the original.[40]

The Portuguese had made themselves so unpopular in Ceylon by the 1590s that they were safe only behind their Colombo fortifications. Even so, a substantial number of half-castes and Christianized Sinhalese acknowledged allegiance to Goa. The Portuguese were able to take advantage of local quarrels to maintain a foothold until 1656, when they gave way completely to Dutch rule. The island's principal export products were cinnamon and precious stones. The Portuguese controlled most of the region where the cinnamon grew.[41]

At the eastern end of the Ganges-Brahmaputra delta between Bengal and Arakan, a series of Portuguese fort captains turned completely pirate during the last quarter of the century. They did a thriving business in slaves with the government of Arakan, which developed its production of surplus rice very substantially on the basis of the augmented labor supply. One Gonsalves Tibão dominated the east end of the delta from 1609 to 1617.[42] Arakan had maintained its complete independence from Burma since 1430. Its fortified capital of Mrohaung, founded in 1433 and fortified by King Minbin a century later, was able to withstand two determined attacks of Burmese armies in 1544 and 1546. For the better part of a century thereafter, Arakan was locally an important naval power. Its King participated actively in the destruction and looting of the Burmese capital of Pegu in 1599, aided by several ambitious Portuguese mercenaries. Otherwise, Arakan functioned more as a part of the history of Bengal than of Burma down to its eventual reincorporation into Burma in 1785.

In 1607, Arakan's King Razagri, angered by a betrayal by Portugal at Syriam, to be described later, broke the power of one Portuguese pirate lair at Dianga Island off the Chittagong coast only to have another appear immediately thereafter. The killing of some six hundred Portuguese at Dianga attracted a punitive attack from Goa in 1615, which nevertheless failed in its attempt to capture Mrohaung. After 1620, Arakanese authorities threw in their lot with the Portuguese slave traders, who operated from Chittagong to make raids on eastern Bengal. The slave market at Mrohaung attracted the attention of Dutch noncompany traders who purchased in Arakan slaves needed to repopulate the various East Indian Banda Islands assigned for their exploitation. In 1629 the Mogul Emperor Shah Jahan attacked a Portuguese pirate nest on the Chittagong coast, but it was not until 1666 that the naval power of the Arakanese-Portuguese pirates was broken and the coastal area annexed to Bengal. The piratical habits developed by the Arakanese long survived the elimination of their Portuguese teachers.[43]

[40] Danvers, 520; Codrington, 104–105.
[41] Codrington, 109–124; Goonewardena, 6.
[42] Hall, *A History of South-East Asia*, 205.
[43] *Ibid.*, 328–341.

The generally profitable trading operations of the Portuguese with the Siamese and the Peguan Mons ran into difficulties after 1539 because of the outbreak of warfare between the Toungoo Burmans and the Mons and subsequently between Burmanized Pegu and Siam. A single trading galleon sent from Goa to Pegu in 1539, under the command of Fernando de Moraes, arrived just as the Burman army and river fleet were closing in on the Pegu capital of the Mons. At the request of the Mon ruler, Fernando took over command of the defending fleet and succeeded in scattering the Burman navy in an initial encounter. But after the capital city of Pegu itself fell to the Burman army and the Peguan boatmen deserted de Moraes, the Burmans cornered and killed him, capturing his crew. On this occasion a larger body of Portuguese troops at Bassein was barely able to make their escape.[44]

Then began a process which was destined to continue for some time. Captured Portuguese were transported into the interior, given Burmese wives (and eventually assigned a section of the royal ahmudan lands), and incorporated into the Burman army as an elite artillery corps. In Siam and Cambodia, as well as in Burma, mercenary Portuguese military adventurers and captives became prized resources for the armed forces. To place the military role of the Portuguese in proper perspective, it is necessary to trace in brief outline the course of the convulsive warfare of the mid-sixteenth century which engulfed Burma, Pegu, Siam, Laos, and to some degree Cambodia.

## Toungoo-dynasty Burma: Bayinnaung's Empire

The crippling of the power of the Ava government as a result of its destruction and occupation by the Mohnyin Shans from 1527 to 1555 afforded a long-awaited opportunity for southward expansion at the expense of the Mons on the part of the Toungoo Burmans. The Shans generally were themselves a spent force as a result of long attrition. King Tabinshweti (1531–1550) of Toungoo augmented his military resources by his initial occupation of the Kyaukse granary area and by the receipt of many Burman reinforcements from ravaged Ava. Pushing down the Sittang Valley, he then overran most of the Irrawaddy delta area by 1535 and captured Pegu itself, as already indicated, in 1539. The rival Shan government at Ava brought temporary assistance to the ousted Mon ruler, who withdrew to Prome, but the Mon state fell apart after the ruler's early death.

In the tradition of the early Pagan rulers, Tabinshweti won over the support of Mon chiefs by honoring their civilized customs and granting them equal status. He then successfully attacked Martaban and annexed the Tenasserim coast down to the Siamese border at Tavoy by 1541. Portuguese mercenaries under one João Cayeyro aided in the capture and despoiling of Martaban. Portuguese gunners also assisted in the subsequent ousting of Shan rulers from Prome and in the consequent Burman recovery

[44] Danvers, 441–447.

of the Minbu-Myingyan irrigated area and the site of old Pagan. Tabin-shweti was crowned as heir of both the Pagan and the Pegu traditions.[45]

After the abortive Burman attacks on Arakan of 1544 and 1546, previously mentioned, preparations were made for an invasion of Siam in 1547–1548 via Tenasserim. The initial Burman attack carried through to Ayuthia, but the Burman artillery contingent of 180 Portuguese under Diogo Soares de Mello apparently found its technical counterpoise in the defense unit of some fifty Portuguese under Diogo Pereira, whose services the Siamese had enlisted.[46] The thwarted Burmans returned without spoil, badly discouraged. The demoralized King Tabinshweti proceeded to lose control of both himself and his kingdom. He was assassinated in 1550.

The threatened disintegration of the Toungoo-Pegu kingdom was stemmed by King Bayinnaung, a brother-in-law of Tabinshweti. During his thirty-year rule (1551–1581), his armies were destined to range over a wide area of Southeast Asia extending from Tavoy in the south to Shwebo in the north, from Ava eastward across the Shan plateau to Chiengmai and Laos, Vientiane, and thence southward down the entire valley of the Menam. In his initial recapture of Pegu from Mon rebels (1551) and his conquest of Ava and Shwebo (1554–1555), he enjoyed the valuable assistance of the artillerymen of Diogo Soares de Mello's band, but the Europeans were probably thereafter a relatively unimportant military factor. An important increment was Bayinnaung's successful enlistment of Shan levies in his armies. His conquests of the Shan states beginning with Ava itself were largely bloodless affairs. Every Burman division had its Shan contingent. His attacks on Siam and Laos were Shan as well as Burman campaigns.[47] He established firm suzerain control over Chiengmai, which he placed under the rule of one of his sons.

All might have been well had the phenomenally energetic Burman ruler been able at this point to curb his megalomania. But Chiengmai opened the way to Ayuthia, which became the primary objective of his am-bition. His first deceptively easy capture of the Siamese capital in 1564 was promptly annulled by a rebellion. His second capture of it in 1569, an action vigorously contested, established Burman control of Siam over a period of about fifteen to eighteen years. But problems began to proliferate elsewhere. Bayinnaung's involvement in the political affairs of distant Laos resulted in several hard-won but futile victories and two disastrous defeats. Each of the latter afforded opportunity for rebellions to spring up elsewhere. The 1570s were largely consumed by repeated and futile Burman expeditions into Laos.

The Burman defeat of Siam also encouraged Cambodia's rulers, Ang

---

[45] Hall, *A History of South-East Asia,* 210–211. Burma's effort to take over Arakan in 1544–1547 was abandoned in favor of the attack on Ayuthia.

[46] Danvers, 486.

[47] Sao Simong Mangri, *Shan States and the British Annexation* (unpub-lished), 63–66.

Chan and Boromoraja I, to attempt to even old scores with Ayuthia. Bayin-naung had therefore to consent to a reestablishment of Ayuthia's defenses by his puppet ruler, T'ammaraja. These fortifications were eventually to be used against the continuance of Burman control. The Siamese, nevertheless, made no further effort to revolt in Bayinnaung's time. At the time of his death in 1581, the Burman ruler was preparing to conquer Arakan, which up to that date had escaped his attention. The campaign was canceled, and Arakanese independence survived for two centuries longer.[48]

Beyond doubt, Bayinnaung's Burma was the most powerful Southeast Asian land state of its day. It provided, however, no threat to the Portuguese, for it possessed no sea power that could in any way challenge that of the Europeans. Its crippling of Siam's military power also eliminated any possible challenge to Portuguese control of the straits from the landward side, even if Buddhist Siam could have managed to cooperate with Islamic Malay sultans in a common effort against the Portuguese. European visitors to the rebuilt capital of Pegu in 1569 marveled at the display of Burman wealth and power. The remarkable Burman ruler found time to build pagodas, to distribute Pali scriptures, and to promote the study of the *dhammathats,* the Burmese rendering of the treatises of the law. He outlawed animal sacrifices to certain spirits, especially as practiced among the Shans, and made the fabulous offer of 300,000 ducats to the Goan viceroy for the Buddha tooth found at Jaffna, only to acquire later from Ceylon a duplicate tooth of dubious validity, along with a Sinhalese bride. The gift tooth he duly enshrined in the Mahazedi pagoda.[49] But the most civilized and prosperous portion of his domain, Mon Pegu, he eventually left exhausted and ravaged, with much of its irrigated ricelands reverting to jungle.

## Siam's Recovery of Independence

The leader of Siam's nationalist independence struggle was Pra Naret, a son of T'ammaraja, Burma's vassal king at Ayuthia. In his youth he had spent six years in Burma as a hostage and was acquainted with Burma's military methods.[50] He had returned to Ayuthia in 1571 and had distinguished himself for his effective and courageous military leadership against the invading Cambodians. His first chance to challenge Burman control came in 1584, when a princely feud in Burma pitted the heir of Bayinnaung, Nanda Bayin, against his uncle, the viceroy of Ava. Pra Naret on this occasion led a Siamese force into Burma in response to Pegu's request for aid, only to discover in the nick of time the nefarious plans of Nanda Bayin to have him killed. Thereupon he collected Siamese prisoners previously taken to Burma by Bayinnaung and returned home. Two other ambitious but futile Burman attempts to retake Ayuthia by cooperative

---

[48] Hall, *A History of South-East Asia,* 212–218.

[49] *Ibid.,* 215–217..

[50] H. G. Q. Wales, *Ancient South-East Asian Warfare* (1952), 118–120.

thrusts directed from Lower Burma and from Chiengmai were made in 1584–1585 and 1586–1587.

Pra Naret was prevented from following up his 1587 victory over the Burmans by his need to end once for all time the threat to Ayuthia from the Cambodians. The latter were obliged to abandon Angkor by 1589. But Siam's independence was assured after 1587. In 1590 the harried Burman King permitted the return of a captive prince of Laos to Luang Prabang as ruler. The latter promptly proclaimed his country's independence of Burma. Pra Naret became titular ruler of Ayuthia upon the death of his father T'ammaraja in 1590, under the title of Naresuen. In 1592 he repulsed a fifth and final full-scale Burman invasion led by the heir apparent to the Pegu throne.

Naresuen used his newly achieved initiative judiciously. He overran Tavoy and the Tenasserim coast in 1593 and then, in response to Mon appeals, raised the Burman siege of Moulmein and captured neighboring Martaban. His next concern was to inflict a paralyzing defeat on the Cambodians. He captured their capital, Lovek, in 1594, and repopulated sections of ravaged Siam with many captives taken from Cambodia. He recovered Siam's suzerain rights over Chiengmai in the very next year when the Burman viceroy had to request his aid against an invasion threat from Luang Prabang. An initial Siamese attack on Pegu failed in 1595, but that city's days were numbered.[51]

The Burma kingdom fell completely apart at the end of the century in an episode which afforded opportunity for Portuguese adventurers to come to the fore. The trouble started between two brothers of Pegu's King Nanda Bayin, one the prince of Prome and the other of Toungoo. When the faltering titular ruler proved unequal to controlling the situation, a general rebellion developed. The powerful Toungoo prince enlisted the cooperation of the King of Arakan in the capture and complete destruction of Pegu in 1599. All semblance of political cohesion vanished in Burma. King Naresuen of Siam arrived too late to share in the booty and was defeated when he attempted to move up the Sittang Valley toward Toungoo. Arakan joined in once more to capture Siam's fleet and to force withdrawal of its army.[52] The captive Peguan King was killed on his arrival at Toungoo. Meanwhile the strong Arakanese fleet occupied the port of Syriam, which the conquerors then placed under the command of a Portuguese mercenary adventurer named Philip de Brito. This event signalized the abandonment of a national kingship including both Mons and Burmans, and Burma ceased thereafter to be an attractive port of call for overseas trade.[53]

[51] Hall, *A History of South-East Asia*, 218–222; W. A. Graham, *Siam* (1912, 1924), I, 193–199.

[52] Ian Macgregor, "A Brief Account of the Kingdom of Pegu," *JBRS*, XVI, part 2 (1926), 99–112.

[53] Hall, *A History of South-East Asia*, 222–223, 324; G. E. Harvey, *History of Burma* (1925), 193–205.

The civilized and prosperous state of Mon Pegu, long highly re-garded as a commercial shipbuilding center, was thus destroyed. Its popu-lation was killed, carried away, or forced into hiding; its buildings and temples were ruined and looted; its roads and waterways were reported clogged with human debris. The Tenasserim coast including Martaban fell under the rule of Siam, which promptly revived its isthmian portage trade via Mergui.[54] Burma's delta ports were thereafter little used. The harbors silted up; shipbuilding ceased; rice fields reverted to jungle. Political leader-ship among the Burmans gravitated to interior Ava, whence the capital was moved in 1635. This event signalized the unfortunate abandonment of the objective of an integrated national kingship including both Mons and Burmans.[55]

## The Twilight of Portuguese Influence

Characteristic of the declining phase of Portuguese influence in Southeast Asia was the proliferation of adventurous escapades on the part of traders and mercenary soldiers of Portuguese descent. One of the most noteworthy was the episode of Philip de Brito as "king" of Syriam, the port of Pegu, from 1599 to 1613. The Portuguese account written several years afterward in Lisbon (1621) attributed the extraordinary events to divine providence and miracle, particularly with reference to the role of de Brito's helper, Salvador Ribeiro de Souza. The account related how three small river craft of de Souza ambushed the entire Burman fleet coming down-stream from Prome, and how twenty-six men with the aid of four wounded drummers allegedly destroyed the entire army camp of the enemy.[56] How-ever exaggerated, the episode was clearly a daring example of opportunist bravado.

Having been left in charge of the Arakanese customhouse at Syriam in 1599, de Brito conceived the idea of building a fortress stronghold in the time-honored Portuguese fashion and of transforming the place into an outpost of the Goan Empire. He received some assistance from the sur-viving remnants of the Mon population, which was hemmed in from Mar-taban by the Siamese and from Toungoo and Prome by Burman enemies. After expelling the governor of Arakan and constructing his fort, de Brito left Ribeiro de Souza in charge and proceeded to Goa to solicit official Portu-

---

[54] E. W. Hitchinson, *Adventures in Siam in the Seventeenth Century* (1940), 12–13. The ten-day portage trip, as here described, ran upstream from Mergui south-eastward across the watershed to Jalinga and thence to Prachuap on the gulf coast. The summer monsoon carried ships thence to the Menam River and upstream to Ayuthia.

[55] Harvey, 193–205; Hall, *A History of South-East Asia*, 222–223, 324.

[56] Macgregor, "A Brief Account of the Kingdom of Pegu," 99–130; F. C. Danvers, *Report on the Portuguese Records Relating to the East Indies* (1892), 20–21.

guese support. Ribeiro and a small group of followers managed from 1599 to 1602 to withstand the land and naval attacks of the angered Arakanese King and his Prome ally, partly by reason of superior defensive tactics, and partly by reason of his enlistment of local Mon support. The Mons offered to make Ribeiro their King, and he accepted. Upon de Brito's return from Goa with a Portuguese commission as captain-general and with six ships containing reinforcements and stores, he took over from the now-disillusioned Ribeiro, who would no longer be party to de Brito's schemes.[57] For more than a decade thereafter Philip de Brito ruled at Syriam. He established a naval patrol off the coast and attempted to force all passing ships to stop and pay toll. Following successive futile attempts to dislodge him, both the Arakan and the Toungoo princes acquiesced in de Brito's assumed role as ruler of Lower Burma between Martaban and Bassein. His son married a daughter of the neighboring Mon chief of Martaban, a vassal to Siam.

De Brito might conceivably have continued indefinitely to enjoy Mon support if he had been willing to forego the plundering of pagoda shrines and efforts at mass conversion to Christianity, policies which presumably were based in part on Goan expectations.[58] Such tactics alienated the Mons, and it was due to the defection of one of the Mon chiefs within the fort that the prince of Ava, King Anaukpetlun, gained entry during a month-long siege in 1613. De Brito's gratuitous attack on Toungoo in 1610, coupled with plunder and arson, had attracted the vengeance of the Burmans. When captured in 1613, de Brito and his officers were summarily killed, and the remainder of the Portuguese garrison, about four hundred strong, were transported inland to several villages near Shwebo as a second elite corps of gunners and musketeers for the Burma army. They were given royal lands and Burmese wives and were permitted to enjoy the ministry of a Catholic priest.[59] The southward advance of King Anaukpetlun continued at this time down to Tenasserim, which was nevertheless successfully defended by the Siamese with the help of Portuguese mercenaries. Portuguese Catholics in Siam had a church and a Jesuit missionary in attendance after 1606. The Siamese Church had been serviced since 1598 from Manila.[60]

The de Brito story in Lower Burma can be matched in Cambodia by that of another soldier of fortune named Diogo Veloso. Early Portuguese missionary contacts with Cambodia, dating from 1555, had encountered strong opposition from Buddhist monks and had been brief affairs. Probably the most exciting result of their entry was the discovery of the ruins of Angkor by two missionaries in 1570. The position of the Portuguese im-

[57] Danvers, *Report*, 20–21. Ribeiro became a hero of Portuguese legend.

[58] Harvey (185–189) tells how de Brito stripped gold and jewels from pagodas and even took temple bells for casting cannon.

[59] Hall, *A History of South-East Asia*, 315–316. Harvey (189) called de Brito a heroic scoundrel, but also adjudged him a more effective ruler than some native princes.

[60] Hutchinson, 21–24.

proved noticeably in 1583–1584, when the Siamese, finally freed from the Burman threat, renewed their relentless pressure on Cambodian Angkor and Lovek. In his extremity, the feeble Cambodian King Satha, who had heard of the potency of the Portuguese mercenaries in the Burman and Siamese armies, decided to enlist some Portuguese help of his own. In connection with the effort, Diogo Veloso and four companions, along with a Dominican padre named d'Azevedo, gained royal favor at Angkor. Veloso married a cousin of the King and became his adopted son; he was placed in command of a kind of praetorian guard at the court. Unfortunately, the first appeals for aid sent to Malacca elicited a negative response. Padre d'Azevedo died in 1589 about the time that Satha shifted his capital back to Lovek, but Veloso accompanied the retreating royal court and continued in high favor.

The inability of Malacca to respond to King Satha's pleas prompted an alternative appeal to Manila, where Spanish authorities were allegedly anxious to gain entry to the Asian mainland for both religious and political reasons. Opportunity for communication with Manila was afforded by the arrival at Lovek in early 1593 of two Spanish soldiers. They had been captured off the Annam coast and had escaped enslavement by fleeing overland to Cambodia. The younger of the two, Blas Ruiz, who had seen previous service in Peru, promptly joined Veloso as a court favorite. Prior to the launching of the final and successful attack on Lovek by the Siamese in late 1593, Veloso was sent to Manila to solicit military aid in return for promised commercial advantages and freedom of missionary operations in Cambodia. The effort failed. Spanish help was not available at the time because Governor Dasmariñas was departing on an ill-fated expedition to the Moluccas, during which he was killed by a mutinous Chinese crew. The mutineers ran off to Annam with the captured vessel. The son of the murdered governor finally prepared a letter for Veloso to take to Satha promising unofficial aid.

The fantastic episode had just begun. The luckless Veloso returned to Cambodia in early 1594 just in time to fall prisoner to Siam's King Naresuen, who had just captured Lovek. Satha and his two sons fled northward to Laos, where the deposed ruler died in 1596. Blas Ruiz and companions were also captured at Lovek and were placed aboard a Siamese prisoner ship for transportation to Ayuthia. Nothing daunted, Ruiz managed to seize the craft and to sail it to Manila, arrived in June, 1594. Meanwhile, the resourceful Veloso gained favor with Siam's King Naresuen and was assigned command of a ship destined also for Manila with a Siamese negotiator and a cargo of benzoin aboard. Ayuthia's instructions to Veloso were to solicit Spanish aid for Siam against an expected renewal of attacks from Burma.[61] No one could doubt the versatility of the Europeans. The last phase of the

[61] B. P. Groslier, *Angkor et le Cambodge au XVIe Siècle* (1958), 19–41; A. Hamilton, *A New Account of the East Indies (1688 to 1723)* (1727), II, 105–114. Hamilton is apparently inaccurate in many details here.

escapade of the adventurous pair will be related in a later chapter in connection with the Spanish effort to intervene militarily in Cambodia from 1596 to 1599.

As a sequel to Veloso's amazing performance, Portuguese influence persisted in Phnom Penh into the early 1700s. An English visitor to Cambodia in 1717 reported the presence of some two hundred Goan Portuguese who still held posts under the Cambodian King, some as interpreters, some as Shahbandars. All of them were enjoying pensions from the ruler. They no longer paid any deference to the exhortations of the resident Catholic padre. Cambodia during the interim was caught inextricably in the crossfire of Vietnamese-Siamese rivalry. Incidentally, two Portuguese monks described the ruins of Angkor Wat under restoration in 1570.[62]

The influence of the Portuguese in Vietnam was somewhat less important than elsewhere. They made contact with the coast on at least four occasions between 1516 and 1540, often enough to name the Mekong delta area Cochin-China to distinguish it from Cochin, India. The trade of Vietnam in the sixteenth century was largely with China and the Liuchiu islanders, the latter trade continuing long after the Tokugawa closed off the trade of Japan proper. Portuguese trade with Vietnam was mainly a shuttle traffic between Macao and the ports of Annam, dealing in firearms and Chinese wares. The Portuguese at Macao found that cannon and firearms were perennially in demand.[63]

## *The Decline of Portuguese Power*

The basic reason for the final collapse of Portuguese power in Southeast Asia was military. Neither Malacca nor the Portuguese forts in the Spice Islands proved able to withstand the superior naval power of the Dutch and English enemies of Portugal's Spanish rulers. Philip II not only neglected the interests of his Portuguese subjects after taking over as King in 1580, but he gratuitously provoked trouble with the Netherlands by interfering with free Dutch access to spice supplies at Lisbon. Because the Portuguese were unable to keep abreast of European improvements in ships, navigational equipment, and personnel discipline, they lost control from 1606 to 1614 of the Malabar Coast shipping, the Malacca Straits, and the Moluccas. But the contest was waged to the end with spirit and tenacity. The Dutch captured Malacca in 1641 after several previous failures at attack and three decades of naval interference. The final siege lasted almost a decade. It involved in the end the Dutch purchase of surplus-rice supplies in both Arakan and Siam in order to deny it to the beleaguered and famine-ridden city. Not until 1638 did the Dutch gain from the Portuguese a foothold on Ceylon, and it was 1658 before the Portuguese withdrew. They were

[62] M. Ghosh, *A History of Cambodia* (1960), 232–238, 243. The Dominican discoverers of Angkor were Lopo Cardozo and João Madeira.

[63] J. J. Van Klavern, *The Dutch Colonial System* (1953), 30–32.

never ousted from Goa or Macao. In the end they simply ran out of the resources and manpower needed to sustain their trading empire, but it took an equally determined European power to displace them.

What would have happened if they had not squandered their limited resources on interminable warfare or had found some more constructive outlet for the energies of the multitude of adventurous spirits among them is hardly a proper topic for historical treatment. It is equally irrelevant to consider the positive or negative effects on their survival as a power of their characteristic crusading and missionizing commitments; without these they would not have been Portuguese. After virtually all political and commercial power had been hopelessly lost, Lisbon and Goa held on tenaciously to their *patronato* monopoly of missionary direction and control throughout Eastern Asia.

What may be historically relevant is a characterization of the importance of certain parts of Portuguese policy. Malacca, despite internal corruption and external interference, retained its role as a potentially profitable entrepôt almost to the very end, a port rivaled in the Orient only by Canton. Nonetheless, Portuguese interference in the normal flow of the spice trade undoubtedly ruined many port merchants of central and eastern Java, victimized the Spice Islanders, and greatly inconvenienced the Gujerati cloth merchants. The latter managed by means of defiance of Portuguese rules, licensing arrangements, and open bribery to keep a fairly substantial flow of spices reaching the Near Eastern cities.[64] Generally, the Portuguese exploited trade instead of developing it. They contributed little or nothing to commercial activity, and their operations were parasitic rather than capitalist and limited to a small volume of costly luxury goods. Their only demonstration of unquestioned superiority was in the military field, frequently to be adjudged a rather dubious contribution.[65]

There remains the fact of Portuguese alienation of peoples through chronic abuse of their power to coerce. The mixed race which took over the Portuguese name after several generations of intermarriage was probably less capable of discipline than Albuquerque's followers, but its members were probably not less arrogant, avaricious, and daring. One of their more candid historians of the seventeenth century left the following comment on the dire sufferings experienced by a shipwrecked Portuguese crew in Natal, Africa:

> *These misadventures, and others which happen daily on the India voyage, should serve as warnings . . . to the fidalgo Captains of Fortresses, for them to moderate their excesses . . . letting the poor live in peace. For the Sun in Heaven and the water in the spring were not given by God for the great alone. . . . Cruelties and wrongs which we see used daily towards*

[64] R. O. Winstedt, *Malaya* (1956), 146; Moorhead, 205–217; W. H. Moreland and A. C. Chatterjee, *Short History of India* (1953), 197–203.

[65] J. C. Van Leur, *Indonesian Trade and Society* (1955), 117–119, 159–166.

*the poor in those fortresses have deeply horrified us. But God is so just, that even though Kings now neglect to punish the culprits, He does it with a far heavier hand.*[66]

A final comment concerns the historical advantages and handicaps derived from the availability of European sources of information beginning with the advent of the Portuguese. The magnificently informative descriptive essay of Tomé Pires, translated and first published under the direction of the Hakluyt Society in 1944, is a major case in point. Three other great contemporary Portuguese historians, who along with Camoens fostered the flowering of the Portuguese language in a kind of delayed Renaissance, contributed their matchless *Decados da Asia.* João de Barros (b. 1496) wrote especially on China, Siam, and Ceylon. Diogo de Conto (b. 1542), who was quoted above, spent fifty years as soldier and writer on India's west coast; he was a salty commentator but enormously industrious. The third was the partly Jewish and only nominally Catholic Antonio Bocarro (b. 1594), who wrote voluminous descriptions of fortresses, cities, and towns of east India.[67] Much else in the way of historical sources continued after 1641 to be collected and preserved at Goa. The indelible Portuguese influence was reflected in the continued widespread use of the Portuguese language in Southeast Asia as well as Goa and Ceylon. To the secular Portuguese historical documents must be added the missionary contributions, linguistic studies, maps, and descriptive items collected under the supervision of the Portuguese patronage system. No longer is the Western student of Southeast Asian history dependent on Chinese records of tributary missions or other more general commentaries. The handicap and the danger also lie just there, that Southeast Asia comes to be represented after the Portuguese intrusion overmuch through European eyes.

[66] Diogo de Canto, quoted in C. R. Boxer, *Three Historians of Portuguese Asia* (1948), 21.

[67] Boxer, 6–28.

PART 4

*European Commercial Dominance*

# CHAPTER 10

# The Dutch

## Commercial Empire

The decline of Portugal's naval power in Southeast Asia at the end of the 1500s, attributable to neglect and attrition, opened the way for European rivals to invade its spice-and-pepper trading monopoly. The leadership was taken mainly by the Dutch, who for a generation had been fighting for their national survival against Philip II of Spain. The action of Philip II in 1594 in denying Dutch access to the spices available at the port of Lisbon left the Dutch little choice but to seek Oriental products for themselves. The English cooperated with the Dutch in challenging Goa's assumed monopoly of the trade of India's west coast, but the English Crown and Company were not prepared, especially after James I's accession, to join the Dutch in any deliberate assault on the position of the Iberian powers in Southeast Asia. In the end the superior financial and naval resources of the Dutch Company combined with greater determination and constancy of purpose elevated the Dutch to a position of unchallenged leadership in the trade of Southeast Asia. Portuguese control was eliminated from both Malacca and Ceylon, and Goa's power was rendered innocuous.

The commercial empire of the Dutch was based on a firm territorial foothold in Java. That island became the hub of a vast trading arc extending from Persia, India, and Ceylon on the west to the Moluccas, China, and Japan on the east and north. Only Spanish Manila, which will be treated in the next chapter, escaped inclusion in the Dutch trading system. It was essentially a business enterprise, in which widely scattered factory centers promoted maximum opportunities for exchange, whereas the Portuguese had conducted merely a collecting operation. Trade between Asian ports received priority under the Dutch system. Eventually, Java became under Dutch leadership the world's center of coffee production through the transplanting of an entirely alien culture. Immigrant Chinese traders came to play an increasingly important role, as both suppliers of Chinese goods and middlemen, in the expanding commercial activity of Southeast Asia. The Dutch Empire declined during the late decades of the 1700s.

## The European Context

Both the English and the Dutch concern with challenging the Portuguese monopoly of trade to the Orient was provoked gratuitously by Philip II of Spain, following his assumption of the Portuguese Crown in 1580. Before then English overseas exploration had been confined primarily to futile efforts to find a northeast or a northwest passage to the fabled markets of Cathay. When these efforts failed, the overland route to China via Russia and the Middle East was explored with similarly discouraging results. England's only substantial surplus for export was woolen broadcloth, which was salable only in the colder climates and was emphatically not attractive to Indians or Southeast Asians.

The completion of Drake's sensational world-circling voyage in 1580, with its cargo of Ternate spices, stimulated the organization of England's Levant Company (1581) and also gave rise to an abortive venture into the South Atlantic by one Captain Fenton under sponsorship of Queen Elizabeth and the Earl of Leicester. The most successful and informed of the early English visitors to Southeast Asia was Robert Fitch, who returned to England in 1591 with a discouraging report on the gloomy possibilities and prospects of English trade in the area. Meanwhile the defeat of the Spanish Armada in 1588 decimated both Lisbon's and Spain's Atlantic naval power and transformed anti-Spanish feeling from a kind of open season for hunting on the part of Devon and Cornwall sea dogs to a national rallying behind Good Queen Bess. After the revived naval efforts of the Dutch from 1595 seriously challenged the Portuguese monopoly, English traders took an active interest in reaching Southeast Asia.[1]

The Dutch were subjected to more direct provocation than the English to end the Portuguese-Spanish monopoly. They lived by trade, and the distribution of Oriental pepper and spices in northern Europe was an essential part of their commercial operations. The original prohibition of Dutch access to Lisbon, issued by Philip II in 1580, was not effectively enforced. False flags were used, and Lisbon asked few questions. The ruling was enforced temporarily after 1585, but another period of tolerance ensued. It was in 1594 that Lisbon was firmly and irrevocably closed to the Dutch. By that time, the Dutch traveler Linschoten had returned from his nine-year visit to Indian and Southeast Asian ports in 1592. He proceeded to publish his *Itinerario* and sailing manual, with maps, in 1595 and 1596. An English translation appeared in 1598. After 1596 Dutch mariners began an uncoordinated but persistent effort to reach the Spice Islands, some proceeding around Africa, some via the Straits of Magellan. Twelve or thirteen expeditions were sent out over a period of five years, including more than three-

[1] William Foster, *England's Quest for Eastern Trade* (1933), 14–46, 60, 79–107.

score vessels. A Dutch fleet in the Java Sea was first attacked by the Portuguese from Malacca in 1597.

By 1599, the route via the Cape of Good Hope and thence directly to the Sunda Straits had attained general acceptance as the fastest and most feasible one for Dutch ships to follow. It bypassed Portuguese Goa, Ceylon, and Malacca, was independent of the monsoon winds, and made direct contact with East Indies islanders who appeared only too happy to cooperate with an enemy of the hated Portuguese. For the returning portion of the twenty-two ships which undertook the 1598–1600 voyage via this route, the profits realized were fabulous.[2] The Dutch established a temporary trading headquarters at Bantam, a pepper port in western Java, and extended their exploratory contacts to Ceylon, Siam, Indochina, Luzon, and Japan.

After peace negotiations between England and Spain had been partly concluded in the late months of 1600, the English East India Company was launched, on the very last day of the year. The peace settlement was very tentative, for neither Spain nor Portugal surrendered its exclusive trading claims; nor did London concede them. The English venture into the Orient clearly depended on Dutch willingness to bear the brunt of Portuguese opposition and also on the probable reluctance of Portugal to court additional opposition by breaking the peace with England. Since the English ships had little to carry as exports marketable in the pepper-and-spice areas, they also counted on the cooperation of Indian cloth merchants to provide them with East Indies cargoes.[3] The English Company was also handicapped by the lack of adequate capital funds; the Dutch East India Company, which was formed in 1602, commanded ten times the assets of its English counterpart.[4] For the Dutch the venture was a full and irrevocable commitment essential to the national interest; for the English it was something of an opportunist affair, falling short of a full commitment both politically and economically. The charter for the Dutch Company, granted by the States General in 1602, combined the resources of six participating chambers of commerce.[5]

## Dutch Victory in the Indies

The Portuguese lost no time in challenging the Dutch intrusion. In spite of the fact that the English blockade of Lisbon in 1599 eliminated any possible aid from Portugal, Admiral Mendoza collected thirty fighting

[2] J. J. Van Klavern, *The Dutch Colonial System* (1953), 36–37. Dutch misbehavior made bitter enemies at Madura and in the Banda Islands.

[3] Foster, 136–184. Downton's voyage of 1614 spent two-thirds of its subscription cost to purchase Spanish rials of eight. Another one-seventh was in broadcloth.

[4] D. G. E. Hall, *A History of South-East Asia* (1955), 224–232. Dutch capital amounted to 6.5 million guilders.

[5] *Ibid.*, 232–235; B. H. M. Vlekke, *Nusantara* (1960), 115–119.

ships from Goa and Malacca for his assault. The results were inconclusive. The attackers failed to drive the Dutch from Bantam or from Ternate, but they did strengthen their hold on alternative spice sources at Tidore and Amboina. The control of the Java Sea fell to the Dutch following a decisive naval victory in 1602. By 1605, however, a Spanish fleet from Manila captured pro-Dutch Ternate and carried its ruler as captive to Manila. Meanwhile the Portuguese garrison at Amboina ran out of munitions and surrendered to the Dutch.

By that time, James I had concluded a definitive English peace with Spain (1604), so that the English spice traders thereafter stood aside as nonparticipants in the continuing Dutch-Spanish conflict over the Moluccas. The English tactics were illustrated in 1606 by Henry Middleton, who worked both sides of the street. He obtained cloves from Ternate in return for rescuing its new ruler and three Dutch merchants from Tidore captors and then dickered with the Portuguese at Tidore for purchase of their spice holdings on the argument that the Dutch would shortly leave them no alternative but to surrender it all.[6] Middleton gained a full cargo in such fashion at the cost of some English prestige. The Dutch Company, engaged as it was in fortifying and defending Dutch holdings, in making treaties and dispensing justice, resented the tactics of allegedly irresponsible English intruders who followed them around making friends of their enemies and threatening to glut the European market for spices. After ousting the hated Spanish from Ternate in 1608, the Dutch in 1610 ordered English ships also to stay out of the Moluccas.[7] But Dutch monopoly claims were based on the terms of a bilateral treaty with the Sultan of Ternate, who had solicited Dutch protection against the Spanish.

The English also encountered difficulties with both Indians and Portuguese off the Indian Malabar Coast. Since Indian cloth from Cambay was an essential item of exchange for the purchase of both spices and pepper, the English Company directed its initial efforts to making arrangements for commercial access to Gujerati ports. Portuguese and Indian opposition was finally overcome by 1613. The Mogul Emperor Jahangir agreed to the location of an English factory at Surat after having his own naval altercation with the Portuguese. A series of bitterly contested Portuguese-English fights ensued when the Portuguese opposed English participation in the Indian cloth market.[8] Goa did not give up easily, for it intrigued later with Jahangir; but the Portuguese cause was doomed.

Dutch-British negotiations conducted in Europe from 1612 to 1615

[6] William Foster, *The Voyage of Sir Henry Middleton, 1604–1606* (1943), xxiv–xxxii.

[7] Foster, *England's Quest*, 198–207; George Masselman, "Dutch Policy in the Seventeenth Century," *Journal of Economic History*, XXI (December, 1961), 455–460.

[8] William Foster, *The Voyage of Thomas Best to the East Indies, 1612–1617* (1934), i–xli.

found the Dutch government far more conciliatory than the Amsterdam Company on the question of England's access to the Indies trade. The conference came to nought when the English insisted on maintaining peace with Spain and refused, therefore, to share the costs of continued anti-Spanish military operations in Southeast Asia, as contemplated by the Dutch. Using cloth and opium as cargoes, the English voyagers, operating after 1614 in joint-stock ventures, developed contacts on their own at Acheh, Bantam, Patani, and Macassar in a sustained effort to obtain spices. The most persistent and daring of the English Company commanders was probably John Jourdain, who ventured directly into the Moluccas in 1613–1614. He offered a premium of 8 rials of eight per bahar (500 pounds) of cloves over the Dutch price of some 50 rials. When some of the smaller of Ternate's vassal islanders accepted Jourdain's generous offer, they were later victimized for violating Ternate's contract to sell to no one but the Dutch. Jourdain thereupon returned and offered to make good the fines assessed by the Dutch. He left the area under Dutch threats but with a full cargo. Jourdain died fighting the Dutch in 1619 at Patani.[9]

British-Dutch relations in the Indies degenerated to open warfare from 1618 to 1620, with the stronger well-directed Dutch forces having the better of the contest. The Anglo-Dutch alliance against Spain, concluded in Europe in 1619, allocated one-half of the pepper and two-thirds of the spice output to the Dutch and called for the assignment by each party of ten naval ships and an equal sharing of both trading and military costs in future ventures. But the agreement was never really applied in the Indies. It encountered the obdurate hostility of the Dutch governor at Jacatra (renamed Batavia), the imperious Jan Pieterzoon Coen, who was blockading Bantam at the time and rendering it unusable by the English. English traders who shifted to the new Dutch port of Batavia found themselves subjected to Dutch rules. Coen subsequently raised the expenses of proposed joint operations, both commercial and military, so high that the English were unable to assume their agreed 50 per cent of the cost. The Dutch "Massacre of Amboina" in early 1623, when more than two-thirds of the occupants of the English factory were executed for alleged conspiracy, ended all further pretense of cooperation. The English shifted their Java headquarters back to Bantam from 1628 to 1682. They also continued to call at the Javan port of Japara until 1652 and at Macassar until 1667. The Portuguese, Danish, and French traders also used Macassar and Bantam for a time.

It was not until thirty years after the Amboina affair, following Cromwell's victorious Dutch war in 1652–1654, that the question of English trading rights in the Indies was again raised and Holland made amends for the arbitrary executions at Amboina. The English Company thereafter could enter the Indies but not to trade with designated ports which were under Dutch monopoly control. The English East India Company did not

[9] William Foster, *The Journal of John Jourdain, 1608–1617* (1905), 241, 271–274, 365–368.

become heavily involved in the quarrel between Charles I and Parliament until after 1647 and maintained throughout the course of the civil war its desultory operations on the fringes of Indonesia. Meanwhile, the Dutch eliminated Portuguese Malacca in 1641 and entrenched themselves firmly in Java and the Moluccas. Spain finally abandoned Tidore in 1663. The avoidance of serious Dutch involvement in Europe's Thirty Years' War left them free to outdistance all native and European competitors in the Asian trade.[10]

## Southeast Asian Setting: The Java Sea

The most prosperous Javan port of call for Europeans in the early 1600s was the pepper station of Bantam on the western end of the island. The wealthy Sultan profited from competitive bargaining for its products, but the port was notoriously badly governed. The staff of the English factory established at the port in 1602, for example, reported that the local Sultan afforded no police protection whatever and himself resorted to blackmail in order to extract forced loans from foreigners. The business area was overrun by disreputable Chinese who were capable of promoting their predatory ends by arson, kidnapping, and direct assault as well as by ordinary thievery. The only feasible protective device available to Europeans was to hire other Chinese, on promise of generous rewards if successful, to protect factory premises. This amounted in fact to a more moderate kind of Chinese blackmail. Despite the bitter rivalry between the English and the Dutch elsewhere, they had to band together for self-protection at Bantam. Alongside the Chinese criminals and counterfeiters were ranged a number of responsible Chinese traders operating a thriving junk trade from Canton and other ports of the Fukien coast. They usually insisted on taking all available Spanish rials back to China, and the Europeans trusted them sufficiently to sell goods to them on credit.

Not all the negative goings on at Bantam were attributable to the Orientals, however. One English factor related that following a drunken revel, a Dutch naval officer fired into the court premises of the Sultan himself, just for fun.[11] Europeans were contributing their share of disorder. The editor of one of the early Hakluyt publications was constrained to defend English Company servants against the allegedly scurrilous charges that they were "an ungodly set of gluttons, drunkards, and miscellaneous debauchees." Such critical recipients of Company hospitality in the Orient, he argued, did not comprehend that such occasions were "part of the high Roman living of their day."[12] Bantam, like Portuguese Malacca and also Batavia later, was

[10] Hall, 244–250.

[11] Foster, *Middleton*, xix–xx, 97–126. The Bantam reporter characterized his arsonist neighbor, a Chinese innkeeper and liquor distiller, as an "offspring of the Divell and heire of hell."

[12] Christopher Birdwood and William Foster, *The Register and Letters of the Governor and Company of Merchants of London* (1893), xxi.

a deadly place for Europeans to live. Dysentery, fever, and scurvy took a terrifying toll of life at all port cities.

It was hardly surprising under the circumstances prevailing at Bantam that the newly appointed Dutch Governor-General Coen decided in 1618 to establish a fortified trading center in western Java independent of Bantam and discreetly distant from the powerful Javan state of Mataram. Mataram had established itself as the successor of the disintegrated Majapahit state in central Java following the conquest of the strong port city of Demak in 1588, an action also associated with Mataram's formal allegiance to Islam. Coen acquired possession of Jacatra almost by default. By 1619, the Dutch port of Batavia was in operation on the site, equipped with harbor, canals for drainage and transportation, and a protecting fort. Coen moved none too soon, for in the same year the aggressive Sultan Agung of Mataram (1613 and later) reduced Cheribon province behind Batavia to vassalage status, along with the northern port city of Tuban. Madura Island fell to Agung in 1624 and Surabaya in 1625. Bantam was the next major prize on Agung's list, and only the tiny Dutch post of Batavia barred the most accessible coastal route leading to the western end of the island. Meanwhile the Dutch took advantage of the time afforded them to consolidate their defensive position.[13]

The task of conquering the ladang-cultivated Sundanese area of western Java, which had for so many centuries defied control by central Java, was undertaken by Mataram in 1628–1629. Batavia was the initial objective. The army of Mataram on this occasion paid a dear price for its ruler's disdain for sea power, which had never been revived after the conquest of his port city enemies. The huge Javanese army avoided the inhospitable interior and attempted to advance along the shoreline, where it was dependent on transportation by sea of the necessary food and military supplies. When the Dutch fleet successfully destroyed Mataram's supply lines, the attack of emaciated Javanese forces on Batavia was easily beaten off. The Dutch thus gained a major victory at trifling cost. Mataram continued to hold the allegiance of its many native vassals and persisted for another fifty years as the leading power of Java. It extended its control to the Bali Strait in 1639 and made an abortive effort to capture that island. But in the end its aggressive power was spent. Mataram was never able to complete the conquest of the western end of the island or to generate enough naval power to challenge Dutch control of the Java Sea.[14]

Most of the labor of construction at Batavia was done by Chinese immigrants, who also fitted actively into the Dutch trading pattern. Governor-General Coen began the practice of leaving virtually all retail trade, including neighboring coastal traffic, to the resident Chinese colony. At Batavia the Chinese selected their own headman, who was responsible for

---

[13] Van Klavern, 26–27; Vlekke, 128–135, 145.

[14] Van Klavern, 46, 49; Harry Benda, "The Structure of Southeast Asian History," *JSEAH*, III (1962), 122–124; Vlekke, 149.

settling civil disputes and for maintaining order within the community. Chinese were also the leading dealers in locally produced rice, sugar, and distilled arrack liquors. They were usually the high bidders for monopoly posts covering the collection of ship dues, bazaar fees, and taxes on salt production. The economic power gained by the Chinese proved in the end to be damaging to the interests of many Javanese.[15] Much trouble would come of Chinese involvement in Java and elsewhere.

The Banda and Molucca islanders bore the brunt of the ruthless assertion of Dutch control as few others were obliged to do. When the entire populations of several of the rebellious islands (such as Lonthor and Run) refused to accept Dutch control, their members were either eliminated or sold into slavery in Java. Elsewhere the surplus spice plants were systematically destroyed whenever there appeared to be danger of overproduction. After 1650 the Dutch ruled that the Banda Islands could grow only nutmeg and Amboina only cloves.[16] The Dutch may have overplayed their hand in the Moluccas economically as well as in physical abuse, for they spent enormous sums in their conquest of the area and in their manning of naval patrols and fortress installations. The nonexpanding spice trade was destined to play a diminishing role in the growing pattern of Dutch commerce.[17]

Indonesian ships using the Java Sea were required to carry a Dutch Company passport describing the cargo and destination of every trip on pain of enslavement of crews or outright extermination. Macassar held out longest against this ruling. As indicated before, it permitted not only English but also Danish, Portuguese, and French ships to call down to 1667 and long served as a rival center of spice trade. After 1667 Macassar's vagrant seamen resorted to piracy and to mercenary employ, as in the case of their participation in Madura's attack on Mataram in 1675. The Dutch also eliminated the south Borneo pirate base of Banjermasin. Macassar's fall in 1667 marked the beginning of a new era of Dutch imperial rule. The Dutch conquered Mataram (1678–1680), Bantam (1682), and virtually all of the eastern islands except commercially unattractive areas like Bali, Lombok, the shores of the Macassar Straits, and northern Borneo.[18]

## Sumatra and Malaya under the Dutch

At the extreme western end of the Indonesian island chain, the advent of the Dutch and the English found the Sultan of Acheh exerting a powerful influence. Taking advantage of his truce with the Portuguese

[15] Writser Jans Cator, *The Economic Position of the Chinese in the Netherlands Indies* (1936), 3–8.

[16] Van Klavern, 45–46. Crop surpluses were destroyed on Ternate in 1650, at Makjan and Batjan in 1656, and at Tidore in 1667.

[17] Hall, 250–251.

[18] Van Klavern, 46–49; Vlekke, 168–172, 200.

(since 1587), he had extended his control through the entire length of Sumatra along both coasts and into Malaya from the Johore frontier as far north as Kedah and Patani, excepting only Malacca itself. Acheh reached its peak of power from 1620 to 1636 when it bid fair to realize the aim of dominating the straits. European visitors in the early 1600s found Acheh glutted with goods, especially Surat cloth, which was purchasable there for little more than it cost in the Bay of Cambay. The Sultan was clearly trying to monopolize the cloth trade to the extent of prohibiting Gujerati access to other Sumatran or Malay ports under Achehnese control. One English commander, badly in need of an interpreter to counter the tactics of grasping and unprincipled local brokers, purchased from the King of Acheh a Portuguese-speaking Gujerati slave well acquainted with the region. Acheh confiscated ships and enslaved the crews of native traders found trespassing in the straits within its claimed preserves. European captains were annoyed at being obliged in the early 1600s to obtain permits at Acheh for pepper trading at such upper Sumatran ports as Passaman, Tiku, Baros, and Preamon, and then only after much haggling.[19]

The Dutch made the original mistake of allying with Johore against Portuguese Malacca in 1606. They quickly discovered that they must keep on good terms, at least for the time being, with the powerful Achehnese. When a Dutch captain staged a foray against the shipping of Acheh, the Company quickly arranged to compensate the Sultan for the loss. While heavily involved in the problems of the Banda seas and in Java (to 1629), the Dutch could do little more than keep Malacca under intermittent attack. The serious blockade began in 1633, and the port was ruined commercially by 1635. But it was another six years before the final assault was successfully undertaken. During the interim, Pahang was attacked by Johore, and the Siamese attempted to take over Kedah and Trengganu on opposite sides of the peninsula. The final Dutch assault was made in cooperation with Johore and Minangkabau forces but not with Acheh, which all Malays except Pahang hated. Portuguese Malacca surrendered in part from starvation, the Dutch having had the foresight to corner the surplus rice of Arakan and Siam to prevent its reaching the beleaguered port. The Dutch nevertheless lost more than one thousand of the twenty-three hundred men in their attacking force from combat or disease.

The Dutch took over a ruined city and a wasting economic asset in Malacca. Most of the trading population had fled the city by 1635. Some seven thousand persons lost their lives during the course of the siege, and the former population of twenty thousand was reduced to sixteen hundred or less at the time of capture. Material destruction was widespread, and the subsequent outbreak of plague provided additional discouragement. Some improvement in trade was realized by 1650 in such locally produced staples

---

[19] Foster, *The Voyage of Thomas Best,* 256–258; Foster, *The Voyage of Nicholas Downton,* xxix–xxxi.

as pepper in consequence of the vigorous assertion of Dutch monopoly controls. The port operated at a chronic deficit nonetheless. It was 1668 before the Dutch were successful in curbing the monopolistic pretensions of Acheh, a development affording opportunity to bring the trade of other west coast Sumatran ports under effective Dutch control. But the peoples of interior Sumatra and Borneo were little affected by the presence of Europeans.

The Portuguese proved to be the only non-Dutch group to make regular use of the port facilities of Malacca. This was necessary for the Goan contacts with Macao and other Portuguese holdings in the Indies. Muslim Indian traders preferred to limit their contacts to the northern periphery of the straits—Acheh, Kedah, Junk Ceylon, and Takuapa. Traders from China had never liked the Portuguese system, and their fellow countrymen operating from Siam and Cambodia wanted free access to Malay tin, which was being extracted in large measure through Chinese initiative. Chinese junks proceeding southward were pressed by the Dutch to visit Batavia rather than Malacca in any case. Semipiratical Buginese operated from the south end of the straits in open defiance of Dutch monopoly claims. The Dutch themselves controlled the Java trade.

Malacca served Dutch interests as a place for the assembly and exchange of cargoes to be used in the interocean trade and as a defense installation to prevent any rival from exercising control at so vital a point. The port failed to develop materially either in population or in volume of trade. In 1660, the once-thriving entrepôt was merely a provincial center of the Dutch-Javanese Empire, with fewer than five thousand inhabitants, one-third of them slaves. In 1660, of the nonslave population 1,470 were Portuguese-Eurasian, 588 were Malays, 547 were Indians, 426 were Chinese, and only 145 were Dutch.[20] A visitor at Malacca during the early decades of the 1700s described the Dutch church located on top of the hill with a flag flying from its steeple, visible to all passing ships. The nearby fort, large and strong, was a full league from the shipping roadstead. Local production was limited to tin, ivory, and fruits. All grain had to be imported because untamed island neighbors, by their thefts and burnings, made agriculture impossible.[21]

The equivocal policy pursued by the Dutch was largely responsible for their failure to develop Malacca into a commercial and financial asset. They wanted to restore the trade of the city but not at the expense of the maximum growth of Batavia. They undertook to monopolize the trade in tin and pepper produced in the straits area by means of treaties imposed on neighboring sultans. But they refused to pay a competitive price for either commodity, especially tin, and failed to provide the naval patrols required for enforcing their treaty claims. They levied a customs duty on

[20] Richard O. Winstedt, *Malaya and Its History* (1948), 47–53.
[21] Alexander Hamilton, *A New Account of the East Indies (1688 to 1723)* (1727), II, 43–45.

imports and exports of 5 and 10 per cent respectively without providing available alternative cargoes for visiting traders. Their patrol of the straits, which was the only service capable of justifying their assessment of the 4½ per cent license fee for the use of the straits, was not sufficient to curb piratical operations. Malay politics, especially around Johore, degenerated into a state of perpetual feuding between Buginese and Minangkabau partisans, with local inhabitants, including the sultan, acting as mere pawns in the game.

Dutch monopoly control of the straits was also limited by agreements made with England in Europe following Cromwell's war in 1654 and in the English-Dutch alliance of 1674 (after repudiation of Charles II's treaty of Dover). English Company vessels were then accorded gratis use of the straits. This concession was reaffirmed after the Crowns of Holland and England were temporarily joined under William and Mary, in 1689. The privileges granted to the English became increasingly important during the course of the eighteenth century.

## Siam, Burma, and Vietnam: Relations with Europeans

Both the Dutch and the English traders received a hearty welcome from Ayuthia in the early 1600s. Siam recovered rapidly from its unhappy experiences connected with the Burma wars of the previous century. Three ports were available for Siamese trade—Mergui on the Bay of Bengal side, Patani in northeastern Malaya, and Ayuthia itself. The Anglo-Dutch rivalry at Ayuthia from 1612 to 1622 was bitterly contested, involving open fighting in 1619. Jourdain was killed at Patani while negotiating his surrender to the Dutch under a flag of truce. The Dutch also outbid the English commercially. A Siamese embassy journeyed to The Hague in 1608–1609, and a treaty was concluded in 1617. The English Company withdrew completely from Siam in 1622.

The Dutch exchanged valuable cloth for Siamese rice and also carried quantities of Siamese pepper and hides to China and Japan. Following Siam's receipt of Dutch military assistance in the early 1630s against Cambodia and rebellious Patani, a Dutch factory of solid brick construction was established at Ayuthia, inaugurating a forty-year period of Dutch trade domination. Batavian trading operations were extended temporarily to Cambodia in 1636, to Tongking in 1637, and to interior Laos in 1641, but with discouraging results. Cambodia and the Dutch were at war in 1643–1644. Until 1674 English interest in the Siam trade was on a purely private basis. The Dutch traders at Ayuthia grew wealthy and strong, contributed handsomely to the court for enjoyment of trading rights, and rode out successive periods of friction.[22] The most serious diversion accompanied a

[22] Hall, 255. Two life-sized statues of Dutch traders dressed in all their seventeenth-century finery can be seen in Bangkok's famous Wat Po.

French intervention in the 1670s and 1680s, to be considered in a later chapter. Private trade was permitted at Ayuthia in surplus and noncontraband items, but the Siamese treasury official (Shahbandar) had first claim on all cargo purchases and provided all export items intended for exclusive sale to foreigners.[23]

Seventeenth-century Burma was almost as uninterested in seaborne trade as the Siamese were in favor of it. The one exception was independent Arakan, where rice surpluses were available for most of the century. Especially after 1635, when the Burma capital was shifted to inland Ava, the problems of trade with Burma became difficult. Both the Dutch and the English Companies were active, but with discouraging results. One Crown-supported English "Association of Merchants" (William Courteen and Paul Pindar) became interested in Ava from 1635 to 1646 outside the East India Company monopoly. Negotiations with Ava proved somewhat less expensive than local bribery, but they were at best slow and arduous. The Ava Court refused to enter into permanent written agreements, so that every new ruler had to be approached *de novo*. Stranded or shipwrecked sailors on Burma's coasts were usually enslaved. The long Irrawaddy River trip to Ava had its hazards, and duties were high. Some profits were nevertheless realized by the English traders, who maintained factories at both Syriam and Ava for a decade after 1647.

During the Anglo-Dutch war of 1652–1654, the Dutch succeeded in halting English trade to Burma, about the same time that Burma itself lost interest. The English factory at Syriam was kept open until 1657 in an effort to collect past debts, while the English factor in charge profited from illegal private trade. In the face of the increasing severity of Burma's export restrictions, Siam's Mergui port attracted much of the Bay of Bengal trade after 1660. England's Syriam factory was reopened briefly in 1680 as a source of saltpeter, stick lac, and musk. The Dutch had meanwhile given up in Burma in 1676.[24]

In 1637 the Dutch also opened a factory at Pho-hien (near Hungyen) in Tongking, where trade had previously been dominated by the Chinese and Japanese. They made commercial contact with the capital at Hué as well. The English gained the right to share Dutch access to Pho-hien and Hué in 1654, but their establishment of factories was delayed until 1672 and 1683. The Dutch thwarted a French effort to locate a factory in Vietnam in 1680, but the trade proved unattractive because rival political factions were forever feuding. Both Companies broke off trade with Vietnam by 1700. Only an intermittent Vietnamese trade in arms with Portuguese Macao

[23] E. W. Hutchinson, *Adventures in Siam in the Seventeenth Century* (1940), 21–40. Hutchinson is apparently in error over the alleged English Company connections with both Cambodia and Siam from 1658 to 1674. See D. K. Basset, *New Light on English Relations with Siam.*

[24] D. G. E. Hall, *Early English Intercourse with Burma, 1587–1743* (1928), 49–60, 69–84, 99, 105–125.

persisted. Even so the seventeenth-century contact with European traders developed in Vietnam a new category of merchants and intermediaries not previously present.[25]

Vietnam's primary political interest during the last half of the 1600s was to increase its domination over Cambodia in competition with Siam. Vietnam nominated a puppet Cambodian ruler after an invasion in 1658 and exercised a dominant influence at Phnom Penh from 1675 to 1710, when Siam again intervened.[26]

## Establishment of Dutch Trading Supremacy

The powers conferred on the Dutch East India Company by the States General extended far beyond its exclusive right to trade in the East Indies. It was empowered to dispense justice, to employ and direct the use of troops, to conclude alliances with native princes, and to conduct diplomatic and commercial relations generally. The seventeen governors of the Company, resident in the Netherlands, were usually hesitant about assuming unnecessary political commitments. They set basic policy objectives, controlled finances, and specified what the nature of the returning cargoes should be. Whereas similar joint-stock ventures operating in a European context functioned as integral elements of a growing competitive economic system, the Dutch East India Company was shielded from domestic competition and was subject to neither legal nor social restraints over what its agents did in Asia. Furthermore, the important decisions in the execution of policy were often made by the men on the spot without any reference to Holland. During the first two or three decades of the existence of the Company, it functioned primarily as an imperial and naval power, not as a trading organization interested in profits. Dividends to stockholders were customarily paid out of capital funds.

The architect of the Netherlands Asiatic Empire was the previously mentioned Jan Pieterzoon Coen, governor-general from 1618 to 1623 and from 1627 to the time of his death from cholera in 1629. His establishment of exclusive Dutch control over the Banda Islands and the Moluccas, a policy fully authorized by the Amsterdam authorities, was carried out with a ruthless thoroughness which earned for him a reprimand at home but not a repudiation of his gains. The Spanish and Portuguese were defeated by 1615, and the English fleet was driven out by 1620. The Spanish held on precariously at Tidore until 1663. Even when ordered to pursue a cooperative policy under the 1619 treaty between London and The Hague, Coen deliberately raised the financial and naval ante so high that the English could not stay in the East Indies game with the Dutch. The costs were high, but so were the stakes.

Coen proposed in general a threefold policy as an essential basis for

[25] Lê Thanh Khôi, *Le Viet Nam* (1955). 285–288.
[26] M. Ghosh, *Cambodia* (1960), 246–251.

successful Company operation. In the first place, the Dutch must dominate the sea lanes of Indonesia and operate from firmly held bases within the area. Secondly, profits must be derived mainly from Asian trade, extending over a wide area from Persia, India, and Ceylon on the west to the Spice Islands on the east and to China and Japan on the north. Finally, a few ships only, richly laden with a carefully selected cargo, should make the long voyage to Europe annually. Although Coen's plans were never fully executed, they set the general pattern of the Dutch commercial empire.[27]

Coen's shift of the Dutch headquarters to Jacatra (renamed Batavia) and its successful repulse of the central Javanese army of Mataram have already been described. The site was originally an unsightly swamp, flooded in the rainy season, surrounded by ladang-cultivating villages, and occupying a sparsely populated region infested by wild animals—tigers, wild pigs, and rhinoceros. The Dutch preferred for reasons of security that the immediate environs of Batavia be uninhabited. Batavia itself was built in large measure by Chinese immigrant labor, supplemented by local contract ("princely-serf") labor and by the enslaved crews of native *prau* vessels seized as smugglers and brought in from the Banda Islands and the Celebes. The Dutch brought stone from Coromandel Coast quarries, obtained teakwood from Japara in east Java, and used local coral stone. Bricks and glazed tile were manufactured locally by the Chinese.[28] Mataram's trading position steadily declined, especially after the Dutch capture of Malacca in 1641 canceled Java's principal rice market. The hostile Sultan later conceded Dutch territorial claims to territories behind Batavia.[29] Central Java rice surpluses were subsequently marketed at Batavia. All traders were well treated at Batavia so long as they accepted Dutch authority over the traffic of the Java Sea and refrained from entering the spice-producing areas.

The construction of Batavia in the Dutch pattern (canals, castle, town hall, church, Latin school, and market place) was completed by Governor van Diemen (1636–1645), who ranks second only to Coen as creator of the Dutch Empire. He also carried through the final reduction of the Portuguese fort of Malacca in 1641. Three other costly undertakings followed: (1) the establishment, in 1652, of a Dutch way station at the Cape of Good Hope, (2) the conquest of the cinnamon-producing areas of Ceylon, virtually completed in 1656, and (3) the crushing of a Spice Island rebellion from 1650 to 1656.

Dutch naval superiority in Southeast Asia was unchallenged by the 1650s. It rested in part on superior economic reserves in Holland, largely unimpaired by the exhausting Thirty Years' War which raged in Central Europe until 1648. The Franco-Spanish war continued in Europe for still another decade. The control of the Dutch owed much to superior mobility of their armed forces, the courage and impetuosity of their seamen, and the

[27] Vlekke (1943), 117–128.
[28] Van Klavern, 39–45.
[29] Vlekke (1943), 125–143.

sturdier rigging, faster speed, and better cannon of their men-of-war. By the 1650s Holland was realizing increasing profits from the Asian trade, developed under Coen's master plan.[30] A temporary setback occurred in 1653–1654 with Cromwell's defeat of the Dutch in the naval war in Europe. The Dutch were obliged to pay an indemnity for the Amboina affair of 1623 and to permit English vessels to resume trading in the Indies. Later clashes with England and France occurred in succeeding decades, but by 1660 the Dutch had become strong enough in the Indies to withstand such stresses and to continue to expand their authority.

## The Conquest of Ceylon

Dutch interest in Ceylon dated from an alliance with Raja Sinha of Kandy against the Portuguese in 1638, a move designed originally to divert a portion of Goa's naval forces from the Malacca blockade. Under this agreement, the Dutch took over permanent possession of Galle and Negombo ports, but left the Portuguese in possession of the strongly fortified city of Colombo and other coastal areas.

Following Portugal's recovery in 1640 of its freedom from the disastrous rule of the Spanish kings, Lisbon made a frantic diplomatic effort to salvage its threatened position in Asia by concluding a peace treaty with the Netherlands, in June, 1641. This was too late to forestall the Dutch capture of Malacca, which had occurred in January, 1641. The treaty was scheduled to come into force one year after signing, but all hostilities were to halt immediately on receipt of the news of the agreement. Molestation of trading ships by both parties was to cease for a period of ten years.[31]

The treaty failed to achieve Lisbon's purposes because the Dutch found excuses to postpone its application until late 1645. The Company first advanced as a prerequisite its demand that the Portuguese in Ceylon withdraw from the cinnamon lands behind Galle. It later alleged the lack of explicit instructions from the House of Orange and finally the delayed receipt of the news of the treaty ratifications. Goa, meanwhile, was subjected to repeated Dutch blockades, and a naval battle was actually fought beween the rival forces off Negapatam in south India in April, 1644. The Portuguese recovered some lost ground in Ceylon when the Kandian government and the Dutch Company differed over the disposition of the cinnamon lands. When the peace was finally implemented in late 1645, the Portuguese offered to divide the cinnamon lands with the Dutch in complete disregard of Kandy's claims.[32]

[30] Van Leur, 188.

[31] Frederick Charles Danvers, *Report . . . on the Portuguese Records Relating to the East Indies* (1892), 44–45. The scope of the treaty included all Oriental states friendly to or in confederation with the Dutch Company. Brazil was reserved for Portuguese commerce.

[32] *Ibid.*, 45–49.

The final Dutch victory in Ceylon was delayed until 1656. A joint Dutch-Kandian attack against Portuguese Colombo in 1652 was badly co-ordinated. Colombo gained a further reprieve because reinforcements could not leave Holland during the course of the ensuing war with Oliver Cromwell's England. But the authorities of Kandy hated the Portuguese more than they feared the Dutch, and Colombo's fate was sealed as soon as aid reached the Dutch in 1655. Following the combined Dutch-Sinhalese victory in 1656, the victors immediately fell to quarreling over the disputed disposition of the cinnamon lands. Kandy would permit Dutch access, but wanted to retain control. After two years more of fighting the Dutch forces controlled not only Galle, Negombo, and Colombo and their hinterland, but also the Jaffna area to the north and adjacent Manar Island as well. Kandy retained control of the interior of the island, from which it could still subject the cinnamon lands to predatory raids.[33]

During the thirty years following the expulsion of the Portuguese from Ceylon, the Company authorities in Holland and in Batavia had great difficulty restraining successive governors of Ceylon, the van Goens father and son, from attempting the complete conquest of the island. This expansionist policy was in direct violation of Company desire to limit political commitments to the needs of trade, since much of the territory to be occupied had no commercial value. One excuse of the elder van Goens, valid from 1668 to 1674, was the need to prevent the enemy French fleet from gaining a foothold in Ceylon.[34] When open war developed with Kandy's Raja Sinha in 1670, Governor van Goens envisaged the prospect of establishing a base of Dutch power in Ceylon and south India rivaling that in the Indies archipelago. The project was blocked for the time being by developments attending Louis XIV's second war against the Dutch (1672–1678). In 1678, the belligerent elder van Goens took over as governor-general at Batavia for three years as successor of Maetsuycker. The Netherlands directors themselves finally intervened to remove the younger van Goens from the governorship of Ceylon in 1679, and Governor-General Speelman took over at Batavia in 1681. This ended the van Goens policy of conquest so long pursued in Ceylon. Even so, the Dutch by 1680 had virtually doubled their 1658 holdings on the island, extending control far beyond any possible strategic or commercial needs.[35]

Dutch rule in Ceylon illustrated the logic of events under which Dutch expansionism found no easy stopping place. The urge for power provided its own motivation. Dutch experience in Ceylon also demonstrated the complete failure of burgher colonization efforts and the general ineffec-

---

[33] K. W. Goonewardena, *The Foundation of Dutch Power in Ceylon* (1958), 6–47, 58–75, 81–129, 155–180, 198.

[34] This French episode will be described in Chapter 12.

[35] S. Arasaratnam, *Dutch Power in Ceylon, 1658–1687* (1958), xiii–xxii, 2–97.

tiveness of the Dutch religious and cultural influence. Several of the treaties negotiated with the Kandian government and nearly all port-city and diplomatic exchanges were communicated in Portuguese. The Dutch settlers generally kept socially and culturally aloof from the native population. Christian missionary efforts were directed mainly toward the reconversion to Protestant Christianity of half-Catholicized indigenous groups, which might otherwise persist in their preference for the Portuguese.[36]

## Dutch Control over Major Indonesian Islands

Dutch control over Sumatra was accomplished largely in connection with Dutch participation in settling local feuds. Direct punitive action against the allegedly treacherous Sultan of Palembang in 1658 carried with it the promise of Dutch protection over the neighboring islands of Banka and Billiton. The Jambi Sultan also gave the protecting Dutch extraterritorial privileges and a monopoly of the pepper trade. European efforts to curb the megalomania of Acheh eventually attracted support from the Minangkabau people, who were accorded Dutch protection in 1662 in return for a monopoly of trade. By 1666, virtually all of Sumatra's west coast was cleared of Achehnese interference.[37] But the presumed Dutch monopoly of the Palembang and Banka pepper trade was far from effective. Chinese junks and those of the Malays carried off as much produce as the Dutch. In 1700 English pepper ships could obtain a full cargo of pepper in the straits merely by bribing the Palembang ruler and also the Dutch factory chief. The profitable Dutch opium trade with Palembang was sharply curbed in 1708 when the ruler restricted imports to a mere three chests per year.[38]

Conquest of the port of Macassar at the lower end of the Celebes was a difficult problem. It was abundantly supplied with cannon by its anti-Dutch European visitors,[39] especially the Portuguese, and it had a long naval tradition. In 1660 the Dutch extracted sweeping promises from the wily Sultan to expel the Portuguese, to stop trading with the Spice Islands, and to cease interfering in the Company's affairs, only to see these pledges repudiated. Finally, in 1666–1667, the vigorous Dutch naval commander, Cornelius Janszoon Speelman, undertook the task of reducing Macassar with indigenous aid. His principal ally was a Buginese force under Aru Palakka of Boni, whose family had been killed under orders of Sultan Hassan Udin of Macassar. Forces from Ternate also assisted the attack in compensation for Speelman's defeat of the Tidore Sultan, rival of Ternate. Macassar fell in 1667 after a siege of four months. The Dutch took over the main fort,

[36] *Ibid.*, 194–235.

[37] Vlekke (1943), 146–154; Hall, *A History of South-East Asia,* 261.

[38] Hamilton, 63–65.

[39] Macassar's fort mounted 272 cannon, and its larger ships carried eighteen guns each.

razed the others, collected a huge indemnity of 1 million rix-dollars (Dutch-coined) plus one thousand slaves, and assumed a monopoly of the trade of the port. In early 1668, a Dutch governor was installed.[40]

The opportunity for Batavia's intervention in the affairs of Java came in 1674, when a Madurese leader, enjoying the backing of irregular pirate refugees from Macassar, defeated the half-imbecile and tyrannical King Amangkurat I of Mataram. Wary of Bantam's designs in western Java, the cautious Governor-General Maetsuycker adopted at first only half measures in response to Amangkurat's plea for help. When Mataram's capital fell in 1677 and the fleeing Amangkurat died, his son, the *Adipati*[41] Anon, became dependent on Dutch assistance. Batavia then had to face the hostile Madurese-Macassar forces. At this juncture, the cautious Maetsuycker died, and the previously mentioned Rijklof van Goens from Ceylon became governor-general, giving the aggressive Speelman strong support. Speelman installed Anon (Amangkurat II) as the puppet ruler of Mataram, while Palakka's Buginese allies and other forces from Amboina under Captain Jonkers ran down the luckless Madurese rebel leader, Trunojoyo. Amangkurat II gave the Dutch free access to Mataram's forts, monopoly control of Java's surplus rice, recognition of Dutch territorial claims in western Java, and control of several northern forts as a pledge of repayment of war costs.[42] Resistance within Mataram ended in 1682.[43]

From the Dutch point of view a reckoning with Bantam was long overdue. The port had survived a number of Dutch blockading operations and had continued to entertain English and other rival European traders. Opportunity was afforded when the Sultan of Bantam in 1677 asserted his claim not only to the hinterland of Batavia, but also to Cheribon state to the east of the Dutch port. Again internal controversy gave the Dutch an easy victory. The eldest son of the Sultan, Haji, angered because he was being passed over in the inheritance, staged a coup in 1680 and appealed to Batavia for aid. Haji's success in the civil war was largely attributable to Dutch support. In the settlement arranged in 1684, the Dutch obtained clear possession of Cheribon and a wide strip of territory extending through to the southern coast of Java. They also acquired as of 1682 exclusive trading rights at Bantam, including the expulsion of all non-Dutch Europeans and their own occupancy of the fort. The heavy war indemnity was waived on condition that Bantam continue to honor its trading agreement.[44] The complete consolidation of Dutch authority throughout Java was deferred until 1705 after the death of Amangkurat II. The treaty of that year, con-

[40] Hall, *A History of South-East Asia,* 261–262.

[41] Note the survival of this Sanskrit term for head of state in the use of Adipadi Ba Maw during the Japanese occupation of Burma in the 1940s.

[42] Van Klavern, 50–52.

[43] Vlekke (1943), 154–163; Hall, *A History of South-East Asia,* 262–264.

[44] Hall, *A History of South-East Asia,* 264–265.

cluded with the new ruler, made fiefs of all lands of western Java and protectorates of all the central and eastern sections of the island. Upon leaving Bantam, the British moved their trading headquarters to Benkulen on the western coast of lower Sumatra.

Portuguese exiles from Macassar and Bantam found asylum either at Malacca, at Macao, or in the remote island of Timor far to the east of Java, where the Dutch were permitted a factory. Portuguese troops in Timor resisted forcibly from 1688 to 1703 the efforts of Macao Portuguese to interfere in Timor's affairs. Local laws and liberties were maintained, and no bishop from the outside was accepted. Timor possessed limited commercial and political importance. The coast was subject to violent storms, and the trade was limited to sandalwood, beeswax, food provisions, and gold.[45]

## The Dutch Commercial Empire

The Dutch commercial empire centering at Batavia was first of all a trading-company undertaking, mercantile in its objectives and secularist in spirit. It was in no sense a crusade, a missionary operation, or a romantic adventure. It found its justifying mystique at the outset as part of a desperate struggle for national survival waged in Europe and also in the heavy financial and personal commitment made by Dutch traders to the success of the enterprise in Asia. Both of these considerations, it was assumed, warranted their exercising extensive powers. Spices were the only items over which they exercised monopoly control. Where the Dutch were ruthless, as in the Banda Islands, their actions were allegedly justified as measures taken in the enforcement of essential rules of trade. They were rarely guilty of banditry or massacre based on greed or religious fanaticism, motives which had at times characterized Portuguese policy in Goa, Malacca, and the Moluccas. Their factories on the Coromandel Coast of India did a thriving business with the local cloth industry and never functioned as semipiratical strongholds. For this and other reasons the Dutch were never hated by indigenous peoples as were the Portuguese.

The Dutch religious and cultural impact was weak for various reasons. The Dutch married and mingled less freely with the local inhabitants than the Portuguese. Dutch concern was focused mainly on trading profits and the control of possessions. In Ceylon and Amboina the presence of an indigenous Catholic population involving political considerations led to Dutch missionary efforts. Large non-Muslim ethnic groups, such as the Menadonese, Bataks, Timorese, and Florese, were also partly Christianized. Few converts to Christianity were made anywhere among the Muslim inhabitants. The Dutch assigned to Christian Amboina a virtual monopoly on clove production to the disadvantage of neighboring Muslim islands. The

[45] Hamilton, 74–77.

Amboinese reciprocated by furnishing an effective supply of troops for the Dutch military service. The Dutch secular policy was generally well received in India, where they got on famously with Coromandel and Bengali business groups. The Netherlanders also found kindred spirits among the business-minded Chinese. In their several missions to Peking Dutch Company agents raised no objection to doing prostrations at court in the fashion customary for tribute bearers.

Dutch policy was particularly successful in Japan, where contacts dated from the accidental arrival of the storm-driven pilot Will Adams in 1600. The Dutch succeeded in convincing the suspicious Japanese that they harbored no ulterior religious or political designs, motives which appeared to characterize contemporaneous Portuguese and Spanish contacts with Japan. The net result was that the Dutch alone were permitted to continue trading with Japan on a limited basis at Deshima Island in Nagasaki harbor after 1641, when all other foreign trading contacts were forbidden. For almost a century, the metals obtained in Japan (copper and silver) were of great importance to the Dutch trading pattern in the Orient.

The trading system of the Dutch was generally a highly skilled and professional operation. They were the leading merchants of Europe—experts at marketing, superior mariners, skilled in banking and insurance. The Company also enjoyed the advantages of abundant cash reserves and continuity of direction. Clothing, food, drink, and supplies for the outgoing fleet were collected from all over Europe, and Dutch ships were made ready in Europe's leading dockyards. The cargo of salable commodities made up an insignificant 4 per cent of the cost of the average voyage; coins and bullion amounted to ten times that amount. Specifications for returning cargoes were prepared two years in advance and based on careful considerations of market conditions and prices. Because of the heavy Oriental drain on Europe's precious metal supplies, the Asian trade of the Company invariably took precedence over the requirements of the home market.

The fleet normally left around New Year's Day and reached Batavia in August or September. From Batavia, Dutch ships meanwhile were scurrying in all directions, visiting Dutch factories located at important trading points, everywhere doing business at a profit and collecting valued items. Cargo for the return journey, assembled at Batavia, was packed with great care and started on the homeward voyage in October or November. In case of war, the fleet often had to circle Scotland in order to reach Amsterdam safely.

The Dutch trade in Asia was a multisided operation planned with equal care. The traditionally staple "splendid and trifling" items of trade of ancient times, such as drugs, scented woods, perfumes, gems, rhinoceros horns, and white cows' tails (for the Moluccas), were now completely subordinated. Spices, pepper, and cloth sent to China procured Chinese wares for the Japanese trade. The Japanese paid in silver, gold, or copper, which had a ready market in India, where more cloth was obtained for the spice

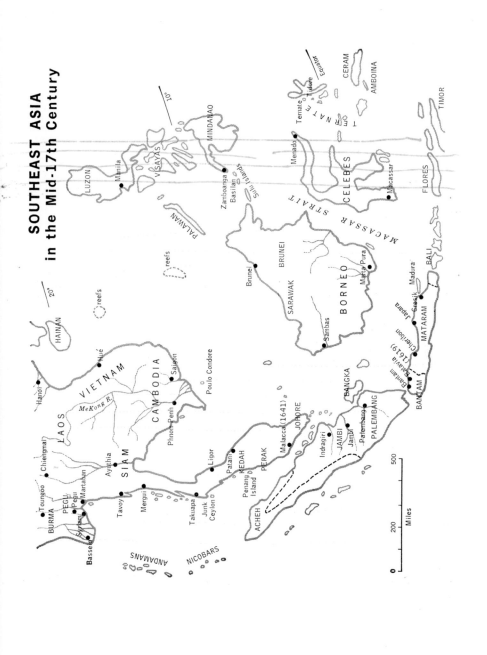

**SOUTHEAST ASIA in the Mid-17th Century**

trade and the next trip to China. Or pepper might be sent to Surat in western India for Surat cloth and on to Persian ports where gold and silver could be had, as well as inferior Persian silks. Food was procured from Java itself, from Siam, and, for a time, from the Arakan coast of Burma. The Dutch introduced into Java the cultivation of sugar for the Asian market and of coffee for the European. They also managed in expert fashion to meet the insatiable European demand for tea which developed in the eighteenth century. The total operation was a competently handled and professional performance.

A third characteristic of the Dutch trading system was that it functioned in a worldwide context. Everywhere the acquisition of Asian bullion through trade was made a primary consideration in order to reduce as far as possible the outgoing consignments of silver from Amsterdam. Chinese silver was obtainable directly until 1661, when the Dutch fort on Formosa was captured by the Chinese renegade Koxinga. After this, access to Chinese ports was denied until the opening of Canton by the Manchus in the 1690s. The previously abundant supply of Japanese silver for export was similarly cut off in 1668; after 1690 the Japanese gold supply dwindled and its price in goods became exorbitant. The Dutch nevertheless continued to obtain enormous supplies of copper from Japan. The metal was highly marketable in India where it was used for coins, weapons, building materials, temple idols and decorations, gongs, utensils, jugs, and wire. Except as a source of metals, the Japanese trade was never particularly profitable to the Dutch, especially after 1700.

Much of the bullion needed for the outgoing trip was Spanish silver, either in bars or rials of eight (8 shillings). The Dutch eventually coined their own rix-dollar to match the Spanish rials. Supplies of silver could be obtained in Hamburg if war prevented access to Spain. The silver obtainable on the China coast was nearly all in Mexican dollars brought over to Manila by the Spanish galleon trade, to be described in the next chapter. It was the steady accretion of bullion coming from Spanish America which lubricated the expanding pattern of world exchange. As a final medium of exchange the Dutch, after 1650, collected enormous numbers of cowrie shells, available in India, for use as small change in Southeast Asia and especially in the West African slave trade. The English obtained their requirements of cowries from Amsterdam.

Thus African and American commercial considerations were involved as well as European and Asian. The market for Asian textiles (cottons and silks) in Europe, amounting after 1700 to more than half the value of the returning Dutch cargo, coupled with the rising demand for tea and coffee, constituted a heavy drain on the European metals. The bullion cargo on outgoing Company ships increased from around 2.4 million florins in 1690, to 5 million in 1700, to 7 to 8 million in 1722–1728. The English Company's heavy involvement in the trade of high-quality Surat cloth to

Europe helped stimulate the successful efforts made during the course of the eighteenth century to devise methods of machine manufacture of cotton cloth. Under the Dutch regime at Batavia, Southeast Asia became for the first time in its history one of the important centers of world trading activity.

## Particular Items in the Dutch Trading System

The staple item of commerce of the Asian trade during the middle seventeenth century was pepper. Most of it came from west Java, lower Sumatra, and the eastern coast of Malaya. The Dutch supplied from 60 to 80 per cent of Europe's needs at the outset and also sold a considerable quantity of pepper to China, India, and Persia. Pepper's importance for the China trade was indicated by the occupancy of the post of Shahbandar at Bantam, the chief pepper port, by a Chinese. Since pepper was not subject to monopoly control, the heavy competition in the trade operated to reduce the margin of profit in Europe and to produce an occasional glut in the market. For the European trade, pepper began to decline in importance in favor of textiles, both cloth and yarn, after 1668. Pepper declined to little more than 10 per cent of the homebound Dutch trade during the 1700s.

The carefully guarded Dutch monopoly of the source of spices made them the most constantly profitable element in the Netherlands trading system. Policing expenses were high, but the price in Europe was around ten times that paid in the islands. Spices netted as a rule around one-quarter of the Netherlands auction proceeds. The price in Asian markets was kept high enough to discourage resale for the European market but not too high to kill the Asian trade. If European shipments were interrupted, the surplus could usually be sold in India. But on a number of occasions in the early eighteenth century, surpluses had to be destroyed in Amboina, Batavia, and even in Amsterdam.

During the second half of the 1600s, the Dutch introduced sugar cultivation into Java. It could not compete with West Indies sugar in the European market, but it captured most of the markets of northwest India and Persia, and was also sold in Japan. The new culture was introduced with a minimum of difficulty by turning the task over to the Chinese residents, who were afforded access to leased land. The Chinese, in fact, were almost indispensable to sugar cultivation.

The Dutch trade in textiles was highly selective. The Dutch got most of their cotton cloth until the early eighteenth century from the Coromandel Coast of India, with Bengal a close second. The cloth was usually produced according to specifications provided by the Dutch, who not infrequently leased shops and set up their own factory premises. Different qualities of cloth as well as various printed designs and bleaching methods were specified to meet the demands of the Indonesian, the Chinese, and the Japanese trade.

Cheaper cottons were in demand for the African slave trade and in the West Indies. Civil wars in India during the early eighteenth century eventually ruined the Coromandel weavers, forcing the Dutch to shift procurement to Bengal. There they encountered after 1740 the sharp competition of the British East India Company. The Dutch trade with both India and China began to lose out heavily after 1770 when the British began the systematic cultivation of Indian opium as a substitute item for the Indonesian and the Chinese trade. The British Company eventually took the lion's share of the high-quality-cotton-cloth trade to Europe from both Bengal and Surat.

Silk yarns and fabrics were obtainable in Persia and Bengal as well as in China. Bengali silk, less prized than the Chinese variety, was still acceptable in Japan, while the inferior Persian cloth was not. The Persian silk trade dropped out of the Dutch Company program after 1682. Amsterdam regularly asked for Chinese silks, but the Japanese market commanded priority consideration for that commodity, especially in view of the uncertainty of the available Chinese supply until well into the eighteenth century. Much Bengal silk went to Europe.

The steadily increasing consumption of coffee in Europe and the almost insatiable demand for Chinese tea in the West accomplished a mild commercial revolution in the early eighteenth century. The Dutch preferred to let Chinese junks deliver cargoes of tea to Batavia, where it could be purchased with pepper or cloth and a variety of special items for little more than the cash price for tea at Canton. However, they were forced by competition of the British and Ostend Companies to enter into the direct Canton tea trade in the 1720s and for a number of years thereafter. The Chinese junk traffic to Batavia was still encouraged. Only slightly less important was the developing coffee trade. From 1686, when the European market for coffee became really important, until 1726, the only source was Mocha in the ancient Sabean country of Yemen in southern Arabia. The supply was limited, and except for the fact that the Turks charged exorbitant dues at eastern Mediterranean ports, English, French, and Dutch trading competitors would have had little share in the profitable trade. Mocha's methods were highhanded, and its cash demands were excessive in any case. An early Dutch attempt to process the Mocha beans at Ceylon proved a failure.

Dutch experimentation with the coffee plant in Java began after 1706. Carefully nurtured plants requiring three to four years to mature were distributed to the village headmen through the regents of Preanger district in western Java. An incentive price of 50 guilders per picul (122 pounds) was paid to the regents at the outset for the delivery of dried coffee beans to Batavia by pack caravans. By 1725, when the production became significant, the delivery price was halved, and it was reduced to 12½ guilders per picul in 1726. Regents kept most of the money and obtained the necessary labor by *corvée* or by tribute-tax exactions. Dutch coffee sales in Europe trebled from 1726 to 1728 and continued thereafter to gain steadily. The

Mocha price broke in 1727 but not before the Amsterdam Company had realized an enormous windfall profit.[46]

The Dutch trading system had its defects, which will be explained shortly, but these must be weighed against the evidence that it was on the whole a highly competent, imaginative, and industrious business operation on a many-sided front. It supervised much of the financing, production, and marketing of commodities over the entire trading arc extending between Persia and Japan. Its major impact in Southeast Asia was on the island section, but the newly generated commercial climate penetrated virtually everywhere. The Philippines alone were excluded from its direct effects, but even there the stream of Mexican silver entering East Asian trade facilitated rather than hindered the objectives of Dutch commercial expansion. The introduction of the two new cultures into Java, sugar and coffee, without disturbing the traditional rice-growing sawah economy of the central and eastern portions of the island was also a notable achievement.

## Dutch Rule in Java: Seeds of Decay

Within Batavia and in its immediate environs, where few Javanese lived, the Statutes of Batavia devised by Governor Maetsuycker in the mid-seventeenth century provided the basic law. In the Javanese-inhabited area, the traditional adat law continued in effect, and Dutch control was only indirectly applied. Social cohesion was thus effectively preserved but at the sacrifice of any important Dutch contribution to indigenous legal and governmental institutions. A principal objective of the Dutch rulers was to enlist the support of native princes and regents. Both parties had an enemy in the fanatic *ulama* religious elite, who advocated the full application of the Koranic system of government and law. One retrograde movement was seen in the Dutch introduction of slavery, previously almost nonexistent in Java. Javanese artistic and literary capacities, which had found fruitful expression eight centuries earlier at Borobudur under Indian cultural inspiration, faltered under the dual blight of Islamic iconoclasm and Dutch economic domination. Religious vitality also fell to a low ebb.[47]

From the outset, the European overlord found it easy to obtain access to a substantial proportion of local production of commercial value (rice, pepper) by exercising the chief's recognized claim to a portion of the labor and normal output of his people. The cultivating villager under this arrangement was not greatly concerned how the surrendered portion of his crop was marketed or to whose profit it accrued. But when alien cultures, such as sugar and coffee, were promoted by exploiting the chief's power to exact labor and services gratis for ends which had no relation to traditional

[46] Virtually the entire foregoing discussion of Dutch trading policy is based on Kristof Glamann, *Dutch-Asiatic Trade, 1620–1740* (1958). For the coffee tribute system see also Van Klavern, 59–63.

[47] Vlekke (1943), 191–213.

habits or needs, the villager inevitably suffered a net loss of freedom. Heavy capital investment, as represented in the Company's development and ownership of all coffee plants, produced an intensification of control over productive efforts whether exerted directly by the chiefs or through the Company's coffee sergeants. The Chinese, until the troubles of 1741, dominated the sugar industry; after this time it also was taken over by the Company. The dynamic aspects of Javanese economy thus came to be alien-owned and directed, with the native chiefs sharing a minor portion of the profits.[48]

The highly successful coffee-tribute system illustrated the problems involved. The control of relations with the regent chiefs of the coffee areas was entrusted to a Commissary of Native Affairs, which directed the work of the coffee sergeants, one being assigned to each regent. The commissary acted as paymaster, lender, provider of consumer goods (salt, textiles, opium), and inspector of cultivation. The agency also directed an elaborate spying system, commanded a contingent of militarized police, and acted also as prosecutor. Access to the coffee-tribute area, which was concentrated in Preanger state near Batavia, was permitted only to holders of official passports. The first abuses developed when the commissary agents began to accept lavish "presents" from wealthy regents under their control. The two groups sometimes connived at the exaction of overweight picul requirements from producers.

A more serious situation emerged after 1760 as a result of loans advanced to inefficient and sometimes spendthrift regents. Company funds available at 3 per cent interest were loaned to regents against the security of coffee deliveries for 9 to 12 per cent. The accumulated arrears of interest payments often amounted in a year's time to the value of the required coffee deliveries. When Company credit was no longer available, the impecunious regents would resort to short-term loans from Chinese lenders at exorbitant rates of interest. Chinese lenders thus could acquire three-to-ten-year domainal rights over particular desa villages, including the regent's claim to labor service and to part of the crops. Thus the most prosperous aspect of Java's export production came in the course of time to profit the regents as well as the village producers virtually nothing at all.[49] It was this highly lucrative coffee-export business which filled the gap in dwindling Dutch Company operations during the latter half of the eighteenth century, when the profits of the Asian trade began to dry up.[50]

The basic cause of the collapse of the Dutch Company was deterioration of personnel and operating standards. Company service usually proved demoralizing, and those who did not wish to be demoralized had to avoid it. Dutchmen entering the lower levels of the service were enlisted all too often from the dregs of Netherlands society—reprobates, bankrupts, thieves,

[48] J. H. Boeke, *The Evolution of the Netherlands Indies Economy* (1946), 1–9.

[49] Van Klavern, 63–64, 67–70.

[50] Vlekke (1943), 188–190.

and others with criminal propensities. Many of the decent settlers tended
to be German immigrants who joined up unwittingly. The Company in its
prime drove its employees very hard, paid them meagerly, and restricted
severely the economic activities of nonemployee Dutch. Company officials
began to earn the major portion of their income from private trading on
the side. Many of them attained a level of wealth and luxury, including
having slaves and servants, which made return to life in Holland unattractive. Corrupt manipulations at Company expense became almost universal,
but they were probably at their worst in India. Well-placed officials at
Deshima, Japan, and in the Moluccas also earned fabulous fortunes. The
façade of legality was maintained by the unwritten rule exempting cargoes
from examination, in cooperation with ships' crews who shared in the profits.
An estimated three-fourths of Dutch trading business became a smuggling
operation. Company directors and the House of Orange itself shared personally in such illegal profits.[51]

In the eighteenth century, Company salaries were customarily discontinued as of no consequence just as soon as an official established a substantial outside income. When Company profits were inadequate, which was
frequently the case, dividends were paid from capital funds, averaging
around 18 per cent per annum. By 1780, and especially following the pun-
ishing war with Britain in the following year, the embarrassed Company's
situation became hopeless. It began to compel its own officials to buy bonds
and to make "donations" annually. These exactions amounted to around
one-quarter of the estimated income of Company officials by 1791. One informed student observed that the Company in the eighteenth century provided a façade behind which prominent Dutch families in difficult straits
sent sons to the Indies to recoup the family fortunes.[52]

The Batavia Hollander was a remarkable species. Only the hardy
survived the rigors of hard work, debilitating climate, and disease, and
these tended to make Java their home. Heavy drinking and smoking were
regarded as measures calculated to ward off disease. Children were usually
reared by slave nursemaids. Bathing was infrequent, and the night air was
considered dangerous. Boys only were sent back to Holland for education;
most girls remained uneducated and became Asianized. Few native Javanese
lived in Batavia or in the immediate environs of the city. The population
included Balinese, Buginese, Malays, Macassars, Amboinese, Indians, and
especially Chinese. The Chinese actually performed most of the servicing
functions and small-scale business until the troubles of 1740–1741 developed. Wealthy Dutchmen purchased country estates, nonproductive
except for cattle and for sugar raised by Chinese, where they lived in
patriarchic luxury replete with servants, slaves, and concubines.[53]

[51] Van Klavern, 67–72; Vlekke, 164–165.
[52] Van Klavern, 67–72.
[53] Vlekke (1943), 164–190; Van Klavern, 56–58.

Batavia's alarming decline apparently started after a disastrous epidemic of malaria in 1732 which inspired the Company's imposition of drastic rules to curtail the irregular trading practices upon which most Dutch residents were dependent for income. Trouble developed in 1740 from the presence of more Chinese in Batavia than could find employment, a situation which impelled the authorities to require that every Chinese acquire a residence permit. Chinese who failed to secure such permits, either by refusing to pay the bribes demanded by Company officials or for other reasons, eventually withdrew to areas adjacent to the city where they organized a small-scale insurrection. Rumor magnified the action into a possible general rising. Under the circumstances, the fearful Dutch population panicked and massacred several thousand Chinese residents of Batavia. Thereupon, an estimated ten thousand Chinese fled the city, producing a sharp decline in economic activity. Europeans took over management of the sugar mills, and Javanese labor had to be conscripted with the aid of the Cheribon Sultan. Meanwhile, non-permit-holding Chinese, variously armed, moved eastward through Java, gathering other Chinese recruits and local allies along the way, all intent on killing Europeans. The rebels were eventually cornered with the help of a force of Madura islanders. A special quarter of the city was eventually set aside for returning Chinese, but even after a thirty-year interval, recovery was still incomplete. Political stresses developing at the time within the Javanese community were fairly well contained.[54]

Official reports from Malacca in 1750 suggested that difficulties were also being encountered in the straits. The Dutch were powerless at the time to punish Buginese pirates who were buying tin from the Sultan of Johore in violation of the Dutch monopoly. On the other hand, some non-licensed traders (mostly Chinese) who were obtaining illicit tin from the Sultan of Kedah had their cargoes confiscated by the Dutch.[55] At the same time, private British traders, licensed from India, were participating in the tin trade at both ends of the straits under immunity from Dutch control. One such British trader in the early eighteenth century allegedly received the offer from his friend, the Sultan of Johore, of the island of "Sincapura" as a present for use as a future center of trade.[56] By the middle of the eighteenth century, the Dutch Malaccan authorities had thus lost effective control over the straits. Pirates operating from the Sumatran side preyed on vessels too weak to fight them off and they were sometimes bold enough to attack the Dutch flag itself. The Dutch similarly exercised only minimal control over piratical bands active off the Borneo coast, and they exerted virtually no control over the western coast of Sumatra where the English

---

[54] Van Klavern, 50–67.

[55] Brian Harrison, "Malacca in the Eighteenth Century: Two Dutch Governors' Reports," *JRASMB*, XXVII (May, 1954), 24–34.

[56] Hamilton, 45.

operated the trading center at Benkulen. Chinese traders with Borneo (cloth for pepper) operated from both Siam and Cambodia.

The Dutch Company's empire had already run its course before the conquest of Holland by French Revolutionary forces gave it the *coup de grace* in 1795. The Japanese trade had long since become unprofitable. Political convulsions in India connected with the breakup of the Mogul Empire and the establishment of British hegemony had ruined the Coromandel trade, and the British themselves took the lead in Bengal. The Dutch problem was that of compounded lack of responsibility at all levels, the Company to its own stockholders and to the Dutch people, the Company's servants to the Company itself and to the peoples affected in Southeast Asia. The entire structure of Dutch trade monopoly in the Indies crumbled after defeat at British hands in 1781 in a war connected with peripheral Dutch involvement in the American Revolution. Meanwhile, so-called country vessels from India, licensed by the British Company and using opium as a principal means of payment, invaded all trading areas of Southeast Asia and also took over much of the China trade at Canton. Competition also developed from Belgian, Danish, and Prussian trading companies and, after 1738, from the Americans. The shift from Dutch to British hegemony in Southeast Asia will be considered in a subsequent chapter.

# CHAPTER II

# Spanish Rule

# in the Philippines

$\mathcal{T}$ he connections between the Philippine Islands and the rest of Southeast Asia before the Spanish conquest were more ethnic than historical. The population was derived from successive waves of migration, the latest coming as recently as the fifteenth century via Borneo, the Great East, and Java. Filipino borrowings from Hindu culture, although by no means absent, were secondhand and superficial in character. Indigenous political institutions and commercial practices were rudimentary, and religion was confined to the worship of ancestral and nature spirits. Islam had penetrated the large southernmost island of Mindanao and parts of Palawan at the time of the Spanish arrival, but it had barely made contact with the Visayas and Luzon.

Spain's contributions were to unify the islands governmentally for the first time, to introduce Christianity on a massive scale with adaptations to the local scene, and to maintain for a period of almost 2½ centuries political and commercial contacts with New Spain in North America. The conquest itself was accomplished with a minimum of violence. Through Manila's lucrative trading connections with Mexico and with China, Mexican silver flowed into the commercial channels of Eastern Asia. Otherwise the Philippines operation was more a royally sponsored Christian mission than a commercial colony. Local government, as well as religious acculturation, was assigned for the most part to various regular orders of the Catholic clergy, into whose privileged ranks the Filipino Christians were denied entry. Another local grievance derived from the minimal economic development achieved during Spanish rule throughout the country generally. Such rebellions as occurred were usually economically and religiously oriented, but they were easily suppressed because never coordinated over a wide area.

Manila was repeatedly attacked or blockaded by the Dutch without success prior to 1648, and it was actually captured and occupied briefly by the British in 1762–1764. Charles III of Spain and a succession of liberal governors initiated a number of reforms later in the eighteenth century, which were never fully implemented and only moderately successful. The first phase of Spanish rule over the Philippines ended with the severance of Manila's commercial lifeline with Mexico during the course of the Napoleonic occupation of Spain. Subsequent efforts at commercial adjustments ran aground, especially after 1842.

## The Pre-Spanish Philippines

The indigenous Negrito peoples of the Philippines, who still number some 10 per cent of the population, were crowded back into the more remote sections of the islands by Indonesian immigrants coming from the south in early times B.C. The newcomers made up a considerable portion of the sawah (wet-rice) cultivators of the northern islands. The word *Tagalog* in Luzon originally meant rivermen, as opposed to hillmen. During the millennium and a half dating from the first or second century B.C., the central Visayan Islands in particular received successive waves (possibly two) of Malay settlers coming mainly via Borneo and speaking languages akin to those of Borneo. They came in outrigger canoes and brought with them familiarity with the use of iron and bronze for implements and weapons, a knowledge of porcelain making and other industries, plus a semblance of law, an alphabet, and rudimentary arts. Filipino contacts with the Śrivijayan trading system were meager, but through the straits channel were transmitted, nevertheless, certain aspects of Hindu culture. A final group of Malay immigrants, coming in the 1400s and 1500s, were the transmitters of Islam. They arrived mainly from the direction of the Spice Islands. The Malays of Mindanao and south Palawan were converted to Islam, but its influence was too brief to spread further northward. The Spanish for the most part left this highly belligerent Moro population discreetly alone, never attempting to exercise any real control over the southern islands.[1]

The description of the people of Ma-i, or Luzon Island, by the previously cited Chinese writer of the thirteenth century, Chau Ju-kua, tells of people who covered the lower part of their bodies with a sarong, who worshipped idol images, and whose chiefs habitually used the white umbrella as the symbol of authority. Chinese trade with the Ma-i was slow and difficult, for vessels from the Fukien coast engaging in it were always the slowest reaching home. Traders dared not risk going ashore, according to Chau, for the people were half savage and every village or island was politically separate, there being no general government. Trade by barter was carried on in front of the chief's house, but the visiting trader had to wait sometimes as long as eight or nine months for payment after the Chinese products had been distributed. Exportable items were wax, cotton, pearls, shells, and betel nuts.[2] Indian cultural connections were indicated

[1] Gregorio F. Zaide, *Philippine History and Civilization* (1938), 24–34; H. de la Costa, *The Jesuits in the Philippines, 1581–1768* (1961), 12–13.

[2] F. Hirth and W. W. Rockhill, *Chau Ju-kua* (1911), 159–162.

by the presence of a number of words of Indian origin as well as the significant use of the white umbrella by the chiefs.

Commercial contacts with Sung China, beginning presumably in the late tenth century, contributed a knowledge of metallurgy, gunpowder, umbrella manufacture, gong making, and silver workmanship, along with the wearing of loose cool garments. The peoples of Luzon received a considerable increment of Chinese blood and some from Japan also. Both elements probably strengthened the native Tagalog-speaking stock.[3] Filipinos also apparently borrowed from the Chinese religiously. The good spirits of the crowded animistic pantheon were those of one's ancestors, represented by idols, and the bad ones were those of enemies. Spirit manifestations of nature, sun, moon, plants, rivers, caves, and animals were also worshipped. Worship ceremonies centered in groves, for the Ma-i had no temples. It was the crudeness of the indigenous religion which provided the opportunity for the missionaries and also their justifying theory that Christianity would serve to liberate the people from the tyrannical enslavement of the devil.[4]

## The Spirit and Purpose of the Spanish Undertaking

The Spanish occupation of the Philippines was undertaken in the militant spirit which characterized the entire Catholic revival following the Council of Trent. Under the leadership of Philip II, the Spanish people, acting presumably as the agents of God's providence, would crush Protestantism in Europe, defend against the Turks, and usher in the millennium by carrying the Gospel to the peoples of America and Asia. The Philippine Islands, like those of the Caribbean Sea in America, would conceivably afford a base for the entry of Christianity into the Asian mainland. But the Asian mission must avoid the brutalities and trampling on native rights which marred Spain's conquest of its New World Empire. The basic interests of the colonists and the natives were not to be regarded as irreconcilable. Philip II rejected repeatedly the suggestions of Spanish captains that a handful of resolute men, variously estimated at several hundred to a few thousand, could conquer China and also Japan, just as the Aztec and Inca Empires in America had been overcome. Military action on a large scale was barred; the Spanish invasion of Asia was to be made on the spiritual level.[5]

In a very real sense, therefore, "the key to the history of the early Philippines is found in the missionary character of the enterprise."[6] The Papacy transferred to the Spanish Crown the administration of the new

[3] Zaide, 41–50.

[4] John Leddy Phelan, *The Hispanization of the Philippines* (1959), 49.

[5] *Ibid.*, 4–5; Zaide, 169–179; William Lytle Schurz, *The Manila Galleon* (1939), 68–70. Proposals for military conquest were vetoed in 1573 and 1586.

[6] Charles B. Elliot, *The Philippines* (1916), 154.

Church of the Indies, and the Crown in turn assigned to the regular clergy the task of Christianizing the natives. The missionaries enjoyed the support of the king in demanding that other interests be subordinated, and even sacrificed if necessary, to promote religious ends. The Crown bore the expenses of the mission and paid the annual deficits of the Manila government. The missionaries tended inevitably, in time, to magnify their own importance. They also solicited royal support for laws designed to protect the natives from oppression and looked upon the powers vested in the governor as designed by implication to promote the primary objective of conversion. In actuality, Spanish policy oscillated between exhibitions of generous concern and truculent avarice.

The ecclesiastics had the ear of the Spanish king from the first and were largely in control of the colony after 1700. The regulars who occupied the missionary frontier accepted the jurisdiction only of the superiors of their several orders, rejecting the Manila bishop's power of visitation. The secular clergy, whose standards of discipline were allegedly inferior, managed the urbanized Christian communities and were alone responsible to the bishops.[7]

## Spanish Conquest and Government

Spain's claims to the Spice Islands were advanced for the first time by Charles V in 1522, following the return of Magellan's voyage. They were renounced reluctantly in 1529 after repeated and costly efforts had failed to establish an effective foothold in the area.[8] But the chain of islands where Magellan himself had met death was claimed by right of discovery. They were first called the Felipinas in 1542, after Charles V's son and heir, Felipe. In this same year the first expedition from Mexico attempted in vain to reach the islands. It was not until after the succession of Philip II as King in 1555 that prolonged preparations, beginning in 1559 and extending over a period of five years, were completed for the occupation of the mission colony. Five ships and four hundred men left Navidad in New Spain in November, 1564, under the leadership of Admiral Legaspi. Aside from the purposes of discovery and conversion of natives, the expedition was directed to obtain information concerning trading prospects and to find a safe feasible route back to New Spain.

The first settlement, made on the island of Cebu in the Visayan region, afforded discouraging commercial prospects. The only exportable product appeared to be cinnamon from Mindanao, largely unavailable because of Moro hostility, and the poverty-stricken islanders themselves provided no market whatsoever for manufactured goods. But the possibilities of trade with China became apparent in the appearance of Moro

[7] *Ibid.,* 154–155; Phelan, 5–8.

[8] De la Torre and Saavedra managed to reach the area in 1527 and 1528, respectively.

praus off Cebu carrying Chinese silks and porcelain. The islanders were incapable of offering serious resistance, and Legaspi's conciliatory but firm policy succeeded in establishing a dependable Spanish base. Legaspi remained in the Philippines until his death in 1572. The return journey to New Spain was accomplished via the difficult westward-blowing North Pacific trade winds, the first time they were ever used. The first partial cargo of cinnamon was of little value, but the ships carried news of the potentials of the China trade.[9]

The subsequent establishment of the Spanish capital at Manila in 1571 did not go uncontested. A Moro fleet attacked the place shortly after the founding, and a more formidable challenge came from a large Chinese fleet in 1574. On the latter occasion, the garrison barely survived and only because fifty reinforcing musketeers arrived in the nick of time. But a lucrative trading pattern was promptly established after the Chinese learned that silver could be obtained for their wares at Manila. Spanish control of the coastal areas was accomplished quickly and bloodlessly for the most part, since no centralized government existed to coordinate pockets of local resistance. The task was largely completed by the time of Legaspi's death in 1572.

Moro resistance in the south was formidable partly because Islam afforded a political and ideological basis for a common defense and partly because the vitality of the indigenous-kingship system contributed greater political cohesion. Terrain, climate, and disease hazards also contributed to the Spanish decision not to undertake the Moro conquest. Moro pirates were a perennial nuisance in the Visayas, but the Manila area was relatively free from their menace, and Spanish trade was unimportant elsewhere. Manila did establish a fort at Zamboanga in Mindanao in connection with Spain's early-seventeenth-century contest with the Dutch over the control of the Spice Islands. Manila did not have enough to gain either commercially or in terms of missionary objectives to warrant undertaking the conquest of the formidable Moros.[10]

The Spanish administrative system as developed in Mexico was transferred intact to the new Philippines province. Its great achievement was to accomplish a unification of the hundreds of island units. The governor-general, the *audiencia* court, and a treasury official at Manila were the direct representatives of the Crown. The audiencia was charged particularly with safeguarding the rights of the state against encroachments by the clergy. Provincial districts and cities were ruled by *corregidores* and *alcaldes mayores*. They had charge of police and militia, the maintenance of roads and public works, and the support of missionary operations on the frontiers. As direct rulers over the people, the feudal *encomenderos* were charged with responsibility for tax and rent collections and for judicial decisions. They were appointed by the Crown as heads of royal fiefs

[9] Schurz, 17–24.
[10] *Ibid.*, 27–28; Phelan, 142–144.

(*encomiendas*), each of which comprehended as a rule several *barangay* villages. Parallelism with Spanish America nevertheless broke down in the encomiendas. They were frequently profitless, partly because of the imposition of elaborate precautions to prevent abuse of power, done usually at the insistence of the clergy.

The first score of years involved food shortages, which prompted resort to illegal exactions by encomenderos. Increased production and the surge of the Manila trade eventually relieved the food problem. It was illegal after 1591 to enslave the Filipino Christians, but labor was exacted from those still in the process of Christianization and under various other compromises. Reform measures of 1595 and 1604 relieved such abuses. A prolonged crisis developed during the first half of the 1600s when Manila suffered repeated blockades and attacks by the Dutch. In several situations of dire crisis, as during the Dutch attacks of 1609 and 1621, as well as around 1648, encomendero exactions of labor, food, and other necessities were harshly imposed. Impressment was used to recruit timber cutters, shipbuilders, crewmen, and munition makers. The Crown took over most of the private encomiendas after 1621.

The military pressure on Manila eased after 1648, when, in the Treaty of Münster, Spain finally conceded recognition of Netherlands independence in return for the cessation of Dutch attacks on Manila. Arbitrary labor exactions were curbed thereafter for the most part, although the government did require at times the compulsory sale by quota assignment of needed products such as rice on an almost gratis basis. The limited number of lay Spaniards who made the annual trip to Manila from New Spain invariably chose to participate in the galleon trade rather than attempt to extract profit from an encomienda grant. The system disappeared entirely between 1721 and 1742. Thereafter tax collections and judicial functions were shared by the alcaldes and the native *caciques* of the barangays.[11]

Caciquism, the exercise of power by chiefs, survived Spanish arrival in the Philippines. Local *datu* chiefs were simply exempted from tribute and installed as petty governors of towns and as *cabeza* headmen of village barangays. The Europeans deprived the chief of some of his former autocratic powers, thus curbing the prevailing trend in the direction of suprabarangay kinglets, a tendency which continued only in non-Spanish Mindanao. Villagers continued to help their chief harvest his rice and build his house and contributed to him a fraction of their produce. But the operation was now supervised by the Spanish, and the tribute was transmitted to the encomendero or the alcalde. A feudal native aristocracy emerged eventually within the ranks of the caciques and provided a necessary link between the village population and the Spanish authorities. Caciquism weighed heavily in the Spanish system.[12]

[11] Conrado Benitez, *History of the Philippines* (1954), 86; Phelan, 9–12.
[12] Benitez, 87; Phelan, 15, 153–161; Costa, 13.

The power of the civilian government was seriously curbed in time both at the center and at the village level by the growing authority of the clergy. The political influence of religious groups reached its peak after 1700, when they actually got the upper hand. The Bishop of Manila was second in authority only to the governor, and a royal decree of 1725 made the bishop ad interim governor in case of the death of the incumbent. The clergy frequently resisted the governor's authority even to the point of inciting vengeful mobs to attack governmental officials, as occurred in 1719. Official and lay enemies of the clergy were also attacked by excommunication and interdict and on occasion through the local Inquisition. Extreme care was taken that no one tainted with Jewish, Moorish, or Protestant leanings be permitted passage to the islands.

The regular orders of the clergy supervised large sections of the population which were outside the bounds of official control. The regulars actually administered 80 per cent of the parishes. Members of a specific order were assigned responsibility for missionary work in a given region and specialized in learning the local languages, so that the regular clergy often constituted the sole means of official communication. They frequently refused to accept direction either from the bishop or from the civilian authorities. Generally speaking, the Spanish lay colonists gathered at Manila, and control over the half-million Filipinos was left to scattered local officials and to the regular clergy.[13]

## *The Chinese at Manila*

Contingent on the hazards of piracy and the supply of silver at Manila, some thirty to forty Chinese junks came to Luzon around March of each year. They unloaded their wares at Parián, the Chinese quarter located just outside Manila's walls, paying a modest 3 per cent harbor dues. They brought a great variety of consumer essentials not intended for the galleon trade, plus their high-quality merchandise. The cargoes included hardware, nails, pots and pans, gunpowder and saltpeter, furniture, jewels, and all kinds of foods, such as grain, pork, fowls, fruits, and nuts, plus livestock. The Chinese traders were often accompanied by craftsmen of all sorts and by a large number of riffraff crewmen and laborers picked up on the Canton wharves. The craftsmen included barbers, tailors, shoemakers, masons, painters, weavers, blacksmiths, along with skilled workers in silver. The Spanish, like the Dutch at Batavia, could not do without Chinese services, and yet the numbers and character of the Chinese constituted a menace.[14]

[13] Bernard Moses, *Spain Overseas* (1929), 71–72.
[14] Schurz, 68–77; Phelan, 12–13. The Jesuit Alonso Sanchez (d. 1593) urged the conquest and forcible conversion of China with the aid of Japanese Christians. See G. D. E. Hall, *Historians of South-East Asia* (1961), 204–205.

By 1600, the Chinese population in Manila's Parián quarter numbered some eight thousand inhabitants, nearly all males. By 1621 Chinese numbered around fifteen thousand and by 1636 around thirty thousand. Many of them neglected to pay the required license fee imposed on all resident foreigners. Others found that it was convenient to marry Filipina Christians, some of them of doubtful orthodoxy, and thus escape the onerous alien tribute and residence-payment requirements. The Chinese headman of Parián was invariably selected from the Christianized group. He exercised wide governmental powers, subject to review in important cases by the local alcalde or by the audiencia court. The few hundred Spaniards occupying walled Manila were in periodic danger of being swamped by the alien Chinese, a fear shared by many of the neighboring Filipinos.

The first serious trouble developed in 1593, when a hired Chinese galley crew which had been impressed into service against the Moluccan pirates murdered the Spanish passengers on board, including Governor Dasmariñas, and ran off with the ship to the mainland. When retaliatory executions were inflicted by the Spanish authorities, several hundred irregular Chinese war junks attacked Manila. A decade later, on the occasion of the visit of a Chinese mandarin, the Spaniards hired Japanese mercenaries to overawe the Chinese, only to succeed in stirring up serious mob rebellion by suburban Chinese *sangleys*. Even the friars were obliged to help organize and direct defense efforts on this occasion. Only artillery fire from Manila's walls dispersed the rebels. Similar crises developed in 1639 and 1662, the latter in connection with Koxinga's threat to attack the islands from his recently acquired Formosan stronghold. In virtually all of these incidents, as in later ones, Chinese imperial and coastal authorities remained almost completely indifferent to the plight of their overseas countrymen, who had abandoned residence in China and presumably allegiance to Peking.[15]

After each rebellion the Chinese were permitted to return to Manila, for the Spanish needed both their trade and their services. An increasing number of Chinese learned in time to appreciate the temporal advantages attending the nominal acceptance of Christianity, including marriage opportunities, residence privileges, and fewer taxes. They sometimes joined the Church in disturbingly large groups; on one occasion, some four hundred were baptized in one day. An audiencia investigation of 1695 reported that Chinese converts made loyal subjects and good Catholics but not very good Christians. Most of the Chinese were a disorderly and demoralized lot, lacking both ethical principles and cultural background. Their presence aggravated the vices of the Filipinos, especially their love of gambling and cockfighting, not to mention laxity in church attendance and observance of fast days. And yet it was the friars themselves along with the merchants, both with vested interest in the galleon trade, who opposed

[15] Schurz, 79–91; Costa, 128–131.

the governor's proposals in the eighteenth century to expel all non-Christian Chinese.[16]

## Manila's Relations with China and Japan

Spanish efforts beginning in 1575 to penetrate mainland China for trading and missionary purposes were unsuccessful. They encountered violent opposition from Macao, where the precariously situated Portuguese jealously guarded their presumed religious-monopoly privileges. Following the belated recognition of Philip II as King of Portugal by Macao in 1583, both Governor Ronquillo and the clerical leadership at Manila advocated the sending of an armed expedition to force China to grant entry to Spanish missionaries despite Macao's opposition. A force of eight thousand soldiers in ten to twelve galleons was regarded as adequate for the task of crushing Chinese resistance and adding the country to the Spanish Empire. The proposal was vetoed by Madrid. Persistent efforts to smuggle Spanish Dominican missionaries ashore eventually aroused the antagonism of the Chinese officials themselves. For a short time, until pushed out by the Dutch in 1642, the Spanish maintained a fort at Quelong on Formosa which served as a base for prospective Dominican penetration into China. Evacuation of the foothold was made necessary partly by the diversion of Spanish military strength after 1637 to an attack against Moro pirates, who were playing havoc with some Jesuit missions in the Visayas. In time Spanish Dominicans did effect an entrance into Tongking and later into China also.

Direct Spanish trading at Chinese ports would have moderated the often-extortionate prices asked by the junk traders at Manila. But the Spanish lacked not only the ships and manpower but also the patience and perseverance requisite to trade with China. A number of desultory efforts made at Chinese ports during the course of the seventeenth century brought little or no profit, and Manila became satisfied to let well enough alone as far as the junk traffic was concerned.[17]

The Manila authorities also failed to establish satisfactory relations with the government of Japan. Commercial relations began in a desultory way around 1586. Lay leadership at Manila wanted to cultivate good relations with Japan partly because of the potentially profitable trade in fine fabrics available there but mainly because Spanish galleons returning to America via the North Pacific route frequently needed a friendly port of call. A number of them were driven aground on Japanese islands, where they usually encountered hostile receptions. The principal difficulty blocking better relations came from missionary zealots, mainly Franciscans, who insisted on accompanying Japan-bound trading vessels from which they smuggled themselves ashore. Suspicions of their intentions were entertained

[16] *Ibid.*, 93–98.
[17] *Ibid.*, 63–65, 71–77; Phelan, 137–139; Costa, 37–50.

by the ruling Japanese shogun, the ambitious General Hideyoshi. Fear of possible Japanese attack diverted Manila's plans to conquer the Moluccas following Governor Dasmariñas's death in 1593. Tensions had reached the breaking point in 1598 when the general died. Hideyoshi was at that juncture undertaking the conquest of both Korea and China.

During the first decade of the new century, Manila's relations with the new shogun, Tokugawa Ieyasu, improved notably, especially after 1604. Following the wreck of a galleon ship near Hirado in 1609, an agreement was signed providing for friendly treatment of Spanish ships along Japan's coast in return for promised Spanish aid in the areas of shipbuilding and mining. Japan did not, however, agree to accept missionaries or to exclude Dutch trade, as requested by Manila. Potential Japanese commercial interest in the Pacific trade was reflected in the unwelcome arrival of two Japanese ships at Acapulco, New Spain, in 1613 and 1616 respectively. Spanish-Japanese relations again deteriorated after 1610. This was due in part to the residence at Hirado of Will Adams and Richard Cocks, Englishmen hostile to Spanish trade. The first was an agent of the Dutch Company and the second of the English. They fanned suspicions of ulterior Spanish designs connected with illegal missionary infiltration. Tokugawan fears were enhanced by the alleged offering of arms by the Spanish visitors to the new shogun's western enemies, especially the Satsuma and Choshu daimyos. Persecution of Japanese Christians as potential subversives reached a peak after the new shogun, Hidetada, took over in 1616. He turned back Spanish embassies in 1622 and 1624, severed relations with Manila, and then expelled all the Spanish friars.[18]

Manila had meanwhile become equally suspicious of its one thousand to fifteen hundred Japanese residents. They had aided the Spanish during the Chinese rebellion precipitated by Spanish truculence in 1603, but became thereafter increasingly resentful of Spanish control. Repeated riots occurred, especially after a 1609 ruling which reserved all Manila trade with Japan to Spanish vessels. Many of the Japanese returned home; others were expelled. The remnant remaining at Manila in 1621 sympathized openly with the Dutch during the siege of that year. A temporarily successful effort on the part of the Japanese to reopen trade with Manila in Japanese vessels in 1631–1632 was abandoned almost immediately. Subsequent hostile relations concerned Japanese pirate operations based on Luzon.[19]

## *Spanish Intervention in Cambodia, 1596–1599*

The preliminary stages of the Spanish-Portuguese involvement in the affairs of Cambodia in the 1590s were described near the end of Chapter 9. Following the collapse of King Satha's regime at Lovek in 1594, the twin

[18] Schurz, 105–114; Costa, 129–131.
[19] Schurz, 116–119; Hall, 200.

Iberian adventurers, Diogo Veloso and Blas Ruiz, found themselves together again at Manila in mid-1595. On the basis of a false rumor that King Satha had recovered his throne, they enlisted the personal and financial support of several Dominican missionaries, notably Fathers Ximenes and Aduarte, to outfit and transport a military expedition to Cambodia. Forgetting that he had arrived in the last instance as the official emissary of King Naresuen of Siam, Veloso assumed the new role of ambassador of Satha's nonexistent court and signed a highly irregular agreement with Manila dated August 3, 1595. The presumptuous document recognized Spain's legal primacy in Cambodia and pledged conversion to Christianity on the part of the King and Queen in return for the promise of a Spanish garrison to back up the agreement. A three-vessel expedition with 120 soldiers aboard under the command of General Gallinato was able to sail by late January, 1596, but it encountered heavy storms. Only the vessel commanded by Ruiz managed to proceed directly to Phnom Penh. Veloso's ship was driven aground on the Mekong delta, and its occupants reached Cambodia by traveling overland. Gallinato's vessel, with a majority of the troops aboard, was driven southward to Singapore, where it awaited the seasonal change of the monsoon winds.

Although the Spanish at Phnom Penh, including Ximenes and Aduarte, were unable at the outset to challenge the superior power of the Cham and Malay mercenaries employed by the usurper King, Srei Santhor, they did not long delay asserting their influence. In April the Europeans attacked and looted several Chinese junks anchored near their quarters, an action which evoked a royal demand to make restitution to the despoiled junkmen. Feigning compliance with the royal order, a band of forty men gained access to the palace on May 12 and 13, murdered Srei Santhor and several of his sons, burned the King's vessels, and exploded his gunpowder magazine. They then retreated to their fortified position to await Gallinato's arrival with the summer monsoon. To the dismay of the conspirators, the arriving Spanish commander disowned the affair as completely disreputable, promised reparations to the injured parties, and departed Cambodia with his entire force in July, 1596.

The ingenuity of Veloso, Ruiz, Ximenes, and Aduarte was far from being exhausted. En route back to Manila, Gallinato was persuaded to skirt the Annamese coast to look for the Spanish vessel brought there by mutinous Chinese in 1593. At the port of Hanoi, Ruiz and Veloso broke ship, obtained an armed escort and guides, and proceeded overland to Laos in search of their friend King Satha. Ximenes went ashore to communicate with Augustinian missionaries in Tongking. When the visiting Spanish were attacked shortly thereafter, Gallinato departed, leaving Ximenes ashore as a kind of hostage; he was obliged to find his way back to Manila as best he could. Most of the expedition returned to Manila by June, 1597, to conclude their costly and futile adventure. A dozen Spanish soldiers aboard a separate junk who were driven southward to Malaya decided later to rejoin Veloso and Ruiz in Cambodia.

When Veloso and Ruiz discovered upon arriving at Vientiane that Satha had died, they persuaded the queen and the prince-heir of twenty years to accompany them back to Phnom Penh and claim the throne. The news of their impending arrival in Cambodia was accompanied by rumors that the Spanish were returning in force. Thereupon the panicked son of Srei Santhor fled, and several leading officials plumped for the protégé of the Europeans, Satha's heir, who was subsequently crowned as Boromoraja II. During the wild disorders which accompanied the ensuing civil war, the Europeans, with the assistance of a small band of Japanese (Liuchiuans), managed to keep control of Phnom Penh. Veloso and Ruiz were made governors of provinces with access to official revenue and fortified positions adjacent to the capital. Friction developed between them along national lines, with Veloso deferring to Malacca and Ruiz to Manila, although any kind of reinforcements would have been acceptable to them. Several ships arrived from both centers in late 1597 and early 1598, but the passengers were missionaries rather than soldiers. The Cambodian adventure took second priority with both Malacca and Manila to the imminent Dutch invasion of the Java Sea and the Moluccas.

While the situation in Phnom Penh remained in precarious balance, Fathers Ximenes and Aduarte at Manila maintained constant agitation for sending another expedition to Cambodia. They denounced the timid Gallinato and called for a holy war in support of the missionary cause. The new governor, Francisco Tello de Guzman, reluctantly agreed to the proposal after the son of ex-Governor Dasmariñas offered to finance the enterprise in return for his own designation as governor of Cambodia. Desmariñas assembled new and old partisans for the venture, and the expedition departed Manila in three ships in September, 1598. Storms took a heavy toll, as had been the case two years before. One ship was wrecked and rendered almost a total loss. The frigate with Ximenes and Aduarte aboard sank in the China Sea. Ximenes lost his life; Aduarte managed to return with survivors to Manila via Macao. The third vessel commanded by Dasmariñas himself put back to Manila for minor repairs and then proceeded to Phnom Penh in October, 1598.

The wild enterprise came to its denouement in 1599. Protracted haggling on the part of the reinforced Europeans to conclude a protectorate treaty with the now-debauched King ran aground in the face of determined opposition. Elements of the court and the mandarins were now being accorded strong support from Siam. A showdown fight developed between the Spanish-Filipino faction and the strong corps of Malay mercenaries in mid-1599. Only one Spaniard and several Filipinos survived the massacre. King Boromoraja II was himself assassinated at the end of 1599, when the mandarins installed a new pro-Siamese ruler. This tragedy of Phnom

Penh marked the end of Spanish interference in mainland Southeast Asia until the Franco-Spanish venture at Tourane and Saigon in 1859–1860. The European community, largely Goan and Portuguese, continued in residence on a commercial-missionary basis until the nineteenth century. During the period of serious galleon losses from 1647 to 1657, Manila contracted for the construction of ship replacements in Cambodia.[20]

## Manila's Relations with Macao and the Moluccas

Spanish-Portuguese relations in Southeast Asia, even during the sixty-year period of their sharing the same king (1580–1640), were characterized more by jealousy than by cooperation. The original settlement of Legaspi at Cebu in 1568 was challenged as an intrusion by a Portuguese fleet of ten ships which laid siege to the Spanish fort for three months in an abortive effort to force Legaspi to evacuate the Philippines. Relations improved somewhat under joint rulership after 1583, when Portuguese traders from Macao were granted temporary permission to bring Chinese wares to Manila. The Spanish came to the aid of the Portuguese garrisons in the Spice Islands repeatedly, in 1584–1585, 1593, and 1603–1604. But except where a common enemy was faced, Moluccan or Dutch, rivalry between the two Iberian nations persisted. When the Portuguese governor at Macao attempted to trade in Chinese products at Acapulco, he was brought to trial before the Case de Contratacion at Seville in 1590. The Portuguese were equally jealous of their exclusive claims to the Moluccas and their patronato monopoly of religious patronage throughout Eastern Asia. Macao also opposed Spanish efforts to trade at ports of China or Japan, especially at times when Portuguese ships were barred from Manila.

Active Spanish-Portuguese cooperation developed for a time after 1605 in the face of the common threat from the Dutch against both the Moluccas and Manila. Macao participated in the Manila trade from 1619 to 1636, sending annually up to ten ships with total cargoes valued as high as 1.5 million pesos. During this period, the Portuguese obtained spices from Manila for the Indian and European trade in return for Chinese wares and Indian cloth. A royal decree ended the arrangement in 1636. In 1640, when Portugal recovered its independence from Spanish rule, Macao sequestered 300,000 pesos worth of Manila's property to cover alleged debts. Manila's limited trade with Malacca and Goa after 1580 was mainly in Indian cloth.

Two considerations apparently prevented Manila from establishing firm control over the Moluccas. In the first place, the Spanish after 1529 consistently conceded Portugal's prior legal claim. This was true even after

[20] B. P. Groslier, *Angkor et le Cambodge* (1958), 38–57. Father Aduarte's *Historia* (1640) reflected his combination of religious zeal and lack of political scruples. See also Costa, 413–415.

the Dutch entry, when Spain intervened from the base at Zamboanga on Mindanao Island to occupy part of Ternate in 1606 and to establish a firm hold on Tidore. Madrid deferred to Lisbon's first claim on the available spices, lest Goa's power should collapse completely. Secondly, Manila was never vitally interested in the spice trade, and therefore demonstrated no constancy of purpose with regard to the Moluccas. Even during the half century (1606–1663) when Spain had access to ample supplies of cloves from Tidore, it failed to develop adequate trading connections for the distribution of the supplies. New Spain itself afforded a very small market for spices, and the Atlantic ports of North America and Europe obtained cheaper spices from Portuguese and Dutch sources. Spain's costly defense of Tidore was abandoned in 1663; the island was evacuated along with the Zamboanga base in the face of the threat of a Formosan attack on Manila. This withdrawal ended Spain's connections with the Moluccas.[21]

Manila's withdrawal from Tidore and Zamboanga, involving the abandonment of islands below the Visayas to Moro and Chinese pirates, marked the beginning of the gradual decline of Spain's Philippines Empire. The vigorous initiative which had characterized the first century was replaced by lackadaisical inertia in later decades. This development paralleled the decline of national spirit and economic vigor within Spain proper. Speculators and brokers in Mexico absorbed an increasing share of the profits of the transpacific trade. Silk producers in Spain registered increasing protest against the traffic in Chinese fabrics obtained via Mexico. Noncommercial wealth in the islands tended to be absorbed by the Church and charitable foundations, which provided in time a principal source of credits for the galleon trade. The continuing flow of silver from New Spain brought profits to a favored few at Manila, but most of it went to Chinese and Indian traders.[22] A closer look at the galleon trade itself is now in order.

## The Manila Galleon Trade

The trade between Manila and Acapulco, New Spain, was carried on in vessels owned by the Crown of Spain and operated under rules drawn up in Madrid, known collectively as the Laws of the Indies. In order to encourage immigration to the islands, all Spanish residents were supposed to share the profits of the trade. About 190 persons, for example, shared in the voyage of 1586. A second consideration was to prevent a few persons from appropriating the lion's share of the profits. The third general objective was to limit the *permissio,* or authorized cargo, to a fixed value in terms of the several staple articles of commerce. This permissio amounted

[21] Schurz, 130–142; Costa, 45–47.
[22] Schurz, 49–54.

to less than 300,000 pesos prior to 1700; it increased to 500,000 in 1734 and to 750,000 in 1774. The idea was to limit the drain on Mexican silver and to protect the Spanish silk industry from ruinous competition with China's products. Chinese silks were provisionally denied entry into Peru in 1587 and were permanently banned from Peru in the formal edict establishing the bounds of the galleon trade in 1593.

In pursuance of the first objective of general participation, *boleta* tickets were distributed widely to the Spanish inhabitants. But single-unit holders, lacking capital, usually sold their tickets for some 125 to 250 pesos. Under conditions of monetary inflation, the price later rose to 500 and even 900 pesos. For the average citizen, trading in boletas was more important than commerce in goods. Ship officers also shared liberally in the boleta distribution.

The system encouraged all kinds of fraud and roguery. The outcome was that fewer and fewer persons actually shared in the galleon profits. Only twenty-six participated in the voyage of 1786, with one person controlling 23 per cent of the space. The ships were invariably overloaded, and the augmented cargo usually ran to 2 or 3 million pesos in value. The Space Allocation Board in Manila included the governor and his attorney general, high Church dignitaries, the City Council, and, after 1700, an increasing number of firms representing major families. The clergy including bishops, cathedral deans, and friars, participated as individuals via lay proxies and also through the charitable foundations, or *obras pias,* acting as banking agencies. Persons lacking capital of their own borrowed from the charitable foundations. The obras pias waxed rich from insurance operations as well as from lending.[23]

The westward voyage was fairly simple. Two ships left per year (later only one) around February or March. They were large vessels, built in Manila as a rule, with three or four decks. The cargo was mainly silver and ballast, with perhaps some Flemish laces and American chocolate. The passenger list was fairly large, including high officials and their families and twenty to eighty clergy who traveled gratis and a number of merchants who were fare-paying passengers. The vessels might also carry from one to four companies of soldiers, many of whom, along with the crews, had been pressed into service. No foreign or unauthorized passengers were allowed passage. The route followed the latitude of Panama westward past the Marshall and Caroline Islands to the Cebu straits in the central Visayan group. Before a full-sail wind, the voyage was usually completed within two or three months.[24]

The cargo assembled for the return journey, which usually started in June, was rich and varied. Few Philippine items were shipped apart from cotton and, eventually, Manila cigars. Some Indian cottons were included,

[23] *Ibid.,* 71–77, 159–190.
[24] *Ibid.,* 32–34, 216–227, 268–275.

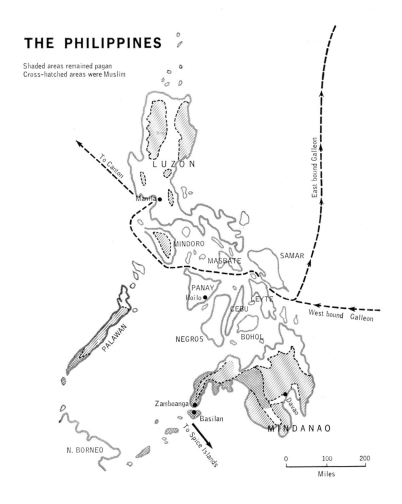

THE PHILIPPINES

Shaded areas remained pagan
Cross-hatched areas were Muslim

To Canton

East bound Galleon

L U Z O N

Manila

MINDORO

MASBATE

SAMAR

PANAY
Iloilo

LEYTE

CEBU

West bound   Galleon

NEGROS

BOHOL

PALAWAN

Zamboanga

Davao

Basilan

To Spice Islands

M I N D A N A O

N. BORNEO

0        100        200

Miles

but the main cargo was in silks. One silk cargo contained fifty thousand
pairs of stockings, along with crepes and gauzes, velvets and taffetas, flowered
silk, heavy brocades, cloaks, robes, and kimonos. There were also bed
covers, Persian rugs, tapestries, table services, church vestments, and hand-
kerchiefs. One seaman's chest reportedly contained eighty thousand combs.
Of less importance were the gold and jewelry, jade and jasper, fans with
ivory and sandalwood handles, thimbles and brass toothpicks, and drugs and
perfumes. Until the year 1700, slaves could also be included in the cargo.
During the two or three months prior to the departure of the galleon,
Manila was a busy place. Goods accepted from the Chinese and properly
packaged were registered for shipment within the limits of the traders'
boletas. Ships had to be repaired and reconditioned in preparation for the

return journey. Food and water for a seven-to-nine-month voyage must be provided and finally the cargo taken aboard.[25]

After threading the straits at Cebu, the eastbound ships could take advantage of the southern monsoon winds up to the 15th parallel of north latitude, but from there on the winds were variable. Hurricanes could be encountered at any time between July and October. Many ships were wrecked on the Japanese islands, and others turned around and returned to Manila. The voyage was both harrowing and exhausting. Cramped quarters amid overweight cargoes were made worse by rats and vermin, water shortages, fever, scurvy, and skin diseases. The best westerly winds, to be found between 32 and 38° N, carried the galleons to the California coast, down which they sailed to Acapulco. The shortest time was seven to eight months; some trips lasted twelve; many ships didn't arrive at all. Faulty construction was partly to blame. The period from 1636 to 1657 was especially bad for the galleon trade. Heavy losses were sustained, and Manila was virtually bankrupted with a million-peso debt. Another difficult period developed after 1714, when Madrid attempted to abolish entirely Manila's trade in Chinese silks.[26]

In appearance Manila was a splendid city, and its glamor persisted long after decline had set in. Following the disastrous fire of 1603, it was entirely rebuilt in stone and tile. The trading aristocrats lived recklessly and luxuriously. They enjoyed leisure for three-fourths of the year with all amenities provided in the way of housing, clothing, food, drink, and servants. The situation bred idleness and sloth, susceptibility to gambling, cheating, and other vices, with little or no attention given to agricultural or industrial development. Chinese managed the retail trade and provided the craftsmen, artisans, and servicing personnel. They also assembled at Manila most of the items for the galleon trade. The Filipinos, kept under control by the police and the Church, provided food and servants. Life at Manila represented in unmatched fashion "the charm of the East."

Difficulties developed mainly from the abject dependence of the entire Spanish population on the annual arrival of the silver fleet. The fortunes of too many were riding on the success of a single year's venture, for a wrecked galleon could ruin a small trader for all time. Unsuccessful fortune hunters, unable to return to New Spain, usually sold their annual boletas and then took to beggary rather than seek a livelihood in a craft or trade. Aside from ex-traders reduced to destitution, Manila's Spanish population also included a large number of disbanded soldiers and rene-gades, who were usually capable of any degree of violence or fraud. An English visitor to Manila in the early eighteenth century commented quite smugly as follows: "If [the country] were in the hands of some industrious nation, it is able to furnish . . . materials to build a commerce . . . but the

---

[25] *Ibid.,* 32–34.
[26] *Ibid.,* 103–104, 265–266.

Spaniards are rich, lazy and proud, and rather discourage than improve trade or engage the natives to be civil and industrious."[27]

## The Clergy and Missionary Operations to 1610

In one important respect, the Spanish shared their civilization with the inhabitants of the islands in a fashion not matched by any other European colonizing power. They contributed a new religious orientation which left a permanent imprint on the entire fiber of Filipino society. Spanish policy differed from the Portuguese in not encouraging inter-marriage and in the consequent development of no large *mestizo* population.[28] Augustinian monks accompanied Legaspi on his original voyage of conquest in 1565. The Franciscans arrived in 1577, the Dominicans and Jesuits in 1581, the Benedictines in 1595, and the Recollects, a branch of the Augustinians, in 1602. Manila became the seat of a bishopric in 1581 and of an archbishopric in 1595. Except within Manila, the regulars surpassed the secular clergy from the outset in both numbers and influence. Many of them in the early years were more interested in the Philippines as a staging point for entry into China and Japan than in the islands themselves.

The cathedral establishment at Manila included a *cabildo* of twenty-seven learned ecclesiastics to assist the archbishop. The bishop's court was surpassed in its jurisdictional authority only by the royal audiencia. The religious establishment also included the Inquisitor, whose authority sometimes rivaled that of the archbishop, plus a number of Rome-appointed judges conservator to adjudicate differences between the several regular orders and the secular clergy.[29]

Secular Filipino priests were permitted entry only into minor posts of the Church, usually being assigned to the more laborious tasks. They were not permitted entry at all into the regular orders. The attitude of the Spanish clergy with respect to their exclusive role in Church affairs was compounded of a sincere regard for maintaining standards, involving scruples about the unfitness of the Filipinos, plus an amalgam of pride, avarice, vanity, and desire for control. The bishops held title to vast estates from which they derived labor services for building purposes, transportation by land and water, and personal servants. Although the bishops on numerous occasions rose to champion the cause of the people against oppression, they were not interested in agricultural improvement on their own estates or in encouraging Filipinos to accept responsibility.[30]

The Augustinian and Franciscan orders, being first on the scene, gained control of a majority of the most lucrative parishes in Luzon, al-

[27] A. Hamilton, *A New Account* (1727), II, 157–159: Schurz, 38–52.

[28] Benitez, 89.

[29] Zaide, 159; Elliott, 219.

[30] Claude Buss in Lennox Mills (ed.), *The New World of Southeast Asia* (1949), 23–26; Phelan, 72–89.

though all of the orders shared in them. The Augustinians were particularly active in *cabacera,* or mission pueblo, development. In addition to village work, the Franciscans operated schools and hospitals, and became very much involved in the attempted penetration of Japan. The Dominicans were particularly interested in the Chinese and in higher education. They worked in the Parián quarter of Manila and manned the Spanish staging point at Quelong in southern Formosa until it was captured by the Dutch in 1642, They founded the University of Santo Tomas in 1611 and the College of San Juan de Letun in 1630. They also established the first printing press in 1602. The Jesuits took over the difficult Moro frontier in the south, a region impoverished and victimized by pirates. They were also interested in education, and contested vigorously with the Franciscans over access to Japan. Benedictines and Recollects were less aggressive.

Within the islands, each order was assigned responsibility for several major linguistic groups, which tended to fix their jurisdictional boundaries. The usual Crown tactic of curbing independence of regular orders by supporting the authority of the government and the secular clergy and by scattering mission assignments was here ineffectual. The regulars alone learned the languages, and their influence was therefore essential for maintaining control. Since title to the parishes was vested in the several orders under the patronato system of assignment, only a determined action by the civil authorities could oust them. No governor dared make a move so destructive of Spanish authority. As recipients of large land grants, the orders assumed the role of encomenderos in many areas. They controlled education in the barangay village units, acted as judges, collected tax tribute, and bought up native-produced surpluses for sale at a profit.[31]

On two matters of policy the regulars were unanimous and adamant. They repeatedly denied the authority of the bishop to exercise his visitation function as provided by the decisions of the Council of Trent. They accepted direction only from superiors in their respective orders. This policy removed 80 per cent of the parishes from episcopal control. In order to protect disciplinary standards, the regulars also refused to admit Christian Filipinos into the orders. This policy was pursued despite the perennial shortage of personnel, for some 250 to 400 resident monks and friars were simply not sufficient to man the many mission stations. After the initially attractive prospect of carrying the Gospel to the matured civilizations of China and Japan began to fade, recruitment of regular-clergy replacements from Spain became increasingly difficult. The cost of transportation and outfitting also taxed the dwindling resources of the royal treasury. The journey itself was arduous and dangerous, requiring often two years' time. A considerable number decided en route to remain in America, and attrition from the effects of climate and disease were heavy both in traveling and in the islands. In the eighteenth century, Crown pressure finally forced the

[31] Zaide, 159; Phelan, 46–49, 84–85.

overburdened orders to use some native priests, but they were never accorded order membership and were denied the emoluments and the prestige of heading a parish.[32] This discriminatory practice was destined to become a principal factor in the eventual stimulation of Filipino national unrest.

## Missionary Methods and Accomplishments

The period from 1578 to 1609 has been called the golden age of the missionary enterprise in the Philippines. Zealous missionaries approached the task with unbounded faith and enthusiasm and aroused a correspondingly enthusiastic response from the people once initial adjustments were made. The encomendero usually prepared the way for the missionary by putting down local resistance and establishing firm control. In the face of the customarily hostile reaction on the part of the adults, the missionaries adopted as a primary object the instruction of the children of the leading families, who were usually surrendered to their care out of parental curiosity or ambition. Such children were receptive to training and indoctrination and also proved effective in transmitting the faith to their parents. If the chief could be won over, then the baptism of virtually the entire community followed. Only the obdurate and hostile were denied baptism. Within less than a decade after 1578, some 170,000 converts had been made. The number was 500,000 by 1622 and 910,000 by 1750. The sons of chiefs were invited to take advanced work in the monastery school.

The problem of instructing the converts was a difficult one. The attempt to employ the *reducción* plan of assembling Christians in large stations, so successfully used in America, was resisted by the Filipinos. Subsistence farmers could not be persuaded to abandon the security of their developed rice fields and their local access to fish and game. They were also reluctant to leave the vicinity of the tombs of their ancestors. The alternative method adopted was to establish a parish headquarters (cabacera) to which the natives could be enticed periodically by the staging of colorful festivals. These included processions, dances, and theater performances along with religious and ritual celebrations. One of the three large annual festivals was in honor of the patron saint of the locality. Between festivals, the cabacera staff would make the rounds of *visita* chapels located in the peripheral regions of the parish. Eventually the hilly frontier beyond the range of the visita was manned by garrisoned soldiers, euphemistically called "active mission" stations, to protect the Christianized population from the raids of the fierce Negrito tribesmen of the mountains.[33]

Religion was propagated in the native tongue but with the key words of the Christian faith kept in Spanish to avoid any identification with pagan gods. The four printing presses operated by the regular orders

[32] Phelan, 31–39, 43–44, 86–87.
[33] *Ibid.,* 44–49, 53–57, 74–75.

published a variety of bilingual catechisms, dictionaries, grammars, confessionals, and language commentaries. The catechisms were for the priests' use only, since all instruction was oral. During the course of nearly two centuries of publishing activity (to 1768), the Jesuit Society alone published around forty works of substantial importance. Apart from the hostile primitive folk of the mountains and occasional rebellions led by self-styled prophets claiming supernatural powers, clerical control was effective in preventing serious resistance except in the southern islands.[34] An interesting commentary on the vogue of Spanish religious nomenclature appeared in a Panay rebellion in 1663. The leader-prophet, who claimed to have been in conversation with mountain demons, adopted the name God Almighty, while his helpers were Christ, the Holy Ghost, and the Virgin Mary, along with numerous named popes and bishops. The outraged Spaniards crushed the rising with unusual dispatch. This rebel tactic of associating traditional religious sanctions, bearing Christian names, with economic unrest continued into the twentieth century.[35]

It is not surprising that missionary zeal was unable indefinitely to maintain itself at the high level demonstrated by the first generation. In the face of dwindling resources, the appalling magnitude of the task, and the imposition of arbitrary barriers, such as the Dutch attacks on Manila and interorder rivalry, acute disappointment set in after 1610. A spirit of apathy, routine, and discouragement replaced the early enthusiasm. Jesuits and Franciscans quarreled over access to Japan; Jesuits and Dominicans differed over education; the dwindling chance of entering China in the face of Portuguese objections was an additional annoyance. Most missionaries continued faithful to their vows and their responsibilities, but the accumulating shortcomings of their roles became increasingly apparent as the century wore on. Even so, the Christianizing process, once firmly established, progressed in spite of difficulties and human frailties.[36]

The first serious disciplinary problems developed within the Augustinian order after 1607. In order to meet its overextended responsibilities, the Augustinians made the mistake of recruiting creole monks from New Spain who were ill-trained and lacking in moral stamina. Offenses included violations of celibacy vows and property thefts. Part of the difficulty stemmed from the lack of moral support capable of being generated by close communal association. Missionaries forced to live in frontier isolation and subject to oppressive climatic conditions and illness required strong will power if they were to avoid dechristianizing themselves. Such violations, even though committed by a small minority, set a demoralizing example to Filipino Christians and also undermined corporate morale. It

[34] *Ibid.,* 56–58; Costa, 620.

[35] David R. Sturtevant, *Nativistic Movements in the Philippines* (unpublished). After a rebellion in 1910 Governor-General Forbes had in jail one God Almighty and three Jesus Christs.

[36] Phelan, 56, 66–76.

required two decades for the Augustinians to restore proper disciplinary standards. A less flagrant offense, but equally destructive of morale over a long term, was the practice of friars dedicated to poverty becoming wealthy landlords and acting the part of bankers and merchants at Manila.[37]

One barrier in the way of improving agricultural methods was the reluctance of the friars to instigate changes in traditional cultivation and labor practices which might disturb their relations with the cabacera headmen, or caciques. Under the dependency system, the chief of the barangay could muster a considerable labor force made up of debt peons, convicted offenders, or captured persons to use in cultivating the communally owned lands. These dependents were not slaves, but they suffered varying degrees of unfreedom and eked out a bare livelihood on their own as share croppers. The war-chief nobles and the freemen ranked between the chief and the dependents. Cultivators generally had little or no incentive to improve production. Efforts to abolish the dependency arrangement in the late 1600s were ineffective because by that time the caciques and the friars themselves had taken over title to the formerly communal lands. If the Mindanao pirates could have been brought under control, production of cinnamon bark, spices, and pepper could have been developed. As it was, only minor production increases were realized in cotton and, in the late eighteenth century, in tobacco.[38]

## *The Filipinization of Christianity*

In spite of the efforts of the missionaries to make a clean break with pagan practices, associations with older worship forms inevitably reappeared. Saints took the place of the friendly spirits; miracles became the new form of magic; images were a substitute for idols. Under a conspiracy of silence, many popular pagan practices persisted, especially in connection with illnesses; the older genii were propitiated under Christian forms. Filipino fondness for daily baths, sometimes immorally staged, vetoed the friars' efforts to make occasional deprivation of the bath an act of penitence. But the love of bathing lent itself to almost boundless faith in holy water, especially for curing illness.

The missionaries were fairly successful in the eradication of polygamy, since the practice had entered only recently with Muslim influence and had developed no deep social roots. The Christian husband was allowed to select from his several spouses the wife he preferred. But the eradication of easy divorce, a traditional practice which had long served to hold down polygamy, was much more difficult. Missionaries also encountered difficulty in eliminating drinking rituals long associated with family celebrations, nature and ancestor cults, and illness. The sacraments were only gradually applied, beginning with baptism. The Eucharist was

[37] *Ibid.*, 33–40.
[38] Schurz, 48–49; Phelan, 20–22, 105–119.

reserved for confessors of several years' standing. Confession and penance were reluctantly accepted by the Filipinos and were therefore ineffective. Confirmation and extreme unction were very rarely given. The practice of selecting godparents for a child from a higher social stratum fitted in with the traditional Filipino kinship patterns and was therefore added to the Christian ritual.

The prevailing Spanish view was that all Asians except the Japanese were basically inferior, inconstant, cowardly, revengeful, and morally weak. The Filipinos in particular copied the vices rather than the virtues of the Spanish. Generally speaking, they absorbed about as much of Catholicism as they could easily digest, which was considerably less than the missionaries would have liked. The digested elements, nevertheless, became an integral part of the Filipino way of life, affording the people a new sense of human dignity, freedom from fear, and elements of social cohesion. The old and the new mingled at the level of the acceptance and comprehension of the Filipino. Christianity in the islands took on a special ceremonial and emotional content, a flavor all its own, markedly selective in its performances. Although indigenous Filipino institutions were inferior in areas of governmental and artistic development to the New World Inca and Aztec, the very lack on the part of the Filipino of a sophisticated indigenous culture made him more able than his American contemporaries to appropriate the essentials of the new faith.[39]

## *Rebellions and the British Occupation of Manila*

Because of the wide differentiation of languages and the fragmentation of the Philippines into numerous island units, periodic expressions of popular unrest were usually localized affairs. Even when sympathetic and simultaneous, they could not be coordinated. The immediate occasion was usually an economic grievance, such as forced labor, cacique exactions, tribute payment requirements, or loss of land. Some such disturbances appear to have centered around more purely political and religious issues. Regardless of cause, the individual or group leadership of a rebellion usually assumed the role of religious prophets appealing on supernatural premises to the traditional predilections of the population.

Related rebellions on Bohol and Leyte in 1621 were cases in point. A demon spirit of the forest allegedly urged the prophets to end Spanish political and economic control, to repudiate Christianity, and to retreat to the protective influence of the hill temples dedicated to the ancestral spirits. Invulnerability was promised. The guns of the foreigners would fail to fire, or if fired fail to kill, and in any case the dead would be brought back to life. Persons imbued with a fanatic faith generated by an orgy of traditionalist magic were usually fearless of death but also completely ineffective militarily. Disillusionment regarding the efficacy of the native

[39] Phelan, 11, 23–26, 53–57, 63–75; Hall, 205–206.

religions as well as the political disintegration of the rebellion followed the inevitable debacle of defeat.[40]

The most serious native rebellion in the seventeenth century started in Luzon in connection with labor exactions imposed during Dutch threats to Manila. Impressed Visayan labor in the Manila shipyards rose in 1649, and the movement quickly spread to their home island of Samar, where fields and homes were abandoned during the course of the fighting. The other rebellion was in the Pampanga section of Luzon in 1660–1661. It developed as an aftermath of the hardships imposed during the Dutch wars and through official efforts to collect unpaid dues of forced labor. This rebellion spread to other islands, where native kings were set up. Missionaries were killed and churches looted. All risings were crushed, and the Pampangans became thereafter the most dependable element of the Filipino constabulary. The Chinese at Parián usually provided a more vulnerable and economically provocative target of Tagalog hostility than did the well-armed Spanish.

Three rebellions can be cited in the eighteenth century. The first began in Bohol Island in 1744, developing from multiple grievances. The leader and several thousand of his followers withdrew into an interior mountain stronghold, where for more than eighty years they resisted Spanish attacks. A more basic issue was raised in a Tagalog rising in 1745–1746 protesting the missionary absorption of communal land for cattle ranches. The third rebellion occurred in 1762–1763, simultaneous with the capture of Manila by British-Indian forces but not coordinated with British designs. The capture was a part of William Pitt's aborted anti-Spanish campaign undertaken at the end of the Seven Years' War. The Filipino rising centered in the Ilokano section of Luzon and involved, for the first time, a real threat to Spanish control. Fortunately for the Spanish, the Pampangan constabulary held firm, and the caciques also rallied to oppose the British and the rebels.[41]

The British-Indian occupation of Manila lasted for some twenty months, beginning in October, 1762. But the conquering forces under Admiral Cornish and General Draper were unable, in the face of Filipino hostility, to extend their control much beyond the bounds of the city walls. A ranking member of the audiencia court, Simon de Anda, refused to accept the governor's decision to surrender and, with the aid of priests and native Christians, mobilized a continuing resistance. Return of the city to Spanish control was arranged by the Treaty of Paris, signed in February, 1763, but the Spanish paid a dear price. The city of Manila was sacked of all valuable treasures, and four hundred houses were burned. An assessed 456,000-dollar indemnity was raised only by raiding the funds of the obras pias. The governor died in January, 1764, and the departing British had to deal in the end with de Anda as acting governor. The occupy-

[40] Sturtevant; Phelan, 147–152; Zaide, 240–241.
[41] Phelan, 145–156.

ing forces returned to India in June, 1764. The damage suffered by Spanish prestige encouraged Filipino uprisings in ten provinces, fortunately uncoordinated. De Anda's forces put them down with some difficulty.

## Reforming Efforts

The shock of the near loss of the islands was the signal for the first serious effort to inaugurate reforms. In the new King, Charles III, the Spanish had a ruler of imagination and one fully in sympathy with the liberal principles of the benevolent despotism of the day. The able new Governor de la Torre repaired the damage to the city and proposed to Madrid a series of far-reaching reforms.[42] The first reformist efforts were directed against the independent-minded and economically dominant regular clergy. The expulsion of the Jesuit Society in 1768 came in conjunction with its general exclusion from the entire Spanish domain. Papal abolition of the society followed shortly thereafter.

A general attack on the position of the friars was launched in 1770, when Simon de Anda became governor in his own right. He enjoyed the full support of Charles III and the backing of the Archbishop of Manila. The indictment alleged commercialism, interference in civil affairs, neglect of spiritual duties, oppression of Filipinos, and opposition to the teaching of the Spanish language. Along with the objective of secularizing friar properties, the archbishop reasserted his titular powers of visitation over parishes manned by the regular clergy. The controversy was bitter. It took a racial turn before its conclusion, with Filipino secular priests contesting the role of the Spanish regulars.

It was one thing to institute reforms on paper and quite another to carry them out in the face of vested interests of long standing. Even with explicit royal sanction for the secularization program, given in 1774, the effort to curb the privileges and wealth of the regular orders petered out. It was virtually abandoned after Governor de Anda's death in 1776. But the racial and national issue was destined to be revived in the following century. Charles III also endeavored without success to abolish the system of hereditary headmen (cabezas) in the barangays. He proposed to make the village magistrates elective and to improve the efficiency of the tax collections. Madrid was too far removed to accomplish such ends.[43]

Following the collapse of efforts to curb the role of the clergy, a serious program designed to make the islands economically self-sufficient was inaugurated. The proposals of the new Governor Don José Basco y Vargas in 1778 included the improvement of agriculture, industry, and commerce. He encouraged the cultivation of cotton, mulberry trees, sugar, tobacco, indigo, and hemp, the mining of ore, and the manufacture of

[42] Zaide, 274–279, 294. The British-Indian government later made an abortive effort in 1773–1775 to take over several of the Sulu Islands.

[43] *Ibid.*, 290–295, 307–317; Phelan, 121–125.

porcelain. With royal approval, he founded the Economic Society of Friends of the Country in 1781. The society continued in operation until 1811, was revived in 1820, and was responsible for establishing an agricultural school at Manila in 1861 and a professorship of agriculture at the University in 1881.

The most noteworthy economic accomplishment was realized in the area of tobacco cultivation. A royal monopoly was established for the commodity in 1780–1782, including controls over production, preparation, and sales. It yielded enormous profits in time, restoring the island's government to complete solvency. During the ensuing century, the islands became the greatest producer of tobacco in the Orient. Even so, the cultivators realized little gain, and in the end corruption and maladministration forced the abolition of the monopoly, in 1881–1882. This and other monopolies, including wine and gunpowder, came to be thoroughly hated by the Filipino people. But the undeveloped agricultural potential of the islands came gradually to be appreciated.[44]

In the area of commercial reform, a new commercial code in 1769 established a corporation of merchants (*consulado*) entrusted with the general supervision of the galleon and other trade. Additional outlets were needed because it was becoming increasingly difficult to dispose of accumulated Oriental goods at Acapulco. Under Governor Basco's leadership the Royal Company of the Philippines was organized in 1785. One-eighth of its stock was purchased by the King of Spain. The Company tried to encourage trade to Spain via Canton, India, and the Cape of Good Hope. In 1789 Manila was opened freely to the world's shipping in Asiatic goods, but the immediate response was disappointing. Outsiders had too long been regarded by Manila as enemies and heretics to feel themselves welcome. By 1795–1796, Chinese and Spanish ships still outnumbered all other arrivals by about 3 to 1. In 1810, one-fifth of the Company's trade was with India, but Indian goods were paid for entirely in Mexican silver.[45] The Company transported very little goods from Europe, and it was unable to break the established pattern of collecting Oriental wares at Manila even though they cost 20 per cent more than at Chinese ports.[46] When the succession of reform governors came to an end in 1806 with Napoleon's occupation of Spain, there was relatively little to show for their desultory efforts.

## The First Half of the Nineteenth Century

The disappearance of Spain's American Empire brought the stream of silver to an end and forced Manila to reorient its trade in the direction

[44] Zaide, 332–335; Schurz, 53–60. The tobacco monopoly produced a half-million-peso profit in 1808 and a 3.5-million peso profit in 1880.

[45] Manila received from Mexico and Peru in 1810 some 2.7 million pesos in silver; of this amount more than 1 million went eventually to India.

[46] Zaide, 332–336; Schurz, 53–60.

of Europe. The last galleon left Manila in 1811, and the last arrival from Acapulco was in 1815. The effect was seen in the port clearances in 1818, when twenty-seven English and American but only twenty-two Chinese and Spanish ships visited Manila. Permission was given for private trading, and the arrival of peninsular Spaniards introduced new ideas and a changed commercial perspective. A dozen or so Spanish firms were in business at Manila in 1840. But the trading pattern for the city disintegrated after 1842, when the British Treaty of Nanking with China opened five additional ports on the South China coast. No longer did the Chinese junks or the foreign traders have reason to resort to Manila. Business died, and Manila was bankrupt by 1850. Little besides the tobacco monopoly was left. Some later gains were made in agriculture, but the general economic situation continued to deteriorate during the remainder of the century.[47]

A French visitor of puritanical leanings reported on Manila discouragingly in 1820. The worthy gentleman was shocked by the habit of the two sexes bathing together and taking naps after dinner lying side by side on floor mats. Everybody smoked "segars," especially the women. Religion, he complained, gave no support to morality, and the Inquisition court was concerned only with outward conformity to orthodox standards. The children of the priests were reared in a convent. The city was, in his opinion, "a habitation unfit for good men. It would be difficult to mention a city where the manners are more corrupt than at Manila; religion is unequal to bridle them."[48]

It is against this evidence of obvious decadence, however much exaggerated in the report, that one must appreciate the disturbing impact of the influx of new waves of regular clergy who invaded the Philippines during the 1820s and 1830s. They were riding the crest of a new surge of missionary enthusiasm characteristic of the ultramontane spirit of post-Napoleonic Europe and comparable in many respects to that of the Counter Reformation. The reconstituted Jesuit Society reentered its old missionary field on the Mindanao frontier, intent on educational advance and on using steam gunboats to corner old pirate enemies. The suppression of many monasteries in Spain in 1835 influenced additional regular clergy to transfer to the Philippines.

The result was to increase the tension between the traditional and the new. Disciplinary standards stiffened markedly, and the old Spanish friction with the Filipino clergy sharpened accordingly. A new regulation issued in 1841 explicitly outlawed regular orders founded by the Filipino community. In 1843 a rebellion, the first of a series extending throughout the remainder of the century, was led by disgruntled native clergy concerned over discriminatory practices of the Spaniards and the lack of edu-

[47] Schurz, 60; Buss, 25–26.

[48] John Crawfurd, *History of the Indian Archipelago* (1820), I, 150, quoting from M. Le Gentil, *Voyages dans les Mers de l'Inde.*

cational opportunity and professional appointments available for Filipinos. Adding fuel to the racial and national discontent was the gathering economic resentment over the enormous landholdings of the clerical orders.[49] The culmination of this controversy will be considered in a later chapter.

[49] Charles Derbyshire, *The Social Cancer: A Complete English Version of Noli me Tangere* (1912), xiii–xviii.

# CHAPTER 12

# Siam and Vietnam

## in the Seventeenth

## and Eighteenth Centuries

*M*ainland Southeast Asian states during the 1600s and 1700s demonstrated sufficient political vigor to resist control by outside powers. In some respects they took advantage of Europeans rather than vice versa. The history of these two centuries therefore must be studied in its own right and not as an addendum to the account of the European impact. Siam, during most of this period, was the strongest and most stable of the mainland states, although this period of its history was not a particularly distinguished one. The state itself survived the rule of several monarchs who were political liabilities personally. The royal succession almost invariably involved palace intrigue if not overt rebellion, accompanied as a rule by the massacre of princely rivals. During most of the 1600s, Siam's rulers sought profitable commercial contacts with European traders and enlisted foreign mercenaries in their service. King Narai was dangerously threatened during the 1680s by a French imperialist intrigue utilizing the high-level political influence of a Greek adventurer. English fortune hunters were also involved. This experience led the Siamese government after 1688 to adopt an isolationist policy with respect to Europeans, which persisted to the middle of the nineteenth century.

Siam's relatively strong position reflected for the most part the weakness of its neighbors. Burma's Ava government was exhausted following Bayinnaung's military efforts of the previous century. Ava managed to hold down the Peguan Mons and to keep control of the Shan plateau as far east as Chiengmai, but the Burmans lived to themselves and did little until the mid-eighteenth century to influence the history of the period. The story of the rise of Burma's Konbaung dynasty after 1740 will be reserved for the next chapter.

During the middle half of the seventeenth century Vietnam was

torn by civil war, north against south. After the pointless feud was eventually abandoned in 1674, the expansionist pressures of the Nguyen government toward the south were absorbed by the hapless buffer state of
Cambodia. The two sections of Vietnam, both highly developed governmentally, tended generally to be suspicious if not hostile to Western contact, the north somewhat more so than the south. Christian missionary
agencies, largely Jesuit and French, continued to function in Vietnam
under great handicaps.

Revival of civil strife in South Vietnam during the 1770s contributed
to a second major French involvement in Southeast Asia, this time under
the sponsorship of a missionary friend of the dispossessed prince, Nguyen
Anh. With French help, Nguyen Anh recovered his throne and succeeded
in uniting the entire country. This unofficial involvement of private adventurers in Vietnam established a tradition of French influence in the
state which found expression in the eventual creation of French Indochina
in the nineteenth century.

## Siam from 1605 to 1670

The successors of Siam's heroic deliverer from Burmese rule, King
Naresuen, who died in 1605, were much concerned with establishing diplomatic and commercial contact with the outside world. Representatives of
the government of King Ekat'otsarot (1605–1610) greeted Dutch and English ship captains at Acheh in Sumatra shortly after the ruler's accession,
inviting both Companies to trade with their country. Dutch trade began
in 1608 and English in 1612. Other foreigners were also welcomed. Portuguese mercenaries serving in the Siamese army were matched after 1600
by the arrival of several hundred Japanese refugees, many of whom were
Christians fleeing from the persecution of General Hideyoshi and the early
Tokugawa shoguns. They came to Siamese Patani as well as to Ayuthia
aboard both Japanese and Portuguese ships. Tokugawa Ieyasu himself
became interested shortly thereafter in trading with Siam as a source of
firearms and gunpowder as well as the usual items of tin and hides. Some
three hundred of the Japanese immigrants were assigned special quarters
at Ayuthia and enlisted as an elite palace guard. They were commanded
by Yamada, one of their own number.

Siam's policy of encouraging outside trade was continued by successive rulers. The fairly obvious motive was to benefit the royal treasury,
since the king assumed monopoly control over all items of foreign commerce, both imports and exports. King Ekat'otsarot imposed a new tax on
ships and markets. But the royal agents dealt responsibly on the whole, and
the Dutch in particular traded profitably, especially after they took over
the traditional Japanese commerce with Ayuthia following the closing of
Japan's ports to all but the Dutch. Another Siamese motive was to en-

courage the revival of the isthmian portage trade, which had long been in abeyance.[1]

The well-intentioned and peaceful-minded King Songt'am the Just (1610–1630) surmounted initial political difficulties and established firm control. He quelled an early protest rebellion by Yamada's guards, who had favored a rival claimant, and then restored their favored status in return for surrender of the P'etchaburi stronghold. He also repelled an invasion from Laos. Then came trouble with Burma over Tenasserim, which was successfully defended for Siam with the help of the Portuguese mercenaries. In the peace of 1618, Siam kept Tavoy but acknowledged Burman suzerainty over Chiengmai in the northwest. During the early 1620s the Dutch traders crowded out their English Company rivals in a viciously waged contest for trade supremacy. The English factory at Ayuthia was closed in 1622 and not revived until almost forty years later, in 1661. Resident Portuguese offended the King by attacking a Dutch ship in 1624, and four years later the entire group of defiant Portuguese was clapped in jail. The pious and ineffective Songt'am was probably best remembered for his discovery and enshrinement at P'rabat of an alleged giant footprint of the Buddha, which became thereafter an important center for pilgrimage.[2]

King Prasat T'ong, who usurped the Siamese throne in 1630 after having poisoned Songt'am and eliminated his two sons, was a criminal person devoid of moral scruples. When the Japanese leader Yamada turned against him, poison was again effectively employed. In 1632, after the Tokugawa shogun had refused to recognize Prasat's usurpation, the King tried unsuccessfully to massacre the entire body of Japanese. The majority made their escape by sea. The Dutch Company, having almost the entire commercial field to itself, managed with great difficulty to keep on passably good relations with the demanding King. It was done at the expense of a considerable sacrifice of dignity (congratulatory letters, etc.), in addition to lavish presents and promised military cooperation against rebellious cities, Patani and Singora. The tension reached the breaking point in 1636 when the drunken King threatened to execute two Dutch prisoners. The Dutch then eased the situation by persuading the queen of Patani, who had survived two attacks, to accept voluntarily the titular suzerainty of Ayuthia. Similar difficulties developed in 1639, 1648, and 1654. In the last instance, the Dutch finally resorted to blockade to bring the King to reason. Prasat T'ong's reign witnessed some creditable reforms, but it exhibited periodic orgies of vindictiveness which counted victims by the thousands.[3] Turpin's possibly overdrawn description of the court itself, based on contemporary

---

[1] W. A. R. Wood, *A History of Siam* (1926), 159–162; D. G. E. Hall, *A History of South-East Asia* (1955), 297.

[2] E. W. Hutchinson, *Adventurers in Siam in the Seventeenth Century* (1940), 35–40; Wood, 166–170.

[3] Wood, 172–181; Hall, 297–301.

reports of missionaries, tells of petticoat intrigue, savage cruelty, and court debauchery.[4]

Following the death of the unlamented King Prasat T'ong in 1656, Prince Narai, a younger son, assumed control, after the usual contest with rival claimants, in 1657. Narai was a vast improvement over his father. He was well-mannered, lively, energetic, unwarlike, friendly. But Narai pursued much the same opportunist policy of seeking to exploit the presence of foreigners for his own ends, and his growing impatience with the Dutch developed into a kind of phobia. It led him in 1659 to invite English Company refugees from Cambodia to reestablish their factory at Ayuthia, promising to waive the required payment of old Company debts. The English factory was revived in 1661; the angered Dutch struck back in 1664 by blockading the Menam River entrance and forcing the King to grant them a new treaty. They exacted among other things a monopoly of the export trade in hides and the prohibition of the use of Chinese and Japanese sailors on Siamese vessels. These two concessions amounted to a virtual assertion of Dutch monopoly over Siam's trade with both China and Japan. Finding that English Company representatives were not willing to be drawn into the morass of the Ayuthia-Batavia feud, Narai eventually looked elsewhere for a counterweight.[5] Meanwhile the English Company found the situation at Ayuthia increasingly unsatisfactory.

Following the Dutch conquest of Macassar in 1667, Narai invited an exiled prince of that city, accompanied by several score of his bloodthirsty followers, to seek asylum in Siam. This experiment in playing up to Indonesian enemies of the Dutch almost ended disastrously when the group proved untrustworthy. Taking advantage of royal favors and interpreting clemency as weakness, the ferocious Macassars in 1686 staged a foolhardy attack on the palace itself, using their favorite weapons of poisoned daggers and swords.[6] Here was no dependable help for Narai. Under these circumstances the King turned finally to solicit assistance from noncompany English fortune hunters and from Holland's powerful European enemy, the French. The course of this episode will be traced later.

Meanwhile, King Narai also became involved in a short and inconclusive war with Burma, consequent on the rise of the Manchu dynasty to power in China. A Manchu army invaded Burma and attacked Ava in 1659 while in pursuit of a Ming rebel prince. Thinking mistakenly that the fall of Ava was imminent, the fearful Burman vassal ruler at Chiengmai asked protection from Ayuthia. A similar request came from the Peguan Mons in Lower Burma. The opportunity was too tempting to refuse. Chiengmai authorities belatedly tried to retract their request for aid after the Chinese had withdrawn, but Siam's armies were already on the move.

[4] M. Turpin, *History of the Kingdom of Siam* (1808), 6–8.
[5] Wood, 190, 194–195.
[6] Turpin, 55–64; Hutchinson, 125–131.

On their second attempt, in 1661, Narai's forces captured and looted Chiengmai. They also staged a deep penetration into Lower Burma in 1662. But it was all to no purpose, for in the end both areas were returned to Burman rule.[7]

These half-hearted expansionist ventures of King Narai were apparently curtailed partly in response to embarrassment associated with a domestic rebellion of Buddhist monks against the impious ruler. The savage crushing of this rising, involving the killing of wearers of the robe, was sacrilege in the eyes of most Buddhist Siamese and entailed further loss of popular support for Narai. The King's rift with the Buddhist hierarchy no doubt contributed also to the friendliness of his reception of successive French missionaries in 1662 and 1664. The missionaries were understandably surprised and gratified over the King's unexpected grant of land for a seminary and his actual assistance in building them a church. They developed a completely unfounded expectation that the opportunist king's gestures made him a likely candidate for conversion. In fact, he was at the time treating a visiting group of Persian Muslim partisans in the same friendly fashion.[8] Developments in the affair will be considered below.

## Vietnam in the Seventeenth Century

Seventeenth-century Vietnamese history was in many respects a repetition of the perennial feuding between north and south in Champa times. Although the Lê dynasty survived as the titular authority, *de facto* Nguyen leadership at Hué and in the south dated from 1558, and Trinh leadership in the north from 1597. The Trinh gained recognition during the 1590s by curbing the troublesome Mac rebels along China's Kwangtung border and were able thereafter to obtain investiture from Peking. The Nguyen-controlled region of the south was less thoroughly Sinicized, including Chinese refugees from Manchu China and other enterprising adventurers, among whom the Confucianist tradition was less strong. Serious trouble between north and south started in the 1620s, when Hué refused to accept the assumed authority of the Trinh over a border province in central Annam.[9]

Most of the initiative in the seven dreary military campaigns extending from 1627 to 1674 came from the Trinh, the stronger of the two rivals in both resources and manpower. But the Annam littoral demonstrated once more the difficulties faced by an invader from the north. The strongest Nguyen defense was a double line of walls above Hué which the Trinh forces failed repeatedly to breach. In the third campaign (1639–1643) the Trinh enlisted the aid of three Dutch men-of-war. When the

[7] Hall, 302; Wood, 191–193.

[8] Turpin, 33.

[9] Hall, 355–356; Jean Chesneaux, *Contribution à l'histoire de la nation vietnamienne* (1955), 43–46.

Nguyen galleys surprised them, capturing one Dutch ship and barely missing taking the other two, Trinh leadership reproached the Dutch for lack of vigor. Batavia thereupon decided to get out of Vietnamese politics and trade. The Trinh armies generally lacked spirit and morale; they fought far from their bases and suffered accordingly from lack of supplies and from illness. The Nguyen defenders, on the other hand, fought on their own soil in protection of their own rice fields. The latter also enjoyed the advantage of better artillery, which they had acquired through trade with Portuguese Macao, especially after 1630. A foundry for cannon manufacture had actually been set up at Hué in 1615 by a Portuguese named Jao da Cruz.[10]

It was this trade with Macao which had opened up all of Vietnam to the penetration of Jesuits and other Portuguese-sponsored missionaries. Some of the Jesuits who were expelled from Japan during the early decades of the seventeenth century came to Vietnam. The mission of Faifo, near Tourane, was established in 1614 by a party of Jesuits who were immobilized at Macao while en route to Japan. They established a similar mission in Tongking in 1626. Faifo was also the center of overseas trade for Chinese, Japanese, and Portuguese. It was to the Faifo mission that the Avignonese Alexander of Rhodes, a gifted linguist, was attached from 1627 to 1630. The remarkable success achieved by Rhodes in the baptism of an alleged sixty-seven hundred Christian converts, including princes at the court, proved to be his undoing. He was denounced by the Trinh government as a disruptive social influence impugning ancestor worship, the imperial cult, and filial piety in general. He and other missionaries were accordingly ordered to be expelled in 1630. Before Rhodes left for Europe he prepared a map, a catechism, and a Vietnamese dictionary.

The prohibition of missionary work in Vietnam was at first not rigidly enforced. The attractiveness of the trade in firearms, cannon, lead, and saltpeter from Macao modified the enforcement of the exclusion order, especially so in the Nguyen section of the country. Rhodes himself managed to return to Tongking several times between 1640 and 1645, when he was definitely and finally banished. It was between 1630 and 1665 that the Nguyen faction was able to build up its military superiority by permitting continuation of the Macao trade, even though this policy permitted the entry of the missionaries. Both Vietnamese protagonists stiffened their exclusionist policies during the 1660s, making the continuance of missionary work extremely difficult. It was the striking contrast between the royal welcome in Siam and the hostility encountered in Vietnam that focused French attention on Ayuthia. The Trinh finally gave up the futile effort to conquer the south after the failure of the seventh campaign in 1674. They concentrated their efforts thereafter on improving their control over the China border areas and in reducing neighboring provinces in Laos to vassal status. The Trinh capital of Hanoi was a populous Venice-like

[10] Lê Thanh Khôi, *Le Viet Nam* (1955), 241–251, 263.

city, with river boats on its many canals paralleling wide paved streets and markets. Heavy taxes imposed on the peasantry provoked rebellions in the second quarter of the 1700s. With the Trinh thus immobilized, the Nguyen meanwhile resumed expansionist efforts against Cham survivors in the mountains and the Khmers of the Mekong delta. For more than a full century after 1674, the two Vietnams remained at peace.[11]

With respect to the shifting of dynasties in China, Trinh Vietnam was consistently pro-Manchu. It recognized the new Ch'ing government in 1664, and Emperor K'ang Hsi sent a friendly return embassy in 1667. Aside from the advantage to be derived from Chinese recognition, the liaison was made closer because the Mac rebels on the border were closely associated with surviving Ming Chinese partisans in Kwangtung province. Ties with the Manchus were strengthened when the Trinh captured the Mac citadel at Cao-bang in 1678. A short time thereafter, a flotilla of fifty Chinese junks full of Ming exiles, including two generals and an estimated three thousand soldiers, appeared at Tourane harbor in South Vietnam asking for asylum. They were sent to the newly occupied areas of the Mekong delta, where one group settled at Mytho and the other at Bien-hoa. They caused Hué some trouble during the next decade, but their settlement contributed to the relentless push into the sparsely populated delta region formerly occupied by the Chams and Cambodians. The last tiny remnant of old Champa was occupied in 1697. The Vietnamese migrants reached the Gulf of Siam in 1700, when a third colony of Chinese was settled at the Ha-tien promontory.[12]

During the century of peace between the two sections of Vietnam, the balance of strength shifted perceptibly in the direction of the south. The north retained the advantage of population superiority and a well-organized governmental structure on the Chinese model. It possessed a broad-based taxation program, a budgetary system, a systematic land survey, and a graded bureaucratic structure. But important weaknessess were present. The economy was static and foreign trade virtually dead. After 1724, the Trinh rulers began putting all government offices up for sale, thus completely undermining official integrity and the Confucianist examination system. Production and internal trade were well articulated, but the landed wealth was concentrated in a limited number of mandarin families. Decline of vigor apparently began in the 1730s; the rulers became increasingly careless and corrupt, and the imposition of additional taxes and *corvée* labor pushed the peasantry into deeper poverty. Rebellion flared from 1739 to 1749, and full pacification was delayed until 1767. The Trinh rulers were clearly losing power long before their final displacement in the 1780s.[13]

[11] *Ibid.*, 264, 285–288, 290–291; Chesneaux, 47–53.
[12] Lê Thanh Khôi, 251, 257, 266–268, 360–362.
[13] *Ibid.*, 253–262.

South Vietnam fared somewhat better in spite of its periodic wars with Siam over control of Cambodia. The elastic frontier in the south afforded opportunity for population movement and expanded economic development. Principal gains were realized in the early decades and at mid-century, when two additional provinces were added. Nguyen bade fair to complete the absorption of Cambodia following the Burman destruction of Siam's Ayuthia capital in 1767, except that a prolonged internal Cochin-China rebellion intervened. This story will be resumed later.[14]

## *Alexander of Rhodes and the French Vicars Apostolic*

The enlistment of the participation of the French Church in the missionary program of Southeast Asia was largely the work of Alexander of Rhodes, the Avignonese Jesuit who had spent a quarter century in the Far East prior to his return to Europe in 1649. He was especially interested in the Vietnamese, among whom he had experienced marked evangelistic success prior to his banishment and whose language he had mastered. After his return the Propaganda agency at Rome published his Latin-Annamese dictionary, a Latin-Portuguese-Annamese catechism, and a map of Annam.

Rhodes advocated three essential proposals to advance the missionary program in Eastern Asia. A concerted effort had to be made, he argued, to train a native hierarchy, from bishops down to priests, if the task of Christianization was ever to be accomplished. This required the enlistment of a group more self-effacing than the Lisbon and Goa archbishops, so intent on maintaining their patronage monopoly. The new leadership must also be more willing than were the regular orders as a rule to turn jurisdictional responsibilities over to native hands. A cadre of missionaries specifically dedicated to this objective would therefore have to be enlisted.

In the second place, Rhodes particularly wanted to enlist the participation of the powerful and influential French Church in the task. France was easily the dominant Catholic power in Europe at the end of the Thirty Years' War, while the two Iberian states were suffering hopeless decline. Portugal had lost out at Malacca and in the Spice Islands, and Spain's influence extended little beyond the Philippines. Finally, Rhodes must find some method of bypassing the patronato claims of the Portuguese through direct papal action. The needed pattern he discovered in the vicariate system, which had previously been employed on at least one occasion in 1636. Vicars apostolic would hold appointment by the Papacy to extinct sees and would enjoy the rank and title of bishops, functioning under the direct authority of the Pope.

Rhodes obtained approval of his plans from Rome in 1653, and the first French vicars apostolic were appointed in 1658. They were selected

[14] *Ibid.*, 269–271.

from a group associated with the University of Paris, both lay and clerical, led by Monsignor Pallu, who himself received the first vicariate appointment. A seminary was established at Paris for training candidates in Oriental languages and other useful subjects in 1663. The Paris Foreign Mission Society (Société des Missions Étrangères) included the seminary, the supporting group at the University, and the missionaries in the field. The program enjoyed the direct approval of the French Court. The first two missionaries of the society left for the Orient in 1658, led by the second vicar apostolic appointee, Lambert de la Motte, the Bishop of Berythe, an extinct see in Asia Minor. His destination was China or Vietnam.[15]

It was quite by accident that de la Motte and his companion, Laneau, ended up in Ayuthia in 1662. Having encountered the virulent hostility of the Portuguese Archbishop of Goa, they contemplated at first the possibility of entering China via Burma, only to be balked by difficulties attending the Burma-China war. They finally crossed the isthmus at Mergui, proceeded to Ayuthia, and then took passage for the Annam coast. The ship was wrecked, and the two Frenchmen found their way back to Ayuthia. Encountering a friendly reception from King Narai, they remained in Ayuthia until the arrival in 1664 of Monsignor Pallu (Bishop of Heliopolis), who had meanwhile been designated vicar apostolic to Tongking. Meanwhile at Paris the French East India Company was revived in 1664 under the direct patronage of Louis XIV, combining two earlier organizations interested respectively in the East Indies and China trade.

Pallu's first visit to Siam lasted only a year, during which he gained favor with the King by assisting in the preparation of defenses for key cities against a Dutch attack expected in 1664, which was actually limited to a blockading operation. Pallu became convinced that Siam rather than Vietnam was the most feasible base for the activities of the society in Eastern Asia and that Ayuthia also could become a center of French political influence. He so reported to both Rome and Paris and obtained an affirmative response to his solicitations for aid from the government of Louis XIV and from the Papacy. A papal bull of 1669 placed Siam and neighboring states under the religious jurisdiction of the new Church at Ayuthia. The French government acted similarly in 1668 following cessation of hostilities with the Dutch and English in Europe.

## The French Intrusion, 1662–1682

French operations in the general area of Southeast Asia during the quarter century following the arrival of the first representatives of the Missions Étrangères developed in three areas—one missionary, the second political, and the third commercial—but all were interconnected.

Earliest on the scene and the most persistent in their commitment were the missionaries. The primary religious interest of Monsignor Pallu

[15] Hall, 302–304, 355–357; Lê Thanh Khôi, 292.

and his associates in the Paris society was qualified to the extent that their program was to be a peculiarly French undertaking. They solicited and obtained the cooperation of the Court at Versailles, French naval forces, and the French East India Company. So pervasive was the idea of a distinctly French missionary effort in defiance of the stultifying Portuguese monopoly that it eventually spread to the Jesuit Society as well. The Jesuit General for France decided in the 1680s after considerable prodding from French Minister Louvois and the confidant of the King, Madame Maintenon, a Jesuit partisan, to associate conversionary efforts in Siam with the establishment of French political control. This decision was accompanied by a shifting of the royal patronage from the Missions Étrangères to the somewhat less inhibited Jesuit order. The shift was not unconnected with the fact that Louis XIV's confessor, Père de la Chaise, was also a Jesuit. The French Jesuit community assumed its autonomy after 1685, and it formally repudiated Portuguese control in 1700. Pending this development and during the first two decades (1660–1682), the direction of the French mission in Siam and its liaison with Paris remained in the hands of the Paris society.[16]

Upon his return to Ayuthia in 1673 after an eight-year absence in France, Monsignor Pallu delivered a personal letter from Louis XIV to King Narai suggesting the desirability of closer political relations between France and Siam. So enthusiastic was Narai's response that Pallu and his associates pressed for an immediate exchange of embassies. This was not possible at the time in view of Louis's Dutch war of 1672–1678. Meanwhile Pallu obtained from the friendly King a grant of land for the mission at Lopburi and permission to establish a seminary at Ayuthia. Three years later the seminary was in operation with one hundred pupils in attendance. A female community known as the Votaries of the Cross was also established. About the same time, a French missionary skilled in medicine obtained assignment as governor of Siam's Puket Island, or Junk Ceylon.[17] Ayuthia thus became the base for French missionary penetration into Cambodia and the two Vietnams.

During the 1670s, the vicars apostolic in Siam and elsewhere began to encounter the rivalry of the Jesuits, who arrived in considerable numbers. Bishop Pallu also aroused the ire of the Spanish Dominicans when he obtained the appointment in 1674 of a Christian Chinese resident in the Philippines named Gregory Lopez as vicar apostolic to China. The angry Spaniards actually arrested Pallu on the occasion of his visit to Manila in 1674, and transported him as a prisoner via Mexico back to Spain. There he obtained release only as a result of the direct solicitation of Rome.

When Pallu again returned to Siam in 1682, he was armed with an explicit ruling approved by the College of Cardinals, dated in 1680, commanding respect on the part of Catholics generally for the authority

[16] Hall, 355–358.

[17] Hutchinson, 43–51; Wood, 195–198; Hall, 303–304.

of the vicars apostolic. He also carried an explicit papal order of 1679 commanding the consecration of Gregory Lopez and directing him to proceed to China to serve as vicar apostolic at Nanking. Dominican pride died hard. It was 1685 before Lopez's consecration was completed at Manila and 1690 before his entry into China was approved. Lopez died in 1691 before entering upon his assignment. The opposition of the Spanish Dominicans was mollified by having the vicariate of Tongking assigned to them in 1693.

Monsignor Pallu's dedication to the religious objectives of the Missions Étrangères was apparently matched by that of his earliest associate in Siam, Monsignor de la Motte. But following de la Motte's death in 1679, the missionary atmosphere at Ayuthia became more politically minded, with the ambitious Jesuit faction setting the tone. Jesuit leaders sought to penetrate to the royal court itself. Their first achievement was to arrange the conversion and enlistment as a Jesuit partisan of a Greek seaman, adventurer, and linguist named Constantine Phaulkon, who became during the 1680s the dominant personality in the Siamese government. This aggressive political trend in missionary policy was strengthened by the pro-Jesuit alignment of the Versailles Court already referred to.[18]

The second and purely political aspect of the French intrusion into the Orient began in 1668 with the sending of a small French fleet. A second and larger fleet sent out in 1670 under the command of Admiral de la Haye was under orders to establish a French base of operations. Ceylon and Banka Island off lower Sumatra were mentioned. Initial plans to enlist Portuguese help to seize the port of Galle in Ceylon from the Dutch fell through, and arrangements were eventually made for cooperation with the Sinhalese government at Kandy against the common enemy, the Dutch. The effort was made in the spring of 1672. Admiral de la Haye, proceeding from the French Company factory at Surat, occupied an offshore island near Trincomalee in eastern Ceylon, where a rendezvous was planned with the Kandian army. The French garrison occupied and fortified the island, but immediately encountered problems of illness and lack of food. The Dutch, stimulated by news of the renewal of war in Europe, reacted promptly and set out to intercept food supplies from Indian ports intended for the French garrison. Within two months, in early July, the dispirited French force, its valid manpower reduced by disease to one-third strength, evacuated the island just a few days before the collaborating Kandian force arrived in the vicinity. The needed French base was eventually established in 1674 at Pondicherry below Madras. Admiral de la Haye's fleet was defeated and captured by the Dutch governor of Ceylon, Van Goens, in September of that same year.[19]

[18] Hutchinson, 68–70; Hall, 355–358.

[19] S. Arasaratnam, *Dutch Power in Ceylon, 1658–1687* (1958), 61–66; Alexander Hamilton, *A New Account of the East Indies* (1727), I, 189.

Efforts of the French government to establish diplomatic contact with King Narai, a policy strongly recommended by Bishop Pallu, were repeatedly postponed. In 1678, near the close of the Dutch war, an eastbound French ship carrying rich presents for the Siamese Court was captured and confiscated by the Dutch. King Narai himself finally took the initiative in 1680 by sending an embassy to France on a returning French ship. But the vessel foundered off the coast of Madagascar, its tragic fate not being known in Siam until 1683. The fates seemed hostile.

French commercial relations with Southeast Asia made almost as slow progress as French political-naval relations. The French established trading connections at Surat in 1668, at Bantam in Java by 1669, and at the fortified post of Pondicherry in 1674. They also made repeated contacts at Tourane and Hué in Vietnam, where missionaries of the Paris society smuggled themselves ashore under the guise of merchants. As a kind of symbolic gesture of accord, one Company ship brought to Hué a present from Louis XIV consisting of two cannons, which were duly delivered by the arriving vicar apostolic. A French factory was established and maintained for a brief period, until the Dutch forcibly intervened. The French used Bantam as an entrepôt base for trading in the Indies until 1682, when the port was closed to all except the Dutch. French missionaries stayed on in Vietnam in spite of difficulties, garnering what satisfaction they could from maligning the reputation of the hated Dutch.

The first French Company representative arrived at Ayuthia in 1680, coming from Surat. He developed a fruitful liaison with the ambitious Constantine Phaulkon, then the mere English-and-French-speaking interpreter for the court but destined to become Siam's Superintendent of Foreign Trade and eventually director of foreign policy. It was the Company representative, backed by the Jesuits, who first proposed that Phaulkon throw in his lot with the French to subvert the independence and integrity of the Siamese state.[20] In 1682, after twenty years of contact with Southeast Asia, the French had little to show for their efforts; and so also had King Narai.

## English Fortune Hunters and Constantine Phaulkon

The English factory at Ayuthia, which was reopened in 1661, encountered discouragements from the start. Part of the trouble was attributable to the Company's unwillingness to make itself a political counterweight against the Dutch as desired by King Narai. Another cause of failure seems to have been the untrustworthy character of Company representatives, who insisted on trading for themselves on the side. The factory operation ran completely aground during the 1660s and had to be revived *de novo* in 1674. But the problems continued much the same. In 1678, Company agents at Bantam sent one George Barnaby to Ayuthia to see

[20] Wood, 195–198; Hutchinson, 43–51.

what could be done to improve the situation. Accompanying him was the thirty-one-year-old Greek, Constantine Phaulkon, whose connections with English traders were of long standing, having started when he became a cabin boy at the age of twelve. He had served acceptably with the Company since 1670 but had resigned in 1678 to try his luck at fortune hunting. In addition to Potts, the head factor of the Company at Ayuthia, Barnaby and Phaulkon became associated with two other resident Englishmen, the brothers White. George White had served as river pilot on the Menam since 1670. His younger brother Samuel arrived in 1675 from Madras, where he had forfeited his caution money by deserting the Company's employ. Samuel had meanwhile become the captain of a Siamese vessel operating from Mergui to transport elephants to India's Masulipatam port in return for Indian textiles.

Relations between Potts and Barnaby at the Ayuthia factory were far from cordial. Barnaby persuaded George White to take service with the Company, and the two employed the precocious Phaulkon to promote their private trading ventures. This kind of operation, which did nothing at all to improve the financial condition of the Company, was heartily disapproved by Potts, even though he himself was apparently no model of efficiency or probity. Potts resented particularly the presence and activity of the incredibly energetic Phaulkon, who mastered Siamese within two years' time; he had previous knowledge of Portuguese and Malay as well as English and French.[21]

In 1680, Barnaby and George White devised a new scheme whereby Phaulkon would enter the Siamese service as commercial interpreter and use his influence to help the English Company oppose the interests of the Dutch. But once having entered the government's service and perceiving the opportunities which it afforded, Phaulkon apparently double-crossed his English friends (according to Potts) and took the side of the Siamese in opposing Company efforts to negotiate an advantageous trading contract. Potts and Barnaby quarreled so violently over Phaulkon and other matters that Barnaby was recalled to Bantam in 1682, shortly before that port was closed to the English by Dutch action. He returned to Ayuthia almost immediately in a private capacity, resuming his cooperation with Phaulkon, who had meanwhile risen to the elevated post of Superintendent of Foreign Trade for King Narai's government. His services to the King in this capacity and as interpreter in connection with visiting diplomatic and commercial missions gave him in time substantial influence over Siam's foreign policy. Before long, Phaulkon obtained the appointment of Barnaby as governor of Mergui, with Samuel White acting as Shahbandar. George White had meanwhile resigned from Company service in disgust and had gone home to England.

The inevitable closing of the unprofitable English factory at Ayuthia was associated with an unseemly quarrel between Company agents and

[21] Hutchinson, 57–62.

Phaulkon, an episode involving quite gratuitously the government of Siam as well. Potts initiated the argument by blaming the burning of the English factory in December, 1682, on his favorite enemy Phaulkon. A special Company agent, honest but overproud, who was sent from Surat in 1683 to make a final proposal of an annual trading contract, tried to ignore Phaulkon in his negotiations. He tried also to persuade the King to stop interloping operations of Barnaby and White from Mergui, for which he held the Greek responsible. The agent's efforts failed completely. He was no match under the circumstances for the former Company underling, whom he was trying to ignore and undermine. The English factory ceased operations in 1684, the agent claiming that a debt of 65,000 pounds was due the Company from Siam's government and from Phaulkon in particular. The subsequent English mission to Ayuthia to solicit payment, sent in 1685, was virtually ignored by the Siamese. The visit coincided with an arrival of an impressive embassy from France.[22]

The denouement in the relations between the English Company and Siam came in connection with efforts of Madras to stop the piratical activities of Barnaby and White from Mergui. These activities were directed mainly against shipping from Golconda state on the Coromandel Coast of India, where Muslim traders had long considered the Mergui trade to be their special preserve. Phaulkon himself had sponsored the plan to use interloper English seamen, easily available, to flood the Bay of Bengal with "Siamese" shipping. But in seeking redress for minor grievances, White's seamen far exceeded the bounds of Phaulkon's authorization and legality itself by capturing seven prizes within the five months from October of 1685 to March of 1686. Phaulkon questioned White's conduct but failed to curb it. Company headquarters at Madras blamed the government of King Narai for the piratical conduct of former members of the English Company.

The embarrassment occasioned for Madras by the operations from Mergui was very real, even though none of its own ships was molested. Indian traders held Madras responsible for the activities of English pirates, and the Company on one occasion went to considerable trouble to recover some stolen pearls for the aggrieved Indian owner. The final decision of Madras to act directly against Mergui was based on a royal proclamation of James II, issued in 1686, forbidding English seamen from serving in ships of foreign rulers in the East. While issuing the peremptory command that White and Barnaby come forthwith to Madras, the Company again presented Ayuthia with the unpaid bill for 65,000 pounds and seized shipping in Mergui harbor pending settlement of the dispute.[23] At the time the Company moved in, Samuel White was preparing to make his escape to England with his accumulated loot in his own ship, using forged seals of the Siamese government to legitimize his ownership.

[22] *Ibid.,* 68–85, 89–91.

[23] *Ibid.,* 125–151; Hall, 309–310.

Captain Weldten, commander of the Madras squadron of three vessels which occupied Mergui port, experienced no difficulty in obtaining agreement with his basic demand that all English quit the service of Siam. In fact the relations between the two English factions were so cordial that they decided to celebrate with a banquet ashore. They failed to reckon with the angry Siamese garrison, which obviously, and with some reason, suspected a considerable degree of collusion in the affair. On June 14, 1687, the evening of the banquet, the Siamese staged a surprise attack. They sank one of the Company vessels and massacred all Englishmen ashore except a few escaping survivors including White and Captain Weldten. White was permitted to sail for England in his own ship, and the Company eventually forgot its debt of 65,000 pounds and its subsequent declaration of war against Siam.[24]

## The Phaulkon-Tachard Conspiracy

After Phaulkon's irreparable break with the English Company, he had little choice but to throw in his lot with the French. King Narai, since the receipt of Louis XIV's first letter in 1673, had regarded the French as the most likely available counterweight to offset the influence of the Dutch. The two were bitter enemies in Europe, and Monsignor Pallu along with other missionaries had encouraged the development of close French ties.

But the conspiracy which was evolved by Phaulkon and Father Tachard, the Jesuit leader, was another kind of affair which the King could not possibly approve. Despite his enormous influence at court, the Greek found himself in a very vulnerable position. His very power, combined with the acquisition of great wealth, attracted the jealous enmity of persons in the government and in the army. Phaulkon's influence rested entirely on his intimacy with the King. Royal backing, in turn, was dependent on the continued physical vigor of the ruler and on Phaulkon's own ability to enlist French assistance without imperiling the independence of Siam. When these conditions disappeared, he was caught in a train of events from which he found no way of escape.

The first suggestion that Phaulkon support the French political intrigue came from a representative of the French Company in 1682, who brought a letter of recommendation from Louis XIV himself. The two became acquainted when the Greek performed his usual role as interpreter for King Narai. Phaulkon would probably have preferred an English alignment if such a policy had been feasible. One indication of his new alignment was his conversion to Christianity by a member of the Jesuit Society, which thereafter claimed his allegiance.

[24] Hutchinson, 134–151; Maurice Collis, *Siamese White* (1936), 303–307.

In 1684, a second, nonnegotiating Siamese mission was sent to France via England, requesting that Louis XIV send an ambassador to Ayuthia with plenipotentiary powers. On this occasion, Phaulkon apparently made a last futile effort through George White to compose his differences with the English Company. The real leader of the Siamese mission, Father Vachet of the Missions Étrangères, presented his much-feted Siamese wards at the Court at Versailles, only to find that Jesuit advisers were in the ascendancy and that the French Court was reluctant to act. His most telling argument proved to be the facts that Phaulkon, the dominant personality at King Narai's Court, was a recent Jesuit convert and that there appeared to be a very real chance to convert the King as well.

The returning French mission to Siam was headed in 1685 by the Chevalier de Chaumont, a converted Huguenot who was fanatically bent on accomplishing the King's conversion. He was escorted by two warships. The large clerical contingent was now headed by Père Tachard, a learned Jesuit scholar. The Missions Étrangères group was represented, but its leaders were now divorced from policy direction. The squadron made stops at the Cape of Good Hope and at Batavia, arriving at Ayuthia in the fall of 1685. At the time Madras was still pressing Siam to honor the English Company debt.[25] The ensuing negotiations proceeded at two levels, one between Chaumont and King Narai, with Phaulkon acting as interpreter, and the other between Father Tachard and Phaulkon. The exhortations of the head of the French mission looking toward the conversion of the King were duly toned down in Phaulkon's transmittal of the conversations. He also put into the mouth of the King a very sensible rejoinder about the value of religious variety. The astute Greek was thus very much in control.

The formal treaty draft concluded in December, 1685, gave France fairly substantial commercial concessions, including freedom to trade, a monopoly in the export of pepper (of which Siam had little), and a partial monopoly of tin. In addition, the Malay port of Singora, near Patani, was to be garrisoned by French troops, presumably as a deterrent against a possible Dutch attack. A French alliance was implied but not explicitly indicated; Chaumont, at Phaulkon's prompting, did make an oral reference to the matter. The dispatch of a French military force was to constitute the earnest of their firm alliance.[26]

The more serious negotiations looked toward the prospective control of the kingdom by the Jesuits. The plans included the French garrisoning of at least two armed fortresses and the infiltration into the Siamese government as governors and heads of fortresses, at Phaulkon's direction, of three- or fourscore able Frenchmen, preferably members of the Jesuit order, but disguised as laymen. Phaulkon undertook to guarantee

---

[25] Hutchinson, 99–121; Hall, 305–306; Wood, 200–204.
[26] Wood, 200–204.

that the next king would be amenable to the acceptance of French aid. The proposed conversion began to look more like subversion. On the return trip to France, a high official at the Ayuthia Court accompanied Chaumont, while Père Tachard carried the proposals worked out between himself and Phaulkon.

The French government negotiators at Paris decided to raise the stakes on both the formal and the informal aspects of the proposed agreement. They asked for more sweeping commercial concessions, including extraterritoriality for French residents. They also proposed to the Siamese representative, quite unsuccessfully, that Mergui be ceded to France as a shipbuilding and naval repair base. This seems to have become the principal objective of French policy. They decided to demand through Tachard that Phaulkon substitute Bangkok and Mergui as the fortresses to be occupied by French troops, since Singora was too remote to be of use to France. Phaulkon was to be compensated by being knighted and made a Count of France. French troops would seize Bangkok if resistance developed to these demands.[27]

The French expedition which returned to Siam in 1687 was top-heavy on the naval side. It included six warships and a troop contingent commanded by Marshal Desfarges numbering only 636 men. The two plenipotentiaries were again accompanied by Père Tachard and fellow Jesuits, plus a representative of the French Company. More than one hundred of the troops were lost by illness on the outward voyage, and many of the five hundred who arrived were ill. Before acceding to the French demand for garrison assignment at Bangkok and Mergui, Phaulkon found it necessary, in order to quiet Siamese suspicions, to require that all French soldiers take an oath of allegiance to King Narai and subject themselves to Phaulkon's own orders. This demand was resented by the French envoys, but their own men were in no condition at the time to contest the order.

When the disposition of the French forces was finally made, the Bangkok fortress garrison was reduced to two hundred men (twelve hundred were needed). One hundred twenty were assigned to Mergui; thirty-five were sent to pursue pirates in the gulf; others provided a small bodyguard for the palace at Lopburi, where Phaulkon resided. More than one hundred others were either dead or invalided. Under the circumstances, the Missions Étrangères turned against Phaulkon, the King's Minister, and the unhappy French envoys must have wondered who was being exploited and by whom. Only Marshal Desfarges and Father Tachard among the French leaders continued to put confidence in the wily Greek. The French treaty in its final form provided more extensive trading privileges, exemption of resident Frenchmen from local courts, and French control of all islands within a 10-mile radius of the port of Mergui. Tachard returned

[27] Hutchinson, 110–121.

immediately to France to recruit the French personnel to be infiltrated into key government posts by Phaulkon. When the news of Phaulkon's death six months later reached France, Tachard reportedly disbanded no fewer than one hundred men whom he had selected.[28]

Phaulkon's downfall in the spring of 1688 was precipitated by a serious illness of the Siamese King. This afforded opportunity for action by the many enemies of the now virtually isolated Minister. They were led by General Pra P'etraja, who had just returned from a victorious campaign in Cambodia. In the crisis, Phaulkon commanded the French garrison at Bangkok to proceed to Lopburi, ostensibly to protect his own pro-Christian candidate for the throne. But General Desfarges, presumably advised by representatives of the Missions Étrangères, refused to obey. He suggested another possible candidate for the throne, and retired to the safety of the Bangkok fortress. Some of the Jesuit fathers joined his garrison. Phaulkon, defenseless, was arrested in May and executed in June, 1688. King Narai also died, on July 11, 1688. The final step was to evacuate the French forces.

The sensible Siamese authorities preferred to negotiate the French withdrawal rather than to incur further enmity and bloodshed by storming the meagerly manned Bangkok fortress. The French garrison at Mergui fought its way out, the survivors making their way to Pondicherry. Arrangements were made for Desfarges to depart via Mergui on Siamese ships in November, 1688, on condition of hostage liability. Hostages and missionaries of the Paris society who stayed behind were roughly handled, especially in 1689 after the returning Desfarges captured and held Puket Island for a time. The vicar-bishop lost his life as a result of this indiscretion. But the persecutions stopped in 1690, and representatives of the Missions Étrangères were thereafter permitted to resume their work. Subsequent negotiations at Ayuthia by Father Tachard in 1689 were unproductive, as were English Company efforts to acquire the use of Mergui. Meanwhile the patient Dutch negotiated a new commercial agreement with Siam and set up business at the old stand.[29]

## Siam after 1688

The story of the seventeenth-century intrigue at the Court of Ayuthia carries more significance than the mere disclosure of events themselves. It affords a close-up look at the atmosphere of intrigue and chicanery prevailing at an Oriental capital-port during the period of Dutch commercial hegemony. The situation reflected, for one thing, the enormous military prestige acquired by Europeans in general both as a source of arms and as persons belligerently expert in their use. This consideration was behind King Narai's dangerous wish to find a French counterpart to the assumed

[28] *Ibid.,* 114, 155–165.
[29] *Ibid.,* 151–152, 160–169, 172–177; Hall, 312–314; Wood, 214–218.

threat of Dutch intimidation. The episode reveals also the narrow line, especially among the English, separating the traders' duties to the Company and the furtherance of their private fortunes. A similarly detailed look at the Dutch trading activities would probably disclose the same situation. The story reveals also the intimate association of Catholic missionary zeal with the objectives of national aggrandizement, as well as the inveterate rivalries existing between competing missionary agencies. The total picture also explains why the cultural and economic contributions of Europeans in such areas as Siam and Vietnam were so meager.

One of the most unfortunate aspects of King Narai's flirtation with foreign adventurers was that it aggravated once more the always-difficult problem of the orderly succession of rulers. The designation of the Uparat, or vice-king, as presumptive heir to the throne, was thereafter in Siam honored more in the breach than in the observance. The rough soldier P'etraja, who overthrew Phaulkon, ended the French threat, and himself usurped control, faced almost interminable rebellions throughout his troubled fifteen-year reign. He earned a reputation for intemperance, cruelty, and moral depravity matched by few other rulers in Siam's history. Successions to the throne were normally accompanied by vengeful palace revolutions, occasionally developing into full-scale civil wars. The decline of Siam's military vigor and discipline was demonstrated in the disgraceful performance of land and sea forces in a fruitless campaign conducted against Cambodia in 1717. In 1733, a group of three hundred annoyed Chinese actually attacked the palace at Ayuthia.[30]

An English visitor to Ayuthia in 1720 described a well-fortified city 10 miles around, located within a great loop of the Menam River. The site was transformed into an island by the digging of a canal connecting the bases of the loop. The city itself was pierced by numerous canals. The guns of entering foreigners had to be deposited at the mouth of the river. The King was reported to be fond of lofty titles and particularly proud of his possession of a sacred white elephant. He traveled in state by elephant cavalcade ashore and by gilded-barge procession on the river. The people lining the route of travel were invariably prostrate at his passing. The highest officials of the realm were subject to his autocratic whim. The Siamese population, on the whole, was described as temperate and well behaved. Marital vows were faithfully observed; parents cared for children and children for aged parents. Both sexes wore their hair clipped around the edges and close-cropped, 2 inches long at the center.[31] Women customarily minded the stalls in the market place. Chinese residents were very numerous. Buddhist temples, some of them massively impressive, were everywhere in evidence in the city and capable of accommodating an estimated fifty thousand monks.

[30] Wood, 219–232.
[31] This same hair style was common in Pegu and Laos.

The position of the European foreigner in 1720 was described as unenviable. The Dutch factory still dealt in skins, tin, and sapanwood intended mainly for the Japanese market, but commercial intercourse under the royal monopoly was becoming increasingly difficult. The suspicion of European traders in particular outweighed the court's interest in either bribes or imported luxuries. A highly irresponsible Persian was apparently acting as Shahbandar. It would be the mid-nineteenth century before Siam's rulers would again welcome the foreigner. The octogenarian French bishop of the Missions Étrangères in 1720 operated a church and a seminary at Ayuthia. But Christian converts were very few and often insincere. The completely renegade Portuguese Christian community was served by priests whose conduct was allegedly scandalous.[32]

Siam's dependencies in the isthmus and northern Malaya were far from prosperous in the early 1700s. The eastern shore of Malaya was the prey of Bugis pirates, whom neither the Dutch nor the Siamese made any serious effort to suppress. Johore sent a tribute mission to Ayuthia once in three years. Trengganu port was closed by a bar for half the year, and the Malay coast as far north as Patani was too disorderly to permit normal trade. A Dutch brick factory at temple-studded Ligor bought up all available tin output. Along the western coast, Mergui was closed to Europeans but available to Coromandel and Bengal traders. The shoreline from Mergui to Junk Ceylon was infested with pirate bands and slave traders, while the resident Chinese who had regularly bought up the Siamese governorships in the isthmus region were so rapacious that local enterprise in tin mining was discouraged. Kedah had discarded its vassalage to Siam, but it was now a poor, isolated state with a capital-port located some fifty miles inland.[33]

## Continuance of French Interest in Southeast Asia

Official French interest in Southeast Asia reached a low ebb during the quarter century following the fiasco of 1688 in Siam. The union of the Crowns of Holland and England in 1689 and the consequent initiation of a Second Hundred Years' War between France and England approximately doubled the resistance which French enterprises might expect to encounter in the Indies. The final two wars of Louis XIV exhausted France and eliminated all possibility of continued royal support either to the Missions Étrangères and the French Jesuits or to the French Company of the Indies.

The bankrupt French Company was revived from 1719 to 1725 under the promotional magic of the fabulous John Law. A prosperous trade developed between Pondicherry and Canton, but if the operation

---

[32] Hamilton, 85–103.
[33] *Ibid.*, 35–41, 81–85.

was to expand, it needed to acquire an interim point of contact on the east side of the peninsula. The Company sponsored an examination in 1721–1723 of the possibilities of Pulo Condore Island, located some 50 miles south of the Mekong delta, but the site proved to be unsuitable. A more favorable report on Tongking was received in 1737. The Vietnam coast appeared to afford the only feasible location for the needed French Company post, a conclusion which received the hearty approval of Catholic missionary interests.

During the period since 1688, the operations of the vicars apostolic had ceased to be an exclusive French affair. The Spanish Dominicans took over the Tongking vicariate in 1693. Following the subsequent wholesale expulsion of missionaries from China as a consequence of the Rites controversy, the Vietnamese field was flooded with new recruits. From 1728 to 1739, the leadership of the vicariate system was assigned to an Italian, even though the Paris society continued active in the operation. Since the Trinh rulers of North Vietnam refused to relax their hostility to missionary work, most of the new missionaries came to Hué and the south Annam coast. Regardless of nationality, however, the missionaries in Vietnam welcomed the proposed establishment of French trading contacts as a means of securing a relaxation of official antagonism to their activities.[34]

Events of the War of the Austrian Succession, particularly Dupleix's conquest of Madras, the principal British Company post in India, afforded the French a long-awaited opportunity to make a forward move in Southeast Asia. Initial contact with the Nguyen ruler at Hué was made by Captain Freil, a nephew of Dupleix, in 1747 on his return from a trading trip to Canton. But before the ruler's encouraging response could be exploited, the French Company lost its temporary ascendancy in India by the restoration of Madras to Britain in the 1748 peace settlement. Nevertheless one Pierre Poivre, an ex-missionary of the Paris society and an ardent advocate of French trading entry into Vietnam, led a French Company mission to Hué in 1749–1750. He succeeded in arranging a commercial treaty with the Nguyen authorities and also acquired information about trading possibilities in Tongking. But upon his departure, he offended the ruler by abducting a useful interpreter, whereupon the King retaliated by expelling twenty-seven French missionaries. Between the difficulties encountered in obtaining the return of the missionaries in 1752 and the problems of establishing trade itself, the project of a French factory in Indochina faltered. The French Company recalled Dupleix in 1754, and the entire French Empire in India collapsed politically during the course of the ensuing Seven Years' War. The French Company itself folded for a second time in 1769, after which the Paris authorities shifted their attention to opposing British interests in the New World.

[34] Thomas E. Ennis, *French Policy and Development in Indochina* (1936), 24–25. Converts in the Tongking mission totaled three hundred or less in 1760. They were far more numerous in South Vietnam.

# The Unification of Vietnam: Pigneau de Behaine

The steady infiltration of Vietnamese refugees and settlers into the Mekong delta area, which met with only a feeble protest from Cambodia and no effective rejoinder from Siam, appeared to be nearing a complete victory for the Nguyen rulers of Hué in the mid-1700s. Cambodia had to surrender claims to additional delta lands in 1749. The emergence shortly thereafter of the aggressive Konbaung dynasty in Burma was sufficient to immobilize Siam on the other side of Cambodia. South Vietnamese forces took over unchallenged control of Cambodia following the Burmese capture and destruction of Ayuthia in 1767. The vigorous reassertion of Thai influence in the capture of Phnom Penh in 1771 by Siam's new leader, P'ya Taksin, was short-lived, for Nguyen forces promptly occupied the city. But just as the Vietnam triumph seemed to be assured, South Vietnam was obliged to face at home the formidable Tay-son rebellion. This new conflict was destined to enlarge its scope and to continue for more than a quarter of a century.

The rebellion initiated by the three Tay-son brothers differed from the dynastic feuding of the previous century in being economically and popularly motivated. It derived much of its support from popular opposition to the exploitive tyranny of kings and mandarins, whether Nguyen or Trinh. Its supporters included merchant groups, peasants, Buddhist and Taoist partisans, and even some of the Moi hill folk. A British visitor-negotiator in 1822 discovered that the Tay-sons even at that late date were still regarded by many as having governed with greater equity and moderation than either their Nguyen or Trinh enemies.[35]

The course of the conflict was tortuous and confused. The Tay-son rebels first attacked Saigon in 1772–1773, but they were obliged in 1775 to proceed northward to dislodge the Trinh armies, which had meanwhile seized Hué. Upon their return to Saigon in 1777, they eliminated virtually the entire Nguyen dynasty, with the notable exception of a fifteen-year-old boy named Nguyen Anh. The prince took temporary refuge in the frontier gulf town of Ha-tien, where resided at the time a thirty-six-year-old French vicar apostolic named Pigneau de Behaine. The two fled the city together, taking refuge on a nearby island in the Gulf of Siam. At this juncture, 1778, both French and British authorities in India recognized the opportunity afforded them by events to win favor in Vietnam by championing the cause of the exiled prince, but neither was free to act. France had just openly allied with the rebelling American colonists.

Nguyen Anh was twice able to rally support and stage a partial recovery of control from the Ha-tien base, once in 1778–1781 and again in 1782–1783. On the second occasion, his French friend returned with him to Saigon. But the Tay-sons retook the city and again hounded the two

[35] Lê Thanh Khôi, 269–272; Hall, 362–363; Chesneaux, 57–63.

out of the country, chasing them from island to island until both sought safety in Siam. A final forlorn effort to return was made in 1784 with Siamese aid. The Nguyen cause seemed hopelessly lost. It was under these discouraging circumstances that the vicar offered to seek aid from French sources. He left for Pondicherry in December, 1784, accompanied by the five-year-old Prince Nguyen Canh.[36]

Pigneau de Behaine had been sent out by the Missions Étrangères in 1765. He had arrived in Cochin-China just prior to the Burmese capture of Ayuthia. Following that disaster, he was put in charge of a missionary college which had evacuated from Siam to Ha-tien, a coastal border town whose control had been repeatedly contested between Ayuthia and Hué. Pirates invaded the town and burned his school in 1770, forcing Pigneau to withdraw temporarily to Pondicherry, where he set up another seminary project. He was made vicar apostolic and Bishop of Adran in 1774, while still in India. He returned to Ha-tien just in time to become again a refugee, this time in the company of Prince Nguyen Anh.

The bishop and the little Prince Canh found no encouragement when they stopped in India in 1785. After remaining in Pondicherry for more than a year, they departed for France in July, 1786, accompanied by a Vietnamese retinue of some twoscore soldiers. They arrived in Paris penniless in early 1787, but their fortunes quickly improved. Through the enthusiastic assistance of the aged Pierre Poivre, the vicar raised a considerable sum of money and got a hearing at court. He eventually obtained from Louis XVI's government a tentative alliance agreement promising French military aid in return for exclusive trading privileges in Vietnam and the cession of Pulo Condore Island and the harbor of Tourane, which would be used as a shipbuilding and repair center. The contemplated military aid of four French frigates and 1,650 men, fully equipped, included a company of artillery and some 250 Indian sepoys. The bishop and his party returned to Pondicherry in May, 1788.[37]

Meanwhile the Tay-son forces had moved northward against the Trinh, capturing Hanoi in 1786. But Trinh elements continued to resist tenaciously in North Vietnam, where they were accorded substantial support from suzerain China. It was not until 1788 that the rebels drove the remnants of the Trinh across the northern Tongking border and carried their naval counterattack to the South China coast. This substantial diversion afforded opportunity for Nguyen Anh, with Siamese help earned by his own enlistment with them against the Burmese in 1786–1787, to return to the Mekong delta, where he again organized his supporters. He was able to recapture the undermanned city of Saigon in September, 1788. The first contingent of French aid reached Saigon shortly thereafter, just in time to help him consolidate his hold.

[36] Hall, 364–368.

[37] John F. Cady, *The Roots of French Imperialism in Eastern Asia* (1954), 11–12; Michel Du'c Chaigneau, *Souvenirs de Hué* (1941), 1–14; Hall, 369–370.

But the aid came from private sources, not from France. Governor Conway of Pondicherry (of Conway Cabal fame), acting under discretionary orders from Paris, was entirely unwilling to honor the treaty terms or to participate in what he regarded as a romantic and dangerous adventure. The redoubtable Pigneau was undeterred. Using funds raised in France and from other French sources, he was able to assemble four shiploads of military stores including artillery and to enlist some one hundred (or more) officers and men as volunteers. By no means all of them were French. The bishop acquired two ships of his own, and Conway provided the frigate *Meduse* and another vessel to escort the final contingents to Saigon, including Pigneau himself in July, 1789.[38]

Exactly how decisive the aid of the French was in achieving the victory of Nguyen Anh is a matter of some dispute between historians. The original verve of the Tay-son movement tended to evaporate following the death in 1792 and 1793 of the two remaining brothers. But the most disparaging estimates of the French role concede that French assistance gave to the Nguyen side superiority in artillery plus valuable assistance in building, equipping, and officering a naval force, which alone permitted the carrying of the war to a victorious conclusion in the north. The reinforcement from the French also did much to lift the morale and expectations of their allies, even though predictions of further aid to come were quite exaggerated.[39] The French contributed aid when and where it was most urgently needed in naval and artillery development and in training and fortifications. The volunteers included at least twenty French officers, highly motivated, expertly trained, and able to direct the labors of other volunteers. One need only refer to the previous history of the effectiveness of casual Portuguese adventurer and mercenary units in Southeast Asian warfare to validate the importance of the performance of the French. They transformed a defensive effort on the part of a struggling vassal prince just returned from exile into a successful campaign to unify all of Vietnam, a task which no previous Nguyen ruler had dreamed of accomplishing.

The total French-led force may have numbered at its maximum strength 360 men. Approximately one hundred were volunteers recruited in India, including men with considerable military experience. An estimated 125 sailors defected from the crew of the *Meduse*. A third contingent of unknown size drifted down from Macao and other ports, drawn from French ships which were forcibly disarmed by British craft during the course of the ensuing war. From one such ship, a naval frigate on a round-the-world voyage, came Jean Baptiste Chaigneau, a twenty-five-year-old

[38] Cady, 13–14; Hall, 369–370; Lê Thanh Khôi, 300, 313–321.

[39] Lê Thanh Khôi (320–321) discounts the importance of the French role on the ground that the Vietnamese did most of the fighting, especially in the later phases. Finlayson's *Mission to Siam and Hué* (1826), 354–355, mentions twenty Frenchmen as having been in the service of Gia Long.

naval officer with his French wife, in 1791. An older naval officer named Vannier, who had come in 1788, had been present at the surrender of Cornwallis at Yorktown and had fought with de Grasse against Rodney. Admiral Dayot built and commanded the Vietnamese navy.[40] The senior military officer was Puymandel, an expert in preparing fortifications and in training methods. A late English visitor to Hué in 1820 marveled at the superior character of the city's fortifications, based on the pattern of Vauban. He commented also on the excellence of the army barracks and the surprisingly effective arsenal for the manufacture of artillery up to 64- and 93-pound calibers.[41] Pigneau himself served the cause indefatigably as organizer, administrator, and Foreign Minister.[42]

Most of the French volunteers left Vietnam by 1794–1795, after receiving news of revolutionary developments in France. Five of the key French officers were still present in 1799 at the time of Pigneau's death; four remained in 1802. Vannier and Chaigneau alone remained after 1809, the first being married to a Vietnamese. Nguyen Anh was apparently able, after 1795, to continue the struggle largely on his own resources.[43] It was not an easy victory. The Tay-sons' fleet was destroyed in 1792, but their main land fortress had to be captured twice, in 1799 and 1801. Hué was first occupied by the Nguyen forces in 1801, and Hanoi, the key city in Tongking, in 1802. In June, 1802, at Hué, the victorious prince proclaimed himself Emperor of Vietnam under the reign title of Gia Long. He obtained Chinese investiture in 1804. His own record as Emperor and that of his successors will be considered in a later chapter.

The Bishop of Adran survived long enough to envisage the final triumph of the cause with which he had so devotedly identified himself. He died after a prolonged illness with dysentery in October, 1799, exhausted by the debilitating climate, his assiduous labors, and disease. He was buried at Saigon with high military honors. A monument marking the grave recorded the ruler's appreciation of his faithful services and personal qualities, and a guard of honor was long posted over the spot.[44] This sad event affords opportunity to end the account of two centuries of confused history of Vietnam and Siam on a somewhat creditable note.

[40] John Crawfurd, *Journal of an Embassy to the Courts of Siam and Cochin-China* (1828), 256. The entire naval contingent contained fourteen or fifteen experienced officers, including two named Forgant and Barizy.

[41] *Ibid.*, 250.

[42] Cady, 14; Hall, 370. For a complete account of the career of Pigneau de Behaine see Charles B. Maybon, *Histoire Moderne du Pays d'Annam; 1592–1820* (1920), chaps. V–IX.

[43] Lê Thanh Khôi, 320–321. Chaigneau, 14–18; Hall, 374.

[44] Hall, 370–371; Chaigneau, 13–14.

# CHAPTER 13

# Burma's

## Konbaung Dynasty

*B*urma's inland-centered state, following the loss of Tenasserim to the Siamese in 1615, ruled the central valleys from Martaban and the delta on the south to Shwebo on the north. The Shan sawbwa princes as far east as Chiengmai were vassals of Ava, but except for border Myosa fiefs and states, Burman control was tenuous and lightly imposed. Shan states to the north and east of Ava were as much under Chinese as under Burman suzerainty. Ava managed to fend off a Manchu invasion in 1658 by surrendering the Ming prince to whom it had given asylum; it retained Chiengmai only because that city preferred light Burman rule to the heavier hand of Ayuthia. Meanwhile, Mon nationalism in the south (prior to the 1730s) glowed only faintly, as fire in the ashes, following the devastation suffered under Bayinnaung. The institutional patterns of Burmese government and society were being crystallized, but vigorous leadership was lacking until the mid-eighteenth century.

Another explosive demonstration of Burman military might, comparable to that under Aniruddha and Bayinnaung, was instigated by a nearly successful effort on the part of the Mons after 1740 to conquer the entire central valley. Finding a leader in the son of a myothugyi of Moksobo (Shwebo), who called himself Alaungpaya, the Burmans reestablished a short-lived empire rivaling in size that of Pagan. It included all the northern Shan states up to the Chinese border, the kingdom of Siam itself for a brief period, the Tenasserim coast, the kingdom of Arakan, with eventual threats in the direction of Chittagong, Manipur, and Assam on the Indian side. This expanding Burmese state eventually encountered effective opposition from Bengal, taken over by Britain's Clive in 1760. This chapter will trace the story of Konbaung Burma up to 1819, prior to the first serious clash with the power of British India.

## *Burma from 1635 to 1740*

The permanent transference of the capital of Burma northward from Pegu to Ava in 1635 meant the surrender of any idea of an alliance with the coastal Mons and Burma's withdrawal from active commercial and diplomatic contact with the outside world. English and Dutch traders who tried repeatedly to establish factories at Syriam and elsewhere found Ava not interested in trade except as a means of exploiting the foreigner or of acquiring prestige and military facilities. Xenophobic hatred of foreigners and a conviction of Burma's own superiority influenced the outlook of the Ava government. A few constructive moves were made by King Thalun (1629–1648). He supervised the compiling of an improved lawbook based on India's ancient Code of Manu. He also made a complete inventory of landholdings within his realm and improved the administration of the royal irrigated lands assigned to ahmudan army units. But weak rulers followed Thalun.

King Pindale (1648–1661) and his brother-successor King Pye (1661–1672) faced serious difficulties on the Chinese border connected with the previously mentioned liquidation of the final expressions of Ming resistance to the new Manchu regime. Ava's first problem was to halt the oppression of the Shan princes along the Yunnan border by the partisans of prince Ming Yung-li in 1650. After the prince finally fled to Burma and was interned at Sagaing in 1658, his own desperate Ming followers, bent on recovering their leader, ravaged all of Upper Burma to the very walls of Ava and south as far as Pagan. King Pye finally had to take over control from the palsied hand of his brother, but he faced the invasion of an overpowering Manchu army, to which he was obliged to surrender the ill-fated prince in 1662. Meanwhile, King Narai of Siam had conquered Chiengmai, as previously indicated, and had penetrated in halfhearted fashion far into Lower Burma. Fortunately for Ava, Narai was lacking in aggressive imperialist designs and obsessed by his growing fear of the Dutch. Chiengmai by itself excluded the Siamese conquerors and again sought alliance with Ava, while Narai evacuated all of Lower Burma except the Tenasserim coast.

The ensuing eighty years of Burmese history constituted a period of stagnation and decline. The reigns were short and punctuated by palace intrigues and mass executions of princely rivals. The last three of the Ava line of rulers were complete nonentities. The kings were mere figureheads, almost palace prisoners; a coterie of royal ministers dominated the government. Burma lost the Kabaw Valley, located west of the Chindwin River, to the Manipuris, whose horsemen inaugurated a series of destructive raids. The enfeebled government was incapable of making an effective rejoinder.[1]

[1] D. G. E. Hall, *A History of South-East Asia* (1955), 318–324.

It was apparently during this period that the chief ministers, or Wungyis (great burden bearers), began to function corporately with respect to policy, administration, and high judicial affairs. The Wungyis were four in number. As a Council they eventually took the name *Hlutdaw* (place of release), adapted from the chamber or courtroom adjacent to the palace wall where their daily sessions were held. Each Wungyi had a younger assistant called a *Wundauk* (support or prop). In the presence of incompetent fear-stricken kings, hardly daring to leave the sacred palace precincts, the Hlutdaw came to exercise virtually plenary authority, unless and until the Wungyis were restrained by the ruler himself. Their responsibilities included foreign policy, army and navy, taxation and expenditure, appeals from the provincial courts, and general administration. For matters which concerned the palace as distinct from the government generally, the ruler was assisted by four *Atwinwuns*, or "interior burden bearers." Such governmental institutions were obviously no substitute for a vigorous ruler, for all ministers were entirely subject to his despotic whim, but the Hlutdaw officials did provide an essential element of stability within the limits of their assumed authority.[2]

Following the disastrous experiences of 1687 and 1688 at Mergui and Bangkok, both the French and British in India became interested in Burma for other reasons than trade. Locked as they were in desperate competition for naval control over the Bay of Bengal, both European Companies needed an accessible port of call for repairs and shipbuilding, especially one capable of access during the period of the northern monsoon. From October to the end of the year, the Coromandel Coast of eastern India was subjected to destructive hurricanes, from which the available open roadsteads offered no protection. The nearest repair base for the British fleet was Bombay and for the French ships Mauritius Island. Burma's port of Syriam offered by contrast not only shelter from the northern monsoon, but also an abundant and cheap supply of teakwood timber and skilled labor. The English Company, therefore, established a repair dock at Syriam in 1709, which it placed under the management of a non-Company person. The dockyard was used until 1743, when it was destroyed by a Mon rebellion, although the Company had shifted its own business back to Bombay in 1741. The French also operated a dockyard at Syriam for more than a decade after 1729. Involvement in Burma's affairs in consequence of measures taken to meet these shipping needs was to cost both Companies dearly in succeeding decades.[3]

Visitors to Lower Burma in the early 1700s reported a most discouraging situation. The once-great city of Pegu was only one-twentieth of its former size. The country around it was jungle, the haunt of wild

---

[2] John F. Cady, *A History of Modern Burma* (1958), 13–17.

[3] G. E. Harvey, *History of Burma from the Earliest Times to 10 March, 1824* (1925), 141–186.

animals, where populous villages had once stood. Deermeat sold for 3 to 4 pence a pound. Apparently the Ava government exercised little actual control outside the main river corridor and Pegu and Syriam. Syriam's limited perimeter was protected by a wall of stone, but four-fifths of the city's population lived outside the wall. Its merchant population included an assortment of Armenians, Portuguese, and Muslim Indians. Pagoda ruins were visible everywhere, but no repairs were being made.

The contrast drawn by observers between the disciplined, kindly, and abstemious Buddhist monks—eating one meal a day and often dwelling, as in Pagan times, in the depths of the forest—and the conduct of the port population was striking. Native women wore scanty clothing, high slit skirts with thighs exposed; temporary marital alliances were easily arranged for foreign visitors; parents allegedly even offered daughters to their temporary guests. European gunners visiting the port were especially popular, being regularly assigned wives for an indefinite stay. Propitiation of evil spirits, especially for illness, was widely practiced. As described by one visitor, a traditional dance to the earth goddess involved a fit-induced shamanistic orgy on the part of a female medium allegedly in communication with the goddess.[4]

Catholic chaplains had been permitted residence in Burma since 1554 to attend the religious needs of captive Portuguese and more recently French soldiers. But the moral standards of the Christian community, which numbered three to five thousand, had sadly deteriorated. Goan priests in particular were described as scandalous and contemptible in their conduct, with "their morals . . . on a level with their intelligence."[5] One chaplain was regularly located at Syriam and one at Shwebo. Two members of the Missions Étrangères had arrived in Lower Burma from Siam in 1689, invited to come by Burman and Mon captives whom they served. The jealous Portuguese residents denounced the Frenchmen as spies and fomented the hostility of the Buddhist monks against the newcomers. They were accordingly taken as captives to Ava in 1693, maltreated physically, and then drowned. Similar hostility was demonstrated by the Goan chaplains against Italian Barnabite priests who came to Syriam in 1721. A bishop Nerini was executed in 1756 at Pegu for being pro-French. Burman xenophobia was later to be demonstrated against the Siamese, Manipuris, and Arakanese, as well as against the British and French.[6]

## The Mon Rising and the Emergence of Alaungpaya

Granted the long history of Mon-Burman antagonism and the demonstrated weakness of the Ava government in the early 1700s, an

[4] A. Hamilton, *A New Account of the East Indies* (1727), II, 18–22, 29–35; M. Turpin, *History of the Kingdom of Siam* (1908), 9–13.

[5] Hamilton, 35.

[6] Harvey, 345–346.

attempted revival of Mon power was inevitable. Opportunity came in 1738–1740 when raiding horsemen from Manipur overran much of Upper Burma to the very walls of Ava. In 1740, a localized rising of Shan and Mon deportees at Ava also tied Burman hands. Mutinous troops in the south thereupon killed the official governor (*Myowun*) of Pegu, after which the Mon rebels seized Syriam and Martaban, massacring all Burmans. They selected as their King an ineffective ex-monk, the son of a previous governor of Pagan. The Mons destroyed all foreign churches and factories at Syriam and gained artillery and gunner recruits by capturing six unsuspecting Ostend Company ships and crews, which chose this inauspicious moment to visit the port. The Mons captured Prome in 1743. They ran into some difficulty with the Burmans in 1747, which caused the frightened monk-king to flee, but eventually resumed their advance under the ambitious Binnya Dala. The Manipuri raids on Upper Burma were curbed by 1749 but not in time to prevent the fall of Ava in 1752 to the Mon armies.

The inevitable Burman counterattack began in the same year as Ava's fall. It was led by the son of a myothugyi headman at Moksobomyo (*myo*=city). The overconfident Binnya Dala left too few troops to consolidate his control in Upper Burma. Once having found a vigorous leader, Burman resistance gained strength rapidly, especially after premature evacuation of Ava by the Mons gave the Burmans an easy victory there in 1753. The victors withstood a counterattack the following year and then freed Upper Burma of Mon control. The Moksobo leader took the reign name of Alaungpaya (embryo Buddha), claimed descent from a fifteenth-century Burman King, and began the construction of a palace-fortress at his home city, renamed Shwebomyo (town of the golden leader). Although Manipuri trouble erupted intermittently, Alaungpaya was able, with the help of increasing Mon disunity, to proceed triumphantly down the river valley, capturing Prome, Henzada, Bassein, and finally Dagon in the vicinity of Syriam by early 1755. He renamed the final acquisition Rangoon (end of strife). Completion of the conquest of Lower Burma was delayed for two years, until May, 1757, while Alaungpaya's forces returned northward to deal again with the Manipuri raiders and to end Shan disaffection. His conquest of the Shan sawbwas as far east as the Salween River reduced them for the first time to complete subservience. His final infliction of terrible vengeance on the Manipuris came in 1758–1759. Alaungpaya incorporated "Cassayer" (Manipuri) cavalry into his army and Brahman astrologers into his court and imported numerous captives to swell the slave markets of Sagaing and Amarapura.[7]

In connection with the final conquest the fortresses of Syriam and Pegu by Alaungpaya, the French Company became heavily involved. Sieur de Bruno, who was in charge of French shipbuilding operations at Syriam

[7] Hall, 324–327, 344–345, 349.

after 1751, apparently developed dreams of repeating de Brito's performance of the early 1600s. Governor Dupleix approved the project and assigned him as resident agent representing Pondicherry in November, 1752. But the support which Dupleix solicited from the Company directors in France for his Burma venture was denied in 1753. Dupleix himself was recalled in the following year. De Bruno nevertheless stayed on, refusing to give up his dream of adding Lower Burma to the French domain. He and eleven other French officers were captured after Alaungpaya's successful siege of Syriam in 1756. Most of the French aid sent belatedly from Pondicherry in response to de Bruno's urgent pleas also fell into Burman hands. The captured de Bruno was forced to dictate the decoy letter which lured two French ships into the river entrance, where they were seized by Alaungpaya. A third French vessel arriving later managed to escape the trap. The original French captives were beheaded. From the captured French vessels the Burmans acquired thirty-five guns, thirteen hundred muskets, and abundant military stores, plus two hundred fighting men to serve as slave troops, duly provided with a priest and Burmese wives. With this valuable increment to its striking power, the Burman army carried through the capture of the Pegu fortress by May, 1757. The event was a grimly bloodthirsty affair.[8]

Meanwhile the worried British officials at Madras, fearful that the French were indeed about to attain the upper hand in Burma, managed to compromise their own relations with proud King Alaungpaya. They seized the island of Negrais at the western end of the delta in 1753; a Company vessel at Dagon got into embarrassing difficulties in 1755; Madras refused to comply with Alaungpaya's request that George II reply personally to a letter from the Burman King. When the Company attempted later to negotiate concerning the authentication of its own delta holdings in 1756–1757, it was exposed to insatiable blackmail demands for arms by the Burman ruler. Madras was completely unable at the time to provide military aid, engaged as it was in a death struggle with the French in India. The British Company was in the process of liquidating its timber stations at Bassein and Negrais when the caretaker remnant of the British staff was massacred in October, 1759. Alaungpaya apparently suspected that he was being played for a fool. False rumors that the British had been connected with a final abortive Mon rising and the jealous vindictiveness exhibited by a French mercenary were contributing factors. After French political power was completely eliminated from India as a result of the Seven Years' War, the urgency for a British counterbalance to French intrigue in Burma no longer existed.[9] The British Company thereupon abandoned the Burma venture.

[8] *Ibid.*, 345–347; Harvey, 229–234.

[9] Hall, 345–349; Harvey, 224–225.

## Capture of Ayuthia and the Chinese Invasions

The end of Alaungpaya's reign came with startling suddenness. The flight of many Mon refugees to Siam prompted his massive effort to capture Ayuthia and to repopulate Lower Burma with Mon and Thai captives. Invading via the Tenasserim area, the Burman army surprised the Siamese, who expected an attack from the north, and invested Ayuthia in April, 1760. But Alaungpaya was himself critically injured by a badly handled siege gun; he died on his way back to Burma. The Siamese campaign was postponed for four years amid the ensuing political confusion attending the royal succession at Ava. A younger son of Alaungpaya finally succeeded and restored order in 1764 under the name of Hsinbyushin. One of his first moves was to shift the capital from Shwebo back to the strategic center of Ava. He then renewed the war on Siam.

The Burman invasion of Siam in 1766 and 1767 was overpowering. Using not only the captive French gunners but also Shan levies and Manipuri cavalry, King Hsinbyushin entered by way of Chiengmai and Vientiane. This army joined hands with another Burma force invading from the south and laid siege to Ayuthia for a second time. A relief army from Laos was driven away. The city held out for more than a year, but was obliged to capitulate in March, 1767. It was thoroughly looted by the victors and reduced to a heap of ruins. Not even the temples and Buddhist manuscripts were spared. Recovery of Siamese independence might have taken a long time had not a diversion come from an unexpected source.[10]

King Hsinbyushin's overambitious projection of Burman power into the Shan and Lao states bordering the China frontier provoked a series of invasions by Chinese armies. They started while the Ayuthia campaign was in progress and continued until 1770. Armies of the Yunnan viceroy were repeatedly halted by Burman-Shan forces at or near the frontier, although at one time the invaders penetrated to within thirty miles of Ava. The rival commanders eventually signed the treaty of Kaungton in 1770, arranging for the withdrawal of the Chinese armies and reopening the caravan trade via the upper Irrawaddy River. Despite Hsinbyushin's objections to the treaty, the subsequent exchange of decennial missions between Burma and China sealed the agreement and inaugurated an extended period of improved relations.

This exhausting diversion to the north permitted Burmese interests in Siam and elsewhere once more to get out of hand. Hsinbyushin felt obliged to stage a conclusively destructive raid on Manipur and then to quell the mutiny of a Mon levy which recaptured and burned Rangoon in 1773. A general exodus to Siam of Mons fleeing Burman vengeance was followed immediately by an attempted Burman invasion in pursuit of the

[10] Hall, 350–352; Harvey, 252–254, 271; W. A. Graham, *Siam* (1924), I, 205–212.

refugees. But Siamese resistance was rallied by a half-Chinese robber leader named P'ya Taksin, who turned back the invading army. The same happened to a subsequent effort at invasion three years later launched by the pious and ineffective son of Hsinbyushin, King Singu (1776–1782). After the defeat of 1776, Singu abandoned the effort at invasion.[11]

P'ya Taksin made full use of the breathing spell afforded by the quiescent policy of Singu to expel the Burmese viceroy and reoccupy Ayuthia in 1778. After eliminating the legal heir to the throne, he usurped control temporarily. Acting on the advice of soothsayers and probably from considerations of his personal safety, he selected Bangkok as the site for a new capital. He obtained from Laos the famous Emerald Buddha image, and it was duly enshrined in the temple area adjacent to the new palace site. P'ya Taksin was ousted from control in 1781 by a coterie of palace nobles. King Rama I, the founder of the Chakri dynasty and also partly Chinese, became the King[12] in 1782, the very year that Singu was replaced in Burma by his vigorous but tyrannical uncle, King Bodawpaya.

## *The Reign of Bodawpaya*[13]

The long reign of King Bodawpaya marked the crucial turning point in the history of Burma's Konbaung dynasty. The ruler was a man of un-questioned personal capacity and princely authority, probably the ablest of the sons of Alaungpaya. At the very outset of his reign he succeeded in rounding out the boundaries of Burma by including the coastal regions of Tenasserim and Arakan. The latter country he occupied in 1784 with little difficulty, taking advantage of internal factional divisions.[14] The doors were open at long last for Burma to develop fruitful and progressive relations with its neighbors around the Bay of Bengal. Bodawpaya in-herited relations of peace and mutual respect with China, as well as a demonstrated military potential which would have made his country virtually unassailable by any enemy intruder. He also had the chance to integrate his country economically and politically by promoting internal as well as foreign trade and by enlisting the loyalty of minority peoples, especially the Mons, Arakanese, and Shans, through taking account of their interests. On one point only his government acted fairly responsibly, namely in his negotiations over border relations with British-held Chitta-gong. But even here a pattern of aggressive belligerency emerged near the

[11] Hall, 353–354; Harvey, 252, 259–260; Graham, 208–212.

[12] Graham, 205–212.

[13] For a more detailed account of the reign of Bodawpaya, see Hall, 502–512, and the introduction of the same author's *Michael Symes: Journal* (1955).

[14] Arthur P. Phayre, *History of Burma* (1883), 180. For more than a quarter century after 1684, the Arakanese Court was at the mercy of a plundering and murderous palace guard.

end of his reign. On almost all of the other counts, Bodawpaya failed to measure up to even minimum expectations. His potentially illustrious rule laid the groundwork for national and dynastic disaster.

The failure of King Bodawpaya can be attributed in large measure to his inordinate personal vanity. For two full decades he refused to recognize that the conquest of Siam, to which his dynasty was committed, was an unnecessary as well as an impossible, even insane undertaking. He invaded the country repeatedly, in 1785–1786, 1794, 1798, and 1802, and ended by surrendering all claims to Siamese territory outside Tenasserim. The last claim to be given up was Chiengmai in 1802. These disastrous and costly campaigns, especially the two in the nineties, entailed the imposition of ruinous burdens on the peoples of Lower Burma in particular. Previously cultivated areas reverted to jungle as Mons, Karens, and Arakanese fled before the rapacious agents of the King. Even after invasions of Siam proper ended, Burman raiders from Tavoy continued for another decade to loot the isthmian trade of Takuapa with Junk Ceylon, attracting counteraction from both Ligor and Trang, with serious losses sustained on both sides. These raids began as early as 1785.[15]

But military exploits were not the only obsession of the King. One of his first decisions was to build a new capital at Amarapura, 6 miles to the north of Ava, a gratuitous and highly burdensome undertaking. He suspected for various reasons that Ava was ill-omened. He must perforce fill the new capital with impressive monuments, contributory to his personal merit religiously and to his glory as a ruler. In addition to the twenty thousand slave laborers whom he brought back from Arakan in 1785, he transported the massively impressive Mahamuni image of the Buddha, one of the most revered in all Burma, across the mountains and up the river to Amarapura. It was housed in the famous Arakan pagoda, the first of Bodawpaya's many pretentious religious edifices. Exactions of slave labor from Arakan continued far into the following decade. The last of his many grandiose pagoda projects was the massive Mingun structure, located across the river and upstream from the capital and planned to tower 500 feet above its foundation stones. The abortive effort left the countryside impoverished without the structure's ever being finished. Some of the King's public works endeavors were useful, for example, flood-control dams and reservoirs, but an exorbitant amount of forced labor was exacted to satisfy the King's personal vanity. His pronounced Bodhisattva aspirations as an emergent Buddha aroused sharp rejoinder from the Burman monastic leaders, but national exhaustion rather than clerical protest brought an end to his building mania.

Under circumstances of excessive expenditures and moody self-concern on the part of the King, a downward spiral of national well-being

[15] G. E. Gerini, *Historical Retrospect of Junk Ceylon Island* (1905), 64–77; Phayre, 215.

began. Thus the new tax registers compiled in 1783 were used, not to distribute more equitably the tax burden, but rather as a basis for imposing additional extraordinary exactions. This had the inevitable effect of discouraging any expansion of economic activity. Excessive demands levied on the Mons and the Arakanese bred resentment and rebellion, followed by savage repression and still heavier demands. Refugees from Arakan fled to Chittagong during the 1790s by the tens of thousands, and the Mons staged a comparable evacuation in the direction of Siam. Even the language of the Mons was proscribed. The timid Karens of Lower Burma hid away in the jungle swamps or withdrew to the hills. The situation deteriorated further when the dispirited King, balked of realizing his military and religious aspirations, began to neglect his governing responsibilities. On the occasion of Michael Symes's mission to Burma on behalf of the British-Indian government in 1795, he noted the extreme devastation of the delta area and Pegu. At the time of his second visit seven years later, he observed that Upper Burma as well had been similarly impoverished by excessive tax and labor demands and by the ruler's almost complete neglect of his duties. Widespread lawlessness had become endemic throughout the countryside.

Down to the time of Bodawpaya, the Shan sawbwa princes, vassal to Burma, had been treated with a considerable measure of respect. They were summoned to the capital to attend royal coronations and annual *pwe* festivals, at which times they were accorded places of honor and status in the royal presence. They wore an eighteen-strand sash, or *salwé*, accorded only to princes of the royal family. In their own capitals they were permitted the use of the white umbrella within their palace *haws* and the golden umbrella outside. Shan princesses were honored in the royal harem. The plenary authority of the sawbwas within their own domains was acknowledged, including powers of life and death. Shan levies served under their own leadership in the king's armies.

Beginning around 1800, Burman garrisons were stationed in the Shan states as far east as the Salween River. They were commanded by a high military officer (*sitke*) with headquarters at Mongnai. The authority of the Shan princes declined as a result of the imposition of direct Burman control. The haws of the sawbwas became shabby and run-down. Internal feuding and lawlessness multiplied; agriculture and trade, for which the Shans had previously been famous, languished. Self-respect and cooperation gave place to a lackadaisical attitude alternating with sullen discontent. The last occasion when Shan contingents served in the Burman armies was in 1825.[16] British control of the Shan States after 1852 came as a welcome escape from Burman misrule for many of the Shans, as well as for the Mon and Arakanese remnants and the Karens.

[16] Sao Saimong Mangri, *Shan States and the British Annexation* (unpublished), 67–73.

## Burma-Bengal Relations

In spite of the development of considerable trouble along the Arakan-Chittagong frontier as a result of the habit of rebel Arakanese to operate from British territory, relations between Bengal and Amarapura down to 1811 were reasonably good. The most serious difficulty developed over the mass flights of nonpolitical refugees during the 1790s. These the British were loath to surrender, even though they constituted a considerable burden on the Bengali authorities. It was one thing to turn over bandit rebel leaders, as was done in 1794, and another to return bona fide refugees from Burman vengeance. The border was closed legally by Bengal in 1800, but passage across the frontier could not be prevented.

The two missions of Michael Symes, in 1795 and 1802, as representative of the governor-general of India achieved generally satisfactory results. The Bengali authorities agreed to extradite criminal refugees and to police the frontier more effectively, while the Burmese Court promised to refrain from making unreasonable demands for the return of all refugees. Between the Symes visits, several official British-Indian Residents carrying chips on their shoulders, especially the importunate Captain Hiram Cox (1796–1798), became impatient and demanding. But neither Burma nor Bengal wanted war, and the Symes agreements were, on the whole, loyally carried out.[17] Bengal at the time was concerned with maintaining good relations with Burma in order to forestall any effort of the French to find a base for naval operations along the Burma coast.

Relations began to deteriorate in 1811, when the son of the original Arakanese rebel leader, who had died in 1803, invaded Arakan province from Chittagong. He actually succeeded in capturing Mrohaung. The rebel's appeal for British protection and the subsequent proof of British laxity in policing the difficult frontier aroused the anger and suspicion of Amarapura authorities. Following the recovery of Burman control over Arakan, Bodawpaya's troops proceeded under orders to cross the Chittagong frontier in pursuit of the rebels. Representations made by Captain Canning, British-Indian representative at Amarapura, did little to relieve the tension. It persisted until early 1815, when the death of the rebel leader ended the immediate crisis. Many of the Arakanese rebels surrendered to Bengali authorities in May, 1815, but Calcutta refused to return them to Burma except on the basis of evidence of their commission of nonpolitical criminal offenses.

The warlike posture of the Burma Court which developed between 1811 and 1815 carried over into the final years of the reign. Burmese aggression against Manipur, Chahar, and Assam from 1816 to 1818 took the form of attempting to elevate to power local princes amenable to Amarapura's control. In June, 1818, the governor (Myowun) of coastal Arakan

[17] Cady, 68–71; Hall, *Michael Symes: Journal,* introduction.

challenged the British Company's control over parts of Chittagong. When Bodawpaya died in 1819, the stage was set for a clash between rival imperialisms, with Bengal as the aggrieved party. British India was no longer under the necessity of maintaining good relations with Burma, as had been the case during the Napoleonic Wars.[18]

## *Konbaung Burma: Government*[19]

A close look at the eighteenth-century Burma government reflects the pattern also found in neighboring Buddhist countries. The assumed divinity of the Burmese ruler was based on the traditional symbols of Indian origin. These included the occupancy of the sacred palace precincts and possession of the essential royal regalia, such as the sacred sword and the white umbrella. The ministrations of Brahman priests were required at coronations, for determination of auspicious places and dates, and in the ceremonial functions of the court generally. By the eighteenth century, however, the Brahmans were usually tawdry Manipuris, although genuine ones from Benares were obviously preferred. The Brahman priests played no part in policy determination. They functioned as individual specialists in royal magic, enjoying the backing of no ecclesiastical organization and serving no literary or cultural ends. All subjects except the chief queen must prostrate themselves in the royal presence, and foreign visitors must remove their shoes in the throne room.

The importance accorded to the proper location of the capital as a contributing factor in the prosperity of the reign was evident in the frequent changes of location under the Konbaung kings. Six new capitals were built within a century—the first at Shwebo, the second and fourth at Ava, the third and fifth at Amarapura, and the last at Mandalay. Strategic necessity involving the location on the Irrawaddy at the mouth of the Myitnge River dictated the general vicinity, but any dynastic misfortune was considered prima-facie evidence that the presumed magical abode of the gods had not been properly ascertained.

The principal advisers of the king, as previously indicated, were the Wungyis of the Hlutdaw Council and, to a lesser degree, the Atwinwuns, or palace secretaries. The Hlutdaw members supervised the general administration in the name of the despotic ruler. Their responsibilities included the appointment of provincial governors (Myowuns) and the four influential chief military commanders, or *Winhmus*. The Myowuns who were posted at frontier entry points, such as the China border and Rangoon, were assigned considerable responsibility for foreign relations. They were the initial negotiators and conducted all visiting diplomatic missions en route to the capital. They also administered the foreign-trade regula-

[18] Cady, 71–72.

[19] Except where otherwise indicated this section is based on Cady, *A History of Modern Burma,* chap. I.

tions. At the palace, most elements came in groups of four. The king had four main queens, four Wungyis, four Wundauks, four Atwinwuns, and four Winhmu commanders.

The credentials of the local myothugyi headmen were authenticated at the palace treasury, or *Shwedaik*. The elaborate system of ahmudan-class royal retainers liable for service in the "professional" army and at the palace was administered by the *Atwinwuns* of the palace, but the military service units (asu) when called up for duty were commanded by the Winhmu. Wungyis could also assume command of the army on occasion. In parts of the country where the village units had been destroyed and the countryside was more or less depopulated, artificial units of township administration under circle headmen (*taikthugyis*) were formed, their titles being also authenticated and filed in the Shwedaik. Petty disputes were settled by mediation at the village level, but important cases, especially in the criminal field, were under the jurisdiction of the Myowuns, subject to appeal to the Hlutdaw. Fief holders (Myosas), including royal princes and other important personages, were directly under the control of the palace, and tenure was dependent on royal favor.

On the ecclesiastical side, the Burma government included the primate, or Thathanabaing, appointed by and responsible to the king. He served as chairman over the Council of the Sanghas, on which were represented all sects of the Buddhist monastic community. Both the primate and the Council acted as agents of the king for the proper control of the clergy, not as a depository of ecclesiastical authority per se. Regional *Gaingyoks* (bishops) functioned in large measure autonomously. They were charged with the direct responsibility of enforcement of the Vinaya discipline among the clergy of their respective jurisdictions. Venerable *Sayadaws* headed important pagoda centers and shrines. These were frequently large institutions supported by gift endowments, including living quarters, library facilities, schools for novices, and pagoda premises. Virtually every village had its pongyi kyaung monastery and school, where the youth received the rudiments of education.

Two other religious arms of the government were composed of non-monks. One person was assigned to be the registrar of ecclesiastical lands (the *Wutmyewun*), and there was an agency, headed by the *Mahadanwun*, which had responsibility for keeping the official roll of all properly ordained monks of reputable standing. By the Vinaya rules and by custom, the monks were not supposed to be concerned with mundane affairs, either material or political, but the Burmese kings had learned from experience to keep the influential Sangha under close surveillance.[20]

The Burma government was most effective as an instrument of justice and order in the region immediately around the capital. Granted a ruler who was willing to curb his personal vanity and ambition, who would select an able Hlutdaw Council and support its considered decisions

[20] Cady, 4–7, 9–14, 16–18.

as to selection of officials and its choice of policies, the government could function rather effectively. The farther away from the capital, the less effective the authority of the Hlutdaw and the more arbitrary and irresponsible the actions of royal officials. These latter included in each province a granary officer and tax collector (*Akunwun*), a police and military official (the Sitke), the shipping inspector and customs officer (*Akaukwun*), and the Shahbandars at ports of entry. The latter were often foreigners. The government's control was apparently weakest in the Myosa fiefs, which were usually left to the untrammeled rapacity of the incumbent.

At the local level, the traditional authority of the hereditary myothugyi was frequently a tower of strength. He identified himself with his people and, under optimum conditions, protected them against unjust treatment. Local government was probably less equitable where the non-Burmans were ruled by artificial taikthugyi headmen. More primitive peoples like the Karens of Lower Burma and the Chins and Kachins bordering the Chindwin Valley and the upper reaches of the Irrawaddy were not integrated into the regular governmental system. The athi, or non-royal-service population, were liable to an annual household tax and to indefinite exactions of labor.

The crowning weakness of Burma's system of government, as with all Southeast Asian governments based on the Indian pattern, was the difficulty of arranging an orderly succession. The Burman arrangement for designating an heir apparent was similar to the Uparat, or vice-king, system of Siam. Burma's *Einshemin* (lord of the eastern house) was often a selected older son of the king by a high-ranking queen. The choice could also fall on a younger brother of the king himself. The incumbent was usually selected well in advance and granted a fairly pretentious court entourage and an armed bodyguard. He was also permitted participation in high governmental affairs, including presiding over occasional sessions of the Hlutdaw. During the period of the Konbaung dynasty, almost as many brothers succeeded as sons. The successions were frequently contested, resulting in princely bloodbaths. The last one accompanied the accession of King Thibaw in 1878. The most responsible representative of the line, Mindon Min, took off the robe of the monk to take over control of the palace.

## Konbaung Burma: Economy and Society

The most serious economic handicap which Burma faced in the early nineteenth century was the commercial and agricultural prostration of the once-prosperous Mon-inhabited Lower Burma delta area. This region, possessing the largest economic potential and the most noteworthy record of civilized achievement, lay devastated and largely depopulated. Neither the resources nor the incentive existed for the restoration of productivity of the area. In order to ensure that grain-short Upper Burma should have access to Lower Burma's rice at moderate prices, the export of that commodity overseas was forbidden. There appeared to be little appreciation on the part of the government of the value of overseas trade. The principal item of trade with India was raw cotton exported mainly via Arakan. The internal trade of Burma along the Irrawaddy River artery provided employment for a large number of boatmen, who moved southward with the help of sails in the winter season and northward during the period of the summer monsoon. But the items of exchange did little to increase the net wealth of either region. In addition to rough milled rice in substantial quantities, Lower Burma sent northward fish products, salt, and European and Indian manufactured wares.

The food output of the irrigated granary areas of Upper Burma—Kyaukse, Minbu, and Shwebo—was absorbed in large measure by the capital itself and by the various regimental service orders (asu) of the ahmudan population. Little effort was devoted to conserving the limited water resources of the dry zone as a means of extending the area of irrigation or to improving the existing facilities. The raising of cotton for export registered a net gain, but the excessive exactions of forced labor and taxes by the king discouraged individual or community efforts to expand production. Petroleum, gold, silver, and precious stones were royal monopolies. The burdens attending the construction of impressive pagoda monuments were probably more than matched by the gratuitous construction of five successive capitals in the Ava-Amarapura-Mandalay area within less than a century.

The trade with China via river boat to Bhamo and thence by mule or bullock caravan was fairly vigorous. Large Chinese caravans also arrived annually via the northern Shan plateau at a market fair located about 13 miles from the capital at the base of the plateau escarpment. The Chinese brought gold leaf for pagodas, silk products, tea, and dried fruits and nuts. They returned with quantities of seeded raw cotton, ivory and precious stones, betel nuts, and, near the end of the period under discussion, large quantities of Bengal opium. A substantial Chinese trading colony assembled at Sagaing across the river from Ava and Amarapura.

An entire suburb of the Burman capital was set aside for the use of Shan traders from the eastern plateau. The most valuable item of Shan trade was livestock, including the better animals making up the Shans' bullock caravans. They took back salt, fish products, and betel nuts. But the Shan states were decadent economically as well as politically, even though the sawbwa princelings held on tenaciously to the tattered symbols of their authority. The proverbial thrift of the Shans was qualified by their mania for gambling. The sawbwas themselves came to derive a major portion of their tax revenues from selling the gambling contracts for several fairs (pwes) per year, each lasting for ten or fifteen days. The results economically and socially were highly debilitating. The Shan chronicles tell a dismal story of interstate feuding, palace intrigues, and rebellions. Many of the minor northern princedoms remained illiterate and heretical (non-Buddhist) down to Konbaung times.[21]

The customary land law of Burma tended to encourage community and family effort rather than individual enterprise. Although the king himself claimed title to all land, continued occupancy was guaranteed to any persons who would reduce unused land to cultivation. Only the royal court and the monasteries could commandeer slave labor for such tasks. For others land reclamation was achieved by community and family cooperation. This meant that hereditary ownership resided in the family as a whole rather than in any particular member and that the title was usually inalienable. Even a member who moved to another locality continued to have a claim to the family estate. The most effective sanction which any village community could apply to check the unsocial activities of a troublesome resident was to exclude him from access to his family patrimony. The family group itself functioned as the agency of social insurance for the care of children and the infirm. The combination of family solidarity and the power of village elders to expel recalcitrant residents was, in areas of established settlement, usually an effective means of curbing serious crime.

Despite the democratic aspects of the Buddhist faith, Burmese society, like that of Cambodia and Siam, was highly structured, and sharp distinctions were imposed. Variations of rank were strictly maintained, especially in the vicinity of the capital. Status at court was indicated by the wearing of the salwé, the golden-colored sash or chain composed of a varying number of twisted strands. The salwé of the king had twenty-four strands, that of the Einshemin eighteen. The lesser princes had twelve, the Wungyis nine, and the lesser Wuns six or three. Rank was also indicated by the number of tiers permitted on the roof of an official's house, by the types of dress, accessories, and accoutrements, including the number and color (white, gold, or red) of umbrellas to be displayed publicly. The use of elephants for transportation was usually reserved for the king and high officials under his authorization.

Status outside the ranks of deified royalty attached to the office rather than to the person, for all rank depended on royal favor. Special modes of speech were required when addressing the king, officials, and venerable *pongyi* (great glory) monks. Wealth alone contributed little to social status, since there was no incentive for its accumulation in a system of collective family ownership of land and taxation based on arbitrary exactions by greedy officials.[22] Among the common people, the asu clansmen were proud of their ahmudan status and their regimental affiliations. All Burmans counted themselves superior to minority peoples. Warfare afforded an outlet for their spirit of daring and self-assertion, otherwise denied to them by the requirement of abject servility to officials.

The cohesive factor in Burmese society, aside from family and com-

[21] Mangri, 10–16, 35, 61.
[22] Cady, 15–16.

munity solidarity, was found in religious enthusiasm and in reverence for the genuinely pious Buddhist monks. The construction of local pagodas and pongyi kyaungs and public contribution to the daily needs of the monks were works of merit and acts of religious devotion. The monks of the local kyaung maintained the village school for boys and were available for consultation by the elders on community matters. Initiation of youth into the Buddhist order by the colorful and solemn *shin pyu* ceremony was a major social event. Every youth usually spent at least one full lenten season in the monastery, but entrance and exit from the ranks of the novice monks were easily accomplished. The major annual festivals and colorful light celebrations were determined by the Buddhist calendar and were often staged on pagoda premises.

Popular dramatic performances (pwes) combined singing, dancing, and storytelling, including ribald puns. Such performances frequently continued throughout the night. Then there were boat races, games, cockfights, gambling devices, and exciting escapades during the dry season. Buddhism contributed to sobriety, hospitality, and literacy and to respect for elders, religious leaders, and teachers. But demonstration of personal honesty at one's own expense was neither expected nor required by popular mores. The popular heroes of Burmese literature came not from the ranks of the kings, but from the humble victims of their tyranny or from the Robin Hood bandits who defied the royal authority. Most villagers knew little and cared less about what happened at court. Kings, along with floods, famine, and the malevolent, were ills to be endured.[23]

The moral authority of the Buddhist Sanghas derived from the reverence and respect which they inspired from the people as a whole. Monks were often used in diplomatic roles when a guarantee of integrity was required. They also intervened on occasion to protect unfortunate or defenseless individuals from the wrath of the king. Many of those so rescued, especially in the case of political prisoners, became slaves of the monastery. But Buddhism as such exerted no real limitation on the absolute authority of the king, which derived from Hindu sanctions and the customary practices of royal despotism. For example, the slaughter of princely rivals at times of accession was considered admissible for security reasons, but many rulers tried to compensate for such damage to their karma by subsequent lavish contributions to works of merit, mainly pagodas. The proudest and most popular boast which any king could advance was that he was a dedicated supporter of the Buddhist faith. The country's history, like that of Siam, provided numerous precedents of princes who retired to the sanctity of the monastery and later emerged as the most devoted of rulers. King Mindon of Burma and King Mongkut of Siam were modern examples. In general, the Buddhist Sangha preserved Burma's traditions of literacy, civilization, and morality.[24]

[23] Harvey, 332–333.
[24] *Ibid.*, 88, 97, 107, 117–118, 158, 166, 199, 233.

A concluding historical note for this chapter on the early Konbaung dynasty concerns the arrival at Rangoon on June 13, 1813, of the Rev. Adoniram Judson, an American and the first Protestant missionary to Burma. He came to Burma after having been excluded from Calcutta by British Company officials, who were hostile to such allegedly mischievous nonsense. Thus began the establishment of the American Baptist Mission. Its early successes were among the Karens of Tenasserim and Lower Burma. Judson, in time, earned the respect of both the Burmese and the British as a scholarly Christian.

# CHAPTER 14

# Establishment

## of British Commercial Hegemony

The establishment of British commercial hegemony in Southeast Asia from 1785 to 1825 was
connected with an eastward projection of the trade of India on a scale
unprecedented in the previous history of the region. It was accomplished in
part by the British Company's absorption of the authority of the dying
Mogul Empire and consequent British domination of the principal ports
of India after 1785. In part it was a result of the steady decline of Dutch
commercial activity during the latter half of the eighteenth century. The
*coup de grace* for Dutch trade in India, and for that of the French as well,
came during the early 1780s when Holland and France became involved
in war with England in connection with the American Revolution. Dutch
Company competition in the East Indies was completely eliminated in favor
of England by 1795, following the occupation of the Netherlands by French
Revolutionary armies.

But the transition to British hegemony was more than an English
Company triumph. The agents primarily responsible for the commercial
revolution of the late eighteenth century were the large numbers of so-called
country vessels operating from India under license by the English Company.
They were built in India, financed by private British funds realized from
business activities in India, and manned by Indian lascar seamen, but they
were commanded by English ship captains. As Dutch claims to monopolistic
control gave way, these "country" vessels based on India took over the lion's
share of the eastern trade, invading European preserves which the Asian
competitors of the Dutch had never dared infringe. Cotton cloth continued
to be a staple export of India, but the new traders added quantities of raw
cotton from Bombay and the even more valuable opium from Bengal,
produced and sold under Company monopoly. The port of Canton was the
principal terminus of British shipping on the China side, where tea, silks,
and porcelains were the exports. Except for the American clipper ships
entering the Asian trade after 1783 and continuing through the French
wars, the British craft had the run of the Southeast Asian area.

British territorial acquisitions in Southeast Asia during the period of the commercial transition were not considerable until near the end of the transitional period. The British acquired Penang Island in 1786 and Malacca in 1795, thus ensuring passage through the straits. Possession of Province Wellesley opposite Penang came in 1800, and the Company took temporary possession of Java under a British proconsul in 1811. Java was surrendered in 1816. More important were the acquisition of Singapore Island, started in 1819 and finished in 1824, and the Company's annexation of two coastal regions of Burma, Arakan and Tenasserim, in 1826. These territorial gains in Southeast Asia were dwarfed by the concomitant expansion of Company territory within India proper.

British hegemony in Southeast Asia was related, therefore, to the larger geographical context extending from India to China. Whereas the Dutch Empire had operated from within Indonesia and had been essentially monopolistic in its character and objectives, that of Britain was based on the enormous resources of the Indian subcontinent and finally functioned virtually on a free-trade basis. These circumstances afforded full scope to the enterprise of the "country" traders and led eventually to abolition of the Company monopoly. By the time Britain's hegemony had been established in 1830, its own machine-made cotton cloth had achieved a quality equal to that of the best broadcloth of Surat, long a primary staple of the Asian trade to Europe as well as to the Far East. Britain's commercial and industrial leadership was destined to continue in Southeast Asia for more than a century.

## *"Country" Vessels, Opium, and British Commercial Supremacy*

The successful promotion of Dutch sales of Javan sugar and Chinese silks on the western Malabar Coast of India, especially after 1730, had a disruptive effect on existing Indian trade patterns. The principal sufferer was Bengal, which had previously marketed substantial amounts of both sugar and cheaper-grade silks on the Malabar Coast. For example, during the two decades from 1730 to 1750 Bengal's trade at Surat declined by 90 per cent; following a moderate revival, it fell even lower after 1760. This situation came to be of direct concern to the British Company following Clive's conquest of Bengal at Plassey (1757) during the Seven Years' War. The Company was saddled with the task of governing a populous province under circumstances of heavy standing indebtedness and continuing military expenditures. A fairly obvious recourse was to utilize the exclusive political power of the British in Bengal not only to collect land taxes but also to revive the trade of the province in a fashion profitable to the Bengal treasury. The most urgent need was to find a commodity marketable in Southeast Asia and China which would obviate the need for continued shipments of European silver to Canton in payment for increasing exports of China tea.[1]

The answer to the problem as far as Bengal was concerned was the production and marketing of opium as a Company monopoly, to be distributed in the eastern seas by licensed "country" traders. Opium had been smuggled into China in a small way by Company ships from Madras in payment for tea as early as the 1730s. The tactic had aroused protests from English supercargoes in China who argued that it imperiled the whole trade at Canton. They cited the imperial decree of 1729 prohibiting Chinese from importing or smoking the drug.[2] From Bengal also the production of opium under secret monopoly of Company officials had previously been carried on in a limited way as a means of private profit. This operation the Company eventually took over. Cultivators in the vicinity of Patna were paid enough to induce them to shift from rice to poppies. Company monopoly of production and sale permitted official control over the volume of the output so as not to depress the price and also afforded a handsome profit from Company auction sales to "country" traders at Calcutta. A substantial amount was regularly allocated to the Dutch for disposition via Batavia, and smaller allotments were permitted for consumption in India and in Britain's deficit Benkulen colony in western Sumatra. Company servants in charge of assignment of contracts also profited personally from their control over the administration of such arrangements.

The transfer of credits from Calcutta to China was accomplished in several ways. "Country" vessel bidders at the Calcutta auctions could either pay in specie or leave with the Company I.O.U. certificates redeemable in silver at Canton. Company agents at Canton could also pay a portion of the cost of their purchases of tea by the issuance to Chinese exporters of Company bills of credit capable of being redeemed in opium by non-company British ship captains. Needless to say, the operation called for a considerable measure of Chinese official connivance. Once begun on a substantial scale, a commercial operation so convenient in meeting Bengal's financial needs and so profitable to the private "country" trader could never be abandoned. Company ships, which were denied the privilege of opium smuggling in order to maintain correct official relations with China, frequently proceeded from Calcutta to Bombay to obtain cargoes of raw cotton, also readily salable in China. After 1773–1774, when markets for west coast Indian goods in Persia dried up as a result of natural disasters, Company ships operating from Bombay also shifted in large numbers to the China trade.[3]

Traffic in opium was not new to the trade of Southeast Asia. Its source during the period of Muslim supremacy at Malacca had been in

[1] Holden Furber, *John Company at Work* (1948), 160–169.
[2] K. Glamann, *Dutch-Asiatic Trade, 1620–1740* (1948), 240–241.
[3] Furber, 164–167.

Arabia, especially Mecca. It persisted on a *sub rosa* basis into Portuguese and Dutch times. For example, a profitable trade in opium on a small scale was carried on by the Dutch Company after 1695 from the island of Bengkalis opposite Malacca, the trade having been taken over from private hands.[4] What was new in the Bengal operation was an aggressive and openly espoused sales-promotion program extending throughout Southeast Asia and along the China coast under the protection of the British Company flag. The trade was usually conducted by European ship captains in charge of heavily armed (twelve mounted guns), copper-bottomed craft of 500 tons or more, serviced by disciplined lascar Indian crews. Improved armament and navigational aids permitted such ships to visit areas where Muslim opium traders had feared to venture. A second important factor in the opium trade was the discovery of the particular susceptibility of the Chinese to the opium-smoking habit. This was the case not only in China proper but also in Chinese colonies scattered throughout Southeast Asia. In spite of spasmodically enforced regulations to the contrary, opium became widely accepted during the latter half of the century as a basis of credit and exchange throughout the trading arc from India to China.[5]

The predominant role of British traders in the commerce of Southeast Asia and the China coast was not fully established until after the emasculation of Dutch competition. As previously suggested, this occurred during the course of the Netherlands' involvement after 1780 in war with Britain in connection with the American Revolution. Until 1780, Dutch ships shared in the coastal trade of India, using ports on both sides of the peninsula, although in gradually diminishing volume. They managed until 1781 to acquire Indian cotton cloth for export through their own native agents, although after 1774 Dutch operations generally had become increasingly dependent on the collusion of English Company servants. For example, the Dutch Governor Ross at Chinsura in Bengal conducted, until the outbreak of war in 1780, a highly profitable private business in Patna opium in cooperation with understanding British contractors. Ross realized 100 rupees profit per chest on the auction of allegedly inferior opium coming into his possession and then overcharged Batavia for its share of the drug, which was frequently delivered in Java by British "country" vessels. All Dutch commercial operations in India came to a fairly abrupt end after 1781.

During the course of the war, Dutch Company property in India was confiscated by the British authorities. The Dutch lost a large number of ships, including all homebound ships and cargoes. No ships dared

[4] A. Hamilton, *A New Account of the East Indies* (1727), II, 65–67.

[5] Furber, 18–23, 167–169. It has previously been noted that the Dutch used opium in Java in part payment to regents for coffee tribute collections. Burmese overland trade with China included opium as a regular item of exchange. Symes reported little or no opium addiction among the Burmese in 1795.

leave Netherlands home ports during the war period, and Batavia tried frantically to dispose of its glut of goods to neutrals. Buginese pirates surprised and almost captured Dutch Malacca in 1784. In the treaty of Paris of 1784, the Dutch renounced all monopoly trading claims so that British traders were thereafter legally free to operate anywhere within Southeast Asia.[6] The Dutch port of Negapatam, India, was ceded outright to the British, its trade being absorbed by nearby Madras. Stripped of ships and other trading facilities and denied access to Indian markets except on British sufferance, the once-lucrative Dutch trade in India died during the latter half of the 1780s. The increased British shipbuilding at Calcutta using Burma teak reflected the change. Calcutta began for the first time to rival the long-established dockyard operations at Bombay. Vessels of 1,000 tons displacement were built in Calcutta after 1791, and one giant ship of 1,300 tons in 1802.[7]

Dutch trader depots in India were kept open after 1785, if at all, only because they still served the private trading interests of the men in charge. But the imposition of reforms by the British Parliament to curb the financial abuses of private British traders, who had frequently used Dutch facilities to transfer their exorbitant profits back to Europe, fell heavily on the Dutch in India as well. All who were in a position to know the facts of the situation realized that the Dutch Company was ruined. The Dutch allowance of seven hundred chests of opium in 1784 was reduced to five hundred in 1786, and by 1789 even this amount had to be purchased from the British on credit. By 1785, a full one-fifth of the stock of the English Company was owned by Dutch investors wise enough to shun their own Company. The bankruptcy of the Dutch Company was fully exposed by 1791. Only the Portuguese trade to Macao in pepper and silk seems to have held its own against the overwhelming British competition.[8]

The predominance of British commerce in Southeast Asia around 1790 can be measured in terms of the number of licensed "country" traders. During the 1780s, this tonnage multiplied six times, concentrating mainly in the Bengal area. Three-fifths of Bengal's imports from the East in 1793–1794, a year for which figures are available, were paid for in opium. A bare majority of the forty-five hundred chests annually offered for sale at the Calcutta auctions went to China. The rest was sold in Southeast Asia for items marketable in China, such as tin, pepper, spices, gold, and coined silver. Five thousand tons of British shipping visited Batavia in 1786, an increase of two-thirds in four years despite expensive port dues. The "country" vessels returned to Calcutta at the conclusion of the trading cycle with full cargoes of Chinese wares, plus Southeast Asian items including spices from the Moluccas, camphor from Borneo, and teak from Burma and

---

[6] D. G. E. Hall, *A History of South-East Asia* (1955), 280.

[7] Furber, 189.

[8] *Ibid.*, 28–30, 82–89, 96–98, 101, 181.

Siam. The regular Company-vessel trade with China carried increasing quantities of raw cotton. Taking advantage of famine conditions in China in 1790, which reduced the acreage of China cotton temporarily, the normal shipment of 50,000 bales of cotton per year was increased to almost 1 million bales, much of which was of inferior grade. Company vessels also carried opium to Southeast Asian ports, especially to Penang and Benkulen and Batavia, amounting to approximately one-quarter of the amount handled by noncompany shipping.[9]

## Strategic Factors: British-French Rivalry

The principal source of political rivalry encountered by the British in India during the last half of the eighteenth century was from the French rather than from the fading Dutch power. Although the French had been theoretically excluded from India politically in 1763, they had kept control of the Mauritius and Reunion Islands in the Indian Ocean and were able from there and through Pondicherry to maintain connections with anti-English Indian princes in the Deccan. During the French participation in the American Revolution, from 1778 to 1783, French agents in India were able to stir up considerable trouble for Governor-General Warren Hastings in Mysore, Hyderabad, and the Maratha states. A French naval squadron operating from Acheh and Mergui actually threatened to blockade Calcutta in 1782–1783 when hurricane damage forced the British fleet to retire temporarily to Bombay. It was this French naval power which also prevented the British from taking over Dutch holdings in Ceylon and the Cape of Good Hope during the course of the American war. The return of the French flag to five "purely commercial" posts in India after the peace of 1783 did not mean that the resourceful enemy of England would not try to revive its dreams of empire in the Orient if opportunity were again afforded.[10]

The Anglo-French contest was reopened on a world scale with the French occupation of the Netherlands in 1795 during the French Revolution and in connection with Napoleon's intervention in Egypt in 1798–1799. Rivalry was reflected in the nonofficial involvement in the civil war in Vietnam by several score Frenchmen who gave spirited support to Bishop Pigneau and his friend Prince Nguyen Anh. French hostility was behind the extensive campaigns waged by Governor-General Wellesley in India, which virtually committed the English Company to the conquest of the entire subcontinent. The contest impinged also on the island of Java, where French and British proconsuls after 1808 vied in the application of reforms and for permanent control. It eventuated in Britain's control of all potentially hostile way stations en route to the East—the Cape of Good Hope, Mauritius, Ceylon, and the Malacca Straits.

[9] *Ibid.,* 173–183.
[10] *Ibid.,* 7–8.

The potential threat of an enemy fleet to Britain's interests in India was repeatedly demonstrated. The French had captured Madras during the War of the Austrian Succession, had besieged the same fort in 1758–1759, and had threatened the blockade of Calcutta in 1783. Each instance emphasized the need to acquire a year-round British naval base in the Bay of Bengal. The problems connected with the temporary British conquest of Manila in 1762–1764 had suggested the desirability of a British base on the eastern side of the peninsula as well, a need supported by the increasing volume of the China trade. In 1773, the British occupied the island of Balambangan about 13 miles off the northern coast of Borneo, but the garrison was wiped out by Sulu pirates in 1775.[11] An even more insistent demand was to control a way station near the entrance of the Malacca Straits to which British ships could repair in time of need. Bintang Island off Singapore was proposed in 1769 by one enterprising "country" vessel captain, Francis Light. The possibilities of both Acheh and Kedah were also explored, especially after the French used Acheh and Mergui in 1783. Such was the background of the decision of the British Company in 1786 to commission Francis Light to negotiate with the sultan of Kedah for the lease of Penang Island a few miles off the Kedah coast. A vague kind of lease agreement was arranged with the Sultan, and Light himself became the first Company official placed by Bengal in control of Penang.[12]

But Penang did not satisfy the needs of British interests either as a trading post or as a naval base. It was too far north to attract trade through the straits or to control the pirate-infested waters. It was too distant from Burma's teakwood supplies to become a shipbuilding center. Nor did a mere lease from the Kedah Sultan confer a clear title, especially since Kedah itself was vassal to Siam. A more firm treaty of cession was exacted in 1791 following a preventive military operation by Light at the time when Kedah was apparently preparing to attack the island for an alleged breach of the lease agreement. Calcutta's interest in Penang increased somewhat after 1797, when tentative plans were formulated to attack Manila. The expedition was canceled out of concern over Napoleon's invasion of Egypt and the eruption under French instigation of anti-British action among the Indian princes of the Deccan. In 1800, a coastal strip about 45 miles long opposite Penang Island, named Province Wellesley, was acquired. The Penang roadstead was used as a port of call for British shipping, both Company and private, and the British territorial claim on the mainland served to cancel any further pretense of Dutch control over Malaya's tin supply. But an effort to cultivate spices on the island was completely unsuccessful. Penang was for the Bengal government a largely

---

[11] The British reoccupied Balambangan temporarily in 1803–1804. This interest in the Sulu Sea foreshadowed a subsequent French effort to occupy Basilan in 1859.

[12] Hall, 422–430.

profitless undertaking. Losses sustained in its operation totaled 81,500 pounds by 1814.[13]

The threat of French intrusion in Southeast Asia was intensified in 1795 when French Revolutionary armies overran the Netherlands. Paris sponsored, as the successor to the Stadtholder's authority, a puppet Batavian Republic, which espoused liberal objectives both governmentally and in trade. From his refuge in England, the expelled Stadtholder placed Dutch overseas possessions under the protective custody of Britain, and London pledged to restore them once peace was attained. Under this arrangement Britain took over with minimal difficulty all Dutch properties in India, the Cape of Good Hope, Ceylon, Malacca, western Malaya, western Sumatra, Amboina, and the Banda Islands. The local Dutch authorities at Batavia disliked the idea of British control quite as intensely as they did the liberal trading proposals of the Batavian Republic in Europe. They kept control of Ternate, Macassar, Palembang, and Banjermasin in Borneo. A British blockade of Batavia, halfheartedly applied in 1800, was suspended out of concern for possible French threats to India from Mauritius and Egypt. The temporary restoration of peace in Europe in 1802 prompted the theoretical return of several occupied Dutch possessions, but revival of the war in 1804 and the creation of the new kingdom of Holland under Louis Napoleon reversed the situation once more.[14] Meanwhile in Holland the Company's debts and assets were taken over by the state, in 1798–1799, and the charter was permitted to expire.[15]

British-Indian concern lest the French obtain a temporary naval base in Burma was responsible in large measure for the two missions of Michael Symes to Amarapura in 1795 and 1803. King Bodawpaya gave no commitment to exclude French ships from Burma's ports, but Symes satisfied himself and also Calcutta that little danger was to be anticipated as long as Bengal and Burma maintained friendly relations. The eventual complete British occupation of the Dutch Indonesian Empire will be described following an examination of trading developments.

## Suggestions for a Pattern of Free Trade

Two new factors appeared in the trading pattern of Southeast Asia during the 1790s. The first was the activity of an increasing number of American ships in the region, and the second was the unavoidable adoption by the Dutch of a policy of free access by outsiders to Batavia. The ending

[13] L. A. Mills, *British Malaya, 1824–1867* (1925), 18–27; Walter Makepeace et al., *One Hundred Years of Singapore* (1921), I, 14–18.

[14] B. H. M. Vlekke, *Nusantara* (1943), 214–219.

[15] Hall, 281–282; Cyril Northcote Parkinson, *War in the Eastern Seas, 1793–1815* (1954), 156–170.

of Dutch Company control by agencies in the Netherlands in 1796[16] led
to the adoption in 1797 of a policy opening Batavia to non-Dutch vessels,
especially American and Danish, for general marketing purposes. The
plan was simply to sell the assembled Asian goods at Batavia rather than
in Amsterdam. Trade with American vessels en route from China to Europe
had in fact been started at Batavia several years earlier. The principal demand for Javanese products in the Atlantic area was for coffee, and Americans proved willing to take unwanted sugar and pepper in order to obtain
ample coffee cargoes. Payment presented some problems because most
of the silver had gone into hiding in favor of Dutch paper currency,[17] but
the plan nevertheless worked well for a decade or more. Batavia realized
such substantial profits from local coffee sales that the treasury was able
to tide over to some extent the subsequent collapse of trade following
Denmark's involvement in the European war in 1807 and President
Jefferson's embargo policy of the following year. The degree of marketing
success experienced at Batavia cast discredit on the entire system of monopoly
on which the Dutch system had traditionally been based. After 1805, Batavia
considered the advisability of opening even the sacrosanct spice trade to all
comers.[18]

American clipper ships began operating in the mid-1780s on a
worldwide basis, setting a strenuous pace. The most vigorous routine was
to take grain, fish, and naval stores to the West Indies for sugar products
and rum, and to proceed thence to Europe for weapons, hardware, woolen
cloth, and metals. The next step was around Cape Horn to the Oregon
coast, where manufactured wares were bartered for Indian furs. The assembled cargo was then transported across the Pacific via the Spanish
galleon route to Canton and there exchanged for tea, silks, porcelain, and
silver. Proceeding thence to Batavia for coffee and spices and on to India for
cotton cloth, the ships continued the circuit around Africa to the Atlantic.
The Americans did not hesitate to sail in the off seasons and were quick
to unload and to acquire new cargo. Their ships were fast and highly
maneuverable, although somewhat smaller than the East Indiamen.

An easier alternative for American ships was to proceed directly
from the Atlantic to Bombay or Calcutta, where they could pick up specie,
raw cotton, and piece goods on credit from private British traders to be
used in the China trade. They proceeded to China via Southeast Asian
ports and then back to India, eventually leaving for the Atlantic with a
varied cargo partly Chinese, partly Javan, partly Indian. Accounts with
British creditor firms in India were usually settled in Europe or in America

[16] Daniel Wilco van Welderen Rengers, *The Failure of a Liberal Policy*
(1927), 13.

[17] J. J. Van Klavern, *The Dutch Colonial System in the East Indies* (1953),
73–75.

[18] Vlekke, 227–229.

after the cargoes were finally sold. This trading arrangement with the Americans had the inestimable advantage for British businessmen in India of facilitating repatriation of earnings to Europe outside the Company monopoly. Officials at the Indian ports required the payment of only moderate port dues under the most-favored-nation clause of the Jay treaty of 1794, while nevertheless stipulating that such vessels must touch at an American port on the return voyage before proceeding to Europe. Some American shippers later improved on this routine by picking up Turkish and Persian opium for trading purposes in Java and China. The same pattern was theoretically available for Danish, German, Swedish, and even Portuguese ships, except that Parliament's regulations dating from Pitt's bills of 1783 and 1784 forbade British subjects to return Oriental products to Europe via noncompany vessels.[19]

Private business initiative in India was also demonstrating the advantages of nonregulated trade, even though in an area not free from criticism. The opium traders, for example, dominated the principal sea lanes by their numbers and their superior initiative, discipline, and belligerency. They sometimes acted little differently from ordinary pirates. The traffic was highly demoralizing and risky, putting a premium on recklessness, speed, and violence. Company officials made no attempt to discipline obviously disreputable craft leaving and entering Calcutta. An English captain and three or four mates, a loyal lascar crew, and a disciplined sepoy fighting unit made a formidable combination. Their teak ships would neither rot nor splinter under fire and would outlast oaken ones 6 to 1. Bombay's ships were somewhat larger, but Calcutta's were more numerous and faster. Native traders at Surat, Bombay, and other ports learned in time to build their ships to resemble the European, often with imitation gun portals, in order to take advantage of the prestige and awe which such ships inspired.

Other forms of business than opium dealing were open to private British enterprise. The insurance services of India, for example, were very largely in European hands. Funds were accumulated largely from the savings of European residents, and confidence was inspired by knowledge that the directors of financing operations had access to the aid of local authorities and some degree of official naval protection, at least in the Bay of Bengal area. The Bombay Insurance Society covered all shipping at that port, and Calcutta had nine separate insurance societies. Banking credits were available to foreign as well as British shipping, especially in such cases as the American trade which facilitated repatriation of earnings to England. British investments in the "country" trade usually earned 8 per cent dividends or better, but the licensed noncompany vessels were strictly forbidden to undertake the trip to Europe.[20]

[19] C. N. Parkinson, *Trade in the Eastern Seas, 1793–1813* (1951), 357–365.
[20] *Ibid.*, 331–336, 340–352, 357–365.

## Problems of the British Company Trade

Official English Company trade with the Orient, in contrast to the more elastic private operations, followed a stodgy traditional routine. Outgoing cargoes from Europe consisted of woolen cloth, salable mainly in China, plus large quantities of copper, lead, Swedish iron, and Spanish silver. They also included naval stores and consumer supplies for British residents, such as the 3 million bottles of Madeira wine taken out in 1805. Such items as machine-made Manchester cloth played little part as long as the Company monopoly was in force. The Company in India, after all, was itself in the cloth business in partnership with Indian weavers. Down to 1810, superior-quality Indian cloth, along with China tea, actually made up most of the returning cargoes to Britain. This was during a period when British cloth production increased no less than nine times (from 1797 to 1810). Saltpeter was another important trading item from India for Americans as for British as long as the war lasted in Europe.

The Company continued to pay regular dividends in Europe while incurring a mounting accumulation of debt in India. Heavy war costs and numerous shipwrecks played havoc with potential profits. At the same time the permitted private remittances under Company certificates honored in London exceeded 1.1 million pounds per year, not counting an undetermined volume of irregular remittances transmitted through various other channels. What came to be known as the "clandestine" trade, mainly via American ships, really represented in considerable measure the earnings from private British investments in India. The adaptable Americans in the Atlantic traffic and the "country" ships on the Southeast Asia–China runs outdistanced the phlegmatic Company ships, which were content to follow a leisurely unchanging rhythm.[21] A new pattern of free enterprise was clearly demonstrating its advantages.

## The Status of British Trade in the Orient to 1820

One of the vulnerable parts of British trade in the Orient was the traffic in opium. It was a perishable commodity which had to be carefully packed and ventilated. The chests were usually wrapped in hides to keep the contents from spoiling. The chests weighed 140 to 160 pounds, and a single ship carried up to five hundred chests. The amount offered for sale at the semiannual auctions in Calcutta was kept fairly constant down to 1799 (around 4,250 chests), when the quantity was doubled. It was approximately doubled again by 1804, after which the amount again remained fairly constant.[22] The increasing price which bidders at the auctions were willing to pay demonstrated that the market was outstripping the supply.

[21] *Ibid.,* 69–82, 331, 357–365.
[22] *Ibid.,* 350–357.

The auction price per chest held at around 750 rupees (1 rupee = 50 cents) until 1801, when it jumped to 1,124. In 1804, increases boosted the price to 1,437, despite the increased quantity available. With the amount kept relatively constant thereafter, the bid price rose to 1,639 rupees per chest in 1811, 1,813 rupees in 1814, and 2,300 rupees in 1817. Meanwhile the cost of production in Calcutta remained around 112 rupees per chest. Thus by 1817 the auction price was approximately twenty times the production cost. Consumers actually paid up to thirty times this cost.[23] This kind of bonanza operation could not be expected to continue indefinitely.

The race to market the auctioned opium was a cutthroat affair. About three-fifths of it usually went to China and two-fifths to Southeast Asia. The process involved collusion with purchasers along many coasts— covert meetings to barter for tin, spices, ivory, pepper, betel nuts, and dollars. The usual method in Java was to bribe the Shahbandar of the port and also the Chinese customs collector, obtaining illicit spices in return. Particular areas were closed to the drug from time to time. Thus Junk Ceylon, which around the mid-1700s had developed a lively trade in opium attracting a disorderly band of Buginese traders, was closed tight by action of the Siamese government in 1784.[24] But generally port officials, offered a suitable incentive, were reasonable and cooperative.

A new situation developed after 1815, when certain American ship captains began obtaining Turkish and Persian opium for purposes of trade in the Orient. Turkish opium began to enter the Javan market in 1818, forcing a gradual decline in the Bengal opium price. The Americans could offer it at the outset for one-third the price of the superior Bengal product partly because they did not have to pay the exorbitant costs of the Calcutta auctions. The price eventually leveled off by adjustment in both directions to about two-thirds that of the Bengal product. Introduction of the cheaper Persian opium into China produced in the Canton price a decline of one-third or more from the 1817 level. Shortly thereafter Malwa opium from India, produced by native princes outside the Company monopoly, also began to enter the Oriental market. This forced the Company to extend its control over parts of western India by military action in an attempt to close off the trading routes from Malwa to the coast. Outside competition continued to undermine the Company's monopoly position throughout the 1820s, eventually forcing a drastic increase in the controlled Patna output in order to make good financial losses due to the decline in the price.[25] The market for opium in China nevertheless appeared to be almost insatiable.

During the first decade of the nineteenth century, the monopoly position of the Indian Company in the European trade was directly

[23] John Crawfurd, *History of the Indian Archipelago* (1820), III, 518–522.

[24] G. E. Gerini, *Historical Retrospect of Junk Ceylon Island* (1905), 54–55.

[25] Parkinson, *Trade,* 350–357; David E. Owen, *British Opium Policy in China and India* (1934), discusses the entire problem.

attacked by British critics both in India and in Britain. Holders of wealth in India, both Company servants and independent businessmen, who wanted to facilitate the transfer of their savings back to England, advocated the privileged participation of "country" vessels in the European trade. The Europe-bound tonnage alloted since 1793 for private noncompany use was not only inadequate but also costly and often little used. To this attack in India on the Company monopoly was added the clamor of traders in Liverpool and Glasgow, who demanded a right to share in the India trade, so long a monopoly of the port of London. The two complainants were uncooperative because the owners of India-built ships wanted to exclude Liverpool and Glasgow from their requested privileged status.

The principal supporting consideration in favor of free trade was the demonstration of superior efficiency and speed by the private "country" traders in the Orient and by American "interlopers" on the Atlantic run. The argument for ending the monopoly also received strong theoretical support from the Manchester school of free traders including the aggrieved Glasgow followers of Scotsman Adam Smith. Liverpool's loss of the slave trade after the 1807 outlawry of the traffic by Parliament increased the urgency of the reformers' demands. When the charter came up for renewal in 1813, the Company was denied the continuation of its monopoly of the British trade to India. Liverpool-Glasgow pressure was largely responsible. The Company was empowered for another twenty years to continue to trade in its own right and to license "country" ships for the trade in the Orient. It was otherwise reduced to a governing agency for Britain in the expanding Indian Empire.

Among the proponents of the cause of free trade were many Company officials like Stamford Raffles, the founder of Singapore, about whom more will be said shortly. Another was a British diplomatist and author, John Crawfurd, who professed to see in the enlightened principles of free trade a solution for what he described as the disgraceful record of the European monopolists in Asia. In his classic description of the Indonesian archipelago published in 1820, Crawfurd presented a scathing denunciation of European dominion, especially Dutch, in Southeast Asia. He cited the native bitterness engendered by the seizure and forced delivery from the inhabitants of marketable goods. His charge that Europeans had been guilty of acts of piracy against competing Asiatic traders was supported by many cited examples of wholesale fraud and violence. He denounced particularly the folly of monopoly and of the denial of free trade as contributing to oppression. The ending of the Dutch monopoly, he argued, afforded an opportunity to bring all previously closed areas, such as the Spice Islands, Japan, China, and Siam, into mutually profitable commercial relations. Trading entrepôts should be established to operate on a free-trade basis. American traders, he pointed out, had acted under no company monopoly, had incurred no political involvements or feuds with the native inhabitants, were paying no heavy military costs, and yet were carrying to Europe a large proportion of the tea and coffee of Southeast Asia and China.[26]

## *Daendels and Raffles in Java, 1808–1816*

The general policy of India's governor-general, Lord Minto, with respect to Java after 1800 was quiescent. He would leave the authorities of the Batavian Republic in charge of Java so long as the French fleet was denied the use of the East Indies. Under these circumstances, the reforms in traditional Dutch practices proposed by such Dutch Liberals as van Hogendorp and Muntinghe were pushed aside by Conservative Governors Overstraten and Nederburgh. The latter maintained that some form of coercion had to be applied on the Javanese population if the production of such exportable items as coffee and sugar was to be maintained. Habits of laziness were allegedly too deeply engrained to be overcome by mere economic incentives. Only by coercion could the trade of Batavia be sustained and a return be made available to the state to cover some portion of the enormous Company debt it had assumed. The governor, his agents, and the native regents of Java continued in control, with minimal changes of an administrative nature.[27] This traditionalist policy might have continued indefinitely if the Batavian Republic in Europe had not been transformed in 1806 into the kingdom of Holland with Napoleon's brother Louis as King.

Louis Bonaparte's appointed governor, Marshal Herman Willen Daendels, arrived in Java in early 1808. He was anything but a Dutch traditionalist. Although of Dutch nationality, he had fought with General Dumouriez in the early years of the French Revolution and later became, as a Marshal of France, a worshipper of Emperor Napoleon. His assignment in Java was to prepare the island's defenses against the inevitable attack by the British-Indian forces. His efforts did not lack vigor. He abandoned most of the Outer Islands, retaining only minimal forces at Macassar and Amboina. Barracks were built for a Javanese army of seventeen thousand men; arms foundries were set up; a military road was laid out along the coast; a fleet of small fast vessels was based on opposite ends of the island. Daendels undertook also to move the island's capital inland for reasons of health and defense. In a misguided effort to improve governmental efficiency, he canceled the authority adhering traditionally in the local sultans and regents by transforming them into salaried officials of the Dutch state, presiding over arbitrarily delimited prefectures and regencies. Daendels thus lost the support of the local aristocracy, whom he robbed of both dignity and self-respect.

[26] Crawfurd, 220–292.
[27] Rengers, 13–19.

Daendels encountered many difficulties. No officers were available for the proposed Javanese army. There was no money to finance his military preparations. His grandiose efforts to increase coffee production threefold ran into the discontinuance of the Danish trade after 1808 and a falling off in American purchases leading to complete embargo stoppage in 1810. A British blockade was finally imposed on Batavia in 1810. Daendels undertook to stave off bankruptcy by selling landed estates to local speculators, mainly Chinese. He supplemented this measure by forced loans and the issuance of paper money. Purchasers of landed estates were granted unlimited rights of exacting *taille* taxes and *corvée* labor in complete derogation of the traditional system of land tenure. Daendels also engaged in several private swindles. After Holland was annexed directly to France in 1810, he outraged Dutch political sensitivities by ostentatiously running up the French flag. He thus succeeded in offending virtually everybody, except perhaps the land-hungry Chinese, by riding roughshod over all resistance.[28]

The fall of Java to the British came in 1811. Daendels was recalled early in the year, managing to return to France on an American ship. The British fleet had meanwhile reoccupied Cape Town and Malacca, and had captured Mauritius Island from the French and Amboina from Daendels's garrison. The new governor, Jan Janssens, who had previously surrendered Cape Town, faced an equally hopeless situation in Java. The British occupied Batavia in August, 1811, and captured Janssens himself in the following month. British conquest was facilitated by the successful subversive efforts of Stamford Raffles from Malacca to turn the native princes against French-Dutch control. Macassar and Palembang were taken over later.[29] Java was destined to endure another spasm of quixotic reform under a British proconsul.

In the personality of Thomas Stamford Raffles, who was the English Company's selection as governor of Java, there appeared in Southeast Asia a new kind of colonial administrator. Raffles was a representative of the British liberal-humanitarian tradition, which had outlawed the slave trade in 1807, canceled the Company monopoly in 1813, and espoused the ideal of economic freedom generally. He was doctrinaire in his convictions. His political and economic views were acts of faith, tenaciously and sincerely entertained even in the face of contrary evidence and essential compromises. Raffles was also a manifest-destiny British imperialist convinced of the intrinsic superiority of enlightened British rule. He justified his aggressive tactics and bridged over his compromises of principle by affirming the innate validity of his ideas.[30] Raffles's liberal instincts and his ardent nationalism coalesced most easily in a kind of phobia against the Dutch colonial system, which he denounced unsparingly as pernicious

[28] Vlekke, 229–237; Hall, 405–411.

[29] Van Klavern, 80–86; Parkinson, *War in the Eastern Seas,* 412–417; Hall, 411–413.

[30] Vlekke, 239–264.

and enslaving. He was determined to demonstrate in Java the superiority of his concept of liberal humanitarian rule to the satisfaction of the Javanese and the resident Dutch, as well as to that of the Company officials in Calcutta.[31]

Raffles was also a scholar in his own right, especially in matters affecting Indonesia.[32] He was one of the first of a long procession of highly literate British civil servants who were to come to the Orient. Associated with him were others of dedicated scholarly interests. John Crawfurd, the ranking member of the British civil service in Java during the six years of Raffles rule, was the author of several valuable works including the massive three-volume *History of the Indian Archipelago* (1820).[33] Crawfurd was a man of more pronounced liberal convictions than Raffles himself. The liberal Dutch reformer Muntinghe also associated himself with the administration of Raffles. It was not accidental that the discovery and the first serious examination by Europeans of the impressive Borobudur monument in Java were undertaken under Raffles's sponsorship.[34] Even the severest Dutch critics of Raffles's five-year rule in Java conceded that there was much less corruption among the British officials serving under his direction than was previously established as standard by the Dutch.[35]

Governor Raffles undertook to introduce several major reforms in Java. In the first place, he centralized the governmental administration in an attempt to free the villagers from the alleged tyranny of their native rulers. He thus continued Daendels's policy of emasculating the power, dignity, and prestige of the princes, making them virtual puppets under European officials. The desa headmen were henceforth to be elected. He also undertook to improve the court system by introducing jury trial, the abolition of torture of the accused, and better treatment of prisoners generally. Debt slavery was outlawed, and a heavy tax was levied on other forms of slavery looking toward its eradication.

Raffles's most difficult undertaking was his attempted introduction in 1813 of the Bengal system of land settlement and taxation. It was based on the *ryat-wari* pattern of free individual land ownership subject to payment of a specified annual tax. Raffles lacked the staff to make the necessary land surveys or to collect the tax. His attempt to make the elected desa village chiefs the recorders of individual holdings and the collectors of taxes pushed the confused headmen entirely beyond their depth. The assessed taxes, amounting to one-quarter to one-half of the annual produce of the land, could only be levied on a village basis, since

---

[31] Rengers, 19, 41.

[32] See Thomas Stamford Raffles, *The History of Java* (1830).

[33] See also John Crawfurd, *Journal of an Embassy to the Courts of Siam and Cochin-China* (1828).

[34] N. J. Krom, *Barabudur: Archeological Description* (1927), I, 32–36.

[35] Van Klavern, 94–95. Also associated with Raffles were the naturalist Thomas Horsfield and the scientist Colin Mackenzie. See Hall, 411–420.

nearly all of the cultivated land was communally owned and administered. Raffles's demand for payment of taxes in cash on pain of forfeiture of title to the land forced the cultivators into the clutches of the Chinese moneylenders. The latter took a mortgage on the land and imposed heavier interest on the peasants than the regents had ever demanded. By an additional ruling that all uncultivated land was the property of the state, many of the rotation crop sites under periodic ladang cultivation were made available for sale to Europeans and Chinese. This was in addition to the steady accumulation in government hands of tax-delinquent land. Only by the sale of lands was Raffles able to counter the mounting deficit.[36] His innovations in land reform and tax collection were thus complete failures.

The exigencies of circumstances forced Raffles to violate his own antimonopoly principles. From the outset he gave preferential treatment to British vessels in Javanese ports. When the Palembang Sultan failed to curb anti-European violence on Banka Island, Raffles made the tin-mining operations on the islands a state monopoly.[37] In the basic coffee-producing area of Java's Preanger province, deliveries continued to be collected in kind, although by Europeans rather than by the regents. But when the ending of the war in Europe in 1814 opened the prospects for vastly increased coffee exports, Raffles forgot all about tax reforms and the abolition of forced labor.[38] Dutch critics have alleged that only after it became evident that Java was to be returned to the Dutch did Raffles attempt to scuttle the coffee-tribute system. It became evident in the end that the peasants preferred the traditional security of communal ownership under the chief's control to unfamiliar innovations which jeopardized title to their lands.

For two full years after the promised return of Java to the Dutch in 1814 Raffles dragged his feet about leaving, while endeavoring to persuade Calcutta to keep control. But Company officials had had enough of grandiose promises and chronic deficits, and they recalled Raffles in August, 1816.[39] Dutch officials returned to Java to pick up the pieces. As a paternalistic autocrat, supremely confident in the correctness of his own liberal ideas and adept at finding excuses when they failed to work out, Raffles had repeatedly overextended his authority. He was far from popular in Calcutta.[40] On leaving Java, he was assigned supervision of the minor pepper station of Benkulen on the south coast of Sumatra and given temporary oversight of Malacca until its return to the Dutch in 1818.

[36] Vlekke, 239–264; Hall, 411–420.

[37] G. C. Allen and A. G. Donnithorne, *Western Enterprise in Indonesia and Malaya* (1957), 21–22.

[38] Rengers, 19–25; Hall, 411–420.

[39] Van Klavern, 87–95; Rengers, 19–25; Hall, 420.

[40] John Bastin, *The Native Policies of Sir Stamford Raffles in Java and Sumatra* (1957), 90–110.

## Raffles at Benkulen and Singapore

The pepper port of Benkulen had been operated by the English Company since 1685, shortly after the Dutch had closed Bantam in western Java to non-Dutch shipping. Although it produced considerable quantities of pepper, it ran a perennial deficit, which was usually met by shipments of rice and opium from Calcutta. The contract system for collecting pepper at Benkulen differed little from Dutch practices in Java, but economic vitality was completely lacking. Company employees made money on the side in pepper purchases and in the forced delivery of food by natives, but the chiefs were indolent and lacking in authority. The one substantial contribution which British occupation made to the area was to end petty warfare.

Within two years of his arrival at Benkulen, Raffles obtained the reluctant approval by Calcutta of his proposal to revitalize pepper production under an incentive system of "free gardens." He advanced loans to the chiefs for the planting of additional pepper plants, waived the customary tribute-delivery requirements in favor of a specified annual tax, and proposed to purchase surplus pepper from private producers. The incentive plan failed to work in the Sumatran context. The loans to the chiefs were not repaid, and the Company in the end had to bolster the chief's authority to force pepper deliveries. In an attempt to counter the widespread failure to pay the assessed taxes, Raffles introduced a system of debt slavery to the Company up to a limit of ten years' duration. Thus many of the objectives so ardently espoused by Raffles in Java, such as reducing the powers of the native chiefs, discontinuing economic coercion, and the ending of slavery, were repudiated at Benkulen. Some reasons for the failure of the Raffles pepper scheme were beyond his control, for the world price of pepper collapsed in the early twenties largely because of extensive American participation in the Acheh market. Nor could Raffles be blamed for Adam Smith's failure to take Sumatra conditions into account. One can understand, however, why after the Benkulen fiasco Calcutta rejected Raffles's advocacy of European colonization in Sumatra as a means of stimulating economic development.[41]

Meanwhile the restoration of Dutch control at Malacca, in 1818 after a decision reached in Europe, made the still idea-pregnant Raffles very unhappy. His own dream and that of Crawfurd for the emergence of a more liberal system of trade in the straits area appeared to be doomed. Malacca was almost past using in any case, for the fort had been destroyed in 1807, and the harbor was neglected. The island of Singapore was a possible alternative site for a free-trade entrepôt, but the Sultan of Riau-Johore who ruled the island was pro-Dutch in his sympathies and affiliations.

But Raffles was not to be deterred. He began negotiating in 1819 on

[41] *Ibid.*, 72–134.

his own initiative with the local chief of Johore, whom he found co-operative. Raffles then engineered the Riau Sultan's replacement by a brother, who promptly accepted an offer of 5,000 dollars a year to approve the grant of land and facilities at Singapore to the British. The Penang governor, angered at Raffles's presumption, refused to "add violence to injustice" by sending the requested troops to support the dubious claim. He favored outright British withdrawal from Singapore.

But a prospect so promising was not to be repudiated out of hand. Lord Hastings, the governor-general of India, feigned opposition to Raffles but nevertheless sent a contingent of two hundred troops to the island as a token defense pending a final decision in Europe. Company directors similarly criticized Raffles for violating instructions and precipitating a *casus belli,* but they deferred their final decision on the basis of Hastings's questioning of the Dutch claim to the island and his emphasis on the urgent need for a free port in the vicinity. Other considerations favoring Raffles's proposal were the need to police the straits and to provide a place where Asians could get a proper price for their produce.

While the question was under consideration, Singapore started functioning as a trading center with very promising results. The population reached ten thousand in 1820, and Asiatic craft alone did a 4-million-dollar business in the first year. Sensing a probable *fait accompli,* Raffles in 1823 concluded a new lease agreement with both the Riau Sultan and the local chief providing for more substantial monthly payments for the use of the island. The cost of the full British title obtained in 1824 was a combined initial payment of 60,000 dollars to the two chiefs plus 2,000 dollars in monthly rentals.[42]

The agreement with the Dutch, which was reached in 1824, called for the exchange of Benkulen for Malacca and the surrender of all Dutch factories in India, plus claims to Singapore and mainland Malaya, in return for British renunciation of future acquisitions in Sumatra and the islands south and east of Singapore. The Dutch kept the Riau Archipelago, and the British assumed suzerainty over Johore. By act of Parliament in 1826, the Straits Settlements were set up uniting Penang, Malacca, and Singapore under a single Presidency operating from Penang. Control was transferred to Bengal in 1830, when Singapore became the administrative center. Much of the remaining territory of the Malay Peninsula was vassal to Siam.[43]

The Dutch were far from happy with the final coup of their long-time *bête noire,* Raffles, in planting a free-trade entrepôt in the very heart of Indonesia. But they were powerless to resist the gesture and were facing at the time serious economic and political problems in Java. Nor were all British free-trade imperialists happy over the alleged gratuitous surrender

[42] R. O. Winstedt, *Malaya and Its History* (1948), 57–61.

[43] Walter Makepeace et al., *One Hundred Years of Singapore* (1921), I, 21–23.

by Britain of future establishments in Sumatra and the Spice Islands.[44] Dutch monopoly practices continued to be severely criticized. The Glasgow East Indian Association, for example, appealed to the British Foreign Secretary, Lord Palmerston, in 1840, to stop Dutch interference with shipments of Indonesian pepper and coffee to Singapore and with British access to the Moluccas.[45] But the division of spheres of influence between the two powers satisfied the essential needs of both and was destined to continue.

On the basis of the highly successful operation of the port of Singapore,[46] the British government adopted as a cardinal objective in Eastern Asia the promotion of free trade. Britain's attainment of leadership in industrial production coupled with unquestioned British naval superiority buttressed the policy. The East India Company's monopoly control of the "country" trade to China and Southeast Asia was canceled in 1833. The opening of all areas of Southeast Asia, as well as China and Japan, became an immediate commercial goal. Southeast Asian history was entering the modern period of intensive economic development as a market for European goods and as a place of capital investment for the production of items needed for the world market.

## The Results of the First Anglo-Burman War, 1824–1826

The First Anglo-Burman War of 1824–1826 witnessed the projection of British influence and control into two coastal areas of Burma, Arakan and Tenasserim. The war was precipitated by Burman occupation of Manipur and Assam on Burma's western border following the accession of the pampered and ambitious son of Bodawpaya, King Bagyidaw, in 1819. The Burman military leader Maha Bandula, in 1822, invaded Assam and from there demanded that the Bengali authorities surrender political refugees to his custody. He was preparing to invade Chittagong also when Calcutta declared war in March, 1824. An expeditionary force of British-Indian troops proceeded to Rangoon by sea, capturing the city in May just before the break of the summer rains. This move had the desired result of forcing the withdrawal of Bandula's forces from the frontiers of Bengal, but the ensuing rainy season made virtually impossible any immediate British-Indian advance northward from Rangoon.

The war lasted almost two years and was a costly one from Calcutta's point of view. The invading forces sustained severe losses from fever and

[44] John Anderson, *Acheen and the Ports on the North and East Coasts of Sumatra* (1840), 1–7, 29–106.

[45] *Ibid.*, 239, appendix XV.

[46] Singapore's trade reached 5.6 million pounds in 1850 and 13.5 million pounds by 1864. See Winstedt, 60–61.

dysentery, which accounted for most of their fifteen thousand fatalities. A spirited Burman army besieged Rangoon until near the end of 1824, but it was no match in the field for the well-armed and better-disciplined sepoy forces supplied by sea. Bandula's army was defeated in April, 1825, and the leader himself was killed. But the dry season was again too far spent for the British to undertake an advance on Amarapura. A second debilitating rainy season was spent at Prome. Meanwhile dissident Mons and Karens in Low Burma, encouraged by the defeat of the Burman army, started a widespread rebellion. The final advance of the British-Indian army northward from Prome during the second dry season was assisted by the introduction of the first armed steamer on the Irrawaddy River.

By the Treaty of Yandabo, signed on February 24, 1826, the Burma government was required to pay a 10-million-rupee indemnity (10 rupees = 1 pound), to evacuate Assam and Manipur, and to cede Arakan and Tenasserim to the British Company. Burma agreed to accept a British Resident at Amarapura, to negotiate a separate commercial treaty, and to refrain from making war on Siam. The execution of the terms was less than satisfactory for the British. John Crawfurd undertook, with meager results, to negotiate the commercial treaty, and the Burma Court made life so unpleasant for the British Resident at the capital that the post was abandoned twelve years later. The Burmans suppressed the Mon and Karen rebels with severity, going so far as to proscribe the use of the Mon language.

During the course of the ensuing quarter century, the British were able to develop Arakan's rice production to a point beyond that realized even in the early 1600s. Moulmein port in Tenasserim also became a rice exporter and the center of a timber and shipbuilding industry. One of the most important results of the war was the curbing of Burman belligerency in the direction of both India and Siam. The war was also a convincing demonstration of the importance of sea power and of the sustained authority behind the combination of British military leadership and India's vast resources of supplies and manpower.[47]

The first Southeast Asian state to recognize the fact of British hegemony in the region of the Bay of Bengal and to come to terms with it voluntarily, granting the full rights of free trade and investment opportunities as demanded, was Siam in 1855. It is to the history of the Chakri dynasty of Siam in the nineteenth century that attention must now be turned.

[47] Hall, 515–520; J. F. Cady, *A History of Modern Burma* (1958), 72–75.

# CHAPTER 15

# Nineteenth-century Siam:

# Rama III and Mongkut

At the beginning of the nineteenth century, Siam was strongly traditionalist and anti-European. It had not forgotten the bitter experiences of King Narai's near-fatal involvement with British and French adventurers in the 1680s. The government had recovered from its spoliation at Burma's hands, but its overseas commerce and its domestic business were almost entirely under Chinese control. After British-Indian power reached Siam's frontier from both the Burma and Malaya sides in 1826, some kind of adjustment had to be made. Under Rama III, the response was minimal and grudging, for he continued to think in traditional terms about the preservation of his autocratic powers and his royal monopoly of trade and the exaction of tributary deference from subordinate vassal states. A continuance of this policy of refusing to recognize the necessity of coming to terms with the rising tide of British influence in particular would have meant, no doubt, Siam's eventual loss of political and economic independence along with the rest of Southeast Asia.

That Siam was able to maintain in large measure its juridical and territorial independence was due to the reorientation of policy given by King Mongkut, who came to the throne in 1851. He had spent the previous quarter century in the semiseclusion of a monastery, where he undertook in a fairly serious way the study of Western science, philosophy, and literature. He attained a passable mastery of English and Latin languages as his mediums of communication with occidental learning, taking advantage of the presence of American and European missionaries as tutorial agencies. As King after 1851, he came to terms with the commercial countries of the West by voluntarily negotiating a series of acceptable treaties with them, starting with Great Britain. The tactic cost his state something of its legal and fiscal independence, but Siam succeeded nonetheless in weathering the initial storm of rising Western influence and power. He also enlisted the assistance of some fourscore technical specialists from the West in many areas of administrative, scientific, and economic development, selecting them from various sources. Although he was handicapped by traditionalist limitations and by personal idiosyncrasies, Mongkut's program set Siam along a new path, which was continued and amplified by his son and heir King Chulalongkorn. This later aspect of Siam's development will be considered in a subsequent chapter along with frontier problems arising from British and French colonial encroachments.

## The Early Reigns of the Chakri Dynasty

The partly Chinese founder of Siam's Chakri dynasty, King Rama I (1782–1809), assumed power amid general acclaim following the collapse of the authority of the eventually insane P'ya Taksin and an abortive *coup* by a usurper. Rama's most urgent task during the first decade of his reign was to reorganize the defenses of his country to withstand the renewed attacks of Burma's King Bodawpaya. As previously explained, these attacks degenerated in time into mere border raids on Chiengmai, to 1802, and against Junk Ceylon and the lower isthmus for a decade longer. Siam surrendered its claim to Mergui and Tavoy after 1792, but with the aid of its Ligor vassal it kept control of the isthmian portage routes and suzerainty over much of the lower peninsula.

Because of the constant Burmese threat, Rama I dared not assert too vigorously his claims to Cambodia. Taking advantage of the strife between the Tay-son rebels and Nguyen Anh, Rama I did manage to restore to power in 1795 Cambodia's King Anh Eng, who had previously taken refuge in Bangkok from the Tay-sons. As the price of Siam's aid, Bangkok annexed several Cambodian border provinces including Battambang, Siemreap (Angkor), and parts of the Korat.[1] A concession was later made, in 1802 following the unification of Vietnam by Emperor Gia Long, permitting Cambodia to acknowledge the suzerainty of both Siam and Vietnam.

Rama II, who acceded to the Siamese Crown in 1809, was not an aggressive person and in fact took little active part in the administration of governmental affairs.[2] When Gia Long established Vietnam's military ascendancy at Phnom Penh in 1812, at a time when Burma seriously threatened Siam, King Rama II was content to gain compensation for Siam at Cambodia's expense in the Korat and along the left bank of the middle Mekong River. The eventual diversion of Burma's interest in the direction of India after 1819, culminating in the Anglo-Burman War of 1824–1826, ended this perennial threat to Siam's security. Rama II's last important act was to depose in 1821 the Sultan of Kedah, who had added the offense of intrigue with the Burmans to his earlier unauthorized cession of Penang and Province Wellesley to the British Company. But Chakri Bangkok discreetly avoided measuring strength with the British-Indian

[1] D. G. E. Hall, *A History of Southeast Asia* (1955), 395–397.
[2] Walter F. Vella, *Siam under Rama III, 1824–1851* (1957), 8.

forces that were shortly thereafter to bring Burma to its knees. Siam was internally strong but wary.[3]

Under the first two rulers of the Chakri dynasty, Siam persisted in its traditional avoidance of treaty relations with European powers, remembering its painful experiences under King Narai. Some concessions were nevertheless being made. A Portuguese trader was permitted after 1818 to act as a kind of Shahbandar to ships of his own countrymen, and a private English trader named Hunter was also admitted. Bangkok negotiated with a British mission headed by John Crawfurd in 1821 but refused at the time to conclude a treaty.[4] A similar negotiation was attempted by the Burney mission in 1825. During the following decade both Protestant and Catholic missionaries entered the country, and treaty engagements were finally accepted in 1833. The story of Siam's eventual voluntary abandonment of the policy of diplomatic and commercial isolation from the West will be deferred until after an examination of the country itself in the early nineteenth century.

## Kingship and Government in Nineteenth-century Siam

The government of Siam under the Chakri dynasty owed much to the institutions of ancient Angkor, and was also similar in many respects to Burma's system. The ruler was a reincarnated deity, a Chakravartin, or universal emperor, and a destined Buddha, or Bodhisattva. He was also the occupier of the sacred palace site. Brahman priests at court performed ceremonial and magical functions but exercised no influence otherwise on governmental administration.[5] The king's person was unapproachably sacred and his authority absolute. He was owner of all the land and also of the bodies of his subjects, who were legally his chattels. His claim to taxes and personal services was thus predicated on actual ownership. Underneath this borrowed system of divine kingship lay traces of the survival of an indigenous Thai concept of the paternalistic responsibility of the ruler for the welfare of his people, a tradition which recovered some vitality during the latter half of the century. The ruler's autocratic control was unqualified. As the incarnation of the authority of the state, the king determined the content of the law, formulated policy decisions, selected high officials, and elevated or degraded social rank. The tax revenues of the state and the king's private purse were the same. Cultural promotion and patronage of Buddhism were closely associated with the enhancement of

[3] Hall, 398–399. Burmese agents negotiated with Minh Mang's government at Hué as late as 1824 for an alliance against Siam.

[4] *Ibid.*

[5] W. F. Vella, *The Impact of the West on Government in Siam* (1955), 320–321.

royal prestige. Economic improvements, such as canal, land, and trade development, were made quite as much to enhance royal revenues and prestige as to promote public welfare.[6]

The consultative Council of the King, called the *Senabodi,* included the heads of the six chief governmental departments. The three most important were the Departments of the North (concerned with Burma frontier defense), the South (concerned with the Malay frontier), and of Commerce and Foreign Relations. The three top officials enjoyed a considerable measure of autonomy in military and revenue matters, and the posts tended to be filled on a hereditary basis. In the four Laotian provinces in the north and in Ligor and Singora in the peninsula, local chiefs usually served as governors. Other Malay vassal sultans paid tribute to the king.[7] The three lesser Departments of the Capital, the Palace, and the Lands were headed by officials who served at the royal pleasure. Judicial, administrative, and revenue functions were not differentiated into specialized services. Court princes, especially the vice-king, or Uparat, were often designated as nominal chiefs of the six major departments, with appropriate access to income sources. Princes were apparently not assigned, as was the practice in Burma, to Myosa fiefs or to provincial governorships, for fear that they might develop a local following. Censors checked on the performance of all high officials and governors, especially those located near the capital.[8]

The functions of the government were limited in scope. It controlled all foreign trade by means of monopolies, customs dues, and tax farmers, and it guaranteed minimal requirements of order and security from external danger. On the other hand, the government took no responsibility for local police protection against bandit outlaws, a function which had to be shouldered by the elders of the local village communities. As in Burma, virtually all civil suits were settled by local mediation. In criminal cases, relatives and neighbors were obliged to answer for offenses committed by a member of the group and also to help apprehend the criminal. Central governmental officials were notoriously rapacious and corrupt, and were therefore avoided by the people as far as possible.[9]

Social status in Siam, as in ancient Cambodia, depended on royal preferment. Princely status eroded away by stages after five generations. The sons of high officials became pages at the palace, while selected daughters of governors and vassal princes joined the royal harem as political hostages. The capital was the focal point of political power, cultural standards, social preferment, and wealth. Popular respect for authority reflected habits of deference which were related quite as much

---

[6] *Ibid.,* 317–320; Wendell Blanchard et al., *Thailand: Its People, Its Society, Its Culture* (1958), 148–151.

[7] John Crawfurd, *Journal of an Embassy to the Courts of Siam and Cochin China* (1828), 372–378.

[8] Vella, *Impact,* 322–327; Blanchard et al., 148–151.

[9] Vella, *Impact,* 327–331.

to the Chinese pattern of family relationships as to the Indian tradition of divine kingship.[10]

Aside from transmitting a portion of the provincial revenues to the capital, governors exacted from the people *corvée* labor on public works, amounting to some three or four months of duty per year, and also military service. These exactions were subjected to little or no oversight from the court. Money payments in lieu of *corvée* were usually accepted, as was the delivery of specialized requirements such as saltpeter, ivory, and sandalwood.[11]

Acting as a cushion between the royal officials and the people, locally resident patrons collected and transmitted the required dues and obligations in the name of the king. The patron was a kind of Siamese version of the Burman myothugyi. The relations between the patron and the Thai freemen were personal rather than territorial and were a two-way affair. In return for services performed, the patron was obligated to protect his clients from rapacity and injustice and to lend them money in cases of dire need. Service dues were registered, and the status of individual males was tattooed on their wrists, the sons being assigned as were their fathers. But a client could change his patron if dissatisfied. If burdened by debt, he could also sell himself and his family into slavery, the patron thereby losing his services. Hence arose the readiness of patrons to protect wards from desperate insolvency. The land was family-owned, each group acquiring claim to as much as it could clear and cultivate.[12]

## Social and Religious Characteristics

Approximately one-third of Siam's population in the early nineteenth century was slave. The master, taking the place of the patron, must deliver the requisite royal dues, while otherwise enjoying exclusive claim to the slave's services. As in Burma, the status of certain categories of slaves, especially pagoda slaves and debtor slaves, could approximate that of the freeman. Prisoners of war were chattels of the king, providing him with slave troops. They usually lived in compact national units, whether Burmese, Laotian, Cambodian, or Malay. Except for the Burmese, who were strictly supervised, the prisoner-slaves lived much the same as the ordinary Thai freemen, except for performing their royal obligations of military service.

The Chinese constituted the only other large alien group. They were active in foreign trade, including opium smuggling, and in many other areas of economic activity. Commercially, Bangkok was a Chinese city. It was often found more economical to hire industrious Chinese to construct public works than to depend on free *corvée* labor. The Chinese paid a poll

[10] *Ibid.*, 322–327.
[11] Vella, *Rama III*, 14–27.
[12] James C. Ingram, *Economic Change in Thailand since 1850* (1955), 12–13.

tax in lieu of personal services, and many Chinese bid successfully for the posts of tax farmers. Their closely knit secret societies (huis) were usually designed for self-protection, but they sometimes became involved in organized crime, such as smuggling and thievery. Chinese-Siamese relations became particularly bad after 1837, and a situation of open rebellion developed for a time in 1848.[13]

John Crawfurd's characterization of the Siamese people, derived from his visit of 1821, was sympathetic and appreciative, in spite of the low opinion which the frustrated British negotiator developed at the official level. He commended the Siamese for being a temperate and peaceful people, obedient, orderly, and not given to vengeance. Their standards of domestic life were high; they were indulgently affectionate and sensitive to filial duties. Divorce was easy, and polygamy was for the rich only. Siamese officialdom he condemned as rapacious, defective in candor and sincerity, and inordinately vain in its assumption of national superiority. Officials were described as abjectly servile toward superiors but disdainful toward inferiors.[14]

A more perceptive modern characterization of the Siamese has described them as committed to Buddhism, easygoing as compared with the industrious Chinese, fun-loving and not worrying about tomorrow, and generous in cases of dire need, especially where merit for karma was to be gained. They also were characterized as essentially a self-centered people, indifferent to problems not involving themselves directly. They were often prone to tell untruth to hide guilt or to gain face or even to spare another's feelings. They conformed well to the moral code in visible, verifiable situations, and were politely tactful and unobtrusive. From the village level up to the king, they were responsive to the requirements of hierarchic status. Although neither efficient nor particularly progressive, they were capable of accommodating themselves to changing circumstances.[15]

Popular religion in Siam contained many elements common to all of the peoples of Southeast Asia. Religion was largely concerned with the placation of mischievous vagrant spirits, basic considerations which pushed the Hindu pantheon, the Naga serpent, and even the Buddha at times into the background. Such animistic beliefs served to elevate to places of importance the spirit doctors, magicians, astrologers, horoscope casters, and dream interpreters. Fever and other forms of illness were equated with devil possessions. Auspicious days were important, as were talismen, charms, and love philters.

At the court level, the Brahman experts functioned in astrology and numerology and in the placation of the spirit world. As a divinity in his own right, the king was presumed to have power to dispel flood or famine, epidemic or natural disaster, and to keep in proper touch with ancestral

[13] Crawfurd, 372–375; Vella, *Rama III,* 14–27.

[14] Crawfurd, 342–349.

[15] Characterizations by Robert Textor and Walter Vella, unpublished.

spirits.[16] Anna Leonowens, the governess at Rama IV's Court, described the alleged execution of three victims on the site of the gateway to a newly constructed fort in order to provide spirit protection. She also reported an all-night cannonade from the palace at the year's end, following the reeling of a sacred cotton thread around the walls, all designed to ward off the mischievous spirits.[17]

Buddhism was also very influential. It was associated with popular festivals and dramatic performances depicting scenes from Indian legends and local mythology. Standards of merit seeking stressed the holy character of the abstemiousness of the monastic life, plus values inherent in pagoda and temple construction and in contributing to the daily needs of the monks. In actuality, the Buddha was usually deified as another member of a variegated pantheon associated with Indian doctrines of karma and transmigration and Hindu cosmology. At the highest Theravada level, Buddhism stressed reverence for the monastic order, devotion to the eight-fold path of righteous living, emphasizing neither sacrament nor ritual. Every man had to work out his own salvation by merciful deeds.[18]

The king's control of the *Sankharach,* or monastic community, was very similar to the pattern prevailing in Burma. A royally appointed primate presided over an executive Council of the Order, which included representatives from the four main sects. To this system, the Siamese added a Buddhist Assembly and four ecclesiastical boards, one each for administration, education, propaganda, and pagoda slaves, and all headed by ministers of high rank. Only theras (teachers) of ten years' standing could conduct ordinations. Two of the higher ranks in the order could be attained only through examinations in the Pali scriptures.[19]

Efforts to raise the standards of the monkhood were generally ineffective. King Mongkut, himself a thera of twenty-seven years' standing, sponsored a return to the purer standards of the Mons and Sinhalese but with little effect outside Bangkok. The popularity of magical and animistic accretions to Buddhism was too formidable to be easily exorcised.[20] Despite such disparaging references as that of Crawfurd to the effect that the attractiveness of the monks' life in Siam was enhanced by their being excused from *corvée* labor exactions, the majority of observers tended to agree that the monastic system contributed to Siam's society valuable elements of moral self-respect, learning, and compassionate concern.[21]

[16] Vella, *Rama III,* 28–31.

[17] Anna Leonowens, *The English Governess at the Siamese Court* (1954), 182–183.

[18] Vella, *Rama III,* 31–42.

[19] Blanchard et al., 99–101.

[20] Vella, *Rama III,* 31–42.

[21] George Finlayson, *The Mission to Siam and Hué* (1826), 106–118. Finlayson accompanied Crawfurd. He found the Siamese monasteries well appointed and the monks friendly.

## Siam's Foreign Trade in 1820

Because Siam had virtually cut off trade with Europeans since 1688, it did not follow that the country was uninterested in commerce or lacking in the means of profitable foreign exchange. Emphasis placed on British dominance of the India-to-China trade and on American and Danish participation in the world commerce of the region (Chapter 14) must not hide the extent to which the Chinese junks had come to monopolize the shuttle traffic along the eastern seaboard of continental Southeast Asia since the collapse of the Dutch Company. A large proportion of the east coast trade at the turn of the century came to center at Bangkok. All visitors to the city around 1820 reported that virtually the entire trading population was Chinese, from the floating bazaars on Bangkok's many canals to the wealthy wholesale-dealer warehouse owners.[22] All vessels in the harbor, whether of Chinese or Siamese nationality, were manned by Chinese crews. They bought and sold at Bangkok with a minimum of restrictions, while other traders encountered weeks of delay, probably due in some measure to impediments raised by jealous Chinese themselves. Siam did welcome the visits in 1818 and 1821 of American vessels bringing firearms for sale.[23]

In 1821, a British visitor estimated that approximately fourscore junks from China traded annually with Siam. About fifty of the smaller ones and several large ones came from Canton. Shanghai was second in importance as the port of origin, and Ningpo was third. The junks traded in the traditional semiannual monsoon rhythm. As early as 1821 a pattern of trade between Singapore and Bangkok was also developing, to the extent of fourteen or fifteen junks annually, trading mainly in opium. Eleven small junks went to Borneo and back, and smaller numbers visited Batavia and Manila. The coastal trade of eastern Malay was largely a monopoly of the King of Siam, his ships calling at more than a dozen ports to gather local products for the Chinese trade. The King exercised first claim on many desirable articles of import. Trade around the Gulf of Siam continued during all seasons of the year. The King also sent two official Chinese-manned junks yearly to Canton, where they enjoyed duty-free entry. Regular tributary missions left Bangkok for Peking every three years.

Most of the ships using the Bangkok port were built in Siam, where construction costs were 25 to 50 per cent lower than along the China coast. They were usually small vessels of around 200 tons displacement, with a few as large as 1,200 tons. They were described as high at the stern and bow, single-decked, and shallow-keeled, with their two to four masts carrying sails of matted bamboo. The holds were divided into some six

[22] Finlayson, 106–118, 194.
[23] Vella, *Rama III,* 115.

to fifteen compartments for cabins and goods storage. Navigation facilities on these ships were poor, and crews were consequently overlarge. The ships carried no pumping mechanisms, and the compass was reportedly housed at the stern in a little temple niche dedicated to protecting deities. English and American ships were several times as fast, sailed in all seasons, and could make three trips while the Chinese were making one.

The Chinese traders nevertheless enjoyed substantial advantages over the Europeans. The most important was their virtually free access to Chinese markets south of Shanghai, where they could obtain tea, porcelains, and silks for much less than the European traders, who were confined to the rigged market of the Cohong merchants at Canton. Chinese traders also possessed a thorough knowledge of Asian markets; owners usually accompanied the cargo and disposed of it at retail prices at ports of call. They were economical and careful in details and skilled in sorting cargo. They handled many items of a traditional character which the Europeans ignored, such as perfumed woods, rhino horns, ebony, benzoin, camphor, and hides. The Chinese were also quick to adjust to new trading opportunities. By 1824, no fewer than forty-four Chinese-manned junks from Siam were calling at Singapore, making Siam the second-most-important Asian user of the port, next to China itself.[24]

As early as 1820 Bangkok was attempting also to make official trading contact with the ports of Bengal, but with discouraging results. The first voyage required eighteen months to complete and incurred a net loss of 24,000 ticals. Part of the loss was due to Dutch exactions made in the straits after the vessel had run aground. Nor were the Siamese able to understand the official communication which the captain had brought back from India. What the Siamese most wanted to get from India was firearms.[25] It was against this background of indicated Siamese interest in Indian trade that the English Company decided to send John Crawfurd on a mission to Bangkok to see what could be done to facilitate commercial exchange.

## The Crawfurd Mission to Bangkok

The Crawfurd mission to Bangkok in 1821 carried a substantial cargo and also some valuable presents for the King, including cloth, glassware, muskets, and a horse. The objective was to arrange a commercial treaty which would afford British access to Siamese ports on a 6 to 8 per cent duty basis, with the privilege of free disposal of all cargo. Crawfurd's first difficulty was with the standing requirement that all vessels entering the Menam River park their guns ashore. His successful insistence that this ruling be waived in his instance aggravated suspicion of his intentions, a distrust which local Chinese traders were only too glad to encourage. Al-

24 Crawfurd, 48–51, 172–184, 408–414.
25 *Ibid.*, 141.

though treated politely on the whole, the mission was subjected to close surveillance and was threatened repeatedly with loss of face. The visitors were excused from the requirement to prostrate themselves in the royal presence but only after they agreed to remove their hats and shoes and sit with their legs under them pointing away from the royal dais. Crawfurd evaded with considerable difficulty Bangkok's demand that court correspondence be conducted with diplomatic representatives of the King of England and not with mere agents of the governor-general of the Company.

Crawfurd negotiated at first with the governor of Paknam, the point of entry, then with the ranking member of the Senabodi, who was the Foreign Minister and master of warehouses. The eldest son of the King looked on. A Muslim Indian Shahbandar and a Portuguese served as interpreters. The general atmosphere of the palace was described as one of arrogance and avarice. The conspicuous presence of Brahman priests was in keeping with the pictures on the walls of the royal passageways of scenes from the *Ramayana* legend. The level of King Rama II's personal interest in the visit is reflected in his unusual request that Crawfurd's Indian tailor dress a 3-foot puppet like Napoleon Bonaparte.[26]

The Crawfurd mission's negotiations dealt with two substantive questions, one having to do with trade and the other with the status of the Sultan of Kedah. On the commercial question, Crawfurd refused to tie his request for a treaty to the Siamese desire for the right to buy firearms at Indian ports, alleging that this would constitute an unfriendly act toward Bengal's friend, Burma, with which Siam was perennially at war. The Foreign Minister, in his turn, refused to consider any preferred treatment for British ships in regard to duties or disposal of cargo unless the trade amounted to at least five ships a year. Crawfurd's arguments concerning the mutual value of free trade in the Adam Smith tradition were completely ineffective.

The other question concerned Siam's demand that the Sultan of Kedah, "the King's slave" who had taken refuge in Penang after having been driven out of Kedah earlier in 1821, be required to answer for his misdeeds in Bangkok. The charges consisted mainly in his having intrigued with Burma in opposition to Ligor's control of the isthmian portage areas. The demand was based on allegations made by the governor of Ligor, which were declared not subject to review. Crawfurd's counterproposal that Siam restore the Kedah Sultan to power so wounded the pride of the Siamese Court that any possibility of successful negotiation on commercial matters was precluded. Crawfurd became convinced, however, that Siam was less strong militarily than had previously been thought and that Penang therefore had little to fear from the Kedah situation. Siam, by inference, had actually conceded *de facto* British title to Penang.[27]

[26] Finlayson, 120, 133, 144–146, 158–159, 265; Crawfurd, 71–103.
[27] Crawfurd, 71–103, 163–174; Hall, 446.

## Rama III and the Burney Mission

The death of Rama II in 1824 opened the way for the accession of Prince Thap as Rama III. He had previously directed a defense force against the Burma threat and had also gained experience in the government department concerned with shipbuilding and foreign trade. Whereas Rama II had given little attention to governmental affairs, being interested in literature, religious monuments, and palace extension, the new King as a mature man of some experience was destined to be more active. Prince Thap's hereditary claim to the throne was weak because of his having been born prior to his father's accession and to a commoner mother. The original Uparat, or heir apparent, had died in 1817, and no successor had been named. Younger princes, approximately half his age, were monkish or inexperienced. A court clique dictated the choice of Prince Thap as Rama III, and the nineteen-year-old Prince Mongkut, the most likely rival, withdrew discreetly to a monastery. The old chief ministers of the Senabodi were kept in power, particularly Prince Prakhlang, who headed the Department of the South and the Foreign Office.[28] It was this new court which faced the accumulated problems attending the outbreak of the Anglo-Burman War in 1824.

The key problem raised for Siam by the Anglo-Burmese War was connected with the British occupation of the Tenasserim coastline, an action which had little or no bearing on the defeat of the Burman armies. Rama III hoped to recover control of Tenasserim, which had been Siamese prior to 1760, in return for assistance to the British-Indian forces in supplies and possibly also militarily. For this purpose, he raised three Siamese armies and staged several anti-Burman raids on the Mergui area. After the British moved in, these armies were recalled from frontier posts, in 1825, ostensibly to attend the formal coronation ceremonies. Bangkok was also concerned with repeated efforts on the part of agents of British Penang to negotiate secretly with the Ligor Raja, whose territory was an integral part of Siam. These were coupled with Penang's opposition to Siam's continued efforts to reestablish its suzerain status over all the Malay sultanates.

British policy toward Siam took two directions in 1824–1825. The concern of Bengal, faced as it was with the burdens of military operations, was to enlist the support of Siam against the common Burman enemy. On the other hand, Governor Fullerton of Penang, aware that Bangkok was pressing the Raja of Ligor to reassert Siamese authority in the straits area of Malaya, advocated a bolder course. He proposed to restore the rebellious Kedah Sultan despite Siamese opposition and to extend British protection to other Malaya states, especially Perak and Selangor, which were threatened by the reassertion of Siamese control. Perak had declared its independence from Siam in 1822 with the support of Selangor.[29]

[28] Vella, *Rama III*, 1–13.
[29] Hall, 446.

Although Governor Fullerton's proposals were out of accord with Bengal's desire to establish good relations with Siam, Calcutta did not disapprove two *faits accomplis* by the Penang authorities in 1825. A bluffed threat of armed intervention by Fullerton succeeded in stopping an armed expedition from the Siamese port of Trang destined for Perak and Selangor. The second action involved the negotiation of a highly irregular treaty agreement between Penang's representative, Captain Burney, and the Raja of Ligor, an action exceeding the authority of both negotiating parties. The agreement promised that Britain would refrain from interfering in Kedah in return for Ligor's pledge to refrain from attacking Perak and Selangor. It is more than probable that Rama III disapproved of this commitment, if indeed he knew about it, for Ligor was preparing to send another small armed force into Perak when Calcutta decided that Burney should proceed as its envoy to Bangkok to forestall trouble with Siam.[30]

Bengal's instructions to the Burney mission were moderately phrased. He was to reassure Bangkok that Britain's occupation of Tenasserim constituted no threat to Siam's security. Fullerton added his own subordinate instructions that Burney should support strongly the independence of the Malay sultanates as opposed to Siam's suzerainty. It is significant that Burney prolonged his visit until months after the Burman war had been concluded and that he did not raise any issues regarding the Malay sultanates and commercial concessions until after the Treaty of Yandabo had been signed in February, 1826. Only then did he make Siam's agreement not to interfere in the Malay states a condition of friendly relations.[31]

It was not to be expected that Rama III would accept Burney's assurances concerning Tenasserim entirely at face value. His suspicions were not allayed by Burney's suggestion during the war that the Siamese might aid Britain as an ally by attacking the authority of Burma in the eastern Shan state of Kengtung. Siam's determination to keep its hands free was strengthened by the report that British officers in Tenasserim had attempted to suborn the Mon commander of one of the Siamese armies by a tentative proposal to establish a Mon buffer state. Having been thwarted by the British occupation in his hope of recovering Tenasserim for Siam, Rama III was determined to concede as little as possible regarding commercial matters and Malaya. At the same time, he dared not invite trouble by rebuffing Burney as Bangkok had rebuffed Crawfurd five years before. The need to avoid a break with the rising Anglo-Indian Empire was especially urgent in view of developing Siamese problems on the Laotian and Cambodian frontiers.

The terms of the agreement reached in June, 1826, were decidedly vague; it labored the theme of reciprocity. The official text was in Siamese. The "independence" of the Malay states was defined in such a way as to

---

[30] *Ibid.*, 447–447; L. A. Mills, *British Malaya, 1824–1867* (1925), 136–155.
[31] Vella, *Rama III*, 109–111, 115–118; Henry Burney, *The Burney Papers* (1910).

permit all the sultans to continue sending to Bangkok the traditional tokens of vassalage status. Both parties agreed to respect the power of the Sultan of Perak and not to attack the state, but the Sultan was not to be prevented from sending the symbols of tribute to Bangkok if he wished to do so. Siam promised not to obstruct the rights previously enjoyed by the British to trade with Trengganu and Kelantan, and Britain on her part promised not to disturb the states in question on any pretext whatsoever.[32] Bangkok refused Burney's offer of 4,000 dollars a year for the withdrawal of Siamese troops from Kedah and the restoration of the Sultan. Siam exacted instead a pledge that Britain would remove the Sultan from Penang (to Malacca) and cooperate in thwarting any future attempts of the exiled ruler to return to Kedah by force. Despite the angry dissent of Governor Fullerton, Bengal accepted these terms as constituting something of a net gain.[33]

In the area of commercial concessions Siam granted very little. The British could trade only in accordance with local custom. They could rent land and build factories if express permission were obtained and resident Britons would be subject to Siamese courts. The exportation of rice was forbidden, as was the importation of opium. A consolidated customs levy based on the depth of a ship's beam was to be substituted for the previous 8 per cent ad valorem duty. Aid was to be accorded to distressed seamen. Recognizing the extreme repugnance with which the presence of a British official at Bangkok would be regarded, Burney did not even try to establish a consulate.[34] Treaty ratifications were exchanged at Trang in 1827.

## The Post–Burma War Period

Tenasserim under British rule was far more important politically than economically, for it served as a lever on both Burma and Siam. It effectively inhibited any renewal of warfare between the two traditional enemies. With the naval and military resources of India behind the otherwise feeble coastal holding, British control denied the use of the most accessible means of transit between the two countries. Siam's desire to recover Tenasserim was tempered, in Burney's opinion, by fear that Britain would demand too high a price for it in Malaya and by concern that its occupancy by Siam would revive the feud with Burma.[35] British control meanwhile was a boon to the local inhabitants, who had been many times victimized by both sides in the interminable quarrel. Calcutta later toyed with the idea of setting up a Mon buffer state or exchanging Tenasserim for Kedah, but the matter was not seriously pushed.[36]

[32] Hall, 448; Mills, 136–152.

[33] Hall, 448–449.

[34] Vella, *Rama III*, 115–121. Burney predicted that any enforced presence of a British consul in Bangkok would breed war within six months.

[35] Burney, I, 157–166.

[36] *Ibid*, 165–166.

Events in Malaya soon overtook the equivocal treaty terms of 1826. Neither side honored its agreement as far as Perak was concerned. The Siamese attempted both by subversion and by direct military intervention to influence the Sultan to revive his vassalage status, which was permitted under the treaty. Governor Fullerton, on his side, sent a small sepoy detachment and a warship to bolster Perak's resistance and to urge the Sultan not to acknowledge Siam's suzerainty. An agent of Fullerton, acting in his customary uninhibited fashion, proceeded to negotiate a completely unauthorized treaty of alliance and protection, conditional on Perak's severance of all ties with Ligor and Bangkok. The Company officials at Calcutta censored the negotiator severely at the time and refused to give formal ratification to the irregular treaty. The net effect of Fullerton's action was nevertheless to cause Siam to abandon its efforts to control the western coasts of Malaya below Kedah. Penang did honor its pledge to oppose any forcible return of the ex-Sultan of Kedah. Return was attempted on repeated occasions during the 1830s. The Sultan was eventually reinstated in 1842 by consent of Siam after renewing in token fashion his vassalage status. Britain took a somewhat less negative view of the efforts of Siam to strengthen its control of Trengganu and Kelantan on the eastern shore during the 1830s.[37]

The tenacious efforts of Bangkok to maintain its traditional primacy in Malaya represented only one phase of the determination of Rama III to halt the serious deterioration of Siam's authority over its vassal tributaries, which had developed during the last years of the previous reign. This trend was clearly in evidence in Cambodia, where Vietnam had assumed a dominant role in the early 1820s, and also in the expansionist tendencies of a prince of Laos. Prince Ahn of Vientiane had aided Siam in suppressing a revolt at Bassac in 1819 and now felt unappreciated and ambitious. In late 1826, when wild rumors were afloat that Britain would make a naval attack on Bangkok, rebel Lao forces under the prince overran the adjacent Ubon and Korat provinces of Siam. The rebellion was short-lived because Ahn lacked resolution and fled to Vietnam at the first signs of the restoration of Siamese authority. Rama's forces captured and despoiled Vientiane, and its territories were parceled out as increments to regular Siamese provinces. The Siamese proceeded to realize additional gains in the Luang Prabang region of Laos and in the trans-Mekong district opposite Bassac, the latter at the expense of Vietnam.[38]

Siam's efforts to recover the upper hand in Cambodia were not immediately successful. They failed in 1833–1834, when a rebellion in Vietnam presented possible opportunity. They were finally successful in 1840–1842, when they were able to find allies against Vietnam within Cambodia itself. King Ang Duong, who was installed by the Siamese in 1842, also obtained recognition from Hué five years later. He was thereafter permitted to send tribute to both capitals. Rama III maintained his predomi-

[37] Hall, 450.
[38] Vella, *Rama III*, 78–9?.

nant influence by accepting the sons of Duong into the Bangkok government for training purposes. He also solicited support in Cambodia itself by championing the preservation of Buddhism against the allegedly hostile threats of Confucianist Vietnam.

The reign of Rama III was effective and vigorous in the traditional sense of reestablishing royal and national prestige and strengthening vassal control. The kingdom was certainly stronger in this sense in 1851 than at Rama III's accession in 1824. But its expansion had been halted in Tenasserim, Cambodia, and Malaya, and the Chakri dynasty was otherwise on the defensive. It was questionable how long the traditionalist policy of opposition to the rising tide of pressure from the outside world could be successfully maintained.[39]

Commercial activities at Siamese ports continued very much the same until the middle thirties. Conditions along the eastern coasts of Malaya got worse rather than better, for Patani was ravaged by civil war, and Trengganu was pirate-ridden. By contrast, the Gulf of Siam was well policed, and its trade was active.[40] British ships rarely visited Bangkok as of 1832 because heavy duties were levied on larger European vessels, while the smaller Chinese junks paid no duty at all. Two or three cloth-laden ships per year came from India's Coromandel Coast. Even the opium market in Bangkok was being preempted by the Chinese ships, which were coming partly from Canton and partly from Singapore. The influx of silver due to Bangkok's favorable trade balance was helping push the country in the direction of a money economy. The government's income was slowly rising, amounting in 1850 to double what it had been in 1824.[41]

The one innovation made by Rama III during the thirties was the negotiation of an American treaty of commerce in 1833, done at Siam's own invitation. The American negotiator, Edmund Roberts, committed the egregious error of failing to bring along appropriate presents for the court, but in this instance it made little difference. Siam's desire for an American treaty was apparently connected with two considerations. One was the need for the regular importation of arms, and the other was to find a makeweight against the threat of a British monopoly. The American negotiation involved neither boundary problems nor other political considerations. The terms of the treaty went only a little way beyond the British treaty of 1826 in providing for most-favored-nation treatment, the moderation of port duties, and permission to establish a consulate. No American consul was sent, however, until 1856. Permission was also given for the entry of American Protestant missionaries, many of whom had already arrived at Bangkok in 1831.[42] There is no evidence that American ships ever took extensive

[39] *Ibid.,* 70–77, 105–108, 141.

[40] George W. Earl, *The Eastern Seas* (1837), 148–155. The Sultan of Trengganu at this juncture was in the final stage of opium addiction.

[41] Vella, *Rama III,* 19–20, 177–178.

[42] *Ibid.,* 122–124.

advantage of the Siamese invitation to trade, but the treaty did provide a basis for a culturally significant Protestant missionary impact.

## The Missionary Impact on Siam

Despite the 140 years of persecution and suppression of Christians in Siam since the French missionary debacle of 1688, at least six churches of the Roman Catholic faith survived in 1828 when Protestant missionary contact was established. A Netherlands Protestant missionary-linguist, Carl Gutzlaff, arrived in 1828. In his three-year connection with Siam, he translated the New Testament into imperfect Siamese, prepared a Thai-English dictionary, and made further Bible translations into Cambodian and Lao. But in 1831 Gutzlaff left for China where he later had a distinguished career in diplomacy as well as in the field of translation. The first American Board Protestant missionaries arrived in 1831 and those of the Presbyterians in 1840. Meanwhile, in 1830, Monsignor Pallegoix of the Missions Étrangères came to revitalize the Catholic missionary program. The programs of the two missions took different channels. The Catholics pursued the familiar pattern of church and chapel ministry of the sacraments, seminary and school training for youth, and the organization of an indigenous monastic order. The American Protestant effort tended in the direction of translation, publication, medical missions, and secular education.[43]

Although neither missionary effort had any important impact as far as the number of converts was concerned, they both contributed materially to the cumulative Western cultural influence. Monsignor Pallegoix has been credited, during his stay of some thirty years in Siam, with eight thousand baptisms; the American Protestants during the same period converted scarcely any at all.[44] The difficulties were many. The climate proved deadly, for one thing, so that the average tenure per missionary was only five years. Missionary knowledge of the Siamese language and culture was limited, and any direct criticism of Buddhism aroused local resentment. Christianity, especially the Protestant variety, was completely alien and almost incomprehensible to most Siamese, and individual seekers found it almost impossible to break with family and community ties.[45]

The American missionaries were nevertheless responsible for many innovations. One started the first newspaper in the Siamese language in 1835. Another, Rev. Jesse Caswell, served for eighteen months as tutor in English and science to the prince-monk, Mongkut, receiving in return permission to use a room at a convenient Wat temple for his own preaching

[43] *Ibid.*, 31–42; Kenneth E. Wells, *History of Protestant Work in Thailand, 1828–1958* (1958), 5–15.

[44] The first American Board convert was made in 1849 and that of the Presbyterian missionaries in 1859. The American Baptists, extending their operation from Burma to Siam, had enlisted several score Chinese converts by 1863.

[45] Wells, 2–4.

and distribution of tracts. Mongkut attended the funeral of Reverend Caswell, in 1849, and later as King erected a monument over his grave. An American medical missionary, Dr. Dan Bradley, was credited with the first smallpox vaccination in Siam in 1839, the King himself receiving vaccination at his hands. Monsignor Pallegoix taught the inquiring Mongkut to read Latin, in addition to giving him instruction in science. The excellent rapport which developed between Mongkut (the future Rama IV) and his Western missionary friends and tutors contributed much to the more sympathetic pro-Western orientation which developed during the course of his reign. Mongkut as a monk-scholar became genuinely interested in the outside world and in science. He even tried to eliminate some of the magic and superstition from Siam's Buddhism of the day.[46] Also among his personal friends were a number of British officials resident at Singapore.

Rama III raised no serious objections to the missionary program until 1848, when he became exceedingly annoyed over the Catholic program in particular. He issued an edict calling for the destruction of all Christian centers of worship and expelled eight Catholic priests. The American Baptist Mission Press was burned out in 1850, perhaps by arson, including a stock of books and a complete new edition of the New Testament. Employees of missionaries were imprisoned in 1850. The royal decree was only partially carried out. But Rama III made no concession on the missionary question in connection with the negotiations of Britain's Balestier in 1849 and James Brooke in 1850. The King was preparing further expulsions when he died in 1851.[47]

Rama III's policy also took a reactionary turn after 1840 in the matter of foreign trade. Largely as a means of profiting the royal treasury and the officials in charge of the foreign-trade monopoly, the government increased the price of exported sugar by 40 per cent. Rama III extended the employ of Chinese tax farmers in an effort to squeeze more revenue from exports of other items, such as sampan woods (for dyes), dried meat and fish, pepper, and edible birds' nests. The King also began to build and operate European-model ships for his own use and that of favored nobles, all of which were duty-free. The long-time British trader at Bangkok, Hunter, became so discouraged by 1844 that he abandoned legitimate trade entirely in favor of opium smuggling, for which he was eventually expelled. The number of British vessels visiting Bangkok in 1849 fell to five only. The reduction of the volume of British shipping appears to have been a major purpose of Rama's discriminatory policy.

When the British Company sent Joseph Balestier in 1849 to seek relaxation of Siam's new trading restrictions, he was treated as a mere trader representative. He tried in vain to bypass the Senabodi and lost his temper over his failure to make direct contact with the King. James Brooke

[46] Vella, *Rama III*, 31–42; Wells, 5–15.
[47] Henri Mouhot, *Travels in the Central Parts of Indo-China* (1864), I, 95–98; Wells, 19–21.

tried again in 1850, this time bringing full credentials from England to-gether with an imposing retinue, plus an unusual measure of ability and patience. It was all to no avail. Brooke asked for a resident consulate, extra-territorial privileges such as China had recently granted foreigners, freedom to trade, purchase land, and worship, and a moderation of taxes. The King declined to listen to his arguments and refused any new treaty. Despite the ominous warning signals which the China war had afforded, Rama III was obviously determined to keep the foreigner out and to preserve his tradi-tional tax-farming method of gaining income.[48]

Rama III's court system—self-centered, interested in preserving its semidivine prerogatives and the prestige of wealth and power and lacking concern for outside commercial opinion—was not destined to survive any-where in Southeast Asia. The same could be said of his system of nominal vassal appendages, over which Siam refused to accept responsibility for policing or control. The minimal demands of the Western traders, which he met in 1826, no longer sufficed in the 1850s. Nor could Bangkok expect for long to resist the impact of Western cultural and scientific innovations. Fortunately for Siam, an appreciation of the world outside had already gained lodgment in the mind of the studious ex-monk Mongkut, who took over the kingship on the death of Rama III in 1851.[49]

## King Mongkut and the Vogue of Westernization

The accession of Prince Mongkut in April, 1851, was arranged by the Senabodi while Rama III was on his deathbed. Two ranking princes, both brothers of Rama II, had previously been eliminated, the first by natural death and the second by execution for treason, and no Uparat had been selected from the eight eligible sons of Rama III. The dying King disliked Mongkut, his half brother, because of Mongkut's nontraditional views and his advocacy of Buddhist reform along the lines of the older Mon pattern; but Rama III was not able to control the selection. The modulation from the monk's robe to the royal regalia of the palace by Mongkut followed a venerable historical precedent. It added the reverence due the holiness of the monk to the symbols of divine autocracy on the Indian pattern. The same precedent was destined to be followed by Burma's King Mindon in the fol-lowing year under conditions of dire peril to the neighbor kingdom. The circumstances added to the awe in which Mongkut was held, which was in turn an effective deterrent to would-be troublemakers. His rapport with the people owed much to his previous daily contacts with them as a mendi-cant and as a pilgrim in the countryside.

Mongkut was forty-seven years old at the time of his elevation to the kingship. He was a self-reliant man, outspoken and fearless, who acted under conviction rather than from expediency. He was an indefatigable

[48] Vella, *Rama III,* 125–140.
[49] *Ibid.,* 141–144.

worker and frugal in his personal wants, but he was full of pleasure as well as business. As a long-time monk, he had no love for war or instruments of war. He lived not as a palace recluse but among his people. Partly from a genuine desire for modernization and partly out of caution, he undertook to reach an accommodation with Western ways and expectations. He opened the doors of his country to outside trade and invited foreign experts into his employ on generous terms covering many areas of the economy, government, and education. He even contributed articles to a Westerner's local newspaper, the *Siam Times*. He always ruled within the context of the autocratic tradition and therefore accomplished little to alter the system of government itself. He was equally conservative respecting privileges of the nobility. All advisers were kept under strict control by the king, who did not even allow scope for his own brother, the vice-king, to accept responsibility or to introduce innovations.[50]

Mongkut's accession marked an abrupt change in the status of members of the foreign missionary community, several of whom were his personal friends. He responded to a letter of congratulation from the French bishop with a gift of money and a cancellation of decrees of banishment hanging over five priests. He also moved to assure the protection of all Christian subjects from persecuting actions by provincial governors. When Bishop Pallegoix returned to Europe for a visit in 1852, he carried letters of regard from the King addressed to both Louis Napoleon of France and to the Pope. Mongkut was on equally good terms with the Protestants. Moving into the palace after twenty-seven years of monastic celibacy and study of the English language, he decided that his chief queens should also learn English. He therefore engaged three wives of American missionaries to teach the language to the ranking women of the palace. This routine lasted for three years, with each teacher devoting two days of each week to the task. A Christian day school for children was organized in Bangkok in 1852. With Mongkut's consent and the permission of the local vassal prince, a Protestant missionary establishment was later started at the frontier city of Chiengmai in 1863.[51]

The urge to westernize was in some respects stronger in the vice-king —Chudha-mani, Mongkut's younger full brother—than in the King himself. The less pious brother had also been passed over in 1824 when Rama III took the throne, but instead of joining a monastery he had become a student of applied science. He was fond of books, scientifically curious, and deplored his country's backwardness. Under Rama III, Chudha-mani had served as superintendent of artillery and commander of Malay infantry, as naval commander in an expedition of 1842 sent against Cambodia, and as supervisor of defensive fortifications on the Burmese frontier. He gained a su-

[50] *Ibid.*, 1–13; Samuel J. Smith, *The Siam Repository* (1869–1874), I, 64–66; John Campbell, *Siam in the Twentieth Century* (1902), 80–91; Abbot Low Moffat, *Mongkut, the King of Siam* (1961), 37.

[51] Mouhot, I, 95–98; Wells, 23–26; Moffat, 13–15.

perior command of English as a result of contact with Americans and with British engineers and served Rama III as official translator of English documents and secretary for English correspondence. He was also a student of navigation, coastal defenses, iron casting, and telegraphy. Admired by foreigners for his sagacious, energetic, and liberal spirit, he was also popular locally as a generous patron of sports and shows.[52]

In his quarter century of effort to find out what made the West so strong, Chudha-mani became enamored of European ways. He collected English books and periodicals. The furniture of his palace situated on the left bank of the river was entirely European, and it became the scene of European-style parties which the missionaries sometimes found uncongenial. He dressed his two wives in pleated European dresses with ruffled sleeves. As a private gentleman, he corresponded widely with Westerners in English. He named his eldest son Prince George Washington but refused to send his sons to a missionary school for fear of their possible conversion to Christianity. His interest in navigation and shipbuilding led him to construct the first European-type vessel in Siam. He later fitted a steam engine to a small river craft. He also developed his own lathe and machine ship and even wrote an essay on watch repairing.[53]

Toward his jealous brother, the King, the vice-king was discreetly subservient. Regulations requiring that he withdraw money from the treasury only on order of Mongkut were a source of irritation between them. He exercised no executive power under Mongkut, and was forced to renew his oath of allegiance twice a year like all other officials in the government. But he alone of all the Siamese need not grovel before the King. Some outside observers regarded the younger brother as more competent in matters of statecraft than Mongkut. Prince Chudha-mani died in 1866, two years before Mongkut. Prince George Washington became the vice-king in 1868, when Mongkut's eldest son took over the throne.[54]

The vogue of westernization which influenced so strongly the Siamese Court after 1851 was also transmitted in some measure to Cambodia. In 1858, a French visitor to the country described the striking contrast between the decadent conditions which prevailed at the King's residence near the coast of Cambodia and the modernist abode of the youthful vice-king, who had spent some years at Bangkok as a protégé and political hostage. On the Cambodian coast, a fat Chinese chief of the pirates had bribed the authorities, including his friend the King, and was carrying on his licensed robbery with complete impunity. Officials were alternately insolent and servile and were consistent only in their open solicitation of gratuities. The Chinese ran the markets and restaurants, opium shops, and gambling halls. At Udong, located above the confluence of the Tonle Sap and the Mekong and twelve days by elephant from Campot port, the youthful vice-king

[52] Leonowens, 186–196.
[53] Smith, I, 61–63.
[54] *Ibid.;* Mouhot, 45–50.

greeted the visitor with a European handshake and regaled him with a European meal replete with a bottle of brandy and topped off with jellies and Manila cigars. The furniture of his apartment was entirely European, including chairs and sofas, mahogany tables, and mirrors, plus a windup music box capable of playing the "Marseillaise" for his visitor. The prince was apologetic that his furnishings project was incomplete, but he promised the visitor that his house would in time be beautiful.[55]

## Siam's New Treaty System

From the outset of his accession, King Mongkut recognized both the necessity and the desirability of revising standing commercial treaties. The crux of the problem was to reach agreement with the powerful British. Less than three weeks after the death of his predecessor, in April, 1851, he wrote to personal friends among British officials in Singapore, acknowledging their congratulatory greetings and indicating how they might continue to address private letters to him via his personal secretary. He also asked that efforts to negotiate a new commercial treaty be delayed for a least a year until the cremation of the remains of Rama III was properly attended to.[56] Bangkok's desire to come to terms with Britain peaceably was undoubtedly increased by the events of 1852, which saw a British-Indian force, acting on little provocation, occupy the central valley of Lower Burma. Bangkok's moves to liberalize trade restrictions voluntarily preceded formal treaty conversations.

Negotiations for the revision of the British treaty were initiated by Sir John Bowring in April, 1854. Bowring had served as British consul at Canton from 1849 to 1852, when he had gone home on leave. He was a noted linguist, a former editor of the *Edinburgh Review,* and the editor of the collected works of Jeremy Bentham. His literary achievements had earned for him the doctor's degree from the University of Groningen. As a disciple of Bentham and Adam Smith, Bowring was an enthusiastic advocate of free trade and harbored an ambition to crown his literary reputation by a notable diplomatic triumph. Knighted on the eve of his departure from England in early 1854, Bowring was sent back to Hongkong as Chief Superintendent of British Trade in China, as governor of Hongkong, and also as British plenipotentiary with power to negotiate treaties with China in particular but also with Japan, Siam, and Cochin-China. His declaration of intent to negotiate at Bangkok was sent from Singapore while en route to Hongkong.[57]

King Mongkut's reply, sent to Hongkong three months later in July,

[55] Mouhot, I, 178–204.

[56] King Mongkut, "English Correspondence of King Mongkut," *JSS,* XXI (1927), 13–15.

[57] John F. Cady, *The Roots of French Imperialism in Eastern Asia* (1954), 114, 120–123.

1854, congratulated Bowring on his knighthood and his new diplomatic appointment and indicated a desire to meet Bowring personally in order to cement more firmly the friendship between their two countries. He asked that several months' notice be given of his intended arrival at Bangkok, including full details as to the size of his entourage. He also suggested that Bowring meanwhile write to him privately concerning the substance of the desired treaty terms so that his Council could begin consideration of them. In response to the suggestion of the King, Bowring sent three private letters in which he explained among other things his alarming intention to bring a British war vessel up the Menam River. Mongkut's reply announced his readiness to receive Bowring and told of his proclamation asking his people to keep the peace and to avoid consternation at the appearance of the warship at the capital. He also broadened his invitation to include the American Minister to China, Robert McLane. The invitation was later extended also to include Townsend Harris, the newly arrived American envoy to Eastern Asia. One aspect of the situation which was gratifying to the Siamese was that Bowring and Harris came as plenipotentiaries accredited by sovereign governments and not as mere representatives of the East India Company, as had been the situation in the 1826 negotiations.[58]

The British negotiation at Bangkok was conducted in the early months of 1855. Bowring took full advantage of his scarlet Groningen doctor's gown when talking to the King about literary and other mutual interests, while his assistant, Harry Parkes, conducted the negotiations. The British gunboat, anchored off Bangkok, delivered repeated twenty-one-gun salutes for psychological effect, and when negotiations ran aground on one occasion, Bowring threatened to delay the gunboat's scheduled departure. Siamese authorities were prepared to meet the British demands in a fashion that would also be satisfactory to the Americans and the French. The most important terms of the treaty granted extraterritorial rights for British subjects, with the right to rent land, to construct residences, and to travel a day's journey inland from Bangkok. British ships should have access to all Siamese ports, and a consulate could be established at Bangkok when the volume of trade reached ten ships a year. The treaty also provided for a single uniform duty on items for export and a maximum 3 per cent duty on imports.

Harry Parkes returned to Bangkok from London in March, 1856, to exchange ratifications. He took the occasion to exact with some difficulty, in an acrimonious negotiation lasting more than a month, additional concessions demanded by London. On this occasion, Parkes lacked proper credentials and insisted on anchoring his gunboat before the city. His new demands included provision for the organization of a proper customs service, for the free export of gold and rice, for the abolition of the government's monopoly in coconut oil, and for the imposition of a fixed nominal tax on British-owned properties. The Siamese also consented in this instance that

[58] Mongkut, 3–17.

the English copy, not the Siamese as in 1826, be made official. A Chinese version of the treaty was later prepared at Hongkong for the use of Chinese traders.[59] The Bangkok government complimented Parkes publicly for his industry and was discreetly private in expressing to Harris its great annoyance over his overbearing tactics.

The American treaty was concluded in the same year and along the same general lines. Townsend Harris was present during and immediately after the bullying performance of Parkes and became thoroughly annoyed himself at being pushed aside. He found the Siamese thoroughly disillusioned and hostile as far as the English were concerned. Siamese officials confided to Harris their fears that Siam was about to suffer a fate similar to that of Burma and asked whether the United States would act to protect Siam.[60] Harris finally concluded his negotiations on May 29 and left soon after for Japan, not even affording time enough for the Siamese government to prepare proper acknowledgment of the letter and presents sent by President Pierce to the King.[61]

The French negotiations with Siam, Cambodia, and Vietnam require further comment. Because of involvement in the Crimean War, Paris gave a tardy response to suggestions from Bowring in 1855, coming via the French Minister at Canton as well as through London, that France send agents to Bangkok to collect the treaty which was waiting for them there. The only French groups genuinely interested in such a treaty were apparently the missionary societies. As the French negotiator, the latter expressed a strong preference for the erratic French vice-consul at Shanghai, Montigny, over the regular French diplomatic representatives to China, Bourboulon and De Courcy. Both were known to be far less enthusiastic than Montigny about giving political support to the missionary cause.

Montigny's original instructions from Paris of November, 1855, applied only to Siam. He was to be content with obtaining the terms of Bowring's treaty except possibly for additional guarantees concerning religious liberty for Siamese Christians and access of French missionaries to the interior. He could consult with Monsignor Pallegoix at Bangkok and could also consider stopping at Tourane en route to China to present to Hué a mild protest against recent anti-Christian edicts, but without committing France to action.

Montigny's mission to Southeast Asia was a comedy of errors. He dallied at Rome so long that he missed his intended transportation via the Red Sea, and did not reach Singapore until mid-May, 1856. Pending the delayed arrival of the sailing vessel coming via South Africa with the presents for the Siam visit, he commandeered the convoy services of two

[59] Cady, 142–143; Mongkut, 15–29.

[60] Cady, 148.

[61] Mongkut, 30–35. The American presents included several framed mirrors, a microscope, a rifle and a Colt revolver, a Webster's Dictionary, maps of the United States, and a picture of the President.

armed French corvettes. He also wrote, through the Missions Étrangères representative at Singapore, to French Fathers Pallegoix and Miche in Siam and Cambodia respectively, asking their assistance in preparing the way for his intended negotiations at Hué in Vietnam. Montigny also added the gratuitous and difficult request that Miche arrange for him to meet the Cambodian King at the coastal town of Campot (in the middle of the monsoon rains). Both missionaries expressed understandable bewilderment concerning Montigny's complete lack of any awareness of the political and physical realities of the situation, but they were unable to deter the prima donna aspirations of the ambitious French consul.

Montigny reached Bangkok on June 10, 1856, and negotiated without difficulty his treaty terms with Siam. By this time Bangkok was ready to do pretty much whatever the foreigners asked. The Siamese consented that missionaries should be permitted to circulate freely anywhere in Siam, to enjoy the right to reside in the interior, and to erect churches and residences, and agreed also that the Siamese Christians be exempt from persecution. While waiting for his missionary collaborators to make arrangements for meetings at Campot and Hué, Montigny remained at Bangkok until September 21. He disclosed his mission to negotiate with the Cambodian King, Ang Duong, to the great consternation of the Siamese. The King in question had apparently sent to the French consul at Singapore via missionary channels a tentative suggestion that he might want to negotiate.[62] But Ang Duong had no intention of queering his relations with his suzerain at Bangkok by dealing independently with the French. Several Siamese agents meanwhile proceeded overland to Battambang while nine others accompanied Montigny by sea, just to be sure he did not succeed in his negotiation. Even more incomprehensible was Montigny's request that Bangkok pave the way for his intended negotiations at Hué, the bitter enemy of Siam.

Montigny dallied off Campot for a month waiting in vain to see the King. He then prepared unilaterally a draft treaty without any reference to the Cambodian messengers who came to announce the King's inability to meet Montigny. The proposed draft treaty was to be transmitted to the King by a missionary. It provided that the King make the Catholic faith one of the approved state religions, grant freedom from persecution to those accepting it, and cede to France a 40-mile-long offshore island claimed by Vietnam. From this island French forces could supposedly protect Cambodia from attacks by Vietnam, as Siam had allegedly requested France to do. Needless to say, King Ang Duong rejected the French proposal as involving him in difficulties with both of Cambodia's suzerain states. The month's delay at Campot, until October 16, made impossible Montigny's passage to Tourane in the teeth of the typhoon-breeding northern monsoon at that season. His vessel had to return to Singapore while the typhoon season passed; his two escorting warships, proceeding earlier, went on to China via Tourane.

[62] M. Ghosh, *A History of Cambodia* (1960), 260–263.

Meanwhile Montigny's advance letter, prepared at Bangkok in early August, had been delivered at the Hué Court by a missionary emissary arriving by one of the French war vessels en route to China. The letter indicated Paris's desire for a treaty and continued French sympathy for the Annamese people despite many hostile provocations. It threatened dire consequences if the friendly French gesture were rebuffed. The transmitting French vessel arriving in September and, encountering resistance at Tourane, seized the citadel by force after the letter was rejected by Hué. But Montigny failed to appear, and the naval officers were powerless to treat with emissaries who were eventually sent to them from Hué. The two vessels finally left for China. When Montigny managed to reach Tourane on January 23, 1857, he was able to do nothing to make good his gratuitous and unauthorized threats.[63]

The exchange of ratifications of the French treaty with Siam was also handled very badly. The treaty was sent to Europe and back to Siam in the hands of casual messengers. On its return it was delivered to the court without any formality or accompanying presents by a resident Portuguese merchant whom Montigny had named titular French consul. The Siamese interpreted this procedure as an intended slight and flatly rejected the treaty. When the officially designated French consul, M. Heutier, reached Bangkok in December, 1857, he was so coldly received that he immediately applied for leave.[64]

No matter how much the Siamese government may have regretted by this time the decision to come to terms with the Western powers, there was no turning back. Denmark and the Hanse cities got their treaties in 1859, Portugal in 1859, Holland in 1860, Belgium, Italy, and Norway-Sweden in 1868, and Germany in 1872.[65] Siam sent an official embassy to Paris in 1861.

## Siam's Modernization Program

King Mongkut followed up his enlistment of the services of wives of American missionaries to teach the women at the court by employing numerous other Europeans to modernize his state. The aforementioned Mrs. Anna Leonowens, a widowed English lady from Singapore, was brought in to teach his princely offspring the English language and the rudiments of Western science, literature, and history. Among Mongkut's sixty progeny, the eldest son Prince Chulalongkorn was one of the most apt of her students. Englishmen were also invited to serve as harbor master and commanders of a mercenary police force recruited in Singapore. King Mongkut assigned to a Frenchman the task of commanding and drilling the royal army. Another Frenchman was the royal bandmaster. An American headed the newly estab-

[63] Cady, 144–155.
[64] *Ibid.,* 149.
[65] W. A. Graham, *Siam,* 216–219; Mouhot, I, 98.

lished customs service provided for in the British treaty. Another foreigner directed the mint. An American missionary, Rev. S. G. MacFarland, wrote the first good English-to-Siamese dictionary and later, in 1878, took over headship of the first government school for the sons of the nobility, known as King's College.[66] Material improvements included the construction of roads, canals, and bridges and the connection of Bangkok with the new Moulmein-to-Singapore telegraph line. Steamers appeared on the river and brick buildings in Bangkok. All told, some eighty Europeans were employed by King Mongkut in one capacity or another.[67] In general the improvements were probably introduced about as fast as the people could appreciate them.

One important result of the European commercial orientation sponsored by King Mongkut was to end the Chinese domination of Siam's foreign trade and bring Chinese economic leadership into a different relationship to the government. From the time of Taksin's interim rule (1767–1782) following the Burmese destruction of Ayuthia, Chinese immigration to Siam had gained enormously. The Chinese population in Siam numbered around 300,000 by 1850. Although economically powerful, the three principal Chinese factions—Cantonese, Hokkien, and Teochiu—were bitter rivals for control over the more lucrative trades and for royal favor in assigning commercial-monopoly concessions.[68] In 1852, the opium-control system was placed entirely in the hands of Chinese opium farmers. The purchasers of monopolies paid to the government the duties which might otherwise have been collected and then recouped such expenditures and bribes through receipts from the local retail sale of the drug.

After the European treaties became fully effective, the economic base of Chinese leadership in Siam shifted in large measure from foreign commerce to the operation of domestic tax and duty farms. These covered principally the manufacture and sale of spirits, opium distribution, and the direction of gambling and lottery concessions. Chinese purchasers of such monopolies could expand their tax-collecting operations as far as the traffic would bear. Chinese groups, via their secret societies, were obliged to pool their resources in efforts to acquire control. Thugs terrorized rivals in order to realize full value from the concessions purchased. Chinese dealers in illicit opium were sometimes turned over to the authorized monopolists (also Chinese) for punishment. During the latter half of the nineteenth century such farmer sources brought in from 40 to 50 per cent of the total state revenues. High officials also realized handsome incomes in bribes from the allocation of tax-farming concessions.

[66] See Wells, 32–35. One of Reverend MacFarland's sons later became dean of the new medical school in 1892; he created a medical vocabulary and wrote textbooks in Thai. Another son invented the first Thai typewriter and served as secretary to a leading government statesman, Prince Damrong.

[67] Vella, *Impact,* 322–324.

[68] William Skinner, *Leadership and Power in the Chinese Community of Thailand* (1958), 4–6.

The use of opium by the Siamese population was meanwhile strictly forbidden, but it was impossible to regulate the smuggling of the drug by foreign merchants who were covered by extraterritorial exemption under the treaties.[69] The same extraterritorial exemptions had to be accorded within the course of a few decades to "protégé" neighboring peoples resident in areas under British, Dutch, and French rule, including Burmese, Laotians, Cambodians, Buginese, Javanese, and Chinese born outside of China. Thus did Siamese sovereignty begin to waste away and her state finances become dependent in some measure on the otherwise-illegal activities of foreign elements.

The key position among the official foreign assistants, that of financial adviser, was perennially held by a selected British appointee. The policy pursued was in line with British views concerning the mutual advantages to be derived from free trade. It was also coupled with the conservative policy of maintaining a favorable balance of trade and abundant reserves in gold and foreign currency as compared with Thai paper money in circulation. Under such policies the making of remittances abroad covering both dividends and salaries never became a problem. One result of the virtual foreign control of monetary policy was to curtail economic-development expenditures and also receipts from trade. Since the Bowring-Parkes treaty limited narrowly the taxation of British properties, this same low rate became generally applicable. The most important result was to retard public works construction, especially in connection with water-control projects in the central Menam Valley. Industrial development was also sharply limited, and Siam's economy continued indefinitely to rest on rice cultivation and timber and tin production.[70] Siam's output nevertheless expanded steadily after 1856 under the impetus of European trade and especially rapidly after 1870. Chinese leadership pushed relentlessly into the upper social levels of Siam and even into the nobility, riding the crest of the wave of business expansion.

There is no evidence that Siam's economic gains extended far beyond Bangkok. A visitor to Luang Prabang in Laos in 1859–1860 found widespread poverty and stagnant trade, with elephants providing the principal means of transportation. The only outside trade of consequence in Laos was the traditional mule caravan traffic to Yunnan, China. Soldiers were barefoot and were armed with crossbow and lance. Siam's northeastern province of Korat was reported infinitely worse off. Chinese bazaar shopkeepers, who represented the only evidence of industry, were themselves addicted to gambling and opium smoking. They found security behind their heavily palisaded compounds from a roving population described as "bandits and vagrants escaped from slavery and prison [who] gather here like

---

[69] *Ibid.*, 5–7; Smith, I, 5–6; II, 26–27.

[70] See James C. Ingram, *Economic Change in Thailand since 1850* (1955), chap. VIII.

vultures and wolves."[71] The westernization process in Siam clearly had a long way to go.

King Mongkut died of jungle fever in August, 1868, contracted while observing a solar eclipse on the western coast of Siam. He passed away philosophically, without fear or complaint, appropriately in pursuit of his consuming desire to learn.[72] One contemporary observer described the king in a kind of obituary of qualified praise as a man who "respected learning . . . and knew the advantages of being able to think, to study, to devise. He was not himself content with the old ways of Siam. . . . It was good as far as it went."[73]

What corrupted Mongkut in the end was the debilitating atmosphere of his court, including the jealousy-ridden sensuality of the harem and the corrosion of character resulting from greed for power and possessions. He became in his later years petulant, vengeful, and cruel, often offensive to his best friends, and beleaguered by real or imagined conspiracies. His temper outbursts were usually vented on palace personnel. He was vulnerable to flattery, but usually not for long. From first to last he was despotic, capricious and fickle, but he nevertheless turned Siam's historical course into a new direction.[74]

## The Accession of Chulalongkorn

The sudden death of King Mongkut in 1868 aroused considerable apprehension and disorder, reflecting the traditional problems associated with the change of kings. Rumors of rebellion were rife, and lawless elements took to counterfeiting and smuggling. An armed English steamer, the *Avon,* moved upstream for security reasons and anchored opposite the British consulate compound. Fortunately the period of perturbation was short-lived, for the Prime Minister asserted firm control in support of the fifteen-year-old heir apparent, Prince Chulalongkorn.[75]

The initial coronation ceremony was described as something of a physical ordeal, especially in view of the prince's feverish illness at the time. Brahman priests were much in evidence in the throwing of holy water on the white-garbed prince, at first from a golden bowl and then in a drenching shower of cold water released from an overhead canopy. This was followed by a procession of priests, Prime Minister and other high officials of government, and high dignitaries of the Buddhist orders, all in turn pouring virtue-giving holy water on the shivering youth. Brahmans presented him with the magical flower-and-leaf symbols. The prince then discarded his wet clothing, donned the golden apparel of the king, and ascended the

[71] Mouhot, II, 105–114.
[72] Campbell, 91.
[73] Smith, I, 50–51.
[74] Leonowens, 200–205; Campbell, 80–91.
[75] Smith, I, 3–5.

octagonal dais to the throne, with Brahman priests crouching on every side, ostensibly instructing him in his duties and responsibilities. Following the administration of the formal oath of office, one of the priests proclaimed the new King as lord of his people, another as lord of the realm (land). The presentation of the insignia of royalty—golden sandals and chain sash, crown, ring, and scepter—was followed by the discharge of a gun salute by both land and naval forces. High dignitaries prostrated themselves before the royal presence and foreign consuls stepped forward to greet the new ruler.[76] For Siam's first modern monarch, it was a striking mingling of old and new, with the old predominating. But change was in the air. The story of the memorable reign of King Chulalongkorn (Rama V) will be considered later.

[76] *Ibid.*, I, 1–2.

PART 5

*Intensive Economic Development*

# CHAPTER 16

# Java: The Development of Dutch Rule, 1830 to 1920

*F*inancial and political difficulties in the post-Napoleonic Netherlands, culminating in the separation of Belgium in 1830, were accompanied by equally serious embarrassments for restored Dutch rule in Java. The demand of the home government that the island's economy be placed on a profitable basis was urgently advanced. The outcome was the institution of the Culture (cultivation) system, under which the Dutch government undertook the systematic exploitation of the agricultural and manpower resources of Java for the benefit of the Netherlands treasury. The Dutch made the native chiefs and princes their accomplices in taking advantage of deep-rooted cultural and political traditions of the people. Exploitation by government monopoly came under sharp political criticism after 1848 in the Netherlands on humanitarian grounds and also from private trading and investment interests who themselves wanted to participate in colonial economic activities. The operation of the official cultivation system was discredited by a virulent exposé of its brutal and exploitive aspects by a resigned Dutch official, the author of *Max Havelaar,* in 1860.

Within the course of the two decades following 1848, the government-sponsored system was abandoned in favor of the so-called Liberal policy. The initiative in the development of the economy of the Indies was thus transferred to private entrepreneurs and promoters, many of them highly versatile. During the later decades of the century, the production for export of a great variety of items increased amazingly, a process accompanied by a rapid increase of the Javanese population. But by the end of the century, the obvious failure of the rapidly expanding economy to benefit the defenseless population forced a modulation of emphasis in the direction of concern for public welfare. This so-called Ethical policy was pursued for almost a score of years, but was ineffective because paternalistic and superficial. Improvement efforts did nothing to impair European control of the economy or the government, which continued to afford little educational opportunity for the people.

Meanwhile the extension of Dutch authority to important portions of the Outer Islands of the archipelago was accompanied by the rapid development of new products in world demand. In developing the most important items, such as rubber and oil production, non-Dutch capital was permitted to participate. The Netherlands Indies reached its peak output during World War I. Events in the postwar period revealed minimal Dutch response to the trend toward self-government, in which nearby India, Burma, and the Philippines set an example. Meanwhile political unrest crystallized among traditionalist elements and two varieties of modernized elite groups, one Islamic and the other westernized and secular.

## The Netherlands and the Indies, 1816–1830

The European settlement following the Napoleonic Wars left both Holland and its Indonesian Empire in a precarious situation. Cape Colony and Ceylon were taken over entirely by the British. The British were challenging Dutch control of the Malacca Straits, and Dutch trading in India was finished. Temporary sovereignty over the former Austrian Netherlands held out the attractive prospect of coordinating the potential industrial output of Belgium with Dutch trade in colonial products, but this goal was not immediately realizable. Tariff protection needed by Belgium to meet British industrial competition clashed with the Dutch preference for free trade. The Dutch government was heavily in debt, and private capital was lacking to prime the industrial and commercial pumps, so that economic prospects did not improve materially. By 1820, Holland faced the decay of its urban areas, forcing the government to undertake extensive resettlement projects. One-seventh of Holland's urban population was on the dole.

The outlook in the Indies was little better. The British, prodded by Stamford Raffles, moved into Singapore Island after 1819, establishing there a new entrepôt center replacing Batavia. By 1821, the Dutch resigned themselves to the loss of Malacca also. The last halfhearted Dutch punitive expedition against illicit spice growers in the Moluccas was made in 1824, marking the end of any serious effort to reestablish a trade monopoly in spices.[1] The production of nutmeg and mace in the Banda Islands defied Dutch control. Indian "country" vessels ranged widely throughout the East Indies islands distributing cloth, cotton, and opium. The Buginese also dealt widely in a great variety of minor products, backed frequently by the credits of the Chinese lenders.[2] A number of outer regions under nominal Dutch sovereignty were really under Chinese economic control, such as the tin island of Banka, the Riau Archipelago near Singapore, and several ports

---

[1] J. J. Van Klavern, *The Dutch Colonial System* (1953), 162–163.

[2] John Crawfurd, *History of the Indian Archipelago* (1820), I, 149–150, 344, 369, 413.

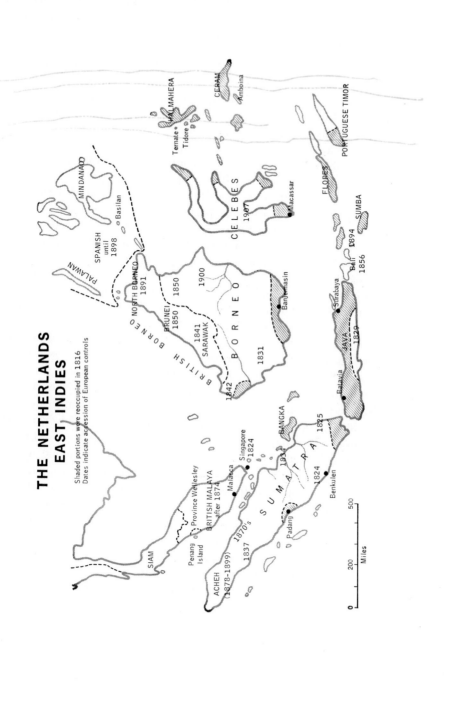

THE NETHERLANDS
EAST INDIES

Shaded portions were reoccupied in 1816
Dates indicate accession of European controls

SIAM

Penang Island
Province Wellesley
BRITISH MALAYA
after 1874

ACHEH
(1878–1899)

1837

1870's

Malacca

Singapore 1824

Padang

Benkulen

1824

SUMATRA

BANGKA

1834

1825

PALAWAN

SPANISH
until
1898

Basilan

MINDANAO

NORTH BORNEO
1891

BRUNEI
1850

SARAWAK
1841

1842

1850

1900

BORNEO

1831

Banjermasin

BRITISH BORNEO

CELEBES

Macassar
1907

FLORES

Ternate
Tidore

HALMAHERA

CERAM

Amboina

PORTUGUESE TIMOR

SUMBA

1894

Bali
1856

Surabaya

JAVA

1829

Batavia

0        200        500

Miles

of Borneo. Palembang was run by a Muslim Arab oligarchy,[3] while the Celebes and Java itself were politically restive. Negotiations with London for a general assignment of spheres of influence were finally concluded in 1824.

The policy adopted in the Indies by the first returning Dutch governor, van der Capellen (1819–1825), was equivocal and ineffective. The basic objective was to encourage free peasant cultivation and to protect the people against abuses. Following the pattern set by Raffles, revenue was obtained by land-rental assessments levied on desa units but payable in either cash or kind. Rejecting a system of direct rule, the Dutch reverted to previous habits of exercising feudal control, under which resident European officials in elder-brother fashion supervised the governing functions performed by the regents and minor hereditary chiefs. Salaried Indonesian officials were meanwhile forbidden participation in business or trade, and desa chiefs were denied the right to hire out their village wards. Neither prohibition was capable of enforcement under the restoration of semifeudal authority. Wherever Dutch control was reestablished in the Outer Islands, the rule of the chieftains was simply confirmed under the umbrella of Dutch sovereignty. This practice entailed in time a number of costly policing operations. Separate courts of law for Europeans were revived in Java, and four new ones were established in the Outer Islands.

Van der Capellen continued and extended the monopolistic coffee-tribute system in the Preanger district, where European planters were now forbidden entry. Those Europeans previously active in coffee production were forced to sell their production to the government at the same low price given to native producers. Chinese and European moneylenders were also excluded from the coffee areas. The postwar boom in the world market for coffee and sugar collapsed in 1822. When van der Capellen voided long-term European land leases in early 1824, the chiefs were unable to repay Europeans for substantial cash advances previously received, apart from exploiting the labor of the cultivators in precisely the fashion forbidden by new Dutch regulations. Batavia was faced, furthermore, with a heavy budgetary deficit due to rising costs of public works, increased administrative expenditures, and extensive policing activities in the Outer Provinces. In this discouraging situation, Governor van der Capellen resorted to the dubious expedient of borrowing the sum of 20 million guilders from the Calcutta banking firm of Palmer and Company, offering as security a lien on the revenues of Indonesia.[4]

In a major effort to end the general economic stalemate, King William of the Netherlands sponsored, in 1824, the establishment of the Neth-

[3] G. W. Earl, *The Eastern Seas* (1837), 133–136, 140–142.
[4] Van Klavern, 97–107; D. G. E. Hall, *A History of South-East Asia* (1955), 461–465.

erlands Trading Society. He put a good deal of his personal wealth into the venture and enlisted private investment by guaranteeing a 4.25 per cent dividend. Although the society was originally planned for worldwide operations, it concentrated after 1827 on the Indies trade alone. It received from the King and the Minister of Colonies at that time a twelve-year contract to purchase all Preanger coffee at controlled prices for purposes of marketing it in Europe. The further plans of the King to use the trading society as a bridge between Belgium's expanding industrial output and Javanese agricultural products collapsed with the independence of Belgium in early 1830. The ensuing civil war added substantially to the Dutch public debt. The new state of Belgium accepted responsibility for only one-fourth of the public debt, so that the Netherlands government became almost desperate for funds.[5]

As if previous difficulties were not sufficient, the Dutch administration of Java found itself engaged from 1825 to 1830 in a costly civil war in the central part of the island. It was a difficult guerrilla affair, long protracted, which added some 20 to 25 million florins to the financial deficit. The causes involved Islamic sensitivities, a disputed princely succession in Jogjakarta state, Javanese hostility to Chinese toll gatherers, and general popular opposition to the restoration of Dutch rule.[6]

Heroic measures for recovery were clearly in order in 1829 when Johannes van den Bosch was selected by the King as the new governor of the Indies. He was directed to execute a previously outlined proposal, designed to obtain from Java, by coercive methods but with guarantees against possible abuses, increased production of items for the export trade. He proposed to abandon the allegedly ill-conceived liberal notions of Raffles and also to discard dependence on private enterprise. He relieved his predecessor, Viscount De Bus de Gisignies, a Belgian, in January, 1830, just a few months before separation of Belgium occurred in Europe.[7]

## Status and Authority in Java

The cultivation system introduced by Governor van den Bosch involved more of Java than the ladang-cultivated coffee-producing areas of the western portion or the low-lying coastal regions previously devoted to sugar culture. It invaded also the densely populated sawah districts of the central and eastern areas of the island, previously little affected by Dutch tribute collections. In order to understand how and why the new system

[5] Van Klavern, 108–115; W. M. F. Mansvelt, *A Brief History of the Netherlands Trading Society, 1824–1924* (1924), 1–15.

[6] Hall, 466–467; Van Klavern, 97–107.

[7] D. W. Van Welderen Rengers, *The Failure of a Liberal Colonial Policy* (1947), 49–75, 90–93, 102.

worked and what its effects were on the people, the general structure of Javanese society must be understood.

The Javanese village or desa was a living social organism, a hallowed religious community of food-crop cultivators, communal in character. To gain the headman's permission to settle, any newcomer to the desa must agree to join in village activities and duties and adopt its customs as binding. The desa supervised all titles to land, houses, and cattle and managed questions of family affiliation, orphan care, maintenance of order, and the supervision of morals. Cohesion was rooted in kinship ties, mutual acquaintance, and participation in time-honored religious ceremonies. Religious customs much older than the formally espoused Islamic faith dictated the performance of desa rites connected with the use of the land and the offering of food to protecting ancestral spirits and local godlings. Essential consumer needs were customarily provided on a self-sufficient basis. Alien traders were not welcome as a rule, and sales to the outside were permitted only by explicit permission. The cultivation of assigned plots of land was carried out by family units, and land escheated to the desa if heirs were lacking. Desas so integrated could usually survive natural disasters and overt political pressures; they proved vulnerable in time to the influence of extended trade and a money economy.

Religion provided within the desa units sanctions and stimuli for the promotion of industry, prudence, order, and punctuality, serving as a kind of substitute for a local police force. Needy persons obtained help and security of livelihood, while neighboring villages, frequently standing in a parent-daughter relationship, assisted each other. Individual prestige within the desa derived for the most part from a person's contribution to community welfare. Accumulation of wealth, especially if accomplished by unsocial means, could be harmful to prestige. Acquisition of possessions beyond one's own needs carried little attraction, and incentive wages and profits carried meager appeal in a situation where leisure was generally preferred.[8]

Since estrangement from such a community was both physically and mentally disturbing, conformity was socially imposed; it did not depend as a rule on a person's deliberate choice or conscience. The automatic acceptance of traditional values and authority, as symbolized in the sacred rites, became the norm for civilized living. The authority of desa elders, the district *Wedana* official, and the regent above him stemmed from the universal acceptance of the same symbols of power. Any rebel claimant to power in this context usually advanced supernatural claims to superior authority; hence the use by rebels of messianic claims, invulnerability, and magic. Where this unconscious, unreflecting acceptance of authority was undermined in favor of a detached or critical examination of tradition, the vitality and strength of the old order drained away. Awareness of this danger

[8] J. H. Boeke, *The Structure of Netherlands Indian Economy* (1942), 14–26, 29–31, 34–35.

lent added strength to the inertia of custom,[9] which reflected an aversion to any unseemly scramble for higher status. A person could attain personal dignity and equality by being what was befitting his position.[10]

Traditional cohesion helped the desas to compete with the alien intruders who dominated their political and economic horizons. The social gap between such aliens, whether Dutch or Chinese, and the Javanese villager was usually unbridgeable. At the port cities, alien Chinese, Indian, and Arab enclaves lived in separate wards under their own chiefs. Indonesian traders could not, as a rule, compete with government monopolies or with the industrious Chinese, who served as lenders, tax farmers, retail merchants, tradesmen, and artisans. In the European-dominated centers, Indonesian residents, torn from their cultural environment and placed in a society lacking the cohesion of the desas, often became demoralized, losing both their sense of values and their personal dignity.[11] It was thus a sound instinct which made the Javanese villager cherish his traditional loyalty to local chiefs.

The Dutch miracle of the nineteenth century in making the island of Java so fabulously productive in the interest of the Netherlands economy was accomplished by exploiting the religious regard of the Indonesian village for his traditional chieftains. Dutch officials, who in theory occupied the position of the divine king, could not actually command acquiescence in their own right. What Batavia did was to utilize the traditional authority and prestige of the regents and the Wedanas, giving to them a minor share in the profits in return for their compliance with Dutch orders. Under this arrangement the chiefs were also strengthened against the attacks of mosque officials and scribes, the custodians of Islamic revelation, who frequently berated the native chiefs for straying from the orthodox path. Dutch officials and the adat (customary) law chiefs were thus more or less allied against the Muslim scribes and the exploited people.

Almost the entire population of Java was involved by the Dutch rulers in agreements made with a few thousand chiefs, each of whom profited personally from the arrangement.[12] The issuance of regulations by the Wedana and the regent concerning the planting of coffee trees, sugar cane, tobacco, and indigo under the cultivation system was only one of their many governing functions. Others included maintaining roads, hedges, palisade defenses, water supply, vital statistics, stream navigation, cattle herds, and land claims. To defy the authority of the chiefs on any matter was both religiously wrong and socially destructive. Popular rebellion under such

[9] C. A. O. Van Nieuwenhuijze, *Aspects of Islam in Post-Colonial Indonesia* (1958), 1–18.

[10] Multatuli (Douwes Dekker), *Indonesia: Once More Free Labor* (1948), 34. Translated by Nicolaas Steelink.

[11] W. F. Wertheim, *Indonesian Society in Transition* (1956), 132–140; Earl, 11–35.

[12] Van Nieuwenhuijze, 41–42; Multatuli, 34–35.

circumstances was virtually out of the question. The van den Bosch system was cleverly conceived, for it utilized Javanese custom for purposes of economic exploitation.[13]

## The Cultivation System in Operation

The plan devised by Governor van den Bosch was basically mercantilist. He would compel the Javanese cultivators, who were assumed to be incapable of responding to wage and price incentives, to devote one-fifth of the cultivated land of each desa to the production of designated export crops, which would take the place of their land-rental obligation. The exports would be handled exclusively by Dutch trading facilities and marketed in the Netherlands, and Dutch industry would enjoy in return favored access to the colonial market. The chiefs would enforce the labor requirements, and European officials would control the site assignments, the harvesting, and the transportation. The operation was concentrated in the sawah-cultivated areas.[14]

The important qualifications and safeguards stipulated at the outset by van den Bosch indicated his full awareness of the probable abuses which would attend deliberate colonial exploitation of the influence of the native chiefs in obtaining peasant compliance. The amount of labor to be exacted was limited, in theory, to that required for the cultivation of an equal area of rice, and villagers were to be accredited with the assessed value of the labor and produce provided by them in excess of their previously remitted rental obligations. A portion of the labor exaction could be used for cultivation, another for harvesting, a third for transportation, and a fourth for factory processing where free labor was unavailable. From the governor-general down, all officials were exhorted to protect the little man from the greed of his chief, including giving a patient hearing to any complaints which hesitant peasants might wish to make.[15]

Between the time of the formulation of the cultivation plan and its full-scale implementation, the secession of Belgium from the Netherlands and the heavy costs of the ensuing civil war in Europe changed the objectives and the context of the proposal. In 1832 van den Bosch was accorded virtual dictatorial powers by the King, and upon the success of his efforts came to depend the rescuing of Holland from bankruptcy. It was no time to raise embarrassing questions at The Hague, and colonial matters were subject to royal decision in any case, being regarded as beyond the competence of the States General. Within a relatively short time, all of the precautionary regulations were forgotten. The Batavia government accorded full scope to the avarice of the native chiefs and the European handlers of

[13] Multatuli, 36, 42–45.
[14] Hall, 468–469.
[15] Multatuli, 37.

the exportable surplus by giving both of them a share of the total profits realized from their several districts.

The methods employed were businesslike. Residencies were required to deliver for export designated produce worth 2 guilders per head of their respective populations. Corporal punishment was inflicted on village chiefs or peasants to enforce compliance. The authorities from the outset claimed at a fixed low price all of the coffee output without conceding any accreditation for overpayments compared with previous land-rent dues. The labor required for the cultivation of sugar cane and indigo usually exceeded by about 50 per cent that required for the same acreage of rice, and the demand for labor tended to grow. In areas adjacent to the sugar mills, considerations connected with transportation and other needs required that virtually all sawah land be devoted to cane. The customary exaction by the chiefs of *corvée* labor on roads, bridges, and new irrigation works also increased, raising the demands for labor on government account in some areas to two hundred days a year. As a final method of exploitation, the old land rentals were also collected in many places, along with high bazaar and salt taxes.

Starting with indigo, sugar, and coffee, government-enforced operations were expanded to include tea, tobacco, pepper, cinnamon, cinchona (quinine), oil palms, cassava, cotton, and cochineal. In some areas rice was classified as an exportable surplus.[16] Indigo, sugar, and coffee were the most important items. The number of coffee trees increased from 116 million in 1833 to 330 million in 1850, commanding the labor of 450,000 adult males. By 1850 sugar cultivation employed 300,000 workers, and indigo another 110,000. Except where a conscientious official exercised self-restraint, safeguards were thrown overboard in an orgy of profiteering.

The profits from the cultivation system were indeed phenomenal. Over a forty-five-year period the Netherlands treasury realized income from Java amounting to some 900 million guilders. The Dutch public debt was retired, and the Netherlands railways were built with the funds. Additional profits went to the Netherlands Trading Society and to private Dutch industry, which marketed an increasing volume of high-priced Dutch cloth in the protected Indies market. The Javanese paid under the system an estimated 40 million guilders more for Dutch cloth than cheaper British manufactures would have cost them. Local contractors in Java, including many Chinese who processed the "surplus" of such commodities, also made huge profits. Dutch authorities made the miracle-working van den Bosch a baron in 1836 and a count in 1839.[17]

The Javanese people were meanwhile denied any means of effective economic or political redress because their own chiefs were heavily involved in the Dutch system. The chiefs maintained a degree of pomp and circum-

[16] Hall, 469–472.

[17] *Ibid.*; B. H. M. Vlekke, *Nusantara* (1943), 265–276; van Klavern, 117–125, 163–164.

stance befitting their traditional roles, and their customary authority was further buttressed by statutory enactments. Unrest first developed in 1843, when the excessive diversion of land and labor from rice cultivation resulted in serious famine. Starvation became widespread in central Java in 1848 to 1850. Lesser grievances included labor assignments distant from one's home, low fixed wages, and excessive exactions by go-betweens. Inherent in the system and not subject to administrative correction was the hemorrhage of wealth from the island in a fashion which the divine-king system had never previously approximated. What was needed in the interest of fair play was to set up an enforceable definition of the legitimate application of the chief's authority. In actuality, villagers were told what to plant, where and how long to work, and what wages they would receive. They were also afforded little or no opportunity for educational adjustment to an alien world to which they were being rendered economically as well as politically subservient. The 50 per cent increase in Java's population which took place during the period of the full operation of the Dutch cultivation system more than absorbed the increased output available for local consumption.[18]

## From Government Monopoly to Private Enterprise

The liberalization of the Netherlands Constitution in 1848, including the assignment of ultimate responsibility for colonial affairs to the States General, produced little immediate effect. The government of The Hague throughout the fifties continued to be dominated by the Conservatives, and especially so in the Colonial Department. The first reform measures were cautiously conceived. The Council of the Indies was first accorded concurrent power with the governor-general in determining policy, and both were exhorted not to oppress the people or deny them sufficient rice acreage to prevent famine. The trade monopoly enjoyed by the Netherlands Trading Society was canceled, although the society continued until the 1890s to transport a high proportion of the commerce of Indonesia.[19] Profiteering actually reached a new high in the fifties, and the peak annual contribution of Java to the Netherlands treasury came in 1866.[20]

The year 1860 marked a kind of watershed. The Dutch abolition of slavery in that year increased the effectiveness of the attacks of the Liberal opposition against the Culture system as a form of semislavery and a denial of the right of economic liberty to Indies Dutch residents as well as to the Indonesians. Critics of the Colonial Department found much ammunition to bolster their attack in the appearance of a novel in Dutch entitled *Max Havelaar, or the Coffee Auctions of the Dutch Trading Company* by Eduard

[18] Hall, 471; Multatuli, 39.

[19] Hall, 490–492.

[20] G. C. Allen and A. G. Donnithorne, *Western Enterprise in Indonesia and Malaya* (1954), 26–28. The Javan contribution alone in 1866 was 32 million florins.

Douwes Dekker. The writer was a former Dutch official of eighteen years' experience in western Java who had resigned in disgust in 1856. Douwes Dekker wrote under the name of Multatuli (borne much). Speaking as one who was outraged over the systematic bullying and plundering of the people of Java, Douwes Dekker got a wide hearing for his flaming indictment. It became in time required reading for Dutch school children above the elementary level. It was a merciless satire on what the writer characterized as the unctuous, hypocritical, and profit-grabbing role of the Dutch residents of Java. It provided political grist for the Liberal Party's Parliamentary attacks on the Conservatives and also aroused private business generally to demand the opportunity to participate in the profitable Java operation.[21] The indictment set forth in *Max Havelaar* was supported by the less emotional writings of another Dutch ex-resident of Java, Isaac Fransen van de Putte, who described the operation of the coffee-contract system and his own experiences in Java as a tobacco planter. After the Liberal Party took over power, van de Putte was made the Minister of Colonies in 1863.

The new policy of the Liberal Party fell considerably short of what Douwes Dekker had conceived as necessary to correct the evils of exploitation in Java. Van de Putte would maintain the flow of income "surplus" from Java to the Dutch treasury but give private enterprise free access to the land and labor of the Indies and raise state revenues from direct taxation. The cancellation of the government's Culture programs in pepper, spices, indigo, tea, cochineal, and tobacco was accomplished by 1866. The more profitable sugar Culture program lasted until 1890 and the coffee program until 1917, by which time Java had pretty well lost the world market to Brazil. Java's sugar output doubled between 1870 and 1885 and had doubled again by 1900. Because the coffee gardens were frequently located in sparsely populated regions, where labor supplies for private operations were unreliable, such areas shifted to tea after 1920.

The States General took over the general direction of colonial policy after 1867, including control over the voting of the Indonesian budget. Several changes were made. Payment of supervisory officials on a commission basis was discontinued, and not more than one-fifth of a cultivator's land could thereafter be used for government crops. The last vestige of compulsory labor for the state in the forest districts was abolished in 1865. A basic agrarian law was passed in 1870 in conjunction with one providing for the free sale of sugar in Java and the gradual ending of the cultivation system in sugar after 1878. Ladang lands and others not permanently cultivated were declared the property of the state and made available for leases of up to seventy-five years. Regularly cultivable lands could be rented from owners for three-to-five-year terms in both the Outer Islands and Java. Indonesian claims to ladang lands located within large leaseholds were transferred elsewhere to the considerable distress of occupants. Employment at

---

[21] Vlekke, 274–288; Van Klavern, 142–147; W. P. Coolhaas in D. G. E. Hall, *Historians of South-East Asia* (1961), 230–232.

wages gained wider acceptance.[22] Legally enforceable labor contracts involving Chinese coolies as well as Javanese were permitted until 1879 and longer than that on the newly developed tin island of Billiton. Entrepreneurial profits drawn from Javanese labor under private enterprise were higher than ever.[23]

In terms of increased output, private enterprise accomplished impressive results. Estates produced in 1875 three times as much in value as had pre-1860 monopolies and ten times as much in 1885. The enormous increase of 66 million guilders in profits realized between 1870 and 1875 reflected also the important contribution to trade made by the opening of the Suez Canal. The food output was protected by forbidding the sale of land by Indonesians to non-Indonesians. The increase in private planting and manufacture was greatest in the sugar and tobacco industries, and extended to the Outer Islands. Land concessions were easily available in eastern Sumatra where tobacco was grown by Javanese labor on a ladang basis, involving a seven-to-eight-year cycle between plantings. Chinese laborers for tobacco cultivation were also obtained on contract from Macao and Malaya; they were eventually replaced by Javanese, after World War I.

New products included copra, palm oil, cassava, kapok, and cocoa. Between 1870 and 1900, Indonesia's exports doubled, its imports quadrupled, and the net export balance grew from 63 million to 81 million. The new imports included mainly capital goods, such as machines, tools, steel for railways (begun in 1873), electronic equipment (telephone and telegraph), and fertilizers. Dutch steamship lines were established after 1870, leading to the development of government-operated coal mining in Sumatra and southern Borneo. Oil production was started as early as 1883, but it, along with rubber, became important only after 1910.[24]

The most aggressive private promoters of business in the Indies were new arrivals from the Netherlands. Released from the mores of their own milieu and impervious to the religious and social claims of what was to them the incomprehensible society of Indonesia, they gave their full attention to moneymaking. The Dutch population increased on the average by a little more than one thousand a year, numbering around sixty-seven thousand by 1900. The Chinese population increased more rapidly than did the Dutch, outnumbering them approximately 3 to 1 in Java and 13 to 1 in the Outer Islands by 1900. The Chinese were less alien than the Europeans but

[22] Van Klavern, 148–151; Allen and Donnithorne, 69–70.

[23] Van Klavern, 160–162. Eduard Douwes Dekker's *Indonesia: Once More Free Labor* was written in 1870 as an embittered rejoinder to gullible Liberals who thought that ending the government's monopolies would solve the problem. Profit seekers were allegedly hypocritical to pretend that they were concerned with the welfare of the Javanese. He even regretted having written *Max Havelaar*. See *Indonesia: Once More Free Labor*, 7, 11, 19, 29, 31–32.

[24] Van Klavern, 157–159; Hall, *A History of South-East Asia*, 493–500.

they also failed to share the indigenous culture, and their superior industry and business ability, combined with clannish solidarity, constituted a formidable barrier to Indonesian business participation. The more inefficient elements of Javanese population, whose total number increased between 1880 and 1900 by almost half a million a year (to 28 million), were swept as day laborers into the Western stream of economic development.[25]

The resulting social situation was somewhat more disturbing in Java than in the Outer Islands. Population increases in Java after 1890 outstripped access to new lands brought under cultivation. Large numbers of wage laborers were recruited by native chiefs acting as contractors and paymasters. Such persons became increasingly divorced from the traditional social order. The youth in particular lacked a tangible or psychological stake in the older tradition and became less amenable to family and community control, demoralized, and anchorless.[26] Abuses connected with wage-contractor operations attracted in time the attention of the government inspectors, which marked the beginning of reform efforts.[27] Where new industries were developed in the Outer Islands, such as rubber, tobacco, oil, and mining, colonial enterprise was frequently entirely alien to the locality. Both labor and capital were imported; the land used had previously been almost entirely waste; the end product was all exported. From such a situation the local population could be completely detached.[28]

It was not so much the economic development per se which disturbed indigenous custom in the Outer Islands as it was the intensification of governmental control which accompanied it. Even the curbing of such unsocial habits as head-hunting, debt slavery, and witch killing tended to impair the effectiveness of social and religious sanctions generally. The displacement of the authority of the chiefs, the collection of money taxes, and novel expenditures on roads, medicines, and hygiene all caused a measure of frustrated distress and confusion, adding to the disruption of community solidarity. Where a trusted official or missionary was present and the disruptive influence of foreign business was not overpowering, the discouraged and confused population would usually listen to lectures or sermons with politeness. They might even find, in time, new meanings for traditional feasts, for reverence toward ancestors, and for other miscellaneous superstitions. Under such circumstances, cultural aspects incompatible with Western standards of government would be sloughed off in time. The task of adjustment was never easy, however, and certain regions of the Outer Islands resisted the Dutch cultural impact in determined fashion.[29]

[25] Boeke; Allen and Donnithorne, 26–28.
[26] Van Nieuwenhuijze, 19–31.
[27] Van Klavern, 152–156.
[28] Boeke, 93–95.
[29] B. J. O. Schreike, *The Effects of Western Influence on Native Civilizations in the Malay Archipelago* (1929), 237–247.

## Dutch Control of the Outer Islands

During the period of the Indies government's concentration on the Javanese cultivation system, minimal attention was given to the control of the Dutch sphere in the Outer Islands or to the suppression of piracy. Until 1870 the Netherlands Trading Society ships used the Sunda Straits for the most part, and the Dutch left the task of controlling the Malacca Straits largely to British authorities on the Malay side. Batavia extended its suzerainty over Bali in the late 1840s; the Dutch took over the tin island of Banka in 1851 and the principal ports of the Celebes in 1858–1859. By that time political rivalries speeded the tempo. James Brooke had become ruler over the Sarawak portion of northwest Borneo in the 1840s as local Raja, and the French were getting interested in Cochin-China. The opening of the tobacco districts in southern and eastern Sumatra from 1856 to 1868 aggravated Dutch friction with the Acheh Sultan, who had once exercised suzerainty in parts of the area. Tobacco development first demonstrated the enormous economic potential of Sumatra. The advent of steam navigation and the opening of coal mines in Borneo and Sumatra made the curbing of interisland piracy increasingly feasible and necessary. If the Dutch expected to keep alive their presumptive claim to the island empire as a whole, they had to accept greater responsibility for its control.[30]

The need to eliminate the operations of Acheh's pirates off the northern tip of Sumatra became urgent following the opening of the Suez Canal in late 1869. After that date, all traffic to and from Europe used the Malacca rather than the Sunda channel. Naval action offshore against the pirates was ineffective without European control of their bases. But before antipiratical operations could begin, the Dutch had to compensate the British for the waiver of their joint pledge given in 1824 to respect the independence of Acheh. The Anglo-Dutch treaty of 1871 abolished differential tariff rates for non-Dutch shipping in the Indies and permitted Singapore to continue trading relations with neighboring areas of Sumatra recently occupied by the Dutch. In return, the Netherlands was granted a free hand to deal with the pirates of Acheh. The bargain also included British acquisition of Dutch holdings on the Gold Coast of West Africa. The Dutch thus paid rather dearly for the dubious privilege of conducting an exhausting thirty years' war against fanatic Acheh. One factor in the outbreak of the war was the apparently unauthorized negotiation of a draft commercial treaty by the American consul at Singapore with the supposedly independent Acheh government. The Dutch-Acheh war started in 1873.[31]

The widespread guerrilla resistance of the Achehnese, sustained as it was by Muslim fanaticism, proved very difficult to quell. Repeated attempts

---

[30] Hall, *A History of South-East Asia,* 493–495.

[31] *Ibid.,* 474–475, 495–496; S. J. Smith, *Siam Repository* (1873), 320. The Acheh Sultan was also a drug addict.

on the part of the Dutch to taper off the costly affair following limited successes and to modulate to civilian control only served to encourage continued resistance. Cholera on occasion took a heavy toll of the Dutch forces. But the most noteworthy casualty was the disappearance of the surplus paid to the Netherlands treasury. War costs absorbed it all after 1877. An attempt to establish, by means of a railway crossing in 1885, a defensible line across the end of the island proved ineffective. A later effort to enlist the aid of a local chief, in 1893, backfired two years later when he defected, carrying virtually all the population with him.

Acheh's submission to Dutch control was finally achieved in 1903 by a combination of relentless military pressure exerted locally and a Dutch effort to make peace with the Muslim world generally, as proposed by the Dutch Islamic scholar Snouck Hurgronje. An Indonesian vice-consul was posted at Mecca, and Dutch assistance was afforded Indonesian Muslims desiring to make the pilgrimage to the shrine. In the meantime, further Dutch military action was required to end disaffection in the Great East and Bali. Governor von Heutsz in 1898 devised a "Short Declaration" to be signed by vassal chiefs, which acknowledged the formal suzerainty of the Dutch. The surviving sparks of the Acheh insurrection were not extinguished until 1908. By that time the Netherlands treasury was making annual contributions to the Indies treasury,[32] and reform efforts were well under way.

## *Ameliorative Efforts and the Ethical System*

The fanatic resistance of Acheh reflected in concentrated form the role which Islam was destined to play as a rallying standard for opposition to Dutch rule. The authority of the chiefs under adat law declined not only by reason of their virtual alliance with the Dutch but also from the continuing attacks by the Muslim scribes on the allegedly worldly practices of the chiefs. Religion provided an arena which Dutch authority failed to penetrate, so that political and cultural resistance came to center increasingly in Islam.

Only in non-Islamic regions where Dutch authority was lightly imposed did Indonesians respond to Christian missionary activity. Protestant objections to pagan religious practices often ran counter to factors contributing to social cohesion. Islam, on the other hand, contributed a sense of personal equality and individual worth within the faith, cutting across differences of local allegiance and racial variations. Christian converts usually aspired to equality with Europeans, whereas Islam challenged both ethnic and caste stratification. Some native Christian missionaries from Amboina enjoyed successes in Pagan (non-Muslim) regions outside Dutch

---

[32] Hall, *A History of South-East Asia*, 495–497; Robert Van Neil, *The Emergence of the Modern Indonesian Elite* (1960), 8–12.

control, involving as a rule collaboration with the local chiefs, but the total Christian impact was relatively slight.[33]

Reforming agitation at the official level began in the 1890s in the lower ranks of the service, especially among long-resident Dutch and Eurasians. They sympathized with the desire of the Javanese to return to the cultivation of rice, a vocation which the people generally understood and preferred. Particularly involved was the need to protect water rights and land access, plus the correction of abuses attending the leasing of sawah land and the contracting for the labor of Javanese workers. Government inspectors began to register complaints entered by the Javanese against the planter class, a practice which tended in time to undermine the disciplinary authority of the employer over his Indonesian labor force. The planters could no longer hide behind the now fast-eroding authority of the native chief.[34] A more general indictment of the results of private enterprise concerned the fact that the rapid increase of population more than absorbed the moderate increment in consumer goods, medical services, and educational facilities.

The new Ethical policy was variously motivated. By 1900, opinion in the Netherlands was generally in agreement that large corporations doing business in Indonesia had become too powerful for the social good and that the government must pursue policies based on the acknowledgment of responsibility for native welfare. Industrial activity of such magnitude could not realistically be expected to be directed by feelings of compassion for the common good, for it was precisely the desire for gain which motivated industry and gave it vitality. The new reforming credo of the twentieth century affirmed that economic freedom, if guaranteed to the Indonesian people as well as to the European, must necessarily benefit all concerned. It was assumed that once the island peoples were afforded the opportunity for self-improvement, they would grasp it with both hands.[35] A more prosperous Indonesia would in the end provide an expanding market for Dutch consumer goods.

More perceptive considerations in support of reform were advanced by the Dutch Islamic scholar Snouck Hurgronje on the basis of experiences in Acheh and elsewhere. He believed that friendly Dutch association with an Indonesian Islamic elite was both feasible and desirable provided the political aspects of the Islamic revival could be curbed. He would therefore discourage Dutch hopes of Christianization, assist Indonesians to make the Mecca pilgrimage, admit educated Indonesians to government service on a wider scale, and sponsor a more active educational program for them, both in the islands and in Europe. Since he was convinced that Islam, however vigorous, could not supply the vitality needed for the creation of a new social order, he insisted that economic and political modernization must

[33] Wertheim, 200–215.
[34] Van Klavern, 168–182.
[35] Boeke, 21, 100–102.

The unfortunate and unanticipated result was to strip the regent chief of much of his adat prestige and also, in time, to compromise the authority enjoyed by the European official himself.

Under the Ethical system, a commendable effort was made not only to instruct Dutch officials about the Indies but also to instruct Indonesian students about Europe. Educational facilities at the village level increased 3½ times between 1909 and 1912; in 1913 some seven thousand schools were in operation with 227,000 students in attendance. The results were nevertheless disappointing. The program lacked adequate funds, and it almost invariably faltered in achieving effective accomplishment because of the apathetic response of the villagers. Superficial Western-type training modified the traditional villager's religious, cosmologic, and adat orientations little if at all, whereas graduates of the First Class National Schools, where most of the funds were expended, exhibited both restiveness and irresponsibility. Subsequent corrective Dutch efforts to inculcate in such schools Christian principles of public concern served only to stir up Islamic resentment. Opportunities to obtain advanced educational training in Europe were limited for the most part to the sons of chiefs and local princes, a group concerned primarily with improving personal and social status. Those who came to experience the uninhibited social contacts available in the Indies Club in Holland and who were at the same time more or less uprooted from their national culture became resentful upon their return to the islands, where comparable equality of status with Europeans was denied them.[40] University education as developed in Java after 1920 was largely technical in character, including schools of engineering, law, agriculture, and medicine. Education in Humane letters was initiated only in 1940. Graduates of such schools were obliged always to be circumspect in political matters if they desired to escape police detention.[41]

## Economic Expansion

While the faltering efforts were being made to promote village welfare measures in the early 1900s, Dutch economic enterprise was achieving marked success in meeting the needs of world markets for plantation and mineral products. Most of the advances occurred in the Outer Islands, where the Ethical policy penetrated lightly and the chiefs, after the Acheh war, accepted Dutch suzerainty with little protest. Indonesia attained an unparalleled level of prosperity during World War I. By comparison with the Outer Islands, Javanese enterprise, although still vigorous, reached a point of diminishing returns. A ruling of 1918 that future long-term land-lease agreements would have to be approved by the villagers concerned as well as by their chiefs brought a prompt end to the obtaining of any further

[40] Van Neil, 41–55, 66–80.
[41] Furnivall, 226–230, 251–262; Vlekke (1960), 320–324.

land concessions.[42] The rapid economic expansion developing in the Outer Islands owed much to the cooperation of government and private industry. The state kept order, developed irrigation facilities, provided medical services, and encouraged experimentation with new crops. The agricultural station of Buitenzorg, located some 25 miles from Batavia, developed new techniques for cultivating cinchona and improved varieties of rubber and coconuts. The government itself operated nearly all of the tin mines and controlled two-thirds of the coal output. Government-constructed railways were 5,700 kilometers long by 1930, while state pawnshops and village credit facilities had expanded at the expense of the Chinese moneylenders. Labor needs in the Outer Islands were supplied by assisting Javanese migration and by active recruitment of Chinese. The use of contract labor began to taper off after 1929, partly as a result of a clause in the United States tariff law of that year prohibiting further importation by America of goods produced by contract labor.[43]

Many private industrial corporations attained enormous size. Only the larger estates could provide experimental equipment and take responsibility for processing and marketing output on a world scale. The production of small holders in rubber, tobacco, and vegetable oils was invariably processed and exported by large Western firms. The transformation of the Amsterdam Trading Society provided an instructive example. It began trading operations in 1879, acquired its first plantation in 1893, abandoned its trading functions in 1910, and by 1929 was managing some twenty-five plantations in Java (sugar, tapioca, fiber) and fifteen in Sumatra (rubber, tea, fiber). Meanwhile the flow of international capital into the Outer Islands— British, German, American, and French—changed the financial picture. A multitude of managing agencies, holding companies, and investment trusts was spawned, which increased ever more widely the distance between Western enterprise and the indigenous economy. Rubber exports occupied first place by 1925, with sugar second. In the context of impersonal relations between the employing firm and the worker groups in the Outer Islands, made up largely of enclaves of alien Chinese and Javanese, the Ethical program became increasingly irrelevant.[44]

## Rise of Sarekat Islam

The most important political event in Indonesia during the second decade of the 1900s was the appearance in 1911–1912 of an organization known as Sarekat Islam. The original sponsors of the group were Muslim Arab and Sumatran merchants, who were seeking to use Islamic sentiment as a weapon against their Chinese rivals in the batik-cloth trade of Java.

[42] Wertheim, 65–67.
[43] Allen and Donnithorne, 28–32, 67–73.
[44] *Ibid.*, 68–73; Boeke, 12–21.

The organization avoided official censure by emphasizing its loyalty to Dutch rule and its sympathy for the Ethical program. The Chinese trader-moneylender class provided at the time a far more vulnerable target for Indonesian attack than did the colonial government. From the start, Sarekat Islam attracted support from the secondary levels of the Indonesian civil service and from Javanese peasants, who seem to have entertained a vague hope of realizing some kind of nationalist ends from membership. The sponsors of the movement were apparently themselves surprised and confused over their unexpected popularity, which reflected nationalist expectations far beyond the possibility of immediate realization. Sarekat Islam was actually a kind of vagrant ship, lacking internal motive power and direction and awaiting seizure by purposeful captains.

Ethically minded Dutch officials, hungry for any evidence to support Hurgronje's dream of the emergence of a responsible Indonesian elite, were inclined to view Sarekat Islam with a measure of enthusiasm. It was certainly an improvement over sheer apathy. It also constituted a substantial gain if compared with periodic nativist movements instigated by self-appointed village prophets who took advantage of natural disasters, such as floods, earthquakes, and volcanic eruptions. Sarekat Islam did not constitute any substantial threat to Dutch rule as long as the Indonesians continued to respect the authority of regents and village chiefs. Authority based on universal sanctions of a cosmologic character was not subject to political challenge. The governor-general nevertheless refused at first (in 1913) to accord legal status to Sarekat Islam on the grounds that the leadership could not possibly control its mass membership.[45]

The role of Sarekat Islam changed as a result of novel circumstances attending the course of World War I. The war slowed down the tempo of the Ethical program, shook Indonesian respect for Europe generally, and discredited the Dutch economically by reorienting trade in the direction of Japan and the United States. Increased wartime prosperity benefited the islanders very little. Consumer prices rose, governmental costs increased along with taxes, and Indonesian labor was powerless to bargain for comparably higher wages and shorter hours. Peasants had to pay a 27-guilder poll tax in lieu of *corvée* labor, plus additional levies on land, houses, and furniture. Religious and student unrest also helped to bring to an end the aura of sanctity which had long been associated with colonial rule. The traditional authority of the regents and the Wedana chiefs was also wearing thin.[46]

Sarekat Islam was the only indigenous nationalist organization which had its sails spread to catch the new political breeze. It was quickly pushed beyond its shallow ideological depth to take on a changing opportunist posture. Its ablest spokesman, the well-intentioned Tjokro, assumed for a

[45] Van Neil, 14–23, 82–100.
[46] Bell, 85–102.

time the role of a messiah, or "righteous prince," mystical in his potency, constituting a symbol of inarticulate nationalist hopes long deferred. He lacked the requisite perspective and resolution for such a heroic role and eventually yielded control to other, more purposeful men. The organization gradually undertook the salutary task of uncovering grievances, a function which attracted in time the sympathetic consideration of Dutch officials. The governor-general, upon reconsideration of the issue in 1916, decided to accord legal status to Sarekat Islam. This action served greatly to enhance its prestige and influence.[47]

A new reformist orientation was introduced into Sarekat Islam after 1915 by the modernistic Islamic scholar Agus Salim, who vigorously denounced the messianic pretensions of Tjokro. Before the new orientation could be fully established, however, the organization was infiltrated by Marxist proponents coming from Holland, who used the organization to attack both colonialism and capitalism. Salim provided the organization for a time with a kind of respectable façade, but the sponsoring anti-Chinese Arab merchants withdrew, as did most of the peasant membership. Faced by a drying up of income resources, Sarekat Islam began to accept protection money from Chinese business enterprises in the form of advertising in the organization's press. The Marxists also began the recruitment of a trade-union membership from the cities to supply a new kind of popular backing. The inevitable rift between Agus Salim's efforts to restore Sarekat Islam's religious character as a modernist Pan-Islamic movement and the endeavors of the Marxists to exploit anticolonialist sentiment and labor-union strikes for political ends developed from 1919 and 1921. The strength of the organizational structure enabled the party to survive the split, but social reformist and religious objectives thereafter were largely taken over by two other modernist groups to be described shortly, one Islamic and the other Western in orientation.[48]

## Collapse of the Reform Program

For a time Dutch Indonesian officials attempted to satisfy the more legitimate grievances brought to light by Sarekat Islam. A Peoples Council, or Volksraad, was approved in 1916, and the practice of forced labor was completely outlawed in 1917. But the leisurely timetable of the proponents of Ethical objectives could not keep pace with the frightening avalanche of demands coming via Sarekat Islam after the emergence of more radical leadership. Small concessions served only to stimulate further expectations. Attacks eventually centered on "sinful capitalism," presumably that which realized high profits and kept the people poor. The wartime attrition of dedicated Dutch civil service personnel also took its toll, while the alarm

[47] Van Neil, 101–107, 111–117.
[48] *Ibid.,* 118–139, 143–153; Benda, 32–55.

of Dutch residents increased. By 1920, most Dutch spokesmen in Java agreed that the Ethical program was dangerous folly.[49]

Inherent contradictions within the Ethical program contributed to its failure. At no time did it contemplate any serious curtailment of Dutch economic privileges and control. Indonesian hostility to Dutch economic exploitation with its associated discriminations and frustrations eventually became articulate, a development which was hastened by the decline of European prestige during the war. The secondary conflict between the Ethically minded Dutch civil service and the less idealistic business group from Holland was, by 1920, resolved in favor of the latter group. A Conservative Minister of Colonies, who took over in the Netherlands in 1919, went through with the establishment of local Councils, as previously recommended, but the Ethical program died.

Meanwhile, the Dutch attempt since Hurgronje's time to encourage an apolitical Islamic revival realized a limited measure of success outside Sarekat Islam. One development was the emergence of a small group of literate modernist Muslims, trained in part at the University of Cairo, which opposed Islamic obscurantism almost as strongly as it disliked Western secularism and Christian missions. Some of the group stressed a back-to-the-Prophet movement, while others urged the assimilation of Western science and history. Although not insensitive to the political and social injustices of the Dutch colonial system, the Islamic modernists also condemned the Indian cultural survivals and the traditional adat law as well. Such sentiments were shared by the educated Indonesian elite, especially in central Java and among the Minangkabau peoples of Sumatra. They organized a Young Muslim League and undertook preaching missions. They also set up modern Islamic schools in both Java and Sumatra, which attracted students from well-to-do families and enjoyed a measure of government support. By the mid-1920s, the movement found a measure of political expression in the Muhammadijah movement based in central Java.[50]

Another characteristic expression of the aspirations of the few Western-trained Indonesians was Budi Otomo (beautiful or noble endeavor), which appeared in 1908. This group was organized along Western lines. It was detached from Indonesian traditionalism and was essentially self-centered rather than nationalist. It espoused the aim of strengthening and rejuvenating Javanese culture to enable it to meet modern demands. Frustrations arising from the group's lack of complete identification with either traditional or European cultures eventually produced a tendency, which became evident by 1914, to adopt the Japanese pattern of using Western methods to counter Western control. Efforts of the moderate leadership to guide the Budi Otomo ship into politically stagnant waters were doomed to failure. The younger, more radical intellectuals prevailed, but not with-

[49] Van Neil, 175–194, 203–207.
[50] *Ibid.*, 56–66, 159–174.

out precipitating defections to both left and right. Moderate elements sponsored patriotic welfare and youth programs in the schools, favored the enactment of reforms along Ethical lines, and participated actively in the Volksraad.

It was within this Europeanized group of Indonesians that Communist spokesmen first gained a hearing. Prominent among them was a Eurasian adventurer and distant relative of Multatuli, also named Douwes Dekker, who became in collaboration with several Dutch associates the leader of an interracial Leftist movement. Douwes Dekker and his Dutch friends were exiled from Indonesia in 1913 to the distress of almost no one. Their tactics had offended Islamic sensitivities and had angered all Dutch residents.[51] It was following this setback that the Communists undertook to infiltrate Sarekat Islam. The Dutch leader of the Communist effort was Hendrik Sneevliet, a member of the so-called Indian Social Democratic Society, which gained a following in the Semarang branch of Sarekat Islam in 1917. Consideration of political developments in Indonesia during the twenties and thirties will be reserved for a later chapter.

## An Appraisal of Dutch Rule to 1920

The history of Dutch rule in Indonesia from 1830 to 1920 affords a demonstration of economic imperialism at or near its technical best. The Dutch multiplied the economic output and commerce of the islands by integrating Indonesian resources with world markets and by encouraging the participation of Western capital generally. They took full advantage of the potentialities of indirect rule, utilizing the authority of the natural leadership of Indonesian society in the interest of order and expanding commerce. They exploited effectively the lack of cohesion within and between the various ethnic, religious, and national groups to forestall the rise of political opposition. The semislavery of the Culture system was corrected in time by the Dutch themselves, and sincere effort was made at official levels after 1900 to stimulate a modernizing trend in cooperation with the Indonesian elite, looking toward a larger indigenous share in both the advantages of economic development and governmental administration. In the crucial test of the beneficence of their rule, the Dutch failed, not apparently from any malicious design or from hypocrisy, but rather because the system which they developed was so completely alien to Indonesian experience and desires. The very success of their financial, production, and marketing operations created an unbridgeable chasm between the alien-dominated economy and effective Indonesian participation. The well-intentioned reform efforts of Ethically minded Dutch officials elicited a disappointingly meager response from those supposed to benefit from the program.

[51] *Ibid.*, 55–66, 159–174.

In Indonesia as elsewhere in potentially productive regions of South-east Asia, the inescapable task of relating the indigenous political and economic order to an ever-broadening world context was far from a painless experience, and it could scarcely have been otherwise. The Dutch demonstration of what could be done in the achievement of pacification and improved economic output and trade was historically significant partly because the enormous population growth which accompanied the process precluded any possibility of reverting to a traditional parochial economy. The tragedy of Dutch colonial rule was that it afforded little indigenous experience in handling such a system and also it tended to exploit and to perpetuate the problems of Indonesian cultural and regional disunity. These problems survived to embarrass the efforts of Indonesia to function as an independent economic and political entity after World War II.

# CHAPTER 17

# Burma under British-Indian

# Rule to 1914

*B* ritish colonial control of Burma was developed as an extension of the larger Indian Empire. Once firmly established in India, the British felt obliged to assume control over confused or hostile border areas such as Burma, which were incapable of withstanding the mobilized power of the subcontinent. India thus became the nucleus of an empire extending far beyond the borders of the earlier Mogul rule. The difference was due in large measure to the complete domination of the Indian Ocean and the Bay of Bengal by British naval power. Some of the projections of British-Indian power were merely adjuncts to trading operations, such as the posts at Aden, the Persian Gulf sheikdoms, Singapore, and Hongkong. Control of contiguous areas, such as Burma, Ceylon, Baluchistan, and the Himalayan frontier, fell in a different category as being essential for India's security. Siam and the Malay sultanates lay outside the security perimeter, but they also gravitated in time toward British-Indian control.

Indians themselves collaborated actively with the British in the development of Burma's economic resources as well as in the conquest. Indian labor built the docks and the railways of Burma, handled its freight, manned most of its industries, and helped harvest the rice crop. Indian businessmen, along with a smaller number of Chinese, dominated important retail trading operations and the financing of agricultural expansion. British capital financed the railways, developed the industries, the mines, and the plantations, and marketed the export surpluses.[1]

On the negative side, British-Indian rule substantially disrupted Burma's indigenous social order and permitted local peoples generally only a minor share in the accrued economic advantages. An Indian-type administration was introduced into Burma along with an alien system of law, land tenure, and taxation. The influx of Indian labor, plus accompanying

[1] Guy Wint, *The British in India* (1947), 20–24.

business, professional, and banking personnel, was probably resented by Burmans more than any other aspect of British rule. As a result of the increasing deterioration of social controls, Burma became by 1914 one of the most disorderly countries of the world. The emerging plural society, with divergent ethnic groups interrelated only on the economic plane, was an unintended but inevitable result of the policy of artificially stimulated economic development under an alien kind of government.[2]

## Burma under Kings Bagyidaw, Tharrawaddy, and Pagan

The British military victory over Burma leading to the Yandabo Treaty of 1826 was achieved mainly because the superior resources of India made possible a sustained campaign running through two rainy seasons. Complete British naval control of the Bay of Bengal, added to the superior arms and discipline of the Indian army, also lay behind the otherwise-tenuous postwar occupation of the Tenasserim and Arakan coastal areas.

Burma's loss of Arakan and Tenasserim, never really integral parts of the kingdom, was not serious in a material sense, and the surrender of suzerain claims over Manipur and Assam was even less so. The one-million-pound indemnity exacted by the treaty was a staggering sum for the government to raise in view of the fact that much of its support was derived from personal services. But the really devastating blow sustained by Burma was the shattering of royal and national prestige. This loss was permanent and irrevocable, affecting adversely the mood of the court, the effectiveness of governmental authority, and the morale of the army. Burma was never afforded an opportunity after 1826 to recover its self-confidence.

The precipitate withdrawal of British forces from Lower Burma in late 1826 (done largely for reasons of health) after the payment of the second installment of the indemnity entailed two unintended consequences. It made impossible the negotiation of any satisfactory commercial treaty, as was attempted by John Crawfurd. It also meant turning over strong points such as Rangoon and Bassein to Burman control, paving the way for eventual Burman recovery of large areas of the delta which had been occupied by Mon and Karen rebels during the late phases of the war. The crushing of the Mon-Karen rebellion was a gruesome affair involving the wholesale destruction of towns and villages and the devastation of the countryside. Some ten thousand Mon refugees fled eastward to British-occupied Amherst district beyond the mouth of the Salween River. The Karens took refuge in hill areas and swamps. Agriculture in lower Burma was disrupted to the point of actual famine conditions, which required rice importations from India. The continued use of the Mon language was proscribed, and a de-

[2] John S. Furnivall, *Colonial Policy and Practice* (1948), 303–312.

liberate program of enforced assimilation was initiated. A final effort at Mon resistance to Burman control flickered out in an abortive rebellion of 1838.[3]

The final decade of the reign of King Bagyidaw after the departure of the British was a frustrating period. He made a persistent but largely futile effort to recover lost prestige by resisting the presence of a British Resident at his capital, arguing that necessary diplomatic relations could be handled by an official of Wungyi rank posted at Rangoon. He finally admitted the British Resident (Major Burney) to Amarapura in 1830 and paid the final installment of the indemnity, all in the forlorn expectation that the British, in return, would restore Tenasserim to Burmese control. Bagyidaw did succeed in negotiating the recovery of control in 1833 of the Kubo Valley, located west of the Chindwin River on the border of the Chin Hills. Thereafter, relations between the British Resident and the court deteriorated progressively until the Amarapura post was finally evacuated in 1839.

The situation within the Burmese Court itself became increasingly demoralized after 1831. The King's deep melancholia involved periodic lapses into insanity, and a clique consisting of the chief queen and her avaricious brother gained wealth and influence. In the rivalry which developed between the predatory court group and Prince Tharrawaddy, brother of the King and Einshemin heir, Bagyidaw became little more than a bystander. The weakening of royal authority and the impending revolt by Prince Tharrawaddy, who was backed by a disreputable personal following, eventually plunged the countryside into a turmoil of chaotic lawlessness.[4]

Tharrawaddy's accession as the new King in a coup of 1837 produced little or no improvement in government and caused progressive deterioration in British-Indian relations. He flatly repudiated the Yandabo Treaty, drove the British Residency from Amarapura, and forced subsequent negotiations to be carried on at Rangoon. He successfully crushed the final Mon rebellion in 1838, and appeared on the verge of renewing the war with Britain around 1840, when a Burmese army of some forty thousand men gathered at Rangoon. An attack on both Tenasserim and Siam appeared likely at a time when British-Indian forces were heavily engaged militarily in both China and Afghanistan. The threat was never executed, partly by reason of impaired army morale and in part as a result of Tharrawaddy's own lapse into insanity by 1842. Internal disorders developed into another civil war in 1844.

One of the sons of Tharrawaddy, Pagan Min, took over control in 1845, following the collapse of the rebellion. His seven years of misrule and neglect of the business of government were further vitiated by his avari-

---

[3] John F. Cady, *A History of Modern Burma* (1958), 72–75. Except where otherwise indicated, this chapter is based on chaps. III, IV, and V of this work.
[4] *Ibid.*, 75–78.

cious and vengeful spirit. He eliminated all royal relatives thought capable of challenging his control. He presided over a thoroughly debauched court. His reign came to an unlamented end during the course of the Second Anglo-Burman War of 1852–1853.[5] The sad deterioration of Burmese kingship during the quarter century from 1826 to 1851 illustrated the vulnerability of the institution of deified monarchy when its sacrosanct status and authority became impaired by irreparable loss of prestige. The Konbaung dynasty never did recover from its humiliation at British hands in 1824–1826. Its performance during the succeeding decades contrasted sharply with the conservatively responsible reign of Rama III in neighboring Siam during the same period.

## British Tenasserim and Arakan

British rule in the Tenasserim and Arakan coastal regions accomplished after 1830 substantial economic and governmental improvements. British control of Tenasserim, as previously indicated, denied the use of this ancient corridor to both Siamese and Burmese armies, whose perennial feuding had brought untold suffering to the resident population. The first British Commissioner, Maingy, was successful in adapting court procedures, both civil and criminal, to Burmese customary law and procedure. He established order, using former Burmese officials including headmen as judges, revenue clerks, and tax collectors, while leaving local policing functions to the villagers themselves.[6]

Trouble developed when Maingy began a costly and burdensome road-construction program in a region which had always preferred water transportation. When *corvée* labor proved unsatisfactory, the Commissioner began the introduction of Indian convict labor, with most unhappy results. Problems also arose when emigrant settlers from Burma opposed British taxes levied locally in cash and insisted that their personal-service obligations were due solely to their own myothugyi chiefs, even though resident at a distance. The most useful early immigrants to Tenasserim were Chinese brought in from Penang.

Commissioner Maingy was replaced in 1835 in response to a demand from British residents for an Indian-type system of governmental courts and administration and the introduction of contract labor from Madras. The new Commissioner, Blundell, had a difficult time. He was embarrassed by the inefficiency of the Company staff, by pressures exerted by English merchants (in rice and teak), and by resident Mons who refused to be ruled by Bengali methods. Standards of official honesty and efficiency in Tenasserim deteriorated after 1842. In spite of such governmental difficulties, the economic development of Tenasserim was maintained, and the population

[5] *Ibid.*, 78–80.
[6] *Ibid.*, 80–81.

grew. Rice acreage increased by 50 per cent from 1845 to 1852, as did the total population. The exploitation of teak timber was wastefully carried out, and by 1850 the most valuable forests in the Amherst area were gone. Timber merchants began eyeing the virtually untouched forests on the Burma side of the boundary.[7]

At the outset the British administered Arakan as an integral part of Bengal, paying little or no regard to local traditions. Relationships between headmen and their followers were ignored, and hereditary chiefship was abolished. The unrest which developed in 1836 as a result of this leveling process was easily put down, and immigration from Bengal increased. Indian labor was utilized for the most part to stimulate rice production. Rice acreage increased about $4\frac{1}{2}$ times from 1830 to 1852, giving full employment to the local population and even attracting laborers from central Burma. Unit acreage taxes were reduced to encourage development of new lands. Akyab became for a time the foremost rice-exporting port in the world. The Arakan district produced a handsome profit for the East India Company, in contrast to the chronic deficit incurred at Moulmein.[8]

## British Rule in Lower Burma

British acquisition of Lower Burma in 1852 up to a line running laterally above Prome and Toungoo was an aggressive move generated by local circumstances and the logic of the imperialist process. Late in 1851 a boastful Burmese governor (Myowun) at Rangoon levied a fine on two visiting British vessels for violating port rules. This was regarded by the British both at Rangoon and Calcutta as in derogation of their prestige. Governor-General Dalhousie of India wanted to avoid an expensive war, but he nevertheless dispatched two naval vessels to deliver an ultimatum for redress and for dismissal of the offending Myowun. The unprepared Burmese government accepted the terms of the ultimatum, but the local tension persisted until British naval guns went off in January, 1852. Dalhousie reprimanded the trigger-happy naval commander but did not repudiate the war which the officer had provoked. A new ultimatum demanding an indemnity to cover war costs, amounting to one thousand times the initially levied fine, was delivered in February, 1852. This was followed by British occupation of strongholds at Martaban, Rangoon, and Bassein in April and May, presumably done to force Burmese acquiescence to the February ultimatum.[9]

Following this minimal demonstration of conciliation and patience, Dalhousie proposed to London in June, 1852, that the occupation of Lower Burma be made permanent in view of the important advantages to be derived therefrom. After a personal visit to Rangoon during the rainy season, the governor-general prepared a final recommendation proposing the uni-

[7] *Ibid.,* 82–84.
[8] *Ibid.,* 85–86.
[9] *Ibid.,* 86–87.

lateral annexation of Lower Burma without bothering to force the acquiescence of Amarapura. This course received prompt approval at London.
Following the capture of Prome and Pegu in the autumn of 1852, a formal
proclamation of annexation was issued by Calcutta in December. The new
province of Pegu included much but not all of the coveted teakwood forest
area.

The guerrilla war came to an end suddenly following a coup in
Upper Burma in early 1853 which deposed the impossible Pagan Min. Disaffection started in the army, but it included also ranking members of the
Hlutdaw. The new ruler, Mindon Min, a half brother of Pagan, was a humane ruler and a sincere Buddhist, who, like his Siamese contemporary, King
Mongkut, had spent much of his previous life in a monastery. He called off
the war in Lower Burma but firmly refused to recognize by treaty the British
acquisition of the lost territory.

After the withdrawal of support by the Burma government, political
opposition to British control in Lower Burma fragmented quickly. Military operations by isolated bands finally degenerated into mere banditry. It
nevertheless required more than four years to bring the region under a
semblance of police control. A direct British administration was then set
up on the model of Bengal, with variations based on experience derived
from Arakan. The boundaries of the old Tenasserim province were extended
northward to include the region between the lower Sittang and Salween
Rivers. The rest of Lower Burma was organized as the province of Pegu.
These two parts plus Arakan were amalgamated in 1862 to become the equivalent of a governor's province in India.[10]

Public revenues in Lower Burma were derived primarily from the
imposition of a tax levied on cultivated lands. Encouragement was afforded,
as previously in Arakan, for the development of new areas of agricultural
land. This policy required among other things the preparation of comprehensive records of landholdings, a laborious and tedious task, in which the
government enlisted the aid of indigenous township officials (*myooks*) and
the circle headmen, or taikthugyis. The myooks, who also supervised tax
collections and adjudicated petty civil and criminal cases, were carefully
chosen from the old myothugyi ranks and from among other men of responsibility and character. They usually enjoyed indefinite tenure. Assisting as
revenue collectors and surveyors were some of the former taikthugyis. They
were liable to close surveillance and to official sanctions against misconduct,
being left little initiative or authority in their own right. The local police
officers (*gaungs*), functioning under the British system, enjoyed neither
authority nor popular respect, while the village headman (*kyedangyi*), the
largest taxpayer, became a man of all work performing a variety of thank-
less village chores.

The new administrative system was highly artificial, but it was perhaps as effective as could have been devised under the circumstances. An

[10] *Ibid.,* 89–93.

almost-complete vacuum of authority had been created following the withdrawal of many myothugyis and higher Burman officials northward. British deputy commissioners in charge of the several districts supervised the work of the myooks and taikthugyis, exercising oversight in all aspects of governmental responsibility.[11]

The economic gains realized during the course of the first two decades of British rule were impressively gratifying. Timber extraction was expanded under regulative control of the Forestry Department. The government assumed title to all teak trees and strictly enforced its leasehold regulations. Rice acreage trebled during two decades, mainly through the granting of gratis title to cultivators who would develop virgin areas. A receipt for the payment of a nominal tax assessment covering the first three to five years was regarded as legally negotiable evidence of a pioneer's land claim either for purposes of sale or as collateral for a loan. The export of rice surpluses to India, a privilege never previously permitted to Lower Burma, quickly put the new Pegu district on a self-sustaining basis financially. Steamboats were introduced on the Irrawaddy River, and railways were eventually built, running up the Sittang Valley as far north as Toungoo and to Prome on the Irrawaddy. After 1868, the Irrawaddy Flotilla Company took over most of the river transportation. Trunk roads and river embankments were constructed at government expense. The population of Lower Burma doubled during the first decade of British rule, and the prosperity of the region began to attract increasing numbers of emigrants from the Burma kingdom itself. Trade between the two Burmas increased steadily.[12]

The improving economic situation was not without some discouraging aspects. The shift to steam navigation on the rivers deprived thousands of river boatmen of their means of livelihood. The price of rice in Upper Burma rose in accordance with competing prices available for overseas exports. Peasant borrowers on land-title security often acted irresponsibly, incurring heavy indebtedness to rapacious Burman moneylenders. The disappearance of the traditionally acknowledged authority of the myothugyi chief, the development of a money economy and a wage-labor system, and the relaxation of religious and social controls, especially in newly settled areas, aggravated the decay of the traditional social structure. Old regulations covering the display of symbols of social status in such matters as houses, dress, and accoutrements disintegrated under conditions of new-found individualism. When a real agricultural boom developed during the 1870s following the opening of the Suez Canal, Indian labor and moneylenders entered the scene with socially demoralizing effects. The confusion was further aggravated by the application of an alien British-Indian system of law and court procedure.[13]

11 *Ibid.,* 93.
12 *Ibid.,* 94–95.
13 *Ibid.,* 95–96.

Religious adjustments under British rule were imperfectly achieved. Official efforts during the late 1860s to integrate the better monastic schools with a tax-supported educational program, including the introduction of additional training in geography, arithmetic, science, and the English language, attracted no cooperation from the monks and were abandoned in the early 1870s. Discipline within the Buddhist monastic order of Lower Burma, divorced as it was from the Royal Court Commissions, began to deteriorate. The new British government refused to recognize and enforce the authority of the Buddhist ecclesiastical code. Dissension and indiscipline in religious circles became progressively worse with the passage of time.[14]

The only important Christian missionary impact was made among the non-Buddhist Karens. The Karens for the most part welcomed British rule, and the Sgaw group in particular responded to the Christian message, especially as presented by the American Baptist Mission. Missionaries reduced the leading Karen languages to writing (using the Burmese script), organized churches, and conducted schools. Educated Christian Karens eventually assumed the leadership of the Karen National Association, organized in 1881. By and large, Buddhism in Lower Burma demonstrated continuing vitality despite signs of internal deterioration and the counterappeal of Christian missionary activity.[15]

## *The Reign of Mindon Min, 1852–1878*

In the person of King Mindon, Burma acquired a ruler similar in many respects to his Siamese contemporary, King Mongkut. Each had spent much of his previous lifetime in a monastery. As sincere Buddhists, both were opposed to war and bloodshed and were determined to maintain peaceful relations with the dominant British-Indian government. Both were serious students of religion and advocated a simpler and purer form of Buddhism. Given the same opportunity, Mindon might have equaled his contemporary's interest in science and in the affairs of the outside world. But his new capital, built at Mandalay, at the outset of his reign, was isolated and did not afford such opportunity as was available at Bangkok for outside contacts. No missionary or other friends were available to teach Mindon the English language. Mindon was less vindictive than Mongkut and was generally respected by the British as well as by his countrymen for his personal integrity, piety, and kindness, and for the sincerity of his efforts to live up to ideal Buddhist standards of kingship. He was also progressive in economic matters. He introduced steamship navigation on the river and encouraged the growth of trade not only with Lower Burma but also with China. The atmosphere of the Mandalay Court, nevertheless, lacked the passion for modernization which characterized royal circles at Bangkok.

[14] *Ibid.,* 96–97.
[15] *Ibid.,* 98–99.

King Mindon was on the defensive; his country was beleaguered politically and economically and was doomed to disappear.

King Mindon's daily routine illustrated the ideal of Buddhist kingship in action. It included a half-hour of morning prayers followed by oral reading of extracts from the Buddhist scriptures. He held a plenary morning audience at nine o'clock, with obligatory attendance of important princes, ministers, and other high officials, for the discussion of reports from provincial governors and other matters relating to domestic and foreign affairs. This was followed by a smaller noon conference covering military matters. The King then spent the early afternoon hours undisturbed in the quiet of his private library reading from palm-leaf manuscripts, parchment scrolls, and books, covering such subjects as religion, philosophy, history, geography, and politics. The scriptures were again read to him at the dinner hour.[16] But even so, his outlook was narrowly circumscribed, and the scope of his possible adjustment to the imperatives of outside forces was severely limited. The kingdom of Burma lasted throughout his lifetime but did not long survive his passing in 1878.

King Mindon refused steadfastly to legalize by treaty the British *de facto* occupation of Lower Burma, and he did not conceal his expectation that the area would some day be restored to Burma. Partly by reason of his own sincere aversion to violence and intrigue, bolstered, no doubt, by his awareness that his own dispirited army was no match for British-Indian forces, he made no effort to take advantage of British involvement during the 1850s in difficulties in the Crimea, the Sepoy Rebellion of 1857–1858, and the ensuing Anglo-French war with China, 1858–1860. His relations with the British Commissioner, Major Arthur Phayre, were conducted on a basis of mutual respect.[17]

King Mindon attempted with little success to eliminate feudal aspects of the Burmese administrative system following recommendations brought back to him by missions sent abroad. He tried in particular to abolish the Myosa system of fief assignments to princes and high officials. He attempted also to end the misappropriation of moneys passing through official hands by instituting a system of designated stipends and salaries. He undertook to raise revenues for the most part from *thathameda* land-tax assessments based on a productivity index for a given area multiplied by the number of households. Collections were never quite sufficient to establish fully his salary-stipend system of payments, for the number of households was seldom reported correctly, and officials continued to enjoy their customary perquisites and fees. The establishment of administrative supervisory posts checked flagrant financial abuses, but they contributed little to revenue. Other sources of income were the royal monopolies of timber, petroleum, precious stones, and the dues levied on trade. Part of the reason for

[16] Thaung, "Burmese Kingship," *JBRS*, XLII (December, 1959), 183–185.
[17] Cady, 100.

revenue shortage was the exemption from taxes of most of the occupants of royal service lands. The high cost of constructing and adorning the new capital located on the allegedly more auspicious site of Mandalay aggravated financial problems. Mindon's economic improvements included the introduction of a system of coinage in 1861.[18]

One serious palace rebellion marred the reign of King Mindon. In 1866, two of his disaffected sons broke into the Hlutdaw chamber and killed the king's brother (the heir apparent) and his supporters, but they failed to capture the King. The thwarted rebels fled to British Burma, but the son of the slain prince then staged an abortive coup of his own. This instance had the unfortunate result of preventing Mindon from designating another Einshemin to succeed himself, a circumstance which produced unfortunate results in 1878. Meanwhile the steady deterioration of the Burma army continued despite the employment of training officers from the outside. The morale of the royal service troops was further undermined by the eventual assessment of the thathameda household tax on ahmudan families not occupying royal lands. Many of the malcontents migrated to Lower Burma, and the integrity of the once-spirited Burmese regiments disappeared. The Burma army of 1878 was a mere shadow of what it had been in 1824.[19]

The principal cause of Mindon's friction with British Burma developed over resentment on the part of Mandalay to the British presumption of suzerain status. The pressure from India was relentlessly applied. A British Resident was readmitted to Mandalay in 1862, and in 1867 full extraterritorial jurisdiction was accorded to this officer over British living in the kingdom. From 1867 on, the British-Indian government adopted as a fixed policy objective the establishment of control over Burma's foreign relations. The treaty of 1867 also granted British steamers the right to traverse the entire length of the Irrawaddy River up to Bhamo, where the caravan trade route to China started.

Mindon attempted to counter the presumed exercise of British foreign-relations control by soliciting diplomatic relations with the United States, Italy, and France. Following the pattern of King Mongkut of Siam in attempting to avoid dependence on a single source of aid, he invited the entry of Frenchmen and Italians as missionaries, engineers, and governmental experts. Relations with British India developed more difficulty in the early 1870s, when British authorities at Rangoon became increasingly insistent on obtaining access to Yunnan. This followed the exploratory French naval mission of Lagrée and Garnier up the Mekong Valley in 1867–1868, to be described later. The pattern of imperialistic rivalry over the assumed commercial opportunities available in Yunnan developed under circumstances which tended to take less and less account of the legalities of

[18] *Ibid.,* 101–102.
[19] *Ibid.,* 103.

Burman sovereignty. The rivalry eased somewhat after 1870 when the Franco-Prussian War eliminated for the time being any threat of official French moves in the direction of western China.[20]

Fully aware of the perils of the situation, King Mindon in 1872 sent to Europe a diplomatic mission headed by a ranking member of the Hlut-daw. The objective was to obtain arms if possible and in any case to establish diplomatic contacts apart from the presumed suzerainty of India. Innocuous commercial treaties were concluded with Italy and France, but the mission was ignored by the British Foreign Office.

An incident at Hanoi in 1873 staged by Francis Garnier and a French merchant aroused British concern, as did the visit of a French emissary to Mandalay in the same year. The tentative promises made to King Mindon by the latter covering the extension of good offices in any third-party dispute involving Burma and the sending of French officers to train the Burma army were both repudiated later by Paris. London's reply was to stage the famous Margary expedition from Shanghai to Bhamo in 1874. It ended disastrously early in the following year when Margary attempted to retrace his journey, accompanied by a small sepoy force. The loyal cooperation of the Mandalay government in the Margary mission, for which it provided a 250-man Burmese escort, was ill repaid. British-India in effect broke off diplomatic relations with Burma later in the same year by prohibiting the British Resident from complying with the traditional requirement of protocol that he remove his shoes at royal audiences. The basic reasons for Britain's change of policy were the presence of a number of French and Italian adventurers at Mandalay and the spate of alarmist rumors concerning French designs on Burma. Mindon's efforts to preserve Burma's independence and at the same time to avoid giving legitimate grounds for offense to British-Indian authorities were at the point of collapse when the good king died in 1878.[21]

## British Absorption of the Burma Kingdom

Granted the dominant position which British India had assumed in Southern Asia, the absorption of the faltering and land-bound kingdom of Burma was only a matter of time and circumstance. That it did not occur in 1878 when the youthful King Thibaw came to power, hemmed in as he was by a disreputable palace clique, was due mainly to the accident of the concurrent development of the Balkan crisis, an Afghan war, and the second Boer War in South Africa. The British took custody of the eligible alternative Anglophile prince of Nyaungyan, and preparations for intervention were far advanced in the spring and again in the summer of 1879. But Indian authorities dared not undertake simultaneous wars on two frontiers. As a precautionary measure the Residency staff was evacuated from Manda-

[20] *Ibid.,* 104–108.
[21] *Ibid.,* 108–110.

lay in September, 1879. The threat of French influence at Mandalay was not yet serious, whereas the Russian threat at Kabul in Afghanistan was immediate and involved the matter of British prestige. Rangoon business groups financed further explorations of the China border in 1881. It was a foregone conclusion that when a later opportunity should arise, British action would be taken against the militarily impotent and highly injudicious palace clique at Mandalay.[22]

Affairs in Upper Burma meanwhile went from bad to worse. The King was a cipher, while his mother-in-law, formerly the chief queen, and her rascal confederate ran affairs for their own private advantage. Far-reaching administrative reforms in the direction of a cabinet-type administration, long in process of development by progressive Wungyis who had visited Europe, had no chance of adoption under the circumstances. All officers were for sale, and banditry and intimidation became widespread. By 1884, rebels held Sagaing, just across the river from the old site of Ava; a Shan rebellion was raging; Kachin raiders were invading Upper Burma in force; a gang of Chinese freebooters sacked and burned Bhamo. Meanwhile the purging of opposition elements at Mandalay continued. The faltering Burma kingdom awaited only the occasion which was to end its existence.[23]

The opportunity for effective British action came in the latter half of 1885, when the anti-imperialist Liberal Gladstone, in power since 1880, temporarily lost control of the Ministry at London to Conservatives Lord Salisbury and Randolph Churchill. French imperialist expansion had, since 1881, absorbed the entire coastal area of Vietnam and parts of Laos. In early 1885, Burma negotiated a commercial treaty at Paris, and a French consul named Haas was despatched to Mandalay in June of the same year. Although apparently acting without authorization, Haas negotiated substantial French loans for Burma's railway-construction needs and the establishment of a bank for currency issues, both to be serviced by oil royalties and river customs. A Burmese official left for Paris in July, 1885, to arrange exchange of ratifications.[24]

It was under these circumstances that the overconfident Mandalay authorities decided in August, 1885, to levy an exorbitant fine of 23 million rupees on the Bombay-Burma Trading Corporation for the alleged illegal export of teak logs on the Toungoo-Pyinmana frontier.[25] Burmese officials of the area were notoriously corrupt, and whether irregular methods had been used or not, the fine partook of the character of ill-concealed blackmail. The trading issue was one probably capable of negotiation if it had been handled with firmness and patience. A responsible Burman Wungyi

---

[22] *Ibid.,* 111–114.

[23] *Ibid.,* 115–116.

[24] *Ibid.,* 118.

[25] British authors disagree as to whether actual bribery occurred. The matter will have to remain undetermined until independent access can be had to Company records.

tried belatedly to reduce the fine to a mere 5 or 10 per cent of the original asking.

The foolish attempt of Mandalay to collect an extortionate fine was the occasion rather than the cause for Britain's sending the short-term ultimatum to Burma in October, 1885. The real cause of the intervention was British desire to eliminate the threat of French influence in Upper Burma. Even the issue of French interference would apparently have been subject to negotiation at Paris in view of the complete disavowal of the unauthorized negotiations of consul Haas by the new French government headed by Freycinet. The imperialistic Ferry had lost power at Paris in March, 1885. Under the circumstances the long-restrained pressure of business interests at Rangoon for action was not to be denied expression.[26]

The decision to annex Upper Burma to India rather than attempt to install an Anglophile ruler in place of Thibaw was virtually decided by default. The only surviving candidate had become a French protégé. Thus, in spite of the genuine concern felt by Rangoon's Commissioner Bernard and other informed officials over the difficulties to be encountered in Upper Burma, the strategically sensitive and commercially minded groups bent on erasing the Burmese Court had their way. London's approval of the proposed ultimatum demands reached Rangoon on October 17. Full mobilization along the main river avenue began two days later, and the twenty-day ultimatum was presented on October 22.

The ultimatum reached Mandalay on October 30. Its key demand was that the Burma government thereafter submit all matters of external relations to the decision of the government of India. The dominant court group sent a defiant reply, and the King made a futile effort to rally his subjects to oppose the "enemies of Burma's customs and religion." British armed steamers crossed the border on November 14. Mandalay fell two weeks later, and Thibaw and his principal queens were taken captive to Calcutta. The elimination of the Burma King and the country's annexation to India on January 1, 1886, was an accomplished fact before the results of the British election of December, 1885, restored a Gladstone Ministry to power.[27]

## Annexation and Pacification of Upper Burma

The misgivings entertained by Commissioner Bernard about the difficulties and unrequited costs to be encountered in Upper Burma were proved correct. British efforts to find responsible Burmans of experience and authority to man the central administration were powerless to prevent deterioration from endemic disorder to overt rebellion. The drift was aggravated by the British application of harsh repressive measures in an attempt to halt the trend toward anarchy. Insecure villagers organized their

[26] Cady, 116–119.
[27] *Ibid.,* 120–121.

own foraging parties. The army's shooting of pillagers, its floggings, and the burning of uncooperating villages eventually incited all armed bands to turn on the British-Indian forces who had despoiled them of king and court. The full scope of the potential resistance was not immediately apparent. The declaration of February 26, 1886, made by Viceroy Lord Dufferin, that Burma would be ruled as an integral part of British India was the beginning rather than the end of the problem.[28]

The only question which came up for Parliamentary decision in London was the loaded one of whether the costs of the Burma operation should be charged to British or to Indian revenues. Prime Minister Gladstone himself ruled that Parliamentary approval for the armed action was not required, since it was allegedly waged for reasons of India's security and not for trade, and that the war was in reality one in defense of India's security and happiness. In any case what had been done could not be undone.[29]

For more than a year after the annexation of Burma to India the situation deteriorated alarmingly. The rebellion spread to Lower Burma and assumed the proportions of a national rising. Many responsible Burmans shed no tears over the elimination of the predatory Mandalay clique, but they usually did not identify the young King Thibaw with that group. They objected particularly to the destruction of the royal court and its symbols of governmental authority, which also left the Buddhist religion without support. Rebel resistance was uncoordinated and incapable of inflicting serious losses on the British forces but also difficult to corner. The sending of Burman recruits and police against the rebels was abandoned in 1887, but continued effective use was made of some contingents of Karen volunteers. The civil war dragged on for five years. Eventually more than forty thousand Indian troops and police were assigned to man hundreds of armed posts distributed along all of the important roads. In the end the expenses of pacification exceeded by approximately ten times the estimated cost of the original military operation. Thus did Commissioner Bernard's gloomy predictions prove all too accurate.[30]

British control of the Shan plateau areas to the east of Burma's central valleys was accomplished with little difficulty. By acting as peacemakers between rival Shan factions and by confirming the authority of the sawbwas and myosas who submitted to British suzerainty, the British pacified the vast area during the course of two dry seasons, 1887 and 1888. Annual-tribute assessments were levied on a five-year basis. The governor of Burma was authorized in 1888 to assign political officers to the area, and the operations of the minimal judicial and administrative services were modified in accordance with local custom. The state of Karenni opposite Toungoo was not included among the Shan States, since it had been accorded the status

[28] *Ibid.,* 126–129.
[29] *Ibid.,* 131.
[30] *Ibid.,* 133–134.

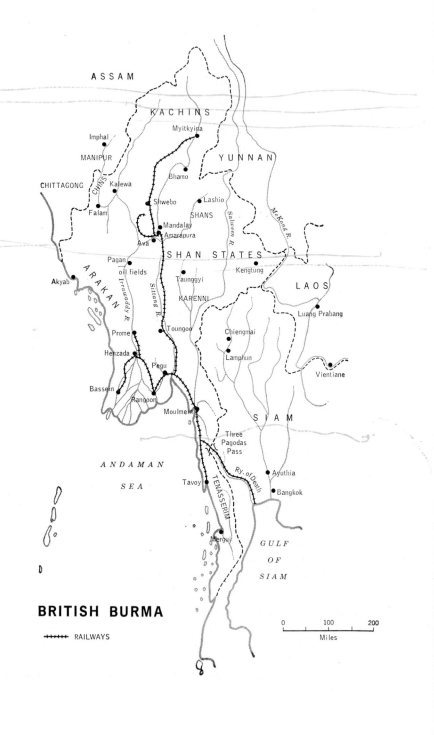

**BRITISH BURMA**

+++++ RAILWAYS

| 0 | 100 | 200 |
Miles

of titular independence from both British and Burmese control by a previous treaty of 1873. The British assumed proprietary rights over all Karenni forests and mineral resources. The chiefs had to maintain order and protect trade, and European residents were not subject to their jurisdiction.[31]

Burma's boundary with Siam was fixed in 1892. The Mekong River became the frontier between French Laos and Kengtung state, which was in subordinate alliance with Burma. The taungya-cultivating Kachin tribesmen of north Burma agreed in 1892 to submit the settlement of their disputes to a British superintendent. Chin tribes to the west of the Chindwin accepted British authority in 1895. Burma's boundaries, except for that with Yunnan, were thus established by 1895.[32] In view of the difficulties encountered during the preceding decade, it is not surprising that the Indian government demonstrated little enthusiasm over the prospect of extending its responsibilities still further eastward in the direction of Siam.

One incidental result of the long struggle for pacification was to stimulate the national awareness of the several Karen groups. They took an active part in suppressing Burman rebels and bandits in their immediate vicinities. Because Burman Buddhist monks participated in the anti-British rising, the Karen Christian communities tended to take the lead in opposing the threat of Burman violence. Here were sown the seeds of the Karen National Union risings which occurred following Britain's withdrawal after World War II.[33]

## The New British Administrative System in Burma

The revamping of the Burma administrative machinery was the work of Sir Charles Crosthwaite, who took over as Commissioner in 1889. The destruction of the hierarchy of royal officials and the discrediting of many taikthugyi and myothugyi incumbents for participating in the rebellion forced a reexamination of the entire system. On the basis of his previous experience in India, Crosthwaite decided to eliminate the upper and intermediate levels of the traditional governmental hierarchy and to accord real power and authority to village headmen (*thugyis*), supervising some seventeen to eighteen thousand village tracts. The court, the Hlutdaw, the various grades of Wuns, the police, judicial, and granary-tax-collecting officials, and the myothugyis of both ahmudan and athi affiliation were all

---

[31] *Ibid.*, 136.

[32] Relations between Upper Burma and China were complicated by the insertion of a stipulation in a treaty of July, 1886, done at the instance of Robert Hart of the China Customs Service, that periodic tributary missions should continue to be sent from Burma to China as in the past. This treaty was modified in subsequent conventions of 1894 and 1897, and the embassies to China were forgotten.

[33] Cady, 137, 139–140.

discarded in favor of an Indian-type system supervised by European district deputy commissioners. Cooperative myothugyi incumbents were permitted to continue in power until their deaths. Britain's policy of direct rule in Burma proper contrasted sharply with Dutch rule in Java.

In return for a 10 per cent commission on tax collections, the village thugyi was asked to serve as a police officer, petty magistrate, and tax gatherer, besides performing a number of side chores. He could commandeer labor to maintain wells, roads, and paths and to establish a village watch. He was responsible for keeping vital statistics, administering sanitary regulations and burial grounds, and guarding against cattle disease. The functions of land surveying and assessment were taken over entirely by the Land Records Department. The plenary authority exercised at the outset by the deputy commissioners was later fragmented into a number of specialized governmental agencies to supervise the judiciary, public works, health, and police.[34]

The introduction of an alien system of law and court procedures was from the Burmese point of view particularly disturbing. Court decisions ceased to have much relevance to Burmese ideas of justice. The new procedures seemed to introduce a game of technicalities and rules, which the not-too-scrupulous legal profession was able to exploit for personal advantages. Truthful evidence, previously obtainable through mediators, proved difficult to arrive at by impersonal court procedures. The new oaths administered to witnesses carried no terrifying religious sanctions comparable to traditional ones. Perjury and bribery became widespread. The increase of court litigation, especially in connection with the rapid turnover of land titles in Lower Burma, was particularly demoralizing socially. It struck at the practice of joint landholding which provided the traditional basis of family integration. In many newly developed agricultural areas, no traditional ownership rights of any kind existed, so that all claims came to depend on the records made by the Land Records Department and its periodic settlement surveys. These procedures had little relevance to customary law.[35]

During the course of the quarter century between the end of the pacification and the outbreak of World War I, the central secretariat at Rangoon came to include a score or more of specialized services. These, for the most part, functioned independently of the general administrative system. After 1897, when Burma was accorded legislative autonomy under a lieutenant governor, an appointive, advisory Legislative Council was introduced. Its minority of nonofficial members included at the outset one Burman and one Shan. The Council membership was expanded in 1909, when two elected members, both British, were introduced, one chosen by the Burma Chamber of Commerce and the other by the Rangoon Trades

[34] *Ibid.*, 143–144.
[35] *Ibid.*, 146–148.

Association. Other appointive members were added by 1920 raising the total to thirty, of which thirteen were non-British. But every action of the Council was subject to the successive vetoes of the local governor, the viceroy in India, and the Secretary of State for India in London. The needs of the British business community and the requirements of the expanding economy received primary consideration. By comparison, efforts to ameliorate Burmese grievances, frequently made articulate only at the instance of sympathetic settlement or forestry officials who were closest to the people, usually encountered difficulties. The municipal corporations functioned almost exclusively through participation of interested Europeans and occasionally of some Chinese.[36]

Burmese who were trained in English, in surveying, and in administrative procedures were admitted by examination to a Class II civil service. They usually served as township myooks or as subdivisional officers or extra assistant commissioners for the districts. The first Burmese deputy commissioner was appointed in 1908, and the first indigenous High Court judge in 1917. The emerging semiwesternized official elite formed a distinct social class, having little in common with their villager countrymen. They were usually not accorded intimate social intercourse with the European group. They maintained large urban households, including nieces and nephews and other relatives, with Indian servants to perform menial tasks. They still found satisfaction in attending religious festivals and in patronizing the pagoda, but they often became politically emasculated and socially isolated by reason of their connections with the government.[37]

British administration of Burma at the upper levels was far more efficient in terms of personal integrity and concern for promoting economic progress than Burmese rule had ever been. British officials frequently elicited respect and occasionally affection. The Indians who came along in the wake of British rule were by comparison neither liked nor respected. At the lower levels of government, abuses of authority still abounded, partly because processes were misunderstood and powers were misused. Relatively few British officials learned the Burmese language well, and only the exceptional ones among them developed a sympathetic awareness of the Burman point of view. The disappearance of the officials of old Burma, from the king down to the myothugyi, robbed the society of leaders who had been the creators of manners and fashions, the patrons of literature, art, and religion. Gone also was expert craftsmanship, responding to the refinements of public taste and to the gradations of status based on Burman standards and values. What made the cultural losses doubly hard to bear was the inability of the people generally to share in the economic advantages realized under British-Indian rule.[38]

[36] *Ibid.*, 149–150.
[37] *Ibid.*, 151.
[38] *Ibid.*, 153–154.

## Circumstances and Incentives to Agricultural Expansion

Whereas the Dutch program of economic expansion in Java in the nineteenth century had been accomplished for the most part by taking advantage of the authority of the native chiefs, British Burma operated from the first on a laissez-faire basis. The Dutch system protected agricultural land from alienation to non-Javanese, while all land claims in Burma were negotiable as mortgage security and hence transferable. Agricultural expansion in Lower Burma was stimulated in large measure by the steady accumulation of private debt in the process of land clearance and development. The debts served progressively to dispossess the pioneer settlers and to send them on to develop still newer areas.

Four essential factors provided the stimulus for agricultural expansion in Burma. (1) The completion of the Suez Canal in 1869 opened for Burma a new rice market in Europe and an expanding triangular trade involving India. (2) The immigration of experienced wet-rice cultivators from Upper Burma was supplemented by (3) the organized importation of coolie labor from India for harvesting purposes after 1870. (4) Abundant cash credits and expert loan administration were provided by the Chettyar moneylender class of south India. The Chettyars obtained their needed funds from the Imperial Bank of India located at Calcutta. They loaned only on fairly good land security and at rates which, although they were high (15 to 36 per cent per annum), were substantially lower than those required by Chinese traders and Burman lenders. The latter groups were usually willing to enter the scene at earlier stages of land development. The expansion of rice production in Lower Burma had been substantial prior to 1870 (in fifteen years 740,000 acres were added), but the average annual increment from 1875 to 1900 was two or three times as great. The traditional economic system of Burma was submerged so quickly in favor of commercialized agriculture that few Burmese could understand what was happening, much less endeavor to adjust advantageously to the new situation.[39]

The government of Burma contributed to economic development by helping finance the immigration of Indian laborers. Eighty thousand entered, for example, in 1883. It also constructed bunds to protect river lands from floods, provided railway and road transportation, and constructed wharf facilities at principal ports. The government also maintained peace and order, kept comprehensive records of landholdings and land transfers, and provided the legal framework for the handling of an increasing volume of litigation relating to transference of land titles. Private firms, British and Indian, ran the rice mills and the marketing services overseas.[40]

According to the Land Revenue Act of 1876, a negotiable "occupancy

[39] *Ibid.,* 157.
[40] *Ibid.,* 158.

right" capable of use as security for a loan could be obtained by paying a nominal tax assessment for a single year. Seldom was a pioneer cultivator able to stay the entire twelve-year period required for full ownership. He usually lost title before the time was up to the Chinese trader or Indian moneylender, or he was simply displaced by the strong-arm methods employed by better-financed and more ruthless promoters, who hired large gangs of laborers and thugs to defend their claims. Displaced or vacating cultivators had the choice of moving on to develop other virgin tracts or of accepting employment under a large operator. Private indebtedness threatened to engulf the cultivators, who had to continue to struggle to keep their heads above water. In a newly developed township, near chaos usually prevailed. Disputes between rival claimants were complicated by a great deal of chicanery in establishing and recording occupancy rights. The Chettyars generally preferred to keep their assets liquid and not to acquire titles to land.

The riceland boom continued with little abatement (except briefly in 1894) until the general depression of 1907–1908. It reached a peak between 1895 and 1900 when some 1.5 million new acres were added in five years. With the collapse of the world price of rice in 1907, an increasing number of cultivators lost their lands and became renter-tenants. Interest rates rose exorbitantly; land rentals remained high; and the fixed land-revenue demands were too inelastic to adjust to depression conditions. The problem of land alienation began to affect Upper Burma after 1908 for the first time. Remedial measures proposed by experienced settlement officials, including sharp reduction of taxes in poor years, provision for cooperative credits to cultivators, standardization of grain measures and qualities of cotton, and cooperative ginning services for cotton producers, were pushed aside by governmental unconcern. Both the moneylenders and the cultivators also suffered from the practice of collusive buying of rice by large British milling firms, which found it highly disadvantageous to bid against each other. The collusive practices started in 1882 and were perfected in 1894, subject to repeated lapses and revivals.[41]

On the basis of 1870 standards, Burma's exports increased fourfold by 1900, ten times by 1914, and fifteen times by 1926–1927. Imports were less than one-third of exports during most of the period, and the absolute gap between them tended to increase.[42] British banking and business interests were also active in a large variety of nonagricultural operations. The government-owned Burma Railways were financed by interest-guaranteed bonds marketed in India. The Irrawaddy Flotilla Company virtually monopolized river transportation. Several British firms were active in the extracting and processing of teak timber. The oil industry got well started by 1908, when a pipeline was laid from the oil fields to a refinery located at the port of

[41] *Ibid.,* 159–162.
[42] Furnivall, 78–92.

Syriam. Much of the advance in mining (lead, zinc, silver, tungsten, tin), in rubber plantations, and in cement manufacture took place after World War I. Except for oil, industries were almost entirely foreign in their labor force and management. They therefore had little impact on the indigenous population.[43]

Repeated proposals were advanced to correct the trend toward alienation of land from cultivator ownership. A number of proposed remedies were borrowed from the British Parliament's "three F's program" of Irish land reform. Several projects proved reasonably effective on a limited scale, but the really thoroughgoing reform proposals designed to obtain permanency of tenure and fair rents presented administrative difficulties and were usually denounced as gratuitous.[44] The precarious status of the cultivator and the socially demoralizing effects of the prevailing laissez-faire policy did not appear compelling to those who assumed that the ever-expanding rice output would in time benefit the people generally. The process of formulating governmental policy was too cumbersome and the chances of veto were too many for the concerned minority of officials to achieve the difficult reforms needed to prevent the Burmese peasant from losing his land. Business interests and Chettyars who were prepared to resist government efforts to end usurious practices were invariably better represented in the Legislative Council than were the cultivators themselves, and the final decisions in any case were not made in Burma. A Cooperative Bank was established for Upper Burma in 1910. Credit societies numbered some 1,250 by 1915, but the cooperative-credit movement experienced difficult times in subsequent decades.[45]

## Cultural and Religious Decline

Decline of Burmese culture under British rule occurred in many areas. Expert craftsmanship lost much of its motivation with the disappearance of the royal court and the bureaucratic hierarchy, and cheaper manufactured imports tended to replace Burmese goods in the market place. High literary competence in the Burmese language gradually disappeared. English became the language of the law courts, the best lay schools, and the higher levels of government, while Hindustani vied with Burmese in the urban bazaars. Monastic discipline also deteriorated. By promising to keep the incumbent Buddhist primate, the thathanabaing, in office and not to interfere in religion, Commissioner Bernard enlisted his aid in the suppression of the disorders of 1886–1887, especially in instances where monks were involved. But Bernard's successors at Rangoon saw no need to accept the

[43] Cady, 163.

[44] *Ibid.*, 164–165. The most thoroughgoing reforms were proposed and sponsored by Sir Frederic Fryer in 1892 and 1896, and by Governor Thirkell White in 1906.

[45] *Ibid.*, 167.

proferred assistance of the Buddhist hierarchy. They refused to support the disciplinary measures of the Sangha, and eventually subjected the wearers of the yellow robe to the humiliating control of the secular courts and the ordinary police. When the last thathanabaing died in 1895, the post was allowed to remain vacant, leaving disciplinary measures to regional and local monastic heads who were denied governmental support.

The relaxation of religious standards was spelled out in widespread violations of monastic vows and in periodic exhibitions of primitive magic. Tattooing for invulnerability was usually connected with sedition. The traditional prestige of the yellow robe survived better than did the actual social and religious contributions made by the monastic community. Its educational functions declined in importance, and the heavy weight of traditionalism within the Sangha itself prevented Buddhism from making any important contribution to the fashioning of adjustments to social order necessitated by the inescapable impact of Western influences.[46]

The decline of religion as a humanizing and integrating social factor was felt more seriously in the south than in Upper Burma. In the latter area, village communities remained effective, and most pongyi kyaung schools continued to function. After 1900, secular schools where English was taught began to attract the children of well-to-do parents, partly because the Western-type training held out vocational opportunities. Such students often developed an attitude of contempt toward the traditional curriculum and a feeling of superiority to their parents. Their exposure to a strange curriculum taught in an alien language, on the other hand, was also frustrating, especially to the majority who failed to achieve passing marks needed to qualify for government posts or for higher-level training.[47]

The average Burman Buddhist was unfitted both by experience and by social mores to compete in the area of business. The profit-motivated Indian and Chinese merchants presented formidable competition, not to mention the British banking, milling, and exporting firms. In both the social and economic spheres, therefore, the new generation of Burmans experienced difficulty in coming to terms with the changing order. A decreasing number of them shared with their parents the nostalgic memories of the good old days of the Burma kings, which were never to return.[48]

## The Problem of Growing Lawlessness

Much of the alarming increase in crime which characterized British-ruled Burma was the work of unemployed wanderers. They often lacked access to land and were resentful of the traditional discipline imposed by the village elders. Youthful groups took to petty theft and then to dacoity

[46] *Ibid.,* 168–170.
[47] *Ibid.,* 171.
[48] *Ibid.,* 172.

(gang robbery) partly to find excitement and partly to obtain funds to bribe the police or to obtain surety guarantees against jail sentences as "bad livelihood" suspects. Another source of trouble and frustration, from the 1870s on, was the presence of contract laborers recruited sometimes from disreputable elements in India. They monopolized labor opportunities in areas of transportation, industry (except in oil), and public works, virtually closing the door to Burmese employment in all economic lines except agriculture.

Crimes of violence among Burmans resident in British-ruled areas began to increase alarmingly after 1880. The growing disorder merged later with the rebellion of 1886–1889. Following the rebellion, the cumulative effects of chronic debt and semianarchy on the expanding agricultural frontier and seasonal unemployment aggravated the trend toward social deterioration. Upper Burma, after 1890, returned fairly quickly to normal conditions of effective community control, in large measure because of the persistence of resident land ownership on a family basis. Such was not the case in Lower Burma.[49]

The problem of coping with growing disorder was a baffling one. Population groups that failed to find remunerative employment during the two long breaks in the agricultural season, after the planting and after the harvest, found excitement and profit in lawlessness. Predatory escapades were accompanied by the increasing incidence of crimes of violence inflicted under circumstances of frustration and anger. Many village communities lacked the traditional facilities for mediating disputes. Also missing was the once-effective sanction of ostracism for unsocial conduct. Expulsion from the community solved no problems under the new circumstances. Severe police and court methods, including the jailing and flogging of offenders, the punishment of uncooperative village communities, and the disciplining of remiss headmen, all had little effect. The more meticulous the policing operations became the more offenses were brought to light. Concealment of crime was easy because intimidated village groups usually refused to give evidence against offenders.

The level of violent crime in 1912 was twice that of 1904 despite all counteracting policing efforts. The Lower Burma divisions of Pegu and Irrawaddy in 1912 accounted for more than half of the serious crime. Responsible British officials, including the governors, were at wits' end seeking a solution to the problem.[50]

The causes apparently lay outside the effective competence of policing methods. The problem was aggravated because police service by Burman constables itself afforded opportunity for illegitimate exercise of power through the use of threats and personal abuse. The traditional hierarchy of social gradations, which had provided the criteria for proper deference toward royalty, court officials, military service captains, and ordinary myo-

[49] *Ibid.*, 173–174.
[50] *Ibid.*, 175–176.

thugyi chiefs and village elders, had largely disappeared. The Buddhist Sangha, which still afforded a means of escape from economic competition as well as an avenue for achieving social distinction, was losing much of its prestige. The upper rungs of the social ladder in government service, land ownership, and business were closed to all but a select minority of Burmese. From the downward trend of social mobility in the direction of eventual equality with the despised *Kala* coolies from India, many persons developed a humiliating and intolerable sense of social degradation and personal abasement.[51]

As social status gradually disintegrated, respect for authority declined and with it the effectiveness of customary restraint on unsocial conduct. Personal prestige was sought by feats of personal daring, including the infliction of violence and the defiance of the police. The attitude of resignation characterizing the Javanese peasant before the onerous demands of village elders and regents was not shared by the spirited Burmans, who found psychological release in lawless violence. With the subsequent rise of nationalist sentiment, lawlessness tended to coalesce with political disaffection, in which all elements of the Burmese community including the monks themselves came to participate actively.

## Renaissance of Burmese Cultural Traditions

The first efforts to reaffirm the traditional values of Burmese Buddhist culture came from a small Western-trained lay group which enjoyed support from a few sympathetic Europeans. Nonclerical schools were sponsored to teach the moral tenets of Buddhism combined with a Western-type curriculum modeled on patterns of the Christian mission school. Supporting Burman societies in Moulmein, Myingyan, Mandalay, and Bassein sought to solicit school funds by advocating the curtailing of excessive expenditures on youth initiatory ceremonies, new pagoda construction, funerals, and marriages. These efforts elicited only a limited response. Monastic schools usually refused to accept any modification of the traditional curriculum. They would not employ teachers for new subjects and refused to keep essential records of attendance and achievement or to accept the oversight of school inspectors. Government-sponsored secular schools eventually filled the gap. Whereas the government-recognized monastic schools outnumbered the lay schools almost 5 to 1 in 1891–1892, government secular schools were in a bare majority by 1910, and in a 60 per cent majority by 1917.

Another expression of the lay revival of Buddhist values was the Young Men's Buddhist Association, organized in 1906. Its objective was to refashion valuable elements of the Buddhist tradition in the context of the best Western learning and standards. The association was neither traditionalist nor antiquarian, and its leadership included several able men of Euro-

[51] *Ibid.,* 177.

pean education. Although at first primarily a student affair devoted to the discussion of religious subjects, the association developed branches in a number of urban centers, which were interested in Burmese art and literature as well. From the outset the organization was suspected in conservative government circles. A General Council of Buddhist Associations began to meet in annual sessions during the course of the second decade of the century. The tendency to shift the topic of discussion to forbidden political subjects was successfully resisted at first, but the political-minded elements eventually found expression. At the close of World War I, the GCBA emerged as an important spokesman for the educated Burmese laity.[52]

A strictly nonpolitical approach to the study of Burmese history and culture was initiated by the Burma Research Society. It was organized in 1909 by a British settlement officer, John S. Furnivall, with the aid of the professor of Pali at the Rangoon University and one of the Burmese sponsors of the YMBA. The society was expressly enjoined from discussing economic as well as political questions so that interested members of the civil service would be free to participate. Its field of interest included all aspects of Burma's cultural history—literature, religion, arts, music, drama, and folklore. Its actual appeal was limited to a relatively small group of Burmese and British, but it provided a meeting place and a medium of expression in its *Journal* for those who shared a sympathetic interest in the preservation and development of Burmese culture.[53]

The Buddhist lay school movement, the YMBA, and the Burma Research Society were all eventually outflanked by more radical expressions of nationalist revival. Events overtook the constructive endeavors of the moderate leaders of the westernized elite long before they had time to realize their objectives. Developments in India, particularly those connected with the Gandhian movement following World War I, forced the pace unduly. Within the time afforded it was simply not possible to achieve an adequate adjustment between an inescapable tradition and the new order relentlessly imposed by contacts with the outside world.[54]

The effects of the intensification of the Western influence upon the Burmans were strikingly different from those in Siam and Indonesia. In Siam, the symbols of governmental and social authority remained unimpaired. The court itself took the initiative in the westernizing process, enlisting the advice and assistance of foreign experts but channeling the currents of change within the boundaries set up by customary law. Because the vitality of the traditional order continued intact, Siam was less hostile to the influence of missionary endeavor, to foreign-language training, and to westernization than was Burma. The Siamese developed no comparable

[52] *Ibid.*, 180.
[53] *Ibid.*, 181.
[54] *Ibid.*, 182.

xenophobia against Indians and Europeans. Economic improvement in Siam was slower but less disruptive and overpowering than in Burma. Community and family ties in Siam remained strong, the monkhood was disciplined and respected, the moneylender and trader were less predatory and powerful.

In Java also the desa village unit remained a closely knit community, secure in its possession of the land and functioning under customary adat law. Crime and court litigation were not serious problems. The application of the Gatherings in Java under the "gentle pressure" of Dutch supervisors may have been debilitating, but it did educate social demand and had its democratic aspects. Peasant debt in Java was softened by government-operated pawnshops and peoples' banks, and by the prohibition of land alienation to foreigners. Clerical unrest was relatively slight; complaints against abuses of authority got a ready hearing; and official corruption was apparently less widespread than in Burma. The Javanese, like the Siamese, supplied most of the labor required for economic expansion, while the Burmese did not.

The Burma system left the people freer to err and also to act constructively as individuals except insofar as they fell under the bondage of unrestrained economic forces and an alien, impersonal law. Educational opportunity was more widely available in Burma than in Java and the trend was correspondingly greater to come to grips culturally with Western governmental and social concepts. Burmese eventually were accorded a far greater role in the central government than were the Javanese. One major grievance of the Burmese against British rule was connected with political association with India, a relationship which persisted until 1937. The country was open to an annual coolie invasion and to the free operation of Indian merchants and moneylenders, all of whom were protected by British-Indian government and law. British administration was arbitrarily efficient in its imposition of improvements, but the multiplicity of governmental services, often serving needs little understood by the people, became to the Burmese villagers a nuisance from which they would gladly be free.[55]

[55] Furnivall, 262–275.

# CHAPTER 18

# Vietnam

## and French Indochina

$V$ietnam was the last of the important states of Southeast Asia to be brought within the expanding circle of European control. French interest in the country was of long standing, going back to the original sponsor of the Missions Étrangères, Alexander of Rhodes, in the seventeenth century and the almost-continuous subsequent history of Catholic missionary connections. The influence of Pigneau de Behaine and the coterie of French officers associated with him in helping to establish the Nguyen dynasty of Gia Long during the 1790s carried over into the second decade of the 1800s. Two French mandarins of high rank were still at Hué in 1819. By the time the French government succeeded in establishing diplomatic connections with Hué in 1821, the friendly Gia Long had died and conservative Confucianists and nationalists dominated the court. Pressures for treaty relations from both the British and French were rebuffed by the new ruler, who inaugurated in 1825 a policy of harassment of Christian missionaries and their converts. Persecution of Christians became violent after 1833, developing into a feud between King Minh Mang and French missionary leaders, who solicited the aid of French naval vessels visiting Eastern Asia.

Official French concern modulated to overt intervention during the time of Louis Napoleon, when a French foothold was obtained in Saigon and adjacent areas. The eventual extension of French control throughout all of Vietnam, Cambodia, and Laos entailed difficulties with the Chinese and the government of Siam. At the outset, national-prestige considerations rather than economic interests were behind the French imperialist endeavor. Systematic development of governmental administration and the exploitation of economic resources began on a mercantilist basis after 1897. Although French scholarship contributed remarkably to the study of the history and culture of the regions within Indochina, the official French policy of cultural assimilation and imperial domination did not help the Vietnamese in particular to make essential adjustments to economic and political contacts with the Western world.

## Vietnam under Gia Long and Minh Mang

Experienced observers who visited Vietnam in the 1820s were impressed with the evidences of a mature civilization. As the humble and distant imitators of the Chinese, the Vietnamese were adjudged to have attained the highest level of culture of any Southeast Asian people. They produced silk textiles and porcelain on the Chinese pattern, as well as cotton cloth. They were also expert in the manufacture of metal objects, especially brassware. The people were described as small of stature, mild-mannered, good-humored and talkative, and not awed in the least by the sight of European visitors. Family relations followed the Chinese model. As the priest of the ancestor cult, the father exercised complete control of his household. Village communities were viable social and economic entities, controlling on a cooperative basis the use of the land and the maintenance of irrigation facilities. The mandarin administration was described as less despotic and oppressive than was government elsewhere in the region, being limited in Vietnam by customary usages of long standing. The visitor observed also that the Chinese-type culture deteriorated as one proceeded southward from Tongking. Cambodian neighbors were regarded by the Vietnamese as outright barbarians, and the Siamese were considered offensively vain. Chinese weights and measures were used only in Tongking and Annam.[1]

Negative aspects of Vietnam society, as reported in 1820, included widespread poverty and disease, which were especially evident in the south and in the hilly areas. In Tongking and upper Annam, the ricelands were so intensively cultivated that the propagation of the malaria-carrying mosquito (*Anopheles*) was inhibited. This was not the case in the less fully developed lands of Cochin-China or in the "slash and burn" areas of the mountainous hinterland.[2] Only in areas adjacent to and within the Mekong delta in the south had Chinese immigrants intruded in the state. Communications were almost entirely by water, along the coastline and via interior canals. But the seafaring population of the lower coasts, where the soil was thin and barren, was wretchedly impoverished. Conscription for both *corvée* labor and military service was imposed on males from sixteen to sixty years of age, subject to customary regulations. Justice was for sale, and the rich attacked the poor with impunity. Opium addiction and lack of cleanliness added to the general incidence of poverty and disease.[3]

---

[1] John Crawfurd, *Journal of an Embassy to the Courts of Siam and Cochin-China* (1828), 482–497.

[2] Pierre Gourou, *The Tropical World: Its Social and Economic Conditions* (1958), 100.

[3] Crawfurd, 496–497; George Finlayson, *The Mission to Siam and Hué* (1826), 325–339; Jean Chesneaux, *Contribution de l'histoire de la nation vietnamienne* (1955), 82–83.

In Vietnam as in neighboring Cambodia and Siam, nobility and mandarin status deteriorated one grade with each generation unless renewed by royal preferment. Both military and civilian mandarins were posted in every province. Each province was divided into several regional departments, and they in turn were divided into prefectures, all mandarin-ruled.

The son of J. B. Chaigneau, one of the surviving French mandarins, has afforded a picture of life of a high official in the capital city. The elder Chaigneau was accorded a fifty-man guard for his residence quarters and house servants to match such elevated political status. The house was roofed with Chinese tiles, furnished tastefully, and equipped for the staging of large formal receptions and the entertainment of guests. Separate quarters were provided for the women. The compound-garden was decorated with flowers and palm trees and surrounded by a bamboo palisade. At court, the two French mandarins were permitted to substitute bows for the customary multiple prostrations required of all others in the presence of the king. Palace ceremonies included royal audiences, musical and theater perform-ances, dramatic ceremonials, and the annual sacrifices to earth and heaven on the part of the king. A handsome temple was dedicated to the royal ancestors. The army included an eight-hundred-animal elephant brigade; 130 elephants were assigned to the service of the royal palace.[4]

The royal city of Hué was itself a fortress stronghold, a mile and a half on a side. Its 30-foot-wide rampart was well cased with masonry and protected at the angles by protruding bastions, each defended by thirty-six guns. The exterior wall was flanked by a moat, and the inner palace citadel was protected by double ramparts. The army barracks were excellently con-structed, and the local arsenal produced guns of good workmanship and various calibers. The impressive fortifications displayed abundant evidence of the assistance afforded by French engineers in its construction. Canals connected the fortress moat with the adjacent river, and branch canals ran also inside the walls. The spacious streets of the city were laid out at right angles. The approaches to Hué by coastal corridor and canal from the nearby port of Tourane (20 miles distant) were well guarded by uniformed soldiers armed with muskets of French design. The city was adjudged in 1820 to be impregnable to attack by an Oriental army.[5]

The building of Vietnam's capital and the establishing of firm govern-mental control throughout his domain were the achievement of Gia Long. He also revived the Confucianist examination system in 1803, promulgated a new legal code in 1812, and began the centralization of the administration. He respected the Catholic faith espoused by his French friends and per-mitted the unimpeded functioning of the missionaries. These were mainly Spanish in the Tongking section and French in Annam and Cochin-China. Six Christian bishops were resident in 1820 plus a large number of indige-nous clergy, who were usually inducted into holy orders around their

[4] Michel Du'c Chaigneau, *Souvenirs de Hué* (1941), 14–44, 54–69.

[5] Crawfurd, 240–256, 343, 350, 360.

fortieth birthday. Christians numbered at the time an estimated 300,000 in Tongking and some sixty thousand in Cochin-China.[6]

Minh Mang, who took over the kingship after the death of Gia Long in January, 1820, followed in many respects the same policies. He further centralized the administration, introduced the definition of three levels of performance for the triennial examinations, reorganized the taxation system, and introduced by 1839 a program of salaries and pensions for princes and mandarins to replace the traditional assignment of fief estates. But the entire emphasis in the official examinations was Confucianist, including knowledge of the classics, prose and poetry compositions, and the memorization of edicts and laws. Partly because of the strongly traditional emphasis and partly because of distrust of the mounting political pressures, from French and British sources especially, Minh Mang turned against the French mandarin friends of his father and eventually against all Catholic missionaries and their Christian following. As a symbol of his traditionalism, Minh Mang sought investiture from Peking.[7]

## Revival of French Contacts

After several abortive efforts on the part of French naval vessels to establish contact with Hué after 1817, the objective was accomplished by a private trader from Bordeaux, Auguste Borel, in 1819. He was welcomed by the two surviving French mandarins, Chaigneau, and Vannier. This first commercial venture was moderately successful financially, and the merchant was encouraged to come again. Chaigneau and his son, Michel, returned to France with Borel for a visit with Brittany relatives whom the elder Chaigneau had not seen in thirty years.

As soon as his arrival in France was known, Chaigneau was called to Paris by the Minister of Marine, who offered him appointment as consul and Commissioner for France at Hué. Louis XVIII, in a personal appeal, made acceptance of the offer a test of Chaigneau's patriotism and capped the appointment with designation of the appointee as a Knight of St. Louis. His duties included responsibility for the safety of persons and property of French nationals in Vietnam. Returning with the same Bordeaux merchant, Borel, Chaigneau was accompanied by his son, Michel, and his nephew, Eugene Chaigneau, and also by Borel's son, Eduard. Four French missionaries and an entomologist named Diard from the Museum of Paris also were in the party. They reached Hué in early 1821.[8]

King Minh Mang was willing that French trade should continue, but he saw no need to negotiate a treaty with a country so distant as France and flatly refused to recognize Chaigneau's status as French consul. The King

[6] Chaigneau, 196–199.

[7] Lê Thanh Khôi, *Le Viet Nam* (1955), 323–332.

[8] John F. Cady, *The Roots of French Imperialism in Eastern Asia* (1954), 15–16; Chaigneau, 206–219. The Bordeaux firm was Balguerie Sarget et Cie.

was aware that if he gave concessions to one of the European powers, all would be pressing for similar privileges. A British-Indian mission of 1821 received the same negative response. But no real problem developed for several years as far as the safety of French residents generally was concerned. Chaigneau actually performed the duties of acting French consul; Borel established a warehouse at Tourane; Diard was permitted to hunt insects to his heart's content. French practices still carried prestige. After the King addressed inquiries to the European visitors concerning the style of French military uniforms, officers of the Vietnamese army appeared with epaulets. Even so, it was easy to perceive that the days of French favor at the Confucianist Court of Hué were numbered.[9]

John Crawfurd was sent to Hué by the India Company in 1821, partly to establish relations with the new ruler but mainly to look over the place and see what the French were doing. The Company mission was respectfully received at both Saigon and Hué, and the French mandarins, who acted as interpreters, were unfailingly kind, polite, and attentive to Crawfurd's needs. The mission was furnished on request with copies of the Vietnamese rules governing foreign trade, and British traders were invited to visit the three ports of Saigon, Tourane, and Faifo; Hué and Hanoi were described as restricted ports. The King nevertheless flatly refused to grant an audience to Crawfurd as the representative of a mere Company and declined to correspond or to negotiate with the governor-general of India on the basis of equality. He even refused to receive the presents brought by the mission. Crawfurd, in turn, refused to accept the King's presents, whereupon the ruler withdrew his own reply to the governor-general. Relations at the end of the mission were far from cordial.

Crawfurd nonetheless succeeded in the principal objectives of his mission. He satisfied himself that French influence was in decline and that the Indian Empire had little to gain and nothing to fear from so poor a country even if France should gain full control. Since every move of the government of India was suspect, he saw no advantage to be gained from pressing for treaty negotiations. Whereas Siam's relations could be handled with advantage through Calcutta, those with Vietnam, he thought, might better be handled directly through the Crown. The essential interests of British trade could be managed, if necessary, through Chinese junks operating out of Canton or Singapore, which would arouse no political prejudice.[10]

Events of the 1820s contributed to the anxieties of Hué. The commander of a French naval frigate pressed in vain for an audience in 1823. In 1824, Minh Mang rejected a proposed alliance with Burma against the common enemy Siam. The Anglo-Burman War which followed and the consequent British annexation of coastal areas claimed by both Siam and Burma were even more disturbing. By 1824, distrust of the Europeans was beyond all dispelling. Vannier and Chaigneau were given leave to depart

[9] Chaigneau, 223–238.

[10] Finlayson, 343, 350–360, 393–395; Crawfurd, 257–277, 306–308, 403.

for France in late 1824. They paid their final respects at the tomb of Pigneau de Behaine at Saigon on their departure. Especially alarming to Hué was the arrival during the late twenties of new French missionaries, the representatives of the ultramontane religious revival in Europe. Persecution of Christians, ostensibly for political reasons, began in 1825; churches were closed and missionary entry was officially denied. Continuing efforts to negotiate a treaty on the part of Eugene Chaigneau as representative of France were finally broken off by Hué in 1830. A visit in 1832 by an American named Roberts, who was also negotiating with Bangkok, added to the mounting pressure. The last high-ranking mandarin friend of the missionaries died in 1832.

Relations between Hué and the French residents of Vietnam deteriorated in a downward spiral of cause and effect during a period of civil unrest involving alleged missionary complicity. A carryover from the Tay-son rebellion occurred in 1826–1827. A Siamese invasion of Cambodia claimed Minh Mang's attention in 1833, as did a rebellion in the south led by the son of a former Marshal of the Left, who had been a friend of Gia Long and Pigneau. The rebel's solicitation of French aid was discovered, and missionary interests near Saigon suffered accordingly. Minh Mang thereupon required all missionaries to assemble at the capital, where they were held as virtual prisoners. Some managed to escape; execution and banishment of the recalcitrant began. Seven French and three Spanish missionaries lost their lives from 1833 to 1840. In the latter year, the King began to adopt a more conciliatory attitude, probably in view of events connected with the Opium War.[11] Christian leadership in Tongking tended in time to align itself with disaffected political elements in connection with the old Lê dynasty. Hué's imposition of more repressive measures provoked in turn more local disaffection and recurring French naval demonstrations.

## *The Missionary Feud with Minh Mang*

The vigorous Catholic revival which characterized the post-Napoleonic period in Europe found expression in the daring missionary penetration of various countries of the Orient, including Vietnam. The missionaries accepted personal risks and sacrifices, were contemptuous of any political barriers imposed, and were also oblivious to the feeling of local alarm which their aggressive actions might arouse. The restored Bourbon government of Louis XVIII assisted in 1816 the reestablishment of the Paris Missionary Society and the Lazarist Society. Both of them resumed their extensive prerevolutionary activity in Eastern Asia. Renewed interest in missionary activity among the clergy of France was matched in the layman-sponsored Agency for the Propagation of the Faith, started in 1829, also predominantly French in character.

The reactionary trend in the Church which marked the reign of

[11] Chaigneau, 230–238; Lê Thanh Khôi, 333–336, 340–343; Cady, 16–17.

Charles X was reversed somewhat in 1830 by some fast footwork on the part of liberal elements within the French clergy. Liberal sentiments were stronger among the mission-sponsoring groups than within the hierarchy of the bishops. Thus a foundation was laid for a partial accommodation between the French Church and the new Orleanist regime of Louis Philippe.[12] It was one of the ironies of nineteenth-century history that the anticlerical Orleanist monarchy should lay the foundation of French colonial intrusion into Southeast Asia by establishing the presumption that France was the protector of Catholic missionaries throughout the Orient. This development was more the product of events than the result of any deliberate decision of the Paris authorities.

The period from 1830 to 1848 witnessed the rapid expansion of French missionary activity in Vietnam despite the absence of official French support and the imposition of the repressive policies of King Minh Mang. Missionaries found the entry into Tongking from Macao fairly easy; officials could be bribed, and concealment in disaffected areas was readily possible. Papal recognition of the primacy of the French Church in Oriental missions came in 1839, when by concordat agreement with Lisbon, the Portuguese "right of patronage" was formally abolished. The Paris Missionary Society was assigned responsibility for a half-dozen vicariates in the Indochina area. They shared Tongking with the Spanish Dominicans operating from Manila. French naval officers on duty in the Orient could not ignore the presence of their missionary nationals since they provided virtually the only tangible evidence of French interest in the region. Missionary personnel on their part welcomed the periodic visits of French naval vessels to the Vietnam coast.[13]

A move which might have broken this vicious circle of rising tension was Minh Mang's abortive effort in 1840 to negotiate at Paris by sending a diplomatic mission consisting of two negotiators and two interpreters. Their arrival in France in November, 1840, afforded opportunity for spokesmen of the seminary of the Missions Étrangères to publicize the harsh treatment suffered by its representatives in Vietnam during previous years. The timid Louis Philippe bowed to clerical pressure in refusing to grant an audience to the visiting embassy. What settlement might have been negotiated is not known. But after having rebuffed a Vietnamese effort to negotiate differences, Prime Minister Guizot, himself a Protestant, flatly refused to acknowledge any obligation on the part of France to protect adventurous Catholic missionaries even though they might be of French nationality. Any prospect of achieving a moderation of Vietnamese policy regarding missionaries, forestalled in any case by the hostility exhibited by them at Paris, was completely dispelled when Minh Mang died in January, 1841, and was succeeded by the far more anti-European King Thieu Tri.[14]

[12] Cady, 28–38
[13] *Ibid.,* 23–26.
[14] *Ibid.,* 32–33.

## *The Basilan Episode*

When Prime Minister Guizot sent the Lagrené mission to China in 1843 to negotiate a French treaty following the Opium War, he authorized naval commanders to afford only such protection of French missionaries as they might be able to give without compromising the French flag. Lagrené was also directed to acquire a territorial foothold at Basilan Island in the Sulu Sea, so that French vessels would no longer be dependent on the hospitality of the Portuguese, the British, or the Dutch. If conditions were found to be favorable, Lagrené was authorized to negotiate a provisional political agreement with the local chiefs or with the sovereign whom they acknowledged. Secrecy was enjoined in view of the expected hostility of the British to any such French move. The possibility of Spanish objection was apparently not anticipated.[15]

The project miscarried badly. On the occasion of the first visit of the French Admiral Cecille to the island with two corvettes in October, 1844, five French sailors who had gone ashore were kidnapped. The French were obliged to ask assistance of the Spanish from Zamboanga in their rescue attempt. Two of the men were later found killed; the other three were ransomed for some 3,000 piasters. The borrowed Spanish gunboat bombarded the palisaded capital of the offending chief, but the Europeans had to withdraw when the tide fell. A second French campaign of seven weeks' duration, using flat-bottom boats obtained at Manila, resulted in the signing of a convention with the Sulu chief acknowledging prospective French proprietorship over the island in return for a promised payment of 100,000 dollars within six months. Admiral Cecille's fleet finally proceeded to Singapore and Batavia before returning to Macao in July, 1845.[16]

The Basilan affair was a damaging blow to French prestige. The expedition had nothing to show for the considerable sums expended and for the humiliation it had suffered at the hands of a minor Sulu chief. Manila protested via Madrid against the French invasion of territory allegedly tributary to Spain. The British were perturbed and mildly amused at the humiliating outcome. The whole undertaking was promptly repudiated by Guizot, who declared that the island was not suitable physically as a base and would be of little help to French shipping in any case.[17]

## *Increased Tension in Indochina*

Prior to the Basilan expedition, both Lagrené and Cecille had received direct appeals from French missionaries in Tongking to intervene in their behalf. A sustained naval demonstration at Tourane or off the

[15] *Ibid.,* 44–45.
[16] *Ibid.,* 57–58.
[17] *Ibid.,* 59.

Tongking coast, it was alleged, would encourage disaffected partisans of the old Lê dynasty friendly to the missionaries to challenge Hué's control. Missionaries argued that, once installed, the new Lê ruler would give France the desired naval base in addition to missionary concessions. In transmitting the appeal back to the Minister of Marine in Paris, Admiral Cecille suggested the desirability of a visit by a Lê representative to Macao or even to Paris to negotiate for French aid. Lagrené was dubious over the probable negative British reaction, but he envisaged a French Tongking as a possible alternative to Basilan. To all such proposals, Prime Minister Guizot gave a flatly negative reply.[18]

King Thieu Tri's hostility was meanwhile aggravated by periodic visits to Tourane by several arrogant French captains. Five condemned missionaries were rescued by them in 1842, as was Bishop Lefebvre in 1845. While the bishop was waiting at Singapore for a chance to return to Vietnam, the local British governor allegedly offered to repatriate him by steamer if he would await the results of contemplated British negotiations at Hué in behalf of religious freedom. Lefebvre's preference to return on his own and to risk a second arrest was hailed by French clerics as an example of patriotic self-denial designed to block British political designs. In 1847, two French naval vessels, one of them commanded by Captain (later Admiral and Minister of Marine) Rigault de Genouilly, took more vigorous action. When they experienced difficulty in obtaining a reply to their letter demanding an end to Christian persecution, they destroyed the native fleet and the harbor forts at Tourane. Rigault was destined to lead the subsequent futile attack on Tourane, in 1858–1859. Thieu Tri responded by offering to pay a reward for the murder of any Europeans within his domain. Soon thereafter he fell mortally ill and was unable to communicate with the more friendly British mission which arrived to negotiate in October, 1847. He died in November.[19]

The increasing agitation in 1847 and early 1848 for sustained French diplomatic action at Hué, coming from Missions Étrangères sources both at Paris and in Tongking, was cut short by the overthrow of the Orleanist dynasty in February, 1848. For some four years thereafter, Paris completely lost interest in East Asian affairs because of overriding political concerns nearer home. Things got worse in Annam. A disgruntled brother of Tu Duc, the new Hué ruler, withdrew to Tongking and eventually headed a short-lived rebellion in 1851. In successive edicts of 1848 and 1851, King Tu Duc decreed the end of all Christianizing efforts and revived the offer of rewards for the killing of Europeans. The missionaries were obliged to go completely underground. Native priests were branded and exiled; two French missionaries were executed in 1851 and a bishop in 1852. Any remedial measures from France had to await the consolidation of Louis

[18] *Ibid.,* 59–60.
[19] *Ibid.,* 73–76.

Napoleon's control and the determination of his policies. Meanwhile Vietnamese nationalism profited from the increasing use of the vernacular language and script in displacement of Chinese, especially in poetry and drama. French intrusion in 1859 apparently cut short a promising development of Vietnamese nationalist culture.[20]

## Louis Napoleon's Decision to Intervene

The Prince-President's susceptibility to Catholic propagandist pressure developed largely from his determination to deny to his Legitimatist political enemies of the Right the backing of the French Church. He restored and protected the Papacy in Rome and turned education in France over to the clergy as the price of their support. He was equally concerned, as the heir of the Napoleonic tradition, with reestablishing French prestige in the world. During the first decade of his regime, he was able to act abroad only in collaboration with his British ally, notably in the Crimean War and in the Anglo-French effort to obtain a revision of the treaties with China. It was the China war which finally afforded him the opportunity to transfer substantial naval and military contingents to the Orient, to be used between innings in the China affair to succor missionary interests in Vietnam and secure a territorial foothold.

The concerted clerical campaign to enlist the armed intervention of France in the affairs of Vietnam was resumed in mid-1852. It came directly on the heels of the news that a second French bishop had been executed. The supporting documents were prepared by eight missionary bishops in the Orient and by French diplomatic representatives at Macao assisted by Father Libois of the Missions Étrangères. The contemptuous treatment being accorded to French missionaries by the Vietnamese state, a petty vassal of China, was denounced as damaging to the honor and prestige of France throughout Eastern Asia, where Catholic influence would always be the measure of French influence. The guilty rulers of Hué themselves reportedly expected retribution, and civilization generally would applaud the Prince-President in an act of humanity in his punishment of such petty sovereigns for their criminal actions. The acquisition of the harbor of Tourane could be obtained either by negotiation or by seizure if necessary, as a means of establishing the toleration of Christianity and the security of European missionaries in Vietnam.[21]

Louis Napoleon's affirmative decision to restore French dignity in the Far East elicited a spate of supporting official memoranda in Paris. The Ministry of Marine pledged enthusiastic cooperation. Tourane was described as a great prize, a valuable entrepôt in time of peace, a useful base in war, a populous and productive center of French influence capable of replacing the miserable remnants of a once-great French Empire in India. Various

[20] *Ibid.*, 79–80; Chesneaux, 97–102.
[21] Cady, 93–99.

considerations postponed action for half a decade, when the issue had to be argued out again. The Taiping rebellion in China presented one diversion, and adequate French naval resources were simply not available in any case until after the conclusion of the Crimean War in 1856.[22] Meanwhile the fiasco of the Montigny negotiations in 1856–1857 at Bangkok, at Campot in Cambodia, and at Hué (described in Chapter 15) reduced French prestige in the area to an all-time low. King Tu Duc's spokesmen at Hué boasted that the French barked like dogs but ran away like goats.[23] Dynastic and naval prestige were thus added as supporting considerations to the agitation of the clergy in favor of intervention.

## The Tourane-Saigon Expedition

Emperor Louis Napoleon decided to take advantage of French participation in the China war of 1858–1860 to acquire a foothold in Vietnam. The original instructions for the expedition, formulated in Paris before receipt of the news of the dismal results of the Montigny negotiation, reserved for later decision the role which Admiral Rigault de Genouilly's fleet should play on the coast of Annam. But the selection of Genouilly as the naval commander was itself indicative of the Emperor's interest in Indochina. Napoleon III in 1857 made himself easily accessible to clerical proponents of intervention and preferred their advice to the negative recommendations made by his own Foreign Office. Some argued that France could claim Tourane under the never-executed 1787 treaty of Pigneau de Behaine, adding that the Vietnamese would welcome French deliverance and turn Catholic. Monsignor Pellerin was more convincing in his disclosure, in a personal interview with the Emperor, of the dire consequences which had followed Montigny's fiasco at Tourane. Little account was apparently taken at Paris of Admiral Genouilly's own warnings that the coercion of Hué would be no easy task and that a substantial force including engineers and artillery would be required.[24] Nor was any attention paid to the far-from-secret information that Tourane harbor had an evil reputation on health grounds.[25] The problems involved were simply never realistically considered at Paris.

It was decided at the last moment to associate the Spanish with the Tourane expedition, since the missionary interests of the Spanish Dominicans were also heavily involved in Tongking. Spanish participation contributed a kind of international character to the affair and also provided a friendly base at Manila from which the French navy could operate. A total of one thousand troops from the Philippines participated during the early

[22] *Ibid.*, 100–101.
[23] *Ibid.*, 153–155.
[24] *Ibid.*, 168, 178–180, 215.
[25] Chaigneau, 229–230.

phases of the campaign, and these were later augmented by reinforcements. One result of Manila's aid was to establish the presumption for more than a decade that Spain had a prior claim to any European gains acquired in Tongking. From the French point of view, the entire operation was an affair not of the Foreign Office but of the Ministry of Marine; Genouilly, who was raised to the rank of vice-admiral on the eve of the operation, commanded both his own and the Spanish forces.[26]

The expedition got under way during the late summer of 1858, following the conclusion of the treaties of Tientsin at the end of the first phase of the China war. The fourteen French ships, including five transports, reached Tourane on August 31, only six or seven weeks before the onset of the winter monsoon rains. Preparations were far from adequate. Only two thousand French troops, many of them African, were available for shore duty. Flat-bottomed boats capable of traversing the rivers and canals were lacking, as well as bridging and other land transport facilities needed for artillery. Precious weeks, during which an attack on Hué might possibly have been undertaken, were lost because a native informer recruited by the accompanying Father Pellerin gave false information concerning an imaginary attack about to be launched by ten thousand Vietnamese troops. A much-needed indigenous labor force promised to Genouilly by the missionaries also failed to appear, and no popular risings occurred, as had been prophesied, in the Christian pro-Lê areas of the north.

Even before the onset of the winter rains, around October 20, the climate had begun to take a deadly toll. The sun was murderously hot; the food became contaminated and the water supply polluted. Dysentery and fever became epidemic, and finally cholera and scurvy developed. Meanwhile shelters, storerooms, and hospitals had to be constructed. By the time the first serious clash took place between the opposing forces on December 21, the French army was already so depleted in strength that minor initial successes could not be exploited. Illness and the rain inhibited any further operations. Other difficulties developed. The admiral quarreled with Monsignor Pellerin and then with his Spanish associates when he decided that the only way to salvage anything from the unhappy situation was to shift attention to Saigon in the south, where the superior French naval power could make itself felt. Neither the missionaries nor the Spanish had any interests to be served at Saigon.

The shift to Saigon was made in February, 1859. After capturing the fortresses and installing a small but well-supplied garrison, Genouilly returned to Tourane in April, 1859. Reinforcements from Europe relieved Vietnamese pressure on the garrison, but cholera quickly broke out among the new arrivals, and the French were still unable to take the initiative against the far more numerous indigenous forces. The prospect for receiving

[26] Cady, 210–211.

any additional help from France disappeared upon Napoleon III's launching of his ill-advised intervention in Italy in May, 1859. This event was followed a month later by the repulse of the European allies at the Taku fort in North China. The admiral tried in vain to negotiate with Hué and then to carry out a bluffing ultimatum threat. He held on at Tourane until October, 1859, where a successor arrived with orders to evacuate the bay. The Franco-Spanish garrison at Saigon managed to survive for another year in the face of a serious siege, until the ending of the second phase of the China war in late 1860 made possible its relief.[27]

## The Making of Peace

The problem of whether to undertake the annexation of Saigon and vicinity or to settle for mere commercial and religious guarantees was seriously pondered at Paris. The discouraged Emperor was ready to scuttle the whole affair. Only Admiral Genouilly's arrival in Paris and the eventual accession as Minister of Marine of the aggressive Chasseloup-Laubat at the end of 1860 turned the decision the other way. Admiral Charner's largely naval relief expedition arriving from China in 1861 cleared the environs of Saigon, but his forces immediately suffered losses from illness. The perimeter of control was further extended when the main body of French army contingents from China plus reinforcements from Manila arrived in April, 1861. Key points in three adjacent provinces were occupied. When initial efforts at negotiation made no progress, the French commander simply announced unilaterally in July, 1861, the annexation to France of Saigon and its environs. The Spanish commander thereupon demanded that control be shared jointly or that France assist in obtaining a comparable foothold for Spain in Tongking. The controversy was shifted to Europe, where Spain finally gave up the contest, emerging in the end empty-handed.[28]

The Hué authorities finally agreed to negotiate with the French mainly as a consequence of the long-delayed outbreaks of rebellion in Tongking. They feared French or Spanish participation if peace was not made. Partisans of the Lê pretender, with Christian Vietnamese support, rose in the spring of 1862 and again in August. The treaty which was signed on June 5, with both European commanders participating, granted to France the control of three Cochin-China provinces plus the island of Poulo Condore, the opening of three ports, freedom of religion, French priority with respect to any future territorial alienations, and an indemnity of 2.8 million taels of silver (4 million piasters). When the Franco-Spanish feuding later came to light, Hué attempted to hold up ratification of the treaty. Thereupon, the allies closed ranks and issued a joint ultimatum in November, 1862, threatening to aid the rebels. They then repelled a final counter-

[27] *Ibid.,* 212–219.
[28] *Ibid.,* 222–223, 268–272.

attack on Saigon. Arrival in February, 1863, of the final contingents of French African and Algerian troops from China and about eight hundred more men from Manila turned the tide and forced Hué's ratification of the treaty in April.[29]

The Vietnamese government made one more diplomatic effort to recover legal control of the Cochin-China provinces. It took advantage of the early difficulties which the admiral-governors encountered at Saigon as a result of their inability to use the ex-mandarins as ruling officials. The former mandarins actually enjoyed no authority in their own right apart from royal authentication, and were lacking in both capacity and inclination to serve the French. The attractive proposal made by a Vietnamese diplomat at Paris was that France should undertake to administer only the three key points of Saigon, Cholon, and Cape St. Jacques and be content with exercising a mere protectorate over the six major provinces of Cochin-China. Hué would pay France a quarter-million-franc tribute annually and concede full French commercial access as well as religious toleration. The treaty was accepted and signed by Louis Napoleon in June, 1864, but it aroused such a storm of protest from naval partisans and other imperialist advocates that the decision was reversed in the following year. The original treaty stood as ratified. The navy assumed thereafter a kind of proprietary interest in the Indochina enterprise.[30]

## The Expansion of French Holdings

In the meantime, naval personnel who were left in charge at Saigon adopted aggressive measures on their own initiative with respect to Cambodia. They had no grievances to correct, for Father Miche and his assistants had not been mistreated. The assumption that the new European arrivals at Saigon had fallen heir to the age-old Vietnamese suzerainty status as regarded Cambodia was a bit premature if not entirely gratuitous. Considerations supporting the imperialist urge were explained by a private French visitor to Cambodia in 1858. He was convinced that the regeneration of Cambodia from its deplorable and defenseless condition could best be accomplished by French control. Slavery would be abolished and peace and security established, and France would thus add another jewel to its crown. It could also find in Vietnam an alternative source for cotton, minerals, tobacco, and sugar. He summed up the case by affirming his desire that "France . . . may be loved, respected, and honoured in the Extreme Orient, as it should be everywhere."[31]

Governor de la Grandière acted to secure the initial treaty at Phnom

[29] *Ibid.*, 268–273; Lê Thanh Khôi, 366–372.

[30] Cady, 274–275; A. L. Moffat, *Mongkut* (1961), 113–117.

[31] Henri Mouhot, *Travels in the Central Parts of Indo-China* (1864), I, 272–277.

Penh in August, 1863. A naval officer, Doudart de Lagrée, visited King Norodom and, with the aid of Father Miche, influenced the King to sign a secret agreement with France conceding French control of Cambodia's foreign relations, the establishment of French consular posts, and the acceptance of a French Resident at the capital. In return, France would undertake to protect Cambodia against Siam's presumed overlordship.

Only the exercise of strong naval pressure at Paris persuaded the reluctant Louis Napoleon to approve the treaty, and subsequently only the threat of actual physical harm to the pacific King Norodom by Lagrée, pistol in hand, forced Cambodia's final ratification. The King's earlier plans to obtain investiture from Bangkok were canceled, and he was crowned by the French instead in June, 1864. King Norodom's vassalage relationship to Siam was thus erased. In July, 1867, Saigon authorities obtained from Siam the recognition of French suzerainty over Cambodia in return for explicit French recognition that the provinces of Battambang and Siemreap (Angkor) belonged to Siam. During the same year, with Rigault de Genouilly acting as Minister of Marine, Admiral de la Grandière at Saigon assumed control over the three remaining provinces of Cochin-China, allegedly to prevent Vietnamese interference in the affairs of Cambodia.[32]

Advocacy of reform measures by a progressive minority at Hué, calculated to meet the rising French threat, ran aground on the shoals of mandarin conservatism. The most promising proposals came from a young Catholic Vietnamese, Nguyen Truong To, who returned from a visit to France and Italy in 1863. Over the next several years he prepared a series of memoranda recommending modernizing reforms similar to those being followed by Siam. Vietnam should cooperate on equal terms with all foreign powers, reducing interior-trade imposts but taxing tobacco, opium, and alcohol and affording tariff protection to new industries. Corruption should be curbed by reducing the number of state officials and by raising salaries of those retained. The army should be reorganized and strategic roadways constructed. Most important of all, the spokesman would enlist Europeans to aid the development of agriculture, industry, trade, and mining, abandon the use of the Chinese script, and translate selected European works in science. Nguyen Truong To succeeded to the extent that he himself was sent to France in 1866 to purchase mining machinery. But time ran out on his endeavors. When the admirals took over Cambodia and the remainder of Cochin-China in 1867, conservative mandarins again assumed complete ascendency at Hué, succeeding thereafter in hiding political realities from the King. Subsequent reforming proposals made in 1879–1881, again citing Siam's example and Japan's successful appropriation of Western methods, were but voices in the wilderness. Vietnam like Burma thus became a casualty of history.[33]

[32] Cady, 275–276, 279.
[33] Lê Thanh Khôi, 362–365.

## Naval Monopoly of Imperialistic Concern in Indochina

The complete unconcern of Emperor Louis Napoleon for the Cochin-China venture after 1861 was characteristic of the French attitude in general during the later sixties and throughout the succeeding decade. The undertaking became associated with fading dynastic prestige, which was not a matter of great popular interest in France. Cochin-China had little or no relevance to missionary interests, and the Missions Étrangères in any case were completely estranged from the Ministry of Marine, especially after 1867, when Rigault de Genouilly became Minister. The unfortunate French fiasco in Mexico was later associated in the popular mind with Saigon as an example of what not to do in scattering limited French forces all over the world in the face of Bismarck's assertion of German hegemony in Europe. News of the expansion of French protection over all of Cochin-China in 1867, for example, aroused no enthusiasm whatever in France. French trade to the Orient was virtually nil and the costs at Saigon were high. The eventual collapse of European France in 1871 discouraged further dissipation of effort overseas. The dominant personality in French foreign policy during the early years of the Third Republic was the Duc de Broglie, a convinced anti-imperialist.[34]

Naval concern for the promotion of French imperialist interests in Southeast Asia found expression at Paris not only in the Ministry of Marine and of Colonies but also in the privately sponsored Paris Geographical Society. Its president was Chasseloup-Laubat, Minister of Marine until 1867, when Genouilly took over the post. It was this society, in cooperation with Governor de la Grandière of Saigon, which sponsored the Lagrée-Garnier expedition to explore the Mekong Valley in 1866–1868. Doudart de Lagrée had distinguished himself in the assertion of the French protectorate over Cambodia, and his younger associate, Francis Garnier, was an equally ardent imperialist. Both were naval officers. The expedition traversed the entire lower and middle reaches of the Mekong River and exited via the Yangtse Valley in China. Lagrée died en route, and Garnier returned to make the final report.

The publication at Paris of Garnier's magnificent two-volume *Voyage d'Exploration en Indochine* in 1873 was sponsored by Rigault de Genouilly. It revealed among other things that the Mekong Valley was unsuitable as a trade channel to western China and that the only really feasible entry was via the Red River Valley of Tongking. If France hoped to compete with the rival British in developing trade with Yunnan, it would have to be through Tongking, hitherto acknowledged to be a kind of sphere of influence of Spain, which had been treated so shabbily in 1859–1861. Garnier prophesied that the opening of the Red River route would

[34] Cady, 277, 279.

make of Saigon an entrepôt rivaling Shanghai in importance. The unquestioned superiority of French culture over that of the peoples of Indochina was, in Garnier's opinion, an added reason why France must not shirk its *mission civilisatrice* in this part of the world. He concluded that if France hoped to avoid national decadence, to absorb constructively the abundant energies of its people, and to forestall the threatening Anglo-Saxon domination of the world, it must be present at all points of the globe. The dominant theme was comprised of personal ambition, manifest destiny, and national pride, buttressed by rivalry with Britain.[35]

Following the completion of his book, Garnier resigned his naval commission and returned to central China. In August, 1873, he was called from Shanghai by Admiral Dupré, governor of Saigon, to take over a daring project in Tongking. The critical situation in North Vietnam had been created by Jean Dupuis, a French merchant in China and an acquaintance of Garnier, who was attempting to open trade with Yunnan. Dupuis had received in Paris some official encouragement from the navy for his venture, but the French government had refused to accept any part of the risk, expense, or liability.

In his dual role as mandarin of the Chinese governor of Yunnan and as a French national, Dupuis forced his way down the Red River and back again with a cargo of arms between late 1872 and March, 1873. He later returned to Hanoi by the same route in May with a 150-man Chinese escort, but was held up this time when he attempted to go back upstream with a cargo of salt. Requests for aid from both Hué and from Dupuis sent to Governor Dupré afforded the opportunity for French intervention. Garnier was accompanied in the proposed "mediation" by threescore fellow adventurers. By seizing Hanoi, Dupré hoped at a minimum to generate sufficient leverage at Hué to force the court to ratify French claims to the protectorate over Cambodia and control over all of Cochin-China, both of which claims had gone unrecognized since 1867.[36]

The outcome of the attempted coup at Hanoi was disastrous to Garnier and Dupuis and to the Christian villagers in Tongking, whose simultaneous risings appeared to be something more than coincidental. The adventurers seized the citadel at Hanoi, but Garnier was killed in a subsequent clash with a Black Flag pirate mercenary band. Dupuis lost temporarily both his vessels and his cargo, and the Christian villages were burned. In view of the negative attitude of the Paris government toward the whole affair, the governor had to disavow Garnier's tactics and to settle for a treaty with Hué acknowledging French sovereignty over all of Cochin-China and for the opening of the Red River route to trade. King Tu Duc undertook subsequently to evade the treaty's implications of French suzerainty

---

[35] Garnier, *Voyage d'Exploration en Indochine* (1873), I; Cady, 281–282.
[36] Cady, 282–284.

over Vietnam by reviving, in 1877 and 1880, the sending of tributary missions to China. The three French consuls who were admitted to Tongking were rendered politically innocuous.[37]

## French Acquisition of Annam and Tongking

Minority agitation within France over the Tongking question refused to die down. Garnier became a martyr to the cause. By 1879, French enthusiasts were clamoring for a protectorate over both Tongking and Siam and for the exploration of the upper reaches of the Irrawaddy. It was not until the 1880s, however, that domestic political problems within France subsided sufficiently to permit the revival at official levels of imperialist interest in Indochina. The project of acquiring Tongking became associated with the contemporaneous interest of Britain in annexing Upper Burma. By the 1880s, also, the partitioning of Africa was well started, so that enhanced international rivalry coupled with a revival of emphasis on the *mission civilisatrice* were able to bear the principal burden of the imperialist motivation. In an effort to divert French attention from domestic political embarrassments, Jules Ferry undertook from 1881 to 1885 to make French expansion a kind of patriotic duty, while also endeavoring with little success to interest French business in the economic stakes involved. A Society of Mines was formed in 1881 to explore the excellent coal resources available near Haiphong.[38]

Events moved rapidly after 1881, when Ferry decided to reduce the coastal area of Annam to protectorate status. In pursuance of this policy and also as a move to end Chinese refusal to accept the treaty of 1874 with Hué, a French military mission headed by Commandant Rivière was sent to Hanoi in 1882. The avowed purpose was to expel Chinese intruders and to counteract the influence of the Black Flag pirates in the area. The mission seized the citadel of Hanoi and occupied the coastal province of Nam-dinh and the coal site at Hon-gay. The mission was challenged militarily, and Rivière was killed. War ensued, with China as a participant. Following French military successes at Hué in 1883, negotiations were undertaken with China at Tientsin. China eventually agreed, in May, 1884, to concede French protectorate claims to Vietnam and to evacuate Chinese forces from the province of Tongking. Then came the ambush of a French force at Bac-Le and France's commitment to a second expensive and unpopular war with China. World opinion turned sharply critical of France. Jules Ferry lost office in March, 1885, amid a chorus of accusations of treason and weakness, just as the second peace with China was signed. This time China conceded French commercial access to Yunnan under a 4 per cent tariff limitation. The treaty obtained ratification in Paris by the narrowest of margins. It was

[37] *Ibid.,* 284–288; Lê Thanh Khôi, 372–379.
[38] Cady, 291–294.

several months following Ferry's fall that the British took over the kingdom of Burma.[39]

For more than a decade after 1885, Tongking provided a club with which the hapless Ferry was belabored by French political opponents. They gloated over the difficulties encountered in administering the region and the unprofitable character of the whole Indochina venture. The French treasury had to make good the perennial annual deficits, which amounted to a total of some 40 million francs from 1887 to 1895. The outlay on Indochina since 1861 was estimated at 750 million francs. Anti-imperialists pointed to Indochina as their favorite example of the folly of expansionism.[40] The naval administrators were indeed having difficulties. Until 1891 virtually no funds were available for economic development. Cochin-China alone enjoyed an effective local administration; rebellion raged in Tongking until 1897. Not until 1897 did Indochina vacate its unenviable status as the place where French colonial performance reached its nadir.[41]

## *The Rule of the Admirals*

The pattern of administration which developed in Cochin-China was a form of direct rule by European officials. The top-level posts were filled with French naval officers and the intermediate ranks with direct transfers from the home civil service personnel. A few of the latter had enjoyed previous experience in Algeria, where assimilation with France was the prevailing policy. There was much of nepotism in selecting the appointees and far too little familiarity with local institutions and language. French officialdom at Saigon tried to develop direct relations with the chiefs of the communes without reference to intermediate native officials or local institutions. The system had scarcely become effective in Cochin-China by 1885 and could not possibly be extended to the newly acquired Annam and Tongking.

The score of Residents-General who served Indochina for short terms between 1884 and 1891 followed no concerted policy. Some gains were made in 1886 during the short seven-month incumbency of Paul Bert, who began to use ex-mandarin officials along customary lines together with an extralegal Assembly of Notables. He discovered how much the Tongkingese disliked Annamese officials, but he died in office before important adjustments could be made. The China border areas remained under military control; much of Tongking continued in a state of rebellion, while coastal Annam was passively uncooperative. Cambodia was ruled indirectly as a protectorate, with little or no attempt on the part of the naval officers in control

[39] Stephen H. Roberts, *History of French Colonial Policy (1870–1925)* (1929), II, 419–433. France employed in Tongking an army of seventeen thousand in 1883–1884.

[40] Roberts, I, 22–26; Alleyne Ireland, *Far Eastern Tropics* (1905), 146–151.

[41] Roberts, II, 433.

to improve governmental administration or to develop economic interests.

The affairs of Indochina for a period of three decades were managed by the French Department of Marine and of Colonies, with the Department of Commerce and the Foreign Office sharing some of the responsibility from time to time. If the French Empire had consisted only of coastal enclaves, the navy might have been a proper agency for administration, but the navy proved unable in Indochina to devise a system of control attuned to varying local needs or to develop coherent economic objectives. The only item of policy on which general agreement prevailed was the mercantilist assumption that colonies in general should serve the advantage of the metropole. With no French capital clamoring for investment opportunities and with chronic deficits met quite grudgingly by the French treasury, funds for economic development were simply not available down to 1891. A major step to correct this situation was taken in November, 1887, when an executive decree ruled that all four units of French Indochina should be brought under the control of a separate Minister of Colonies through a governor-general, who alone would represent the authority of the Paris government. Actually the navy was not displaced until 1894, when Special Commissioner de Lanessan became the first governor-general, bridging the shift of control. The change signified the demonstration of a more serious concern on the part of the French government.[42]

The first substantial administrative improvement was realized under de Lanessan, who arrived in 1891 entrusted with plenary powers to deal with the nearly desperate situation. France either had to exercise control or get out. Bandit pirates infested the China frontier; rebels controlled all but two coastal provinces of Tongking. The flood of functionaries from France more than absorbed the earnings realized from the rice exports of the south. De Lanessan devised a uniform system of administration for Annam and Tongking, ruling through a native mandarinate under the imperial oversight of Hué. He put the control of local militia under the mandarins as a means of restoring a semblance of order. He obtained money for railways, for port development, and for roads from loans and from local taxes. Revenues increased by almost 90 per cent during his four years of office. But the task was far from complete when he left in 1895, and the two years intervening before the arrival of Governor-General Doumer in 1897 were wasted.[43]

## French Control of Laos, 1893

Before the naval administration bowed out of the picture, it staged one more political coup, this time at the expense of Laos and Siam. The original Lao state of Lan Chang (1353 and later) had included boundaries

[42] Roberts, I, 28–29; Charles Robequain, *Economic Development of French Indochina* (1944), 9–10.

[43] Roberts, II, 437–451.

extending from the Annam cordillera and the Black River on the east and north to the watershed of the Menam system on the south and west. The state was Buddhist and Indian in its cultural orientation and was Thai in its language and leadership. Lan Chang had broken into three segments after 1697, with Vientiane in the center being ruled by a prince enjoying support from Hué, and Luang Prabang and Champassak, to the north and south respectively, under nominal vassalage to Siam. After 1778, Vientiane accepted vassalage to Siam as well as to Vietnam.

The Laotian people proper were confined almost exclusively to the valley of the Mekong River and its major tributaries in a continuous pattern of settlements. The backcountry was inhabited by a variety of hill-cultivating tribesmen, some of them akin to the Laotians, others closer to the Khmers and to peoples of South China. The Laotians proper were identical with the people of Chiengmai and Chiengrai in northwestern Siam. They used the Siamese script based on Pali and borrowed new words from the Siamese. The Laotians were sometimes mistreated by the Siamese, but they completely distrusted the Vietnamese and had little in common with them either historically or culturally.[44]

During the middle half of the nineteenth century, Siamese suzerainty in Vientiane was briefly challenged by Vietnam. After resistance was crushed, the country was largely depopulated and annexed directly to Siam by Rama III in 1836. A heritage of hatred was thus incurred. The rulers of the other two Lao kingdoms of Luang Prabang and Champassak were little more than Siamese governors after 1860.[45] When the French threat from Tongking became really serious in Luang Prabang in 1885, a Siamese army entered the state under the pretext of suppressing Chinese bandits and ended by carrying away the royal viceroy to Bangkok as a hostage.

In the 1885 agreement between Siam and France, the superior claim of the former state to Laos was recognized implicitly in Bangkok's agreement to permit France to establish a vice-consulate at Luang Prabang. This concession nevertheless proved to be an opening wedge for French control. The tactic adopted by the French consul for Laos, Auguste Pavie, was to encourage local resentment of Siamese overlordship and to organize sentiment in favor of a French protectorate. On one occasion, the consul protected the aged viceroy and his family when the Siamese forces fled before threatening Chinese bandits. This subversive effort in Laos came to a head in 1893 when the retiring French naval regime, backed by a belligerently aggressive colonial party in Paris, staged a final effort in behalf of French expansionism and prestige.[46]

The French coup was planned and executed in disregard of the legalities of the situation and with the obvious intention of annexing as

[44] Frank M. Le Bar and Adrienne Suddard, *Laos* (1960), 6–15, 37–43.
[45] *Ibid.*, 10–15.
[46] *Ibid.*, 15–16.

much territory as possible at the expense of Siam. The initial move was to assign consul Pavie to Bangkok as resident French Minister in early 1892, after he had prepared Laos for French protection. Pavie's appointment was accompanied by French feelers at London to see what objections the British would be likely to raise. When it became apparent a year later that London would probably do nothing to protect Siam's trans-Mekong territories except insofar as French action might impinge on British Burma's Kengtung claims, the French expansionists moved rapidly forward. The expulsion of two French agents from Siam in February, 1893, became the pretext for the official authorization from Paris of a demand for reparations. Pavie forthwith laid claim to the entire left bank of the Mekong River and demanded the immediate evacuation of Siamese defensive installations. Instead of responding to Siam's appeal for help, the London government counseled Bangkok's acceptance of the French requirements and supported the subsequent French demand for surrender of a captured French commander of one of the several columns invading Siam on the Mekong frontier. The next move of the navy and Pavie in July, 1893, was to send gunboats up the Menam River to Bangkok, this time in complete disregard of contrary orders from Paris, the previously agreed treaty terms, and the mild protest of the British naval commander.

From the British point of view, the European situation in 1893 warranted taking few chances. Anglo-French friction was rife in many colonial areas in Africa. France was busily cementing an alliance with Russia, Britain's enemy in Asia, and the Kaiser had just dismissed Bismarck. Only when the French raised their demands on Siam to include Luang Prabang as well as Vientiane and Champassak did Britain protest and exact from France assurances that a buffer area would be negotiated as soon as Siam had met French demands.

In the face of a French blockade of the Menam, King Chulalongkorn, broken in spirit and disillusioned, accepted the French requirements in late July, 1893. Meanwhile the French had increased their demands to include their indefinite occupation of the port of Chantabun as surety guarantee, plus Siamese evacuation of both Battambang and Siemreap and a 25-kilometer strip extending along the right bank of Mekong. French negotiators made persistent efforts thereafter to compromise further the sovereignty of Siam. Once the treaty with Siam was concluded, Minister Pavie promptly laid claim to territories in the Luang Prabang area regarded by Britain as part of Kengtung. A compromise was finally arranged in January, 1896, whereby Britain conceded that the Mekong River should be the northeastern boundary of Kengtung in return for a firm guarantee that France would not infringe Siamese control of the central Menam Valley. The whole situation continued to rankle between the European rivals until the conclusion of the Entente Cordiale of 1904.[47] France evacuated Chantabun in 1904 and gave

[47] D. G. E. Hall, *A History of South-East Asia* (1955), 603–610.

up in 1907 a measure of extraterritorial control for its Asian subjects. But Siam finally had to surrender both Battambang and Siemreap in 1907, as well as territories west of the upper Mekong, to buy peace with France.

During the course of the 1893 crisis, the governments of both London and India acted to curb the aggressive tendencies of the Straits Settlements authorities to annex the vassal states of Siam in north Malaya. Such action would probably have opened the floodgates to unlimited French aggression and the possible complete obliteration of the state of Siam. Siam's total losses on her eastern boundaries from 1893 to 1907 totaled some 96,000 square miles; much of it was valueless to France.[48]

Under French rule in Laos, only the king of Luang Prabang retained his royal title and prerogatives. The rest of Laos, including Champassak, Vientiane, and Xieng Khouang, became in reality French provinces. A *Resident Superieur* was stationed at Vientiane, the administrative capital, exercising indirect control over the kingdom of Luang Prabang and direct control over the remaining eight administrative provinces. The French acted to control finances and to abolish slavery and eventually took the initiative in health and sanitation services; otherwise they honored local custom and the authority of the local chiefs. Except for the strong objection raised to the proposed annexation of Laos to Vietnam, the original basis on which French annexation had been predicated, the population of Laos remained quiet and relatively unimportant politically.[49]

## The French Administrative System for Indochina

The fashioning of the definitive French administrative system in Indochina was largely the work of Governor-General Paul Doumer, who held office from 1897 to 1902. Doumer was a troublesome Radical Party deputy in Paris, and was presumably sent to Saigon partly to get him out of the way. He was nevertheless a man of imagination and financial experience and had a high capacity for organization and decisive action. He had to cope with a proliferating bureaucracy in Cochin-China, both inefficient and corrupt, with a disaffected body of mandarins in Annam, with a fearful and restive situation in Tongking, and with a stagnant Cambodia. His task was to devise a consistent line of action to replace the previous lack of concerted objectives and general confusion. His greatest achievements were in providing transportation and in fashioning a unified administration without insisting on uniformity of its disparate segments.

In Cochin-China, Doumer raised money from loans and taxes for the construction of roads, canals, port facilities, and railways. He reduced the number of officials, coordinated the legal system along French lines, and introduced a Colonial Council elected in part by French citizens. Approval

48 J. Crosby, *Siam: The Crossroads* (1945), 59–60; Thomas Fitzsimmons, *Thailand* (1957), 233–234; Hall, 610.

49 Le Bar and Suddard, 16–18.

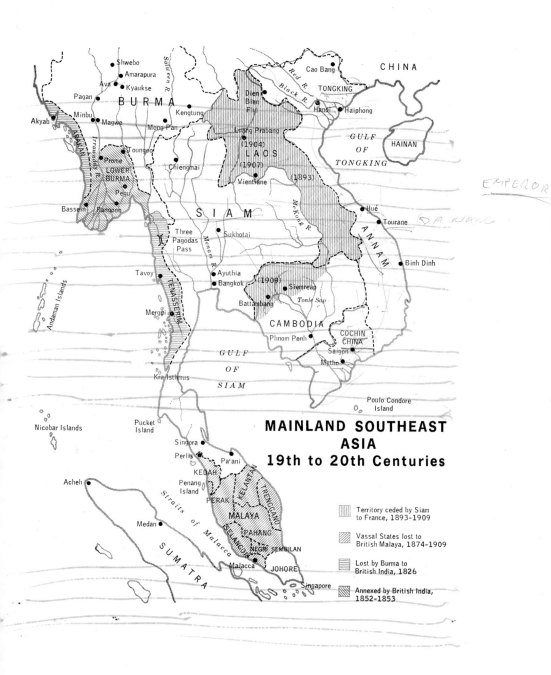

ξ TONKIN.
TÔNGKING

EMPEROR

DA NANG

# MAINLAND SOUTHEAST ASIA
## 19th to 20th Centuries

CHINA

Cao Bang
TONGKING
Hanoi    Haiphong

GULF
OF
TONGKING

HAINAN

Shwebo
Amarapura
Ava  Kyaukse
Pagan
BURMA
Minbu
Akyab  Magwe
Kengtung
Mong Pan

Dien
Bien
Phu
Luang Prabang
(1904)
LAOS
(1907)
Vientiane
(1893)

Red R.
Black R.

Toungoo
Prome
LOWER
BURMA
Pegu
Bassein  Rangoon

Chiengmai

SIAM

Three
Pagodas
Pass
Sukhotai

Tavoy

TENASSERIM

Ayuthia
Bangkok
(1909)

Battambang

Mergui

GULF
OF
SIAM

Kra Isthmus

Hué
Tourane

ANNAM

Binh Dinh

Siemreap
Tonle Sap

CAMBODIA
Phnom Penh

COCHIN
CHINA
Saigon
Mytho

Poulo Condore
Island

Andaman Islands

Nicobar Islands

Pucket
Island

Singora
Perlis   Pa'ani
KEDAH
Acheh        Penang
Island
PERAK
MALAYA
Medan        SELANGOR
NEGRI SEMBILAN
Malacca  JOHORE
Singapore

KELANTAN
TRENGGANU

PAHANG

Straits
of
Malacca

SUMATRA

| | Territory ceded by Siam to France, 1893-1909 |
| | Vassal States lost to British Malaya, 1874-1909 |
| | Lost by Burma to British India, 1826 |
| | Annexed by British India, 1852-1853 |

from Paris for executive proposals was needed to override local French objections. He left intact the imperial-mandarin administrative structure initiated in Annam and Tongking by de Lanessan but assumed control over the finances of both regions. A council of Ministers in Annam functioned under the general supervision of a French *Resident Superieur*. In Tongking, the French *Resident Superieur* exercised autonomous control over the mandarinate, while management of local taxes, schools, and charities was left to the communes. In Cambodia, he undertook to end slavery and other abuses and to promote agriculture by providing settlers and capital, while leaving the royal government intact and attempting to revitalize cultural traditions.[50]

Basic in Doumer's reform scheme was the division of revenues and budgetary allocations. The central budget was supplied by general revenue and customs collections. It provided funds for technical services and the centralized Departments of Public Works, Communications, Agriculture, Mines and Industries, and Judicial and Civil Affairs. Each of the five territorial units formulated its own budget and derived revenues from direct land taxes, the poll tax, and licenses for the sale of such items as alcohol and opium. Tax collections eventually improved, and the chronic deficits disappeared. Local administration, except in Cochin-China, functioned largely along traditional patterns.[51] The whole system was skillfully devised.

In order to stimulate economic development Doumer added to the number and the functions of chambers of agriculture and of commerce in the four provinces penetrated by French business. The chambers helped select the Conseil Superieur, a largely official body which reviewed budgetary allocations, defense problems, public works and economic-development proposals, and legislation and administration generally. The chambers were also represented on provincial Councils, and they functioned as operating agencies to prepare and let contracts for authorized public works projects, to collect port dues, and to run the docks at principal ports. A Chinese Chamber of Commerce represented petty traders in Cochin-China. Doumer solicited a 200-million-franc loan for railway construction and devised plans for constructing some 1,700 kilometers of railways over a ten-year period. The commerce of Indochina more than doubled during Doumer's incumbency, and trade with France trebled. Much of the gain was in rice exports and railway-equipment imports.[52]

The deficiencies of Doumer's system were twofold. It was mercantilist in character, intended primarily to promote the interests of France rather than Indochina. Indochina thus served to provide jobs, trade, and investment opportunities for Frenchmen. Connections were severed with neighboring Oriental markets and sources of supply to a degree characteristic of no other part of Southeast Asia. Economic dependence bred social

[50] Roberts, II, 415–459.
[51] Robequain, 10.
[52] Roberts, II, 451–459; Ireland, 152–159.

disequilibrium and cultural decline. In the second place, it afforded no scope or encouragement for the expansion of native industry or agriculture. Traditional industry and craftsmanship declined. Only large holders with capital could compete in the new economic fields. Attempts to encourage sharecroppers and native proprietorship usually ran aground on the absence of clear definition of land titles, which was needed if the land was to be used for mortgage security. By 1902, Europeans had taken over almost 200,000 hectares of land on which were eventually developed, mainly after 1910, tea, rubber, and coffee plantations. Sugar-cane production had started before the French arrival. Areas of mining and industrial development were confined to the anthracite coal mines of Hon-gay, rice mills in the south, and some silk mills, distilleries, cement works, and electric-power installations. Little or no iron, textile, or sugar manufacture was developed.[53]

Noteworthy progress was later made under the governorship of Albert Sarraut (1911–1917). He ended some of the bureaucratic blight of French functionaries, who numbered almost fifty-seven hundred by 1911, by requiring language study on the part of prospective officials and by opening the lower ranks of government service to Vietnamese. When he took over, some nine-tenths of the officials were ignorant of the local languages. He also began the general development of flood-control measures by government action. He made further adjustments of the law codes of Cochin-China in the direction of French standards, and he made concessions to local custom in other parts of Vietnam.

The difficulty of ameliorating the bureaucratic and mercantilist aspects of colonial administration in Indochina stemmed largely from the elaborate machinery for policy control developed in France itself. A multitude of consultative Councils and commissions, mostly unpaid, represented the self-interest of businessmen, ex-officials, and politicians concerned with colonial matters. The Ministry of Colonies itself was divided into six major departments, including General Administration (with four branches); Economic Concerns (with eight branches); Civil Servants and Accounts; Military, Police, and Medical Services; Education (under joint control of the Minister of Interior); and the corps of Inspectors of Colonies. The Conseil Supérieur des Colonies was a cumbersome advisory body of some 150 members, consisting of a High Council of ex-ministers and former colonial governors, an Economic Council with seven sections, and a Legislative Council. It included French-elected delegates from colonial areas, but represented on the whole the dead weight of inertia—stodgy, diffused, and ineffective. French chambers of commerce and agriculture of the various colonies were represented in the Agence générale des Colonies, and the former Geographical Societies of France survived in the Union Coloniale Française, with ten geographical sections.

[53] Roberts, II, 479–490; Chesneaux, 158–164. Rice production increased by some 47 per cent between 1900 and 1920, but per capita consumption fell.

The viewpoint of the indigenous population was unrepresented in France except for nominal representation in the Chamber of Deputies. But French Parliamentary control of colonial policy was also virtually nil. A Colonial Council, eventually set up in Indochina after World War I, included ten native representatives, elected from an elite constituency, in a total of twenty-four members. The body's decisions could be annulled by the governor's Privy Council, which included only two native notables among twelve.[54]

## The French Cultural and Political Impact

The distinguishing characteristics of the French colonial impact, culturally and politically, were derived in large measure from its motivation in pride of culture and national influence. Cultural interests were demonstrated in the establishment of the École Française de l'Extrême Orient at Hanoi in 1898, which contributed so handsomely to the study of pre-European Southeast Asian affairs. But the colonial peoples had to be taught to admire France and its ways and to appreciate the boon of being associated politically with France. These ends were difficult to reconcile with mercantilist rule. From the British-aristocratic point of view, France paid too little attention in the selection of colonial officials to such factors as gentlemanly breeding, social antecedents, and demonstrated personal authority. The British India civil servant in Burma, for example, affirmed his own ego, did not unbend easily, dressed for dinner, shared his sentiments sparingly, and was usually satisfied with inspiring respect rather than affection. The French, by contrast, adopted an attitude of camaraderie, often did not maintain social distance, treated the natives indulgently as children, and wanted all to share French habits, ideas, and sentiments. They accordingly failed to command respect.[55]

Cochin-China differed sharply from the other four units of French Indochina in that it was a colony, directly ruled by French officials and dominated by French enterprise. The strength of the European impact was also enhanced in the south because traditional Confucian culture was far less firmly entrenched there than in the northern areas, which alone had experienced a thousand years of Chinese rule. French standards also influenced significantly several urban centers in Tongking, where a considerable fraction of industry was concentrated. The Annamese coastal area connecting Cochin-China and Tongking afforded little opportunity for French enterprise, and the strength of traditional social and governmental standards was also greater because of the persistence at Hué of the ceremonial rites of the Vietnamese Court. The French impact in Cambodia outside of Phnom Penh was slight, and it was even less in Laos.

[54] Hesketh Bell, *Foreign Colonial Administration in the Far East* (1926), 136–147, 156–162; Roberts, I, 133–135, 141.

[55] Bell, 174–180; Cady, 294–295.

Difficulties developed from the impossibility of making brown-skinned Frenchmen out of the Vietnamese and keeping them subservient at the same time. Naturalization was available only to those who could speak French, or had served ten years in the public services or army, or had married French wives, or had acquired Legion of Honor recognition. Cambodia and Laos presented somewhat less cultural displacement, for the functioning of Buddhist vernacular schools continued undisturbed. Cochin-China was thoroughly Gallicized, but its native economic leadership was Chinese. It was Vietnam that caused the difficulty, especially after World War I, when direct contact with French civilization stimulated new viewpoints and ideas.

Elementary schooling in Vietnam areas by 1920 was available to one boy in twelve and to only one girl in a hundred. Secondary school facilities were very narrowly limited, with the largest high school in Hanoi providing, in 1925, room for only five to eight hundred students in the face of a growing demand for entry. Only a few of the secondary students were permitted to take French, which was prerequisite for entering the University of Hanoi. The University, established by Governor Sarraut in 1917, started out with a liberal curriculum. Its administration became frightened of student unrest and had shifted by 1923 to concentration on practical industrial subjects. Even so, its eleven industrial schools had less than eleven hundred students in 1923, and the student-faculty ratio was 3 or 4 to 1. The teaching staff at all European-type schools were predominantly French. Indochina thus took no chances with possibly disloyal schoolmasters and teachers. The most serious problem of all was encountered among Vietnamese students who went to France, for they were usually beyond controlling when they returned.[56]

The disturbing cultural impact of French rule was widespread but limited in depth. The authority of the village notables was impaired, lessening social cohesion. The villager who had to live at a distance from the bones of his ancestors came in time to question somewhat the potency of ancestor-spirit gods. Particularly serious among the more sophisticated was the discrediting of the ancestral rites buttressing the authority of the ruler. The educated tended to find an alternative to the traditional sanction of political power in the French Declaration of the Rights of Man and a Citizen or in the American Declaration of Independence. For the most part, however, traditional spirit cults continued unimpaired in their authority.[57]

Opposition to French rule after 1900 centered in Vietnam and especially in Tongking. The general feeling of frustration, combined with a sense of trampled pride of race and culture, stimulated hatred of Europeans

[56] Bell, 203–209.

[57] Kenneth P. Landon, *Southeast Asia: Crossroads of Religion* (1947), 192–193.

and Western ways. But this sentiment was long disparate and uncoordinated. Much of the resistance was based on traditionalism, led by those who were convinced of the superiority of indigenous standards and disdainful of alien ways. At the other extreme were the youthful rebels recruited from the westernized minority, unattracted by the traditional but still unable to participate satisfactorily in the new order. A third urbanized and progressive group, some of them Christian, developed real appreciation of individualism and of French culture generally, but they were nevertheless opposed to French rule which denied them liberty, equality, and fraternity. A few became interested in Marx. By the end of World War I, Tongking was alive with vociferous demands for political reform, but the voices were so badly organized that the authorities felt they could ignore them with safety.[58]

[58] Roberts, II, 474–479. For a devastating critique of French historical writing on Indochina, see Chesneaux's chapter in D. G. E. Hall, *Historians of South-East Asia* (1961), 231–244.

# The Straits Settlements

# and British Malaya

After being detached from the Dutch Indies by Stamford Raffles in 1825, Singapore developed during the remainder of the century into a great commercial entrepôt for all of Southeast Asia. To the traditional pattern of exchange between India, Southeast Asia, and China, the British added the expanding output in cotton textiles and metals of their own domestic industries. Chronic British complaints over Dutch trading restrictions and pirate suppression ended during the 1850s following the clear demonstration of Singapore's hegemony and the eventual liberalization of Dutch trading policy. The Dutch and the British actually decided to cooperate in the face of threatened European and American intrusions.

The British took little interest in the disorders prevailing within the several sultanates of the Malay Peninsula until the 1870s, when the tin output by Chinese miners became important commercially. Treaty arrangements provided for posting British Residents in the four principal tin-mining states, which were grouped into a Federation in 1895. Johore became a full protectorate in 1914, and four additional Unfederated States were acquired by treaty with Siam in 1909. After 1910, rubber was added to tin as a rapidly expanding export item from Singapore. British authorities, functioning more or less through the sultans, supplied governmental and transportation needs for the developing economy. The voluntary entry of Chinese labor on a large scale going back to 1820 and the regulated recruitment of Indian coolies after 1910 for the rubber industry created a multiracial society which was denied any prospect of integration. Partly because of ethnic diversity, British authorities were tardy in promoting education, self-government, and a common citizenship. Fabulously profitable Malaya was eventually overtaken by external events, including the contagious nationalist movements of India and China and the conquest and occupation by Japan.

## The Straits Settlements Trade

The political entity of the Straits Settlements, created in 1826 by the union of Penang, Province Wellesley, Malacca, and Singapore, was conceived at the outset purely as a center of trading activity. Singapore became the administrative center in 1832. The straits had long attracted large numbers of Chinese junks, which brought raw silk and cheap Chinese wares to exchange for forest products of Malaya, Sumatra, and Borneo, salable in the China market. Observers at Penang in 1821 described the many Chinese junks present in the harbor and Chinese laborers and craftsmen doing most of the work at the port city. In the course of the next five years, Chinese attention shifted almost entirely to Singapore. Aside from its role as a center of Chinese trade, Singapore came to serve as a distributing center for British and Indian products (textiles, opium, and metal goods), as an entrepôt to attract traders from the many ports of Southeast Asia, and as a policing center and place of call for English Company trade with China.

Official India Company policy was to avoid interference with the Malay sultanates. Calcutta wanted to do nothing to imperil the profitable China trade or to incur costly trouble with Siam, itself a vassal of China. This cautious policy was qualified somewhat after 1833, when British-manufactured textiles were beginning to capture the traditional markets of the India-made cloth and Manchester was clamoring for freer entry into the vast market of China. After the opening of additional China coastal ports in 1842, Singapore had to share with Hongkong and Shanghai the task of distributing British and Indian wares. Even so, virtually all such goods passed through Singapore harbor en route to China.

The Straits authorities in general and officials at Penang in particular were inclined to be aggressive in matters relating to the Malay Peninsula. They repeatedly sought permission to take advantage of opportunities to extend the perimeter of British control, only to have their requests vetoed in Calcutta and London. Commercial prospects with the Malay sultanates were not regarded as sufficiently promising to warrant intervention to curb existing conditions of confusion and anarchy. As long as British trading interests were not adversely affected, Indian authorities were glad to leave the Malay headache to Siam. Efforts to cultivate spices, sugar, and pepper in Penang and on the adjacent mainland failed because of soil deficiencies and plant blight. India's control over Straits policy came to an end in 1858 after the mutiny episode, but the Secretary of State for India in London retained authority until 1867. Colonial Office control after 1867 made little immediate difference at first, but the perspective changed noticeably following the opening of the Suez Canal in 1869. It was the development of tin mining after the middle of the century on the initiative of Chinese immigrants which forced the reluctant abandonment of the British hands-off policy in 1873–1874.[1]

The development of Singapore as a free port greatly reduced the use of the Malacca Straits by Chinese and Indonesian traders. By 1840, Singapore was visited during the course of a year by an estimated 150 to 250 Chinese junks and by some 200 Buginese praus. Passage through the pirate-infested straits was left for the most part to the less vulnerable British and Dutch vessels. In the middle 1830s, Singapore's exports were virtually the same as its imports, except for foods locally consumed. Large annual imports from China included an item of 140,000 Spanish dollars, providing a medium of exchange which continued available for a number of decades. Chinese vessels also brought to the entrepôt goods from the ports of Siam, Cambodia, and Cochin-China. American traders brought another 90,000 dollars to Singapore, making possible the transfer of around 200,000 dollars annually from Singapore to India. Buginese traders imported goods worth some 800,000 dollars to Singapore. More than half of Singapore's 800,000-dollar trade in gold dust came from Malaya itself. The annual opium trade from India amounted to some 5.4 million dollars (1 million pounds sterling); it was surpassed only by the British-Indian cloth trade of 7 million dollars (1.4 million pounds sterling). Dwindling Dutch trade in spices via Singapore in 1840 was surpassed in value about 3½ times by the piddling traffic in edible birds' nests.[2]

## Piracy and Its Suppression

The British were at first inclined to deal with piracy only as it might interfere with the delivery of native goods to Singapore or with Britain's own trade with China. They left to the Dutch the responsibility of controlling lawlessness on the western shores of the straits. Native craft generally preferred the lenient Dutch pass system to the more rigorous application of British naval control. Armed British action against pirates could often be construed, in any case, as in violation of Dutch or Siamese sovereignty. The four principal groups of pirates were themselves mutually hostile. They seldom attacked European craft, but native vessels were highly vulnerable. A Boston sailing vessel, the *Cashmere,* was nevertheless attacked and robbed in 1835 only a few miles from Singapore, and several of its American passengers were thrown overboard.[3]

The straits pirates usually operated small boats of 8 to 10 tons, propelled by paddles. They mounted swivel guns at the bow, stern, and center

[1] Nicholas Tarling, "British Policy in the Malay Peninsula and Archipelago, 1824–1871," *JRASMB,* XXX, no. 179 (1957), 9–10, 13, 30–32, 46–47, 70–80.

[2] Lennox A. Mills, *British Malaya, 1824–1867* (1925), 186–198.

[3] Tarling, 14–18, 28; T. J. Newbold, *Political and Statistical Account of the British Settlements in the Straits of Malacca* (1839), I, 36–39; Kenneth E. Wells, *Protestant Work in Thailand* (1958), 16–18.

and operated them from behind musketproof wooden screens. The crews were armed with muskets and blunderbusses. Some six to twenty praus would cooperate in attacking becalmed victims, boarding simultaneously at the sound of a loud gong. They operated as far north as Mergui on the Bay of Bengal side and also along the eastern entrances to the straits. Many of the Buginese traders and the Chinese as well who visited Singapore on legitimate business doubled as pirates when opportunity afforded. Singapore usually offered no objection to the disposal of piratical plunder at the port.

The most feared of all the pirates were the Sulu Balanini and the Mindanao Ilanun. During the first half of the century, these groups operated between northern Borneo, the southern Philippines, and the Moluccas. Their ships were large, managed by 40-to-150-man crews, propelled by slave oarsmen, and heavily armed. They ranged at times far and wide and feuded bitterly with the Malay pirates, who resented any poaching on their territory. Of Asian craft only the largest Chinese vessels could resist the northern Borneo pirates, and, in their home territory, the latter did not hesitate to attack European ships. The prevalence of piracy was to some extent a matter of European definition of what was legal. Many of the rules established by the Dutch and the British were arbitrarily imposed. In 1851, for example, Singapore objected to the execution by Pahang authorities of several Chinese pirates who were also in the habit of trading legitimately at Singapore.[4]

The suppression of the pirate nuisance was undertaken seriously after 1837, when the first armed steamers arrived in Southeast Asia. The Dutch took up the problem along the Sumatran coasts and the north shores of the Java Sea; the British operated around Malaya and northwestern Borneo; the Spanish policed the Sulu Sea. By 1847, the pirates were still discreetly active although clearly in retreat. The arrival of the French fleet at Basilan in 1844 and off the Vietnam and China coasts during the late 1850s exerted an added deterrent effect. The Spanish used armed steamers in the formidable task of bringing the Balanini and Ilanun bands under control. By 1860, most of the pirate strongholds had been suppressed in the Malacca Straits, although casual acts of piracy continued. But by that time virtually all the native craft except the persistent Buginese had also been eliminated as traders by the competition of European ships, both sailing and steamer.[5]

## British-Dutch Relations: Borneo

For a quarter century after the founding of Singapore, relations between the Straits Settlements and the Dutch were acrimonious. The Dutch planned originally to make Riau Island at the eastern end of the straits a

[4] Tarling, 28, 55, 62–63; Mills, 214–230; Newbold, I, 36–39.

[5] Tarling, 47–54, 65; Mills, 230.

rival entrepôt to Singapore. Riau was declared a free port in 1828, and its authorities assumed control over the main passages leading to Sumatran ports. Governor Fullerton of Penang favored grabbing Riau despite the explicitly negative terms of the Dutch treaty, but he was overruled. The Dutch plan faltered after 1830, when the loss of Belgium's cloth output denied the Dutch any real chance to compete with Britain in the vital textile field. During the course of the next two decades, trade rivalry tended to get mixed up with suzerain claims and antipiracy measures. The pass system used by the Dutch implied vassal status for the holder and tacit submission to restrictive Dutch trade regulations. Singapore objected most to the preferential Dutch duties against British trade with Java and the alleged Dutch interference with the access of native island craft to Singapore. Tension reached a peak during the forties.[6]

Neither the British nor the Dutch were greatly interested in exercising control in northern Borneo. It was unattractive commercially and was the home grounds of the ferocious Balanini pirates. An earlier English Company occupation of Balambangan Island in 1773 had ended disastrously in the complete destruction of the settlement by the Sulus. The terms of the Anglo-Dutch treaty of 1824 reserving to the Dutch sphere the islands east and south of Singapore may or may not have been intended to refer to north Borneo. British annexation of Labuan Island off the northwest Borneo coast and the private coup by James Brooke in Sarawak in the 1840s were actually used by London as bargaining considerations to persuade the Dutch to liberalize their trade policies. Brooke's move into Borneo, with its implied threat of the extension of British interference into other unadministered parts of Indonesia, forced the Dutch to reconsider their policy. Aside from bargaining with the Dutch, the principal interest of the British in northwest Borneo was connected with the protection of the eastern flank of the China trade. Antipiratical measures could be used to challenge Dutch territorial claims and thereby bolster Britain's central concern for free access to Dutch Indonesian ports.[7]

The principal agent in the Borneo episode was the British adventurer James Brooke, a second-generation East India Company official. At the age of thirty-four, Brooke inherited a modest fortune, purchased a well-armed steam yacht, and proceeded to Singapore, arriving in 1831. He first went to Borneo in 1839, where he helped Raja Muda Hassim of Brunei put down a rebellion. In compensation from the grateful Sultan, he received in 1841 a grant of powers of government over Sarawak (as a kind of fief). Brooke paid 500 pounds per year to the Sultan as "tribute tax." Brooke's next move was to solicit armed support from Singapore and Calcutta. He proposed to end piracy and local plunder in the vicinity of Sarawak, to improve his state's finances, and to stimulate trade with Singapore. Brooke also hired an agent named Wise to work in London in an

[6] Tarling, 22–28, 86–102, 136–138.

[7] *Ibid.*, 143–150, 186.

effort to prod the Foreign Office to annex Labuan Island, where coal needed in the China war was supposed to be available. Labuan was accordingly annexed by Britain in 1846.[8]

For a time Brooke's star was in the ascendancy. London appointed him agent to the Sultan of Brunei in 1844 and afforded him support by sending a naval force to attack the pirates of the area. In 1847, Brooke was knighted by Lord Palmerston's government, appointed British Commissioner and consul-general to Brunei, and also named the governor of Labuan Island. In one or the other of his several capacities, he was authorized by Palmerston to conclude treaties on the Brunei model covering an indefinite region extending to the east. In the early 1850s London also commissioned him to conduct negotiations with Bangkok.

The Dutch moved to counter the activities of Brooke by sending a punitive expedition of their own against the Sulu pirates in 1843–1849. They then accepted London's hint that territorial rivalry could be eased if Holland would reduce its trade restrictions in the Indies. The advantages of Anglo-Dutch cooperation became more apparent after an American agent negotiated a most-favored-nation treaty with Brunei in 1845. The trend was strengthened following the French intrusions into Vietnam in the late fifties.

In 1852, London began to curb Brooke's ambitious plans. It decided to back Spain's asserted claim to the Sulu Islands, negating thereby a previous treaty between Brooke and the Sulu Sultan. At the same time London deprived Brooke of his Labuan governorship and sent out a commission to examine his doings in Sarawak. When faced by London's mild criticism for using British naval forces to promote personal ends, Brooke defiantly proclaimed the independence of Sarawak, with himself as Raja. The independence of Sarawak was eventually conceded by Britain in backhand fashion, in 1862 when London accredited a consul to the government of Raja Brooke. On at least two occasions (1858 and 1868) Brooke offered to transform Sarawak into a British colony, provided he could be repaid for personal expenses previously incurred. He died in 1869, leaving his throne to a nephew, Charles Brooke.[9]

The gradual liquidation of British-Dutch friction in the face of possible rival interlopers in Southeast Asia continued through succeeding decades. In 1853, the Great East was officially opened to all European trade; after 1857, British trade was also welcomed at Javan ports. Further concessions were made in 1865, and the commercial *rapprochement* was firmly established in 1871 by formal treaty. Britain conceded the broad sweep of Dutch sovereignty over the Indies islands, including all of Sumatra, in return for Dutch surrender of a holding on the Gold Coast of Africa, the reduction of tariffs, and the opening of additional Indonesian ports to

[8] *Ibid.,* 190–192.
[9] *Ibid.,* 193–205.

British trade. British steamers thereafter swarmed into the islands, and the Dutch, themselves previously tardy in the adoption of steamer service, began to use similar vessels, many of them built, financed, and serviced in England. Eventually the Dutch welcomed outside capital generally in the development of the Indies economy.[10]

## Origins of British Chartered-company Rule in North Borneo

Brooke's venture in Sarawak was the beginning rather than the end of private adventurer operations in northern Borneo. An American named Moses, an ex-naval officer and pretended U.S. consul, arrived from Singapore in 1865. After obtaining from the Sultan a ten-year cession to a northerly section of Brunei, conditional on promises which were never honored, he proceeded to Hongkong where he sold his dubious claim to two other American merchants. Pooling their meager capital assets of 7,000 dollars, they formed the American Trading Company of Borneo in October, 1865, and established a settlement on the Kimanis River, about 60 miles north of Labuan, where they hoisted the American flag. Using imported Chinese labor, they built a stockade and a jetty and cleared some 90 acres of land. But things soon went badly. One partner left and the other died, leaving the colony to perish from starvation. Approximately a decade later, in 1876, a renegade British trader named Cowie, an arms dealer, set up a trading station on the nearby Bay of Sandakan near the Sulu Archipelago.

Partly to forestall such irresponsible dealings, the financially reputable British merchant firm of Dent Brothers, with some official encouragement, entered the situation in 1876. Using as its agent an Austrian previously connected with the American Company, the Dent group negotiated another lease from the accommodating Brunei Sultan. In return for strategically placed bribes and a guaranteed 15,000-dollar annual rental, Dent acquired claims to an extensive area of largely worthless land running entirely across north Borneo. Since part of the region was under the nominal control of the Sulu Sultan, a second negotiation of 1878, this time with official British backing, cleared the title to the region from the Sulu point of view. In return for 5,000 dollars a year, the Company obtained the right to arbitrate local disputes and to veto any future land transfers. At the time, the Sultan was under heavy attack by the Spaniards, who took over his Sulu Island possessions.

The British government then moved in. A Resident was located on the east coast of the Company holdings, and a consul was posted at Sandakan Bay. Attempts of the jealous Charles Brooke and Cowie to stir up rebellion against the British Company, which became chartered

[10] *Ibid.,* 153–175; G. C. Allen and A. G. Donnithorne, *Western Enterprise in Indonesia and Malaya* (1954), 212–224.

in 1881, were smothered by official British rebukes and subsidies. Thus was the north Borneo political vacuum filled, further interloping prevented, and pirate leaders pensioned off. Spain's claims in the Sulu area proper were fully conceded by Britain in 1885, as were the Dutch rights elsewhere in Borneo, in 1891 and 1921.[11]

## The Role of the Chinese Immigrants

All observers of conditions in the Straits Settlements during the middle half of the nineteenth century emphasized the important role being played by the Chinese. The Malays themselves were largely a fishing and maritime people, and miserably poor. They were nevertheless militarily vigorous and therefore contemptuous of the industrious Indian and Chinese, with whom they were quite incapable of competing in the economic field.[12] The Indian settlers were described as shrewd, avaricious, and industrious if well paid, but they were also usually unable to match the superior energy and business talents of the Chinese. By 1820, the Chinese operated much of the interisland trade, conducted the tax-farmer operations, and performed all construction work as carpenters, masons, and blacksmiths. John Crawfurd declared in 1820 that had it not been for China's law prohibiting the emigration of Chinese women, "we should long ago have seen the principal portion of the archipelago colonized by them."[13] In Malaya the Chinese were to find one of their most attractive opportunities.

As early as 1821 at Singapore, industrious Chinese were doing most of the development work in farming, construction, and lumber acquisition. By 1833, the Chinese constituted the largest ethnic group at Singapore, and they had begun to penetrate into the interior as tin miners and traders. At the entrepôt, they numbered 8,500 compared to 7,130 Malays and 1,760 Indians. They were entering Singapore at the rate of 5,000 to 8,000 per year, most of them as penniless immigrants bound to work for fellow Chinese who had financed their passage costs. Many Chinese residents learned passable English, and a few became well-to-do. The petty feuding of their rival secret societies (huis) was of little apparent concern to the authorities. A visitor concluded that "their industry and perseverance have mainly contributed to the present flourishing state of the settlement."[14]

[11] K. G. Tregonning, *Under Chartered Company Rule: North Borneo, 1881–1946* (1958), 4–8. In 1962, Manila advanced a residual claim of Philippines sovereignty over North Borneo.

[12] O. G. Finlayson, *Mission to Siam and Hué* (1826), 70–74. R. O. Winstedt (*Cultural History,* 135) says that the Malays refused to count work as a virtue and that "what the European moralist regarded as time lost, the Malay regards as time gained."

[13] John Crawfurd, *History of the Indian Archipelago* (1820), I, 132–137.

[14] G. W. Earl, *The Eastern Seas* (1837), 361–374.

The Chinese influx continued to mount decade after decade. Of Singapore's 82,000 population in 1858, the Chinese numbered no less than 50,000. The Indians (11,735) had by then surpassed the Malays (10,900). Many of the Chinese came during the 1850s and 1860s as part of the nefarious coolie traffic originating from minor ports on China's Fukien coast. Both Chinese and European ships participated. The four to six hundred who were usually crammed on a single ship sometimes rioted and invariably suffered considerable loss of life en route to the destination. Arriving at Singapore, the controllers of the traffic, themselves Chinese, would sell the indentured services of the passengers to the highest bidders, also Chinese. The latter often paid from five to six times the cost of passage. British authorities eventually eliminated the worst features of the kidnapping tactics at the ports of origin, but the traffic continued unregulated otherwise. The feuding secret societies in Malaya were generally left to settle their own differences. The traffic was almost entirely male, creating social problems of large dimensions which were added to the normal vices of the Chinese. A French visitor to Singapore in 1858 counted eighty-seven Chinese spirit merchants, plus eleven for arrack liquor, and 144 licensed opium-smoking houses.[15]

The political impact of Chinese immigration in the Malay Peninsula was almost as important as the economic. Problems developed largely in connection with Chinese penetration into the interior for the mining of tin. Tin had long been extracted in a small way from Negri Sembilan, but in 1848 rich new fields were discovered at Larut in Perak state. Other new workings were uncovered in later decades in regions extending along the western slopes of the peninsular mountain divide. Chinese entry in large numbers generated an increasing amount of friction between sultan and sultan, Malay and Chinese, and, even more seriously, Chinese and Chinese. British trade greedily absorbed the increasing tin output, but the Straits government down to 1872 ruled that persons electing to penetrate into the interior did so at their own risk.[16]

## British Intervention in Peninsular Malaya after 1874

Down to 1871, London's negative attitude toward accepting responsibility for maintaining order within the peninsular states was attributable to the view that Britain's interests east of India were confined primarily to the control of the trading channels to China. Holland's predominance throughout most of Indonesia was conceded, as was Spain's sovereignty in the Sulu Archipelago, but British authorities wanted to forestall the possibility of another power's encroachment in the area of their primary concern. Gladstone's first Liberal Party Ministry, in particular,

[15] Samuel J. Smith, *The Siam Repository*, II (1870), 8–9; Henri Mouhot, *Travels in the Central Parts of Indo-China* (1864), I, 37–38.

[16] Allen and Donnithorne, 38–43, 148–157.

was at the outset deaf to pleas from straits merchants to end the disorders in Malaya and to protect local trading interests. A somewhat broader interpretation of imperial responsibilities for exercising effective control within the British colonial sphere, including Malaya, was accepted after 1871. The likely prospect developed that interested parties would take advantage of prevailing disorders to establish footholds infringing on priorities theretofore unchallenged. The mere rumor, for example, that France or Germany was interested in Malaya was sufficient to alter the tone of British policy.

The disorderly situation within the tin-mining region along the western coast of the peninsula became aggravated after 1868. A civil war broke out in Selangor; a disputed succession to the sultanate developed in Perak; a sanguinary feud between rival Chinese mining factions flamed in Larut. The cautious governor of the Straits Settlements, Sir Harry Ord, conforming strictly to his instructions, refused to intervene overtly in order to improve conditions. At the end of his governorship in 1873, the direct appeals by interested straits merchants including representative Chinese to the Colonial Office, combined with London's altered mood, resulted in the selection of the vigorous Governor Sir Andrew Clarke. The selection was made by Gladstone's tottering Ministry, which resigned in January, 1874.

The new governor took full advantage of his permissory instructions to endeavor to restore order without bothering to consult the Colonial Office or even to report developments as they occurred. In early 1874, after the accession of Disraeli to power in London, Clarke intervened to negotiate a conclusion of the Larut war by ending the succession controversy in Perak; he also liquidated civil war in Selangor. Naval blockades of river entrances proved effective because food shortages prevented the assembly of large Malay forces. Three British Residents were sent to the affected areas with authorization to do more than simply give advice. The measures worked well except in Perak and Sungai Ujong, where political explosions occurred.[17]

Once started, British intervention tended to expand. The first Resident to be sent to Perak offended the puppet Sultan by tactlessly interfering with local customs respecting religion, feudal dues, and slavery. He suffered assassination in 1874. Thereupon two thousand Indian troops invaded the state to punish the offenders and to beat the uncooperative Malay chiefs into sullen submission. When these developments were reported to London, Disraeli indicated full approval. Under the new protectorate regimes, land-rent regulations were introduced, the duties of the village headmen were defined, bankruptcy and anarchy were ended. Perak attracted a population of some eighty thousand Chinese by 1890. The posting of British Residents was initiated with Negri Sembilan and Pahang

[17] C. D. Cowan, *Nineteenth-Century Malaya* (1961), 66, 99, 144, 212; C. Northcote Parkinson, *British Intervention in Malaya, 1867–1877* (1959), xvii–xix, 82–114.

states in 1888. A separate protectorate arrangement was set up for Johore in 1895, to be revised in 1914, when an "adviser" was accepted.[18]

A major political development occurred in 1895, when the four treaty states were grouped together as the Federated Malay States. The Federation was placed under a Resident-General located at Kuala Lumpur and exercising administrative authority through a centralized bureaucracy. The governor of the Straits Settlements doubled as the High Commissioner of the Federation. Four additional states were acquired in 1909 through a treaty of cession with Siam: Kedah, Perlis, Kelantan, and Trengganu. By that time Siam's suzerain rights in the peninsula had worn thin, and it was evident that Bangkok was incapable of administering and developing the states along modern lines. Siam had actually borrowed a British civil servant as adviser in Kelantan in 1903.[19] London, in 1909, surrendered to Bangkok a fraction of British extraterritorial rights in Siam and granted a 4–7 million-pound railway loan. The 1909 treaty was not popular in Siam, but the Muslim populations of the four Unfederated States expressed no regret over being freed from Siamese Buddhist rule. Administration in the Unfederated States continued along traditional lines.[20]

The governmental machinery for the Malay Federation included a Federal Council which included representatives of the four sultans and four nonofficial appointees (three British, one Chinese) in addition to the four Residents, the Resident-General, and the governor. The Council modified somewhat the independence and powers of the Resident-General in the direction of increased control by the Federation's High Commissioner. The Residents took an active interest in providing roads, railways, credit facilities, land alienation, and experimental research. They sometimes used tin-mining revenue to meet the needs of the newly developing rubber plantations.[21] The authority of the sultans, which the British at first tried to respect, gradually eroded away as the Malay proportion of the population dwindled and foreign investments increased. Malays got favored treatment in admission to the lower ranks of the civil service, but many indigenous political and legal institutions were abandoned. In the four Federated States where rubber and tin production was concentrated, British investments totaled about 200 million dollars by 1914. The Malays then numbered only 26 per cent of the total Federated States population.

Subject to the overriding authority of the Colonial Office, the governor and the Resident-General exercised arbitrary power in Malaya, since the several state Councils along with that of the Federation were only

[18] R. Winstedt, *Malaya and Its History* (1956), 62–76; Mills, 171–184.

[19] S. W. Jones, *Public Administration in Malaya* (1953), 17–20, 32; N. Ginsburg and C. F. Roberts, *Malaya* (1958), 435–440.

[20] J. Crosby, *Siam: The Crossroads* (1945), 50–52. Siam's four southernmost provinces after 1909 still included 670,000 Muslims.

[21] J. Norman Parmer, *Colonial Labor Policy and Administration in Malaya* (1960), 1–10.

advisory in character. The administration was efficient and generally impartial; local business interests were regularly consulted; elementary education was initiated in three vernacular languages besides English. The Chinese were responsible for about three-fourths of the tin output in 1913, although British dredging methods were gaining acceptance. The superior prosperity enjoyed by the Chinese bridged over their resentment regarding political preference given to the Malays. Proverbially the Chinese seemed not to care who held the cow so long as they did the milking. Malay farmers were usually mired in a morass of debt to the more astute Chinese trader.[22]

## Effects of Closer Contacts with Europe

The opening of the Suez Canal in late 1869 transformed within a short time the commercial outlook of all Southeast Asia along with that of other parts of the Orient. It made economical the marketing of a larger quantity and a greater variety of goods in both directions. The Mediterranean route had actually been used since 1840, when Britain's Peninsular and Oriental Steam Navigation Company inaugurated passenger and light freight service via the Sinai isthmus and the Red Sea. Consul Montigny en route to Bangkok had used this service in 1856, and Britain moved many of its forces for the China war in 1857–1859 via Egypt and Suez. The new canal made feasible the shipment to Europe of bulkier items, such as rice and sugar, and eventually new commodities like palm oil, mineral oil, and latex. The completion of telegraphic communications to Europe added another useful facility.

British shipping realized the greatest initial advantage from the opening of the canal partly because of its having been the pioneer in the use of steamers for the Asian trade. Disraeli's coup of 1875 in buying up the canal shares of the impecunious Egyptian khedive gave Britain a substantial element of control of the waterway. The Dutch, by comparison, had made little use of steamers prior to 1870, and American clipper ships continued in service long after steamers became standard equipment for the British. British industry, furthermore, was almost a full generation ahead of European and American competitors. Seven new British shipping lines were started within fifteen years after the opening of the canal. They were eventually joined in the 1880s by the German Norddeutscher Lloyd, by the French Messageries Maritimes, and by new Dutch, Italian, and Swedish lines.[23]

The surge of European commercial activity in Southeast Asia inevitably affected adversely the traditional role of local traders. Among the Southeast Asians, the Buginese alone survived the competition after 1875. Their praus continued to carry goods between Singapore and the Outer

[22] L. A. Mills (ed.), *The New World of Southeast Asia* (1949), 174–183.
[23] Allen and Donnithorne, 210–212.

Island markets of the Indies. Macassar harbor was improved and managed to retain its commercial importance. Chinese junks, after 1875, gave up their share of the immigrant passenger service to Southeast Asia, leaving it entirely in the hands of British steamers for more than two decades thereafter. In 1899, the Norddeutscher Lloyd began a schedule of passenger service from Swatow to Singapore and Bangkok. Chinese vessels continued to participate in the assembling and distribution of goods at Singapore, and small European steamers became progressively more important in the Southeast Asian trade.[24] By 1920, the Singapore trade as it affected the Indies was almost exclusively a Chinese and British operation. By 1926 the total annual trade of the Straits Settlements amounted to 264 million Spanish dollars, exceeding that of all other British colonies combined. It had been a mere 5 million in 1830.

It was not by entrepôt operations alone that Singapore was able to maintain its position as a leading trading mart of Eastern Asia. Calcutta and Bombay in India, Hongkong and Shanghai in China, and ports of Japan, all of them servicing an expanding export industry, presented formidable competition. Nor was the use of steamers an unmixed blessing for Singapore. Such vessels were no longer dependent on the rhythm of the monsoon seasons which had contributed so much in earlier days to the importance of Śrivijaya, Malacca, Batavia, and Singapore itself.[25] What was needed for Singapore's continued prosperity and what British enterprise provided was an enormously increased output of exportable commodities within Malaya itself. A substantial gain in food production was also realized although never in quantities commensurate with the rapid increase of population. The Straits and Federation governments contributed the requisite orderly conditions—a legal framework covering land surveys, ownership, tenure, and drainage rights, plus railway transportation, low initial taxes, health provisions, and arrangements for obtaining an abundant supply of cheap labor.[26]

## Increased Tin and Rubber Production

As previously indicated, most of Malaya's tin output prior to 1912 was produced by Chinese miners. After that year, when a rise in prices permitted the economical exploitation of ores less easily accessible, European firms registered major increases in production. The new dredging and hydraulic methods required large-scale capital outlays, whereas the Chinese continued to obtain ores from pumping operations in gravel pits. During the course of the ensuing quarter century, to 1937, European output of tin increased more than tenfold and accounted for three-fourths of the total of 77,000 tons a year, whereas the Chinese mines registered no

[24] Tarling, 84–85.
[25] Winstedt, *Malaya and Its History,* 109.
[26] Parmer, 249.

appreciable gains. British mining firms employed large numbers of Chinese laborers and supervisors. The Department of Mining regulated water rights and problems of silting. Tin-export duties became a large item in the revenues of the Federated States.[27]

Following the failure of early experiments in growing pepper and spices in British Malaya, agricultural development had centered on sugar, pineapple, and coffee production. The first two were cultivated with moderate success under Chinese direction. European coffee plantations developed during the 1890s but only to the extent of 47,000 acres and some four thousand workers. The problem of labor recruitment became serious after 1900, since the Malays preferred fishing and subsistence agriculture to regimented employment. Chinese miners and sugar growers competed with coffee planters and the public works agencies of the government for the services of available coolie labor from south India. The very rapid development of rubber plantations after 1910, when the market price soared to 12 shillings a pound, greatly aggravated an already difficult labor-shortage problem.

Regulated recruitment of Tamil laborers from Malaya dated from 1884, when the initial Indian Immigration Ordinance was passed. It established the terms of indentured service and regulated the operation of employment premises, with an assembly depot functioning at Negapatam from 1892 under control of a Straits official. In 1898–1899, indentured terms for Indian laborers were shortened and minimum-wage scales were established. British planters hired their own recruiter agents after 1904, as the government did for its construction needs. Subsidies to steamer passenger service facilitated worker transportation from India.

Recruitment of Chinese workers was never the concern of the Malay government. In spite of known abuses, lodging-house agents were permitted, virtually without regulation, to control recruitment and to assign wages and terms of service. After 1910 indentured contracts were made no longer legally enforceable, but the actual Chinese practices were unaffected. Governmental regulation would have meant becoming involved in the activities of the mysterious Chinese secret societies and in policing a morass of Chinese violence, opium dispensing, and gambling operations. There was also the difficulty of devising any workable agreement with successive governments in China, which obviously cared very little down to the twenties what happened to overseas emigrants. Malay labor policy was therefore concerned almost entirely with immigrant Indians.

Earlier ventures into agriculture were dwarfed by the development of the rubber plantations. British adaptation of the rubber tree began as early as the 1870s, and the first estate in Malaya was planted in 1897. Since six to seven years were required for trees to become productive, only well-financed firms able to wait for returns on their investment could

[27] Allen and Donnithorne, 149–157.

participate. The Department of Agriculture began more serious research in problems of rubber growing after 1905. As a rule, the land was leased on a thirty-year basis, and the jungle growth was cleared under contracts with Chinese laborers. Indian labor was used for planting and tending the estates. The rubber program got under way vigorously after 1910, and by 1913 Malaya's plantation output surpassed that of Brazil's wild trees. Operating between the Rubber Growers Association in Great Britain and the Malay Planters Association were the merchant firms and brokers who provided the managing agents for the large rubber companies. The plantation area had expanded to 1.4 million acres by 1922 and to 2.1 million acres by 1940, with four-fifths of it British-owned. It was the Malay Planters Association which became most directly involved in the labor-management problem.[28]

When the staffing of the rubber plantations first became an urgent problem, from 1907 to 1912, the planter group began recruiting Indian workers. Indians were more amenable to police control than were the Chinese, and there was no point in encouraging greater Chinese preponderance than already existed. The Tamil Immigration Fund Ordinance of 1912 provided that the users of Indian labor, including the Federation government, should contribute to the cost of recruitment in proportion to the numbers employed. Payments from the fund, after 1913, covered costs of transportation, including food costs at the assembly depots. The Immigration Committee licensed *kangany* recruiters in proportion to the number of workers needed in a given year. The number of licensees increased to some eight thousand in 1927, when a peak of 120,000 laborers were brought in. The depression years of 1929 and 1930 showed a net surplus of Indian departures over arrivals; during the thirties around 76,000 net entries occurred annually. In 1938, the entire kangany arrangement was discontinued. The system had avoided some of the problems connected with indentured labor, outlawed after 1910, and was generally successful in realizing its goal of obtaining an adequate but not overnumerous supply of Indian labor.[29]

The regulations for the use of contract Indian labor formulated from time to time by the Federation government were actually enforced in a very casual manner. A law of 1909, passed at the insistence of the London authorities, prohibited wage withholding to cover the costs of consumer goods (truck foods) supplied by employers to laborers. But enforcement was left pretty largely to the planters themselves. The basic Labor Code of 1912 did little more than summarize prevailing standards at Singapore as to hours, contract validity, overtime and task-job pay, mining regulations, and housing and hospital care. In response to planter protests, the High Commissioner promised that employers would be consulted in the actual application of the code. The code was extended to the Straits Settle-

[28] *Ibid.,* 43–44, 108–117; Parmer, 5–10, 15–37.
[29] Parmer, 35–48; Ginsburg and Roberts, 316–319.

ments in 1920. The controller service employed by the Department of Labor to supervise the code usually made it a point to keep on cordial terms with the Planters Association. The basic concern was to forestall embarrassing complaints from India or London but otherwise to do nothing to hamper the prosperity of the expanding rubber plantations.[30]

Some fairly significant changes were made in the labor code in 1923 in response to the Indian Emigration Act passed the previous year by the new postwar government of India. The disciplinary powers of employers were reduced; free repatriation was to be made available after one year; the wage standard was improved; and requirements were indicated for schooling of children and for maternity benefits. The revised code was later reamended after consultations with the planters, and it was enforced by the controller with the same lack of enthusiasm previously displayed. Overzealous champions of the code could usually be curbed by planter appeals to the High Commissioner. Controller cadets were counseled officially to be equally concerned with the welfare of laborer and employer on the dubious assumption that no essential conflict of interest existed between them. Popular controllers were made honorary members of the Planters Association on retirement.

The principal abuses developed in connection with wages and with the theoretical right of workers to shift employers. In slack times planters reduced wages; in good times they kept the standard-wage scale undisturbed by adding bonuses and living allowances. The right to shift employers was effectively hampered by holding back wages, by refusing to accept notices to quit, by pressure from the kangany, and by collusion among employers. Desultory efforts made by the Indian government down to 1937 failed to achieve any material improvement.[31]

## Depression and the End of the Kangany System

Two postwar periods of depression, one in 1921–1922 and the other in 1930–1932, created serious unemployment problems for Indian and Chinese workers in Malaya. During the first period, some sixty thousand were unemployed, two-thirds of them Indians. The decrepit were cared for; some workers were absorbed on public works projects, and many of the destitute Chinese returned home on their own. The problem eased quickly in 1922. The great depression produced far more serious repercussions. The collapse of rubber prices in particular from 2 shillings, 10 pence per pound in 1927 to 9 pence per pound in 1929 and to a mere 2 pence per pound in 1932 illustrated the vulnerability of an economy dependent entirely on world markets for a few commodities. Plantations had to be maintained up to minimal standards even if no markets were available. Daily wages of Indian workers were cut back by more than half, from around 48 cents

---

[30] Parmer, 116–122.
[31] *Ibid.,* 141–158, 166–188.

(2 shillings) a day in 1927 to 23 cents in 1932; other economies were made, and company reserves were tapped. Some seventy-five thousand Chinese, mainly the decrepit, were repatriated at government expense; monthly quotas were imposed to limit Chinese male immigrant entries. Repatriation of Indians was tried for a time in 1930 but was abandoned on complaint from the planters except in cases where work at viable wages was simply not available. Serious unemployment came to an end in 1933, but no marked improvement in wages occurred until near the end of the decade.[32]

The failure of the Federation government to enforce the minimal provisions of the labor code during the thirties eventually became the concern of Congress Party politicians in India. During the depression the controller made a show of firmness in demanding subsistence-level wages of 30 cents per day, or $7.50 per month. He was opposed by the High Commissioner, who heeded the pleas for reductions from both the Rubber Growers of London and the Planters Association in Malaya. Wages rose to 28 cents a day in 1934 and to 35 cents in 1935. But time had run out on the kangany system. Criticisms made by the Indian Congress Party press were echoed by the Central Indian Association of Malaya, a not-too-representative group made up of business and professional men organized in 1936. Following the grant of full self-government for India in 1937, a visiting Indian delegation investigated the situation in Malaya at first hand. Belated employer efforts to meet criticisms by introducing wages of 45 to 50 cents a day were to no avail. In June, 1938, the Indian government canceled the entire recruitment system.

Efforts on the part of the planters to find an alternative source of labor in Java were overtaken by World War II.[33] The Indian population of Malaya, which numbered 22 per cent of the Federated States total in 1931, registered no substantial net gains thereafter. In contrast to the Chinese, Indians tended not to be venturesome and politically minded, unwilling to leave familiar and assured connections.

## Malays and Chinese

Although the Malay proportion of the total population within the area of British control had declined from 51 per cent of the total in 1911 to about 44 per cent in 1931, the indigenous peoples were by no means a negligible economic and political factor in the interwar period. They looked down on the Tamil coolies and had very little in common except on the economic level with the clannish Chinese. Intermarriage with either alien group was opposed by the Muslim Malays; the worship of idols by Indians and the eating of pork by Chinese were symbols of Islamic aversion. English-educated Malays were becoming politically conscious and articulately anti-Chinese. The superior political position of the Malays was

[32] *Ibid.,* 187–212, 222–248; Allen and Donnithorne, 235–239.
[33] Parmer, 45–47, 56–57, 78, 108–113, 192–221.

matched by their established position as agriculturalists and food producers. Along the eastern coast the population was 90 per cent Malay, and the area as a whole was 30 per cent self-sufficient in food. Assisted by Sumatran immigrants, the Malay peasants had contributed greatly to an eightfold expansion of food production.

As fishermen and farmers, the Malays were less vulnerable economically than their alien neighbors who had settled along the western coast since 1850. Behind their Muslim faith were age-old religious rituals associated with their agricultural vocation and their fisherman's role. Malay roots ran deeper into the cultural milieu than did those of the Indians and Chinese, and the Malays could aspire to political partnership with the British in a fashion which the others could not match.

Malay dependence on the Chinese trader and moneylender was generally prevalent. As a farmer, the Malay was perennially in debt to the Chinese trader for the acquisition of needed buffaloes, tools and equipment, and labor. As a fisherman also, whether at Malacca, Kelantan, or Trengganu, the Malay used Chinese credits for the purchase of boats, consumer needs, and equipment and then as a debtor was obliged to sell the entire catch below the current price to the Chinese trader, who marketed the product. Some 200,000 small-holder rubber planters (including Javanese) also operated on Chinese capital and sold the smoked sheets to Chinese dealers. Malays began to take the place of Indians on the rubber estates only after World War II.

The Chinese were admittedly indispensable to the economy, but the Malays were also firmly placed socially and also not willing to abdicate their political priorities. Traditionalist Malays could depend on the tenacity of their religion and culture and the resulting social cohesion, which was unmatched by the uprooted aliens. Representatives of the educated Muslim elite who were not members of feudal families were nevertheless caught in a trap. Any advocacy of centralization and democratization of the government might easily result in the political domination by the already economically potent Chinese. The Malay elite, therefore, would deny equal political rights to the Chinese until the Malays themselves could achieve a greater measure of economic and social progress. Decentralization of power, as desired by the Colonial Office after 1920, and a policy of devolution to indigenous political control played into Malay hands.[34]

The Malay Chinese were strong numerically and economically but weak in social cohesion and in political awareness. They numbered in 1931 some 39 per cent of the total population, including the Straits Settlements, and more than 44 per cent at the end of World War II. The increment was due in large measure to the arrival of large numbers of Chinese women immigrants during the 1930s, after the quota was placed on males. One-third of the 2.6 million Chinese inhabitants were by 1947

[34] Mills, *British Malaya*, 24–27; Ginsburg and Roberts, 192–210, 373–384, 432–435, 455–460.

Malay-born. But their division into linguistic groups and feuding clans prevented political cohesion, while single-minded concern for personal economic gain exerted a demoralizing influence culturally on the transplanted Chinese. Family ties and ancestor cults weakened, and belief in demons, patron-saint spirits, and heroes, such as the Ming Admiral Cheng-ho, provided poor substitutes. The very laissez-faire policy of the government encouraged the proliferation of Chinese criminal propensities, including intimidation within the community, gambling, and the opium mania. With the coming of women immigrants in the 1930s, girl slaves and prostitution were added to Chinese vices.[35]

The characteristic apolitical attitude of the Malay Chinese began to change around the middle 1920s with the accession of the Kuomintang to power in China. In contrast to the traditional attitude of Peking, which had paid no attention whatever to the plight of overseas Chinese, the new Nanking regime made every effort to solicit political and financial support for the south ocean (*Nanyang*) group. Dr. Sun Yat-sen himself had spent some time in exile at Penang and had developed a strong following among the resident Cantonese. During the period of prominence of the Soviet agent Borodin in the party, from 1923 to 1927, the Kuomintang organization in Malaya, acting on directions from Shanghai, followed the official Communist Party line, especially so among the Hainan and Hakka clan factions. The policy was strongly anti-British, and supporting activity was accordingly declared illegal down to 1930. Even after Borodin was obliged to leave China in 1927, Communist elements remained strongly entrenched within the Malay Kuomintang. Radical Chinese nationalists challenged British measures to restrict immigration in 1930, but most resident Chinese paid as little attention as possible to the political agitators.

After 1930 the so-called Malay Communist Party, almost entirely Chinese, tried with little success to enlist membership from other ethnic groups. Some leaders suffered arrest and deportation. After 1935 the Communists fomented strikes and boycotts in the transport field and on the naval-base construction site back of Singapore, as well as at mines, on plantations, and in the crafts. The most valid economic targets of grievance were abuses of contractor authority, practices which were almost a century old, but the strikes were suppressed as allegedly politically inspired. After the Sianfu incident in 1937, the Malay Communist Party dutifully adopted Moscow's popular-front hostility to the Japanese; after 1940 it abandoned completely the strident anti-British agitation. The British authorities did make a beginning in 1940 and 1941 in trade-union legislation and the establishment of industrial courts, thus taking some responsibility for the welfare of urban Chinese labor.[36]

[35] Victor Purcell, *The Chinese in South-East Asia* (1951), 269–281, 325–354; Mills, *New World,* 188–190.

[36] Ginsburg and Roberts, 455–460; Parmer, 122–165; Purcell, 325–356.

## Conclusions on British Malaya

Although in retrospect it is not difficult to perceive that the colonialist role in Malay had started to decline by 1940, the achievements realized during the short period of British occupancy of the peninsula were truly remarkable, especially so in the economic field. Taking over one of the most unpromising segments of Southeast Asia in terms of resources and population, an area almost completely neglected during two centuries of Siamese and Dutch hegemony, the British made it productive and prosperous. The per capita net annual product attained an estimated $310 by 1940. Exports from the colony exceeded its imports in value by some 21 per cent. The total per capita trade of Malaya exceeded that of Burma (second in Southeast Asia) by a ratio of 8 to 1, that of Siam (third) by 18 to 1.[37]

Britain's mercantile achievement at Singapore was accomplished under an enlightened policy of unfettered trade, which functioned without forced deliveries, price fixing, or other discriminatory restrictions. The products of the forests, mines, plantations, and farms of all Southeast Asian peoples found opportunity for sale in a free competitive market at the entrepôt, where capital equipment and consumer goods from every corner of the world were also made available. The necessary pacification and administration of interior regions of the peninsula, where mining and plantation development occurred, were accomplished with a minimum of arbitrary governmental coercion and with little or no interference with the cultural traditions of the indigenous inhabitants. Banking and commercial facilities of Singapore, worldwide in their connections, shared the financial role after 1932 with the large Overseas Chinese Banking Corporation.[38]

British Malaya nevertheless suffered from the limitations of the liberal ideal which it largely exemplified. The rapid growth of population at Singapore and within the western third of the peninsula was a forced-draft operation which produced many problems. It tapped the vast human reservoirs of overcrowded China and India in a fashion largely oblivious to considerations of social welfare and political progress, both of which were traditionally associated with the liberal ideal. The indigenous Malays were swamped economically, unable to meet the strenuous competition, and the alien immigrants were exploited with tragic efficiency. This was often done by compatriots—especially in the case of the Chinese, many of whom became in consequence pretty badly demoralized. The initial improvement in per capita income, arising from increased capital investment and trade, petered out in time. Collusion between the British business community, which held an estimated 260 million dollars in investments and

---

[37] J. R. Andrus, *Burmese Economic Life* (1947), 114–115; Benjamin Higgins, "Review Article," *Pacific Affairs,* XXXI (1958), 74–87.

[38] Allen and Donnithorne, 200–209.

82 million dollars in bonds, and friendly British governmental agencies prevented any effective application of accepted minimal standards for fair treatment of laborers. Chinese capitalists, also holding an estimated 200 million dollars in equities,[39] were completely unregulated in their exploitive treatment of fellow Chinese laborers and Malay debtors.

The easy liberal assumption that population growth and rising per capita output would result automatically in improved social standards was simply not relevant in Malaya. The resulting plural society was culturally bankrupt, lacking accepted norms of conduct, shared values, and effective social controls. Equally inapplicable in Malaya was the principle of political liberalism which condemned arbitrary governmental agencies, lacking responsibility to the interests and wishes of the people ruled. The Colonial Office at London was usually far more concerned with improving labor standards in Malaya and preserving some degree of responsible local autonomy than were the intermediate authorities in India, Singapore, and Kuala Lumpur. This democratic concern present in English society was diluted by exposure to contrary points of view en route to Malaya. The faint stirrings of uncoordinated political unrest present in Malaya during the 1930s were not sufficiently demanding to suggest the need for qualifying the overriding authority of the High Commissioner at Singapore in the interest of developing responsible self-rule.

[39] Mills (ed.), *New World,* 184–190.

# PART 6

# Political Reform and Nationalist Revival

# CHAPTER 20

# The Philippines:

## From Spanish to
## American Rule

Spanish efforts after 1815 to maintain the role of Manila as an Oriental entrepôt, even though cut off from Mexican silver, proved unsuccessful. The city came to grief at mid-century as a result of the opening of additional Chinese treaty ports following the British war of 1840–1842. Spain endeavored thereafter to develop the agricultural resources of the islands, but with little success except for tobacco. The establishment of direct relations with Spain facilitated the arrival of private European trading groups and of peninsular clergy as well. The new arrivals usually deprecated existing Filipino standards not only in the economy and government but also in the church. This emerging situation generated increasing friction between Filipino nationalists and the Spanish, who continued jealously to guard their privileged economic and social positions. Unrest came to center in three areas—among the peasants occupying the friar-owned lands of Luzon, among the Filipino clergy who were resentful of Spanish refusal to accept them as equals, and especially, in the small circle of educated Filipinos who visited Europe. The novels of José Rizal, published after 1887, dramatized the indictment of a dying Spanish system apparently incapable of self-criticism or improvement.

The more or less accidental intervention of United States naval forces at Manila during the Spanish war of 1898 inaugurated a new era for the Philippines. The apparent incapacity of the Filipinos at the time to assume the responsibilities of independence and the probability that some other power would take over control if the islands were cast adrift influenced Washington's decision to stay on, despite nationalist resistance in the archipelago, and Democratic Party criticism in America. American rule liquidated the friar landholdings, eliminated clerical influence in the government, and vastly improved health and educational facilities.

The Philippine products of American capital and business initiative were accorded free entry into the American market, but a Filipino Legislature, mindful of the friar-land problem, insisted on limiting the size of private American landholdings. The promise of eventual Philippine independence, implied at the outset and made explicit in the Jones Act of 1916, tended to become somewhat less sure after World War I. The policy was revived in the early thirties under changed economic and political circumstances attending the great depression. The Tydings-McDuffie Act of 1934 provided for an autonomous Commonwealth government, which emerged in 1936 under a Constitution of Filipino authorship. The ten-year transition to complete independence was interrupted by World War II. The alleged combination of "two hundred forty years in a Spanish convent followed by fifty years in Hollywood"[1] contributed to the Philippines characteristics which were not shared by other nations of Southeast Asia.

## Spain's Faltering Effort to Revive the Philippines

After 1815 the Philippines ceased to be an extension of Spanish America and were obliged to develop direct economic and cultural relations with Spain itself. In succeeding decades, peninsular Spaniards, both traders and clergy, came to Manila in increasing numbers, bringing fresh energy and new ideas. The islands were accorded limited representation in the Spanish Cortes. But the changes realized were not extensive. The regular clergy continued as before to resist the authority of both Madrid and the Bishop of Manila. The monks and friars claimed the credit for establishing Spanish rule and Christian culture in the islands and considered themselves to be the best judges of methods calculated to preserve their achievements. Suppression of some monasteries in Spain after 1835 influenced additional numbers of dispossessed monks to migrate to the Orient. Representatives of the revived Jesuit order replaced the Recollect fathers in the difficult Mindanao area and exerted a stimulating effect on educational efforts generally.[2]

For several decades after 1815, the port of Manila gave promise of economic vigor under the stimulus of private trading activities. A dozen Spanish commercial firms were involved in the Manila trade by 1840. The port afforded a place where Chinese and Indian traders could gain access to Spanish silver and to Chinese wares outside the bounds of the restrictive Co-hong trading system at Canton. The Manila trading operation broke down disastrously during the late 1840s when Chinese goods became easily available at several newly opened ports, especially Shanghai. Simultane-

[1] Robert E. Elegant, *The Dragon's Seed, Peking and the Overseas Chinese* (1959), 285.

[2] Charles Derbyshire, *The Social Cancer* (1912), xiii–xviii.

ously the stream of silver from Europe dried up, and the islands entrepôt was insolvent by 1850. This collapse occurred just when the advent of steam navigation was stimulating the development of new trading patterns for both Europe and Asia.[3]

Additional problems developed meanwhile for Manila in the southern islands. The French gesture at Basilan in the Sulu Archipelago in 1844 forced Manila to make good its claim of sovereignty over the area. Beginning in 1848, steam gunboats were introduced in a sustained policing effort directed against the southern pirates. The Spanish captured the Sulu fortress of Jolo in 1851, but they failed to occupy the interior of the island. Their burdensome operations in the Sulu Sea dragged on inconclusively for more than a quarter century. When the Sultan of Sulu finally agreed to acknowledge Spanish suzerainty in 1878, it was via a negotiated agreement. Spain paid an annual cash subsidy to the Sultan and his advisers, and also accorded him special religious guarantees, succession rights, and trading privileges. Even so, Spanish gunboats continued to chase the Sulu pirates for a long time thereafter. In 1885, as previously noted, Spain surrendered its claim to British North Borneo in return for British recognition of Spain's sovereignty over the Sulu Islands.[4]

Manila's costly and profitless participation in the French interventions at Tourane and Saigon from 1859 to 1863, described in Chapter 15, underscored Spain's inability to compete effectively in the emerging imperialist rivalry.

## Development of Nationalist Resistance

Filipino political and social unrest centered after 1815 in the rich Tagalog areas of Luzon, where friars held most of the valuable land titles. The newly arrived European clergy also encountered increasing challenge to their preferred social and political prerogatives. Decline in celibate discipline exposed some of the clergy to damaging attack on moral grounds. The native clergy were particularly discontented over inferiority of status in terms of education and job opportunities, especially when regulars from Spain started taking over favored parish assignments. After 1840, educated Filipinos openly denounced the reactionary friars as racially bigoted and as the enemies of economic and political progress. Malcontent clergy staged an overt rebellion in 1843 with a view to forcing the Spanish to liberalize their policies. The critical newspapers *El Diario de Manila* and *El Commercio* appeared in 1848 and 1850 respectively. The early leaders of the Church secularization movement (as against regular-clergy control) were Fathers Peláez and Opolinario. The first was a Filipino-Spanish educator,

[3] Claude Buss in Mills (ed.), *New World of Southeast Asia* (1949), 26.
[4] W. Cameron Forbes, *The Philippine Islands* (1928), 46–47.

editor, and scholar, and the second was a frustrated Filipino cleric rejected for membership in a friar order.[5]

Behind the façade of clerical feuding, which reflected the mounting anti-Spanish feeling of the middle nineteenth century, was the basic peasant problem. Villagers who were entangled by debtor bondage and unable to develop new landholdings of their own because of the extent of friar claims to undeveloped land oscillated between contrasting moods. One alternative reaction was a posture of indolent passivity which sought to ignore the hostile world outside, while the other response was aggressively violent. The belligerent reaction frequently developed in a context of nativistic revivalism, messianic in its claims and objectives and magical in its methods. Belief in charms, amulets, and symbols of invulnerability deriving from pre-Spanish traditions found no corrective in the miracle-saturated Christian milieu. The resulting bandit raids were directed mainly against Spanish and mestizo landlords. In central Luzon, the friars became the embodiment of the enemy group, and leadership over such religio-political aberrations was often assumed by malcontent Filipino clerics.[6]

The many-headed Colorum movement which developed in the mid-nineteenth century symbolized the growing unrest. Its founder and first martyr was Father Opolinario de la Cruz of Tayabas province. Following his rejection for membership in a friar order at Manila in 1841, Opolinario proceeded to form his own brotherhood, the Colorum, in which Spaniards and mestizos were explicitly denied membership. Although the character of the organization was essentially religious and social, it developed heterodox ideas and eventually ran afoul of the police. When Opolinario and his followers were finally captured by a Spanish patrol, the leader's body was dismembered in gruesome fashion, presumably to disprove his supernatural pretensions. Surviving remnants of the Colorum retired to the caves of a volcanic mountain fastness, where they founded their "New Jerusalem." Christian names and terminology were used by the rebels, but the doctrines and rites were of pre-Spanish origin. The fame of the organization led other rebel groups to assume the same name, a practice which continued in vogue throughout the remainder of the century.[7]

Political unrest in the Philippines gained momentum after 1869. Revolution in Spain connected with exiling of Isabella II occurred at the same time that the opening of the Suez Canal brought all of Europe much closer to the Orient. Filipino students began to visit Europe in greater numbers. A republican Spanish governor enjoyed a brief tenure

[5] Derbyshire, xix–xxii; Gregorio F. Zaide, *Philippine History and Civilization* (1939), 319–327; George A. Malcolm, *The Commonwealth of the Philippines* (1936), 61; D. G. E. Hall, *Historians of South-East Asia* (1961), 210–212.

[6] David R. Sturtevant, *Nativistic Movements in the Philippines: A Study in Protest Patterns* (unpublished), 2, 6–8.

[7] *Ibid.*, 9–10.

at Manila, and an increasing number of liberal Spaniards began to arrive. Serious trouble developed in 1872 in connection with an army mutiny, a movement with which restive elements of the native clergy were found to be associated. The executed priestly leaders of the rebels were all able scholars, and their names were added to the growing list of national martyrs. The rising tide of nationalist liberal unrest took as its principal target the conservative landholding religious orders. The friars came to symbolize Spanish arrogance and depreciation of the Filipinos. Economic malcontents also attacked the official monopoly of tobacco cultivation and trade, which persisted under the Spanish system. Suppressive measures were severely and continuously applied by the government from 1872 to 1898.[8]

## The Influence of José Rizal

The most articulate and penetrating critic of Spanish rule in the Philippines was José Rizal-Mercado y Alonso. He was born in 1861, the son of a friar-land tenant in Luzon. His parentage was Filipino, but with distant Spanish and Chinese connections.[9] As a precocious student of languages and literature at the Jesuit Ateneo de Manila and the Dominican University of Santo Tomas, Rizal left for Spain in 1879 to undertake further study in philosophy and medicine. He commanded the effective use of four Western European languages and traveled extensively about the Continent. His first literary achievement was his editing of Morgas's sixteenth-century classic, *Sucesos de las Filipinas* (*Events in the Philippines*), which emphasized the pre-Spanish cultural attainments of the islanders. In Barcelona and Madrid, he came into contact with a modern liberal Spanish opinion, which was denied expression in the Philippines by the persistence of friar influence. He belonged for a time to the Masonic Order, where he found sympathy for his anticlerical views. While in Europe, he also became acquainted with Marcelo H. del Pilar, the Filipino champion of complete separation from Spain and the founder of the Filipino nationalist movement. Some contemporaries regarded del Pilar as the more forthright and intelligent of the two.[10] Rizal himself did not disparage Spain's contributions to the development of the islands and rejected radical or violent measures, while trying to accomplish governmental and land reforms by peaceful means. But he saw no hope for his homeland unless the reactionary friar domination was broken. He undertook to promote that end by writing several propagandist novels based on Filipino life.

Rizal's *Noli me Tangere* (*Touch Me Not,* or *The Social Cancer*) was published in Berlin in 1887. The title, taken from St. Luke's Gospel, implied a subject too sensitive for discussion. The setting of *Noli me Tangere* was the stagnant backwater society of Manila, represented as mired in

[8] Derbyshire, xiii–xviii.

[9] Malcolm, 110. Rizal may have had some Japanese ancestry as well.

[10] Malcolm, 106.

petty jealousies, injustices, superstitions, and hypocritical fraud. This vulnerable situation was subjected to the disturbingly liberal contacts of modern Spain and Europe transmitted in the personality of a returning expatriate. The islands society was pictured as unable to come to terms with such influences from the outside and as condemned to die slowly of its incurable malady. The forces of injustice which had previously made a victim of the father of the hero also relentlessly pursued the son, who protested in vain against the mad violence which was breeding disaster for all. The heroine, who was herself the illegitimate daughter of a friar, preferred a nunnery to the travesty of false love following the death of her lover-hero. Rizal did not hesitate to expose the faults of his fellow Filipinos in his attack on what he regarded as a sinister combination of false religion, vice, and greed. Although proscribed in the Philippines, copies of *Noli me Tangere* circulated secretly and were widely read. A second novel by Rizal entitled *El Filibusterismo* (*The Reign of Greed*), published at Ghent in 1890, was equally mature and forceful, but it lacked some of the appeal of his earlier one.[11] Through the personalities of de Pilar and Rizal, rising liberalism in the Philippines owed a debt to Western Europe.

As much as any other single factor, *Noli me Tangere* crystallized the nationalist movement in the Philippines. After living briefly at Hongkong and in Cuba, Rizal returned in 1892 to Manila. He was promptly exiled to a small Jesuit mission on the northern shore of Mindanao. The Philippine League (La Liga Filipina), which he initiated in 1892, limited its tactics to nonviolent petitioning and was for this reason poltically ineffective. The larger nationalist revolutionist movement, for which his name and photograph became a symbol, fell under the control of primitive and sanguinary leaders, whose objectives and methods he did not condone. Magical Colorum groups took up the cause as did the so-called Association of the Sons of the People, or Katipunan, organized by Andrés Bonifacio. The initiatory rites of the Katipunan included a blood covenant binding on all members. Sharing the leadership of the Katipunan with Bonifacio and eventually displacing him was the magnetic and colorful Emilio Aguinaldo, a partly Chinese ex-schoolmaster of Cavite, a town near Manila.[12]

Serious rebellion began in Luzon in August, 1896. A Katipunan plot to assassinate all Spaniards and their sympathizers was uncovered, and the panicked Europeans staged a slaughter. Rizal returned to Manila on the eve of the outbreak en route to Cuba, where he had volunteered his services as a physician. Although at first exonerated by the governor from responsibility for the plot and allowed to proceed to Spain, he was subsequently arrested, returned to Manila for trial, and condemned to die. In the execution of Rizal on December 30, 1896, Spanish authority on

---

[11] Derbyshire, xxv–xxxvii, and the body of the novel; Malcolm, 110–112.
[12] Malcolm, 106–107.

the islands virtually ensured its doom, for Rizal was the national hero. The official suppression of his statements condemning the mad rebellion—statements made in order to avoid embarrassment for miscarriage of justice—actually backfired against the government. Desperately furious, the Tagalog revolutionaries rallied under the leadership of Aguinaldo. The two-year rising was eventually contained by the authorities, and the truce of Biak-no-bato was concluded in 1898. Aguinaldo agreed to go into exile, and the Spanish paid a monetary indemnity to the nationalists. Madrid's belated offers to institute municipal reforms and to establish a consultative assembly served only to fan nationalist feeling and to emphasize the spectacle of Spanish vacillation and panic.[13]

Catholic apologists have pointed out that Rizal's indictment of Spanish rule in the Philippines was distorted in its failure to depict a single priest as a dignified and attractive person. His motives were admitted to be patriotic, but his books were criticized as pathological in tone and propagandist in content. The same apologists emphasized Rizal's return to the Church prior to his execution. They also argued that the norms which he applied so devastatingly to the Philippines were derived from Christianity itself. They placed the real blame for deteriorating conditions on the arrival of venal and ignorant officials sent out by liberal Spain after 1869.[14] This rejoinder was not particularly convincing. There was clearly enough truth in Rizal's indictment to arouse a sympathetic response from his people and to accord him the martyr's role in Philippine history.

Philippine nationalism also found expression in a schismatic religious movement headed by Father Gregorio Aglipay, who was excommunicated in the 1890s following his condemnation of foreign domination of the Church. Aguinaldo made him vicar general of the nationalist army, and in 1902 he assumed the role of supreme bishop of the new Independent Filipino Church. The new order enlisted only Filipinos as clergy, permitted them to marry, conducted services in the local dialects, and itself participated actively in national political affairs. Efforts of the Dominican order, made during the course of the rebellion, to sponsor a militant countermovement known as the Guards in Honor of Mary were completely ineffective, although most Filipinos remained loyal to the traditional Catholic faith. When the Americans arrived in 1898, Filipino nationalists were virtually unanimous in their demand to liquidate friar landholdings and to send the Spaniards home.[15]

[13] *Ibid.*, 92–93, 113–114.

[14] Jesus Maria Cavanna y Monso, *Rizal and the Philippines of His Day* (1957), 1–44, 196–198.

[15] Malcolm, 307–310; Sturtevant, 12–13. The Independent Filipino Church was particularly strong in the Ilocano-speaking region of northern Luzon. In 1918, it included 1.4 million communicants, 310 priests, and ten bishops.

## American Annexation of the Philippines

The intrusion of American naval power into the political affairs of the Philippines in May, 1898, in connection with the Cuban war was as much a surprise to the people of the United States as it was to the Filipinos. It was engineered by a small coterie of naval expansionists led by Captain Mahan, Senator Henry Cabot Lodge, and Undersecretary of the Navy Theodore Roosevelt. This group took advantage of the opportunity afforded by the Spanish war to establish an American foothold in Southeast Asia. Secretary Roosevelt's unilateral sponsorship of the naval mission of Admiral Dewey to the Far East and the orders dated April 25, 1898, directing the admiral to destroy the Spanish fleet in Manila Bay precipitated a train of events which resulted in American annexation of the entire archipelago.

The American decision was made in the context of a feverish world-wide expansionist competition, which had just witnessed German and Russian occupation of important port facilities in North China and a threatened German entry into Southeast Asia as well. One factor in the American decision was Britain's active support of Washington's initiative to serve as a counterweight to the German and Russian advance. A more important factor was the unseemly imperialist enthusiasm generated within patriotic circles in America, including Protestant missionary partisans and expansionists generally, who saw in the situation the hand of God beckoning America to a glorious "manifest destiny." Dewey hats, Dewey cocktails, and "Dewey for President" agitation became the rage following the admiral's victory in Manila Bay on May 1. Investor and trading groups later joined the "manifest destiny" chorus, attempting to rationalize on economic grounds the contagion generated by the imperialist virus.[16]

Roosevelt's initial contention that possession of the islands would bolster America's political and economic stake in the Far East was factually specious. The entire Far East continued to account for only a tiny fraction of America's foreign trade. Within less than a decade, Roosevelt himself acknowledged that the islands constituted the Achilles' heel of America's position in Eastern Asia, calling for heavy naval commitments in deference to Japan's growing influence in the region. Hawaii and Panama were related positively to American security interests; the Philippines were not.[17] The Democratic opposition, led by William Jennings Bryan, adopted an anti-imperialist position at the outset and continued thereafter to make political capital of the difficulties encountered.

The American political position in Manila Bay was heavily com-

[16] A. Whitney Griswold, *The Far Eastern Policy of the United States* (1938), 34–35.

[17] *Ibid.* See also Paul Clyde, *The Far East* (1953), 264–279.

promised by Admiral Dewey's action in summoning the recently exiled Aguinaldo from Singapore to Hongkong in an effort to enlist Filipino cooperation in the destruction of Spanish authority in the islands. The Katipunan leader reached Manila Bay on May 19, and within little more than a month's time he was again at the head of the revived nationalist revolutionary government of 1896–1898. The eight thousand American troops required to capture the Manila fortress, with the aid of Aguinaldo, were sent over in July, 1898, before any final decision had been reached in Washington concerning the disposition of the islands. Manila fell on August 13, a few hours after Washington's signing of the peace protocol with Spain. The subsequent treaty ceding the islands to the United States accorded Spain a 20-million-dollar indemnity. Dewey insisted that he had made no promise or political commitment to Aguinaldo, but the collaborating patriotic Filipinos thought that they were fighting for political freedom. When they learned otherwise, they resumed their rebellious role, bitterly disillusioned. The definition of the political status and the civil rights of the islanders was left for the American Congress to determine.[18]

About 3½ years of military effort were required to subdue the Filipino rebellion and a considerably longer time to conquer the Moros. Aguinaldo fell out with his former associate in the Katipunan, Bonifacio, and was himself captured in 1900. He then took an oath of allegiance to the United States and tried to persuade other rebels to do the same. One of the officers of his army, Felipe Salvador, maintained guerrilla resistance for almost a full decade. Virtually all overt rebellion ceased by 1907. As a law-abiding but unrepentant nationalist, Aguinaldo continued to be a popular political figure. He was accorded a pension by the Philippine Legislature in 1920, and he subsequently made several abortive efforts to challenge the political leadership of Manuel Quezon. Aguinaldo desired to improve the lot of the common man as well as to obtain early independence.[19]

While the rebellion was being put down, the American government hesitatingly decided to retain control of the islands. The President concluded that the Filipinos at the time were incapable of maintaining independent status and that if essential improvements were to be realized, American authority would have to be asserted throughout the archipelago. The Filipinos were meanwhile denied full rights as American citizens, such as jury trial and the right to bear arms, and they must submit to American control while being prepared for self-government. The President's decision to keep the islands was barely sustained by the treaty-approval vote in the Congress, and it faced serious challenge in the ensuing national election of 1900. When military rule was discontinued in 1901, a concerted effort was launched by the President's Civilian Commission and (after 1903) by

[18] Malcolm, 61–63.
[19] *Ibid.,* 114–117.

Chief Commissioner William Howard Taft to win the confidence, respect, and cooperation of the Filipino peoples. From the outset, however, America's role in the islands was apologetic and lacking in convincing political justification.

## Beginnings of Self-government and Land Reform

The pattern of United States rule in the Philippines was set by Taft, first as Commissioner from 1901 to 1904, then as Secretary of War under President Roosevelt, and finally as President in his own right, 1909–1913. Taft abolished army rule, proclaimed equality of rights for all Filipino citizens, decreed the separation of church and state, and accorded freedom of press and assembly. Acting under the Organic Act (Cooper Act) passed by the Congress in 1902, Taft staged the first local elections in 1903, which provided the means of consulting with Filipino opinion in matters relating to municipal and village government. A further step was taken in 1907, when a general Assembly was elected on a restricted literate-taxpayer-suffrage basis. The office of governor-general was set up in 1909. Taft allocated from the outset large appropriations for improvement of educational and health facilities. He honored the customary laws of the conquered Moro tribesmen but otherwise established a uniform law code, to be interpreted in large measure by Filipino judges.[20] Conservative Filipinos of ability were admitted to membership in the Commission in 1901; their first Cabinet assignment came in 1908. Subsequent appointments of Filipinos were made to the executive Departments of Justice and Finance, and to the Labor Bureau. An *ad hoc* Council of State was instituted as advisory to the governor-general after 1909, including among others the speakers of both houses of the Legislature and leaders of the majority party. Eventually all Cabinet posts save that of Public Instruction came to be manned by Filipinos, although the Cabinet continued, in the American tradition, responsible to the governor-general rather than to the Legislature.[21]

The Philippines Assembly which was elected in 1907 was accorded from the outset a substantial voice in determining domestic legislation, in the definition of financial and land policies, and in judicial administration. Accompanying the inauguration of the 1907 Assembly, Secretary Taft committed the American government to a policy looking toward complete independence, pending the development of indigenous capacity to conduct public affairs, to maintain order, and to accord equal protection to the rich and the poor. Under the governor-general appointed by President Wilson in 1913, the appointive Philippines Commission functioned as the upper house of the Legislature under a Filipino majority; thus both houses of the Legislature possessed native majorities. The policies inaugurated by Taft

[20] R. A. Smith, *Philippine Freedom* (1938), 18–31.
[21] Malcolm, 72–73, 98–100.

from 1901 to 1913 did not satisfy impatient Filipino nationalists, but they did afford a basis for cooperation and orderly progress.[22]

It became apparent very early in the occupation that if the Americans were to gain the confidence of the peasant residents of Luzon in particular, they would have to curb the political influence of the clergy and liquidate the landholdings of the friars. On these demands public opinion was virtually unanimous. Friar lands comprised some 430,000 acres, one-half of them located in the vicinity of Manila. They included some of the best agricultural areas, which were customarily leased to tenant cultivators at profitable rates. Residual friar claims to adjacent undeveloped land often blocked the efforts of industrious peasants to gain possession of farms by clearing land and reducing it to cultivation. Also objectionable to the Filipinos were the wide powers wielded by the clergy in various activities of local government. These included the keeping of vital statistics, the administration of health regulations and prisons, and some measure of police control. Friars regularly censored municipal budgets, influenced taxation policy, directed public education, and largely controlled the partitioning and utilization of Crown lands. The proposed reforms involved the revamping of local-government machinery, liquidation of friar-land titles, and orientation of public instruction toward democratic ends under secular control.[23] American objectives were essentially political rather than economic, for at stake was the confidence of the Filipino people in the *bona fides* of United States rule.

The task of curbing the powers of the religious orders was made difficult by their intransigent attitude, especially that of the new papal delegate sent to Manila in early 1900, Archbishop P. L. Chapelle of New Orleans. He declared that American military authorities must not only reestablish friar control over their traditional holdings but also accord military protection of their legal rights. He challenged the declared policy of separation of church and state and offered the services of the clergy in the time-honored fashion for promoting pacification. Chapelle also claimed clerical jurisdiction over former Crown lands, plus control over schools, orphanages, and pawnshops as well as churches. He made no positive response to Taft's proposal that friar lands be purchased by the government and sold in small-holding lots to occupying tenants. Peasant unrest mounted alarmingly when, in the absence of any guaranteed American protection, friars began to move back to reoccupy their former holdings.

The hands of the American Commissioners were greatly strengthened by the terms of the Organic Act of 1902 (Cooper Act), which declared that friar lands constituted the public property of the Philippines government and were to be made available for sale, conveyance, or lease with preference

[22] Shirley Jenkins in J. F. Cady et al., *Development of Self-Rule in Burma, the Philippines, and Malaya* (1948), 84–87.

[23] Garel A. Grunder and William E. Livezey, *The Philippines and the United States* (1951), 112–124.

given to actual occupants. After further abortive negotiations at Rome and Manila, an agreement was finally reached with Bishop Chapelle's Italian successor for the purchase of a major portion of the friar lands for 7.24 million dollars, the money being acquired by the sale of 4 per cent bonds. Minor segments of friar lands escaped sale because agreements on the price were never reached. The purchase price was 2.5 million under what Church authorities asked but was double that of the appraised value as of 1898.[24]

The administration of the purchased friar lands, including surveys, appraisals, sales, and rentals, proved troublesome and time-consuming. Many of the Filipino tenants challenged the legal title of the government and objected to paying for lands claimed as their own by right. The government eventually sustained substantial losses in the retirement of the bonds. The initial regulations for disposal of friar lands required that sales be limited to 16 hectares (40 acres) for individual purchasers and to 1,024 hectares (2,470 acres) for corporations—rulings with which the Philippine Legislature after 1907 indicated full agreement. It resisted later American pressure for scrapping the imposed limitations in the interest of more rapid economic development and proposed instead that friar-land policy be applied to the entire 60 million acres of undistributed public lands.

In 1916, the unsold friar lands and the public domain generally were finally assigned to the Philippine Legislature for disposal, with the original rules pertaining to friar-land sales made applicable to all. Opposition from large-scale American investors to this regulation was blunted by the support of the policy on the part of competing American sugar-beet interests and by continuing anti-imperialist sentiment within the Democratic Party. Filipino legislators, remembering their previous difficulties with the friars, were clearly determined to countenance no revival of absentee-alien landlordism. They were not averse to Filipino control of large estates. One result of the policy was the final limitation of the cultivated area to a total of 7.5 million acres, a fraction of the estimated 20 million acres of tillable land available for improvement.[25]

## Social-improvement Efforts

The declared objective of the American government dating from the appointment of the first Philippines Commission was to rule in the interest of the prosperity, peace, and happiness of the Filipino people and, as far as possible, in accordance with their customs. One of the first major efforts in pursuance of this commitment was to improve health conditions. Infant mortality in 1898 ran as high as 80 per cent in some areas, and the annual death rate in Manila was between 40 and 50 per thousand. Contagious diseases such as tuberculosis, malaria, leprosy, smallpox, cholera, typhoid, plague, beri-beri, and dysentery took a heavy toll. The task was made more

24 *Ibid.*, 124–130.
25 *Ibid.*, 130–136.

difficult because the suspicious villagers resisted vaccination, the use of cholera serums, and quarantine against plague. Expensive improvement of water supplies and sewage-disposal facilities had to be undertaken. Eventually some one thousand dispensaries and forty hospitals were established, plus a dozen leprosariums. Progress came in spurts. The important gains realized from 1901 to 1914 were not sustained thereafter, when American supervision was relaxed. The health program was revitalized under stricter discipline after 1921. The annual death rate in Manila fell to 23 per thousand by 1914 and to very satisfactory 12 per thousand by 1935. Continued heavy infant mortality in the provinces kept the general death rate high. The inoculation of carabao for rinderpest eventually obtained reluctant peasant acceptance.[26]

The equally determined American effort to develop a system of universal, free, and secular education at the primary level met a Filipino demand long articulate and unsatisfied. Even though around one-third of the central budget was regularly allocated to public education, school facilities failed to keep pace with the demand. Difficulties were encountered initially in the required use of English as the medium of instruction and in the utilization of American textbook materials. A large brigade of American teachers was imported at the outset to man the schools. As late as 1915, Americans still comprised one-tenth of the elementary teachers and higher proportions at other levels. Divisional superintendents of education were predominantly American until the 1930s, and both the allocation of funds and the application of instructional controls were centrally administered. Public schools were little affected by political currents. The expanding use of English provided in time a lingua franca for the ten or more major language groups; its use surpassed that of Spanish by the mid-thirties, affording an effective window from which to view the outside world. Constitutional documents, state papers, and official messages were all published in English. Although about three-fourths of the students dropped out of school at the fourth grade, literacy rose from 20 per cent in 1898 to about 40 per cent by 1940. Schools also functioned as centers for basic health education.[27]

In addition to the older Spanish universities, Santo Tomas of the Dominicans and the progressive Ateneo de Manila of the Jesuits, the Protestant Silliman University appeared in Oriental Negros province along with several other private schools at advanced levels. The government's University of the Philippines eventually capped the educational structure, developing ten or more professional colleges and branch campuses outside Luzon. Politics tended to invade the Manila campus.[28] The Departments of Education and Health were joined in 1916, and the Cabinet Minister in charge remained an American long after the Filipinization of other execu-

[26] Smith, 54–62.
[27] *Ibid.*, 41–54.
[28] Malcolm, 285–296.

tive branches. Under American rule, as under the Spanish, Filipinos continued to be insulated from cultural contacts with their Southeast Asian neighbors.

Despite the common allegiance of 80 per cent of the islanders to the same religious tradition and the cohesive influence of widely shared political and educational experiences, genuine nationalism developed shallow rootage in the Philippines. The period of anti-Spanish feeling of the late nineteenth century was too short and too varied in its impact to generate any sense of oneness between peoples of the separate islands speaking different dialects and possessing no older unifying political tradition. Most of the urban Spanish-speaking, property-holding elite accommodated themselves in time to the new regime and became qualifiedly pro-American culturally. The rural population, on the other hand, learned little English, distrusted local-government agencies and central government, and resisted modernization. As elsewhere in the Indies, basic loyalties were directed toward kinship groups or at most toward limited community units, with little awareness of national affiliation or citizenship in evidence. The majority Christian group had very little in common with Muslim neighbors in the southern islands, who became, partly for this reason, a matter of special concern to some of the American Commissioners.[29] The ruling "Spanish" group and the cacique leaders in the village *barrios* were, as always, covetous of their wealth and social position, and became expert at political manipulation and nepotism. Disdainful of the peasants, they took full advantage of the political opportunities afforded them under the new order, while nursing their national pride, so often wounded by tactless Americans. Such a situation generated little national or social cohesion. The American undertaking to develop a self-governing democratic citizenry had a long way to go.[30]

## Problems of Economic Development

During the first decade of American rule, economic advances were limited. The treaty with Spain prevented the United States for ten years from passing any tariff regulations favoring American ships or goods, although an export tax was levied on basic Philippine products sent to other countries than the United States. When legislative action finally became possible in 1909, a quasi-mercantilist policy emerged. Free trade for the mutual exchange of American and Philippine goods was provided, while new duties were levied on Philippine imports from countries competing with the United States. Advantages thus afforded to American investors and importers overweighed protests coming from Commissioners and from other concerned spokesmen in the islands. A virtual American monopoly of Philippine trade resulted, which served greatly to accelerate the role of

[29] *Ibid.*, 90. Particularly noteworthy was the work of Frank W. Carpenter among the Moros as governor of Mindanao and the Sulu country after 1913.
[30] Smith, 31–41.

American firms in developing sugar, tobacco, lumber, vegetable oil, and hemp production. An ameliorative move was made in the Underwood-Simmons Tariff Act of 1913 by the abolition of all export duties. Subsequently, the Jones Act of 1916 permitted the Philippine Legislature, subject to the approval of the President, to enact its own tariff relations with outside nations.[31]

By the end of the second decade, American domination of the islands' economy was well advanced. Investment figures eventually surpassed a quarter of a billion dollars, and they would doubtless have gone higher if the land-acquisition limitations previously mentioned had not constituted a barrier. Many large American operations were allied with wealthy Filipino interests, while much of the manufactured hemp cordage was processed in Japan. Mining developed as an important item of the economy in the 1930s. The United States ultimately absorbed three-fourths of Philippine exports and provided about 85 per cent of the imports.

Expanding production provided tax revenues for building and road construction as well as for health and educational services. Otherwise the village cultivators profited little, since no serious attempt was made to promote agrarian reform. Heavy peasant borrowings at exorbitant interest rates continued to be the rule here as elsewhere in Southeast Asia. Tenancy increased and with it exploitation by absentee owners. Rice production, caught in the pinch between the landlord and the Chinese miller, failed to keep pace with the growing demand.[32] An agricultural bank established in 1906–1907 for the ostensible purpose of making credit more easily available to the small farmer failed of its purpose. This was attributable in part to peasant inertia, but part of the failure was due to the lack of branch agencies conveniently located and the fact that the government neglected to advertise the advantages of the scheme. The funds made available through the bank were actually used, not by small farmers, but by large users of capital for such purposes as the building of sugar centrals. It continued to be easy for the small holder to lose his farm and virtually impossible for the tenant to purchase the land which he cultivated. The Hukbalahap unrest following World War II derived basically from the failure of American rule to solve the problems of land alienation and absentee ownership.[33]

The period of expanding Philippine productivity down to 1930 witnessed a threefold increase (from 40,000 to 120,000) in the resident Chinese population. Legal bans against Chinese entry, designed to protect the native trader and laborer, were circumvented. Sons of legally resident Chinese were permitted entry, but many more were smuggled in. Here as elsewhere in Southeast Asia, Chinese took the lead in construction work and local trade. A Chinese Chamber of Commerce, developed after 1904, provided a forum

---

[31] Grunder and Livezey, 110–111.

[32] Smith, 66–68.

[33] Grunder and Livezey, 93.

for political discussion. It also contributed charitable services and business aids and exercised within the community effective regulation over wages, credits, and other factors of competition. Freed from the arbitrary exactions suffered under Spanish rule, the Chinese by 1932 dominated the wholesale business, controlled three-fourths of the retail trade, owned the same proportion of the rice mills, and financed much of the rice crop and timber extraction. They evaded the regulation forbidding alien ownership of land by marrying Filipinas and taking out deeds in their names. Chinese contributed an estimated three-quarters of the local business taxes and owned investments totaling by 1940 an estimated 100 million dollars. Early high standards of Chinese probity in business tended to deteriorate in time.[34]

## *The Process of Filipinization*

Taft's commendable concern as expressed officially in 1908 that the Philippines be prepared for popular self-government and not be turned over to any aristocracy which might appear capable of maintaining control implied a long-continuing process of preparation. To achieve such an end, he maintained that traditions of good administration would have to be established under firm American control; native personnel must have opportunity to gain experience in government and in politics, and time must be afforded to capitalize on the constructive results of public education. Railways, highways, steamer service, and muncipal reforms had to be provided not merely for economic reasons but also as a means of ending provincial isolation. Convinced that the Filipinos could in time be taught self-government, Taft hoped that the United States would remain long enough to educate the entire population, to make general the use of the English language, and to afford training in the protection and exercise of political rights. Only then did he believe that independence could be safely granted.[35] The problem was to make an early beginning and still be able to control the pace of events.

A substantial start was made in the Filipinization process by the election of a popular Assembly in 1907. The Organic Act of 1902 provided that as soon as two years of peace had elapsed after the taking of a general census (completed in early 1905), general elections could be authorized. These conditions were adjudged fulfilled in March, 1907, and the election was accordingly scheduled for July 30, 1907. Suffrage eligibility, based on taxpayer and literacy standards, was restricted to a mere 4 per cent of the population as a whole. The proportion of voters was higher in the cities, where educational services were better and earnings higher. The overwhelming election victory of the Nationalist Party pledged to seek immediate inde-

---

[34] Victor Purcell, *The Chinese in Southeast Asia* (1951), 569–641; Malcolm, 354–356.

[35] Grunder and Livezey, 84–88, 96–99.

pendence was a foregone conclusion. An earlier pro-American Federal Party had died, and the position taken by the alternative Progressive Party in 1907 that independence should come as soon as Filipino ability for self-government was established involved the unacceptable admission of present incapacity. The first Assembly convened in October, 1907.[36]

The perennial Speaker of the Assembly and the leader of the Nationalist Party until 1922 was Sergio Osmeña, a young law-trained Sino-Filipino of Cebu. He was a man of personal integrity and patriotism, a sincerely religious person who kept his promises and his appointments. As a careful student of parliamentary law and procedure, he was scrupulously fair in the exercise of his official duties, conducting the affairs of the Assembly with dignity and decorum. Although possessed of ample private means, he lived modestly and above scandal. Osmeña's great political contribution was to integrate into a coherent pattern the scattered, divergent, and undisciplined elements of Filipino national unrest. He eventually yielded leadership of the party to Manuel Quezon, the master Filipino politician, who started as the majority floor leader of the 1907 Assembly. Quezon served as Resident Commissioner in the United States during much of the first Wilson administration, and was President of the Philippine Senate in 1922.[37] Although rivals within the party, the two men continued to share the political limelight until the outbreak of the Japanese war in 1941, when they were respectively President and Vice-President of the Commonwealth. The irony of the situation was that most of the men who assumed unchallenged leadership in Philippine politics of whatever party constituted in actuality the very kind of aristocratic oligarchy which Taft had deprecated. A man of the people such as Aguinaldo had little chance for success in contesting the political power of the organized political machines.

A major concern of the Filipino *politicos* who were running the Assembly was to reduce the number of Americans in the public service and to replace them with nationals. By 1920, Americans in the service numbered 1 in 25 and by 1933 only 1 in 60. Many of the American civil service incumbents were eased out by granting liberal retirement allowances for those who retired early. Similarly the Spanish clergy were largely replaced, so that by 1930 eight of the eleven bishops of the Catholic Church were native Filipinos. At every annual session of the Assembly, the legislators approved without dissent a formal resolution affirming the desire and the capacity of the Filipino nation for independent status and its willingness to accept the relevant obligations and responsibilities. Copies of the resolution were regularly sent to the American Congress, accompanied by propagandist appeals to the American people asking for support of Filipino political aspirations.[38]

[36] *Ibid.*, 98.
[37] Malcolm, 172–177, 219–222.
[38] *Ibid.*, 101–106, 307–308.

A new era in the Filipinization process was opened with the Democratic Party victory in the American presidential election of 1912. Democratic Party leaders adopted a somewhat equivocal attitude. Prior to Wilson's election in 1912 and also after the Republicans regained control of Congress in 1920, the Democrats were far more outspoken in their advocacy of immediate independence than they were during the intervening period when they had to accept responsibility for decisions. In accord with the party's traditionally anti-imperialist position was the appointment by President Wilson of Francis Burton Harrison as the new governor-general. Harrison undertook to accelerate the process of independence by affording increased opportunities to the Filipinos in the exercise of power. Whereas Wilson was convinced that the islands were not yet ready for independence (that end was always *almost* in sight), Harrison thought that the event was imminent and that the experience to be gained in governmental participation overbalanced the inevitable deterioration of services entailed in such areas as the health program, public works, and finances. The four new American members appointed to the Philippines Commission were all, like Harrison, lacking in previous contact with the islands. But the greatest change in the Commission was the increase of Filipino membership in 1913 to a majority of five, and the selection of incumbents who reflected the viewpoint of the Nationalist Party leadership. Wilson was apparently influenced in this action by the view that the existence of a Legislature of two houses with diametrically opposite points of view and each with a veto over the acts of the other was a travesty of parliamentary procedure. General-appropriation measures, for example, had failed of enactment in 1910, 1911, and 1912, so that the governor-general in each instance had been obliged to certify the previous year's budget, as was permitted by law.

A similar element of equivocation was also apparent in the Jones Act of 1916, the principal constitutional enactment of the new Democratic regime. The preamble to the act, which paid deference to the traditionally doctrinaire anti-imperialist position of the party, was in several respects inconsistent with the body of the act itself, especially if viewed in the context of the circumstances of its passage. The preamble explicitly denied the intention of the American people in 1898 to conquer the islands. It affirmed the purpose of the Congress to recognize the independence of the Philippines as soon as a stable government could be established; it also declared the desirability of according to the Filipinos, as a means of preparing them for independence, as extensive control as possible of their domestic affairs consistent with the exercise of United States sovereignty. In actuality, the Congress refused to approve an amendment suggesting a tentative date when Philippine independence would be granted, and also reaffirmed the governor-general's complete control of the executive branch and his plenary right of veto over legislative enactments.

What Governor-General Harrison did was to pay more attention to the preamble than to the act itself. He actually abdicated certain executive powers reserved to him in the body of the act by permitting Senate approval of all Cabinet appointments, including that of the vice-governor. The latter was named by the President himself to head up the Department of Education and Health. Harrison also entered no firm rejoinder to the Filipino contention that his veto power should be reserved under the terms of the preamble for items which threatened to impair the sovereign authority of the United States. In the course of seven years, he used the veto only five times.[39] Filipinos assisted in drafting the Administrative Code of 1916, a task which lay clearly within the prerogative of the governor-general. In view of the fact that the Congress indicated no intention of granting early independence, such tactics only created gratuitous difficulties for both Harrison and his successors.

As a man completely devoid of racial prejudice, the new governor-general cultivated the friendship of many Filipinos and thereby incurred the fierce enmity of most resident Americans who accused him of being the pliant tool of his "little brown friends." In most policy matters which were brought before the Council of State, he leaned heavily on the advice of Filipino leaders. The civil service list was 29 per cent American in 1913 and only 4 per cent American in 1920; it became limited pretty largely to education and health, public works and land-survey services, and technical fields such as forestry and fisheries. Harrison argued that the admitted deterioration of service standards consequent on the withdrawal of American supervision was overbalanced by the value of the governing experience gained. Persons who knew Harrison characterized him nevertheless as a good administrator who could be firm when occasion demanded.[40]

Whatever may have been the advantages or shortcomings of the Jones Act and of its application by Governor-General Harrison, the law continued as the basic constitutional document until the middle thirties and constituted a charter for the progressive realization of self-government in the islands. Its promises and spirit could hardly be reconciled with the alleged status of the islands as a basis for the exercise of American political and economic influence in the Far East.[41] It provided for an elective Senate to serve as the upper house of the Legislature; it extended the franchise to literate males who paid a minimum of $15 taxes; it accorded to the Legislature wide scope of decision including the crucial matters of taxation and expenditure, subject always to the seldom-used veto of the governor-general. By 1920, the government was being run by Filipinos, and the political power exercised by nationalist leaders carried with it genuine vitality, even though frequently misused in minor breaches of trust.[42]

[39] Grunder and Livezey, chap. IX; Smith, 78.
[40] Malcolm, 77–78.
[41] Griswold, 450.
[42] Jenkins, 84–87.

## The Regime of General Wood

Although the status of the Philippines was not an issue in the 1920 election victory of the Republican Party, the conduct of the affairs of the islands inevitably came under critical review by the new Harding administration. An investigating mission headed by General Leonard Wood and ex-Governor-General Cameron Forbes reported the existence of maladministration, political confusion, and governmental instability. The word "instability" was in the key to the indictment, for "stable government" had been advanced in the Jones Act as the criterion for self-government. The meaning of the term was vaguely broadened by General Wood to include everything from administrative inefficiency to international insecurity. General Wood indicated his acceptance of the proffered post of governor-general at the conclusion of his investigation. He returned to Manila with a Republican Party mandate to retrieve the situation. Wood's background as a military man, combined with his habits of mind and general temperament, made him unable to sympathize with the ardent desire of the Filipino nationalists for an increasing measure of self-government. He was personally convinced that American withdrawal would constitute as much a disaster for the welfare of the Philippines as for United States prestige and influence in the troubled Orient. He acted also under psychological frustrations connected with his having been bypassed for overseas duty as a general during World War I and as an unsuccessful presidential aspirant in 1920.[43]

Governor-General Wood's basic quarrel with Filipino nationalist leaders concerned their persistent efforts to limit his executive veto powers over legislation to nondomestic matters relating only to the exercise of the sovereign authority of the United States. This was a viewpoint which Harrison's policies had encouraged but which he had never explicitly conceded. Wood was determined to resist any diminution of his plenary executive authority as defined in the Jones Act. He used his veto no fewer than 126 times during his incumbency. No compromise was possible on this issue, for Wood was turning the clock back and the tactics of the nationalists were governed by the political impossibility of retreat. No candidate for election could advocate anything less than the progressive increase of self-governing rights and early independence, whatever his personal opinions might be.

The occasion for the open break came in late 1923. It involved efforts of indigenous members of the advisory Council of State, instituted by Harrison in 1918 and including the speakers of the two houses of the Legislature as well as Cabinet members, to force the hand of the governor-general. In an endeavor to establish their claim of quasi-responsibility to the political authorities in the Legislature rather than to the governor-general, the Council resigned en masse. General Wood thereupon permitted

[43] Grunder and Livezey, 162–166.

their resignations to stand, entrusted routine duties of the several departments to undersecretaries, and sought policy counsel from an extralegal
group of his own composed largely of military personnel. Washington
firmly supported Wood's position.

Differences also developed on economic matters. Filipino opinion
opposed Wood's recommendation that responsible persons be permitted to
lease for twenty-five-year periods, with renewal privileges for an equal term,
areas up to 50,000 acres (80 square miles) in size for economic purposes. The
Legislature was even more opposed to his suggestion that Mindanao and
the Sulu area be made available for large-scale American rubber-plantation
development. The governor-general successfully asserted his unilateral control over a number of state-owned corporations established in Harrison's
time. These involved a National Bank, the Manila Railway, and a National
Development Company interested in coal mines, cement plants, and the
operation of a number of bankrupt sugar centrals. Harrison's Board of
Control, which had previously voted the government stock in these state
corporations, had included the speakers of the two houses of the Legislature.
Wood abolished the Board and with bland inconsistency affirmed his strong
opposition to all kinds of governmental involvement in business.

After repeated Filipino appeals to successive American Presidents in
opposition to Wood's policies produced only negative results, the exasperated nationalist leaders began pressing the American Congress to interfere
by modifying the Jones Act. Several reform measures were brought up for
desultory consideration by the Congress in 1924, but the reform effort completely died out following the election victory of President Coolidge later
in the same year. The Filipinos then began to supplement the activities of
their Resident Commissioner by a privately financed press bureau and with
annual speaker missions, taking full advantage of the Filipino flair for
political oratory. The administration tried to quiet the furor over the embarrassing political impasse in Manila by sponsoring its own investigation.
The resulting report, although not overtly hostile to Wood's total program,
did decry the existing loss of mutual confidence and the general's use of
military advisers. It failed of positive accomplishment.

## Sequel to the Wood Era

The deadlock was eventually resolved by the death of Wood from a
brain tumor in August, 1927. Henry L. Stimson became his successor. Cooperation with legislative leaders was restored, but the Filipino nationalists
were more determined than ever to gain control of their own affairs. On
the American side the acrimonious controversy had the effect of generating
a substantial undercurrent of unfriendly feeling toward the Filipinos as
being overdemanding and ungrateful, a sentiment which was subsequently
exploited by conservative American economic interests seeking freedom

from Philippine competition.[44] The Philippines were destined to witness an even more erratic demonstration after 1929 of the capacity of American policy to swing from one extreme to the other.

One accompaniment of the political furor generated by General Wood's assertion of executive authority within the government was a resurgence of religiously oriented popular rebellions. After 1907, expressions of overt rebellion had almost completely disappeared. By 1924 the psychological climate had changed for the worse. Part of the problem dated from the immediate postwar period, which had witnessed an increase of peasant involvement in debt in central Luzon and rising popular unrest relating to accelerated political change and governmental inefficiency. After 1924, there was popular anxiety over whether excessive American concern for so-called stable government and the security of the islands implied the intention of indefinite continuance of American protection.

Magical nativism blossomed in two fairly remote areas in 1924. The Bucas Grande rebellion developed in the southern Visayas, centering around an alleged resurrection of José Rizal. It was coupled with an ominous warning of doom for the world in general except for the protected inhabitants of Bucas Grande. The rising was effectively crushed by the constabulary and a naval unit, but secret-society groups within the area continued to spawn similar eccentrics for half a decade thereafter. The second rising was headed by Florencio Intrencherado, who apparently gained his initial following by correctly predicting a volcanic eruption. From 1924 to 1927, he set himself up as Philippines Emperor, collecting 3 pesos membership fees from followers and establishing a regal headquarters replete with uniformed attendants, gold sword with bejeweled scabbard, and golden crown. In addition to his vague promise of refuge from impending storm, he advocated repeal of the head tax and achievement of Philippine independence. The captured leader was adjudged insane in 1927, but his followers continued to urge, logically enough, that land records be burned, that the wealth of the islands be more generally shared, and that the goods of the Chinese and Japanese traders in particular be seized. The subsequent anti-Japanese Hukbalahap movement in central Luzon during World War II was similarly rooted in the soil of peasant disaffection, although organized on somewhat more modernist lines. Religious fanaticism remained closely allied in the minds of many with opposition to landlordism and to foreign economic and political control.[45]

Increasing Filipino concern over the economic threat of Japanese settlers related to their increasing participation in the Manila trade, their substantial settlements in the hill-station area of Baguio in northern Luzon, and their development of an even greater stake in the Davao district of eastern Mindanao. Resident Japanese immigrants numbered some twenty

[44] *Ibid.*, chap. X.
[45] Sturtevant, 14–22.

thousand by 1936. In the Davao area they controlled 80 per cent of the trade, including copra and hemp production and the deep-sea-fishing industry. The substantial Japanese-speaking community of Davao ran its own system of internal government within that of the province, including maintenance of its own educational and health facilities.[46]

The sterile atmosphere of controversy which had characterized the period of the Wood regime actually prepared the way for the restoration of Filipino political cooperation with Governor-General Stimson. Stimson was appointed by President Coolidge on the recommendation of Chief Justice Taft, but only after Quezon had requested Taft's intervention in the matter and had persuaded Stimson to agree to accept the nomination if it was forthcoming. One condition of Stimson's acceptance was his exaction of a pledge of cooperation by Filipino nationalists in the Legislature, coupled with his own insistence that the governor-general's role be purely administrative and not be allowed to become involved in the independence question.

During his brief one-year stay in Manila, prior to his being summoned to Washington as President Hoover's Secretary of State, Mr. Stimson avoided controversy and political discussion and succeeded in enlisting the confidence and good will of the leaders of the Legislature. He appointed his Cabinet from members of the majority party and only after consultation with its leaders. Another move in the direction of parliamentary responsibility was the admission of Cabinet members to the floor of the Legislature. He revived the Council of State and expanded its membership to include the majority floor leaders of both houses. The same cooperative relationship persisted under Stimson's successors, even though the opinion of the American business community in the Philippines continued to be antinationalist and highly critical of official policy. After Stimson's return to Washington as Secretary of State, he forestalled for a time threatened congressional cancellation of Philippine trading rights, but his influence was not strong enough in the end to defeat the growing demand to exclude the islands from the American trading area.[47]

## *The Attainment of Philippine Self-rule*

The decision of the American Congress to grant full self-government to the Philippines was in large measure the cumulative result of the agricultural depression in the United States which began prior to the stock-market crash of 1929. American policy had committed the mercantilist error of encouraging the importation from the islands of sugar, vegetable oils, and cordage in competition with hard-pressed United States producers. The allied influence of American sugar interests, including those centering in Cuba, the American Dairy Association, and the producers of cottonseed oil and cordage fibers, simply demanded an end to the favored position

[46] Malcolm, 356–360.

[47] Grunder and Livezey, 184.

accorded to imports from the islands. The traditional anti-imperialist sentiment within the Democratic Party thus suddenly acquired support from
conservative quarters. At the same time, the sentiments of those concerned
with the discharge of America's responsibilities for world peace, and especially for stability in the Orient, were more than balanced by the wave of
isolationist feeling, intent on abdicating all overseas commitments, which
engulfed large segments of American opinion during the early thirties.
Labor opposition to Filipino immigration also contributed in a minor way
to the change.

Instead of the islanders gaining their political freedom, there was an
American declaration of economic independence from the Philippines. In
the new situation, congressional resistance to Filipino independence pleas
evaporated, and an actual threat developed to the islands' economy from
the proposed abrupt cancellation of essential commercial ties with the
United States.[48] The American people, apart from that select number who
owned invested capital, discovered that they had no real stake in the Philippines. Profits from American trade were regarded as negligible in comparison
to the cost of governing and defending the islands.

Events moved fairly rapidly after 1929. A Philippine independence
resolution appended as an amendment to the Smoot-Hawley Tariff Act of
1929 failed passage in the American Senate by a mere nine-vote margin.
Ten other abortive proposals were subsequently advanced as preludes to the
Hare-Hawes-Cutting Act which was finally passed by the Democratically controlled Congress of 1932. President Hoover's veto of the 1932 act was
promptly overridden by the Congress in early 1933. The measure was transmitted to the Philippines for approval by the Legislature or by a convention
to be specially elected to consider the proposal. Complications arose in
Manila when the Filipino leaders who had sponsored the bill in Washington
—Osmeña, Roxas, and Osias—returned home triumphantly to claim credit
for their achievement. Manuel Quezon was in no mood to permit his political rivals to reap such easy gain, so the act became a political football.
Quezon and his partisan followers engineered the Legislature's rejection of
the measure in October, 1933. Some opponents, like Aguinaldo, fought the
bill because it fell short of immediate independence, while others were
critical of its trading stipulations, its immigration restrictions, and its provision for the retention of American military and naval bases.[49] Critics
hoped to fare better under the newly elected Democratic administration.
The situation in both Manila and Washington became very confused.

When the negotiations were transferred back to Washington, Quezon
himself headed the Filipino mission. After several months of frustrated
efforts, a face-saving compromise was finally engineered by Senator Tydings

[48] Jenkins, 79; Malcolm, 101.
[49] Griswold, 450–451; Malcolm, 120–125; Jenkins, 79; Grunder and Livezey,
220–221.

and President Franklin Roosevelt. Explicit provision for American naval bases was omitted from the bill under agreement that the matter be made the subject of later negotiations, and provision was also made for the reversion of the extensive army installations comprising some 300,000 acres to Philippine ownership as soon as full independence was achieved. Otherwise the new Tydings-McDuffie Act duplicated its predecessor. Supplementary acts of Congress set up temporary quotas covering duty-free cordage and sugar imports and an excise tax on coconut-oil imports; they also assigned to the islands' treasury some 50 million pesos derived from the American processing tax on sugar plus a considerable portion of the excise levy on coconut-oil imports. Full application of the United States tariff regulations against Philippine products was later postponed, in 1938. The Tydings-McDuffie Act was accepted by the Philippine Legislature in May, 1934, in an atmosphere of elation tempered by some sober patriotic concern. It was too late at this juncture to contemplate anything short of eventual complete independence.[50]

## Application of the Tydings-McDuffie Act

The act of 1934 authorized the Filipinos themselves to assemble a convention to draft the new Commonwealth Constitution, subject only to several general limitations. The instrument must provide for a republican form of government, include a liberal Bill of Rights, acknowledge the continuance of United States sovereignty for a ten-year interim period, and guarantee the protection of American interests pending the complete withdrawal of American control. The Bureau of Insular Affairs of the War Department would act as intermediary between the two civilian governments in routine matters, and the ultimate authority of the American President would be represented and symbolized in the person of a High Commissioner. The act accorded to the High Commissioner sweeping powers as the representative of the President. He could intervene, whenever necessary, to preserve order and stability, to safeguard property rights and financial solvency, to control trade and immigration regulations, and to maintain American defense installations. Such powers were rarely needed and even more sparingly used. In any case, the political context in which the High Commissioner found himself made it virtually impossible to exercise any sovereign authority. He had a minimal American staff, had to vacate the Malacañan palace, and had to concede that the political initiative lay entirely with the Commonwealth authorities.[51]

The draft Constitution for the Philippines was completed in February, 1935, and submitted to President Roosevelt for approval. It was then ratified by the islands' electorate, on May 14, 1935. American standards were followed in the provision for separation and balance of powers between

[50] Malcolm, 125–132; Grunder and Livezey, 221–224.
[51] Malcolm, 98–100, 369–374; Jenkins, 79–86.

the executive, legislative, and judicial branches of the government. Sovereignty was declared to reside in the people, from whom all governmental authority allegedly derived. Involuntary servitude was outlawed, and social justice was designated as a basic concern of the government. The Constitution became operative on November 15, 1935, by proclamation of President Roosevelt. Full independence was scheduled for July 4, 1946. Quezon won the ensuing presidential election, along with Osmeña as Vice-President, and the former moved into the Malacañan palace. The windfall revenues from the refunded excise and processing taxes on sugar and coconut oil encouraged at the outset an orgy of expenditures on public works, with the usual pork-barrel abuses. This veritable champagne spree on a permanent beer income carried disquieting overtones. Equally disturbing were the political trends under President Quezon toward centralization of power and one-man, one-party control.

A serious proposal to reconsider the whole subject covered by the Tydings-McDuffie Act came from the American High Commissioner Paul V. McNutt, in 1938. He pointed out Filipino agreement with the view that eventual application to Philippine products of the American tariff would be ruinous to the islands' economy and added that American withdrawal from the Orient could entail disastrous political consequences. But no responsible Filipino leader would consider McNutt's concrete suggestions that the United States retain indefinite control of currency and public debt and foreign relations, including tariffs and immigration. The impossibility of a compromise arrangement at the expense of full independence was conceded in 1939 by McNutt's successor, Francis B. Sayre.[52]

The preparation of Commonwealth defenses was entrusted to Field Marshal Douglas MacArthur, who had served previously as Chief of Staff at Washington. He instituted a schedule of enlistments of some forty thousand trainees per year to continue over a ten-year period, besides developing a mosquito navy of torpedo boats and an air force of sixty planes. Neither General MacArthur nor the Commonwealth authorities appear to have taken with sufficient seriousness the imminent threat of Japanese invasion. But in any case the islands were incapable of defense against any all-out Japanese assault without American assistance, which was unfortunately lacking when the crisis came.[53]

## The Assessment of American Rule

A number of things can be cited on the credit side of the American record in the Philippines during the short four decades of control. Among them were the improvement of educational and health facilities and the establishment of peace and order, a stable currency, better prisons and more humane penal laws, and an independent judiciary worthy of public

[52] Smith, 78–87, 97–105.
[53] Griswold, 450–451.

confidence. Systematic land registration ended uncertainty of titles, and the troublesome friar-land claims were liquidated. The islands enjoyed favored access to profitable American consumer markets, plus the expenditure by the United States government of an estimated billion dollars of which more than half was devoted to civilian needs. This was in addition to the 300 million dollars of American investment in the islands' economy. Filipino wages were high by Oriental standards; workmen enjoyed an eight-hour day and compensation benefits. These advantages were partly offset by high living costs, so that labor discontent was growing at the end of the thirties. The virtual American monopoly of Philippine trade made the islands increasingly dependent on the United States economically while contrary policies were being pursued favoring political independence.

Despite the admitted gains, most candid observers agreed that American control had failed badly when judged by administrative standards set by other effective examples of colonial rule. This was due in large measure to inexperience and to violent oscillations of policy. Overt encouragement of Filipino nationalist expectations undercut the effectiveness of American supervisory control, which was required if efficient standards of administration were to be attained. Little governmental attention was given to problems of economic exploitation, partly because the nationalist elite who shared power with the Americans after 1907 were largely lacking in genuine concern for popular welfare. Virtually all the capital investments in banking, shipping, industry, and the export trade were foreign-controlled, and aristocratic Filipinos were the landlords. The 99 per cent indigenous population controlled only 30 per cent of the retail trade, while the 1 per cent foreign population paid 80 per cent of the government taxes. As in other areas of Southeast Asia, the increased wealth derived from Philippine resources benefited relatively few of the Filipinos.[54]

Some observers professed to see, as a result of the impact of American culture, an undermining of the code of Filipino moral behavior, which had never been particularly high. The traditional love of show, pleasure, and gambling and the relaxation of social controls in the direction of vice and dishonesty were the basic factors cited. American jazz music, cheap literature, and the general encouragement of extravagant living allegedly aggravated the trend. But such judgments are difficult to authenticate. Secular education may have weakened somewhat the Christian religious sanctions to proper conduct. It obviously did not dispel credulity and superstition, as demonstrated in the continued rise of religio-political imposters and prophets.

The debits and credits of American rule reflect characteristic faults and values of Western patterns generally. An ebullient American nationalism responded overenthusiastically to the "manifest destiny" imperialism of Theodore Roosevelt and Admiral Dewey. This was counterbalanced by a genuine guilty conscience over keeping any colonial people under un-

[54] Malcolm, 85–88, 278–280.

willing subjection. Hence came the early efforts of Taft to enlist nationalist cooperation in the governing process. This first contradiction was aggravated by the gratuitous intrusion of American political partisanship as evidenced by the contrasting and equally doctrinaire policies of Wilson and Harrison on the one hand and Coolidge and Wood on the other. A characteristically naïve American faith in the efficacy of elections and party politics afforded to the Filipino elite considerable experience in jockeying for power, but the process fell considerably short of providing a sound basis for a democratic society, whether politically or economically defined. The genuine American concern to promote social well-being and increased productivity was measurably vitiated by laissez-faire commitments which vetoed in effect any concerted effort to protect Filipinos from the exploitation of native landlords, alien moneylenders, traders, and processors. The evidence adds up to a convincing demonstration of the difficulty of conducting colonial administration along democratic lines. It may also be noted, in passing, that contrary to the Marxist dogma that imperialism was a projection of capitalist pressures, economic considerations had no important bearing on the establishment of American rule, and they contributed substantially to American withdrawal.

# CHAPTER 21

# Siam from Chulalongkorn

## to World War II

$\mathcal{D}$uring the latter half of the nineteenth century, Siam bowed to the irresistible pressure from maritime nations of the West and voluntarily curtailed its sovereignty by accepting treaty limitations on its fiscal and judicial autonomy. It agreed in 1855–1856 to a 3 per cent tariff, to free interior access for both traders and missionaries, to curtailment of taxation of tangible foreign-owned assets, and to extraterritorial exemption of resident foreigners from the jurisdiction of Siamese courts. Both King Mongkut and King Chulalongkorn subsequently "bent to the wind" by surrendering territory in the face of aggressive French demands, thus avoiding at considerable sacrifice of land and prestige an unequal test of military strength with the European power. At the same time, Chulalongkorn in particular used foreign advisers from many nationalities to modernize governmental administration, to liberalize and reform the legal system, and to realize economic improvements. Reform efforts were hampered by much dragging of official feet and a corresponding degree of frustration on the part of conscientious European advisers.

Despite official resentment over the enforced surrender of border areas to France prior to World War I, Siam sided with the Allies during that struggle. Bangkok took full advantage of anticolonial sentiment developing throughout Eastern Asia after the peace treaties and shifted its principal dependence for international support from Britain to the United States. With the help of American foreign-affairs advisers, Bangkok renegotiated its unequal treaties during the 1920s and thereby recovered full sovereignty. In 1932, westernized politicians and army leaders staged a coup which ended the age-old system of royal absolutism. The symbols and reality of authority remained intact during the course of political gyrations in Bangkok, and a Western-type Constitution was drawn up as a kind of democratic façade. Siam's rulers again adjusted the changing Asian balance of power in favor of Japan during the later 1930s.

## King Chulalongkorn as Liberal Reformer

For about five years following Prince Chulalongkorn's elevation as King in 1868, at the age of fifteen, ministers from the previous reign continued to direct the affairs of the Siamese government. During this interim period, the young King made himself known to his own people and to Asian neighbors. He staged formal state visits to Singapore, Batavia, and Semarang in 1871 and made a subsequent journey to Penang, Burma, Calcutta, and overland to Delhi. At each place visited, he contributed gifts for literary and charitable causes. He conferred with leaders of the Burmese Sangha at a memorable meeting on the platform of the Shwe Dagon pagoda in Rangoon, and was entertained on the same visit as the guest of the British Chief Commissioner. He returned to Bangkok overland by the isthmian route. On the eve of his second and final coronation in 1873, at the age of twenty, he put aside his royal robes for a fortnight and assumed those of a monk in a monastery located within the palace walls.[1]

The new King was a dignified and enlightened individual possessing genuinely liberal sentiments. One of his first acts was to end the requirement of prostration of his subjects in his presence. He abolished slavery by a decree of 1874 which provided that all children born of slave parents would be free at the age of twenty-one. Complete abolition came in 1905. To advise him in the field of government he established two Councils of State. The King himself presided over the higher one, composed of princes and nobility who advised him on revenue measures and factors contributory to the loyalty of his subjects. The lower-level Privy Council was set up in 1874 as a consultative semilegislative organ lacking executive functions. It enjoyed no substantial authority but was responsible for bringing important facts and considerations to the attention of the court. A palace school, established in 1878, set a pattern for state support of secular education generally, although popular education long remained the concern of monastery and missionary schools. A government printing office provided modern school text books and published the weekly *Royal Gazette*. A procession of state scholars, averaging about three hundred annually and including many of the princes, was sent abroad to study.[2]

A number of miscellaneous reforms amplified the program. The Siamese calendar was refashioned on the European pattern; Sunday eventually became a legal holiday, in 1899. Free vaccination was provided to stem cholera epidemics. A decree guaranteeing freedom of the press was honored even to the point of permitting nonlibelous criticism of the King. An American ex-missionary, turned editor, published a series of

---

[1] Samuel J. Smith, *Siam Repository* (1869–1874), III, 297, 313, 323–348; IV, 96, 224, 234, 268; and V, 515.

[2] Wendell Blanchard et al., *Thailand: Its Peoples, Its Society, Its Culture* (1958), 152–155.

periodicals in English and in Siamese. An early royal announcement of religious toleration in 1871 was renewed as a formal edict in 1878, reflecting the degree of friendship obtaining between the court and the missionaries.[3] The support accorded by court circles for the King's reforming program was something short of enthusiastic, for influential conservative ministers were ambitious to keep control. Modernization efforts left the population as a whole largely untouched. In the end, the King's accomplishments fell short of the early promise of his reign, for it proved easier to issue decrees than to alter engrained custom.[4]

Siam's elaborate program of public works was accomplished with the aid of a variety of foreign technicians. A new royal palace was constructed between 1876 and 1880 and was furnished largely in the European style. Electric lights were installed at the palace in 1894. Other new public buildings included a treasury, a customhouse, a museum, a post-and-telegraph center, army barracks, hospitals, and European-style residences to accommodate foreign advisers. Foreign technicians provided a fortified arsenal and a dry dock at Paknam near the mouth of the Menam River. French engineers made a comprehensive survey of Siam's coasts. They included a report on the feasibility of a canal across the Kra isthmus, a project much opposed by Singapore. Railway construction was completed by a German firm in 1900; the line ran from Paknam to Bangkok and extended thence northwest to the Korat plateau, a total of some 200 miles. Telephones, electric lighting, and a tramline were installed in the capital, and telegraph communications were established with French Saigon. Steamboats operated on the river for both freight and passenger service. Basic irrigation canals were dug, and a racecourse was laid out.[5]

## Problems of Administrative Adjustment

Paradoxically enough, Chulalongkorn's personal status as King was a substantial barrier to his own modernization process. Despite the King's liberal inclinations, ability, and masterful temperament, he was in large measure a captive of the traditions of Siamese kingship, which were inimical to thoroughgoing reform. The King of Siam was still the legal possessor of the land and its people, omnipotent, omniscient, always right, and venerated as a demigod. No official dared to contradict or displease the King, but the ruler himself tended to be satisfied with personal subservience rather than to demand efficient performance of duties. Completely

[3] Kenneth Wells, *History of Protestant Work in Thailand, 1828–1958* (1958), 360–365. The new periodicals included the *Siam Repository,* the *Siam Weekly Register,* the *Siam Directory,* and the *Sayahm Samai.*

[4] Walter Vella, *The Impact of the West on Government in Siam* (1955), 334–340.

[5] A. J. Loftus, *The Kingdom of Siam: Its Progress and Prospects* (1891), 616; Vella, 361–364.

absent from the system was any possibility of bridging the gap between the sacrosanct palace government and the people generally. Rulers continued to be one of the perennial evils to be endured. Governmental inertia and the lack of capacity for efficient conduct of business were cited by observers at divergent ends of the social spectrum. The splendor of the palace itself and the adjacent Wat Pra Kian were tarnished by slovenly care. Elsewhere in Bangkok, the Chinese quarter was described as completely devoid of orderliness; filthy roadways were polluted with carrion and festering drains, and streets were choked with rickety vehicles and cook stalls. Receivers of stolen goods offered watches, curios, and even pistols for cheap sale.[6]

Evaluations of government agencies during the nineties reflected the frustrations of the foreign observers. A British education officer characterized the palace itself, paradoxically, as the object of popular loyalty and the cause of the absence of patriotism, as the fountainhead of good laws and of bad rulers. In short, it was called a center of thieving officialdom, idleness, frivolity, and intrigue. Reverence for tradition condoned official corruption and injustice. Any overvigorous application of westernized reforms threatened to revolutionize such a system, and the court as a whole was simply not radically inclined. Governors outside Bangkok followed traditional standards by "eating" their provinces and resisting Western-sponsored innovations. Official peculation was accepted as the customary procedure if done in proper moderation. Salaried officials, who eventually replaced the hereditary governors, were an improvement, but they usually lacked understanding of their duties and were not always honest. Siamese justice came in for particularly severe criticism, as follows: "The Minister of Justice . . . was beautifully impartial in the way he imprisoned the complainant, the defendant, and all the witnesses [he] could get, including the mothers and wives of those [he] could not get. . . . People . . . with remarkable selfishness . . . turn their backs and refuse to see or help innocent men."[7]

Foreign advisers on short-term assignment at Bangkok were understandably impatient to get things done. They encountered maddening periods of delay, popular lethargy, and occasionally outright official jealousy and opposition. The plethora of flattery, cajolery, begging, and threatening required to obtain results was particularly annoying. It was much to the credit of foreign advisers that they did achieve some positive results, and that their total performance was unmarred by any noteworthy betrayal of trust. Examples were numerous. One German adviser developed a really efficient Post and Telegraph Department; another supervised the construction of the first 90 miles of railway; a third German teamed with a Briton to eliminate promotional scandals and corruption in the Department of Mines. Danish drillmasters struggled to discipline the lackadaisical army

[6] H. W. Smyth, *Five Years in Siam* (1898), 17; Lillian Johnson Curtis, *The Laos of North Siam* (1893), 10–16; Vella, 349–350.

[7] Smyth, 18–32.

and a small cavalry unit astride what one observer described as several score "jovial Siamese ponies." The Danes did a little better with the navy, but with neither service did they have a free hand. The higher service commands were occupied by princes previously sent to Europe for training. The army was really intended to keep the Chinese population under control and to aid the police, for it faced no neighboring enemy forces and would have been useless against the Europeans. An Italian headed the school for military cadets.

A British settlement officer with previous experience in India developed during the 1880s an excellent land-survey program for northern Siam, working in the face of enormous difficulties both topographical and human. Educational advisers struggled to improve the superficial and dawdling methods of the Wat schools. They found that discouragingly little money was available for public education after the costs of overseas scholars were defrayed. Some of the elite who returned from study in Europe were so far alienated from the traditional order that they neither enjoyed status nor had capacity to assist.[8]

## The Reforming Program of Prince Damrong

The foreign-adviser program achieved a new dimension of importance after 1892–1893 in the context of the threat to Siam's independence posed by French aggression. Prior to that time, foreigners had been used only as technicians and specialists; after 1892 they were brought in at the top levels of the administration where policies were determined. The disillusioned King and his entourage apparently came to realize after 1893 that they could not depend indefinitely on British protection and must themselves take responsibility for putting governmental affairs in order. The moving spirit in this endeavor was Prince Damrong, the younger half brother of the King. Damrong had earlier been Minister of the North and had also been responsible for educational policy. He possessed both industry and organizing capacity. As the principal adviser to the King, he took care of critical matters connected with the French crisis of 1893, and then undertook the task of reorganizing the entire governmental system.

As the titular Minister of the Interior, Prince Damrong replaced the four traditionally disparate types of provincial units with a uniform system based on the British pattern developed in Burma. The provinces were replaced by circles, each headed by a Commissioner, who supervised the performance of nonhereditary governors. Circles were subdivided into districts, communes, and ten-village units. Village headmen were elected as the titular heads of these "decade" units and were responsible for reporting crimes and for registering the population. The Commissioners reported directly to the Ministry of Interior and shared with the governors responsibility for selecting local officials for the districts and communes. Damrong's

[8] *Ibid.*, 24–32.

other important innovation was to establish a Cabinet of Ministers to replace the older palace Senabodi. The principal Ministries of Finance, Justice, Foreign Affairs, and War were customarily headed by princes. New functional agencies for public works, education, agriculture, and mines and forests usually required a higher degree of technical competence. The traditional officers of the royal household, palace, and royal services were also incorporated into the Cabinet.

Except for the fact that foreign advisers were employed to assist each of the several ministries, the new arrangement well illustrated the French adage that the more things were changed, the more they remained the same. Cabinet posts, particularly when occupied by princes, continued to be treated as lifetime appointments or sinecures. Incumbents often did not take their administrative responsibilities very seriously. Subordinate posts were filled with personal retainers, and revenue increments were often spent without accounting to the Minister of Finance.[9]

British advisers in Bangkok outnumbered those of any other nationality, being especially effective in the fields of finance, police, education, land surveys, and mining. Improvement realized in financial administration from 1896 to 1903 doubled the receipts of the central treasury without increasing rates of taxation. All tax revenue had to be deposited with the treasury and an accounting made of all expenditures. The wasteful tax-farming system was sharply curtailed after 1907. A substantial railway loan was raised in 1903, and a still larger loan for railways was obtained from Britain in 1909 in connection with the surrender of Siam's claims to four Malay provinces. The new bookkeeping procedures were far from popular with officials, and as late as 1900 the royal civil list still absorbed one-eighth of the total budget.[10]

For ten years a Belgian adviser named Jaquemyns assisted Prince Devawongse in the crucial area of foreign affairs. He brought to the task an expert knowledge of international law and previous experience with Lord Cromer in Egypt. Regular Siamese legations were established at Paris, London, Washington, St. Petersburg, Berlin, and Tokyo. Jaquemyns arranged a settlement of the crisis with the French in 1892–1896 and began negotiations to reduce the abuses of extraterritorial privilege. Jaquemyns also served as general adviser to Prince Damrong. He was succeeded in the role as Foreign Officer adviser by a series of three Americans, international lawyers expertly trained. The last of the three, Francis B. Sayre, completed the renegotiation of Siam's treaty system.[11] Belgian advisers in the Ministry of Justice also accomplished important improvement in courts and prison reform. They helped establish a law school in 1897, and brought provincial judges under centralized control in 1903. Assisted by French lawyers, they completed a revision of the Penal Code in 1908 and undertook the revamp-

9 Vella, 342–349; Smyth, 24–32.
10 J. G. D. Campbell, *Siam in the Twentieth Century* (1902), 176–177.
11 W. A. Graham, *Siam: A Handbook* (1924), I, 308–311; Vella, 340–343.

ing of the entire code system to provide a satisfactory basis on which extra-territorial rights could be canceled. Advisers to the army were able to obtain in 1904 the discontinuance of the traditional recruitment of army units from prisoner-descendants fighting under local chiefs or patrons.[12]

Beginning with the arrival in 1889 of Dr. James W. McKean, American Protestant missionaries contributed substantially to medical advance in Siam. With some government assistance, McKean produced quinine pills, initiated vaccination for smallpox, and set up a leprosarium. Dr. Edwin C. Cort of Johns Hopkins (1908 and later) initiated a training school for doctors and nurses at Chiengmai in connection with a mission hospital. These two and other doctor associates were later decorated by the Siamese government for their services.[13] Provision of a proper water supply by 1907 ended the harrowing threat of cholera at Bangkok.

## Aspects of Siam's Economic Development

Siam was in a position after 1870 to share substantially in the vast expansion of European trade which followed the opening of the Suez Canal. Its principal new exports were rice, teakwood, and tin, added to the traditional sale of hides, cattle, and forest products. The centennial of the founding of Bangkok, staged in 1882, afforded opportunity to display the products of all regions of the kingdom. British firms were very active as traders and also in the timber field and tin mining. British-made cotton cloth and hardware constituted the bulk of consumer-goods imports. Opium importation, much of it illicit, was second in importance to cloth. The government was powerless under extraterritorial limitations to halt the demoralizing traffic and, in fact, could not afford to sacrifice the revenues derived from the purchase by Chinese of opium-farmer monopolies. A number of British branch banks were established in Bangkok from 1888 to 1894, and the French Banque de l'Indochine began operations there in 1897. British steamer lines provided most of the Siamese shipping facilities until 1900, when the North German Lloyd began to supply half or more of the tonnage serving Bangkok.

For a number of reasons, Siam's economic development reached a kind of plateau around 1893. Surplus rice available for export amounted to half a million tons in 1893, but the amount failed to increase substantially thereafter for almost a decade. French aggression in that year interposed political and psychological handicaps, but the economic malaise was more fundamental. The principal limiting factors were the lack of an abundant supply of cheap labor and the nonavailability of funds for investment in agricultural and transportation improvements. The abolition by 1905 of slavery and *corvée* obligations reduced the common-labor supply. Chinese

[12] Vella, 344–349.
[13] Wells, 79–82; J. Crosby, *Siam: The Crossroads* (1945), 42.

residents preferred the vocations of craftsmen, traders, and mill operators; the Siamese were wedded to cultivation. Credits available to the peasants for agricultural needs, normally derived from kinship and patron sources, were not sufficient to finance major irrigation and development schemes. The government was unable to raise the needed funds by loans or revenues mainly because inelastic tax rates governed by treaties going back to 1855 continued in force at arbitrarily low figures. Land taxes amounted to only an estimated 5 to 10 per cent of the annual output. Customs duties were similarly limited by treaty to a nominal 3 per cent ad valorem tax. The treaties thus served to apply brakes to Siam's economic progress.[14]

The cautious financial policies of the government were buttressed by the insistence of successive British financial advisers that ample reserves in bullion and foreign currencies be kept in hand to cover the currency in circulation. In justification of such caution, advisers argued that financial responsibility lessened the risks of foreign intervention, citing Egypt as an example. It was nevertheless true that a tight-money policy put a damper on economic expansion in Siam in crucial areas of rice production and marketing, transportation facilities, and industrial development. Ample currency reserves were maintained to protect foreign trade and investments and to expedite the payment of earnings from invested foreign capital. The revenue gains realized after 1897 from the establishment of more efficient collection and auditing procedures were absorbed by expanding needs for foreign aides, courts, police, and education, so that very little was left over to finance capital improvements.

British policy made a few concessions only. A moderate increase in 1905 in the tax to be levied on British-owned properties (which effectively established the maximum rate) permitted the doubling of land-tax revenues, but the rates were still very low. The British refused repeatedly, in 1905 and 1908, to consent to increases in the 3 per cent customs rate set by the 1855–1856 treaties or to permit an excise tax on items for export. Even after the eventual treaty revision in 1926, London insisted that the duties on major items of British import remain for another ten years at 5 per cent only and that the British financial adviser must consent to all foreign loans. The net result was the retardation of Siam's economic development and the government's continued dependence for income on the sale of gambling, liquor, and opium licenses.[15]

A comparison of the social effects of the disparate rates of economic development in the almost-identical economies of Siam and Burma may be instructive. Both emerged as rice-exporting states, with minor dependence on teakwood and mineral production. By 1900 Siam's rice exports were falling rapidly behind Burma's, and teak production was less than half.

[14] James C. Ingram, *Economic Change in Thailand since 1850* (1955), chap. III.

[15] *Ibid.*, chaps. IV and V.

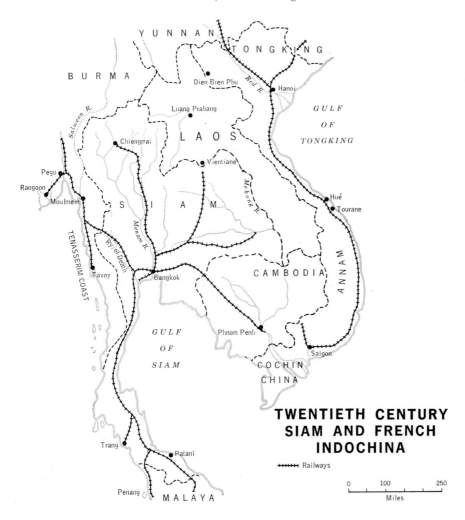

**TWENTIETH CENTURY
SIAM AND FRENCH
INDOCHINA**

╊╊╊╊ Railways

0          100          250
Miles

Some three-fourths of the arable land in the Menam Valley remained undeveloped in 1900, and Siam was far behind Burma in rail and road transportation facilities. In 1902, a retiring British education officer argued
with some measure of justification that British rule could transform Siam
in half a generation, multiplying its wealth.[16] But facile judgment is decep-
tive. British rule in Burma obtained maximum stimulation to economic
development by arbitrarily removing legal and social barriers. Burma
profited economically from an unlimited supply of financial credit from
British and Indian sources, plus the importation of abundant coolie labor
from India. The total output and the profits realized were correspondingly

[16] Campbell, 25–32.

impressive, but it may be doubted that the Burmese people were any better off than the Siamese in consequence.

Siam, with all of its economic and political handicaps, enjoyed the advantages derived from the preservation of the integrity of its traditional political, social, and cultural patterns. For one thing, the expansion of rice cultivation in the lower Menam Valley did not involve, as was the case in the Irrawaddy delta area of Burma, the displacement of old and established political and cultural centers comparable to Mandalay. The Siamese cultivator also usually retained the ownership of his land because he borrowed moderately from patrons and kinsmen and limited his consumer demands largely to things which he himself could produce or could afford to buy. Siam suffered no orgy of lawlessness comparable to Burma's and was less vulnerable than Burma to the vagaries of world markets. No alien labor or landlord groups developed in Siam, apart from the Chinese, whose commercial role was essentially constructive. Continuing effectiveness of royal authority and the persistence of a considerable degree of local autonomy preserved order and kept the social fabric intact. On balance, the advantages may have favored Siam.

## The Successors of Chulalongkorn

King Chulalongkorn's long reign of forty-two years came to an end in 1910. He was succeeded by a British-educated prince named Wachirawut, who was crowned as Rama VI. His conduct and his bizarre interests aroused both opposition and dismay in Bangkok, casting serious doubt in the minds of many on the advantages to be derived from Oriental absolutism with a European flavor. Rama VI was a dilettante writer and dramatic actor, entirely uninterested in matters of governmental routine. He depleted the privy purse of the palace by extravagant expenditures on tours and state functions and imposed no curbs on official corruption and inefficiency. He ignored the advice of official councilors and encouraged instead the influence of flatterers and a coterie of youthful courtiers. He abolished the extensive harem and settled for a mere five selected wives. He offended the regular army by showing favoritism to a personal bodyguard known as the "Wild Tiger Corps," whom he provided with clubhouses, a drill hall, uniforms, and a rugby football team. Although he strongly opposed the idea of constitutional democracy, his erratic conduct did much to discredit a capricious absolutism. Army-officer plots were uncovered in 1912 and 1917. The King's emphasis on compulsory secular primary education did not square with his similar stress on Buddhist revival as an antidote for Western influence. His nationalist emphasis also widened the rift with resident Chinese.[17]

Rama VI continued the use of foreign aides, with few departures

---

[17] Graham, 223–225; Vella, 351–356; Crosby, 19–20.

from the previous pattern. British advisers still predominated in such important areas as finance, judiciary, commerce, agriculture, health, and irrigation. Frenchmen advised on legislative enactments and in the area of legal-code reform. Italians were employed for public works and Americans in the field of foreign policy. German participation was eliminated during the course of World War I, and the practice of using foreigners began to taper off at the end of the war. Siamese policy in 1914 was sympathetic to the German side, partly from resentment over losses of territory to the British and French. But the King's influence was on the side of neutrality, and after America's entrance in 1917, Siam followed the time-honored policy of joining the winning side. The government sent one thousand volunteer soldiers to France, and thus earned a minor voice at the peace conference.[18]

When Rama VI died in 1925, he was succeeded by a younger brother named Prachothipok, as Rama VII. The new King entertained liberal sentiments governmentally and acquiesced in the outlawry of polygamy under the new law code by himself having only one wife. Unfortunately he was a weak personality, lacking in intellectual capacity and incapable of implementing his ill-defined convictions. He advocated constitutional government and parliamentary procedures, but he permitted the High Council to become a virtual monopoly of princely incumbents who were firmly opposed to democratic reform. He contributed little personally to the most noteworthy achievement of his reign, the renegotiation of the treaty system, which will shortly be described. Rama VII offended the nobility, the army, and the bureaucracy by a series of economy measures. He reduced the number of circles from eighteen to ten, thus eliminating many high-level posts. He established a new Civil Service Law in 1928 but exempted the princely bureaucrats from its application. He also abolished the Department of Royal Pages, which had long afforded advantages for the sons of nobles. He wanted to repudiate the ancient theory of absolutist monarchy, but he failed to promote popular understanding of such a policy or to enlist in its support any substantial element of the political elite. Enforced economies in departmental and court expenditures during the depression period greatly weakened his position.

The end came in 1932 when a small group of several score westernized promoters attacked the monarchy. Rama VII weakly submitted to their seizure of control, refusing to use the police power to put them down or to initiate a substitute reform program of his own. Having completely lost control, he returned to Europe for eye surgery in early 1934. A year later he denounced the emerging regime as undemocratic and militaristic and then abdicated in favor of a ten-year-old nephew schoolboy then living in Switzerland. Impotent regents took over palace affairs,[19] and the monarchy was reduced to a symbol only.

---

[18] Graham, 223–228.
[19] Crosby, 19–20, 24–31; Vella, 351–356.

## Revision of the Unequal Treaties

The British treaties of 1855–1856, which provided the basis for fiscal limitations and extraterritorial claims in Siam, carried no time period after which revision could be sought. Modification could only be made by mutual consent, and it was not in the interest of British traders and investors to permit changes. Serious problems developed in connection with the claims advanced by the British and French for the enjoyment of extraterritorial rights on the part of their colonial protégés neighboring Siam. Exemption from Siamese law and court jurisdiction was claimed in time not only by nationals of Burma, Malaya, and Indochina but also by resident Indians and Javanese and by Chinese born outside China in colonial Southeast Asia. The increasing numbers involved aggravated the problem. Extraterritorial privileges meant that registered aliens holding "foreign papers," sometimes forged, could participate, for example, in narcotics smuggling and illicit gambling, with Siamese courts prevented by treaty from taking any corrective action. Exemption claims were later extended to cover the application of police regulations as well as basic law.

The problem can be illustrated by reference to the rule of 1883 covering the application of Siamese law along the borders of the Shan States of Burma. Burma's Shans and other frontier aliens enjoying British-national status could be tried in the courts in the Chiengmai area only with the resident British consul present. The consul was empowered to make "suggestions" to the judge and could also evoke out of the Siamese courts any case involving a British subject. He could also hear an appeal from any Siamese conviction of a British subject. This 1883 rule was made to apply to all British residents in Siam in 1909. In 1899, Britain renounced protégé status for great-grandchildren of European parents and for grandchildren of Asian subjects, concessions which did very little to curb the abuses of the system. The French adopted a similar supervisory policy in 1904 for Siamese court cases involving French subjects from provinces in northern Laos. French consul observers could "assist" the judge or call out the case to be tried before an international (Franco-Siamese) court.

Siam's escape from these legal disabilities was painfully slow. A slight gain was registered in treaties concluded with Japan (1898) and Russia (1899), which made the ending of extraterritoriality conditional on the completion of legal reforms. In 1907, the French surrendered tax exemptions and extraterritoriality for any newly registered French subjects resident in Siam. French Asiatic subjects meanwhile continued to enjoy within Siam all rights of Siamese citizens.[20] In 1909, when Britain acquired full title to the four Malay sultanates, it also waived extraterritorial rights for newly registered British subjects. Pending the promulgation of a revised

[20] Francis B. Sayre, "The Passing of Extraterritoriality in Siam," *American Journal of International Law*, XXII (1928), 70–79.

Siamese legal code, Siam was obliged by the 1909 agreement to pay the salary of the British "adviser" designated to sit in any court of the first instance where a British subject was a defendant. If a European was involved, the "adviser" could insist on compliance with his advice by the judge. Meanwhile the Royal Code Commission, under expert French direction, worked to complete the drafting of the new law code.[21]

The first breakthrough came in 1920, when the revised American treaty provided for the surrender of extraterritoriality as a matter of right, without requiring any *quid pro quo*. This concession had been promised Siam by President Wilson at the Versailles Conference in response to Bangkok's urgent plea for treaty revision. In cases where Americans were defendants, the United States consul could still evoke cases until five years after the date of the eventual promulgation of the new code, but "advisers" no longer sat in the courts. Cases so evoked would, in any case, be tried under Siamese law. The American treaty also renounced all fiscal and tariff restrictions and provided for the termination of the treaty after ten years on the submission of one year's notice by either party.[22]

The task of obtaining general acquiescence for treaty revision according to the pattern set by the American treaty was undertaken by the aforementioned Francis B. Sayre, a son-in-law of President Wilson, who served from 1920 to 1927 as Siam's Foreign Office adviser. His first success was achieved in March, 1924, when Tokyo agreed to a treaty along the line proposed by Sayre as a means of facilitating access for Japanese goods to Siam's markets. The initially encouraging response of France produced no immediate results. The crux of the problem was Britain's attitude, for Britain had most at stake in its long common frontiers with Siam and its virtual domination of Siamese trade (30 per cent of exports and 67 per cent of imports). London refused to move until all treaty states agreed to accept its 1909 policy as a minimum, and no fewer than eight European states refused at first to make any concession whatever. Despairing of productive negotiations at Bangkok, Sayre in 1925 undertook a roving diplomatic mission to the European capitals, a move which in the end proved effective.

The completion of the new French treaty in February, 1925, came at a time when authorities at Hanoi were seeking to make corrective adjustments of Indochina's Mekong River boundary with Siam. The two treaties were negotiated in the same context, but they were separate documents. Paris agreed that French rights with respect to evocation of court cases involving French nationals and international court procedures would terminate five years after the promulgation of the new legal code. France specified that tariff increases imposed by Siam must apply to all states with no compensatory concessions allowed, that future differences would be arbitrated, and that the treaty would be subject to termination after ten years. The frontiers treaty signed in August, 1926, set up a 25-kilometer demilitarized zone on

[21] Graham, 223–225.
[22] Sayre, 80–82.

each side of the Mekong boundary sectors, which would be administered by a joint permanent High Commission. French nationals who were ethnically Siamese and living along the borders would continue to enjoy rights of residence and property ownership under Siamese law. The High Commission would examine leasehold problems and formulate rules governing water diversion, fishing, and navigation along the river. Siamese nationals resident in Indochina would enjoy reciprocal rights identical to those accorded to French nationals in Siam.[23] The liberal character of this border-relations treaty was in sharp contrast to previous French agreements imposed on Siam.

The British treaty concluded in July, 1925, was Sayre's major triumph. It involved obtaining the concurrent acquiescence of the Foreign Office, the Colonial Office, the India Office, and the Board of Trade. The treaty specified that British advisers at law courts would be withdrawn forthwith and evocation rights would end with the completion of the legal code. Treaty rights previously granted to residents along the Burma and Malaya boundaries were retained, and commercial rights of British subjects in Siam were fully and explicitly guaranteed on a most-favored-nation basis. With respect to contemplated tariff increases, the treaty provided that "moderate" levels, to be determined by a separate arbitration agreement, would be applicable for ten years in the principal categories of British imports. A rate of 5 per cent was thus established to cover cotton yarns, textile fabrics and manufactures, and iron and steel products, including machinery and spare parts. Five other European treaties were concluded by Sayre in 1925 and four more in 1926. In recognition of his services, Sayre was accorded by Bangkok the honorary title of *Phya Kalyan Maitri*, which was only one grade below the highest title of nobility of *Chao Phya*.[24] The United States took the lead in finally abrogating all of its special treaty rights in Siam in 1937, and others followed suit in 1939.[25]

One factor which may help explain the rather sudden conversion of European governments to the acceptance of the complete juridical independence of Siam was the emergence in 1925–1926 of the militant Kuomintang nationalist regime in China. Prior to 1925, the Peking authorities had maintained no consular agent in Siam and had given no heed to complaints of Chinese living in Siam. Advent of the Kuomintang government and its claim to the active allegiance of all Nanyang Chinese carried serious implications when Nanking raised the question of negotiating for Chinese consular jurisdiction over all 3 million of the Chinese residents of Siam. A political threat was thus added to the already-ominous Chinese domination of local economic activities.[26]

[23] Sayre, 82–85; and *Siam: Treaties with Foreign Powers, 1920–1927* (1928), 97–116.

[24] Sayre, "Extraterritoriality," 85–88; and *Siam: Treaties,* 132–147.

[25] Thomas Fitzsimmons, *Thailand* (1957), 235–237.

[26] Crosby, 70–76.

The Chinese affirmation of the *jus sanguinis* principle for citizenship as grounds for denying the right of alienation even for Chinese born outside China had first been raised at Bangkok in 1909–1910 at a time when strikes and riots had temporarily paralyzed the entire economic life of the capital. Between 1910 and 1925, both ethnic groups came to regard the preservation of nationalist identity as a condition of survival. The Siamese canceled some of the original advantages enjoyed by the Chinese in owing no personal obligations to the king and in being required to pay fewer kinds of taxes. The increased immigration of Chinese women to Siam during the 1920s slowed down the process of assimilation, although males continued predominant by a ratio of 4 to 1.

Further restrictions imposed by Siam during the 1920s on Chinese vocations and economic status and on the use of Chinese-language instruction in the schools aggravated the militant spirit of Kuomintang nationalism. This sentiment was particularly strong in Canton and the Fukien cities, whence came most of Siam's Chinese population. Although well-to-do Chinese were usually fairly easy to assimilate in Siam, the majority group refused to accept the full responsibilities of Siamese citizenship and demanded the restoration of their special tax status. After the Bangkok revolution of 1932, friction intensified. Many Chinese schools were closed, and the Siamese undertook with limited success to limit Chinese immigration to some ten thousand per year.[27]

## The Revolution of 1932

Monarchial government apparently lost out in Siam because the Western-educated elite including the King himself lost faith in it. The fourscore "promoters" who seized control of the government on June 24, 1932, were recruited from westernized malcontents who denounced as unprogressive both royal absolutism and princely privilege. Worried at the outset over the possibility of British or French intervention to restore to power the friendly monarchial faction, they devised a constitutional façade as a kind of shield and also espoused a number of liberal Western-type reforms. These included freedom of the press, social equality, education for all, graduated income tax, equalization of bureaucratic salaries, a competitive civil service, lower postal rates, and suspension of the unpopular land tax. In actuality, they preferred more direct means of control to constitutional representative government. The economies of democratic nations were virtually paralyzed by the world depression at the time, so that totalitarian patterns attracted attention in Siam as elsewhere.[28]

The liberal author of the 1932 coup was Pridi Phanamyong, a French-educated lawyer, half Chinese. While a student in Paris, he had quarreled

[27] Victor Purcell, *The Chinese in South-East Asia* (1951), 103–158, 167–208; George William Skinner, *Chinese Society in Thailand: An Analytical History* (1957).
[28] Crosby, 45–49.

vigorously with the princely Siamese Ambassador. He eventually returned to Bangkok in 1928 as a lecturer in the Law Academy, where he attracted a youthful following. Under conditions of world depression, mass poverty, Siam's vulnerability to the vagaries of world markets, and the virtual Chinese domination of its domestic economy, Pridi advocated a planned economy. Government operation of the economic system would allegedly help end the Chinese strangle hold, provide employment, capital needs, and marketing facilities, and reduce the discord between employers and labor. The government should even purchase agricultural land for redistribution by the issuance of state bonds. Gains to be realized in popular welfare, educational opportunity, and prosperity would, Pridi argued, more than compensate for the loss of private economic freedom.[29] Pridi's original scheme of government would vest power in the dictatorship of the People's Party. Party members only could be candidates for election to the party Assembly; the latter would elect the president, who in turn would select the fourteen-member executive committee; the committee, in turn, would appoint the ministers and promulgate the laws. Pridi's borrowings from the Soviet were obvious.

Siam's Constitution as finally drafted in December, 1932, departed in a number of respects from the early Soviet pattern advocated by Pridi. It attempted to restore some measure of prestige to the Crown by paying deference to the royal court and by reserving minor items for the king's prerogative. At the same time princes were excluded from membership in the State Council, which now took the place of the proposed Executive Committee. One-half of the membership of the Assembly was to be elected by indirect suffrage; the other half was appointed by the ruling party. A completely elective Assembly was promised within ten years. The Cabinet was to be responsible to the Assembly, but old budgets could apply if new ones were not voted. This Constitution lasted unchanged until 1946, when it was first altered by Pridi's Free Thai Party to permit Prince Seni Promoj, previously Ambassador to Washington, to take over briefly as Foreign Minister.[30]

The Constitution was clearly the creation of power-hungry officials, both civilian and military, who fashioned it primarily as a means of legitimizing before the outside world their seizure of power. It was based on no articulate popular demand, although provincial members of the Assembly developed a vested interest in it. The new Siamese word invented for the Constitution was widely regarded as the name of a usurping prince. The people as a whole were completely uncomprehending and indifferent. Villagers continued to be royalist at heart, and the government's prestige derived from popular respect and reverence for the King and officialdom as the symbols of social values and nationality. Rama VII's initial decision to accept the new order cushioned the transition, as did the absence of any tra-

[29] Vella, 360–365, 373–381; Crosby, 192.
[30] Fitzsimmons, 155–157; Vella, 371–373.

dition of revolt against royal authority. The presence of the King in his palace preserved the sanctity of traditional religio-magical symbols. Because the Constitution established no firm patterns of administration and set no effective limitations to the exercise of power, the new regime was open to shameless abuse and violation of trust.[31]

## The Course of the Revolution

The balance of power within the revolutionary regime gravitated during 1933 into the hands of conservative military leadership. Pridi's radical economic plan was denounced as communistic by both the court and the army, and he was forced into temporary exile in June, 1933. Communism was explicitly outlawed, and it became associated in the popular mind with radical Chinese and Vietnamese nationalists. An abortive royalist coup in October, 1933, which attempted halfheartedly to exploit the issue of communism afforded opportunity for the political emergence of Colonel Luang Pibun Songgram, the army officer who suppressed the rebellion. Both Chinese and Vietnamese Communists were exiled from Siam, and the issue died down in the later thirties. Pridi was exonerated of alleged Communist affiliations in 1934 and returned to the Cabinet as successively Minister of Interior, Foreign Minister, and Finance Minister from 1934 to 1938. It was he who completed the negotiations liquidating the unequal treaties. He was the idol of the young intelligentsia.[32]

Siam's government from 1933 to 1938 was headed officially by the tactful and popular Phaya Bahol. Until he was forced to retire because of ill health, he managed to persuade rival factions to cooperate. Army groups continued to be influential in the Cabinet, and the new conservative Assembly elected in 1937 was respectful of army influence. The government opposed princely influence in politics, and it officially canceled the six traditional grades of hereditary titles. It also abolished land and capitation taxes and levied a nominal 1 per cent tax on income and a 2 per cent tax on business. The treasury continued to draw its principal sources of revenue from opium sales, customs and excise levies, fees, licenses, and fines. The new nationalistic emphasis dealt harshly with the Chinese, who faced discriminatory taxes on income, shops, banking operations, and amusements. The Chinese were prohibited from functioning in twenty-six designated professions which were explicitly reserved for the Siamese. The use of the Chinese language for school instruction was forbidden. When the Chinese tried to escape by accepting Siamese citizenship, the government raised naturalization standards by specifying literacy, wealth, and army service requirements. After 1940, Japanese influence helped fan official anti-Chinese sentiment.[33]

---

[31] Fitzsimmons, 13–14, 167–169.

[32] Crosby, 101–104; Virginia Thompson and Richard Adloff, *The Left Wing in Southeast Asia* (1950), 51–58.

[33] Vella, 381; Purcell, 167–208; Crosby, 21–22.

Partly as a corollary to the anti-Chinese emphasis in the economic field and partly from motives of personal avarice, the new government began to participate actively in business ventures. These included paper factories, textile manufacture, distilleries, sugar and tobacco processing, oil refining, and silk production. Many of the projects operated at a chronic loss because of inefficient management, poor accounting, erratic output, and poor quality. Only in specialized areas such as tobacco manufacture, where the materials were easily available alongside a substantial local market and where the processing was relatively simple, were the government projects financially successful. Rubber production began to make important gains after 1934. Government railways, telegraphs, and electric-power installations, operating under routines previously set up by European advisers, were reasonably efficient. The use of European advisers was nevertheless drastically reduced.

Nationalism in Siam differed from its manifestations elsewhere in Southeast Asia by being positive rather than negative, more imperialist than anti-imperialist. Having used Western European and American help to modernize their country's legal system and to regain their political and economic independence, Siam's leader sought in the 1930s to take advantage of the still more modern systems of single-party rule, nationalization of industry, and authoritarian political control on the fascist or Japanese model. Siam's "promoters" thus followed the traditional bandwagon psychology. They "bent with the wind" to get in on the winning side of World War II, betting at first on a Japanese victory and then shifting sides in 1944 when the odds swung the opposite way.[34]

## *Pibun Songgram and Siam's Fascist Orientation*

The retirement of Premier Bahol in 1938 because of ill health permitted the elevation by the promilitarist Assembly of Colonel Pibun Songgram as Prime Minister. Pridi and other civilians remained in the Cabinet for a time but under army control. Pibun was the leader of a military faction hungry for glory, revenues, and governorships. An attempted assassination of the leader permitted the group to take vengeance on political enemies in late 1938. Pibun was himself a political opportunist, ambitious personally, a jingo militarist, and a modernizer. His westernizing fads included advocacy of the adoption of family names, the wearing of hats and shoes, the use of "hello" in greetings, and such alien notions as industriousness. He also stressed pride of Siamese race and culture almost to the point of making Buddhist enthusiasm synonymous with patriotism. Adding to the older nationalist principles of opposition to the Chinese, Pibun's clique sponsored a Pan-Thai movement for the absorption of irredentist Thai peoples. As a symbolic gesture of his imperialistic ambitions, he changed the official name of the country in 1939 to Thailand, after Muang Thai (land

[34] John Coast, *Some Aspects of Siamese Politics* (1953), 9–10.

of the Thai). Acceptance of Japanese tutelage from 1940 encouraged both his anti-Chinese and his expansionist policies.[35]

Pibun's imperialist plans included the reannexation of several provinces on the Cambodian frontier, plus the trans-Mekong region, several of the easternmost Shan States of Burma, the Tenasserim coast, the lost Malay sultanates, and Penang Island. He was considerably more discreet in his agitation for the recovery of British-held territory than for regions controlled by the fading power of France. In 1939–1941, Pibun pushed aside his foreign advisers and devoted one-third of the national revenues to military preparations. His first overt move followed the collapse of France in 1940, when Hanoi authorities were obliged to accept a minor revision of the 1926 boundary treaty. Shortly thereafter, he asserted Siam's claim to all of Laos down to the Cambodian border plus three provinces of Cambodia. These territories were actually annexed during 1941, under Japanese "arbitration" awards.[36]

Thailand's alignment with Japan owed more to the logic of events than to any single climactic decision. Japanese trade with the country during the 1930s increased until it was second only to Britain's. In 1933, Siam abstained from voting in the League of Nations' censure of Japan over Manchuria. After 1938, Pibun developed a militant youth organization fashioned along Japanese lines and devised a national code of honor called *wiratham,* adapted from Japanese *bushido.* The code was a curious combination of disparate elements. It emphasized nationalist partisanship and loyalty and economic efficiency and industry, together with Buddhist principles of peace, gratitude, trustworthiness, and respect for the young and infirm.

Japan's active wooing of Thailand reached a crescendo after 1940 with emphasis on "Asia for the Asiatics," the "Greater East Asia Co-Prosperity Sphere," and a common reverence for the Buddhist faith. A full-fledged Japanese Embassy was established at Bangkok, and two new consulates were set up at Singora in the Malay southland and at Chiengmai in the north. Japanese "fishing craft" with polished brass naval fixtures began to make frequent visits along both sides of the lower peninsular coasts. Some of the Siamese were disturbed by Japanese presumption; others took bribes. Pibun and his army associates were obviously preparing to gamble that Japan's was the winning side. A few of those in authority may have shared with the ex-foreign advisers some nostalgic memories of King Chulalongkorn.[37]

[35] Crosby, 82–91; Lennox A. Mills (ed.), *New World of Southeast Asia* (1949), 246–256; Vella, 388–389.

[36] Crosby, 92–99, 111–115.

[37] *Ibid.,* 62–69, 91; Vella, 382–389.

# CHAPTER 22

# Burmese Nationalism

# between the Wars[1]

Between the two world wars Burma witnessed the emergence of nationalist sentiment at several distinct levels. The educated Anglicized elite, led at the outset by spokesmen of the Young Men's Buddhist Association, demanded that Burma share fully the dyarchy reforms in London devised for British India. Once Burma's participation in these reforms was belatedly conceded, the same elite participated fairly actively in the elections for the Legislative Council and in Council proceedings. At a lower social level, nationalist resistance to foreign rule drew substantial inspiration from the noncooperating tactics of the Congress Party in India, which boycotted elections. The popular movement also owed much to the radical pongyi agitators, led by the Anglophobe U Ottama. One nationalist faction revived primitive superstitions concerning invulnerability and divine kingship and precipitated an overt rebellion in 1931. Substantial groups in the popular movement were strongly anti-Indian. They repeatedly gave vent to their racial prejudices by attacking defenseless Indian residents of Lower Burma during the course of the 1930s.

A third level of nationalist agitation, intermediate between the other two, developed among students of the University and secondary schools. Student leaders calling themselves *Thakins* (masters) were usually recruited from the half-westernized youth who lacked economic or political stakes in the *status quo*. They preferred westernized political methods to the primitive magic of the rebels of 1931. They were also unwilling to compromise their nationalist aspirations for favored positions within the government, as was not uncommonly done by adult political leaders.

The leading political personality during the 1930s was Dr. Ba Maw, who oscillated between the three levels. He made a temporary alliance with the pongyi-led rebels and boycotters in 1931–1932, then entered the

[1] This chapter has been developed, in shorter form, from "The Renaissance of Burmese Nationalism," part III of the author's *A History of Modern Burma* (1958), 185–426.

government and became Burma's first Prime Minister under the 1935 Constitution, and, when driven from power in 1939, enlisted the support of the student nationalists. It was Dr. Ba Maw and the Thakins who shared limited power during the Japanese occupation from 1942 to 1945.

The wide divergence of opinion between the various levels of nationalist political expression made it difficult for the British authorities to ascertain what the Burmese really wanted in the nature of a common-denominator pattern of reform. The problem was also aggravated by the inevitable delays involved in Parliament's constitutional legislation covering imperfectly understood and rapidly developing situations remote from Europe not only geographically but also in terms of political realities. London's problem was also complicated by the inevitable involvement of Burma with plans for political reform in India. It was to the credit of British policy that, through a process of consultation and compromise, genuine political and constitutional progress was achieved despite the frustrations inherent in the confused political situation.

## Emergence of Burmese Nationalism in World War I

Developments connected with World War I changed the political outlook of Burma in a number of ways. In the economic field, disorganization of the rice-export trade due to wartime shipping shortages, combined with several poor growing seasons, produced serious agricultural unrest. Popular resistance to land alienation and to various types of tax assessment became widespread throughout Lower Burma. In more prosperous Upper Burma, a disquieting increase in crime developed during the war period. Collusive practices by British milling firms in the purchase of rice aggravated the impoverishment of the Lower Burma cultivator.

At the political level, currency was given during the course of the war to various expressions of Allied war aims, including President Wilson's affirmations concerning rights of self-determination. More important was Burma's awareness of actual political developments in India, which provided ready-made objectives and procedures for nationalist political agitation. But nationalism in Burma was never an integral part of the Indian movement. It developed generally within the matrix of indigenous religious and cultural sensitivity. The first popularly comprehensible expression of nationalist sentiment in Burma developed in 1916–1917 in connection with the prohibition of the wearing of shoes on pagoda premises. The agitation was sponsored by a politically minded faction of the Young Men's Buddhist Association. The original nonpolitical leadership of the YMBA was outflanked at the end of the war not only by westernized politicians but also by the various factions of the emerging General Council of Burmese Associations, which displaced the older Buddhist council in 1921.

In the initial expressions of Burmese nationalism, popular hostility was directed strongly against the alien Indian and Chinese populations.

More time was required before anti-British feeling became articulate and organized, since the definition of issues developed in connection with events. The apparent mistake of postwar British reform policy, which was not ungenerous, was to permit unrest to become vocal at social levels incapable of finding solutions for basic economic and political grievances through the newly provided Legislative Council.

Part of the inspiration of Burma's new wartime outlook came from the ambitious plans of the colorful lieutenant governor, Sir Spencer Harcourt Butler. He inaugurated a multisided program of economic and building expansion, which included the projection of an autonomous University of Rangoon. The new and progressive Burma which he envisaged would require the full cooperation of Briton, Indian, and Burman in a spirit of mutual trust. He did not contemplate that the new order would necessitate any revision of government controls. These would continue to function within the ideal of popular loyalty to the "commonwealth system" as a whole. The Governor's persistent emphasis on the combination of educational advancement and empire loyalty carried for many Burmans the disquieting implication that the proposed University and the Anglo-vernacular school system in general were conceived as instruments of political indoctrination.

## Postwar Reform Proposals

As announced by Secretary Montagu in 1917–1918, the official British program for postwar Indian reform promising the progressive realization of responsible government was not conceived as applicable to Burma. The reported prevalence of political apathy within Burma and the apparent widespread desire of Burmans to be disassociated from India counseled that a separate and different scheme be devised. This apparently sensible proposal got off to a particularly bad start because the alternative Burma reforms suggested by the new lieutenant governor, Sir Charles Craddock, gratuitously offended Burmese sensitivities. He declared that Burma was incapable of exercising the degree of self-government planned for India because Burmans lacked experience in representative government at the village level and advanced educational training for higher levels of control. Village Councils had been operative in India since 1882 but not in Burma. Craddock concluded that self-government in Burma should be restricted for the time being to the functioning of district Councils elected indirectly by circle boards which village-taxpayer voters selected initially. Representation at the center would be severely limited, under the Craddock scheme, until such time as experience and political education warranted making further advances.

Craddock's cautious proposal provided the stimulus for the very kind of political restiveness which he had hoped to avoid. The pride and self-respect of the Burmans demanded that they be accorded reforms on the same scale as India. When the Gandhian boycott of the emerging dyarchy regime developed in India, the proposed reforms were similarly rejected in Burma. The local-government scheme devised by Craddock was included in the final arrangement for Burma, and proved to be wholly unsatisfactory.

It was unfortunate that the actual enactment of the Burma reforms was delayed for several years beyond the introduction of the reforms in India proper. Alternative proposals for broadening the suffrage and for transferring additional governmental functions, such as forestry and education, to Burman control had to be worked out in a Reforms Committee investigation. During the interim period of delay, informed Burman political opinion crystallized into a demand for a Constitution patterned on that of independent Ireland rather than on the India reform model. Rather than incur the additional delay and uncertainty which the preparation and passage of an entirely new Constitution would have entailed, Burma's spokesmen finally agreed to go along with a modification of the India scheme, although some other political status entirely separated from India would probably have been preferred. Thus political events in Burma began to outrun London's fairly leisurely timetable.

While the constitutional-reform proposals were still in gestation, the opening of the new University of Rangoon in December, 1920, afforded the occasion for a widespread student strike instigated by the politicians. Discontent focused on the efforts of the British-appointed University governing agencies to stiffen preparatory standards and to free the University from political interference. Passing standards for University graduation were sharply raised in early 1920, and attendance at campus classes was thereafter required of students. Passage of the University Act in August, 1920, was carried through in defiance of unofficial Burmese protests, which alleged that Britain was withholding self-government because of the paucity of University graduates while simultaneously raising standards and removing the University from Burmese control. Governor Craddock's rule as ex officio Chancellor of the University aggravated popular distrust and hostility. The organization of a politically motivated student strike at both the University and preparatory levels in late 1920 was encouraged by the Gandhian boycott tactics launched in India earlier in the same year. The strikers succeeded in closing virtually all secondary schools as well as the University.

The student strike was generally barren of constructive results educationally, although it generated an abortive effort to set up a rival system of national schools, privately supported and free of governmental control. Only a few of the national schools survived. The most important political results of the strike were to impress the nationalist cause on the awareness of all the parents and students affected and to establish a tradition, for better or for worse, of student participation in political affairs. It was during the course of the schools strike that the General Council of Buddhist Associations adopted the more inclusive name of the General

Council of Burmese Associations. Some five hundred local branches of the GCBA appeared, and by 1922, when the dyarchy reforms were ready to be introduced, politics had become a preoccupation of all education-minded peoples of Burma. The national schools system failed of realization, but the political furor generated by the strike stimulated popular hostility to the dyarchy reforms, which were inaugurated in 1923.

The decisions of the British-appointed Reforms Committee in 1921–1922 ran sharply counter to the advice offered by nonboycotting Burmans and by understanding British civil servants, such as John S. Furnivall. Critics questioned the imposition of unwanted circle and district Councils, originally proposed by Craddock, which were to be saddled with onerous duties relating to health, sanitation, and vernacular education. The failure to include revenue measures within the competence of Burmese ministers responsible to the Councils was also challenged, as was the provision for communal representation. Mr. Furnivall questioned the wisdom of introducing at the outset a broad-based taxpayer franchise. He favored reducing the number of qualified voters by some 60 per cent, thus eliminating a multitude of people lacking interest and experience in voting. He would give more real powers to Burmans of substance and education, who would themselves be free to decide if and when the suffrage should be broadened. In the end such important responsibilities as general administration, law and order, land-revenue collections, labor regulation, and finances were actually reserved, in accordance with the India plan, for ministers responsible to the governor alone.

Under the prevailing political climate, the dominant elements of the GCBA group were committed to the negative task of boycotting and wrecking the new dyarchy system. The firebrand leader of the boycotting group was U Ottama, an India-trained Burman politician masquerading as a pongyi monk. A coterie of his Anglophobe followers, many of them also pongyis, captured control of numerous village athin units of the GCBA. U Ottama was subjected to successive prison sentences for seditious utterances in 1921 and 1924, but the action only served to increase his popular following. Eventually many of the Western-educated politicians, in the absence of any substantial middle-class following, found it advantageous to accede to the wishes of the political pongyis. The official prohibition of political participation by village headmen robbed the village athins of the responsible local leadership which the headmen might have provided. Headmen became the objects of attack as the alleged stooges of the government. Subversive political activity tended to coalesce with criminal lawlessness in a baffling cycle of social disintegration.

When the first circle-board elections were held in 1922, twenty-one westernized leaders of the GCBA defected from the majority boycotting element and decided to seek membership in the Legislative Council. The so-called Twenty-one Party adopted the alternative tactic of the anti-

Gandhian Swaraj Party in India, which was to penetrate the provincial Councils in order to publicize its nationalist home-rule demands. The Burmese people generally entertained no confidence in the electoral system as such, and little pressure was required to restrict participation in the initial election to a mere 7 per cent of the eligible voters. This percentage improved but little in subsequent election contests.

## The Operation of the Dyarchy Constitution

Burma's Constitution of 1922 provided for a Legislative Council of 130 members. Fifty-eight of them were elected from general constituencies, twenty-two from special communal and other groups. Two of the Governor's Burmese ministers, who were entrusted with administrative responsibility for agriculture, excise taxes, health, public works (except irrigation), forestry, and education, were responsible to a majority of the Council. Other ministers in charge of general administration, policing operations, land revenue, and financial and labor policies were responsible directly to the governor. The central government of India retained control of external relations and defense, currency and coinage, communications and transportation services, income tax, and criminal and civil law. The governor exercised direct personal jurisdiction over Burma's peripheral hill areas. He also enjoyed the power of veto over legislation and could, if necessary, certify essential budgetary expenditures. The governor's control over budgetary allocations limited severely any discretionary power enjoyed by ministers administering those transferred areas assigned to Burmese ministers responsible to the Council.

Generally speaking, Burma's dyarchy-reform scheme generated very meager popular support. Elected circle Boards and district Councils represented no articulate opinion. The voting system was itself a novel and unwelcome experience made more so because suffrage was based on the payment of unpopular household and poll taxes. The 93 per cent boycott of the first election itself constituted in fact an impressive rejection of the entire dyarchy system. Crucial matters of public concern involving police, courts, taxation, and finance were not under Council control in any case. The district Councils became a haven for political grafters, and the central Council proved incapable of undertaking any positive constructive action. Personalities overshadowed political principles, and cohesion was lacking even among nationalist elements.

Sir Harcourt Butler, who was assigned to a second governorship over Burma to introduce the new system, succeeded in attracting at the outset the cooperation of able Burman leaders to man the transferred ministerships, but the honeymoon period passed quickly. Burman sensitivities were offended by the discontinuance of recruitment of Burmans for the army in favor of Karen, Kachin, and Chin elements. The national opposition in the

Council attacked the policing system by proposing crippling budgetary cuts, alleging political discrimination by the police. Individual and party differences developing within the Council usually had little relevance to the issues which governed popular political attitudes outside the Council. The resident British business community, thoroughly exasperated, came to condemn as mischievous and trifling all politically motivated Burman activity.

The nationalist movement in Burma at the grass-roots level divided in 1924–1925 into two principal factions, one led by westernized persons and the other by the traditionally minded pongyis. The first had a stake in the survival of the British-fashioned hierarchy and operated within the context of a radical political opposition. The group could not in any case countenance the conspiratorial and superstition-ridden tactics of the political pongyis. By contrast, the latter group undertook in 1924 to promote an abortive antitax and anti-Chettyar-moneylender campaign backed by oath-bound village athin members. Participants resorted to physical intimidation and violence and confidently prophesied on astrological grounds the downfall of British rule in 1925. Following a physical clash between the two rival factions at Mandalay in August, 1924, both of them splintered into subunits. These included the pongyi-dominated traditionalists and two other rival boycotting elements of the GCBA, plus the more progressive urban-oriented Home Rule, Swarajist, Nationalist (the Twenty-one), and Independent Party groups.

The Home Rulers joined the parties that were participating in the 1925 elections for the Legislative Council. About 16 per cent of the eligible voters took part, compared with 7 per cent in 1922. The resulting nationalist faction in the second Council was itself rent by personal rivalries, and Council members remained almost completely out of touch with the boycotting village athins. The Independent faction within the Council divided into a conservative progovernment Burman group and a non-Burman communal faction, which joined conservative Burmans in cooperating within the government's heterogeneous majority. Meanwhile the pongyi-led athins continued to agitate for nonpayment of taxes, a movement which modulated eventually in the overt Saya San rebellion of 1931–1932.

In view of the heterogeneity of the membership of both the second and third Councils, a functioning situation was maintained by the government only by studiously refraining from introducing difficult or contentious proposals no matter how urgent was the need for reform. For this reason, much-needed legislative proposals designed to halt land alienation failed of enactment during the prolonged period of the one-third decline in Rangoon paddy prices, from 1926 to 1930. The price collapse was aggravated by collusive buying practices of the British rice-exporting firms. Nationalists in the Council agitated without success for repeal of all direct taxation, proposing to cover the loss of revenue by reduction of payments on Burma's outstanding public debt to India. They undertook also to obtain preference for Burman candidates in the civil service employ. The public for the most part was completely apathetic toward Council proceedings.

The inefficient and frequently dishonest operation of the local and district Councils attracted the downright hostility of the villagers in most regions. Public services in the fields of health, public works, and vernacular education, for which the local Councils were held responsible, were correspondingly badly served. District Councils, like the Legislative Council, were answerable to no local public opinion interested in reviewing official performance. The performance standards of the governing committees of the threescore municipalities of Burma were also adversely affected. The new system deprived the committees of the helpful participation of European members, so that conditions deteriorated rapidly after 1924. By 1926–1927 only 5 per cent of the municipal committees were adjudged officially to be satisfactory in their performance, as compared with 65 per cent from 1919 to 1923. An even more alarming deterioration of the functioning and prestige of the headmen at the village level was correlated with the rising tide of political unrest and crime. The more active were the police, the more crime was uncovered; police baiting became a kind of popular outdoor sport.

## The Simon Commission Investigation

The efforts of the Simon Commission in early 1929 to review the workings of the governmental reforms in Burma were hampered by direct Indian Congress Party instigation of continued boycott tactics. Indian interference included a visit to Burma by Mohandas K. Gandhi himself. The boycott agitation found support in the various factions of the GCBA, which were now influenced to demand nonseparation from India for fear that a separated Burma would receive no concessions at all. The atmosphere at the time of Simon's arrival in Burma was further disturbed by the death in prison of a pongyi political offender, U Wisara, who had undertaken a hunger strike as a protest against his being denied the use of the monk's robe. The more articulate lay-controlled Burma for the Burmans League, which represented westernized elements of Rangoon, took a more reasonable line. The league advocated separation from India and curtailment of Indian immigration and moneylender operations along with freedom from pongyi political domination and the disciplining of disorderly clergy. There was little in the immediate situation or in the record of the previous six years of dyarchy rule to encourage the conclusion that the reforms had been constructive or salutary.

The record of the investigation of Burma's governmental problems and aspirations made up a substantial portion of the Simon Commission's seventeen-volume report. It reflected all phases of resident British opinion. Government servants endeavored to find some common ground with intelligent nationalist opinion, and chamber of commerce spokesmen also produced a labored affirmation of their qualified support of Burma's legitimate political aspirations. At the opposite extreme of British opinion were the ill-tempered denunciations of any move in the direction of home rule by the *ad hoc* Association of Professional and Business Men. The only consideration on which the British community was apparently in full agreement was the desirability of Burma's separation from India. Their consensus served to confirm the fears of many boycotting nationalist groups that Britain intended to deny to a separated Burma some measure of the self-government intended for India. Conservative Burman members of the Simon Commission itself took umbrage at many of the damaging allegations made by the British opponents of constitutional reform.

The articulate Burmese nationalists testifying before the Commission were also strongly in favor of separation from India. The Burma for the Burmans group demanded separation even at the possible cost of retarded self-government, although it expressed confidence that home rule for Burma could eventually be achieved apart from Indian support. The more inclusive Separation League went further, and prepared a detailed constitutional proposal for a "Burma Free State" modeled on the British and Irish systems. Burma's educated elite were clearly not willing to tag along with India's pattern. The period of the Commission's activities in 1930 also marked the appearance of the youthful Dobama, or Thakin, Party which was destined to achieve leadership during and following the Japanese occupation.

A particularly disquieting aspect of the Commission's procedure, from the Burman point of view, involved the careful attention given to minority-group opinion—Karen, Shan, Anglo-Indian, and Anglo-Burman. The Commission gained no comparable awareness of the vehement distrust of British policy being generated among the majority antiseparationist nationalists. It finally recommended a new and properly suitable Constitution for separated Burma, but it failed to reaffirm specific assurances previously advanced by the local Rangoon authorities that Burma's new Constitution would approximate in any case the one proposed for India. The report itself added to the widespread suspicion of London's intentions by identifying the resident British business and professional community as the most determined political opponents of Burmese nationalist aspirations.

The ineffectiveness of the negative boycotting program of the timid and distrustful antiseparationist group and the general lack of any official program of positive action geared to Burma's needs and traditions afforded opportunity for more violent forms of Burman frustration to find expression. These were directed at the outset against defenseless alien Chinese and Indian residents, mainly usurious shopkeepers and moneylenders, but also against the highly unpopular Indian immigrant laborers.

## Xenophobia and Rebellion, 1930–1931

Social and political discontent in Burma reached the breaking point in 1930–1931. A principal factor in village unrest was the collapse between 1926 and 1930 of the price for rice paid to the Burman cultivator. Depressed paddy prices put the cultivator at the mercy of the usurious Chinese shopkeeper and forced the somewhat reluctant Chettyar community to foreclose mortgages on some 2 million acres of developed paddy land. Economic prostration, which obliged the closing down of industrial plants, forced a larger number of Indian workers to seek employment as cultivators and rural workers in competition with dispossessed Burman peasants. A controversy between rival Burman and Indian dock workers at Rangoon, in May of 1930, became the occasion for Burmans throughout the Rangoon area to attack Indian residents indiscriminately. Racial tensions were exacerbated a month later by a prison riot at Rangoon directed against the new Indian superintendent. Burman attacks on Chinese traders and shopkeepers, which started at Rangoon in January, 1931, were followed by local rioting against Indian agriculturalists in the lower Sittang Valley. The comparative absence of direct Burman economic and social contact with the resident British employer and business groups prevented at the outset the development of analogous conflict with Europeans.

Latent resentment against various aspects of British rule eventually amalgamated with general social and economic unrest. The peasant cultivator was squeezed between the British rice millers and Indian and Chinese usurers. The hated capitation tax was being assessed and collected in Lower Burma by the same British government which permitted the continuing influx of Indian immigrants.

The anti-British Saya San rebellion, which began in late 1930, drew its inspiration from traditional rather than contemporary aspects of the Burman political tradition. Saya San, an ex-pongyi from Shwebo, proclaimed his destiny to rule as Burma's King. He revived the entire panoply of royal regalia and the religious symbolism of kingship, including the sacred palace precincts, the white umbrella, and the galon, or Garuda, bird of Hindu mythology. Also in evidence was the lore of astrologer and tattoo artist, the alleged potency of magical amulets and charms, and the presumed enlistment in the service of the new King of the spirit of a murdered British forestry officer. Taxation and land alienation provided the economic bases for popular appeal, but superstitious factors predominated.

The rebellion was foolhardy in the extreme, for the rebels lacked firearms and munitions. The Saya San effort was of necessity a highly secretive affair. It was in no sense a mass rising, much less the result of elite instigation. The forthright spirit of the rebels, nevertheless, was highly contagious; military suppression only encouraged the barrage of continuing Burman agitation within the Legislative Council in support of certain issues raised by Saya San and in condemnation of repressive police measures. The capture and trial of Saya San afforded opportunity for the ambitious Dr. Ba Maw, a European-educated Burman, to gain political prominence in the Dreyfus tradition by serving as legal counsel for the rebel leader. Another emerging Burman politician, U Saw, adopted the galon bird symbol for his own private party. The sheer audacity of Saya San's self-appointed role as the ruler of a resurrected Burman kingdom stimulated the admiration of Burmese nationalists, even though the educated elite condemned the madness and obscurantism of the venture. The heat of the frenzied rebellion welded a connecting bond between hitherto disparate elements of the population, although it made little or no contribution to the resolution of particular political differences.

The British authorities muffed the apparent opportunity afforded in 1931 to reduce tensions through some affirmative action to end several root causes of discontent, especially those connected with tax distress and land alienation. The problem of undertaking any effective reform program was admittedly aggravated by reason of Burmans' distrust of each other and by the customary tendency of politicians to clamor for impossible goals in order to gain personal followings. The people themselves doubtless suspected the motives of many of the political leaders, but they gave their confidence to other less sophisticated groups equally irresponsible. At the local level, the rebellion reduced greatly the authority of the village headmen. Political agitators and the criminally lawless collaborated in promoting the disintegration of governmental authority at the village level.

## The Problem of Burma's New Constitution

The first India Roundtable Conference, which convened in London from November, 1930, to January, 1931, gave scant attention to Burma's affairs. The official representatives of the Burma government, including the governor, Sir Charles Innes, all favored the Simon Commission's recommendation for a separate Constitution for Burma. Burma's separation from India was therefore taken for granted and was declared officially not open for further discussion. Unheeded were the warnings of the Burman representatives that the majority antiseparationist opinion unrepresented at London would cause serious trouble unless explicit assurances were offered that Burma's new Constitution would be no less advanced than India's.

The British government promised only that Burma's prospects for constitutional advance would not be prejudiced by separation. Sir Charles Innes flatly contradicted the Burman insistence concerning the need for explicit guarantees if substantial popular unrest were to be avoided. The governor's entire role at London carried the unfortunate implication that he personally was opposed to Burma's political advance, an impression which was intensified in his subsequent dealings with the Saya San rebels following his return to Rangoon. It was nevertheless agreed that a special Burma Roundtable Conference should be held a year later at which all political elements in Burma would be represented. The sending of the actual invitations to the Burma Roundtable Conference was delayed until August, 1931.

The London Conference of 1931 permitted a full airing of Burma's exaggerated expectations for early self-government. Burman and British participants operated from completely different premises. The former assumed that they were assembled to negotiate the terms of the new Constitution, while the latter were concerned only with affording a hearing for various views regarding reforms whose definition would rest in the end with the untrammeled judgment of the British Parliament. The extreme demands advanced by Burman spokesmen for immediate recall of Governor Innes and for the establishment of a system of parliamentary rule by a cabinet completely responsible to an elected legislature were undercut in the end by the announcement of the nature of the conclusions reached by the concurrent India conference. These included acknowledgment of the need for important safeguards and reservations covering external relations, defense, and financial responsibility.

But the results were far from satisfactory. Studied efforts which were made by several spokesmen at the conference to quiet the fears of the antiseparationists concerning the possibly limited nature of intended British concessions were largely negated by the Burma conference chairman's bland affirmation that Burma would receive a constitution suitable to its needs, whether superior or inferior to India's. The most effective Burman rejoinders to British cautiousness combined the insistence that only a government commanding the confidence of the people could get at the roots of social disease and enlist popular cooperation in their correction. It was also argued that it was safer to move forward, even though somewhat prematurely, than to arouse further discontent by denying deepseated popular expectations.

The generous concluding statement made by Prime Minister MacDonald went much further than the conference itself to satisfy Burman spokesmen. The Prime Minister proposed to set up a Burmese regime separated from India and fully responsible to an elected parliament in the previously reserved as well as the transferred subjects. Unfortunately, MacDonald's statement carried far less assurance to the antiseparationist factions back in Burma than to those who heard it. The most controversial aspect of the statement concerned the desirability of letting the Burmese electorate decide whether or not it favored separation from India to permanent and unconditional political association with India. The issue so stated was so heavily loaded in favor of separation and so vigorously backed by resident British interests at Rangoon, that distrustful Burman opponents professed to perceive ulterior motives behind the proposal. There was, after all, no compelling reason to deny the possibility of Burma's secession from India in the future.

Actually the result of the election referendum held in 1932 was an overwhelmingly majority victory for the antiseparationists. The net result was highly unfortunate. London found it impossible to abide by this decision when the reforms were finally approved in 1935. The determination of the future status of Burma was unduly delayed, and the election contest elicited a maximum of partisan furor and a minimum of judicial appraisal. Indian navigation interests and Congress Party agents, along with Dr. Ba Maw, did their utmost to stir up Burman hostility to the idea of separation. The only positive result of the furor was to end the futile policy of election boycott. Credit for the generous character of the eventual British decision was largely canceled by the difficulties inherent in London's handling the affair at such long range.

## Burma's Separation from India

The attempt of the antiseparationist Legislative Council elected in 1932 to resolve the question of separation or federation along alternative lines from those proposed by the London government quickly ran aground. Both unconditional federation and separation on London's terms were successively rejected. Dr. Ba Maw eventually engineered a unanimous vote in favor of federation on condition that Burma be permitted the right to secede at a later date by action of its own legislature. This proposal ignored London's sovereign constitutional authority. It probably also went beyond what responsible Indian leadership was willing to concede to Burma. Such a precedent might work to paralyze the entire Indian federation. During the course of the Legislative Council session, Dr. Ba Maw also advanced the mischievous proposal that the court condemnation of Saya San be made an election issue.

London continued to urge that the Council reexamine the alternative proposals officially set before it and submitted a summary description of the proposed separated Constitution as the basis for such action. Dr. Ba Maw replied by obtaining passage of a new resolution calling for convening a representative conference to formulate a Constitution capable of automatic development approaching fully responsible government for Burma as a separated entity. But when a special session of the Council actually assembled in 1933, the same mercurial antiseparationist leader plumped for unconditional federation with India. This was an apparent move to align his following completely with the revolutionary movement in India which opposed all of London's proposals. As a consequence the antiseparationist movement splintered and its agitation subsided in the course of the special session. Further abortive consultations between a selected Burmese delegation, including GCBA leaders and Dr. Ba Maw, and a

Joint Select Committee of the British Parliament took place in late 1933. In the end it was left to authorities in London to formulate the new Burma Constitution in the absence of any clear expression of opinion from Burma. The prolonged consultative procedure may have promoted Burman understanding of the constitutional issues involved, but the 6½ years required for decision between the visit of the Simon Commission in 1929 and the final approval of the Constitution by Parliament in 1935 sacrificed valuable time. It was 1937 before the Constitution actually went into effect.

## Burma's Constitution of 1935

One unfortunate element of Burma's Constitution of 1935 was its denial of immediate control by Burma over immigration and tariff policies. This ruling was made out of deference to British and Indian commercial and industrial interests, and in disregard of major considerations supporting Burman desire for separation from India. All members of the Cabinet were made responsible to a majority of the largely popularly elected House of Representatives, but this concession was balanced by the establishment of a Senate, half of it appointed by the governor and half elected by the lower house. Only wealthy and presumably conservative Burmese were eligible for Senate membership. The governor still retained power to administer peripheral hill areas as well as to control defense, foreign relations, and monetary policy. He was responsible for maintaining order, preserving financial stability, protecting minority groups from discriminatory treatment, and safeguarding the interests and integrity of the public services. He could also assume emergency dictatorial control if governmental authority was threatened. Such constitutional prerogatives were not subject to discussion by the Parliament, and no legislative proposal touching constitutional matters and criminal-trial procedures could be introduced into the Council. The governor's general veto over ordinary legislation was also shared by London if it acted within a year of the date of passage. Separated Burma assumed responsibility for 7.5 per cent of India's total public debt, two-thirds of which was represented by the government-owned railway system.

Burma's Legislative Council accomplished little from 1932 to 1936. While the formulation of the new Constitution was taking place in London, all major decisions were actually made by the governor. The potentialities of the proposed reformed Constitution were concealed by the spectacle of politicians within the Council engaging in mock heroics while vying for selfish political preferment. Rifts within the ranks of the antiseparationist majority, which were based largely on personal considerations, were never healed. Few persons besides aspirants to office appeared to be greatly interested in the 1936 elections. The only important political event of the period was the University strike of 1936, which brought the youthful

Thakin, or *Dobama,* Party into national prominence. Participants in the 1936 student strike were destined to become Burma's political elite in the postwar period.

The popular mood in Burma was further damaged by conditions of economic depression. Ameliorative acts concerning land alienation and debt conciliation ran firmly aground in the Council; one-fourth of the paddy land of Lower Burma changed hands through mortgage foreclosures between 1930 and 1936. The foreclosed areas would have been much larger except for the general policy of the Chettyar community to scale down peasant indebtedness in situations where substantial payments could continue to be made. Land taken over by the government for nonpayment of taxes usually reverted to jungle. In many agricultural areas, the cultivators' savings and jewelry as well as their land titles were lost. But even so, little starvation or abject destitution developed in the naturally productive countryside. The rate of land alienation leveled off after 1936 and then receded slowly.

As previously indicated, the period of 1933–1936 witnessed the rise to political leadership of two highly disparate individuals. One was the clever European-educated Dr. Ba Maw and the other the meagerly trained but unscrupulously cunning U Saw. Both men were destined to serve as premiers under the new Constitution, and both were political opportunists. Ba Maw was consistently Leftist and Anglophobe, whereas U Saw gave full leash to his uninhibited urge to power. U Saw's tactics included knifing erstwhile political friends, taking pay for Japanese propaganda to be disseminated through his Rangoon newspaper, and collaboration with British authorities after 1939 in suppressing the nationalist political disaffection led by Dr. Ba Maw and the Thakins.

## The Student Movement and the Thakins

The emergence of the student movement as a political factor and the organization of the youthful Thakin Party both dated from the early 1930s. The schools strike of 1920–1921 and the subsequent abortive effort to inaugurate a system of privately supported national schools had established the tradition that higher education was a matter of nationalist political concern. An impetus was given to student political activities at the University by the construction with privately contributed funds in the late 1920s of a University Student Union building on the Rangoon campus. There, in the time-honored British tradition, wide freedom was accorded for the discussion of public affairs. The Student Union became, in time, the headquarters of student agitation for the entire country.

Because the University students themselves were drawn from a limited European-oriented segment of the population, the prewar student movement was not a matter of broad popular concern. Its organizational roots ran back into the many English and Anglo-vernacular high schools from which the University membership was drawn rather than the village athins of the nationalist GCBA. The movement nevertheless brought together for intimate acquaintance potential student political leaders from all parts of the country. The role of the University Student Union also gained importance from its accessibility in Rangoon to the interference of politicians of the several nationalist parties.

The aggressive spirit of the student movement owed much to the frustration experienced by the vast majority of students in their efforts to obtain diplomas and suitable employment. The ablest of the honors students, who could aspire to entry into the India or Burma civil service, usually remained discreetly circumspect politically so as not to embarrass their future-employment prospects. But many failed the examinations, and jobs were few during the depression even for successful degree candidates. About 40 per cent of the candidates taking the ordinary B.A. examinations regularly failed to pass, and the number of failures for the second-year Intermediate University tests was even higher. Passing marks for students taking the lower level high school final tests were earned by only one-third of the candidates, and in many schools the average of passes was much lower. Diplomas carried some job prospects for the successful, but the limited degree of westernized learning absorbed by the majority of failures in the examinations was generally valueless. The sophisticated atmosphere of the University alienated many of Burma's youth from parental authority. The student movement was therefore as much a product of an artificial and ill-adapted educational regimen as it was an expression of the rising tide of political disaffection. Many students developed a genuine interest in contemporary aspects of world affairs and in socialism, which were excluded from the curriculum.

Two fairly distinct national student organizations, the Dobama group and the All Burma Youth League, amalgamated in 1935 to form the Dobama Asiayone, or We Burmans Association. Members adopted the habit of addressing each other by the term *Thakin* (master), which was roughly the Burmese equivalent of *Sahib* in India. The term became a symbol of youthful defiance of British rule and an affirmation of faith that Burmans were destined to be masters in their own country. The Thakins were, as a rule, dedicated nationalists, disdainful of fellow students who aspired for entry into the civil service and also hostile to middle-class politicians who mouthed nationalist slogans for the purpose of enhancing their political fortunes. The Thakins were effective in organizing their fellow students in the important high school centers. They were generally distrusted by villagers, and their efforts in the late thirties to organize Burman workers were equally unsuccessful.

The intellectual fare of many of the student nationalists included the writings of China's Sun Yat-sen, the Sinn Feiners of Ireland, Nietzsche, and Karl Marx, along with Strachey's *Theory and Practice of Socialism*. Dobama Asiayone spokesmen were revolutionary in spirit but were essentially nationalist rather than Marxist in character. They criticized Burmans who aped the British and denounced the dishonest landlords who exploited cultivators quite as heartily as they condemned the European proponents of capitalist imperialism. They were generally prepared to accept aid from any quarter, even from fascist Japan, to achieve their nationalist ends.

The historically memorable student strike of February, 1936, near the close of the school year, was precipitated by the Thakin leaders who had won control of the Rangoon University Student Union during the previous year. Their efforts to arouse student hostility were assisted by an exhibition of unbending British "face" on the part of the University College authorities. Following several malicious public attacks on a member of the teaching staff, the president of the Student Union, Thakin Nu, was expelled, and the union secretary, Thakin Aung San, who doubled as president of the All Burma Student Movement, was also disciplined. Student strikers thereupon closed off entrances to examination halls by lying across entryways. The strike spread quickly to leading high schools, making it necessary to postpone all school examinations as well. The emphasis shifted in due course to a demand for the reform of the University Act of 1920, which had placed the governance of the institution in the hands of a nonpolitical Council. Some Legislative Council politicians saw the chance to make political capital from the strike by embarrassing Dr. Ba Maw, then the Minister for Education. The examinations were finally held in June, 1936.

The University Act was later amended (in 1939) in partial compliance with Student Movement and nationalist demands. The Chancellor was to be elected thereafter by the Legislative Council, while the revamped University Council could derive only a minority of its members from the University staff or the civil services. The victory of the student-strike leaders of 1936 was a fateful one in several respects. It made possible the infiltration of the University Council by politicians, a move which carried baneful consequences for the educational standards of the institution, especially in the postwar period. The Thakin associates in the 1936 strike became the champions of Burmese nationalism against both the British and the Japanese, and they took over the political leadership of independent Burma after 1948.

## Burma under the 1935 Constitution

The election campaign of 1936, the first held under the new Constitution, aroused little popular enthusiasm and produced highly inconclusive results. The apparent party winner was an alliance composed of five groups of office-seeking politicians led by U Ba Pe, which won the largest single bloc of forty-six seats. Dr. Ba Maw's new popularly orientated Sinyetha, or Poor Man's Party, advocated many land-reform and credit proposals which Burma's peasants ought to have wanted, but it failed dismally to win their confidence or support. The Sinyethas won only sixteen seats. A remnant of the old boycotting GCBA won twelve places, the Thakins three only. Successful Independent candidates numbered around seventeen, while the remainder of the 132 seats went to representatives of communal and of business and labor groups. The Ba Pe coalition broke up because the Cabinet offered too few places to satisfy its ambitious members, and the resourceful Dr. Ba Maw qualified as Burma's first Prime Minister. His first Cabinet of 1937 was a heterogeneous grouping of disparate elements including two of Ba Maw's followers, one dissident from Ba Pe's group, one member of the GCBA contingent, a Karen, and an Arakanese. In order to attract the needed support of British and business representatives, the new Premier held in abeyance the radical socialistic proposals included in his original Sinyetha platform.

Burma's brief experience with responsible parliamentary government from early 1937 to the end of 1941 was too short to accomplish solutions for basic economic problems, but it did produce, for the first time, a wholesome sense of reality in public affairs. The new regime afforded valuable experience in parliamentary procedure and an opportunity for a Burman-controlled legislature to come to grips at long last with such urgent problems as land alienation and cultivator credit. As a rule, the titular ministers of government left the administration of their respective departments to the permanent staffs and concentrated their own efforts on keeping political fences in repair. Generally speaking, the government-supporting factions demonstrated a gratifying sense of responsibility, while opposition groups acted with almost complete irresponsibility. The small Thakin contingent was an exception to the latter allegation.

The absence of any genuine relationship of political factions to the general electorate contributed an unscrupulous tone to the political infighting which characterized the Parliament. Personal attacks against Cabinet members by legislators were punctuated by periodic no-confidence motions, while the columns of the vernacular press afforded opportunity to vilify opponents and to fan popular passions. The encouraging consideration of such genuine problems as agricultural reform, improvement of village administration, immigration regulations, tax changes, and educational policy did not, unfortunately, produce results of sufficient consequence to dispel the traditional suspicion that government continued as always to be an essentially predatory agency. This salutary if somewhat painful and unproductive experience in self-government was aborted by the occupation of Burma by the Japanese in early 1942.

The most substantial achievement of the Ba Maw government was its sponsorship of a series of able reports covering problems of agricultural financing, tenancy, and land alienation. A Tenancy Act which became law in May, 1939, was designed to make tenancies more secure and to end the evil practice of annual leases let at unfair rates. Rental obligations were to take second priority legally to more essential payments for wages and the servicing of crop loans. A subsequent Land Purchase Bill undertook to halt the transference of title to nonagriculturalists and to facilitate recovery of titles by cultivators. Unfortunately administrative problems connected with the execution of both reform measures prevented their actual implementation within the short period of time available to the government. Additional measures intended to halt land alienation and to provide agricultural financing were debated for several years, only to be overtaken prior to their passage by the Japanese war. The tenancy-reform effort ran aground on the impossibility of providing the large number of persons competent to determine fair rental standards, who would be needed to care for the thousands of examinations called for by tenants. Landlords usually found ways to keep rent reductions to a minimum. Amendments proposed in March, 1941, to correct obvious deficiencies in the original Tenancy Act were blocked by the property-minded Senate.

## From Ba Maw to U Pu

The incessant efforts of opposition groups in the Parliament to bring down Dr. Ba Maw's government included the deliberate instigation of anti-Indian riots in July, 1938. U Saw's newspaper, the *Sun,* exploited for the purpose the republication of a book written by a Burma Muslim attacking the Buddhist faith, which allegedly insulted the Burman race and religion. The Young Pongyi's Association took up the protest and precipitated anti-Muslim rioting in Rangoon. The furor spread rapidly and came to include as targets all Indian groups. The frenzied attacks were deliberately fanned by political opportunists. Physical violence was accompanied by widespread looting of Indian homes and shops. Emergency security measures imposed within the Rangoon area included the temporary outlawing of U Saw's paper.

The eventual report of the special Riot Inquiry Committee attributed the outbreak to irresponsible political agitation intent on poisoning Burman-Indian relations and on aggravating tensions relating to unsolved problems of land tenure, Indian immigration, and moneylender control. Underlying factors were the acknowledged distrust of the police by virtually all classes of the population, a consideration which enlisted public opinion generally, including village thugyis, on the side of the rioters. Instead of apologizing for his role in promoting the frenzy, U Saw boldly attacked Premier Ba Maw in the legislature for negligence in suppressing the offensive book and for the generally unpopular role played by the police. Responsible elements within the Parliament managed to defeat by a narrow margin a no-confidence motion submitted in connection with the issue.

Ba Maw's Ministry finally succumbed to mounting difficulties in early 1939. A disturbing revival of student strikes and demonstrations in 1938, instigated by the Thakins, was accompanied by similarly sponsored industrial strife. One University-student demonstrator was beaten to death by a policeman in Rangoon, and a pongyi-led student mob in Mandalay ended in the death of fourteen rioters. Such incidents afforded ostensible justification for the European bloc in the House of Representatives to shift its support from Premier Ba Maw to the alternative faction led by U Pu and U Saw, which it did in February, 1939. The ousted Premier tried in vain to revive his shopworn Sinyetha program. Finding himself unable to establish any effective rapport with the masses, he took advantage of the outbreak of the European war in September, 1939, to ally with revolutionary Thakin groups in a deliberately subversionary program which eventually landed many of the participants in jail.

Meanwhile, under Premier U Pu, efforts to examine important problems of governmental administration were continued. A study of village administration came up with a report advocating election of village headmen by three-year-resident-adult suffrage. The headmen would also be subject to removal from office by deputy commissioners on petition of three-fourths of the village-tract electorate. Headmen would be assisted in judicial matters by village committees elected on a five-year tenure basis, and there would be improvements in village-policing facilities.

This village-committee report was followed by an even more searching examination of the prevalence of bribery and corruption at middle and lower levels of the civil and police services. In an effort to diagnose a disease and to prescribe a remedy, the hearings were conducted under the chairmanship of an outstanding British-Indian civil servant on a confidential basis, without the disclosure of names of either informers or accused. The ascertained causes of corruption were of long standing. The prevalence of official intimidation and bribetaking which was brought to light had apparently been aggravated by the multiplication since 1900 of specialized government functionaries concerned with health, engineering, and taxation and other regulatory agencies. Evidence justified the conclusion that half to three-quarters of subordinate court magistrates made a lucrative business of selling justice, that police standards were even worse, and that excise officials were almost 100 per cent corrupt. Remedial proposals included the payment of more adequate salaries to minor officials and closer official inspection and popular surveillance. Burman members proposed the revival of traditional oath-taking ceremonies and the practice of conducting legal proceedings in open-court (*coram rege*) ceremonies in full view of the public as well as participants. The realistic report added a highly disturbing dimension to the problem of administering any reform legislation however wisely conceived.

The political situation in Burma in the late thirties was also directly affected by developments in neighboring India and China. Overt Burmese sympathy for the objectives of the India Congress Party was confined for the most part to the Thakins and to Dr. Ba Maw's following, but all important developments in British-Indian relations exerted an inevitable influence on the eastern shores of the Bay of Bengal. Japan's initiation in 1937 of an effort to conquer all of China found Burmese opinion generally pro-Chinese. Some of the Thakins echoed anti-imperialist agitation emanating from Indian Communist sources and began examining the general applicability of Marxist principles to Burma's economic and political problems. In general but with notable exceptions, the revolutionary nationalist movement in Burma was prepared to accept assistance from virtually any quarter, including even the Japanese, for the achievement of its political ends.

Outbreak of war in Europe in September, 1939, exerted a sobering effect politically. It produced an abrupt ending of Thakin-sponsored school strikes and the temporary suspension of other inflammatory tactics. Reconsideration of nationalist policies led to the sponsorship of a "Freedom Bloc" program by Dr. Ba Maw and the Thakins. As a condition of Burman cooperation with Britain in the European war, the bloc demanded (1) Britain's recognition of Burma's right to independence, (2) preparations looking toward convening of a constituent assembly, and (3) the subjection to Cabinet supervision of the special authorities reserved to the governor. Dr. Ba Maw became the acknowledged leader of the new ultranationalist coalition, but Thakin Aung San was general secretary and other Thakins were prominent in it.

The Freedom Bloc spokesman put Premier U Pu sharply on the defensive by demanding that he adopt their program, to which the wily U Saw also gave general assent. All "progressive" elements were exhorted to subordinate ideological differences, including Marxist inclinations, to the united effort to exact major political concessions from the war situation. Popular Freedom Bloc appeals of a treasonable nature produced by mid-1940 the jailing of numerous leaders including Dr. Ba Maw and Thakin Nu. Meanwhile Dr. Thein Maung, Ba Maw's chief lieutenant, visited Japan. Upon his return, he presented in a series of widely circulated newspaper articles Japan's claims to the leadership of Asia. Most of the Thakins continued, however, to be emphatically pro-Chinese in their sympathies.

U Pu's government eventually collapsed, in September, 1940, as a result of its pledge of unqualified support to Britain's war effort, which he gave following the German victory in Western Europe and the British tragedy of Dunkirk. Opposition to the war policy by Freedom Bloc spokesmen became the basis for their incarceration, which action the opponents of Premier U Pu used in the Parliament as a basis for the renewal of their political attacks. U Pu's Ministry might have weathered the storm except for the defection of U Saw's following in the final critical stages of the debate. It was U Saw himself who succeeded in forming the new Cabinet. He patterned his tactics on those used by Dr. Ba Maw in 1937 in attracting support from minority groups, plus the British members and several dissident representatives of the previous government.

## *The Ministry of U Saw, 1940–1941*

Premier U Saw's domestic policy was to curb radical agitation by the rigorous exercise of emergency powers and to give positive support to Burma's defense measures. At the same time he appealed for nationalist support on other grounds. He proposed to Burmanize the civil service and thus reduce administrative costs, to introduce free compulsory primary education, to found a Buddhist university, to protect minority rights, and to replace English with Burmese as the medium of instruction at Rangoon University. The enthusiasm with which he suppressed internal unrest stemmed from the opportunity which this policy afforded him to put down all political opposition. He pushed through the conviction and imprisonment of Dr. Ba Maw and other Freedom Bloc spokesmen, later extended their sentences beyond the original year, curbed antiwar agitation in the press, and eventually imprisoned even such opponents as U Ba Pe, who was not promoting subversion at all. Pro-Japanese articles previously appearing in U Saw's own newspaper abruptly disappeared, and he even reopened the Burma Road to pro-Chinese arms traffic in October, 1940. Thakin Aung San and some thirty other Thakin leaders escaped the surveillance of U Saw's police force and fled the country. They eventually returned as Japanese collaborators to team up with Dr. Ba Maw in the Japanese-sponsored government during the wartime occupation.

U Saw's one major diplomatic accomplishment was to negotiate an agreement with India in July, 1941, conceding Burma's right to limit Indian immigration in return for preferential treatment for Indian goods entering Burma. But the Japanese war developed before the treaty ratifications were exchanged. Plans to Burmanize the higher levels of the civil service were vigorously pressed by U Saw, ostensibly as a means of making good the revenue losses incurred by his popular cancellation of direct capitation and household taxes. For such a Burmanization policy he enlisted the support of virtually all politicians, including even the most Anglophile. Effective British control of Burma's governmental administration was eroding rapidly under the stress of essential wartime compromises with U Saw. The outbreak of war in the Far East in late 1941 completed the collapse of British authority.

# CHAPTER 23

# The Netherlands Indies

## between the Wars

The labored Ethical policy of the Dutch was replaced after 1920 by a cautious progam of administrative reform looking toward a selective application of varying degrees of local autonomy within the Indies. The most tangible evidence of increasing self-rule was the establishment of a Peoples Council, or Volksraad, but it was instituted mainly to satisfy the demands of European residents. The Volksraad actually exercised little substantive authority, and the lower-level Councils which were introduced into Java alone were purely advisory in character. Exhibitions of political radicalism during the latter twenties and early thirties influenced Dutch officialdom, both in Holland and in Batavia, to reject proposals for any further constitutional advances and to revert in time to a rigid policy of repression. Any talk of independence was regarded as treason, and even the use of the term "Indonesian" was forbidden. The unprecedented degree of prosperity prevailing during the middle twenties, which came to a peak in 1928, relieved some of the economic tension, but the collapse of the world markets for Indonesian products after 1930 created a grim situation for both the European entrepreneur and the indigenous population. Unemployed laborers returned to Java from the Outer Islands, and much of the agricultural economy reverted to a subsistence basis. Dividends dried up, and the great corporations used up their financial reserves. The traditional "open door" trading policy of the Indies also became a casualty of the depression, as cheap Japanese goods threatened to capture consumer markets. Nationalist unrest was kept under control partly because it was many-sided and not coordinated; it covered the entire political spectrum and included many disparate religiously oriented and island groups. Even so, pressures mounted steadily. The moderate nationalists who cooperated with the Dutch in the Volksraad became sufficiently articulate by 1936 to request Holland's consideration of constitutional reforms. This proposal was flatly rejected by The Hague in 1939, and even after the flight of the Dutch government to England in 1940, no substantial proposal for constitutional change was forthcoming. The Dutch dream of indefinite continuance of control, in cooperation with an expanding educated Indonesian elite, evaporated long before the invading Japanese armies arrived in 1942.

## Postwar Administrative-reform Proposals

The postwar modulation from the Dutch emphasis on the social-welfare objectives of the Ethical system to a program of gradual administrative reform reflected a change of mood and circumstances. The two policies differed markedly in motivation and objectives; they were alike only in their essentially cautious and paternalistic approach. Official Dutch concern prior to 1920 was to stimulate the development of Indonesian leadership in behalf of constructive social and economic ends. After 1920, constitutional concessions were accorded in grudging response to a rising demand for increasing nationalist participation in the government and for freedom from Holland's control. The rising tide of political agitation owed much to increasing educational activity, both European and Islam-centered, and to the measure of recognition given during the war years to Sarekat Islam as a recognized channel for the crystallization of national aspirations and grievances. By 1920, what was left of the vitality of the once-urgent Dutch concern for welfare tended to shift its emphasis to the gradual increase of cooperation by educated Indonesians in matters of governmental administration.

A number of wartime events contributed to the willingness of the Dutch population in both Holland and the Indies to consider constitutional changes. Reorientation of the export trade of the Indies in the direction of the United States and Japan, amounting by 1918 to about 22 per cent of the total, tended to reduce Holland's prestige and to put the Dutch on the defensive. The preoccupation of Britain and France with European affairs after 1914 and that of America also from 1917, coupled with the increasing wartime assertiveness of Japan throughout the Orient, carried disquieting overtones. If Japan should undertake to project its interests southward, the only possible recourse for the Netherlands Indies would be to enlist a conscript Indonesian army. Even the mildest of the Javanese nationalists made it clear that an enlistment campaign would be resisted in the absence of Dutch commitments to accord a substantial measure of self-government to the islands' people. President Wilson's advocacy of self-determination added support to the generally revolutionary climate which developed in Europe from 1917 to 1920. Dutch authorities began to consider several proposals for active Indonesian participation in administrative affairs, a move which they had previously deemed impossibly dangerous.

The reluctant decision of The Hague to introduce administrative changes of a moderate character, including a system of advisory representative agencies at various levels of control, was reached in 1918. The reforms were planned to begin in Java and be extended gradually to the Outer Islands. An official Commission on Reforms eventually made recommendations in 1922. The need for caution was underscored by the observed tendency of nationalist sentiment to become increasingly radical on both the political and economic fronts, as was evidenced by Sarekat Islam's criticism of "sinful capitalism." Conservative circles usually attributed this disturbing trend to the encouragement coming from a coterie of agitators and from irresponsible statements broadcast by the American and Soviet governments.[1]

The only prewar experience in self-government in the Netherlands Indies had been popular participation in a very modest system of Councils initiated in 1903 in selected regions and municipalities. Dutch administration continued the traditional practice of combining bureaucratic supervision and indirect rule, utilizing the tradition of popular respect for the authority of the prijaji officialdom and village chiefs. In most areas of Java (Surakarta and Jogjakarta were exceptions) Dutch Residents and their assistants, who were responsible to the governor-general, functioned in cooperation with salaried Javanese regents selected from the chief class. The regents provided liaison with the people and were amenable to Dutch supervision. Behind this supervisory façade, functional agencies administered such responsibilities as education, health, agriculture, and public works. The postwar reform proposals contemplated the establishment of new regency and provincial-level advisory Councils with potential capacity for development into fully autonomous administrative agencies. In the Outer Islands, where the local sultans' authority persisted under the indirect rule of regional governors in all matters not affecting Dutch interests, it was contemplated that a longer time would be required before the Council system would be applicable.

## The Volksraad

The Peoples Council, or Volksraad, which was approved in 1916 and started in May, 1918, developed mainly as the result of the pressure of Dutch residents in the Indies and became only belatedly a part of the indigenous reform proposals. Dutch settlers objected strenuously to continued arbitrary direction of Indies affairs from the Netherlands and demanded for themselves a substantial share in the determination of policy. A majority of the Volksraad at the outset was European, partly elected and partly appointed, but Indonesians, Indo-Arabians, and Indo-Chinese were represented in numbers almost equal to the Europeans. Most of the elected members were chosen by the existing regional and urban Councils. Appointed membership with the Volksraad included recognized leaders of

[1] Bernard H. M. Vlekke, *Nusantara* (1960), 340–347, 354–355.

minority groups, some of whom were critics of the government. Under the new arrangement, the governor-general of the Indies needed the concurrent approval of The Hague authorities only on decisions of major importance. He was required to consult the Volksraad and to seek its approval on such important topics as the establishment of the separate schedules of the annual budget.[2] The Volksraad could suggest desirable reforms, but it provided little opportunity for free expression of the views of the nationalist opposition.[3]

Minor changes in the character of the Volksraad were introduced at various times during the 1920s, enlarging somewhat the appointed membership and eventually granting to the Indonesians (in 1922 and 1928) a thirty-to-twenty-five majority over the Dutch membership in a total of fifty-five seats held by these two major groups. The election of members of these two groups was accomplished in the end by action of completely separate electorates very small in size, an arrangement which precluded any possibility of real political cooperation. The number of European electors averaged around 550, while the number of Indonesians qualified to vote started at 452 in 1924 and never exceeded 1,530. Most of the Indonesian electors were members of the new regency and provincial Councils. As finally crystallized after 1931, twenty-two of the sixty members of the Volksraad were appointed by the governor-general, including ten Europeans, ten Indonesians, and two of the five foreign Asians.[4]

As a legislative organ, the Volksraad was a feeble agency. It could initiate and amend legislative proposals, petition for the redress of grievances, and put questions and interpellate, but it could not enact law under its own authorization. Nor did it have the right to institute investigations. If the governor-general and the Volksraad failed to agree on a specific legislative proposal, the matter could come up for consideration again six months later. After this period had elapsed, the Crown retained authority either to veto the proposal or to legislate by decree. Royal authority (The Hague) included all matters relating to defense requirements, foreign relations, and final budget approval. Press censorship was limited to matters affecting "public order," a term which the Dutch authorities were free to define. Dutch publications circulated freely, but freedom of political expression and association was omitted from basic civil-rights guarantees.[5] The Dutch justified this ultracautious policy on the grounds that nationalist sentiment was both inarticulate and imperfectly organized, hence ineffective and capable of being ignored. They particularly wanted to avoid in the Indies such expressions of political unrest as were taking place at the time in India, Burma, and the Philippines.

[2] *Ibid.*, 362.
[3] *Ibid.*, 361–363.
[4] *Ibid.*, 362–363, 385.
[5] *Ibid.*, 422–423.

## Administrative Reform at Lower Levels

The general program of administrative reform as outlined in the recommendations of the Commission on Reforms was incorporated into the new Netherlands Constitution of 1922. It made possible the progressive development of a system of democratic reforms for the Netherlands Indies. Starting in Java and to be extended as soon as feasible to the Outer Islands, a uniform system of provincial governments was planned. The appointed governors of the newly projected provinces would serve as chairmen of local Councils organized on the general pattern of the Volksraad. Governors would also act as executive heads of Boards of Deputies composed of salaried officials supervising the several functional departments, including water supplies, irrigation, and electric-power installations. Senior resident officials, prior to the establishment of the full provincial system, would continue to exercise in their designated areas arbitrary executive authority as before. Selected portions of actual or potential provinces which were deemed ripe for reform, such as municipalities and regencies, could be designated immediately as autonomous units, each having its own advisory Council to assist in making decisions. Any such autonomous organs could be suspended or suppressed in instances of gross neglect of duties or failure to cooperate.[6]

In applying the reforms to Java, the older regional units were abolished in favor of five new administrative provinces, three of them established immediately (West, Central, and East Java) and the other two (Surakarta and Jogjakarta) in 1928. Fragments of these provincial units and parts of Madura as well were designated as autonomous regencies; such units totaled around fifty by 1930. Electors for the regency Councils, who must be at least twenty-five years old, numbered approximately one for each five hundred inhabitants. They voted for three members each according to a complicated system of proportional representation.[7] Only a bare majority of the Council members were elected. The regent himself or his Patih minister presided over the sessions of the regency Council, but with a nonparticipating Dutch observer present. Most of the regents resented having to work with the Councils, for their existence undermined traditional authority. A British observer of one session of a regency Council in the mid-twenties noted the ominous psychological impact of a minor incident when, on the motion of a schoolmaster member, a committee consisting of four members was selected instead of the three-member group that had been officially proposed.[8]

[6] A. D. A. de Kat Angelino, *Colonial Policy*, vol. II, *The Dutch Indies*, (1931), 382–384.

[7] *Ibid.*, 385–391.

[8] Hesketh Bell, *Foreign Colonial Administration in the Far East* (1926), 18–39.

Apologists for the cautious Netherlands Indies program of administrative reform underscored the immediate advantages of the system in terms of stability and responsible guidance, and also its long-term possibilities for indigenous training in self-government.[9] Dutch proponents argued in 1930 that since any specific reservation of governmental functions to the islands authorities would not in any case prevent friction, it was better to give to the Indies the potentially complete right to manage their own affairs and to Holland the same measure of right of preventive and repressive guidance and control. Such a policy alone, it was alleged, could preserve the "strength which can only be found in consciousness of the duties of leadership." Dutch leadership would thus "voluntarily . . . limit the extent of its powers as a tutor in accordance with the progress of the pupil towards freedom and capacity to govern."[10] The speciousness of this kind of rationalization was fully demonstrated when time ran out on the leisurely Dutch program.

## Economic and Social Developments during the Twenties

The big economic advance in Indonesia after World War I was made in the almost-virgin territory of the Outer Islands, with special emphasis on tobacco, oil, rubber, and tin production. International capital participated actively. Chinese contract labor was widely used, with some increment of Indonesian labor after the middle twenties. More than half of Indonesia's 1¼ million Chinese came to live outside of Java. Outer Island peoples, such as the Sumatran Minangkabau and residents of the northern Celebes, contributed as small holders to the expansion of rubber and copra production. The oil industry as it developed in southern Sumatra and eastern Borneo maintained world connections in terms of financing, production, and marketing, all of which had very little relevance to the local economy. Much the same could be said for Dutch banking operations, geared to service Western trade and enterprise. Tin and copra production increased during the twenties by 50 per cent; coal and oil output and production of sugar and tea doubled, and rubber cultivation increased by 200 per cent. In 1928–1929, some 500 million guilders in dividends were paid on international capital investments in Indonesia, which totaled around 4 billion guilders. That the Indonesian population shared to some extent in this bonanza was demonstrated by the fact that no less than fifty-two thousand pilgrimages to Mecca were made in 1927,[11] although the disparity in profit distribution between indigenous and foreign populations was enormous.

[9] Kat Angelino, 654.
[10] *Ibid.,* 420.
[11] Vlekke, 366, 374–375.

Economic prosperity had a negative effect in terms of progress in self-government. The assumed possibility of indefinite improvement of popular welfare based on increased output and trade made Dutch businessmen increasingly hostile toward allegedly gratuitous constitutional quibbling. The promises to enlarge the powers of the Volksraad were accordingly put aside, and all nationalist agitation of an uncooperative character was suppressed as treasonable conduct.[12] The larger industrial combinations, British, American, and Dutch, continued to pay low wages, while they contributed little save their moderate tax contributions to the needs of the people or the government. Capital funds required for economic expansion during the 1920s were provided in large measure from current earnings. The size of many of the operations extended far beyond the scope of Indonesian or even Chinese participation. The Chinese shared somewhat in the sugar cultivation, but other crops demanding intensified care, such as indigo, tea, cotton, tobacco, and cocoa, were developed in plantations largely under European control. The only important development in improvement of working standards was the elimination of penal sanctions for enforcement of labor contracts for tobacco cultivation in 1932 and for rubber in 1940. Both actions were influenced by United States tariff regulations prohibiting access to the American market of the products of forced labor.[13]

## The Impact of Modernization

Western influences impinged on Indonesian life with increasing effect during the interwar years. The intensification of agricultural production in Java and improved health facilities combined to produce an enormous increment in the population of the island, which reached about 40 million by 1930. Cultivators of new cash crops throughout Indonesia became involved in a money economy and developed new wants in gadgets, bicycles, medicines, items of clothing, and schooling. Laborers working in mines and industries or on plantations distant from their home desas were initiated into a new world of wage compensation and private debt. For many of them, the traditional shadow plays, religious rites for planting and harvesting, and life-cycle patterns derived from ancient custom became little more than childhood memories lacking in vitality. Persons living in close and continuous contact with an alien environment thus became increasingly divorced from traditional cultural values.

The principal agency of social change affecting the Indonesian people during the boom period from 1915 to 1930 was the expanding Dutch plantation system. It included such commodities as sugar, tapioca, sisal, tea, cassava, and coffee in Java, plus rubber and tobacco in the Outer Islands.

---

[12] *Ibid.*, 365–367.

[13] J. H. Boeke, *The Structure of Netherlands Indian Economy* (1942), 22–49; W. F. Wertheim, *Indonesian Society in Transition* (1956), 104–116.

Plantation lands located near the processing establishments were leased from peasant proprietors for periods of around twenty years, absorbing often as much as one-quarter of the cultivable land in the vicinity of the mills. Indigenous civil servants and village chiefs acted as go-betweens for procuring land leases and seasonal labor as needed. Improved methods of plant selection and cultivation, including the scientific fertilizers, could be applied under supervision to plantation land in a fashion impossible to duplicate on the estates of private cultivators, who were virtually crowded out of the sugar industry after 1920, when the Dutch mills refused to buy their cane.[14]

If the plantation system had been permitted to function indefinitely without the drastic interruption occasioned by the depression of the 1930s, a complete reorganization of the peasant economy of Java might have resulted. The emerging pattern included an upper stratum of rural yeomanry, consisting of landlords and chiefs who profited from lease rentals and from their services to the Dutch in providing leases and labor needs. The seasonally employed peasant, working for coolie wages on the plantations or in the mills, kept one foot in his rice paddy, to which he returned in the off season. Such peasant labor was not organizable as a proletarian worker group. Thus the Dutch plantation supervisor geared his production and marketing operations to the world economy but kept the plantation workers and millworkers subjected to control patterns not differing greatly from those functioning under the nineteenth-century cultivation system. Opportunities for Indonesians to operate as entrepreneurs were kept to a minimum, and the indigenous social order was preserved to facilitate the continued profitable exploitation of land and services. The vast gains realized in production and also the benefits of welfare measures implemented during the boom period before 1930 did little more than employ more people; there was little or no increase in general per capital income.[15]

When the world market for plantation products collapsed in 1930, the distended but still resilient Indonesian social order reverted to a traditional pattern of subsistence agriculture, which proved completely incapable of response to the revived economic stimuli developing during the later thirties. The depression actually broke the back of the budding middle class in Java, and the Chinese moneylenders, with an assist from the Arabs, took over the necessary credit and marketing functions connected with agricultural production. Embarrassed Dutch millowners again enlisted the aid of village chiefs and civil servants to free themselves from unexpired leases of land no longer needed now that plantation output had to be drastically curtailed. Aside from the sharp reduction of native living standards arising from the cancellation of rentals and wage employment, the casualties included the closing of Muslim schools and the loss of prestige

---

[14] Clifford Geertz, *The Social Context of Economic Change: An Indonesian Case Study* (1956), 29–35, 46–47.

[15] *Ibid.,* 37–42, 49–50.

and power on the part of the indigenous bureaucracy and village chiefs who had cooperated with the Dutch. The ensuing vacuum of Indonesian leadership was quickly filled by the emerging modernized nationalist elite drawn in part from unemployed persons in the lower levels of the bureaucracy and in part from educated student circles. The Dutch responded by repressing the nationalist political unrest and then endeavored to counter it by stimulating the conservative cultural nationalism of the literati.[16]

The disintegration of the Javanese bureaucratic literati, or prijaji, began during the 1920s, when they were first subjected to the intensified impact of resident Dutch society. The inherited standards and morale of the prijaji class were derived in large measure from the Hinduistic court culture of the inland Javan kingdoms, which stressed polite behavior, a mystical orientation in religion, and refined tastes in art, music, and dancing. Javanese district officers customarily appropriated the prerogatives of petty kings, and their office staffs kept aloof from the peasant population. The weakening of the integrity and unity of the prijaji class during the twenties was especially apparent in the growing ranks of the holders of new kinds of jobs, such as accountants, technicians, and clerks, who tended to copy the Dutch and to take over the role of cultural middleman as mediators of the intrusive alien civilization. Only the top-level prijaji, who retained a substantial stake in the preservation of the traditional order, kept their inherited standards intact. The modernistic second-level prijaji provided most of the nationalist political leadership, diverging sharply from the conservative standards of the upper-level bureaucrats, who were for the most part willing to continue cooperating with the Dutch.[17]

Political differentiation within Java took on a particularly complicated pattern. Religiously, the population was divided into the *santri* faction centering in coastal Java and the *abangan* faction strongest in interior central Java. The first emphasized the Islamic elements in the prevailing syncretic animist, Hindu, and Mohammedan cult, while the second tended to play down the Islamic influence. In rural areas, the santris often differed little from their abangan neighbors, but the rift was sharper among the urbanized and modernized elite. The santris included the businessmen, the traders, mosque officials, and the Muslim scholars, who themselves covered the entire spectrum between the modernistic puritanical Muhammadijah to the ultraconservative Nahdatul Ulama. Whereas the upper-level prijaji abangan were conservative and nonrevolutionary, as previously indicated, the nationalistic and modernistic lower-level white-collar prijaji provided the political leadership for both the Nationalist Party and the Communist Party. Aside from the general fact that the village chiefs and the cooperating bureaucracy lost political and social influence, the Javanese political structure was hopelessly fragmented between

[16] *Ibid.*, 52–61, 92–94.
[17] *Ibid.*, 84–92.

urban and rural elements, santri and abangan partisans, traditionalist and modernist protagonists in terms of cultural and religious orientation. The crystallization of anti-Dutch sentiment during and following the war bridged over such rifts for a time, but they were destined to survive, along with regional loyalties characteristic of the Outer Island peoples, to bedevil the postindependence period.[18]

In the Outer Islands, the dichotomies between the rural and the urban population and between the traditional and the westernized segments were somewhat more clean-cut and less complicated. The growing number of indigenous traders and small-scale rubber farmers began to resent subservience to the traditional authority of the chiefs quite as much as they disliked the less vulnerable European and Chinese economic domination. Within the indigenous trading community, business ability and wealth became the new criteria for social status. The traditional social stratification disappeared among the Christian Amboinese and the Menadonese of the northern Celebes. The able Minangkabau people of Sumatra began to contribute substantially to the modernist Indonesian intelligentsia. Many of the educated secularized elite, following their disillusionment with the Communist-infiltrated Sarekat Islam of the 1920s, gravitated toward the new nationalist parties, while the educated Islamic group tended to affiliate with Muhammadijah and other santri Muslim organizations. Most modernized Indonesians adopted the black fez headdress, used a sophisticated form of the Malay dialect, and frowned on marriages with Europeans.[19]

Dutch cultural contributions outside the economic field were limited. The Dutch encouraged the adaptation and application of customary adat law to modern needs, and they contributed something to the revival of Indonesian literature. After 1900, Dutch scholars such as Krom, with official encouragement, began the systematic study of classical archaeological remains. But the Europeans failed to share their own language, literature, and culture with Indonesian colonial peoples to any marked degree. The simplified Malay dialect which became the lingua franca of the island empire contained more Portuguese and Arab words than Dutch. Servants were not encouraged, as a rule, to use Dutch in addressing their masters, and offspring of Dutch residents themselves often failed to attain fluency in the mother tongue. The Dutch made no contribution to Javanese art, architecture, or literature comparable to that of ancient India. Obsessed as they were after World War I by the threat of incipient nationalist upheaval, the rulers made no sustained efforts to direct popular energies into constructive or creative cultural channels.[20]

An examination of the educational program developed by the Dutch

[18] *Ibid.*, 109, 120–121, 125, 137–138.

[19] Wertheim, 8–14, 89–101.

[20] G. H. Bousquet, *A French View of the Netherlands Indies* (1940), 43–57, 84–92.

will illustrate one facet of the problem. On the eve of World War II, elementary schools in Indonesia provided facilities for some 2.3 million students. Slightly more than 2 per cent of these persons continued to the intermediate level, and secondary graduates in any given year averaged around eight hundred students only. The heavy cost of education above the primary level was an important deterrent, although many parents and students made enormous sacrifices for educational purposes. Educational advancement opened up limited job opportunities in government service and also as clerks, mechanics, and engineers and as overseers in plantations and industry. The Dutch continued to fill 93 per cent of the high posts of the government, while the percentage of Indonesian incumbents at all levels of administration increased from a modest 30 per cent in 1928 to some 42 per cent in 1938. Three-fifths of the educated Indonesians worked for the government, and most of the Javanese participants in the growing number of cooperative-credit societies were officials of the government.

The meager facilities which were provided for advanced educational training were predominantly vocational in character. The total attendance at the university level for the Indies generally was around eleven hundred, including a substantial number of nonindigenous students. The Agricultural School at Buitenzorg, dating from 1903, was essentially a research institution, concerned with improving seeds, plant varieties, fertilizers, and water facilities. After World War I, colleges of technology (1919), law (1924), and medicine (1926) were established, but they were accessible to a very limited number of students. Thus in 1941, all of Indonesia possessed only three hundred trained doctors.[21] Persons like Sukarno, who possessed an engineering degree, formed the nucleus of the new secularized elite, small in number but increasingly influential politically.

## Political Fragmentation

The most characteristic aspect of the political complexion of the Netherlands Indies in the twentieth century was the severe fragmentation among all elements of the population. Dutch officials wanted complete autonomy of administrative control, and resident Europeans and Eurasians wanted more authority for their elected representatives. European-born Dutch controlled mining and foreign trade, while locally born Europeans dominated the sugar industry, the utilities services, and postal agencies. Domiciled Europeans usually advocated business and industrial development within the Indies, using indigenous personnel. Dutch representation within the Volksraad reflected, therefore, widely divergent views. On the extreme Right, the Vaderlandsche Club, which appeared in 1929, opposed all

---

[21] D. G. E. Hall, *A History of South-East Asia* (1955), 641; Amry Vandenbosch in Lennox Mills (ed.), *The New World of Southeast Asia* (1949), 93–112; Wertheim, 140–152.

expressions of nationalist sentiment. An even more extreme profascist European group appeared in 1934.[22]

With regard to both legal status and political affiliations, Indonesia's 1¼ million Chinese residents occupied an equivocal position. Chinese residents were subject to Dutch courts in civil matters, but until 1917 they were theoretically answerable to Indonesian police and customary adat law in criminal cases. Because they proved far more capable than the Javanese of responding to the opportunities afforded by a European economy, the Chinese constituted for a time the primary target for the attacks of Sarekat Islam nationalists. Indonesian-born Chinese who departed from the islands for periods of more than three months had to register if they wished to retain their status as Dutch subjects. In the consular treaty with China concluded in 1910, the Dutch were permitted to define the citizenship status of Chinese residents of Indonesia, who were of little or no concern to Peking. The coming of the Kuomintang regime to power in 1926–1927 marked an abrupt change. The new Nanking authorities affirmed emphatically that under the *jus sanguinis* principle Chinese allegiance was inalienable. Pride of race and culture prevented the resident Chinese from developing any sense of political loyalty to Indonesia, and yet they themselves were divided by language and other differences. They attained a larger semblance of cohesion after 1931 from a general sharing of anti-Japanese sentiment.[23]

The indigenous population of the Indies also was fragmented into scores of distinct ethnic and linguistic groups, whose geographical, historical, and cultural orientations were often quite divergent. Islam vied with emerging secularist nationalism as a cohesive factor, and yet neither was effectively organized and articulate. According to Islamic standards, a sharp line separated unbelievers from the believing community, the House of (*dar ul*) Islam, but traditionalists tended toward rigidity while westernized modernists favored making essential adjustments to the standards of the outside world.[24]

The Achehnese for example, were fanatically traditionalist, whereas the other leading Malay people on Sumatra, the Minangkabau, were inclined to be reformist in spirit. Many Outer Islanders were strongly anti-Javanese by tradition and by historical associations. Starting frequently among residents of such groups in Java itself, non-Javanese nationalist organizations were spawned in various regions of Sumatra, Madura, Amboina, Minahasa, and Timor. All were intent on preserving their ethnic and cultural identities. They included some women's organizations as well. Thus

[22] G. C. Allen and A. G. Donnithorne, *Western Enterprise in Indonesia and Malaya* (1954), 32–34; Vandenbosch, 84–85; J. S. Furnivall, *Colonial Policy and Practice* (1948), 230–236.

[23] V. Purcell, *The Chinese in Southeast Asia* (1951), 441–554; Allen and Donnithorne, 32–34.

[24] C. A. O. Van Nieuwenhuijze, *Aspects of Islam in Post-Colonial Indonesia* (1958), 66–86.

Indonesian nationalists could not easily agree on the tactics to be followed to attain self-government or on what to do with it once achieved.[25]

Orthodox santri Muslims tended to regard as idolatrous abomination any harking back to past evidences of pre-Islamic cultural and political achievements—Mataram, Śrivijaya, Kediri, etc. The Muhammadijah modernists, by contrast, owed much to rationalist and social-service trends in the Islamic faith emanating from the University of Cairo, where their leadership had studied. They emphasized religious education and personal commitment in preference to dependence on formal rites. They affirmed the obligation of Muslims to pay a percentage of crops, income, or capital to charity and undertook to establish libraries, hospitals, missions, and charities, as well as modern schools. Although the Muhammadijah challenged the role of the scribes as the definers of orthodoxy and was also anti-Dutch, the organization was neither Leftist nor otherwise radical in a political or social sense. Nevertheless, Dutch authorities usually preferred to aid the orthodox opponents of Muhammadijah, especially after it began in the mid-twenties to replace the fading influence of Communist-infiltrated Sarekat Islam. The Muhammadijha reformist movement (it was not a political party) modulated to a somewhat more orthodox position during the 1930s to provide a nucleus for the wartime Masjumi Party.[26]

In the face of the threatened attrition of their influence, the orthodox Muslim scribes countered in 1926 with the organization of the Nahdatul Ulama. They maintained a persistent challenge to the modernizers until the Japanese occupation of World War II, when the invaders attempted to use the scribes for Japan's own purpose. The Dutch generally avoided antagonizing the scribes in particular by following an opportunist policy of accommodation which lacked positive cultural objectives. They thus sought both to prevent religious unrest from taking a political turn and to keep their opponents divided.[27]

## Sarekat Islam, Communist, and Nationalist Parties

As virtually the only popular expression of Javanese anticolonial sentiment during the period immediately after World War I, Sarekat Islam found itself infiltrated by Communist organizers, who undertook to exploit the nationalist movement for their own ends. Marxist slogans proved useful in attracting mass support. For several years (1918–1921), Marxists exercised full control of the militant Semarang branch of Sarekat Islam, and local membership in the two organizations was concurrent.[28] Under the energetic leadership of the Dutch Communist Sneevliet and his Indonesian collabora-

[25] Vlekke, 360, 364.

[26] Wertheim, 205–215, 218–220; Van Nieuwenhuijze, 41–49; Harry Benda, *The Crescent and the Rising Sun* (1958), 61–99.

[27] Bousquet, 2–8, 12–21.

[28] Vandenbosch, 80–85.

tor, Semaoen, the newly formed Social Democratic Association of the East Indies attracted a number of radical Indonesian nationalist members. The association hailed the formation of the Comintern in 1919, and maintained contact with successive Comintern congresses. Shanghai connections were established in 1920, when the Indonesian Communist Party (PKI) affiliated formally with the Comintern, an action taken by the exiled Sneevliet. Temporary alliance between Communists and Sarekat Islam, allegedly in support of national independence and representative democracy, faded after 1921, mainly because Communist policy disliked Pan-Islam and advocated violence as a political tactic. After 1921, Communist organizers shifted attention to the labor-union field, which they attempted to monopolize. The complete break with Sarekat Islam conservatives came in 1922, when the Communists began encouraging the defection of radical nationalist elements from the older organization.[29]

The PKI clearly overplayed its hand from 1924 to 1926 in a doctrinaire effort to sovietize Javanese villages and processing factories. Communists tried with little success to appeal to peasants on the basis of communal traditions of land ownership under adat law; also they established cells in the labor organizations of mills, sugar plantations, and mines. The development of Marxist schools was undertaken by Tan Malaka, while Alimin took over the task of organizing seamen and dock workers as part of the Pan-Pacific trade union centering at Canton. The controversial trend in the direction of resort to violent measures, combined with clashes over policies and personalities, eventually produced rifts within the group itself in 1925–1926. A premature Communist rising, launched in November, 1926, despite the objections of Moscow, was thoroughly crushed. The party was thereupon outlawed; its leaders were exiled, and the Communist movement in Indonesia was quiescent for some fifteen years. Sarekat Islam meanwhile was discredited by its association with the Communists, and it also lost strength. The 1926 rebellion fiasco left the political field open for secularized Indonesian nationalists, but it also stampeded Dutch opinion to demand an end of "soft" governmental policies.[30]

Student-sponsored study clubs took over the leading role politically following the collapse of Sarekat Islam and the PKI. Indonesians who had been to Europe had examined with interest the postwar achievement of freedom for Ireland, Poland, and the Baltic and Arab states, and some of them developed considerable enthusiasm for Moscow's anticolonial agitation. The Indonesian Nationalist Party (PNI) was formed in 1929 by two educated Javanese—Sukarno, an engineer, and Tjipto, a physician—both of them members of the Bandung Study Club. Sukarno's inspiration came in part from the example of India's Congress Party and its program of mass pressure through noncooperation. He demonstrated unusual ability as a

[29] Vlekke, 355–359.

[30] Virginia Thompson and Richard Adloff, *The Left Wing in Southeast Asia* (1950), 163–167.

popular orator and as a fashioner of effective slogans and symbols (a flag and a hymn). He was arrested by the Dutch police near the end of 1929 and interned on Flores Island, later at Benkulen in Sumatra. During his absence, another Indonesian party was organized along much the same lines by Dr. Sartono. In 1932, the pro-Marxist Sutan Sjahrir and Mahammed Hatta (both Minangkabau) returned from Europe and sponsored a moderate Socialist Party. Efforts of the two in cooperation with Sukarno, who emerged briefly from detention during the same year, to unite the two student nationalist movements only brought on Sukarno's second incarceration in 1933. Sjahrir and Hatta were later assigned to penal camps in 1934.[31] Sukarno's heroic reputation as a nationalist leader was probably enhanced by the close attention paid him by the reactionary Dutch Governor-General De Jonge (1931–1936). Except for their promise for the future, the PNI and the Socialists probably merited less concern at the time than the worried authorities gave them. Membership in the PNI was narrowly limited; its social roots were shallow; it was not coordinated with Muslim dissidence. Not until the period of the Japanese occupation did the student nationalist leadership attain widespread popular recognition.[32] Burma's Thakin Party profited similarly.

Official Dutch policy after 1931 placed all nationalist leadership under surveillance and even interfered with political communications of a critical nature between Indonesia and the Netherlands. "Revolutionary" meetings were outlawed, and even use of the term "Indonesia" was adjudged subversive. A few cultural nationalists like Devantoro and the Muhammadijah leaders were permitted activity along religious and educational lines. Devantoro alone sponsored some 250 struggling Tamon Siwa schools. Dr. Sartono's study group later repudiated noncooperation in favor of more immediately constructive methods, and was also accordingly granted a measure of tolerance. The authorities in 1935 permitted a resumption of freedom of assembly for all parties which were willing to accept representation in the Volksraad. The moderate so-called National Parliamentary Group, which was formed from the Volksraad membership, managed to function in a cautious fashion.[33]

## Economic Collapse and Remedial Measures

The economy of the Netherlands Indies suffered a disastrous blow as a result of the world depression of 1929–1934. Export goods derived from both European plantations and from non-European estates as well were hard hit by the collapse of world markets. The large estates were able to cut costs by amalgamation, and some of them continued to export goods at re-

31 Vlekke, 371–373, 379, 383–384.
32 Vandenbosch, 80–85.
33 Vlekke, 379–385.

duced prices; indigenous producers usually abandoned export crops and shifted to subsistence agriculture, especially rice. Total production fell off by one-half during the depression, and the value of exports declined as much as 75 per cent. Government plantations, which had earned a profit of 54 million guilders in 1928, lost 9 million guilders in 1932. Unemployment and low wages in the Outer Islands forced around 100,000 Javanese laborers to return to their already-overcrowded home desas.

Remedial measures were difficult and inadequate. The arable land available for Java's huge population averaged only around 2 acres per family, but pauperism and misery were by no means limited to the Javanese. Crops everywhere were frequently mortgaged for several years ahead to cover peasant indebtedness. Sugar exports were hardest hit, falling to one-third of the former volume and commanding prices as low as one-sixth those of 1928. Prices of imported consumer goods remained relatively high. Payments on foreign-capital account were maintained only at the cost of heavy reduction of imports and consumer living standards. An Industrial Bureau was set up in 1936 to direct recovery efforts. The Dutch authorities contributed 25 million guilders to facilitate the moving of Javanese to the Outer Islands, and twenty-five thousand improved looms were distributed to assist the expansion of the domestic weaving industry. Some recovery in private-garden output of copra, pepper, maize, rubber, and kapok was realized.[34] The burden of debt was reduced in 1936 by currency devaluation, and the approach of World War II eventually revived the markets for Indonesian oil, rubber, and tin.[35]

The Indies government was obliged during the 1930s to abandon the policy of open trade pursued since the middle of the previous century. Production quotas were established for tea, rubber, and sugar to guard against glutting the market, and sales and shipping controls were introduced. Import discriminations, directed mainly against cheap Japanese goods, covered classifications including both national origins and types of goods. Japanese goods comprised more than 30 per cent of the total imports for Indonesia by 1934 and then declined to 25 per cent. The coasting trade throughout the Indies in all commodities was reserved for Dutch ships. No substantial revival of trade took place until 1939–1940.[36]

## Official Rejection of Reform Proposals

Under depression conditions and in the face of police surveillance and the growing Japanese threat, some Indonesian groups adopted a cautious attitude. Representatives of the right-wing Budi Utomo and other anticommunist parties deliberately pursued a "cooperative" policy. Na-

[34] *Ibid.*, 386–390.
[35] Boeke, 22–29; Allen and Donnithorne, 34–39; Wertheim, 104–116.
[36] Allen and Donnithorne, 39–51, 72, 94; W. H. Van Helsdingen, *Mission Interrupted: The Dutch in the East Indies* (1945), 193–201.

tionalist expectations were discreetly phrased, and in some quarters an authoritarian trend appeared. By contrast, spokesmen of the radical Gerindo group, which included the crypto-Communist Amir Sjarifuddin, began to attack colonialism and capitalism generally. In spite of the carefully restricted voting system, elections to the Volksraad in both 1935 and 1939 reflected the rising tide of nationalist feeling and a sharpening of racial antagonisms.[37]

The trend toward radicalism was hastened by the Dutch rejection of a moderately phrased request, approved by the Volksraad in 1936, for constitutional reform. The resolution asked that a conference be convened to draft a plan for gradual modification of Indies-Netherlands relations in the direction of autonomy for the islands within the framework of the Dutch Constitution. The immediate hostility voiced by Dutch members of the Council at the time was echoed subsequently in the blandly negative reply of the Minister of Colonies, delivered three years later. He affirmed that continuance along the established path of decentralization and administrative reform was preferable to any radical alteration of constitutional relationships. Only the gradual appearance of a sound basis for autonomy at lower levels, he affirmed, would afford opportunity for similar developments at intermediate levels and finally at the center.[38]

After the failure of the moderate approach, Indonesian nationalist groups within the Volksraad closed their ranks to form in May, 1939, the *Indonesian* Political Concentration. They had finally dared use the forbidden word, but their tangible gains were minimal. They managed, by November, 1940, to obtain consent from the exiled Dutch government to set up a commission to deliberate and to accumulate relevant political data for the government to consider later at the appropriate opportunity. The report of the commission, as eventually published on December 8, 1941, the very day (in the Far East) of Pearl Harbor, conceded that Indonesians would in the future share more largely in the administration of the colony; but it also insisted that the existing rights of Dutch residents and foreign Asians must, in accordance with their social and economic influence, continue undisturbed.[39]

The Parliamentary Concentration coalition, meanwhile, had set forth a five-point program of demands. The official designation of the island empire should henceforth be Indonesia. An Indonesian should regularly occupy the post of lieutenant-governor, and indigenous applicants should be eligible for assignments up to the level of assistant directors of the administrative departments of the government. Indonesians should also be appointed to membership on the Council of the Indies in Holland. Finally the coalition demanded the election of a new chamber of peoples' repre-

[37] Vlekke, 392–394.
[38] *Ibid.*, 394–395.
[39] *Ibid.*, 395–396.

sentatives by universal adult suffrage to function as a lower house of the legislature along with the existing Volksraad, acting as a senate.

The harried Dutch authorities in England eventually agreed on June 16, 1941, to convene a conference composed of prominent persons from all four parts of the Netherlands kingdom (two of them in the West Indies) to study the problem of postwar constitutional adaptations. Some of the members were later designated, but the conference was never convened.[40] Apparently some moderate nationalist elements, fearful of the Japanese, were ready in 1939 to settle for a ten-year schedule of reforms such as the United States had given to the Philippine Commonwealth. A bold attempt by the Dutch at this juncture to enlist Indonesian political and military cooperation might have made a difference in the long run. But Dutch colonial authorities were afraid to arm the Indonesians for defense of the empire and hoped in some fashion to ride out the approaching storm. At the end of 1941, most politically minded Indonesians welcomed the arrival of the Japanese. Among the first steps of the invaders was to liberate Sukarno, Sjahrir, and Hatta from police detention. The rebellious Acheh nationalists were in full revolt against the Dutch before the Japanese ever attacked.[41]

[40] *Ibid.,* 396–398.
[41] Hall, 633–636; Wertheim, 73–75.

# CHAPTER 24

# French Indochina

## from 1920 to 1941

*T*he mercantilist character of French rule in Indo-china developed greater rigidity in the course of the interwar decades as capital investment increased and trading potentials became more clearly apparent. The administrative system was largely direct, even in those areas where traditional forms of government were retained as a façade. French civil servants monopolized most governmental posts in Cochin-China; French capital and management, with an assist from resident Chinese, controlled and directed the colony's economic-development program. Tentative wartime promises of a larger degree of Indochinese participation in the government were later ignored. Political and economic unrest was not coordinated, however, and the flood of French investments after 1924 substantially reduced unemployment. The French kept educational opportunity at advanced levels to a minimum, partly for political reasons. A large accumulation of European financial reserves sought a haven in Indochina after the mid-twenties to escape the deterioration of the French franc, a development which enabled colonial business enterprise to withstand the shock of the depression. Production standards were fairly well restored in Indochina by 1935. The historic southward migration of Vietnamese from Tongking and Annam into Cochin-China and neighboring Cambodia continued steadily under French rule. Meanwhile, the absence of legitimate means of expression of political discontent contributed to the emergence of Communist leadership of the nationalist cause, in the person of Nguyen Ai-Quoc and others.

## Development of the Mercantilist Program

Although national prestige and the honor of the navy were the touchstones of the early phases of French imperialism in Southeast Asia, its later development was based on more tangible considerations. Moral and psychological support continued to be derived from assumptions concerning the intrinsic validity of France's civilizing mission and its manifest destiny as a world power, but the substance of the operation after 1900 became increasingly economic. French taxpayers tired of making perennial deficit contributions to the Indochinese treasury, and they insisted that the colony stand on its own feet financially. French manufacturers were equally determined to monopolize all available colonial markets and to forestall the development of any competitive industry and commerce within Indochina. With the French-dominated Chambers of Industry and of Agriculture in full control, development plans were coordinated and no foreign capital except that of France was permitted entry.

The mercantilist trading system had the inevitable effect of undermining native industries, which could not long withstand the competition of duty-free French goods. Once-prosperous pottery manufacture, basket making, and silk and cotton weaving all languished, as did oil extraction, starch manufacture, and woodwork. The indigenous population lacked both the capacity, in terms of capital and technical experience, and the requisite official permission to develop alternative lines of economic endeavor. Thus the one country of Southeast Asia with a fairly high potential for industrial development, through its possession of coal, iron, and other minerals, textile resources, and abundant labor capable of disciplined factory regimentation, was industrially limited largely to the processing of rice, sugar, tobacco, and tea products. Substantial amounts of tin, zinc, and coal were found in northern Tongking along with smaller supplies of wolfram, lead, antimony, and manganese. Two-thirds of the anthracite-coal production of Tongking was regularly exported, and the production of cement, brick, and tile was narrowly limited to local needs. Mining development starting in 1904, all French-owned-and-managed, was aborted by World War I, and although revived during the twenties, it never recovered from the subsequent depression. Industrial workers outside the mines numbered only eighty-six thousand persons during the 1930s.

In the steadily expanding pattern of Indochina's total trade after 1900, exports gained progressively over imports. Cochin-China rice constituted the principal item of export, reaching 2 million tons by 1937. But this rice was inferior in quality to that of Burma and Siam. More than half of the income realized from rice sales abroad went to traders and carriers, with the cultivators realizing a meager 26 per cent.[1] Considerably more than half of the imports consisted of manufactured items. They included many things needed by the resident French community, such as metals, machinery, electrical equipment, vehicles, fuel oil, paper, and wine. Tariff rates which were made applicable after 1921 to all imports competing with free-entry French goods were prohibitively high, and in the stringent period of the 1930s French trade assumed monopoly proportions. A coordinated development program geared to the French economy, cheap labor, and arbitrary trade controls contributed to what one observer described in the 1920s as a

[1] Charles Robequain, *Economic Development of French Indochina* (1944), 128–136, 284–304, 344–348.

"conspicuous triumph of French colonization, unrivalled economically in the French Empire."[2]

Individuals of influence close to the scene were aware that the rigid application of mercantilist controls did not serve the interest of the Indochinese people. The critics included Governor Doumer, who served at the turn of the century. He made repeated but futile efforts to obtain for Indochina freedom to adjust to its own natural trading environment, especially with China and Japan. Paris was too distant and too susceptible to opposing political and economic influences to appreciate the importance and feasibility of Doumer's sensible proposal. All Indochina's imports from Asian sources, even those not competing with French products, were heavily taxed, and no reciprocal advantages were accorded to Vietnamese products in French markets. Herein lay the main difference between French policy and that of America in the Philippines. The central government of Indochina drew its principal sources of revenue from customs and excise dues borne by the consumers. After World War I in particular, French economic interests became far more influential in determining trading policy than were the demands of the unrepresented consumer. A ruling was finally achieved in 1928 permitting colonial proposals regarding trade to become operative unless overtly vetoed by Paris, but this was rendered of no effect when depression conditions strengthened even more the tendency toward economic assimilation with France.[3]

## The Dominant Role of Alien Residents

About 72 per cent of the 20,500 professionally identifiable French subjects resident in Indochina in 1937 were pensioners of the government, 53 per cent in the army or navy and 19 per cent in civil service employ. Some 30,000 of the total number of 42,000 French citizens were of pure European descent; the rest included varying mixtures of Asian and African blood. Only 2,000 persons were assimilated as French citizens from the indigenous population. Approximately 2,200 Europeans were employed in trade, banking, insurance, and transportation; the missionaries numbered 629. Here as elsewhere, the French colonies provided satisfaction for what one observer aptly described as the French predilection and ambition for government service. French colonists were only half as numerous in proportion to the total population as were the Dutch in Indonesia. But only 20 per cent of the Dutch were employed in government or armed services, while 72 per cent of the French were so connected. Indochina provided a leisurely, relaxed existence for European residents; about 60 per cent of them were of

[2] S. H. Roberts, *History of French Colonial Policy (1870–1925)* (1925), II, 490–498; Robequain, 243–283, 305–343.

[3] Robequain, 128–136; H. Bell, *Foreign Colonial Administration in the Far East* (1926), 210–226. Taxes on salt, opium, liquor, matches, and rice were important central revenue sources.

more than five years' tenure, and 26 per cent had resided more than fifteen years.[4]

Although living costs for Europeans were high, salaries in Indochina were the envy of other French colonial services. Officials drew regular civil service pay, including houses and furnishings based on French standards, plus colonial allowances and two-thirds pay as retirement compensation. During the 1920s colonial allowances were calculated in francs but paid in piasters at the artificial rate of 3 to 1. The actual value of the piaster was around 12 francs, so that the allowances often exceeded the value of the regular salary pay. French citizens could be tried only in all-French courts located at Hanoi and Saigon. The local population was outwardly subdued and tranquil. European observers and participants regarded Indochina as an outstandingly successful endeavor in imperial rule, as well as a matchless source of wealth for France.[5]

The other alien group which profited from French rule in Indochina was the Chinese. Here as elsewhere in Southeast Asia, the Chinese performed useful economic functions, especially in newly developed regions of Cochin-China, where four-fifths of them resided. They lived cheaply, learned the local languages readily, understood the people, and were adaptable, good-humored, and industrious. Third-generation Chinese were usually assimilated, strengthening the native stock. They nevertheless generated a great deal of local hostility by their monopoly of trade and their usurious tactics. They operated through secret societies and were very adept in evading governmental regulations. They virtually cornered the Cochin-China trade in rice, copra, and fish and dominated the river traffic. They similarly infiltrated Cambodia and Laos as traders and usurers. The Chinese enjoyed no comparable opportunities in crowded Tongking, where they were most unwelcome. The national heroes of Vietnamese history had gained fame by resisting the Chinese invaders, and Tongking was a border region. The Chinese population for all Indochina reached an estimated 420,000 in 1931. The roots of the Chinese were not very deep as a rule, and many of them returned to China during the depression years. An entirely different group began to return in the middle thirties, when they again numbered a substantial 326,000. The proportion of Chinese women to men increased from 68 per cent as many in 1928 to 80 per cent as many in 1938.[6]

## General Characteristics of French Rule

The trend of French administration of the Indochinese federation was clearly in the direction of centralized control, although important differences remained between the several parts. Cochin-China was governed from the

[4] Robequain, 21–38.

[5] Bell, 181–189.

[6] Robequain, 38–44; Victor Purcell, *The Chinese in Southeast Asia* (1951), 207–254.

beginning as a colony under direct French rule, highly bureaucratic and centralized. The retention of the Imperial Court at Hué, with its ritual functions and the mandarinate bureaucracy serving both Annam and Tongking, provided a semblance of reality for the alleged policy of indirect rule. Psychologically the façade was itself significant, although in actuality French provincial officials interfered whenever necessary to adapt administrative operations to the execution of determined economic policies. Some political unrest developed among peasants in Tongking over the failure of the French to end alleged abuses of the corrupt mandarinate, which was undermining the traditional autonomy of the elders of local communes. All provincial budgetary authority was absorbed by the governor-general, including the right to incur public debt by borrowing funds. The objectives of French economic policy varied from region to region. Land alienation from cultivator control, almost nil in Tongking, reached an estimated 75 per cent in Cochin-China, where European plantations were located.

The King of Cambodia, by the Convention of 1884, accepted the authority of the French *Resident Superieur* in both constitutional and administrative matters, receiving in return a civil list for palace expenses. Palace and court functionaries along with Cabinet ministers at Phnom Penh preserved the illusion of royal authority and national independence. A graded bureaucratic civil service replaced the old Cambodian nobility and hereditary incumbents, many of whom were removed from their home territories to avoid complications. A Central Consultative Assembly, dating from 1913 and composed mainly of Residency councillors and high officials, was permitted to express policy opinions, but the agenda of the Assembly was restricted to approved economic and social questions to be discussed in nonpublic sessions. Only minor items of concern were actually approved for discussion, and no significant political discussion was permitted.[7] Fiscal and judicial administration was reserved for French officials only. No pretense was made of administrative autonomy or of genuine indirect rule in Cambodia. The Residents kept order and managed the local officials. Revenues were officially collected, and the King could not borrow money without obtaining French permission. He also surrendered all claims to royal lands.

Most of the Lao country was also under the direct rule of French officials, although frequently they exercised authority through the local chiefs. No effort was made to revive the three former royal families of Vientiane, Xieng Khouang, and lower Laos, their former territories being grouped into eight newly delineated provinces. One prince was named as governor of Bassac. Only the King of Luang Prabang in the upper Mekong Valley retained his royal title and prerogatives as a protected monarch. In such important areas as fiscal policy, policing authority, and trade, Luang Prabang was administered by the *Resident Superieur* at Vientiane. The northern areas bordering Yunnan were ruled under military control by

[7] Robequain, 38–44.

the French. In the eight administered provinces of Laos, French influence was exerted mainly in judicial and educational matters, and in the eventual development of health and sanitary facilities. Otherwise, local custom was respected. The cooperation of the local elite and the tribal chiefs was enlisted in matters essential to such French objectives as order and trade.

The French encountered a minimum of difficulty with the Lao peoples. The abolition of slavery led to one prolonged rebellion from 1900 to 1907 among the Kha tribesmen, who had long kidnapped Vietnamese for sale on the western side of the mountain divide. Ethnic and historical considerations kept Laos almost completely separated from Vietnam and Cambodia. French proposals to annex Laos to Annam for economic and administrative reasons, for example, were abandoned in the face of strong Laotian objections. The people distrusted the Vietnamese even when the latter served only as laborers and as minor functionaries in government employ. The Vietnamese population to the east of the mountains was apparently too presumptuous, too energetic, and too aggressive to fit casual Laotian standards.[8] Cambodians, in turn, were regarded disdainfully by the Lao as effete and lacking in vigor.

The French made substantial efforts to knit their Indochinese Empire together by improved transportation facilities. A meter-gauge railway line from Saigon to Hanoi, a distance of more than 1,000 miles, connected the Red River and Mekong delta centers of population. It was completed in 1913 at very considerable cost. Difficulties of roadbed maintenance and of tunnel, bridge, embankment, and fill construction were aggravated by pilfering, high labor turnover, and the scourge of malaria. A major northwestward railway extension from Hanoi to Yunnanfu in China tapped the profitable South China trade, and shorter radiations extended outward from Saigon and Hanoi. The Indochina railways eventually totaled 3,000 kilometers. French holders of railway bonds received guaranteed interest rates, and French industry profited from supplying the rails, rolling stock, and other equipment. Fourth-class passenger service was widely used by the people for the transportation of market produce, including pigs and chickens as well as fruit and vegetables. High maintenance costs and the competition of coastal shipping and trucks, plus periodic interruptions of service due to floods and typhoon damage, made the railway lines generally unprofitable. They nevertheless served essential objectives of economic unification and security.[9]

Other transportation facilities included roadways constructed at two points across the cordillera from the coast to the Mekong Valley and extending into northern Laos. Paved roads eventually covered 36,000 kilometers all told. River traffic, as well as drainage, was facilitated by the con-

---

[8] Frank M. Le Bar and Adrienne Suddard (eds.), *Laos: Its People, Its Society, Its Culture* (1960), 16–18.

[9] Robequain, 89–98.

struction of dikes in the Red River Valley and by dredging operations in both major delta areas. The ancient canal system paralleling much of the Annam coast fell into disuse. Location and entry problems prevented the two major ports of Saigon and Haiphong from developing entrepôt status. The approach to Haiphong was hampered by excessive silting and that to Saigon by a tortuous channel. The commerce of the largely Chinese city of Cholon neighboring Saigon had access at high tide via a barge canal to Saigon's 25 kilometers of docks, where forty ships could be serviced simultaneously. Much of Saigon was a European kind of city, with paved streets, sidewalk cafes, modern residences, and office buildings. Roadways served the French-developed plantations behind Saigon, and water transportation provided access throughout the Mekong delta and approaches to Phnom Penh, the Cambodian capital. This was largely a French-constructed city built on made land. Cambodia's inland railway and road connections were mainly in the direction of Bangkok.[10]

## Postwar French Gestures at Reform

The substantial Vietnamese participation in the European phases of World War I included fifty thousand workers and an equal number of riflemen. Colonial sources also subscribed several million francs in war loans. Such cooperation inspired Governor-General Sarraut in 1917, in imitation of contemporaneous British promises regarding India's future, to reaffirm French dedication to the rights of man and to the widely acclaimed civilizing mission. In April, 1919, on the eve of his departure for France to become the Minister of Colonies, Sarraut promised to give attention to increasing the popular representation in colonial Assemblies, to be combined with enlargement of the electoral base and an expansion of educational facilities. Such needs became less urgent to him when he viewed them from Paris, even though popular unrest in Annam was clearly on the increase.

Articulate middle-class and student disaffection dated from around 1905. At that time, Vietnamese nationalist representatives made contact with such famous anti-Manchu Chinese reformers as K'ang Yu-wei and Sun Yat-sen. Secret political societies, organized on the Chinese model, appeared in Vietnam by 1910, and a republican League for the Restoration of Vietnam was organized in 1912–1913. An abortive nationalist rising occurred in early 1916. By the early twenties, a moderate Constitutional Party advocated middle-class representation in the colonial Councils and the relaxation of trade restrictions.

The official French response to the medley of reform proposals was actually minimal. At the local-village level, Governor-General Long (1919-1923) replaced the old reactionary Councils of Notables with elected administrative Councils, each having its own budget of expenditures to administer. The new system became effective in some two thousand villages

10 *Ibid.*, 98–116.

by 1925. But the governor-general also doubled the number of European officials, all of whom received increased pay and allowances. In a decree of 1922, he also changed the character of the colonial Councils instituted in 1897 by increasing the number of Vietnamese representatives and by providing for individual-taxpayer suffrage. The electing College of Delegates had previously been chosen from local Councils of Notables. A French majority of twelve to fourteen members was preserved as compared to ten natives, and the powers of the Councils remained in any case purely advisory. Some twenty-one thousand electors qualified under the new scheme. The governor-general retained full responsibility for determining federal policy, and the colonial authorities assumed a somewhat larger measure of local autonomy apart from Paris in economic, fiscal, and defense matters. Needless to say, these cautious gestures at reform fell short of satisfying popular political aspirations, which became particularly vocal in Annam and Tongking.[11]

Subsequent French governors-general accomplished little in the way of reform. Hopes were raised temporarily in 1924, following the leftist victory in the French elections, but the proposals for enhanced representation advanced by the new Socialist Governor-General Varenne ran aground against the determined opposition of the resident French colonists. Varenne did introduce on a consultative basis the office of Inspector-General of Labor and also canceled the surviving remnants of imperial power at Hué relating to traditional court rites and pardons. Such minor concessions served only to fan nationalist demands. Varenne was succeeded in 1928 by Governor-General Pasquier, a career functionary. His principal innovation was to introduce into Cochin-China a Grand Economic and Financial Council on the Tunisian model, composed of twenty-eight French and twenty-three Indochinese representatives selected from financial and trading interests. Under the presidency of the governor-general, the new Grand Council could make decisions on loans and indirect taxes.[12]

One reason why the French felt free to ignore the problem of introducing a greater degree of self-government was that the vast majority of the Vietnamese, especially those living in crowded Tongking, gave prior consideration to the dominating fact of hunger. The popular desire to share in the postwar economic prosperity produced by the flood of French capital was a far more compelling issue than were the poorly articulated proposals for political reform. Particularly strong was the popular demand, unrealized, for greater educational opportunity. As of 1923, Indochina's eleven industrial schools accepted only 1,091 students, and the University fewer still. Unfortunately also, the expanding economic situation denied popular participation to the Vietnamese except in the role of common laborer.[13]

[11] Roberts, 474–479; Jean Chesneaux, *Contribution de l'histoire de la nation vietnamienne* (1955), 183–201.

[12] Lê Thanh Khôi, *Le Viet Nam: Histoire et Civilisation* (1955), 398–405; Chesneaux, 202–205.

[13] Roberts, 474–479.

## Postwar Economic Development

The most important aspect of Indochina's history during the interwar period was the vast scale of economic development resulting from the outpouring of French capital. The total French investment by 1914 already amounted to almost a half billion gold francs, or 100 million dollars. About half of it was in mining and industry and the rest in transportation, electric power, and forestry, and plantations. Wartime inflation brought an end to the traditional circulation of Spanish and Mexican silver as the medium of exchange along the Pacific coast of Asia, and piaster bank notes of the Bank of Indochina became the established currency in the colony.

In the course of the 1920s, the stability of the value of the piaster as compared with the depreciating French franc transformed Indochina into a refuge for increasing amounts of French savings. With powerful financial interests directing the flow of investments, an estimated total of 2.9 billion new francs found their way to Indochina between 1924 and 1930. Rubber plantations constituted the largest single item of development (700 million), with mining second (654 million), and industry third (606 million), plus an additional 500-million total in tea, coffee, sugar, cotton, and cocoa plantations. Banking resources in Indochina reached about 750 million francs. The expansion of the economy permitted the bank itself, by discounting loans at 8 to 12 per cent, to expand its lending capacity to some six or eight times its actual piaster capital. It also provided funds for agriculture-credit banks and for Chinese and Chettyar lending agencies. With very few exceptions, the indigenous peoples lacked the capital, the technical aptitudes, and the planned assistance needed to adjust to the impact of such overpowering economic forces.[14]

The inexorable trend in Indochina was to transfer liquid French assets into tangible property which would escape loss by currency depreciation. Especially after the 1928 devaluation of the franc, the burden of debt owed by the colony in French francs to French creditors was greatly eased. Subject to established rules regarding size of holdings and the improvements required, land grants for plantations were made available to French subjects only, including protégés but not the Chinese. Land acquisitions to highland areas north of the Mekong delta frequently violated the traditional access right of hillside (rai) cultivators, who normally used such lands only one or two years out of twelve. Particularly suitable for rubber and tea was the arc, 20 to 40 kilometers wide, of "red lands" formed from lava flows around 200 meters in elevation circling the southern end of the cordillera. Some 200,000 hectares (2.47 acres per hectare) in this region were made available in 1924 outside the restricted rai reservations of Moi tribes. Local labor could be used for clearing the land, but most of the workers had to be brought from Tongking. French capital also invested heavily in ricelands, five-sixths of

[14] Robequain, 154–177.

which were located in Cochin-China. The total development of French plantations, accomplished mainly between 1924 and 1930, amounted to some 532,000 hectares. Other French funds were used to develop European-style urban amenities in Saigon, Hanoi, and Phnom Penh.

The economic going, especially in rubber production, was not all smooth. The costs were heavy, and the laborers were often ill and unhappy away from home. The depression of 1929–1930 hit much of the rubber acreage before the plantations were productive. The low-income point came in 1931, when the price was only one-fifth that of 1929. In the end, an expanding market for rubber output was assured in France, since Indochina alone of all the French colonies produced the commodity. Rubber exports increased six times between 1929 and 1938. With the assistance of bank credits and government aid drawn from an indemnity fund accumulated after 1931 in part from a tax on French imports, the rubber plantations were able to survive. The piaster was pegged to the franc in 1931 at the low figure of 10 francs to 1 piaster. Labor contracts for work on plantations continued enforceable in law, and contract laborers were obliged to obtain permits to travel any distance from places of employment.[15]

The close coordination of economic and political controls in Indochina greatly aided French efforts to withstand the depression. The governor-general did not hesitate to incur additional public debt in order to maintain the general economy. He also acted vigorously to force obstinate creditors to scale down outstanding debts. Reductions ranged as high as 47 per cent on capital and 75 per cent on interest obligations. Land banks took over many estate loans. Through credits made available by the Bank of Indochina to substantial borrowers the average capital losses were reduced to one-quarter of the equity holdings. Losses in plantations were greater than in industry or trade. Credit advances reached a peak in 1933, and predepression production levels were regained by 1935. By 1936–1937, new French investment funds for Cochin-China amounted to 100 to 150 million francs a year.[16]

## Effects of French Rule on the People

The first four decades of the twentieth century witnessed the continued southward expansion of Vietnamese peoples into Cochin-China, mainly at the expense of older Cambodian residents. The Moi and the Lao peoples also proved unsuitable as employed workers. The Vietnamese came to outnumber the Cambodians by about 13 to 1 in Cochin-China, while this ratio was approximately reversed in Cambodia proper. Cambodians reacted occasionally in retaliatory violence. Vietnamese colonization was deterred somewhat by the threat of malaria, by reluctance of many to sever ancestral ties, and by still-potent religious taboos, but economic pressures to migrate

[15] Bell, 210–224, 276–283; Robequain, 182–218.
[16] Robequain, 150–154, 166–177.

were inexorable. In six Tongking provinces, the population density reached a fantastic four hundred persons per square kilometer, more than twice the maximum density in any part of rural Cochin-China. Much of the voluntary migration to the Mekong delta was via native sampan, but contract labor also entered actively into the situation after 1924. Averaging around fifteen thousand a year, the movement of Tongkingese reached a peak in 1927; it fell off sharply during the depression.

Contract labor from Tongking was also available for French use in mines and plantations developed in the New Hebrides and New Caledonia Islands of the Pacific. Regulations established by the Inspection Générale du Travail after 1927 limited the contract duration to three years and also fixed standard requirements for wages, medical services, and working hours.[17] A considerable number of indentured laborers were caught at Noumea in the New Hebrides by the outbreak of the Far Eastern war in 1941.

The superior industry and adaptability of the Vietnamese and the Chinese were clearly demonstrated in the development of Mekong delta rice fields. New paddy-land development in the delta area had to cope with high water and salt-tide invasions. Canal construction and drainage facilities were carefully planned, usually on a rectilinear pattern. Rice acreage in the area quadrupled between 1870 and 1930, and the annual surplus of 1.5 million tons of rice was perennially the principal export item from Indochina. European capital entered actively into rice-land development after 1920. Among all of the migrant Tongkingese as well as among the displaced Cambodians, indebtedness was widespread, while the landless and footloose experienced a weakening of older mores and family ties. The general wage level averaged one-third of the Moroccan and one-thirteenth of the French standards. Even the elite were restless from denial of educational opportunity and government jobs.[18] The apparent surface calm in Cochin-China was deceiving.

Among the hill folk, the Moi tribesmen who inhabited the mountain divide south of the latitude of Hué were the most directly affected by French rule. They lived traditionally by rai cultivation and by trade in medicinal items and luxury forest products. The French established military posts in the Moi area and brought in the Tongkingese as plantation workers, market gardeners, and government employees at lower levels. Some of the Moi were subjected to forced labor in the clearing of new plantation lands, which were subtracted as a rule from their ancestral rai-access holdings. The Moi also lost their market for medicinal products and were otherwise exposed to outside economic pressures which they were powerless to withstand. Some American Protestant missionary work was permitted among them in an

[17] *Ibid.*, 45–60.
[18] *Ibid.*, 60–74; Charles A. Micaud in Lennox Mills (ed.), *New World of Southeast Asia* (1949), 225–229.

effort to ameliorate somewhat their illiterate and backward state.[19] The Meo and other hillside-cultivating folk to the north of the Moi were less seriously disturbed by French rule.

The situation in Cambodia proper preserved enough of the vitality of the traditional social order to resist disruptive forces from the outside. The King in his palace represented the symbols of authority despite his political subservience to the *Resident Superieur.* Court routines were carefully maintained, and the King still signed ordinances over the countersignature of the *Resident Superieur.* He continued to be the supreme head of the Buddhist religion for Cambodia, including a Minister of Religion as one of his six Cabinet members. Public education was almost entirely Buddhist-oriented and was conducted under joint direction of the Minister of Public Instruction, the village headmen, and the Buddhist monkhood.

Village headmen elected by the local taxpayers were officials of all work in Cambodia and wielded genuine authority. They directed the local police, registered strangers, and staged preliminary court hearings for alleged offenders. Other responsibilities of headmen included vital statistics, tax collections (*corvée,* land and poll taxes, market licenses), and the maintenance of buildings, local roads, and postal deliveries. The headmen also certified the respectability of monastic candidates and helped enforce attendance at pagoda schools. A special training course in codified customs and procedures conducted in the École de droit at Phnom Penh was required of lawyers and judges serving in the native courts. The inertia of historical tradition was destined to carry Cambodia, and Laos also in much the same way, through the colonial experience with the traditional society intact even though losing vitality.[20]

## *Beginnings of Nationalist Agitation in Vietnam*

The first resistance to French rule, which developed in Vietnam in the late 1880s, was led by disgruntled mandarin elements. Opposition was instigated by the regent for the boy Emperor at Hué in 1888. The regent was deported to Algiers, whereupon his partisans withdrew to the Lao country. All serious resistance was quelled by 1894, although remnants held out in remote areas for more than a decade thereafter. Because this type of traditionalist rebellion in behalf of the revival of the power of the Nguyen dynasty was completely devoid of concern for political and social reform, it enlisted correspondingly meager popular response. Political awareness on a national scale hardly existed in Vietnam during the early decades of French control. The tradition of resistance to Chinese control dating from the tenth-century liberation was strong in Tongking and Annam. But in modern times, political controversies had turned on dynastic rivalry, or north against

[19] George Condominas, "Aspects of a Minority Problem in Indochina," *Pacific Affairs,* XXIV (1951), 77–82.
[20] Bell, 246–269.

south, with occasional popularly supported outbreaks such as the Tay-son rebellion of the late eighteenth century.[21]

The nationalist awakening of the twentieth century drew its inspiration from several outside sources. At the turn of the century, some observers who were aware of what was happening in Siam and Japan began to stress modernization as the key to successful resistance to the West. Russia's defeat at the hands of Japan in 1905 greatly strengthened the conclusion that Western aggression could best be contested with Western tools. Political considerations thus supported the demand on the part of Vietnamese youth for modern educational facilities, a pressure buttressed by personal and family ambition for advancement. Contrariwise, official wariness was doubtless responsible in some measure for the failure of French authorities to encourage secondary and university education. Only 1 per cent of the half-million elementary pupils ever reached the high school, and the few who qualified academically for study in Europe had to obtain special permits to go overseas.[22]

Nationalist inspiration came also from China, especially from Kuomintang elements, following the downfall of the Manchu regime. After 1917, Canton became a center for organizing Vietnamese anti-French sentiment. Experiences of individuals in Europe connected with World War I contributed even more to the nationalist cause, for during the course of the struggle, some 100,000 Vietnamese soldiers and laborers saw service in France. These persons, along with students, witnessed French nationalism at white heat and also made contact with French Socialists and others who criticized imperialism. This experience did not end with the war, for as late as 1927 the Verdun fortress was manned largely by Vietnamese troops. French contacts also enhanced appreciation of the advantages to be derived from the technical and scientific aspects of Western civilization. To many dedicated Vietnamese nationalist resistance to imperialism was realistically possible not on traditional and cultural grounds but rather with Western tools. The most modern pattern for many of them during the postwar decades appeared to be the Communist technique of anticolonial revolution and modernization.[23]

For many years, Vietnamese nationalist sentiment continued to be poorly organized and inarticulate. The first authentic leader was Phan Chou Trinh, a nonrevolutionary reformist-agitator. He petitioned Governor Paul Beau in 1906, for example, to arrange that an end be put to the oppression by corrupt and reactionary mandarin officials and that educational facilities be expanded. The response of the authorities at the time was completely negative. Trinh then started a school of his own at Hanoi, in 1907, patterned on modern and liberal lines. It was suppressed by the authorities

[21] George Kahin (ed.), *Governments and Politics of Southeast Asia* (1959), 323.

[22] Lê Thanh Khôi, 380–385; Robequain, 13; Roberts, 498.

[23] Kahin, 324–355.

nine months later. In 1915 Trinh found himself in Paris, where he was detained by the police on suspicion of pro-German intrigue. An abortive coup by Trinh's supporters in Vietnam in 1916, which enjoyed some support from the Court at Hué, resulted in the French installation of a new Emperor. Trinh was not allowed to return to Vietnam until 1925, where he died within a year.

The second Vietnamese leader was a democraaic and antimonarchial revolutionary named Phan Boi Chau, a contemporary of Trinh. Chau dreamed of organizing an Asiatic alliance against the West. He visited Japan and also made contact with a kindred Chinese revolutionary named Sun Yat-sen. He established a revolutionary headquarters in Hongkong in 1906 and participated in a short-lived League of Eastern Asia started in 1908. His Japanese contacts apparently fell through following Tokyo's conclusion of a French treaty in 1907, which provided for the exclusion of anti-French agitators from Japan. Later contacts with the Chinese nationalist Hu Hanmin at Shanghai following the overthrow of the Manchus in 1911 were productive of no positive results. Persistent pamphleteering in behalf of liberal republican principles led to Chau's arrest at French request by Chinese police in Canton. He was eventually released in 1917 when Sun Yat-sen's Kuomintang took over the city. He was apparently involved in pro-German intrigue during the latter phases of World War I. Arrested again by the French at Shanghai in 1925, he was kept safely in prison until his death in 1940.

Chau's efforts were connected with the appearance in Tongking in 1927 of the radically anti-French Quoc-Dan Dang or Nationalist Party, which was modeled on the Kuomintang and maintained contacts across China's Kwangtung province border. The party sponsored an abortive attempt on the life of the French governor-general in 1929, and shortly thereafter it staged a short-lived rebellion. Police repression reduced it to a state of complete impotence from which it did not recover until near the end of World War II. At this stage (and later) the party was apparently too Chinese in its organization and sponsorship to attract widespread nationalist Vietnamese support.[24]

Thus nascent nationalism in Indochina developed within both an Asian and a European context, with but scanty reference in either case to traditionalist considerations. The underground ferment was confined in very large measure to Tongking and Cochin-China, the only two regions which were influenced to any marked degree by the French colonial impact. In 1933, the new Emperor Bao Dai was put forward by the French authorities as an alleged champion of moderate constitutional reform, with the Catholic leader, Ngo Dinh Diem, enlisted as the temporary secretary of the Reforms Commission. Disappointingly little was accomplished. Although the

[24] C. A. Micaud, 225–226, 234; Chesneaux, 212–215. Victims of the 1933 rising included an estimated seven hundred persons executed and three thousand arrested, according to Chesneaux.

Socialist Party victory in France in 1936 brought about the release of a number of political prisoners, some liberty of association, and moderate wage increases, these improvements were short-lived.[25]

## Emergence of Communist Leadership

The Communist movement led by Nguyen Ai-Quoc was unimportant numerically during the 1920s, compared with the Kuomintang-sponsored Nationalist Party of Tongking. Nguyen's original given name was apparently Nguyen Van Tranh. Born in central Vietnam in the early nineties, he became a ship's cabin boy in 1911 and spent the next several years traveling in the Mediterranean Sea and the Atlantic and Indian Oceans. During this time he mastered French and developed some facility in other European languages. He became acquainted with English during a four-year stay in London (1913–1917), when he labored as a cook in a hotel kichen. He also worked secretly on the side to develop an anticolonialist group called the Overseas Workers. Shifting in 1917 to Paris, where he earned a livelihood as a retoucher in a photographic studio, he came in contact with a group of pacifist, anticolonialist French Socialists. He began contributing to *Le Populaire* and other Leftist periodicals. It was apparently at this time he changed his name to Nguyen Ai-Quoc, Nguyen the Patriot.

As a journalist-agitator, Nguyen Ai-Quoc espoused a program for Indochina that was more liberal than Marxian. It included self-rule, civil liberties, equality of rights, opposition to feudal survivals (*corvée* and *gabelle*), and an end to French mercantilist policies in Indochina. His intellectual orientation included the reading of Hugo, Zola, France, Tolstoi, Dickens, and Shakespeare. He was in 1920 the first Vietnamese member of the French Socialist Party, but he was later attracted to the Third International when it adopted a strongly anticolonialist position. He became a contributer to the Paris Communist paper *Humanité,* started a short-lived journal of his own, *Le Paria,* and began the preparation of a book entitled *La Proces de la colonisation française,* published in Paris in 1926.

Nguyen Ai-Quoc's attendance at the Fourth World Congress of the Comintern at Moscow in 1922 began a new phase of his anticolonialist career. He became a member of the Comintern's Bureau for Southeast Asia. He attended the so-called University of Workers of the Orient in Russia for a time in 1924, and in 1925 was assigned as an interpreter for Borodin, the Russian agent and adviser to the Kuomintang at Canton. While at Canton in 1925, he made contact with Vietnamese exiles and sponsored the Thanh-Nien, or Association of Revolutionary Annamite Youth. He returned with Borodin to Russia in 1927 following the failure of the Communist coup in China. He again made his way back to the

[25] Roberts, 474–479, 498; Bell, 227–240; Chesneaux, 216–221.

vicinity of Tongking in 1928, where he eventually was designated as Moscow's Communist organizer for Southeast Asia.

Later phases of Nguyen Ai-Quoc's prewar revolutionary career are obscure. He lived in Siam for a time in 1928–1929 under a monk's disguise. He later made contact with the anti-French Kuomintang partisans in Yunnan, China, but found them to be also strongly anticommunist. He was nevertheless able to continue in China his indoctrination of Vietnamese exiles. He was called to Hongkong in 1930 to settle a rift between two Leftist factions. The outcome was the organization of the Communist Party of Vietnam. Shortly thereafter, the organization helped touch off a minor army mutiny, which led in turn to strike demonstrations in urban centers and an abortive peasant rising in Tongking. For a short time, soviet-type councils were set up in two of the northern provinces. The risings were crushed by the police with great severity. He escaped to Hongkong where he was imprisoned as a revolutionary from 1930 to 1933; he was finally released by a British court for lack of evidence against him. The superior organization of the Vietnam Communist Party enabled it to survive and to resume underground operations in 1933. Police surveillance nevertheless prevented its growth in membership. He undertook after 1936 to follow Premier Stalin's popular-front tactic of cooperating with anti-fascist elements including the French authorities. A Trotskyite faction, centering in Cochin-China, opposed such cooperation and assumed the role of Communist leadership in Vietnam at the time of the outbreak of World War II.[26]

Nguyen from the outset favored cooperation with anti-French nationalists of all affiliations, hoping no doubt that his group would be able in time to indoctrinate them as Communists. He returned to Moscow in 1936–1937 and then came back to China, where he again suffered imprisonment by Kuomintang authorities from 1940 to 1942. After the China-sponsored Dong Minh Hoi (Vietnamese Nationalist Party) group proved unsuccessful in establishing sources of military intelligence in Japan-occupied Indochina, Nguyen Ai-Quoc emerged as the recognized leader of the nationalist exiles, taking the new name of Ho Chi Minh. He received assistance from both the Kuomintang and the Americans in launching an anti-Japanese movement in Tongking late in World War II. He and followers were flown in by American planes during the final year of the war and were provided with arms, munitions, and communication equipment. His Viet Minh army met with little resistance from the retiring Japanese, and he was able to establish a semblance of control over seven provinces of Tongking by the time of the Japanese surrender in August, 1945. Ho's following among Vietnamese nationalists generally was widespread. He was unmatched as an experienced revolutionary leader, an excellent linguist, intelligent, ascetic, dedicated, and withal an indoctrinated

[26] Virginia Thompson and Richard Adloff, *The Left Wing in Southeast Asia* (1950), 21–28.

Communist who could at times be implacably firm.[27] The entire nationalist spectrum was, of course, much broader than Ho's Communist clique, for it included the rival Chinese-sponsored Dong Minh Hoi, the Trotskyites, and religious groups like the Catholic, the Cao Dai, and the Hoa-Hao. The outcome of the contest for control was by no means determined in 1945, but Ho was already strategically placed.

[27] Bernard Fall, *Le Viet-Minh 1945–1960* (1960), 20–37.

# CHAPTER 25

# The Japanese Conquest

# and Occupation

*J*apan's conquest and occupation of Southeast Asia from 1941 to 1945 constituted a watershed of great importance in the modern history of the region. Japan's achievement of military and industrial supremacy in Eastern Asia after World War I afforded the opportunity for its aggressive role in World War II. Expansionist tendencies were enhanced by a spirit of manifest destiny and by the patriotic cult of Emperor worship. The stage for the invasion of Southeast Asia was set by the early German victories in Europe in 1940–1941 and by Japan's own destruction of America's Pacific fleet at Pearl Harbor, which stripped Southeast Asia of effective naval defenses. Japan asked for and received little military assistance from the peoples of the region, but Tokyo's grandiose plans to develop a Greater East Asian Empire required the enlistment of cooperation from the "liberated" peoples. Japanese undertook to aggravate all evidences of anti-Western sentiment. They emphasized the slogan of "Asia for the Asiatics"; they affirmed Nippon's destined role of leadership; they also advanced labored claims of religious and cultural identity with various elements of Southeast Asia's populations. When a year and a half of such tactics produced insufficient returns, Tokyo began to make guarded political concessions calculated to appeal to nationalist sentiment. Meanwhile the brutality of the Japanese soldiery and the army's complete disregard of the economic interests and personal sensitivities of local peoples poisoned relations everywhere.

Japan could count on no support from Southeast Asian peoples when faced by the Allied counterattack in 1944–1945. The net result of the occupation was, nevertheless, to stimulate nationalism to the point that the restoration of stable colonial rule proved impossible after the Japanese had been expelled. An important factor in the new situation was Britain's granting of freedom to India, which destroyed the basis of Britain's long-maintained hegemony in Southeast Asia. Another incidental development was the emergence during the course of the war of communism as an important revolutionary influence.

## Steps in the Development of Japan's War Commitment

Down to the time of the Munich agreement of September, 1938, which revealed the weakness of France and Britain in the face of the German threat, Japan was mainly concerned over a possible second war with the Russians over Manchuria and Mongolia. After Munich suggested the possibility of German-Russian involvement, Tokyo's plans with respect to Southeast Asia became less hesitant. Canton was captured in October, 1938; Hainan Island was taken in February, 1939, and the Spratley Islands were taken in March. These gains provided Japanese bases far along the road toward Singapore. The Russo-German pact of August 23, 1939, revived for a time Japan's apprehensions concerning possible trouble with the Soviet Union, but the ensuing outbreak of war in Europe completely immobilized France, Holland, and Britain. The diversion of American concern toward European developments and away from Eastern Asia plus the possibility of Germany's achievement of a complete victory over the colonial powers of Western Europe raised Japan's hopes that her goals in the south seas might be achieved without a major war.

Meanwhile Japanese preparations in the Southeast Asian region had been pressed since 1935. Official and nonofficial spies were active throughout the area, to India, and beyond. Many were the volunteer representatives of the numerous patriotic societies which spawned in Japan during the 1930s. Japanese settlers at Davao in the Philippines, as previously indicated, took Filipina wives, acquired titles to land in their names, and undertook an extensive colonizing development. Japanese agents examined important military and topographical aspects of the Philippines and the Malay Peninsula. Contacts were also made with nationalist leaders in a number of countries, and special study was devoted to political and cultural cleavages generally. Selected visitors from Southeast Asian countries were invited to Japan for indoctrination purposes.

The timetable of events became ominous after 1940. Pibun Songgram's government at Bangkok signed nonaggression treaties with Britain, France, and Japan, in June, 1940. Two months later, Vichy France, under pressure from Hitler, agreed to permit Japanese occupation of Tongking, a development which was simultaneous with Japan's conclusion of a military alliance with the Axis Powers. Bangkok became greatly concerned immediately thereafter with obtaining assurances from France that Thailand would recover possession of Battambang and Siemreap provinces and cis-Mekong Laos in the possible contingency of the loss of French sovereignty. When the French government refused to comply, Bangkok made it a condition of ratification of the nonaggression treaty with France that it return the two enclaves on the right bank of the upper Mekong River, which had been taken by France in 1904 and 1907. Against the advice of the American government, Bangkok, on November 23, 1940, resorted to an undeclared war to occupy the territory in question. Two months later, a truce was arranged through Japanese "mediation," and a treaty conceding the Thai demands was signed with the helpless Vichy regime in March, 1941. Thailand later made labored efforts to convince Washington that it wanted to pursue a neutral policy and did not intend to profit from the application of Japanese military pressure. It nevertheless did not hesitate to accept additional territory at the expense of British Malaya and Burma, as well as Indochina, during the course of the Japanese occupation.

Japan's southward move came nearer after the conclusion of Tokyo's neutrality pact with the Soviet Union in April, 1941, which was followed two months later by Hitler's attack on Russia. With the Russian front immobilized, Japan moved to occupy all of Indochina in July, 1941, leaving the regular French administration intact to maintain routine governmental services.

While waiting for the world situation to develop to its liking, the Tokyo government made two futile attempts to negotiate an agreement with Dutch representatives for voluntary Indonesian cooperation in the "Co-Prosperity Sphere" plan. Japanese wanted free access to strategic materials, uninhibited immigration privileges to all of Indonesia except Java, and full control over the commercial and industrial operations which would be developed. The Dutch stubbornly refused to accede to these demands, collected a small naval force, and began belated plans to assemble Indonesian defense volunteers. The attack on Pearl Harbor on December 7–8, 1941, triggered Japan's well-planned blitzkrieg against Southeast Asia.

## Japanese Objectives and Plans

The principal economic attractions for Japan in Southeast Asia were the available coal, minerals, oil, and rubber, plus rice surpluses and the trade potential. The region was admirably suited in every way to supplement Japan's own limited resources and to afford full scope for Japan's technological services, trading, and banking facilities. Japanese ambitions appear to have been focused mainly on Indonesia and Malaya. Burma and Thailand at first were of peripheral importance, except insofar as their control might be needed to liquidate British interests in Malaya. The expected German victory in Europe, it was hoped, would ensure the independence of India, so that no invasion of the subcontinent was contemplated at the outset. Tokyo also wanted to close off Chungking China's access to military supplies via both Tongking and the Burma Road.

Japan's assumption of leadership in Eastern Asia was based on a realistic estimate of her predominance not only in the military field but also in the areas of governmental organization, economic development, and technological competence. Japan alone was presumably capable of eliminating

European colonial control in Southeast Asia and of giving the region a rational and effective political and economic organization. Tokyo proposed the establishment of a "Greater East Asia Co-Prosperity Sphere" in which the yen would become the medium of exchange and the Japanese language the lingua franca. The various peoples of Southeast Asia would exercise varying degrees of autonomy but would all be assimilated to the Japanese Empire as vassal political and economic units. Western prestige must be completely discredited, and Japan would emerge as "the leader, the protector, and the light of Asia." Premature nationalist aspirations in Southeast Asia would have to be dampened and the pro-Kuomintang Chinese elements in Southeast Asia victimized and cowed. Special preparations were made to develop rapport with the Buddhists of Burma and Thailand, with orthodox Muslims in Indonesia, with the anti-Chinese Malays and anti-British Indians, and with Christian Karens in Burma and Christian Filipinos. The slogan "Asia for the Asiatics" would attempt to capitalize on anti-Western sentiment in all areas and at all social levels.

## The Japanese Conquest of Southeast Asia

Japan's main army was already poised in Cochin-China when the war began in December, 1941, Pibun's failure to interpose more than token Siamese resistance to the invaders opened the way to a two-pronged attack on Singapore and Rangoon via Thailand. The British at Singapore lost both air and sea control following the sinking on December 9 of two capital ships sent to prevent a Japanese landing on the northern Malay coast. The substantial but widely dispersed British-Indian forces proved no match for the trained Japanese army, with its planes and three hundred tanks, which approached Singapore from the landward side. The time was too short to send in reinforcements even if they had been available. The city surrendered on February 15 after its water supply had been cut. British captives were imprisoned and pro-Kuomintang Chinese, especially those who were known to have contributed to the Chinese Relief Fund, were victimized by the thousands. Captive Indian troops, on the other hand, were well treated and encouraged to organize the so-called Indian National Army, which the Japanese planned to use in the prospective invasion of India. The small Dutch naval forces put up a courageous resistance for a time, but the Indies islands themselves surrendered without a struggle.

Burma proved to be equally indefensible. The Japanese invaded via Tenasserim coast passes behind Moulmein and Tavoy accompanied by the thirty trained Thakin collaborators, led by Thakins Soe and Aung San. The Burmans' role was to develop liaison with the people, to provide interpreters and jungle guides, and to attempt to take over governmental responsibilities in "liberated" areas as the invading army advanced. The Thakins eventually rallied several thousand anti-British nationalists recruited from youth groups and the political pongyis, but their military role was of little consequence. The Burmese peoples generally were frightened and awestruck witnesses of events entirely beyond their control.

The defending British-Indian forces offered their first resistance to the invaders in the Thaton peninsula to the west of Moulmein, but with no success. They were repeatedly outflanked by Japanese contingents, and the premature destruction of the bridge across the lower Sittang River forced the abandonment of irreplaceable military equipment. When the Japanese threatened to close off the northern escape routes, Rangoon was abandoned on March 7, and a general retreat began in the heart of the hot season. British forces retreating up the Irrawaddy Valley had to push their supplies ahead of them and were encumbered by large numbers of Indian refugees also endeavoring to escape to India. A Chinese army, belatedly invited to participate and under the titular command of General Joseph Stilwell, protected for a time the parallel route up the Sittang Valley. The two forces managed briefly to join hands above the Pegu Yoma divide, but neither was able to withstand the pressure of the victorious Japanese. Air cover was provided for the British army at the outset of the campaign by the American mercenary Flying Tiger Corps enlisted by General Claire Chennault, but its planes were destroyed on the ground shortly after the evacuation of Rangoon.

The whole Burma front collapsed when the Japanese invaded the southern Shan States via Karenni and threatened the Chinese communications in the rear. The demoralized Chinese forces became a looting rabble, and the British-Indian army withdrew via the Chindwin Valley and the Chin Hills to Indian Manipur. General Stilwell's smaller group retired via the Hukawng Valley in the Kachin country to the north. Less than five hundred Burman soldiers fought with the British armies, along with some seven times as many Karen, Chin, and Kachin troops. The people generally made no effort to impede the retreating army, but they were left with the unenviable task of coming to terms with the victorious Japanese.

There was no escape at all for the fledgling Philippines Commonwealth army, which had been trained and commanded by General MacArthur. It was cut off by sea by forces from Japan's Formosan bases and suffered the loss of its air force on the ground at the outset of the campaign. The defenders held out in the Bataan peninsula north of Manila Bay until April 9 and on Corregidor Island until May. Filipinos and Americans died together from malaria and malnutrition as well as at the hands of the Japanese. General MacArthur and President Quezon and Vice-President Osmeña of the Commonwealth were evacuated by submarine. Japan's "Greater East Asia" propaganda developed less appeal in the already self-governing Philippines than in any other country of Southeast Asia, despite the fact that most of Quezon's clique later collaborated with Japan.

## Japanese Policies in General

Japanese efforts to elicit or to coerce the cooperation of the strategically placed national groups within occupied Southeast Asia operated at
several levels. Generally applicable was the emphasis on "Asia for the
Asiatics," Japan as "leader, protector, and light of Asia," and the "Greater
East Asia Co-Prosperity Sphere." Relations with the peoples of the southern region were placed under the direction of the Greater East Asia Ministry. It set up an ambitious program of cultural-exchange missions to
Japan, including visits of political leaders, socially prominent individuals,
and foreign students. The study of the Japanese language was pushed in
every country, and every means was employed to destroy the prestige and
influence of Western colonialists and their institutions.

Beyond the limits of such generally applicable propaganda programs, the Japanese followed a highly selective approach with particular
peoples. To the Burmans and the Siamese, the invaders were also loyal
Buddhists. General Suzuki in Burma posed to the gullible as the returned
Myingun prince of the Konbaung dynasty and also took the name of Bo
Myogo, or "Colonel Thunderbolt," in deference to an old Burmese proverb
about the end of British rule being marked by a lightning bolt striking
the pagoda spire. In Java the Japanese became the proponents of Islam, the
allies of the scribes in encouraging study of the Koran, and the instrument
of Allah's vengeance against the heretic Dutch. In Thailand, Malaya, and
Java, the invaders were the enemies of the exploitive Chinese, from whom
they exacted monetary contributions and whose monopoly control of trade
and usury they destroyed. Christian Karens in Burma were visited by Japanese who posed as fellow Protestant Christians, and Catholic Japanese
sought similar rapport with Filipinos. With Indian soldier captives and
civilian groups, the Japanese posed as the friends of India's freedom. They
sponsored so-called Indian Independence Leagues in Malaya, Thailand, and
Burma and an associated Indian National Army. It was only after these
tactics proved to be ineffective that Tokyo broadened the appeal for local
support in certain critical areas to include tentative promises of national
independence.

Generally speaking, the Japanese army preferred not to become involved in governmental problems as long as it had full access to transit
rights and transportation facilities and to food and other supplies needed
for military purposes. Where the local authorities were permitted to retain
control of the administration, as in French Indochina and Thailand, Japanese propagandist efforts were somewhat less intensive. Because the early
anti-Japanese movements in Indochina, both Chinese and Communist-
inspired, were also anti-French, the European authorities accepted the
responsibility of putting them down. Thailand bore the burden of Japanese
supply requisitions, to the extent of some billion and a half of yen credits

and some 300 million newly printed baht. Japan provided no opporunity to redeem this new currency in goods from Japan. Otherwise the Siamese were little affected by Japanese interference. The Malay sultans were also little disturbed, while the Malay Chinese bore the brunt of Japanese outrage and spoliation. In no part of the conquered region did the Japanese efforts to ingratiate themselves falter more hopelessly than in the Philippines. The depth of Filipino resistance and the complete lack of any sense of gratitude for their "deliverance" from American rule shocked, chagrined, and angered the Japanese. Since their assumed divine mission to lead Eastern Asia was incapable of compromise, the Japanese reacted with calculated arrogance and cruelty. The puppet regime set up under the leadership of José Laurel fooled no one and attracted no popular support. Laurel himself refused to follow the example of Thailand and Burma in 1943 by declaring war against the Allies, although such a declaration was forthcoming in 1944.[1]

## Japanese Tactics in Indonesia

Japan's efforts to attract support from conservative, apolitical Muslim circles in Java merit special consideration. Preparations began as early as 1933, when Japanese students were sent to the Near East to study Islam and to make the Mecca pilgrimage. The Japanese Islamic Association was organized in Tokyo following their return, and an Islamic World Conference was sponsored in the Japanese capital in 1938. Attending Indonesian delegates, with expenses paid, were apparently impressed by talk of the divine Japanese Emperor-Caliph. The prewar target of Japanese propaganda in Java was the Islamic Federation or Council (called MIAI), organized in 1937 at Surabaya. It represented both the reformist Muhammadijah and the conservative Nahdatul Ulama groups. Their espoused objectives were the promotion of religion and prosperity and the study of the Koran. Remnants of the old Sarekat Islam organization joined the MIAI in 1939. The movement challenged Dutch rule on religious rather than political grounds, objecting also to the use of adat instead of Koranic law. When the Japanese arrived in 1942, the army was accompanied by Haji-robed (Mecca-pilgrim) Japanese allegedly interested in Islamic research and by soldiers who attended Muslim prayers in the mosques.[2]

In line with Tokyo's long-term objective of transforming the valuable Indies into a Japanese colonial empire, the invaders undertook at the outset to foment opposition on religious grounds to heretical Dutch rule, while discouraging advocacy of independence per se. European residents were publicly humiliated and placed in concentration camps. Tokyo

---

[1] R. A. Smith, *Philippine Freedom, 1946–1958* (1958), 105–110.

[2] Harry Benda, *The Crescent and the Rising Sun* (1958), 61–99, and "Indonesian Islam under Japanese Occupation," *Pacific Affairs*, XXVIII (1955), 350–361.

apparently believed that conservative Muslims would ask a lower price for their cooperation than would the westernized nationalists. The Japanese attempted, therefore, to make particular use of the MIAI and the Muslim scribes at the desa level. Selected scribes were subjected in units of three-score at a time to training courses of two weeks' duration stressing Japanese culture and leadership, the GEACPS ideal, along with the need for Koranic and Japanese language studies in the schools. The task of the scribes was to keep the villagers cooperative and under control. The basic responsibility of the MIAI was to facilitate food requisitions and to help recruitment for the labor battalions and for volunteers for Peta, the Japanese-recruited army. For a time, the MIAI was permitted to publish a periodical. The more politically minded Islamic groups, including Sarekat Islam and the Young Islam League, were forcibly suppressed by the Japanese in September, 1942.

Efforts of the Japanese to enlist cooperation of the MIAI finally ran aground in late 1943, when they refused to accede to a number of MIAI demands. These included the construction of a great mosque, the establishment of an Islamic university, and the development of an Islamic treasury empowered to collect tithes and to disburse funds for the relief of popular distress. The Japanese then turned to the sponsorship of a less religiously fanatical Masjumi Party, which was organized in late 1943. This move coincided with the disappearance of the prospect of an early Japanese victory.[3]

The secular counterpart to the religiously oriented Japanese program involved the establishment, in the spring of 1943, of a puppet political organization, ostensibly autonomous, known as Putera. Sukarno and Hatta were persuaded to head it, while other nationalists including Sjahrir set up a parallel underground movement which could work in collusion with Putera leadership if opportunity was afforded. As the price of their limited degree of political freedom, Indonesian nationalists undertook to assist the Japanese in mobilizing the economy, the military labor force, and the auxiliary Peta army, which was to be officered by nationalists selected by Sukarno. Within a year and a half, the Peta numbered an estimated 120,000 men, but Putera never developed popular peasant backing. It became suspect by the Japanese in late 1943 and was abolished along with the MIAI. In March, 1944, the Japanese tried again by setting up a Peoples Loyalty Organization, retaining Sukarno and Hatta as a convenient façade. The organization was accorded little or no political leeway prior to 1945. The one cultural concession made by the Japanese was to encourage the use of modernized Malay as the Indonesian lingua franca.

The Japanese propaganda effort in Java was largely self-defeating. Negative ideological factors included the asserted divinity of the Emperor, implicit Japanese claims of racial and cultural superiority, and the reli-

[3] Benda, *Crescent,* 103–119, 134–149; C. A. O. Van Nieuwenhuijze, *Aspects of Islam in Post-Colonial Indonesia* (1958), 48–49, 109–112.

giously offensive requirement that all should develop the habit of bowing toward Tokyo. An abortive attempt to ban the use of the Arabic script in favor of the Japanese also aroused intense religious resentment. Indonesian nationalists were offended by the increasing Japanese use of the prijaji chiefs who were adat-oriented and had long been allied with the Dutch. Such ideological friction was intensified by the brutality of the military police (Kempeitai), and by the requisitioning of labor battalions and food grains sorely needed by the Javanese themselves. Indonesian laborers, to an estimated number of 300,000, were used in Malaya and as far east as New Guinea.[4]

The Japanese-sponsored Masjumi Party, or Consultative Council of Indonesian Muslims, was really a political organization functioning under a religious guise. Although theoretically dedicated to the establishment of an Islamic state under the leadership of Allah, the Masjumi included only the less fanatic elements of the old MIAI and the moderately indoctrinated body of village teachers. In conjunction with the scribes, the Masjumi was utilized by the Japanese to keep the people under control and to support defense preparations against the eventuality of Allied counterattack. The occupying authorities really had little alternative to their dependence on the cooperation of the Masjumi and the scribes. The angry temper of the people was reflected in a west Javan rebellion of February, 1944, which developed over hostility to rice requisitions. Simulated religious fervor proved to be no substitute for food.[5]

The collapse of the Tojo government in Japan in mid-1944, following Japanese military reversals, forced a change of policy in the direction of a more active enlistment of nationalist assistance in Indonesia. A qualified promise of independence was held out in September, 1944; religious controls were relaxed; support was accorded to the previously requested Islamic university, coupled with a proposal to publish the Koran. Meanwhile religious traditionalism was appealing less and less to the emerging youthful leadership. The Peta army group was disrespectful of traditionalist controls, and, despite its exposure to Japanese indoctrination, became openly anti-Japanese in the end. A Young Pioneer Corps, sponsored by the secularized nationalists, helped shift the balance in a modernist direction. Thus the Masjumi group was finally pushed off the center of the political stage in the spring of 1945, when the Japanese made their first concrete move to implement the promise of independence. A student conference staged in June, 1945, issued the first call for full independence. Sukarno and Hatta finally attained political ascendancy when the Independence Preparatory Committee was formed on August 14, 1945, on the very eve of the Japanese surrender.

Indonesian religious elements eventually split three ways. Reformist

[4] Benda, *Crescent,* 120–132.
[5] Van Nieuwenhuijze, 49–52; Benda, *Crescent,* 149–168.

groups stayed with the Masjumi Party, the doctrinally conservative leadership affiliated with the Nahdatul Islam faction, and fanatically militant religious elements turned to Darul Islam. Intensified religious partisanship fanned by the Japanese occupation thus survived in Indonesia to confuse political alignments after the achievement of independence.[6] Japanese endeavors to generate anti-Dutch political resistance included at least one overt effort of a Japanese naval intelligence officer to enlist and train a Communist group to oppose the Allies' return. The group was assembled from the non-Stalinist Subardjo-Tan Malaka branch of the party. The emphasis was on anticolonialism, anticapitalism, and anti–United States propaganda. The fairly obvious intention was to split the Indonesian Communist Party, which constituted a possible ally of the returning Western forces in accordance with official Moscow policy.[7] No comparable propagandist program was attempted by the Japanese naval command in the Great East or by the separate Japanese army command placed in charge of Sumatra.

Chinese residents everywhere in Indonesia were forced by the Japanese to register at the cost of about $100 a head and to carry passports indicating their compliance. Many Chinese establishments had previously been looted, during the interregnum of 1942. Eventually the Japanese military afforded some measure of protection to Chinese groups out of deference to the puppet Wang Ching-wei regime in China.[8]

## Japanese Policy in Malaya

Japanese propagandist policy in Malaya was equally calculating but was differentiated along ethnic lines. To the Malays, the invaders pressed home the sense of disillusionment deriving from the failure of Britain to protect them, while also fanning communal hostility toward the Chinese. In return for preferential Japanese treatment, most Malays cooperated in both governmental and military matters. They were negatively impressed by Japanese brutality, but were themselves happy to escape what the Chinese were suffering. The administrative structure of the sultanates was kept intact, except that Japanese advisers replaced the British. District advisory councils, with half of their members appointed by the Japanese, were set up for the purpose of reflecting local attitudes and to provide information. Japanese proposals to unite Malaya and Sumatra administratively, apart from Java, were eventually abandoned in 1944 in the light of the negative response from both areas.[9]

But the Malays did not come off scot free. They were forced by hardship, as were the Chinese, to move toward self-sufficiency in both food

[6] Benda, *Crescent,* 169–194; and "Indonesian Islam," 350–361.

[7] George McT. Kahin, MS notes.

[8] V. Purcell, *The Chinese in Southeast Asia* (1951), 551–568.

[9] N. Ginsburg and C. F. Roberts, *Malaya* (1958), 44–46, 441–442.

and consumer goods. Malays were also brought into the rubber plantations to replace Indian laborers. Material losses throughout Malaya were heavy, particularly in connection with the railways and the tin mines. The war experience also had important psychological effects. Youthful Malay "patriots" derived from their unaccustomed military participation an exaggerated sense of their own importance and political competence. Attitudes of Malay belligerency characteristic of the days prior to the British pacification in the 1870s reasserted themselves. Experience in fighting also served to revive the pre-Islamic cults of invulnerability and other forms of primitive magic latent in the submerged cultural awareness.[10] The supine attitude of the docile Tamil laborer and the grubbing acquisitiveness of the prosperous Chinese were destined to be challenged after the war by the revived political spirit of the Malays. Malay nationalist sentiment was also stimulated by resentment over Japan's arbitrary assignment to Thailand of the four northern sultanates—Perlis, Kelantan, Trengganu, and Kedah—which the British had acquired in 1909 .

As previously indicated, the Chinese of Malaya suffered grievously at the hands of the Japanese. Some renegade collaborators worked for the Kempeitai, but many of those who had actively supported the China Relief Fund following the Japanese attack on China in 1937 were massacred or drowned in the straits. Chinese womenfolk were violated on a grand scale. Here as elsewhere, the Chinese communities were systematically milked by forced loans and property requisions. Such treatment drove many of the younger Chinese to support the activities of actively violent anti-Japanese partisans, who took refuge in the Malay jungle. The partisans called themselves the Malay Peoples Anti-Japanese Army (MPAJA).

As the telltale word "peoples" suggests, the MPAJA was led for the most part by Chinese Communist agents. This group had fomented labor troubles at the outset of the "imperialist" war of 1939–1940 and had otherwise tried to impede British operations. It changed over to the British side and called off the strikes after Hitler's attack on Russia transformed the conflict overnight into a "peoples' war." During the Japanese occupation, the MPAJA was assisted by the British army, which parachuted into the jungle European and Chinese agents, along with arms and communication equipment. Toward the end of the war, systematic MPAJA sabotage had the rail traffic in Malay badly demoralized. This group was destined to resume its anti-British tactics following the surrender of the Japanese.[11]

The Japanese treated with marked favor most of the Indian community in Singapore and Malaya, especially the captured troops and civilian leaders. Virtually all of them became involved in the Japanese-

[10] G. C. Allen and A. G. Donnithorne, *Western Enterprise in Indonesia and Malaya* (1957), 46–48; William Holland, *Asian Nationalism and the West* (1953), 289–298.

[11] V. Thompson and R. Adloff, *The Left Wing in Southeast Asia* (1950), 129–131; D. G. E. Hall, *A History of South-East Asia* (1955), 689.

sponsored Indian Independence League (IIL) and the Indian National Army (INA). Many of the members of the IIL, not only at Singapore but also at Bangkok and Rangoon, contributed funds either voluntarily or under conditions of ill-disguised duress. Some Indian laborers were used on the "death railway" running from Bangkok to Moulmein via Kanburi. But the enterprise was a two-way affair, for the Indian nationalists were trying to use the Japanese quite as much as the Japanese were exploiting the Indians. The prearranged leader of the league was Rash Behari Bose, a Bengali expatriate long resident in Japan, who was brought to Singapore in 1942. He was plainly a Japanese stooge and enjoyed no influence. A captured Sikh army captain, Mohan Singh, played the key role in the first period as head of the INA. The Japanese apparently contemplated a seaborne invasion of the Coromandel Coast of India, using the INA supported by the funds of the IIL as a kind of decoy. The coast was actually open to invasion during the latter half of 1942.

The Japanese plan miscarried partly because Tokyo refused to meet the demands of Captain Mohan Singh. He wanted a categorical public statement by Prime Minister Tojo to the effect that India's future independence would not be compromised, and he wanted an armed Indian force placed under his personal command large enough to be capable of independent military action. He also demanded that Subhas Chandra Bose be recalled from Berlin to replace the Japanese stooge, R. B. Bose. Mohan Singh and his personal followers were taken into custody when they started to disband the INA. They were sent to a prison camp in New Guinea, where they were eventually released by General MacArthur's advancing American forces. The undertaking had virtually collapsed by the time Subhas Bose, a genuine Bengali revolutionary and ex-president of India's National Congress Party, was brought by German submarine to Penang in June, 1943, in an effort to revive the Indian Independence movement. Meanwhile the chance for successful seaborne attack had faded.[12] Later phases of the Indian National Army story will be treated in connection with Japan's attempted overland invasion of Indian from Burma in 1944.

In contrast to the favored treatment accorded to Indian prisoners of war by the Japanese, the lives of British prisoners taken at Singapore were expended wantonly in the forced construction of the "death railway." Few of the Europeans survived the ordeal of heat, disease, overwork, and malnutrition.

## Burma under the Japanese

Members of the so-called Freedom Bloc who had been imprisoned by U Saw's government after 1939, including ex-Premier Ba Maw, Thakin Nu, and the Communist Than Tun, plus the Thakin group that had defected to the Japanese, constituted the political leadership in Burma

[12] Hall, 690; Holland, 289–298.

during the Japanese occupation. Premier U Saw's visit to London on the eve of Pearl Harbor failed to obtain confirmation of Burma's dominion status after the war, and he was detected trying to defect to the Japanese while en route back to Burma. He was accordingly arrested by the British in Egypt and detained in Uganda for the remainder of the war. A handful of the conservative Burman Cabinet members were evacuated with Governor Dorman-Smith to Simla, India, where the Burma government-in-exile was set up.

The "thirty heroes," led by Thakin Aung San, were never in a position to attach any conditions to their assistance to the invading Japanese. They could only gamble and hope for the best. Their actual military role was unimportant, and they stirred up more trouble in their attempted governing roles in the "liberated areas" than they solved. This was especially true among the delta Karens. The collaborators did contribute to the impression fostered by the Japanese that their "liberation" of Burma enjoyed nationalist backing.

From being considered peripheral to Japan's plans in 1940, Burma was actually transformed by 1942 into the principal front-line military position of Japan in Southeast Asia. The situation was far from promising from the Burmese point of view. Transportation facilities, both railways and river steamers, were largely destroyed during the course of the British withdrawal, as were many of Burma's cities. The Japanese army command was in no mood at the outset to advance any concessions of an economic or political nature. Military needs had absolute priority. The army monopolized the available productive and transport facilities, requisitioned cattle and other supplies as needed, assembled thousands of forced laborers, flooded the countryside with printed currency, and rode roughshod over the sensitivities of the people. The enormous rice surpluses in Lower Burma were not only denied sale abroad; no facilities were made available to transport rice upcountry, where a serious food shortage developed. Nor could Upper Burma's cooking oils and cotton find their way south. The Japanese decision at the outset was to postpone even the qualified type of independence contemplated within the "Co-Prosperity" scheme. The army also assumed exclusive control within the Shan States.

The initial Thakin, or Baho, regime gave place during the summer of 1942 to a puppet government headed by Dr. Ba Maw. His party followers and the more acceptable members of the Thakin group also participated. Ba Maw's personal ambition, Anglophobia, and administrative experience and intelligence qualified him for the task. His contempt for democratic procedures and his appeal for "one party, one blood, one voice, one command" were in essential agreement with Japanese principles of arbitrary government. But nothing could counteract the bad manners of the Japanese soldiery. They slapped Burmese elders who attempted to reach accommodation with them; they converted sacred pagoda premises into slaughterhouses and latrines; they treated the monks of the Sangha with contempt as being both useless and lazy; the Kempeitai army police acted with callous brutality here as everywhere.

The situation deteriorated rapidly. Dr. Ba Maw himself was obliged to support the Japanese demand for assembling some thirty thousand forced laborers for military needs, including the building of the Burma end of the "death railway." Some 2 million acres of paddy land went out of cultivation; almost no Japanese consumer goods entered Burma to match the flood of printing-press money. Japanese contractors from the several Zaibatsu combines assumed control over various phases of the plan to put Burma's economy on a self-sufficient basis. Under the circumstances, the efforts of the Greater East Asia Ministry to picture Japan as a fellow Buddhist country, as the "leader, protector, and light of Asia," produced a particularly hollow reaction in Burma.

It became clear by January, 1943, that Burma's people would not support any offensive or defensive measures of the Japanese army unless they were given a tangible political stake in a Japanese victory. Following the failure of Britain's first Arakan offensive in the spring of 1943 and in the absence of any promise from London of postwar self-government or independence, both the Burmans and the Japanese were ready to come to some kind of *modus vivendi*. An Independence Preparatory Committee was accordingly set up in the late spring under the presidency of Dr. Ba Maw. It included most of the responsible Burman leaders, who were obviously prepared to do the best they could for the country in a thoroughly bad situation.

The Constitution which was drafted contained a number of democratic features, even though they were rendered completely inoperative by Japan's plenary emergency powers. Dr. Ba Maw became the Adipadi (derived from the Pali-Sanskrit term for head of state), and the achievement of Burma's "independence" was duly celebrated on August 1, 1943. One of the first acts of the Adipadi was to declare war on the United States and Britain as demanded by the Japanese. The new Cabinet enjoyed the appearance of autonomy, and within the limits permitted by the Japanese in matters of nonmilitary concern, it did exercise something of the reality of control. It was drawn mainly from Sinyetha (Ba Maw's party) and Thakin ranks, but it also included other Burmans of tried integrity and administrative experience.

Adipadi Ba Maw made a sustained effort to qualify as Burma's ruler according to traditional symbols and standards. He undertook to maintain the prestige of both his office and of his person in his strained relations with the Japanese military. He asserted and made good Burma's claim of sovereignty over the Shan States, but not until after the Japanese had ceded two border states, Kengtung and Mongpan, to Thailand on July 4, 1943. Dr. Ba Maw succeeded in establishing friendly and fruitful relations with Premier Tojo, whom he met in Singapore in July, 1943. This relationship stood him in good stead on several subsequent occasions in connection with his running feud with Japanese military commanders in Burma. He did what he could to shield his countrymen from Japanese abuse short of imperiling his own political position.

The Adipadi nevertheless overreached himself in several ways. He took the title of *Mingyi* (great prince or king) and revived some of the ritual and symbolism of the traditional royal court. He brought to Rangoon a quantity of the "soil of victory" from King Alaungpaya's home city of Shwebo, in which to plant a sacred tree on the shore of Rangoon's Royal Lake. His personal ambition provided his principal vulnerability, for he allowed himself to be used enough by the Japanese to ruin his political future as a Burman. He also sacrificed his status as a westernized, European-educated Burman by playing up to the political pongyis, by play acting as King, and by calling in the astrologers on occasion. Although he staked his own future on a Japanese victory, he did not expose his associates in the Cabinet who were plotting against the Japanese.

Adipadi Ba Maw developed cordial relations with Subhas Chandra Bose, the leader of the revived Indian Independence League and Indian National Army. Bose shifted his headquarters from Singapore to Rangoon in October, 1943, changing the name of the organization to Azad Hind (free India). He began vigorous preparations to participate in the proposed conquest of India. Burma Indians contributed a substantial 150 million rupees to the cause, of a total of 215 million collected. But the INA was never permitted a genuine military role. It participated in token fashion in the Arakan campaign of 1944 but with minimal effect. At the very end, the INA, like the Burma National Army, turned on the Japanese, against the wishes of Bose, who was killed in a postwar airplane crash in Formosa while fleeing to Japan.

## British Defeat of the Japanese in Burma

Allied preparations for the counterattack from India on the Japanese position in Burma were begun with the establishment of a South-East Asia Command at the Quebec Conference in August, 1943. Lord Louis Mountbatten was named the supreme commander and General Stilwell of the United States was the deputy commander. In view of the lack of Allied naval power in the Bay of Bengal and the extreme difficulties of the terrain for any overland invasion, Mountbatten was much less anxious to get on with the task than was Stilwell. For the American commander, the early recovery of Burma was important to afford a means of easier access for military supplies to China, which was regarded until rather late in the war as the theater where the final struggle against the Japanese would probably be waged. Stilwell's major task was to train a Chinese army in northeastern India, which, with American aid, would drive the Japanese from northern Burma and thus restore road communication with Kunming via the prewar Burma Road. Meanwhile, the American airforce flew the dangerous "hump" route to Kunming carrying essential military supplies. The sounder British tactic, as far as Burma's recovery was concerned, was to assemble the necessary resources in India and wait for the Japanese to overextend themselves.

The Japanese started their gamble in the dry season of 1943–1944 when they undertook to invade India. It was their hope to capture Imphal in Manipur, to move northward to the Brahmaputra Valley of Assam so as to cut the supply lines of General Stilwell's operation at Dimapur, and then to penetrate Bengal. Once Bengal had been reached, they expected to exploit the enormous popularity of Subhas Bose, head of the INA, in his home province and to foment a general anti-British rising. A second minor Japanese thrust entered the Chittagong coastal area of Bengal via Arakan. Here Indian INA forces were used from the outset in an attempt to suborn isolated contingents of the Indian army.

The Japanese operation was vigorously pressed. Imphal was surrounded but managed to hold out with the help of American airdrop support diverted from the China run. The invaders were stopped short at Kohima in Assam on the way to Dimapur. The Japanese logistic problem in Manipur, especially in the absence of air support, was very great from the outset; it became quite impossible of solution once the rainy season began in late May, 1944. In the Arakan theater, the attempted use of the INA decoys failed completely, partly because many of the empire troops engaged in the region were from British Africa. The Japanese retreat from India, once started, became a rout. With the British Empire forces in pursuit and the American-Chinese forces proceeding southward down in the upper Irrawaddy Valley from Myitkyina, which Stilwell had captured in late 1944, the Japanese were unable to make a stand until the central plain of Burma was reached in early 1945.

Although the Allied army had air support which the Japanese had lacked, it faced the prospect of the same kind of disaster which had overtaken the Japanese at Imphal as far as supply lines were concerned. If the Allies were prevented from reaching Rangoon before the rains broke at the end of May, 1945, their only salvation would be a difficult seaborne attack against the Irrawaddy delta, an enterprise which was vetoed in February as not being feasible. It was in this context that the defection of General Aung San's Burma National Army to the Allied side in late March, 1945, became significant.

The Anti-Fascist League, organized secretly by Thakin members of the Ba Maw government together with the Communist Thein Pe in India, established contact with Simla in late 1943. The objective of the league was to attain self-rule for Burma, and it was prepared to strike the Japanese in the rear at the opportune time whether or not in conjunction with the counterattacking British forces. Mountbatten's eventual decision to regard the BNA as a *de facto* ally was highly unpopular with Governor Dorman-Smith and the conservative Burmans of the Simla government-in-exile, who regarded the Thakins as traitorous turncoats. But the need to reach Rangoon by early May was militarily imperative. As a result of the Burman army's attack on the Japanese rear in the Sittang Valley sector, coupled with coordinated action by separate Karen units organized by the British Force 136 group in the delta and in Karenni, all beginning on March 28, the British advance toward Rangoon was greatly accelerated. In one period of five days, some 150 crucial miles were covered, compared to a labored few miles per day previously. Rangoon was evacuated by the Japanese on April 22, and they made their final stand at Pegu on April 30 and May 1.

For a second time, the courage and daring of General Aung San paid off, in that he became the recognized leader of the Burmese nationalist movement. Because Lord Mountbatten, as Allied commander, faced the still-formidable task of eliminating Japanese control from the rest of Southeast Asia, using Burma as his principal base, he decided to continue to regard the Anti-Fascist League as a military ally. Once in the open, the league greatly enlarged its membership to include virtually all shades of nationalist opinion. Neither Premier Churchill nor Governor Dorman-Smith was happy with Mountbatten's decision, but Clement Attlee's Labor Party government came to power in London during the summer of 1945, and the governor did not take over power in Burma until October. It was then too late to challenge the political influence of Aung San without running the risk of fomenting a wholesale Burman rebellion. Under existing circumstances, no one could be sure that the Indian and African majority of the British Empire occupation forces could be depended upon. In the end, the governor's proposal, made in early 1946, to arrest Aung San and his key supporters was vetoed by Premier Attlee. Burma's independence followed in the wake of similar developments in postwar India.[13]

## Thailand and the Japanese Occupation

Premier Pibun Songgram's tactic of seemingly hesitant collaboration with the Japanese succeeded to the extent of sparing Thailand the material devastation experienced by Burma, but his pro-Japanese policy was far from popular. The Japanese flood of worthless currency used in payment for supplies produced an eventual tenfold increase in the cost of living measured in terms of the baht.[14] An orgy of corruption and dishonesty developed in connection with the inflation, involving official underhand dealings with Japanese authorities. Pibun's government, under Japanese encouragement, intensified the persecution of Thailand's Chinese population during the period of the occupation. Some popular enthusiasm was aroused over the acquisition of the cis-Mekong enclaves in 1940, but

[13] For a detailed discussion of the period see J. F. Cady, *A History of Modern Burma* (1958), chaps. XII, XIII, and XVI.

[14] In 1945, it took 22 Thailand baht to match the also-devalued American dollar, compared to 3 baht in 1941.

very little appreciation developed in connection with Thailand's later territorial acquisitions at Japanese hands. These included Battambang and Siemreap from Cambodia, Kengtung and Mongpan from Burma, plus Perlis, Kedah, Kelantan, and Trengganu from Malaya.

The Thai anti-Japanese movement centered in Pibun's arch-rival, Pridi Phanomyong. As previously indicated, Pridi resigned as Finance Minister at the time of the Japanese invasion and withdrew temporarily to northern Thailand. He returned later to Bangkok under a protecting assignment as regent to the King. With the influential support of Nai Direk, Pridi approved secretly the action of Thailand's Ambassador to Washington, Prince Seni Promoj, in refusing to deliver his government's declaration of war against the United States. Promoj denounced the declaration as unrepresentative of the will of the Siamese people. Between the three, the Free Thai movement was furtively born. American agents were smuggled into Thailand and housed in a European prisoner camp in Bangkok under Thai control. From here they communicated regularly with Allied intelligence agencies in Colombo by short-wave radio transmitters.

The change of government at Bangkok came in the summer of 1944, ostensibly over the proposal of Pibun to build an alternative capital at Pechabun in northeastern Thailand. The site was probably intended as a detached center from which the government could undertake the eventual resistance to the continuance of Japanese control. Pibun himself had learned to distrust the Japanese and their much-publicized GEACPS plans, and his own police chief was also broadcasting regularly to Lord Mountbatten's headquarters in Ceylon. The cornerstone of the new Pechabun capital was laid in April, 1944, but the site was an impossible, malaria-infested location. Pibun's defeat in the ensuing Assembly vote of August 2 technically came over the proposed change of capital site, but in reality it was probably the result of military reverses suffered by the Japanese in the Pacific. Pibun's resignation permitted Pridi's Free Thai group to come to power with Nai Khuang Aphaiwong as Premier.

Thus again Thailand was seeking the customary accommodation with the dominant foreign power, which now appeared to be the United States. In contrast to London, Washington had refused to take seriously Bangkok's declaration of war.[15]

Following the end of the war, Prince Seni Promoj was brought back to Bangkok to serve for a short time as Premier, until January 1, 1946, when the difficult treaty with Britain was signed. American support permitted Bangkok to escape the penalty of its hostile policy toward England. The Thailand Constitution had to be amended in this instance to permit a prince to occupy such a high office. Prince Seni was clearly beyond his depth politically and withdrew willingly from his high responsibility. Pridi continued

[15] W. Vella, *The Impact of the West on Siam* (1955), 382–389; John Coast, *Some Aspects of Siamese Politics* (1953), 21–26.

as kingmaker until November, 1947, when Pibun returned to power in a bloodless coup.

## The Rise of Communist-led Nationalism in Indochina

In terms of material losses and political confusion, Indochina probably suffered from the Japanese occupation least of all the countries of Southeast Asia. Foreign trade was paralyzed except in rubber exports, of which the Japanese continued to take up to 50 per cent of prewar export figures, but no serious civil strife, famine, or epidemic developed. Because the regular French administration continued in power until the spring of 1945, little opportunity was afforded to anti-French nationalists to organize resistance comparable to that developing in Java and Burma.[16] Such disaffection as occurred came from Communist sources operating from both within and outside the country.

Throughout most of the first two years of the European war, Communist policy in Indochina as elsewhere ignored the Japanese threat, concentrating on attacking the colonial power and its "imperialist war." Such groups fomented popular risings in Indochina in November, 1940, directed mainly against the French. The French authorities, who were apparently fully informed of events, put down the rebellion effectively without asking any Japanese aid. Ho Chi Minh's group had to withdraw to South China for reorganization following this initial failure. Full orientation of Ho's group toward the Allied side and against Japan followed the Nazi invasion of Russia in June, 1941. Here as elsewhere, the conflict then became a "peoples' war."

The Vietnamese anti-Japanese movement was far from unified. Ho's Viet Minh League with its base in South China was broadly nationalist but contained a hard-core Communist nucleus. It formed for a time an uneasy coalition with a Kuomintang-sponsored group of Vietnamese nationalists known as the Dong Minh Hoi. The Chinese-sponsored group was probably more anti-French than was Ho, who envisaged the possible future control over Vietnam by Nationalist China as a much greater danger than the fading French control. In any case the two China-based groups eventually became bitter rivals. The uncompromisingly revolutionary Trotskyite Communists, who were especially strong in Cochin-China, refused to cooperate with the local Moscow-sponsored group led by Tran Van-Giau. Both operated underground. The Viet Minh League enjoyed the advantage of an external base, plus Ho's vigorous leadership and his wide reputation.[17]

As previously indicated, Ho Chi Minh's group in South China ob-

[16] Charles Micaud in Lennox Mills (ed.), *New World of Southeast Asia* (1949), 225.

[17] Thompson and Adloff, 28–31.

tained from the American Office of Strategic Services in late 1944 assistance to reenter northern Tongking in an effort to establish an effective anti-Japanese front. The Free French and China's Kuomintang authorities at the outset also cooperated with the effort. With the assistance afforded, the Viet Minh League was able to gain control of seven northern provinces of Tongking by August, 1945. They won largely by default, since legal French authority disappeared during the spring of 1945 after being ousted by the Japanese, and the Japanese themselves subsequently began withdrawing from remote areas. Ho convened a Viet Minh Congress immediately following the Japanese surrender, and was himself elected president of the executive Peoples National Liberation Committee. His leadership was recognized by virtually all nationalist Vietnamese, including the Cochin-China Trotskyite radicals. The Emperor Bao Dai abdicted in favor of Viet Minh on August 25, entrusting to the successor regime the care of the bones of his ancestors. Bao Dai thus surrendered the symbols of imperial authority.

Difficulties developed for Ho when the Nationalist Chinese military forces, acting under Allied authorization, entered Tongking to take the surrender of the Japanese in northern Indochina above Hué. British forces took the surrender in the south of Indochina. The occupying Chinese ignored Ho's pretensions as head of a *de facto* government and put forward their rival Dong Minh Hoi organization to handle the necessary liaison with the people. Thus was the stage set for a three-cornered contest between the French, who were assisted by the British to return to Saigon, the Chinese nationalists, who were undertaking to establish a puppet regime in the north, and the Viet Minh League, which represented, in spite of its Communist connections, the majority nationalist sentiment, both anti-Chinese and anti-French. Unfortunately for the preservation of American rapport with the Vietnamese nationalists at this critical juncture, the death of President Roosevelt left the determination of State Deparment policy in the hands of senior career Foreign Service officers with an exclusively Europe-oriented outlook. Ho's requests for American support of Vietnamese nationalist aspirations went unheeded in Washington. He eventually turned for aid to the rising power of the Communist Chinese in spite of his genuine fear of Chinese domination.[18] American policy later became hopelessly entangled with the impossible efforts of France to recover colonial control.

### Filipinos and Japanese

General MacArthur's landing on the island of Leyte in the central Philippines in October, 1944, was welcomed by virtually all Filipinos. The reconquest of the islands and the contemporaneous destruction of the Japanese fleet not only rescued the Filipinos from bullying exploitation; it also

---

[18] Bernard Fall, *Le Viet-Minh* (1960), 43–48; Ellen Hammer in Lawrence K. Rosinger (ed.), *The State of Asia* (1951), 232–235.

doomed the Japanese hold on the rest of Southeast Asia. With the Philippines in American hands, the long-range submarine operations which had already decimated Japanese shipping in the South China Sea could be greatly intensified. The possibility of an American landing in French Indochina from the Philippines obliged the Japanese in the spring of 1945 to scuttle the French administration, opening the way for the Viet Minh entry. General MacArthur enjoyed the full support of the Islanders. The bogus independence afforded by Tokyo to the opportunist regime of José Laurel carried no appeal whatever in view of the already-realized Commonwealth status under the Americans and the unequivocal promise of independence after the war.

Guerrilla resistance to the Japanese had persisted in many parts of the Philippines throughout the course of the occupation. The most formidable operation was that of the Hukbalahaps, or Peoples' Anti-Japanese Army, functioning on the fringes of the central Luzon plain. The movement was partly Communist-led, and drew some of its peasant support from deep-seated hostility to the cacique landlords, who had long dominated the agriculture and the politics of the islands. The Chinese Communist partisans, militantly anti-Japanese here as in Malaya, joined hands with the Huks. The leader of the Huk army, Luis Turuc, had been a Communist since 1939 only, while the rebels as a whole were mainly peasant-oriented. During the war, the Huks and other rebels provided asylum for refugees and for American intelligence agents landed by submarine; they also contributed generally to keeping Filipino hopes alive. The common front against the Japanese was marred to some extent by the feud going on within the Chinese community, reflecting the strident Kuomintang-Communist rivalry within China proper. Each group informed on the other.[19]

Returning from America in the wake of the United States forces was Vice-President Osmeña of the prewar Commonwealth government. President Quezon had died in 1944. Osmeña headed the provisional government until elections could be held. The material destruction suffered by the islands during the two campaigns was exceeded in Southeast Asia only by that of Burma. The social demoralization resulting from the two interregnums was also great. But the political future of the islands was not in doubt, so that the Philippines did not undergo a postwar political revolution such as Burma experienced. Even more important was the absence of any need to fight for independence, as was the case in Indonesia and Indochina. The postwar Hukbalahap rebellion, calling itself the Peoples' Liberation Army, continued for a number of years to defy the restored Commonwealth authorities, with Communist leadership attempting to exploit genuine peasant grievances. It came to an end through the understanding approach of President Magsaysay in the 1950s.

[19] Russell Fifield, "The Hukbalahap Today," *FES*, XX (1951), 13–14; Purcell, 642–645.

## Summary of the Effects of the Japanese Occupation

One of the significant effects of the Japanese occupation of Southeast Asia from 1942 to 1945 was to demonstrate to the people concerned that Oriental domination could be infinitely less humane and understanding than European colonialism with all of its shortcomings. As one Burman put it, "The British exploited our wealth, while the Japanese sucked the marrow of our bones." The Chinese army intrusions into Upper Burma early in the war and into North Vietnam to receive the surrender of the Japanese both degenerated into wholesale looting. European prestige was damaged but not destroyed.

A corollary political result of the common suffering sustained at the hands of the Japanese was to heighten nationalist sentiment everywhere. In Indonesia, Burma, and Indochina, in particular, the war experience elevated to power a new stratum of youthful political leadership. The novel experience of military activity, long denied under colonial pacification, bred not only a spirit of youthful assertiveness but also enhanced self-confidence. The new mood had some measure of validity for the few who had really shouldered responsibilities for the first time; it bordered on reckless overconfidence for other elements of the new elite.

Because all of the peoples of Southeast Asia went through a common ordeal under Japanese rule, the reality of their community of interests emerged more clearly than before. Historic antagonisms and rivalries were not destroyed, but Southeast Asian neighbors did learn to know each other better and to escape the narrow channeling of their relations with the outside world through the imperial metropole alone. They even began to think in tentative fashion in terms of regional cooperation, although such efforts could become meaningful only in a larger world context. The various types of resistance which the Japanese encountered demonstrated that the peoples of the area were far from the pawns or ciphers which Tokyo had tried unsuccessfully to manipulate. Even in the presence of overwhelming military power, subjugation and control over all of Southeast Asia proved to be no simple and easy undertaking.

The economic losses of the war were staggeringly heavy. They reached a peak in Burma and the Philippines, which were both twice fought over. But elsewhere also, the deterioration of harbors, communication and transportation facilities, public utilities, mines, and factories was very great. The peasants suffered loss of a large fraction of their cattle and buffaloes from Japanese requisition and from disease; millions of acres of paddy and plantation land reverted to jungle. Cholera, plague, and smallpox added to the heavy loss of life from forced labor and malnutrition. The war also demonstrated how vulnerable the economies of Southeast Asia were in their abject dependence on outside markets and sources for consumer goods. The postwar period was destined to see in every country the projection of ambitious and often ill-considered attempts at forced-draft development of a diversified industrial economy. Sanguine hopes that the elimination of colonial exploitation would solve the problems of poverty and political instability were destined to be dashed. Actually wide rifts—ethnic, cultural, and economic—which had long been bridged over by colonial control were laid bare along with evidences of revived historical antagonisms.

Not all of the changes which developed in Southeast Asia during World War II were due to the influence of the Japanese. The ending of British rule in India terminated British hegemony in the area by destroying its essential base. The elimination of French and Dutch power in Southeast Asia was in large measure a result of the German occupation of the homelands, an event which would have produced profound effects regardless of the Japanese. Europe's abdication of world leadership in a second disastrous war in successive generations was after all the major political event of the first half of the twentieth century. Developments in Southeast Asia necessarily reflected its influence.

# CHAPTER 26

# *Relevance*

## *of the History*

$\mathcal{I}$t is manifestly impossible within the limits of this volume, already long, to consider in meaningful detail the important historical developments which have occurred in Southeast Asia since the end of World War II. Furthermore, the little more than a decade which has elapsed since the new states achieved independent status has scarcely afforded the necessary time for evaluation. Monographic studies covering particular aspects of Southeast Asian development and others written on a country-by-country basis are legion, and several general accounts are also conveniently available.[1] No attempt will here be made, therefore, to carry the historical narrative beyond the end of the war in 1945.

What will be undertaken in this chapter is an assessment of the relevance of basic historical considerations, both traditionalist and modern, to the developing postwar situation. One of the most important positive historical developments—indeed, it is second only to the nationalist resistance to colonialism in all forms—is the powerful impulse toward modernization. This development is rooted in the effects of Western contacts experienced during the colonial period and also stems from experiences gained during the course of the Japanese occupation. Characteristics of social and political change will be described; then the scope of the continuing Western influence will be estimated. At the same time, a number of traditional cultural habits and values which continue to demonstrate vitality can be identified. These operate to condition the acceptance of the new modernized order which is being promoted by the westernized elite. Historic rivalries and feuds have also reemerged since the European withdrawal, along with reversions to traditional patterns of arbitrary exercise of governmental authority.

Two inescapable facts apparently veto the possibility of Southeast

[1] George McTurnan Kahin (ed.), *Governments and Politics of Southeast Asia* (1959) is perhaps the most satisfactory account, replacing the older Lennox Mills (ed.), *New World of Southeast Asia* (1949).

Asia's returning to precolonial standards of economic livelihood and govern-ment. One is the area's vast increase in population since 1850; this will necessitate the maintenance of contact with world markets and outside sources of needed consumer goods and industrial supplies. Intelligent in-digenous leadership recognizes that Southeast Asia must continue to seek aid from the industrial states. The second fact is the intrinsic importance of the area strategically and as a prime source of items needed in world trade; this importance forces world powers to take an active interest in the politi-cal fortunes of the area. The emergence of a strong China championing the Communist cause in Asia and determined to reestablish its long-term suzerain status over the peripheral states to the south constitutes an addi-tional postwar development. Thus an understanding of recent events within the region must depend on efforts to relate its long historical and cultural traditions to the positive factors inexorably working for modernization, however slow and halting may be the process of change.

## Characteristics of Social Change

The principal agencies of cultural change in Southeast Asia since the mid-nineteenth century have come from the highly industrial states of the West. They took over the direction of colonialism from chartered companies, from European monarchs, and from the traditional cultural in-fluences emanating from India and China. European control brought to an end the feuding which had long prevailed in Southeast Asian dynastic rivalry and interstate relations. The Western colonial governments usually enlisted the cooperation of elite minority groups, including the Chinese in the economic sphere, and also promoted changes of basic importance in the social structure generally. The new colonial regimes set up frequently artificial frontiers, which sometimes fragmented national and ethnic en-tity. Indigenous cultural, economic, and educational associations were channeled toward the respective metropoles.

The total effect of this colonializing process has been variously as-sessed. At one extreme is the emotionally colored nationalist idealization of the classical pre-European period, coupled with condemnation of exploitive imperialism as the root of all evils. At the other extreme lie the espousal of the "white man's burden" and affirmations concerning the generally beneficial effects of Western rule. Both points of view contain elements of truth. Generally speaking, the colonial system's achievement of better standards of health and governmental administration and the major eco-nomic improvements in transportation and communication, plantations and mines, industry, trade, and banking were designed to serve foreign needs quite as much as indigenous wants and interests. The resident peoples failed to share fully in the benefits of progress realized under colonial rule—partly because they were unable to match the economic experience and financial and political resources of alien competitors, and partly because population increases which accompanied improved order and sanitation prevented any significant rise in per capita income. On the other hand, the postwar program of aid to underdeveloped countries seems to indicate that the white man's burden has simply assumed a different form. In Southeast Asia the most significant historical fact of the last century has been the direct confrontation, both under colonialism and since its liquidation, of differing economic, political, and intellectual orders, combined with the enforced orientation of the region as a whole to a larger world context both culturally and economically.

The several colonial regimes of Southeast Asia could probably have withstood for some time the pressures of incipient nationalist demands had the Japanese intrusion not precipitated an abrupt ending of European control; the Philippines were an exception, for there the schedule for freedom had already been set up by America. Yet the inevitable modulation to self-rule was only a matter of time and circumstance in any case. Political events in India and China and the rapid expansion of Japanese trade and industrial potential were important and inescapable elements of the changing Eastern Asian scene.

The strength and character of impinging forces of modernization were highly disparate, varying from area to area even within the same colonial system. In few countries was nationalist sentiment sufficiently well integrated and coordinated prior to the Japanese occupation to be effectively applied. Practices of indirect rule in Annam, Laos, Cambodia, Malaya and British Borneo, the Outer Islands of Indonesia, and the peripheral states of Burma left much of the traditional order unchanged and unadapted to the trend toward modernization. Indirect rule also tended to retard the development of genuine nationalist sentiment. Even within the more highly developed areas, the available educational opportunities were monopolized in large measure by the sons of elite groups, who were inclined to be conservative. The radicals were found mainly among frustrated students who had nothing at stake in maintaining the colonial *status quo*. Burma's Thakins were a prime example, and the study groups in Java were another.

Alongside the emergence of the youthful nationalists could be observed, even under indirect rule, the gradual erosion of the traditional prestige of the older elite. This usually developed before the radical nationalists could develop new credentials of authority and establish close rapport with anti-Western members of the population. Social disintegration was particularly acute in newly cultivated areas where rice, tobacco, rubber, and tea plantations attracted large numbers of migrant laborers. The vacuum of leadership thus created was sometimes filled by religious fanatics, such as the pongyi monks and Saya San in Burma, the Ulama scribes of Indonesia, and the self-appointed messiahs of the Philippines. Such obscurantists usually lacked any positive sense of political direction, any genuine nationalist aspirations, and any real understanding of the problems to be solved.

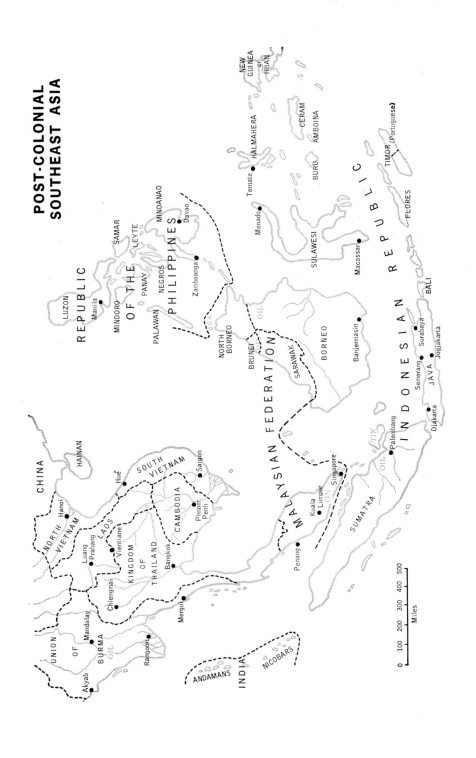

POST-COLONIAL
SOUTHEAST ASIA

The Japanese intrusion not only discredited European prestige and dislodged Western economic controls; it also demonstrated the need for diversified industrial development. It had the further political effect of encouraging youthful nationalists to assume both political and military leadership, especially in Burma, Java, Minangkabau Sumatra, and Vietnam. Youthful nationalists gained confidence and organizational cohesion by cooperating in the several independence struggles. It is fairly obvious that most of the economic and social ills of Southeast Asian countries were aggravated by the Japanese intrusion; and it is equally clear that the hurried postwar withdrawal of the colonial authorities handicapped recovery efforts, especially in governmental administration and the economic field. Thus the exaggerated expectations of the champions of freedom and modernization were usually doomed to serious disappointment.[2] The intrinsic political impact of the occupation was much less extreme in Malaya, much of Indonesia, Thailand, Cambodia, Laos, and the Philippines.

## The Scope of the Western Influence

The Western influence on twentieth-century Southeast Asia was not limited to economic and governmental development. It included an expanding acquaintance with science and its technological applications to such practical needs as communication and transportation, electric power, water supplies, soil conservation, and medicines. It involved, in urban centers, the influx of Western movies, forms of music, and picture periodicals and often some acquaintance with Western literature. The contagion of Western ways was also reflected in such innocuous customs as shaking hands and the use of chairs, hats, utensils, the Christian calendar, and Christmas cards. Western-style newspapers, banking and commercial practices, and typewriters and business machines were essential accretions to the new order.

Technological assistance and other forms of economic aid, often given gratis or on favorable terms at the government level, contributed much during the postwar years to educational needs, health, and agricultural improvement. These services had previously been the concern only of colonial governments or missionary agencies. Christian missionaries continued to demonstrate certain nonprofit institutions and ways of Western civilization, such as hospitals, leprosariums, schools, boy scouts, language transcription, and relief of distress. But the funds at the disposal of the private missionary societies were dwarfed by huge government grants. The Christian converts, except in Catholic areas of the Philippines and Vietnam, were limited pretty largely to minority groups, such as the Karens of Burma and the Menadonese and Amboinese of Indonesia. Southeast Asian peoples generally appreciated the friendly helpfulness of the Christian

[2] Harry Benda, "The Structure of Southeast Asian History," *JSEAH,* III (1962), 127–138.

ethic, but their admiration of the West tended to focus on automobiles, radios, phonograph records, airplanes, sewing machines, and agricultural aids. Greater ease and speed of travel brought the two worlds infinitely closer together in the postwar decades.[3]

The westernized minority which collaborated in promoting cultural adjustments comprised in no country as much as one-tenth of the population. The final results may, nevertheless, prove to be more significant than the historic processes of Indianization and Islamization, which were also accomplished by elite minorities. But the process of great change is always confusing and sometimes painful. Tension between the old and new persisted not only between contrasting parts of the population but also within the minds of the elite themselves. The new leadership retained emotional attachments to traditional customs and sought to appropriate only such Western ideas and processes as could be accommodated with local desires and experienced values. The masses adjusted by fitting new practices into the context of traditional cultural concepts. Spirit doctors sometimes enhanced their prestige by passing out sulfa drugs indiscriminately to the allegedly spirit-infested ill, and the American Dr. Dooley found it advantageous to have a spirit doctor accompany him in his deeds of mercy in postwar Laos. The atomic theory was exploited in Burma to support the Buddha's affirmations concerning the unsubstantial character of matter. Thus the vogue of things Western tended to penetrate, often in a superficial way, into both remote village communities and urban circles. Traditionalist reactions developed from time to time in all areas, but they seldom totally repudiated the seductive influences from abroad.[4]

Generally speaking, many of the people who came to appreciate Western achievements did not share the underlying social and intellectual premises involved or demonstrate the disciplined efficiency necessary for realizing economic desires. A completely unprepared candidate for a Burma medical degree appeared before the examining committee for his eighth consecutive time fortified only by assurance that eight was his lucky number. Peasants used fertilizers and improved seeds without diminishing in the least their propitiation of the earth spirits and their faith in the capacity of the shaman priest to improve fertility. Educated members of the elite described themselves as living in a house of two stories, one traditional and one Western, with no stairway connecting them.

Contradictions were manifold. The Cao Dai of Cochin-China sought in eclectic fashion to incorporate the best items of every creed despite their mutual inconsistencies, including monotheism, spirit mediums, ancestor worship, and a Pope. Burmans accepted gratefully medical books sent by the World Health Organization, but refused to interfere with religious taboos against the taking of life of mosquitoes, rats, and flies, which demon-

[3] For a thoughtful discussion of this theme, see Kenneth Landon, *Southeast Asia: Crossroads of Religion* (1947), 165–172.

[4] *Ibid.,* 202–203.

stratively transmitted disease. At the same time, the Association of Burmese Medical Practitioners made little or no progress in systematizing indigenous practice in order to eliminate quacks and poisonous concoctions.[5] Such problems probably did not differ greatly from those which the prescientific Western world itself had to solve to emancipate medical practice from accumulated superstitions. The strength of the effect of the Western world on Southeast Asia probably increased as a result of the ending of colonial tutelage. But the initiative was being taken by national leaders themselves, who determined what they wanted and decided where to get it.

## Persistence of the Traditional

To what extent did the basic capacities, characteristics, and inheritances of Southeast Asian peoples hold them back from achieving the modernist goals espoused by their postwar leadership? A major difficulty lay in the fact that the life of the average person was lived in a context of a world of spirits—some of them cosmic, some knavish and capricious—upon the proper propitiation of which prosperity and individual well-being allegedly depended.[6] In Christianized countries like the Philippines, the miracle-impregnated milieu differed mainly in the alleged presence of benevolent godling saints who rendered timely assistance against the evil spirits. As previously pointed out, the tenacious persistence of hillside-cultivator society related to its intricate involvement in religious custom. Indigenous medical practice and spirit worship generally went hand in hand. Amulets, charms, and magical tattoo patterns were widely regarded as potent. These indigenous beliefs merged with traditional faith in Indian astrology and numerology at higher social levels. Buddhist pagoda premises guarded by their fearsome-looking griffins were allegedly free from evil spirits.

It was also difficult to westernize peoples, however hospitable and intelligent, who perceived no particular virtue in excessive industry looking toward the accumulation of wealth and who lacked training in the ordered discipline of the modernist tempo. It was not necessarily an indictment of the culture of the Malay, for example, to observe that what the European regarded as time lost, the Malay considered time gained; but the difference was socially and economically significant. Spirit or ancestral shrines were still maintained in most homes. Social security in Southeast Asia continued to be rooted principally in the family system.

Tensions between the traditional and the modern took different guises in the several countries. In Vietnam, industrial employment and urbanization did much to weaken ancestral cults, since the portable spirit

[5] *Ibid.,* 172–192; *Bama Khit,* Rangoon, Dec. 6, 1949; *Oway,* Rangoon, Dec. 9, 1949.

[6] Tibor Mende, *South-East Asia between Two Worlds* (1954), 8.

tablets hardly took the place of ancestral bones. Belief in spirits and sorcery, by contrast, suffered little or no impairment. The proper observance of ancestral rites was regarded as especially important in the office of the Emperor, because the wisdom and aid of the royal clan was traditionally a guarantee of good crops and national welfare generally. Hence arose the distress of conservative-minded partisans when the Gallicized Emperor Bao Dai on August 22, 1945, at the time of his abdication, consigned the care of the royal temples to the nationalist Communist regime of Ho Chi Minh. The sophisticated minority of Vietnamese who questioned traditional spirit cults was very small.[7] A Swedish-American archaeologist tells of his prewar success in allaying popular anxieties by employing a Taoist priest, who was allegedly expert in spirit control, to guarantee that the spirits of a mound being excavated would cause no trouble.

In the northern Malay states, where Islamic orthodoxy was particularly strong, older traditions protruded at many points. Spirit mediums often enjoyed high social status and generous incomes, frequently making their varied incantations in the name of Allah. Shamans made the Mecca pilgrimage. Sabbath observance, attendance at weekly services in the mosque, and the memorization of selected passages from the Koran did not inhibit the faithful observance of pre-Islamic rites. The onset of the planting season witnessed the customary traditional slaughter of sacrificial animals, and the shamans officiated as always in the transplanting and harvest rites. The blade of a hidden ritual knife, furtively wielded, cut the first stalk of ripened grain. Animist offerings also persisted in the fishing industry in connection with boats, nets, and the sea spirits.

Hindu influences also survived in Muslim Malaya. Hindu temples, figures, and relics may have suffered destruction from Muslim iconoclastic zeal, but the Malay words for fasting, teacher, heaven, and hell were still Sanskrit in origin. Hindu ritual was openly practiced in the enthronement of the sultans, as was also the case in coronations in Buddhist Siam and Cambodia. Traditional shadow plays depicting the *Ramayana* legend used Hindu invocations, usually with an Islamic creedal addendum, which served to legitimize the rite. Hindu purification ceremonies in the life-cycle rhythms still involved references to Śiva and to *Sufi* Muslim godlings.[8] Whereas Islam itself posited the principle of democratic equality within the faith, mainly as a protest against caste stratification, surviving nobility status in Malay related to pre-Islamic traditions. Muslim scribal influence in Java also derived in part from indigenous magico-religious notions.

A central problem in Indonesia, as elsewhere, was the reexamination of traditional forms and selective evaluation of Western culture in the light of local needs and world conditions. Actual innovations were largely improvisations and trial-and-error adaptations not based on any

[7] Landon, 192–200.

[8] N. Ginsburg and C. F. Roberts, *Malaya* (1958), 226–233, 316–346.

such deliberate appraisal. Within the context of the principles of Muslim brotherhood and communal village adat traditions, democracy had potential appeal to Indonesians, although the postwar governmental pattern was far from clear. In considering political and social problems, Islam used a scholastic rather than an inductive approach, thus avoiding the risks of making rational comparisons. Not subject to question was the truth of the Koranic faith and the unity of the Islamic community, which could not encompass the idea of the neutrality of the state between true and false religions. The Western principle of freedom of religion was anemic in comparison to the spiritual potency of Islam. Modernist Indonesian leadership as represented in President Sukarno, for example, tended to avoid offending orthodoxy while blunting the sharpness of religious sectarianism.[9]

The polarization of modernist and traditionalist views, which occurred throughout Southeast Asia, created many problems. It usually increased youthful disrespect for teachers, elders, and family control, leading at times to a repudiation of basic moral and social standards. Modernist solvents thus threatened to destroy the traditional past before any constructive deposit from the West could be appropriated. Postwar educational standards were generally lower than prewar. Informed Burman observers have estimated that it may take a generation or more to recover the not-excessively-high instructional levels of the prewar period. Premier U Nu's asserted confidence in the nation's ability to blend the old and the new revealed an awareness of the problem, even though the affirmation itself was little more than an act of faith. "We can be faithful to our past, yet live consciously and gladly in the twentieth century. We can be proudly independent, yet a willing partner in the community of nations. We can blend successfully the religious values of our heritage with the benefits of modern technology."[10] Such aspirations were more easily affirmed than realized.

## Historic Rivalries and Relationships

The roles of the postwar independent states of Southeast Asia were also heavily conditioned by history in their relations with each other, especially when they were immediate neighbors. Siam's tradition, dating from the time of Rama Khamheng in the thirteenth century, was to seek accommodation with the dominant outside power in the area. At first this meant China; then came Ayuthia's flirtation with the Dutch and French in the nearly disastrous experience in the seventeenth century. The policy was resumed in 1850, with Britain in the favored position until Japan ap-

[9] C. A. O. Van Nieuwenhuijze, *Aspects of Islam in Post-Colonial Indonesia* (1958), 86–108, 180–181.

[10] Union of Burma, Economic and Social Board, *Pyidawtha, the New Burma* (1954), 8; *The Progress,* Rangoon, Aug. 8 and Dec. 5, 1949.

peared on the horizon in the 1930s. After World War II, the United States of America was accorded the leading role, presumably until such time as China or India or Japan might again establish primacy in Southeast Asia.

Historic rivalries also carried over. Siam's political traditions included hostility to the Burmese, the Cambodians, the Vietnamese, and northern Malays. Hostility between hill peoples of the Indochina cordillera and the Vietnamese was also traditional. The rivalry of North Vietnam and South Vietnam had a long and painful tradition behind it. The jealousies existing between the various peoples of the Indonesian archipelago, long held in abeyance by Dutch overlordship, were almost sure to reemerge in time unless some generous arrangement for local autonomy could be devised. The persisting feud between Christian and Moro peoples in the Philippines reflected another long-established tradition. Burma's Karens, Shans, and Arakanese feared the prospect of Burman rule.

Interregional rivalries and differences did not immediately erupt into open conflict in every situation, but the potentiality of strife was present. Such factors have helped to prevent meaningful integration of Southeast Asia both politically and economically. Security needs and complementary economic relationships in capital, technology, and commerce would seem to encourage, then, the development of associations outside the region in a larger world context. But it became urgently necessary, after the recovery of independence, that the Southeast Asian peoples should come to know each other better and to share their cultural achievements and social aspirations. A basis for wholesome competition in nonpolitical achievement must be sought. The several countries did agree at Bandung in 1955 to resist any revived imperialist threat from whatever quarter, but the greater probability was that each would try individually to stay out of harm's way while seeking aid, if and when needed, from outside the region itself.

Historic relations of Southeast Asian peoples with India and China also established certain presumptions which affected postwar developments. Demographic pressures from both giant Asian neighbors may be expected to increase, but the favorable conditions for Indian and Chinese immigration to Southeast Asia which prevailed under the period of European dominance no longer obtain. Politically vigorous native governments generally kept the upper hand despite the superior industry and business ability of the Chinese. A special situation existed in the Federation of Malaya and Singapore, where the Chinese constituted a plurality and where Islam made the assimilation of ethnic groups difficult. The Malaysian Federation agreement of 1962 redressed the ethnic balance. The most decidedly anti-Chinese governments were those functioning more or less under American protection—the Philippines, South Vietnam, and Thailand. Under Pandit Nehru's leadership, India's diplomatic and cultural influence continued to be strong, but any direct political or economic impact on Southeast Asia by India remained only a remote possibility. The Indian immigrant was generally more strongly disliked than the Chinese.

## The Problem of Chinese Relations

The most important outside political factor with roots in the historic tradition was China's time-honored assumption of suzerainty over peoples living beyond its southern borders. This was associated with the "ineffable and softly arrogant" Chinese consciousness of superiority over all other peoples and countries. The attitude, instinctive and racial rather than ideological, is some two thousand years old.[11] It still conditions the policies pursued by a resurgent China in relation to Southeast Asia, and has also influenced the responses of the people of the area. The Chinese have been the particular enemy of the North Vietnamese, whose fear of political domination from China persists among all shades of nationalist opinion including the Viet Minh. Except when both are faced by a common danger, the Communist affinity between Hanoi and Peking may be regarded as superficial by comparison.

The Burmese have been determined since the war to maintain friendly relations with China by refraining from the mistreatment of resident Chinese and by trying quite sensibly to avoid making their land again a battlefield. A Burmese proverb runs, "The grass is trampled when buffaloes fight." Rangoon was grateful during the 1950s that Red China did not exploit the Kuomintang provocation developing within Burma's eastern Shan States, and became correspondingly suspicious of United States failure to restrain Formosa, which seemed to threaten to embroil Burma in conflict with China. Article 3 of the Burma-China boundary treaty, concluded in 1961, pledged nonaggression from both sides and registered Burma's agreement not to permit its territory to be used for future military operations again China. Peking may be expected to pursue similar diplomatic objectives with other Southeast Asian states. Indonesia adopted a similar policy of promoting accord with Communist China. The islanders received in return a concession from Peking granting for the first time permissory Indonesian citizenship for Chinese residents of Indonesia. The Indonesian Communist Party became more directly affiliated with Peking than with Moscow. The presence of eight to ten million overseas Chinese in Southeast Asia adds to the urgency of Peking's still-unfulfilled objective to reestablish some semblance of its historic overlordship.

It cannot be assumed that any overt effort on the part of Red China to dominate Southeast Asia by arms would be passively accepted within the region. The other side of the coin of traditional Chinese suzerainty is the historic tradition of successful Southeast Asian resistance to actual physical domination. The Communists of neither Vietnam nor Burma would welcome Chinese military invasion. In the long run, ideological factors may well play only an incidental role in China's future political relations with Southeast Asia.

[11] *The Times of London,* Aug. 20, 1961.

The attitude of the overseas Chinese toward Red China differs markedly from that of the indigenous population. The former welcome a strong China which can protect them against discriminatory treatment, often in spite of Peking's Communist character. In leftist Rangoon bookstores during the 1950s, Chinese Marxist literature went begging, while reproductions of Chinese masterpieces of painting had a wide appeal. Cultural and racial pride among overseas Chinese far outstripped their Communist enthusiasm. Chinese Communist propaganda has for the most part concentrated on trying to attract the positive support of Nanyang Chinese in preference to improving Red China's relations with most Southeast Asian Communist parties. Java may be an exception. Peking's agencies have consistently sought control of the schools and the press and of the sources of business credit. The official Chinese Commission on Overseas Affairs included, from 1949, representatives from Southeast Asia. It was also concerned with encouraging cash remittances to China from the area in foreign currencies and sending students back to China for advanced study. This kind of Communist program appeared to relate more directly to bridging political divisions among the Chinese themselves than to any plot for the overthrow of indigenous nationalist regimes. This was true particularly when the local governments were willing, like the regimes in Burma and Indonesia, to come to terms diplomatically.

## *The Potency of Traditional Symbols of Authority*

Despite the repeated shuffling of ruling cliques at Bangkok, the authority of Thailand's governmental structure demonstrated more stability than any other in Southeast Asia during the postwar period. No seriously disturbing events developed from the series of political somersaults. The elected Parliament served mainly to afford patronage opportunities for provincial leadership. The Parliament building itself was situated appropriately apart from the real seat of authority and seemingly vied with movies and filling stations in Bangkok as a superficial symbol of modernization. Meanwhile, the royal princes retained their social prestige and served usefully in the diplomatic corps as well as in the professions and in education. The continued presence of the King and the symbols of royal authority in Bangkok contributed much to the authority of the government, and the traditional inertia behind the bureaucracy was an additional stabilizing factor. The popular potency of royal prestige was demonstrated briefly in the mid-1950s when the King was allowed for a brief time to tour the countryside. So unreserved was the people's expression of allegiance that the military leadership promptly put the ruler back into his palace cage. The development in time of an increasingly articulate educated middle class could provide Thailand with the civilian leadership needed for a genuinely democratic system of government. This prospect was admittedly distant, but the continuing vitality of traditional symbols of authority apparently afforded time for an evolutionary approach, even though solutions to some basic problems were being postponed.[12]

Postwar problems in Thailand were manifold. They were related to the domination of government by military cliques, the decline of popular participation in administrative functions at local levels under pressure of increasing interference from the center, the prevalence of official corruption, and the general inefficiency of governmentally administered economic monopolies. Efforts to develop a dynamic state-planned economy ran aground on the lack of capital and experience in business matters and technology and the indiscipline and ineffectiveness of the Bangkok administration. A principal source of postwar government income was the state monopoly of rice exports at a time when world prices far exceeded those in Thailand.

The same persistence of the traditional symbols of authority was present in Cambodia, Laos, northern Borneo, and the Federation of Malaya. Even during the confused civil war in Laos, the three opposing parties were all represented by princely spokesmen. Except for Malaya, these countries demonstrated little or no prospect of progress toward increased popular participation in government. In Malaya, the several political tensions developing at various levels—sultan's authority versus popular elections, rivalry between Malays and Chinese, and friction within the ranks of the dominant Malay-Chinese Alliance Party itself—gave promise of persisting indefinitely. But the postwar acceptance in Malaya of a plan for self-government, to be progressively achieved, was a tribute to British tutelage and a victory for a peaceful and orderly approach to a baffling problem.

In the Philippines, the constitutional structure was well established before the war. Following a near collapse of democracy under the arbitrary Quirino regime (1948–1953), the Filipino electorate demonstrated in the 1953 election that it could, with vigorous popular leadership, make its wishes effective. An entrenched party was turned out of office, and a reform administration was installed without inciting rebellion or violent protest. Under pressure from Filipino politicians to attract voters' approval, political aspirants must of necessity continue to take some cognizance of popular desires. Until the nearly identical Filipino party organizations can be rescued from the control of entrenched politicos, who are little concerned with reform measures, the peasants will probably be unable to generate genuine enthusiasm for democratic processes.

## *Waning Symbols of Authority: Burma and Vietnam*

In the three states which experienced revolution in the postwar period—Burma, Indochina, and Indonesia—the problem of sustaining

[12] Rupert Emerson, *Representative Government in Southeast Asia* (1955), 145–150; John Coast, *Some Aspects of Siamese Politics* (1953), 41–58.

governmental authority took different forms. The modernizing elite leaders in all three had to start virtually from scratch. Lacking both the traditional credentials of ruling status and substantial economic power, they assumed authority arbitrarily but tried at the same time to enlist popular backing of their programs. This contradiction in political principles was particularly evident in the centralized direction of programs of planned economic development, which presumably could not wait for the leisurely processes of persuasion and popular consent. While attempting to elicit a mass following to make good their lack of ruling credentials, the new elite exploited to the full their patriotic reputations to justify their exercise of arbitrary power.

The approach varied with personalities and circumstances. Premier Nu of Burma buttressed his position of leadership within the Anti-Fascist Peoples' Freedom League (AFPFL) by establishing rapport with the Burmese population as a patron and devotee of Buddhism and as one who shared popular traditions and folklore. His inefficiency as an administrator, coupled with the emergence of tensions within the AFPFL elite involving both personalities and policies, led in 1958 and 1962 to impositions of army control as the only apparent means of maintaining national unity.

A sharp contrast was presented in the character of the successor governments within French Indochina. Following Emperor Bao Dai's abdication in 1945, communism and anti-imperialist nationalism became solidly entrenched in North Vietnam, operating through the agency of party dictatorship. French cultural alignments were gradually displaced by connections with Moscow, except for the continued use of the French language and regard for French scholarship. The contrasting regime of Ngo Dinh Diem in South Vietnam after 1954 was artificial, partly because Ngo was Catholic and felt obliged to use relatives and friends in key positions in the government. He also incurred the hostility of the French by his acceptance of assistance from America. France had preserved its cultural attachments with the educated minority of Cochin-China even after French political influence evaporated. In postwar Laos and Cambodia, the local authorities welcomed continued French aid for a time, but the rift was unavoidable. Titular rulers continued to exercise real authority despite novel political developments. French businessmen continued active in Cambodia, and several hundred French teachers served in Laotian schools as late as 1960.[13]

## Postwar Government in Indonesia

The problems faced by President Sukarno's government in the Republic of Indonesia in relation to traditional standards of authority were in

[13] Bernard Fall, *Le Viet-Minh* (1960), 336–349; *The Times of London,* Aug. 1, 1949, 11.

many respects similar to those of Nu in Burma. Sukarno's republican regime lacked rootage in customary law and in traditional religious symbolism. Comradeship in armed revolution and in politics did not authenticate the claims of the youthful ruling clique to the bona fide allegiance and submission of many of Indonesia's peoples, who sensed a difference between such "ordinary" people and the traditional princely-ruler class. Those in the lower branches of the ruling bureaucracy paid such abject deference to superiors who were responsible for decisions that individual initiative was virtually eliminated. Younger officers of the army, by contrast, often acted independently of their commanding officers, a habit carried over from their rebellious role in fighting Dutch control. Ethnic schisms developing within the army also impaired discipline, and the army tended also to ignore civilian authority.[14] After the elapse of a decade, traditional social habits and personal jealousies served to dry up much of the postwar nationalist idealism. The new Indonesian elite thus developed little or no identification with the worker and peasant population, especially in the Outer Islands, and tended to become in some regions almost as alien as the Dutch had been. As morale sagged and declared objectives went unrealized, the original fervor gave way to disillusionment and self-seeking.

Democracy held out little prospect of improving the situation in Indonesia in view of the multiplicity of Indonesian parties and the divergence of interests.[15] Economic output declined because investment funds were lacking, and the entrepreneurial functions previously performed by the Dutch and the Chinese went unattended. Lacking also was the disciplined regimentation needed to restore prewar levels of production.[16] President Sukarno became in time an advocate of a centralized program of "guided democracy" in an endeavor to exploit the revolutionary fervor of Communist partisans, who also opposed particularism and multiparty rule. His *Pantja Sila* ideal included faith in Allah and devotion to nationality, humanity, democracy, and social justice; but the precise meanings were unclear, and implementation was sadly lacking. Sukarno's attempt to bridge the chasm between Islam and communism incurred the inevitable risk that he would alienate both sides and thus compromise the achievement of any espoused objectives.[17] Within this highly unstable situation the Indonesian army remained strongly anticommunist and politically important, while the moderate Socialists enlisted no popular following.[18]

[14] B. H. M. Vlekke, *Indonesia in 1956: Political and Economic Aspects* (1957), 8–9.

[15] James H. Mysberg, "The Indonesian Elite," *FES,* XXVI (1957), 38–42; Emerson, 24–40.

[16] W. F. Wertheim, *Indonesian Society in Transition* (1956), 120–131.

[17] Van Nieuwenhuijze, 180–243; Emerson, 24–40; Leslie Palmier, "Sukarno the Nationalist," *Pacific Affairs,* XXX (1957), 101–119.

[18] Statement by Soedjatmoko.

## The Political Future of Southeast Asia

Whether democratic government can take root and survive in South-east Asia is a moot question. A helpful carry-over from the colonial period was the idea that progress toward self-government and independence was to be measured in terms of increased popular representation in elective assemblies. But nationalism, once in control, was more likely to express itself in traditional than in alien patterns of government. Because no popular demand for democratic liberties existed in Thailand, for example, constitutions and elections provided little more than an empty façade, a pretense of modernization. The resulting attitude of political apathy and passivity on the part of the Thai population generally afforded opportunity for dictatorship and authoritarian direction.

In many areas where the traditional basis of rule by hereditary chiefs and divine rulers had worn thin, single-party rule and dictatorship became likely alternatives to a democracy which commanded little popular confidence. In situations where the Western elite were largely absorbed into the bureaucracy, the gap between the governors and the governed was likely to remain unbridged. Until a politically active middle class should appear, possessed of articulate ideas as to what could and ought to be done, the cause of political liberty and freedom of speech, press, and religion would hardly survive to constitute an urgent objective of political aspiration.[19]

Faced with the postwar threat of Communist intrusion into Southeast Asia, Western governments tended to follow the negative tactic of supporting the traditionalist enemies of the Communist system. Such a policy often ignored the need for constructive adjustments between the old order and the new through the selective appropriation of useful elements of Western culture. If such essential adjustments were blocked by traditionalist barriers, the proponents of a radical version of modernization would inevitably undertake to sweep such hindrances aside.

Marxism commended itself to many progressively minded persons in Southeast Asia as an ultramodern short cut to industrialization. The centuries-old liberal British, American, and French systems seemed old-fashioned by comparison. The U.S.S.R. accomplished an impressive economic transformation within a generation; democracy and private capitalism, by contrast, seemed to lack positive direction and also left traditionalism undisturbed. The more rapid Communist techniques of economic and political regimentation could presumably avoid the compromises inherent in the more gradual processes of democratic adjustment. An effective regional pattern of integration covering both economic and security needs might conceivably provide a framework for utilizing much-needed outside assist-

[19] Emerson, 166–170; M. N. Roy, "Democracy and Nationalism in Asia," *Pacific Affairs,* XXV (1952), 140–141.

ance free of the dangers of revival of imperialist control. The Southeast Asia Treaty Organization (SEATO), which was sponsored by Western governments and included only two countries of Southeast Asia, did not fully meet this requirement.

## Epilogue

Historical study involves the conviction that events of the past can become meaningful if viewed interrelatedly in proper time perspective. It demands the careful description of related phenomena placed in chronological sequence and interpreted in broad contexts. If prepared objectively and judiciously, such historical knowledge can contribute to better understanding, and from understanding can presumably come vision and wisdom. In other words, the ultimate truth of history is qualitative in character; it is more than an accumulation of facts. It is always relative and approximate in character rather than definitive or absolute, since deeper insights always await perception in the light of additional evidence. Relativity is particularly characteristic in a field of study as new as the history of Southeast Asia where many interpretations are in dispute. The regional approach does provide a useful and necessary context, even though the approach may seem to involve some overlappings and frequent artificial inclusions and limitations.

If historical truth so developed possesses value in its own right, the West can expect to learn *from* Southeast Asia as well as *about* Southeast Asia. When the Burma Buddha Mission was launched in 1950 for the purpose of strengthening and purifying the faith at home and propagating it abroad, the Rangoon press declared that the world's great religions must join hands in the endeavor to curb moral degeneracy and irreligion, greed, anger, ignorance, and the threat of war.[20] The potential gains in cultural interchange were regarded as obvious. Great possibilities also await intercultural relations in literature and art, now that the creators of Borobudur, Angkor, Pagan, and Ayuthia are free to give expression to their valuable insights and talents. Similarly the ideals of Hindu philosophy and Buddhist monasticism have conditioned many thoughtful Southeast Asians to seek happiness, not by the restless acquisitive effort characteristic of the West, but by curbing personal needs and desires. The furniture of life must not be permitted to overwhelm the spirit. Some of them have questioned the ethical legitimacy of an industrial society, with its use of advertising to stimulate desire, the anonymity of its regimented labor, and the unrestrained rivalry for profits and survival.

One of the wisest of modern Indians stated the issue with moving eloquence, as follows:

[20] *New Light of Burma,* Rangoon, Oct. 6, 1950; *The Burman,* Rangoon, Oct. 8, 1950; *Bama Khit,* Rangoon, Dec. 27, 1950.

*In these carnivals of national materialism are not the western peoples spending most of their vital energy in merely producing things and neglecting the creation of ideals? And can civilization ignore the law of moral health and go on in its endless . . . gorging upon material things? . . . Pride . . . breeds blindness in the end. Like all artificial stimulants, its first effect is a heightening of consciousness and then with increasing doses it muddles and brings exaltation that is misleading. Europe has gradually grown hardened in her pride of all her . . . habits. . . . This is why she is growing incapable of imparting to the East what is best in herself and of accepting in a right spirit the wisdom of the East. . . . Those who gloat over their extension of dominion over foreign races gradually surrender their own freedom and humanity to organizations necessary for holding peoples in slavery. The doom which is waiting to overtake them is as certain as death, for man's truth is moral truth, and his emancipation is in the spiritual life.*[21]

Another observer has suggested that the steppingstones are too far apart to facilitate a smooth transition from traditionalism to modernism in Southeast Asia. Those who seek to use the stones face the danger of falling between. But if faltering nations are able to establish their historical and cultural bearings, they can rise in midstream and resume their way, however painfully, toward a promising future. Perhaps the end result will be something quite new—the combined product of Western inspiration and the genius of the peoples of Southeast Asia.[22] It is to the hope that something can here be contributed to requisite perspective and understanding that this study is dedicated.

[21] Rabindranath Tagore, quoted in D. M. Brown, *The White Umbrella* (1953), 112–113. Used by permission of the University of California Press.

[22] From Landon, *Southeast Asia: Crossroads of Religion* (1947), 202–203.

*Chronology*
*of Historical Developments*
*by Regions and Countries*

| | ROME and INDIA | BURMA'S MONS, PYU | MALAY ISTHMUS |
|---|---|---|---|
| 0 | Heavy trade, Mediterranean eastward | Mon contacts with south India and Telingana; Thaton as capital | |
| | Vespasian halts export of bullion | | |
| | Indian trade shift to Southeast Asia | Use of Meklong River portage route | |
| | | | Portages: Takuapa to Chaiya |
| | Roman missions cross Southeast Asia en route to China by sea | | Trang to Ligor Kedah to Patani |
| | | Pyu Śrikshetra | |
| 200 | Pallavan influence | Overland trade with China | |
| | | | Origins of states: Tun-sun |
| | | Cultural borrowing from India | Kolo P'an P'an |
| | Gupta influence, peak of Indian culture | | Increased Indianization |
| 400 | | Appearance of: | Funan control includes the isthmian region and shores of Gulf of Siam |
| | | Vishnu cult Buddhism Divine kingship | |
| | | Mon influence to Haripunjaya and Lavo | |
| | Impact of Chola Tamil influence | | |
| | Decline of Gupta Influence | Pyu control of Arakan and Irrawaddy Valley | |
| 500 | Pallavan (Telegu) influence from India's Deccan | | |
| | | | Emergence of independent: Dvaravati |
| 600 | | | Tambralinga |
| | | | Lankasuka |
| | Pala rule in north India; Nalanda | Rising Mon power in Lower Burma | |

| FUNAN to CHENLA | CHAMPA and VIETNAM | MALACCA STRAITS | JAVA and INDIES | |
|---|---|---|---|---|
| | | | | 0 |
| Mythical Kaundinya I | Vietnam under Han China control | | | |
| Port of Go Oc Eo in lower Mekong delta | | Pirate-infested and little used | | |
| | Champa founded (K'iu-lien) | | | |
| | | | | 200 |
| Fan Shih-man | | | Poss-ŭ China trade | |
| | | Kedah port | | |
| Fan Hsun | | | | |
| | Fan Yi | Palembang on lower Sumatra | Taruma in West Java | |
| Chu Chan-t'an | Fan Fo Bhadravarman | | Purnavarman in West Java | |
| | | | | 400 |
| | Fan dynasty rulers, seven of them | | | |
| Kaundinya II | | Fa-Hsien's journey via Java or Borneo | | |
| Jayavarman | | | | |
| | | | Indianization of Java | |
| | | | | 500 |
| | Rudravarman I | Predominance of Kedah-Lankasuka state | | |
| | Sambhuvarman | | | |
| Chenla's Bhavavarman I | | | | |
| Funan collapses | | | | 600 |
| Chenla's | | | T'ang China encourages trade revival | |
| | | Palembang and Malayu trade | | |
| Isanavarman I | | | | |
| | Bhadresvaravarman | | | |
| Jayavarman I | | Śrivijayan Empire I-ching's visits | Simo, central Javan ruler | |

| | INDIA and WEST | PYU, MONS, BURMANS | CAMBODIA |
|---|---|---|---|
| 700 | Pala (Nalanda) influence in north India | Arakan state | Land Chenla in upper Mekong Valley |
| | | Nan Chao Shans press from Yunnan | Multiple states in Water Chenla |
| | | Śrikshetra falls | |
| 800 | | | Jayavarman II (from Java?) |
| | Development of Arab-Persian trade to China | Fall of Pyu capital Halingyi to Nan Chao Shans | |
| | | | Devaraja cult established |
| | | Burman intrusion at Kyaukse granary | |
| | | | Impact of Nalanda culture |
| | | Burman expansion to Minbu and Shwebo granaries | |
| | | | Yasovarman I |
| 900 | | Mon rule in Lower Burma from Thaton | Yasoharapura founded (Angkor site) |
| | Negapatam shrine in south India for Indies pilgrims | Burmans found Pagan capital | Rajendravarman II Jayavarman V |
| | | | Banteay Srei Phnom Bakeng Champa wars Sujita at Lavo |
| 1000 | Islam reaches northwest India | Mon Confederacy of Ramanyadesa, disrupted | Suryavarman I from isthmus and Lavo |
| | Tamil Cholas take Ceylon and attack Śrivijaya | | Khmer monuments: Takeo |
| | | Emergence of Pagan dynasty | Phimenakas Baphoun |
| | | Aniruddha | |
| | | Close Ceylon connections | Rebellions and popular unrest |
| | Revival of Negapatam shrine | Thiluin Man and the Ananda temple | |
| | | Myazedi inscription in Pyu, Mon, Burmese | |
| 1100 | Gujerati cloth to Java for spices | Cansu I and the Thatpyinnu temple | Suryavarman II Angkor Wat |

| ŚRIVIJAYA | JAVA and INDIES | CHAMPA and NAM VIET | CHINA | |
|---|---|---|---|---|
| Trading empire | Sanjaya and the Śailendras | Vikrantavarman I and II of Champa | T'ang dynasty Encouragement of seaborne trade | 700 |
| Buddhist center | Forays against Champa | | | |
| | | Nam Viet under T'ang rule | | |
| | | Indravarman I | | 800 |
| | Kedu Valley monuments Borobudur Chandi Mendut Chandi Pawan | | | |
| | | | Persian and Arab traders in South China | |
| Śailendra rule from Java | Śaivite kingdom of Mataram | | Persians sack Canton | |
| | | Indravarman II of Champapura | | |
| Modulation to Śiva cult | | | | |
| | | | | 900 |
| Decline of China trade | | Independence of Nam Viet from China | Decline and collapse of T'ang rule | |
| | Sindok, ruler of east Java | | | |
| | | Temporary vogue of Buddhism and Javan art and religion | | |
| | The Prabanan shrines | | Emergence of Sungs | |
| Revival of China trade; Sungs | Dharmavamsa vs. Śrivijayan trade policies | Feuding along the Annam coast | Canton trading agency established | |
| Javanese attacks are defeated | | | Śrivijayan and Javan embassies | |
| Loss of north isthmus to Cambodia | Downfall of Mataram by Śrivijaya | | | 1000 |
| Chola attacks from south India | Emergence of Airlangga's Kediri | Annamese capture of Cham Vijaya | Active promotion of Southeast Asian trade | |
| Revival of empire at Jambi | Development of Molucca-Indian spice trade via the Sunda Straits | | | |
| Decline of Śrivijayan political influence | | Khmer capture of Vijaya | Decline of Sung trade with Southeast Asia | 1100 |

| | BURMA | SIAM | CAMBODIA |
|---|---|---|---|
| 1150 | "War" with Ceylon | | Angkor destroyed by Chams |
| | Cansu II and the Gawdawpawlin | | Jayavarman VII avenges the Cham attack |
| | | Thai-Shan intrusions southward from China | |
| | Sulamani pagoda | | Annexation of Champa for a time |
| 1200 | Natonmya's Htilominlo temple | | Angkor Thom and Bayon |
| | | Sukhotai founded | |
| | Mongol threats and invasion | Fall of Nan Chao | |
| | | | Loss of Menam Valley and isthmus to Siamese |
| | Fall of Pagan; Wareru over Mons; Shan brothers' rule at Kyaukse | Rama Khamheng founds state of Siam | Indravarman III |
| 1300 | | | |
| | Ava founded | Ayuthia founded by Rama T'ibodi | Thai invasion to Tonle Sap and Angkor area |
| | Kings Binnyu to Razarit at Pegu | | |
| | | Siamese attack Khmers | |
| 1400 | Independence of Arakan | | |
| | | Boromoraja Destruction of Angkor | Angkor area abandoned |
| | | Boromo Trailok | Lovek as capital |
| | Mohnyin Shan tribes harass Ava | Thai suzerainty over Malay states | |
| 1500 | | | |
| | Mohnyin Shans destroy Ava | | |
| | Toungoo dynasty | | |
| | Tabinshweti | | |
| | Bayinnaung | | |
| | Capture of Pegu | Burmese invasions | Temporary return to Angkor |
| | Attacks on Siam and Laos | Ayuthia recovers Angkor | Escapades of Veloso and Ruiz |

| MALAYA-SUMATRA | VIETNAM-CHAMPA | INDONESIA-PHILIPPINES | CHINA | |
|---|---|---|---|---|
| Decline of Śrivijaya | Chams destroy Angkor | | | 1150 |
| | Jayavarman VII takes vengeance on Champa | | Sung decline | |
| | | Collapse of Kediri | | 1200 |
| Disintegration of Śrivijaya | Champa annexed to Cambodia temporarily | | Mongols dominate North China borders | |
| | | Emergence of Senghasari in east Java | Mongol conquest of Nan Chao and Hanoi | |
| Jambi's leadership | Kublai's army captures Hanoi | Kertanagara's rule Mongol invasion of Java | Conquest of Sungs by Kublai | |
| Visit of Polo and the Mongol fleet | Defeat of repeated Mongol invasions | Majapahit displaces Senghasari | Mongol attacks on Southeast Asia | |
| | | | Decline of Mongol influence in Southeast Asia | 1300 |
| Muslim entry into ports of Sumatra: Pasai, Pedir, Kampar, Acheh | Vietnamese press southward at expense of Champa | Gaja Mada era Majapahit pressure on: Bali, Madura, Sunda | Mings replace the Mongols | |
| Founding of Malacca Paramesvara Chinese fleet visits | | Rising power and trade of north Javanese port cities | Cheng-ho's seven voyages to Southeast Asia and Indian Ocean | 1400 |
| Kedah and Patani turn Muslim Tun Ali of Malacca Tun Perak | Final collapse of Cham Vijaya Chams try to turn Muslim to get aid | Javanese commercial connections with Malacca trade in cloth and spices | Mings lose interest in Southeast Asia | |
| Tun Mutahir | | Decline of Majapahit | | 1500 |
| Portuguese capture Malacca | | | Mings rebuff the Portuguese contacts | |
| Attacks by: Acheh Javanese Johore | Vietnamese invade the Mekong delta | Javanese attack Portuguese Malacca Spanish at Manila | Macao to Portugal | |
| Portuguese peace with Acheh | | Interior Mataram dominates Java | | |

| | INDIA | BURMA | SIAM-CAMBODIA | VIETNAM |
|---|---|---|---|---|
| **1600** | Portuguese in Macao, Ceylon, Bengal islands | De Brito episode | | Prolonged feuding, Trinh versus Nguyen |
| | | Burman Ava versus Mon Pegu | Dutch-Chinese trading predominance | Alexander of Rhodes and French mission |
| | Shah Jahan and the Taj Mahal | | | |
| | European trade dominance; Dutch take Ceylon | | Cambodian vassalage to both Siam and Vietnam | Feuding finally ends |
| | | | French missions | Shares vassalage over Cambodia |
| | | Revival of Pegu | Phaulkon affair | |
| | British at Madras and Bombay | | Isolationist policy | Ming refugees to Mekong delta |
| **1700** | Collapse of Mogul power in India | | | |
| | French take Madras temporarily | Mons overrun Ava | Siamese control over Laos areas | |
| | Robert Clive versus French and Bengal | Alaungpaya and the Konbaung dynasty | Burman wars and destruction of Ayuthia | Pierre Poivre episode |
| | Licensed "country" vessels in China and Southeast Asian trade | Siam invasions Ayuthia destroyed | | Tay-son rebellion |
| | | Chinese invasion repelled | | Pigneau de Behaine and Nguyen Anh |
| | Hastings to Cornwallis to Wellesley | Conquest of Arakan | The Chakri dynasty: Rama I | |
| **1800** | | Symes's missions Bodawpaya to Bagyidaw | Rama II | Emperor Gia Long |
| | Bentinck | | Crawfurd mission | French influence declines under Minh Mang |
| | | First British war Loss of Arakan and Tenasserim | Rama III | |
| | | | Burney mission; American treaty | Thieu Tri to Tu Duc |
| | Dalhousie | Second British war Loss of Lower Burma | Rama IV (Mongkut); Bowring treaty | French at Tourane and Saigon |
| | Sepoy Rebellion End of Company rule | Mindon | French assume suzerainty over Cambodia | Rule of the admirals |
| | | Lower Burma as India province | Rama V (Chulalongkorn) | |
| | Opening of Suez Canal trade | Rapid agricultural development | Modernization with foreign advisors | Lagrée and Garnier |
| | | China trade issue; Thibaw and third war | | Tongking control |
| | | | Loss of Mekong areas to France | Pavie and Laos de Lanessan |
| | Indian Empire includes Burma kingdom | Annexation and pacification | | Doumer's role |
| | | Economic development | | |

| MALAYA | NETHERLANDS INDIES | PHILIPPINES | CHINA-JAPAN | |
|---|---|---|---|---|
| | | | Tokugawa rule | 1600 |
| Portuguese Malacca declines in favor of Acheh, Siam, and Dutch traders | Dutch end Portuguese spice monopoly | Spanish at Ternate | Decline of Mings | |
| | Batavia founded, defended against Mataram Java | Periodic Dutch attacks on Manila | Manchu dynasty | |
| Dutch capture Malacca and Portuguese Ceylon | Dutch control of Sunda area of Java | Missionary failure in China and Japan | Chinese intervention in Burma | |
| Dutch neglect Malacca trade | Conquest of Java, Macassar, Moluccas | Importance of clergy in local government and land-holding | Emperor K'ang Hsi | |
| Sultanates are vassal to Siam | Pattern of Asian trade develops | The galleon trade | Rites controversy | 1700 |
| | The coffee-tribute system | | Missionaries expelled from China | |
| | Strife with Java Chinese | | The Co-hong trade system at Canton | |
| | | British capture Manila | Growth of opium trade from India | |
| British acquire Penang Island base | Bankruptcy of Dutch Company | Charles III and reforms | | |
| American participation in Southeast Asia, China, India trade | Involvement in the American war | Tobacco-culture monopoly | MacCartney mission to China | |
| | End of the Dutch Company | Severance of connections with New Spain | | 1800 |
| British occupy Malacca and straits | Daendels in Java | | Amherst mission | |
| Raffles founds Singapore | Raffles in Java | Direct ties to Spain | | |
| The Straits Settlements | Dutch recover Indies except the Malay Peninsula | Anticlerical nationalism | Opium War; opening of Chinese ports | |
| Clearing piracy from the straits | Culture system of production | Colorum and Katipunan rebellions | Opening of Japan | |
| | British Sarawak, Brunei, North Borneo | Manila bankrupted | Arrow war | |
| Chinese-Malay feuding | *Max Havelaar* Liberal policy introduced | José Rizal | Meiji restoration | |
| | | Aguinaldo | | |
| British intervention in tin-area sultanates | Dutch war with Acheh for a quarter century | United States defeat of Spain | Sino-Japanese War Japan in Formosa | |
| Federation of Malaya formed | Inception of the Ethical policy | Annexation of islands | | |

| | INDIA | BURMA | SIAM | FRENCH INDOCHINA |
|---|---|---|---|---|
| **1900** | Congress Party development | The YMBA | Loss to France of: Laos and Mekong enclaves | Economic development on mercantilist lines |
| | Minto-Morley Reforms | Burma Research Society | Battambang Siemreap | French take from Siam: Mekong enclaves |
| | | | Surrender of Malay suzerainty claims | Battambang Siemreap |
| | Cooperation in World War I | Governor Harcourt Butler | Sides with Allies in World War I | French bureaucracy |
| | | | | Chambers of commerce and agriculture |
| | Montagu-Chelmsford reforms | | Dilettante Rama VI | |
| | | Governor Craddock's reform plans | | Lack of self-government concessions |
| | Amritsar | | | |
| **1920** | Dyarchy reforms | Dyarchy application | | |
| | Gandhian boycott | National schools strike | Sayre and recovery of treaty equality | Heavy French franc investments |
| | | The GCBA and boycott of dyarchy | | Suppression of nationalism |
| | Simon Commission report | | Rama VII's reforms alienate many | |
| | Roundtable conferences | Saya San rebellion | The 1932 coup | Communist influence Nguyen Ai-Quoc Trotskyites |
| | | London conferences | | |
| | Constitution of 1935 | Constitution of 1935 University strike Governments under: | Pibun's orientation toward Japan | Recovery from depression |
| | Congress Party governments | Dr. Ba Maw U Pu U Saw | | Vichy acceptance of Japan's demands |
| **1940** | Congress boycott of war | Thakins and the Freedom Bloc | Recovery of French annexations with Japan's aid, plus Malay and Shan States | French suppress anti-Japanese nationalism |
| | | Collaboration with the Japanese | Japanese occupation | American and KMT aid to Ho Chi Minh |
| | Japanese invasion | The AFPFL moves against Japanese | | |
| | Partition of India, Pakistan | AFPFL collaboration with Mountbatten | Free Thai movement; Pridi for Pibun | Viet Minh versus Dong Ming Hoi |
| | | | | Ho versus France |
| | | Aung San to Nu | Pibun returns to power | Bao Dai fiasco |
| | End of British raj | Independent Burma | SEATO affiliation | Dien Bien Phu |

| MALAYA | NETHERLANDS INDIES | PHILIPPINES | CHINA-JAPAN | |
|---|---|---|---|---|
| Unfederated states; cancelation of Siamese suzerainty | Ethical policy introduced | Suppression of Filipino resistance | | 1900 |
| | | Taft's commissionership | Russo-Japanese War | |
| Start of rubber plantations | Plantation development in: Rubber Tobacco | Elections and the Legislature | Fall of Manchu dynasty | |
| Tin-mining expansion | Oil extraction Copra | Osmeña's leadership | | |
| Labor recruitment, Indians and Chinese | Darul Islam | Harrison's role | Japan's twenty-one demands | |
| | Volksraad reform | The Jones Act | | |
| | End of Ethical policy emphasis | Decline of administrative standards | Japanese commercial and political predominance | |
| | Administration reform pattern | Wood-Forbes report | Washington Conference | 1920 |
| Rapid economic expansion | | Wood versus Quezon | | |
| Increased control of Federated States | Outer Island development emphasis | | Period of party governments in Japan | |
| | Communist infiltration of Darul Islam | Stimson for Wood | | |
| | | Depression opposition to Philippines trade privileges | Manchurian incident | |
| Depression problems | Sukarno and the PNI Depression doldrums Dutch suppression of nationalism | | Lytton Commission report | |
| | | Hare-Hawes-Cutting Act to Tydings-McDuffie Act | Japan military attacks China | |
| | Economic recovery | | KMT resistance | |
| Ending of Indian labor recruitment | | Philippines Commonwealth | Japan's emphasis shifts to Southeast Asia | |
| | | | Occupation of Indochina | 1940 |
| Conquest by Japan | Japanese pressure | Conquest by Japan | Japan's conquest of Southeast Asia | |
| | Japanese occupation | Hukbalahap rebels | | |
| | Sukarno and Hatta collaboration | | "Greater East Asia Co-Prosperity Sphere" | |
| Alternative postwar plans | Two Dutch police actions | American reconquest Independence: Roxas | Defeat of Japan | |
| Malayan independence and Federation | Merdeka for Indonesia | Quirino Magsaysay | Communist victory in China | |
| Malayasian Federation to include British Borneo | | | Red China's Southeast Asia pressure on Nanyang Chinese | |

# Selected Bibliography

## I. References and Guides

Echols, John Minor: "Southeast Asia," in George Frederick Howe et al. (eds.), *The American Historical Association's Guide to Historical Literature,* Macmillan, New York, 1961, 319–334. 270 entries, annotated.

Embree, John F., and Lillian O. Dotson: *Bibliography of the Peoples and Cultures of Mainland Southeast Asia,* Yale, New Haven, Conn., 1950. 833 pp. Complete in humanities field, with over 12,000 items; of limited use in history.

Hall, D. G. E. (ed.): *Historians of South-East Asia,* Oxford University Press, Fair Lawn, N.J., 1961. 342 pp. A critical appraisal of basic works in the field.

Irikura, James K.: *Southeast Asia: Selected Annotated Bibliography of Japanese Publications,* Yale, New Haven, Conn., 1956. 544 pp. 965 titles; fully annotated with author index.

*Journal of Asian Studies Bibliography.* Began as a section in each issue of the earlier version, known as the *Far Eastern Quarterly,* 1941–1946. Issued annually as one of the four numbers, 1947–1952. Published as no. 5 of each annual volume since 1952.

Kennedy, Raymond (ed.): *Bibliography of Indonesian Peoples and Cultures,* Human Relations Area Files, New Haven, Conn., 1955. 663 pp. Not annotated. Revised by T. W. Maretzki and H. T. Fischer. Corresponds roughly to Embree and Dotson, covering the islands area.

Lundy, Frank A.: "The Dutch East Indies: A Bibliographical Essay," *PHR,* II (1933), 305–320.

Talbot, Phillips (ed.): *A Selected Bibliography: Asia, Africa, Eastern Europe, Latin America,* American Universities Field Staff, New York, 1960. 534 pp. Some 220 entries on Southeast Asia are included, 90–110. Well selected and evaluated.

## II. Books and Periodicals

Albuquerque, Affonso de: *The Commentaries of the Great Affonso D'Albuquerque, Second Viceroy of India,* Hakluyt Society, London, 1875–1884. 4 vols. Translated from the Portuguese edition of 1774 with notes and an introduction by Walter de Gray Birch.

Allen, George Cyril, and Audrey G. Donnithorne: *Western Enterprise in Indonesia and Malaya,* Macmillan, New York, 1957. A basic descriptive study.

Anderson, John (1745–1845): *Acheen and the Ports on the North and East Coasts of Sumatra,* W. H. Allen, London, 1840. An eyewitness account.

———: *Mission to the East Coast of Sumatra in 1823,* Edinburgh, 1826.

Anderson, John (1833–1900): *English Intercourse with Siam in the Seventeenth Century.* Kegan Paul, Trench, Trubner, London, 1890. This standard study has been corrected at numerous points.

Arasaratnam, Sennappah: *Dutch Power in Ceylon, 1658–1687,* Djambatan, Amsterdam, 1958. A scholarly study.

Bastin, John: *The Native Policies of Sir Stamford Raffles in Java and Sumatra: An Economic Interpretation,* Oxford University Press, Fair Lawn, N.J., 1957. A rejoinder to Raffles worshippers.

———: "Sir Stamford Raffles' and John Crawfurd's Ideas of Colonizing the Malay Archipelago," *JRASMB,* XXVI (July, 1953), 81–85.

Begbie, P. J.: *The Malayan Peninsula, Embracing Its History, Manners, and Customs of the Inhabitants,* Vepery Mission Press, Madras, 1834. Of limited value.

Bell, Hesketh: *Foreign Colonial Administration in the Far East,* London, 1926. A good comparison of Dutch and French systems by a Briton familiar with Africa.

Benda, Harry J.: *The Crescent and the Rising Sun: Indonesian Islam under the Japanese Occupation, 1942–1945,* W. Van Hoeve, The Hague, 1958. Thoughtful and informed.

Benitez, Conrado: *History of the Philippines,* Ginn, Boston, 1954.

Bernstein, David: *The Philippine Story,* Farrar, Straus, New York, 1947. Especially valuable for 1941–1947. Corrects optimistic American estimates of the situation.

Birdwood, George, and William Foster (eds.): *The First Letter Book of the East India Company, 1600–1619,* Hakluyt Society, London, 1893.

Blair, Emma Helen, and James A. Robertson (eds. and trans.): *Philippine Islands (1493–1898),* A. H. Clark, Cleveland, 1905. 55 vols. Translation of original MS in European languages. Invaluable for the Spanish period. E. G. Bourne's "Historical Introduction" is useful.

Blanchard, Wendell, et al.: *Thailand: Its People, Its Society, Its Culture,* Human Relations Area Files, New Haven, Conn., 1958. Descriptive rather than historical.

Boeke, Julius Herman: *The Evolution of the Netherlands Indies Economy,* Institute of Pacific Relations, New York, 1946. Stresses unique features of the Indonesian economy.

———: *The Structure of Netherlands Indian Economy,* Institute of Pacific Relations, New York, 1942. Analyzes the desa, or village community, economy as an evolving institution important in its own right.

Bousquet, B. H.: *A French View of the Netherlands Indies,* Oxford University Press, Fair Lawn, N.J., 1940. Translated by Philip E. Lilienthal.

Boxer, Charles Ralph: "Cornelius Speelman and the Growth of Dutch Power in Indonesia, 1666–1684," *History Today,* VIII (March, 1959), 145–154.

———: *Three Historians of Portuguese Asia: Barros, Couto, and Bocarro,* Hongkong, 1948. An excellent appraisal.

Braddell, Roland: "Notes on Ancient Times in Malaya," *JRASMB,* XX (June, 1947), 161–186; (December, 1947), 1–18; and XXII (March, 1949), 1–16.

Briggs, Lawrence Palmer: *The Ancient Khmer Empire,* American Philosophical Society, Philadelphia, 1951. The most comprehensive treatment, subject to minor corrections.

———: "Dvaravati, Most Ancient Kingdom of Siam," *JAOS,* LXIII (1945), 98–107.

———: "The Origin of the Śailendra Dynasty," *JAOS,* LXX (1950).

———: "The Syncretism of Religions in Southeast Asia, Especially in the Khmer Empire," *JAOS,* LXXI (1951), 230–249.

Brown, Donald Mackenzie: *The White Umbrella: Indian Political Thought from Manu to Gandhi,* University of California Press, Berkeley, Calif., 1953. An interpretive summary.

Burnell, A. C., and P. A. Tiele (eds.): *The Voyage of John Huyghens van Lin-*

*schoten to the East Indies,* Hakluyt Society Publications no. 70 and no. 71, London, 1885, 2 vol.

Burney, Henry: *The Burney Papers,* Vajirnana Library, Bangkok, 1910–1914. 5 vols. (Reprinted from the Originals in the India Office.)

Buttinger, Joseph: *The Smaller Dragon: A Political History of Vietnam,* Frederick A. Praeger, New York, 1958. Valuable for its footnotes and bibliographic comments. Otherwise propagandist in tone.

Cady, John F.: *A History of Modern Burma,* Cornell, Ithaca, N.Y., 1958. A standard account.

———: *The Roots of French Imperialism in Eastern Asia,* Cornell, Ithaca, N.Y., 1954. Covers in detail French policy from 1840 to 1860.

Campbell, John Gordon Drummond: *Siam in the Twentieth Century: Being the Experiences and Impressions of a British Official,* London, 1902.

Casparis, J. G. de: *Inscripties Uit de Cailendra-Tijd: Prasasti Indonesia, I,* A. C. Nix, Bandung, 1950.

———: *Selected Inscriptions from the 7th to the 9th Century A.D.: Prasasti Indonesia, II,* A. C. Nix, Bandung, 1956.

Cator, Writser Jans: *The Economic Position of the Chinese in the Netherlands Indies,* Oxford University Press, Fair Lawn, N.J., 1936.

Cavanna y Monso, Jesus Maria: *Rizal and the Philippines of his Day,* Manila, 1957. A Catholic rejoinder to emphasis on Rizal's anticlerical reputation.

Chaigneau, Michel D'uc: *Souvenirs de Hué,* Shanghai, 1941. Relates to the early nineteenth century.

Chassigneaux, Edmond: *L'Indochine: Histoire des colonies françaises,* Paris, 1932, V, 311–599. Volume 5 of G. Hanotaux and Alfred Martineau (eds.), *Histoire des colonies françaises et de l'expansion de la France dans le monde.* Excellent study.

Chesneaux, Jean: *Contribution à l'histoire de la nation vietnamienne,* Editions Sociales, Paris, 1955. Stresses economic and popular factors including leadership of the Viet Minh regime. Mildly procommunist in emphasis.

Chou Ta-kuan: "Memoires sur les Coutumes du Cambodge," *BEFEO,* XI (1902). Translated by Paul Pelliot. Republished in book form in Paris, 1951.

Christian, John Leroy: *Modern Burma: A Survey of Political and Economic Development,* University of California Press, Berkeley, Calif., 1942. Anglophile, but informative.

Chula Chakrabongse, Prince of Siam: *Lords of Life: The Paternal Monarch of Bangkok, 1782–1932,* Taplinger, New York, 1960.

Clodd, Harold Parker: *Malaya's First British Pioneer: The Life of Francis Light,* Luzac, London, 1948. Well documented and readable. Good chapter on conditions in Malaya in late eighteenth century.

Coast, John: *Some Aspects of Siamese Politics,* Institute of Pacific Relations, New York, 1953. A realistic analysis.

Codrington, Humphrey William: *A Short History of Ceylon,* Macmillan, London, 1929.

Coedès, Georges: *Les États Hindouisés d'Indochine et d'Indonésie,* E. de Boccard, Paris, 1948. A basic interpretation of the pre-Moslem period.

———: "Necrologie Pierre Dupont (1908–1955)," *BEFEO,* XLIX (1959), 637–638.

———: *Les Peuples de la Péninsule Indochinoise: Histoire—Civilisation.* Dunod, Paris, 1962.

————: *Pour Mieux Comprendre Angkor,* Adrien Maisonneuvre, Paris, 1947. 2 vols. Excellent.

Cole, Allan B.: *Conflict in Indo-China, and International Repercussions: A Documentary History, 1945–1955,* Cornell, Ithaca, N.Y., 1956. A useful compilation.

Collis, Maurice: *Siamese White,* Penguin, Baltimore, 1936 and 1940. Also published as *White of Mergui,* Faber, London, 1945.

————: *Trials in Burma,* Faber, London, 1938. The best work of Collis.

Colquhoun, Archibald Ross: *Across Chryse: Being a Narrative of a Journey of Exploration through South China Borderlands from Canton to Mandalay,* S. Low, Marston, Searle, and Rivington, London, 1883. 2 vols.

Cortesão, Armando (ed.): *The Suma Oriental of Tomé Pires: An Account of the East from the Red Sea to Japan, Written in Malacca and India in 1512–1515,* Hakluyt Society, London, 1944. 2 vols. Invaluable as a source.

Costa, H. de la: *The Jesuits in the Philippines, 1581–1768,* Harvard, Cambridge, Mass., 1961. Thorough and well written; from Jesuit sources.

Coupland, Reginald: *Raffles of Singapore,* Oxford University Press, Fair Lawn, N.J., 1926; 3d ed., 1946. Highly readable.

Cowan, C. D.: *Nineteenth-century Malaya: The Origins of British Political Control,* Oxford University Press, Fair Lawn, N.J., 1961. A definitive account of the early 1870s.

Craig, Austin: *Lineage, Life, and Labors of José Rizal, Philippine Patriot,* Philippine Education Co., Manila, 1913. Excellent.

Crawfurd, John: *History of the Indian Archipelago,* A. Constable, Edinburgh, 1820. 3 vols. Appreciative of potentialities of the Javanese if placed under enlightened rule.

————: *Journal of an Embassy from the Governor of India to the Courts of Siam and Cochin China,* H. Colburn, London, 1828. Account of an abortive English mission to Siam and Vietnam.

Crosby, Josiah: *Siam: The Crossroads,* Hollis and Carter, London, 1945.

Curtis, Lillian Johnson: *The Laos of North Siam,* The Westminster Press, Philadelphia, 1903.

Danvers, F. C.: *The Portuguese in India. Being a History of the Rise and Decline of Their Eastern Empire,* India Office, London, 1894. 2 vols.

————: *Report . . . on the Portuguese Records Relating to the East Indies Contained in the Archivo da Torre do Tombo, and the Public libraries at Lisbon and Evora,* India Office, London, 1892.

Derbyshire, Charles: *The Social Cancer: A Complete English Version of Noli me Tangere from the Spanish of José Rizal,* World Book Company, Tarrytown-on-Hudson, N.Y., and Philippine Education Co., Manila, 1912.

De Silva, Calvin R.: *Ceylon under British Occupation, 1795–1833: Its Political, Administrative and Economic Development,* Colombo, 1942. 2 vols. Covers a wide range of sources; reasonably accurate.

Devilliers, Philippe: *Histoire du Vietnam de 1940 à 1952,* Editions du Seuil, Paris, 1952. A standard account.

Dobby, Ernest H. G.: *Southeast Asia,* University of London Press, London, 1950. Geographical study.

Douwes Dekker, Eduard: *Indonesia: Once more Free Labor,* Stanford, Stanford, Calif., 1948. Translated by Nicholaas Steelink.

————: *Max Havelaar,* The Hague, 1860. 2 vols.

Du Bois, Cora: *Social Forces in Southeast Asia,* 2d ed., Harvard, Cambridge, Mass., 1959.

Dupont, Pierre: "Les Buddha dits d'Amaravati en Asie du Sud-Est," *BEFEO,* XLIX, part 2 (1959), 631–636.

————: "Études sur l'Indochine Ancienne: I. La Dislocation du Tchen-la et la Formation du Cambodge Angkorien, VIIᵉ–IXᵉ Siècles," *BEFEO,* XLIII (1943–1946), 17–55.

————: "Études sur l'Indochine Ancienne: II. Les Débuts de la Royauté Angkorienne," *BEFEO,* XLVI (1952), 119–176.

Dupuis, Jean: *Le Tonkin de 1872 à 1886: histoire et politique,* Paris, 1910. A primary source but far from dispassionate.

Earl, G. W.: *The Eastern Seas; or Voyages and Discoveries in the Indian Archipelago in 1832-33-34,* London, 1837.

Elegant, Robert S.: *The Dragon's Seed: Peking and the Overseas Chinese,* St Martin's, New York, 1959.

Emerson, Rupert: *Malaysia: A Study in Direct and Indirect Rule,* Macmillan, New York, 1937. The first adequate history of modern Malaya.

————: *Representative Government in Southeast Asia,* Harvard, Cambridge, Mass., 1955.

Ennis, Thomas E.: *French Policy and Development in Indochina,* The University of Chicago Press, Chicago, 1936. Orderly and useful, but with limitations.

Evans, Ivor Hugh Norman: *Papers on the Ethnology and Archeology of the Malay Peninsula,* Cambridge, New York, 1927.

Fall, Bernard: *Le Viet-Minh, La République Democratique du Viet-Nam. 1945–1960,* Colin, Paris, 1960. Useful but not definitive.

Ferrand, Gabriel: *Abu Zaid Hasan: Voyage du marchand arabe Sulayman en Inde et en Chine redigé en 851,* Paris, 1922.

————: *L'Empire Sumatranais de Çrivijaya,* Imprimerie Nationale, Paris, 1922.

————: *Relations de voyages et de textes geographiques arabes, persan, et turcs relatifs à L'extrême orient du VIIIᵉ au XVIIIᵉ siècles,* Paris, 1913–1914. 2 vols.

Finlayson, George: *The Mission to Siam and Hué, the capital of Cochin-China, in 1821–1822,* J. Murray, London, 1826. The author accompanied Crawfurd.

Firth, William Raymond: *Malay Fisherman: Their Peasant Economy,* Kegan Paul, Trench, Trubner, London, 1946.

Fitzsimmons, Thomas: *Thailand,* Human Relations Area Files, New Haven, Conn., 1957.

Forbes, William Cameron: *The Philippine Islands,* Houghton Mifflin, Boston, 1928, 2 vols.; 2d ed., Harvard, Cambridge, Mass., 1945. The second (one-volume) edition carried the story to 1941.

Foster, William: *England's Quest for Eastern Trade,* Hakluyt Society, London, 1933.

————: *The Journal of John Jourdain, 1608–1617,* Hakluyt Society, London, 1905.

————: *The Voyage of Nicholas Downton to the East Indies, 1614–1615,* Hakluyt Society, London, 1939.

————: *The Voyage of Sir Henry Middleton to the Moluccas, 1604–1606,* Hakluyt Society, London, 1943. Foster edited many other volumes for the Hakluyt Society.

Furnivall, John S.: *Colonial Policy and Practice,* Cambridge, New York, 1948; New York University Press, New York, 1956. A comparative study of Burma and Netherlands India.

————: *Educational Progress in Southeast Asia,* Institute of Pacific Relations, New York, 1943.

————: *The Governance of Modern Burma,* Institute of Pacific Relations, New York, 1958.

————: *Netherlands India: A Study of Plural Economy,* Cambridge, New York, 1939 and 1944.

Garnier, Francis: *Voyage d'exploration en Indo-Chine, effective pendant les années 1866, 1867, 1868,* Department of Marine, Paris, 1873.

————: *Atlas de Voyage d'exploration en Indo-Chine: Deuxième partie,* Department of Marine, Paris, 1873.

Gaudel, André: *L'Indochine française en face du Japan,* Paris, 1947. A detailed argument on the necessity of French collaboration with the Japanese.

Geertz, Clifford: *The Social Context of Economic Change: An Indonesian Case Study,* M.I.T., Cambridge, Mass., 1950.

Ghosh, Monomohan: *A History of Cambodia,* J. K. Gupta, Saigon, 1960. Must be used with care.

Giles, Herbert Allen: *The Travels of Fa-hsien, 399–414 A.D., or Record of the Buddhist Kingdoms,* Cambridge, 1923. Reprinted Routledge, London, 1956.

Ginsburg, Norman, and Chester F. Roberts: *Malaya,* University of Washington Press, Seattle, 1958. A useful summary.

Glamann, Kristof: *Dutch-Asiatic Trade, 1620–1740,* Danish Science Press, Copenhagen, The Hague, 1948. An excellent description.

Goonewardena, K. W.: *The Foundation of Dutch Power in Ceylon, 1638–1658,* Djambatam, Amsterdam, 1958. A scholarly treatment, abutting Arasaratman's study.

Gourou, Pierre: *Land Utilization in Indo-China,* Institute of Pacific Relations, New York, 1945 and 1947.

————: *Les Paysans du delta tonkinois: Étude de geographie humaine,* École Française, 1936.

————: *The Peasants of the Tonkin Delta: a Study of Human Geography,* Human Relations Area Files, New Haven, Conn., 1955. A revision of the French edition of 1936. Gourou's works are standard.

————: *The Tropical World: Its Social and Economic Conditions and Its Future Status,* Longmans, London, 1958.

Graham, W. A.: *Siam: A Handbook of Practical Commercial and Political Information,* A. Moring, London, 1912 and 1924. 2 vols.

Grimes, A.: "The Journey of Fa-hsien from Ceylon to Canton," *JRASMB,* XIX (1941), 76–92.

Griswold, Alfred W.: *The Far Eastern Policy of the United States,* Harcourt, Brace, New York, 1938.

Groslier, B. P.: *Angkor et le Cambodge au XVI^e Siècle d'après les sources portugaises et espagnoles,* Presses Universitaires, Paris, 1958. Groslier opens up a new phase of the history of Cambodia.

————: *Recherches sur les Cambodgiens,* A. Challamel, Paris, 1921.

Grousset, René: *The Civilizations of the East,* Knopf, New York, 1931–1934. 4 vols. Translated by C. A. Phillips.

————: *De l'Inde au Cambodge et à Java,* Monaco, 1950.

————: *Histoire de l'Extrême-Orient,* Libraire Paul Geuthner, Paris, 1929. 2 vols.

Based on best monographic and periodical materials, with a monumental bibliography.

———: *In the Footsteps of the Buddha,* Plon, Paris, 1929; George Routledge & Sons, London, 1932. The earlier edition is in French.

——— et al.: *L'Asie Orientale de Origines au XV<sup>e</sup> Siècle,* Paris, 1941.

Grunder, Garel A., and William E. Livezey: *The Philippines and the United States,* University of Oklahoma Press, Norman, Okla., 1951. A very useful summary.

Hall, D. G. E.: *Burma,* Hutchinson's University Library, London, 1950. Reliable and impartial.

———: *Early English Intercourse with Burma, 1587–1743,* Longmans, New York, 1928.

———: "From Mergui to Singapore, 1686–1819," *JSS,* XLI, no. 1 (July, 1953), 1–18.

———: *Historians of South-East Asia,* Oxford University Press, Fair Lawn, N.J., 1961.

———: *A History of South-East Asia,* Oxford University Press, Fair Lawn, N.J., and St Martin's Press, New York, 1955 and 1960. The standard record of political chronology. Excellent bibliography.

———: *Michael Symes: Journal of His Second Embassy to the Court of Ava in 1802,* G. Allen, London, 1955. Excellent editing.

———: *The Study of Old Indonesian History,* London, 1961.

Hamilton, Alexander: *A New Account of the East Indies (1688 to 1723),* J. Mosman, Edinburgh, 1727. 2 vols.

Hammer, Ellen J.: *The Struggle for Indochina,* Stanford, Stanford, Calif., 1954. Well written, but reflects a strong anticolonial bias.

Harrison, Brian: "Malacca in the Eighteenth Century: Two Dutch Governors' Reports," *JRASMB,* XXVII (May, 1954), 24–34.

———: *South-East Asia: A Short History,* St Martin's, New York, 1954. A good brief survey.

Harvey, Godfrey E.: *History of Burma from the Earliest Times to 10 March 1824, the Beginning of the English Conquest,* Longmans, New York, 1925. Concerned mainly with dynastic affairs and marred by anti-Burmese bias.

Hayden, Joseph Ralston: *The Philippines: A Study in National Development,* Macmillan, New York, 1942. A standard study.

Heine-Geldern, Robert: "Conceptions of State and Kingship in Southeast Asia," *FEQ,* II (November, 1942), 15–30; republished by Southeast Asia Program, Cornell University, Data Paper No. 18 (1956).

———: "Sudostasien," in George N. Buschan, *Illustrierte Volkerkunde,* Stuttgart, 1923, vol. II.

Hirth, Friedrich: *China and the Roman Orient: Researches into Their Ancient and Medieval Relations as Represented in Old Chinese Records,* Kelley and Walsh, Shanghai, 1885.

———: and W. W. Rockhill (trans.): *Chau Ju-kua: His Work on the Chinese and Arab Trade in the Twelfth and Thirteenth centuries, Entitled Chu-fan-chi,* St. Petersburg, 1911.

Holland, William (ed.): *Asian Nationalism and the West,* Institute of Pacific Relations, New York, 1953.

Hoontrakul, Likhit: *The History of Siamese-Chinese Relations,* Bangkok, 1953.

Hourani, George Faldo: *Arab Navigation in the Indian Ocean during the 9th and 10th Centuries,* microfilm only, The University of Michigan Press, Ann Arbor, Mich., 1952.

————: *Arab Seafaring in the Indian Ocean in Ancient and Early Medieval Times,* Princeton, Princeton, N.J., 1951. The peak of Arab activity came around the tenth century. Very readable in spite of compression of detail, but possibly in error in its account of earliest trade.

Hutchinson, E. W.: *Adventures in Siam in the Seventeenth Century,* Royal Asiatic Society, London, 1940. This covers the Phaulkon episode.

Ingram, James C.: *Economic Change in Thailand since 1850,* Stanford, Stanford, Calif., 1955. A superior study.

Ireland, Alleyne: *Far Eastern Tropics: Studies in the Administration of Tropical Dependencies,* Houghton Mifflin, Boston, 1905.

Irwin, Graham: *Nineteenth-century Borneo: A Study in Diplomatic Rivalry,* M. Nijhoff, The Hague, 1955. Covers 1809 to 1888. Critical of London's cautious policy.

Jacoby, Erich: *Agrarian Unrest in Southeast Asia,* Columbia, New York, 1949. Good on the Philippines.

Jayne, Kingsley Garland: *Vasco da Gama and His Successors,* Methuen, London, 1910.

Jones, S. W.: *Public Administration in Malaya,* London and New York, 1953.

Kahin, George McTurnan (ed.): *Governments and Politics of Southeast Asia,* Cornell, Ithaca, N.Y., 1959. 531 pp. Partly supersedes Mills et al., *The New World of Southeast Asia.*

————: *Nationalism and Revolution in Indonesia,* Cornell, Ithaca, N.Y., 1952. Some anti-Dutch bias. Best account of Indonesian nationalist movement.

Kat Angelino, Arnold Dirk A.: *Colonial Policy,* M. Nijhoff, The Hague, and University of Chicago Press, Chicago, 1931. 2 vols. Abridged translation by C. J. Renier. Vol. I covers principles of colonial administration, and vol. II describes Dutch policy in the Indies. An outstanding work, but an apologia for Dutch methods.

Kennedy, Raymond: "A Survey of Indonesian Society," in G. P. Murdock, *Studies in the Science of Society,* Yale, New Haven, Conn., 1937, 267–297.

Kerr, George H.: *Okinawa: The History of an Island People,* Tuttle, Tokyo, 1958.

Klaproth and Londresse, *The Pilgrimage of Fa Hian,* Calcutta, 1848. Translated from J. P. A. Remusat, *Foe Koue Ki, ou relations des royaumes Bouddhiques,* Paris, 1836.

Klerck, Eduard Servaas de: *History of the Netherlands East Indies,* W. L. and J. Brusse, Rotterdam, 1938. 2 vols.

Krom, Nicolaas Johannes: *Barabudur: Archeological Description,* M. Nijhoff, The Hague, 1927. 2 vols. This is the standard work.

————: *Hindoe-Javaansche Geschiedenis,* 2d revised ed., The Hague, 1931.

Landon, Kenneth P.: *Siam in Transition,* Shanghai, 1939. 328 pp. Author relied heavily on Le May.

————: *Southeast Asia: Crossroads of Religion,* The University of Chicago Press, Chicago, 1947.

Lanier, L.: *Études historiques sur les relations de la France et du royaume de Siam de 1662 à 1703,* Paris, 1883.

Launay, Adrien: *Histoire générale de le Société des Missions Étrangères depuis sa fondation jusqu'à nos jours,* Paris, 1894 and 1920. 3 vols. The best account from the Catholic point of view.

Le Bar, Frank M., and Adrienne Suddard (eds.): *Laos,* Human Relations Area Files, New Haven, Conn., 1960.

Le May, Reginald Stuart: *An Asian Arcadie: The Land and Peoples of Northern Siam,* Cambridge, New York, 1926.

Lê Thanh Khôi: *Le Viet Nam, Histoire et Civilisation: Le Milieu et l'Histoire,* Les Éditions de Minuit, Paris, 1955. The best history by a Vietnamese scholar.

Leonowens, Anna: *The English Governess at the Siamese Court,* Boston, 1870 and 1873; Roy Publishers, New York, 1954.

Levy, Roger: *French Interests and Policies in the Far East,* part I, *A Century of French Far Eastern Affairs,* Institute of Pacific Relations, New York, 1941.

Loftus, Alfred John: *The Kingdom of Siam: Its progress and prospects,* London, 1891. Loftus was hydrographer to Chulalongkorn.

Luce, Gordon H.: "Burma's Debt to Pagan," *JBRS,* XXII (1932), 120–127.

————: "Economic Life of the Early Burmans," *JBRS,* XXX (1940), 283–335.

————: *Mons of the Pagan Dynasty,* Rangoon, 1950. Luce is the leading British authority on Pagan Burma.

Lyautey, L. H. G.: *Lettres du Tonkin et de Madagascar, 1893–9,* Colin, Paris, 1884 and 1920. 2 vols. By a leading French militarist-imperialist.

Macgregor, Ian A. (trans.): "A Brief Account of the Kingdom of Pegu," *JBRS,* XVI (August, 1926). By an anonymous Portuguese writer of the early seventeenth century.

————: "Notes on the Portuguese in Malaya," *JRASMB,* XXVIII (May, 1955), 5–41.

———— et al.: *Papers on Jahore Lama and the Portuguese in Malaya: 1511–1641,* London, 1957.

Majumdar, Ramesh Chandra: *Ancient Indian Colonies in the Far East: I, Champa* Punjab Sanskrit Book Depot, Lahore, 1927; Baroda, 1955.

————: *Ancient Indian Colonies in the Far East: II, Suvarnadvipa,* Dacca, 1937–1938; Baroda, 1955.

————: *Hindu Colonies in the Far East,* Calcutta, 1944.

————: *Kambuja-Desa; or an Ancient Hindu Colony in Cambodia,* Madras, 1944.

Makepeace, Walter, et al.: *One Hundred Years of Singapore,* J. Murray, London, 1921, 2 vols.

Malcolm, George A.: *The Commonwealth of the Philippines,* Appleton-Century, New York, 1936. A particularly useful account by an American judge.

Mansvelt, W. M.: *A Brief History of the Netherlands Trading Society, 1824–1924,* The Hague, 1924.

Marrison, G. E.: "The Chams of Malacca," *JRASMB,* XXIV (February, 1951), 90–98.

————: "The Coming of Islam to the East Indies," *JRASMB,* XXIV (1951), 28–37.

————: "Persian Influences in Malay Life (1280–1650)," *JRASMB,* XXVIII (March, 1955), 52–68.

Marsden, W.: *History of Sumatra,* J. McCreery, London, 1783 and 1811.

Maspero, Georges: *Le Royaume de Champa,* G. van Oest, Paris, and Brussels, 1928.

————: *The Kingdom of Champa: A Translation of Chapter I of Le Royaume du Champa,* Yale, New Haven, Conn., 1949. Maspero is the leading authority on Champa's history.

Masselman, George: "Dutch Policy in the Seventeenth Century," *Journal of Economic History,* XXI (December, 1961).

Masson, André: *Hanoi pendant la période héroique, 1873–1888,* Paris, 1929. Excellent account from French point of view. Covers the Dupuis-Garnier episode.

Maybon, Charles B.: *Histoire Moderne du Pays d'Annam, 1592–1820,* Typographie Plon-Nourrit, Paris, 1919 and 1920. Best work on Annamese-European relations.

Mills, Lennox A.: *British Malaya: 1824–1867,* Methodist Publishing House, Singapore, 1925. A sound study.

——: *Malaya: A Political Appraisal,* The University of Minnesota Press, Minneapolis, 1958. Less useful.

—— et al.: *The New World of Southeast Asia,* The University of Minnesota Press, Minneapolis, 1949.

Moffat, Abbot Low: *Mongkut, the King of Siam,* Cornell, Ithaca, N.Y., 1961.

Mongkut, King: "English Correspondence of King Mongkut," *JSS,* XXI (1927).

Moorhead, Francis Joseph: *A History of Malaya and Her Neighbors,* Longmans, New York, 1957. vol. I. Covers to end of the Portuguese period, 1641.

Moreland, William H., and Atul Chandra Chatterjee: *A Short History of India,* Longmans, London, 1953. A useful short history.

Moses, Bernard: *Spain Overseas,* Hispanic Society of America, New York, 1929. A standard account.

Mouhot, Henri: *Travels in the Central Parts of Indo-China, Siam, Cambodia, and Laos during 1859–60,* J. Murray, London, 1864. 2 vols. A firsthand account.

Multatuli. See Douwes Dekker.

Mya Sein, Daw: *Administration of Burma: Sir Charles Crosthwaite and the Consolidation of Burma,* Rangoon, 1938. Good on the period from 1877 to 1890.

Mysbergh, James H.: "The Indonesian Elite," *FES,* XXVI (1957), 38–42.

Newbold, T. J.: *Political and Statistical Account of the British Settlements in the Straits of Malacca,* J. Murray, London, 1839. 2 vols.

Nguyen Khac Kham: *Characteristics of Vietnamese Culture,* UNESCO, New York, 1960.

Nilakanta Sastri, K. A.: *South Indian Influences in the Far East,* Bombay, 1949. Covered by countries.

——: "Śri Vijaya," *BEFEO,* tome XL, face 2 (1941). Published separately at Madras in 1949.

Owen, David E.: *British Opium Policy in China and India,* Yale, New Haven, Conn., 1934.

Parkinson, Cyril Northcote: *British Intervention in Malaya: 1867–1877,* University of Malaya Press, London, 1959. First volume in the Malayan Historical Series. Intensive scholarship; documentation is a bit careless, sometimes fictionized.

——: *Trade in the Eastern Seas, 1793–1813,* Cambridge, New York, 1937. A good introduction to study of naval history in the East, 1803–1810, and an interesting interpretation of British policy.

——: *War in the Eastern Seas, 1793–1815,* Cambridge, New York, 1954. Well written.

Parmer, J. Norman: *Colonial Labor Policy and Administration: A History of Labor in the Rubber Plantation Industry in Malaya, 1910–1941,* Augustin, Locust Valley, N.Y. 1960. A scholarly study of Indian labor recruitment.

Pelzer, Karl J.: *Pioneer Settlement in the Asiatic Tropics,* The American Geographical Society, New York, 1945. Mainly geographical.

Phayre, Arthur P.: *History of Burma,* Trubner, London, 1883. A superior British account.

Phelan, John Leddy: *The Hispanization of the Philippines: Spanish Aims and Filipino Responses, 1565–1700,* The University of Wisconsin Press, Madison, Wis., 1959. An excellent account.

Pieris, Paulus Edward: *Ceylon and the Hollanders, 1658–1796,* American Ceylon Mission Press, Colombo, 1947.

———: *Ceylon: The Portuguese Era, Being a History of the Island for the Period 1505–1658,* Colombo Apothecaries Company, Colombo, 1913–1914. 2 vols.

Pires, Tomé: *The Suma Oriental of Tomé Pires,* Hakluyt Society, London, 1944. 2 vols. Translated and edited by Armando Cortesão.

Polo, Marco: *The Book of Ser Marco Polo, the Venetian, Concerning the Kingdoms and Marvels of the East,* J. Murray, London, 1871, 1903, and 1929. 2 vols. Henry Yule's translation revised by Henri Cordier.

Prawdin, Charol Michael: *The Mongol Empire: Its Rise and Legacy,* G. Allen, London, 1940 and 1954. Translated from the German by Eden and Cedar Paul.

Purcell, Victor W. W. S.: *The Chinese in South-East Asia,* Oxford University Press, Fair Lawn, N.J., 1951. Informative but rather partisan. Borrows heavily from other accounts.

Raffles, Thomas Stamford: *History of Java,* Black, Parbury, and Allen, London, 1817 and 1830. 2 vols.

Ray, H. C.: *History of Ceylon,* vol. I, part I, *From Earliest Times to 1505,* Ceylon University Press, Colombo, 1959.

Ray, Nihar-ranjan: *Brahmanical Gods in Burma,* University of Calcutta Press, Calcutta, 1932.

———: *An Introduction to the Study of Theravada Buddhism in Burma, from the Earliest Times to the British Conquest,* University of Calcutta Press, Calcutta, 1946.

———: *Sanskrit Buddhism in Burma,* Amsterdam, 1936.

Reeve, W. D.: *Public Administration in Siam,* London, 1952. Deals with forms rather than with political realities.

Rengers, D. W. van Welderen: *The Failure of a Liberal Colonial Policy: Netherlands East Indies, 1816–1830,* M. Nijhoff, The Hague, 1947.

Rizal y Alonso, José: *The Reign of Greed,* Philippine Education Co.., Manila, 1912.

———: *The Social Cancer,* World Book Company, Tarrytown-on-Hudson, N.Y., 1912.

Robequain, Charles: *Economic Development of French Indochina,* Institute of Pacific Relations, New York, 1944. The best account of French colonial policy.

———: *Malaya, Indonesia, Borneo and the Philippines: A Geographical, Economic, and Political Description of Malaya, the East Indies, and the Philippines,* Longmans, New York, 1954. Translated by E. D. Laborde.

Roberts, Stephen Henry: *History of French Colonial Policy (1870–1925),* King, London, 1929. 2 vols. A standard treatment.

Runciman, Steven: *The White Rajas: A History of Sarawak from 1841–1946,* Cambridge, New York, 1960.

Sayre, Francis Bowes: "The Passing of Extraterritoriality in Siam," *American Journal of International Law,* XXII (1928), 70–88.

———: *Siam: Treaties with Foreign Powers, 1920–1927,* Bangkok and Norwood, Mass., 1928. Sayre directed Siam's foreign-policy negotiation during this period.

Schrieke, Bertram Johannes Otto (ed.): *The Effect of Western Influence on Native Civilizations in the Malay Archipelago,* G. Kolff and Company, Batavia, 1929.

————: *Indonesian Sociological Studies: Selected Writings,* W. van Hoeve, The Hague, 1955–1957. 2 vols.

————: *Ruler and Realm in Eastern Java,* The Hague, 1960.

Schurz, William Lytle: *The Manila Galleon,* Dutton, New York, 1939. A useful book based on the archives of the Indies and on travelers' accounts.

Skinner, William: *Chinese Society in Thailand,* Cornell, Ithaca, N.Y., 1957.

Smith, Robert Aura: *Philippine Freedom, 1946–1958,* Columbia, New York, 1958.

Smith, Samuel J.: *History of Siam, Reign of H. M. Somdetch P'ra Narai, 1651–1682,* Bangkok, 1880. A basic source.

————: *The Siam Repository, Containing a Summary of Asiatic Intelligence,* Bangkok, 1869–1874. 6 vols.

Smyth, H. Warrington: *Five years in Siam,* J. Murray, London, 1898.

————: *Notes of a Journey on the Upper Mekong, Siam,* J. Murray, London, 1895.

Soedjatmoko: *An Approach to Indonesian History: Towards an Open Future,* Cornell University, Southeast Asia Translation Series, Ithaca, N.Y., 1960.

Steinberg, David J., et al.: *Cambodia: Its People, Its Society, Its Culture,* Human Relations Area Files, New Haven, Conn., 1959. Good on modern problems of social and economic reform; overconcerned with cold war and deficient in its grasp of Cambodian politics.

Taboulet, G.: *La geste française en Indochine: Histoire par les textes de la France en Indochine des origines à 1914,* Adrien Maissonneuve, Paris, 1955–1956. A valuable source collection.

Takakusu, Junjiro: *I-Ching (634–713): A Record of the Buddhist Religion as Practiced in India and the Malay Archipelago,* Oxford University Press, Fair Lawn, N.J., 1896. 2 vols.

Tarling, Nicholas: "British Policy in the Malay Peninsula and Archipelago, 1824–1871," *JRASMB,* XXX no. 179 (1957).

Than Tun: "The Buddhist Church in Burma during the Pagan Period," unpublished Ph. D. thesis, University of London, London, 1955.

————: *A History of Burma, A.D. 1300–1400,* Rangoon, 1959.

————: "A History of Burma down to the End of the thirteenth century," *NBW,* Aug. 23, Sept. 27, Oct. 25, and Nov. 29, 1958.

————: "The Legal System in Burma, A.D. 1000–1300," *Burma Law Institute Journal,* Rangoon, I (June, 1959).

————: "Luce's Contribution to Burmese History," *NBW,* Jan. 24, 1959.

————: *Religion in Burma, A.D. 1000–1300,* Rangoon, 1958.

————: *Religious Buildings of Burma, A.D. 1000–1300,* Rangoon, 1958.

————: "Social Life in Burma, A.D. 1044–1287," *JBRS,* XLI (1959), 37–47.

Thaung, Dr. Daw: "Burmese Kingship in Theory and Practice during the Reign of King Mindon," *JBRS,* XLII (December, 1959), 171–185.

Thompson, Virginia, and Richard Adloff: *The Left Wing in Southeast Asia,* Sloane, New York, 1950. Useful on postwar politics.

———— and ————: *Minority Problems in Southeast Asia,* Stanford, Stanford, Calif., 1955. Breaks new ground; thoroughgoing.

Tibbets, G. R.: "Early Muslim Traders in South-East Asia," *JRASMB,* XXX (1957), 1–44.

Tinker, Hugh: *The Union of Burma,* Oxford University Press, Fair Lawn, N.J., 1957. Excellent on postwar Burma.

Tregonning, K. G.: "American Activity in North Borneo, 1865–1881," *PHR,* XXIII (November, 1954).

————: *Under Chartered Company Rule: North Borneo, 1881–1946,* University of Malaya Press, Singapore, 1958.

Turpin, M.: *History of the Kingdom of Siam and the Revolutions That Have Caused the Overthrow of the Empire up to A.D. 1770,* Bangkok, 1908. Translated by B. O. Cartwright from the original Paris edition of 1771. A useful source.

Vandenbosch, Amry: *The Dutch East Indies,* 3d ed., University of California Press, Berkeley, Calif., 1942. Good on Dutch administration prior to World War II; rather pro-Dutch in tone.

Van Helsdingen, Willem Henri (J. J. L. Duyvendak): *Mission Interrupted: The Dutch in the East Indies and Their Work in the XXth Century,* Amsterdam, 1945.

Van Klavern, J. J.: *The Dutch Colonial System in the East Indies,* The Hague, 1953. An excellent reference.

Van Leur, Jacob Cornelius: *Indonesian Trade and Society: Essays in Asian Social and Economic History,* W. Van Hoeve, The Hague, 1955. Pleads for an Indonesian-centered approach. Follows Max Weber's thesis.

Van Niel, Robert: *The Emergence of the Modern Indonesian Elite,* W. Van Hoeve, The Hague, and Quadrangle Books, Chicago, 1960. Based on Dutch and Indonesian sources; incisive and lucid covering to 1927.

Van Nieuwenhuijze, C. A. O.: *Aspects of Islam in Post-Colonial Indonesia: Five Essays,* W. Van Hoeve, The Hague, 1958.

Vella, Walter F.: *The Impact of the West on the Government of Siam,* University of California Press, Berkeley, Calif., 1955. Well done.

————: *Siam under Rama III, 1824–1851,* Augustin, Locust Valley, N.Y., 1957. Virtually the only available study of the period.

Vlekke, B. H. M.: *Nusantara: A History of the East Indian Archipelago,* Harvard, Cambridge, Mass., 1943; revised ed., Quadrangle Books, Chicago, 1960. Probably the best single-volume account, largely rewritten in 1960 edition.

Wales, H. G. Q.: *Ancient South-east Asian Warfare,* B. Quaritch, London, 1952.

————: "Archeological Researches on Ancient Indian Colonization in Malaya," *JRASMB,* XVIII (1940), 1–45.

————: *The Making of Greater India: A Study in South-east Asian Cultural Change,* B. Quaritch, London, 1951.

————: *The Mountain of God: A Study in Early Religion and Kingship,* B. Quaritch, London, 1953.

————: *Prehistory and Religion in South-east Asia,* B. Quaritch, London, 1957.

————: *Towards Angkor in the Footsteps of the Indian Invaders,* Harrap, London, 1937. Wales breaks new ground but rides some theories hard and is not always dependable.

Wells, Kenneth E.: *History of Protestant Work in Thailand, 1828–1958,* Church of Christ in Thailand, Bangkok, 1958. A useful study by an American missionary.

Wertheim, Willem Frederik: *Effects of Western Civilization on Indonesian Society,* Institute of Pacific Relations Secretariat Paper no. 11., New York, 1950.

————: *Indonesian society in transition: A Study of Social Change,* New York and The Hague, 1956; 2d revised ed., W. Van Hoeve, The Hague, 1959. A useful study, mildly Marxist in tone.

Wheatley, Paul: *The Golden Khersonese,* University of Malaya Press, 1961. Useful revision of thesis (below).

———: "The Historical Geography of the Malay Peninsula before A.D. 1500," Ph. D. thesis, University of London, London, 1958.

———: "The Malay Peninsula as Known to the Chinese of the Third Century A.D.," *JRASMB,* XXVIII (1955), 1–23.

Willmott, Donald Earl: *The Chinese of Semarang: A Changing Minority Community in Indonesia,* Cornell, Ithaca, N.Y., 1960. A searching analysis of the Indonesian Chinese community.

Wilson, H. H.: "Account of the Foe Kue Ki, or Travels of Fa Hian in India, Translated from the Chinese by M. Remusat," *JRAS,* V (1839), 108–140.

Winstedt, Richard Olof: *Britain and Malaya, 1786–1941,* Longmans, New York, 1944.

———: *Malaya and Its History,* Hutchinson's University Library, London, 1948 and 1956.

———: *The Malays: A Cultural History,* revised and enlarged ed., Philosophical Library, New York, 1950. This is the best of Winstedt's books.

Wint, Guy: *The British in India,* Faber, London, 1947. A brilliant characterization.

Wolters, O. W.: "Chen-Li-fu, a State on the Gulf of Siam at the Beginning of the 13th Century," *JSS,* XLVIII (November, 1960), 1–351.

———: "The 'Po-ssŭ Pine Trees,' " *BSOAS,* XXIII (1960), 323–350.

———: "Tambralinga," *BSOAS,* XXI (1958), 587–607.

Wood, William Alfred Rae: *A History of Siam to A.D. 1781, with Supplement,* T. Fisher Unwin, London, 1929; revised ed. The Siam Barnakich Press, 1933. A standard account.

Worcester, Dean Conant, and Ralston Hayden: *The Philippines, Past and Present,* Macmillan, New York, 1914 and 1930. A basic work by members of the Philippines Commission.

Yule, Henry. *See* Marco Polo.

Zaide, Gregorio F.: *Early Philippine History and Culture,* Manila, 1937.

———: *Philippine History and Civilization,* S. E. Macaraig, Manila, 1938.

———: *Philippine Political and Cultural History,* Philippine Education Co., Manila, 1953. 2 vols. Zaide is a popular Filipino historian.

# Index

A Famosa fort, 176, 187
*Abangan* faction in Java, 536
Abreu, Antonio de, 177
Acapulco, galleon trade with, 248
  Japanese ships at, 241
  Portuguese trade to, 244
Acheh, 81, 179, 211
  attack on Malacca, 182
  Chinese trade with, 160
  Dutch friction with, 368
  megalomania of, 182
  pepper trade of, 164
  and Portuguese, 181, 182
Achehnese, commercial development of,
  6
  and Dutch, 219
Achehnese Muslims, 171
Achehnese traditionalists, 539
Adams, Will, 241
Aden, British post at, 380
  opium from, 161, 162
Adipadi Baw Maw, wartime role of,
  576, 577
Adran, Bishop of, 282, 284
Aduarte, Father, at Phnom Penh, 242,
  243
African troops, French use of, 417
Agence générale des Colonies, 431
Aglipay, Father Gregorio, 465
Aguinaldo, Emilio, role of, 464–465, 467
Agung, 209
Agus Salim, 376
Ahn, Prince, of Vientiane, 337
Airlangga, King, 82
  accession of, 135
*Akunwun*, 298
Akyab, Indian movement into, 4
  port of, 18
Ala 'u 'ddin, Sultan, 158
Alaungpaya, King, 285, 289–291
Albuquerque, Alfonso de, 173, 175, 176,
  181

Alexandria, Oriental trade of, 26
Alexandrian merchants, 27
Algerian troops, French use of, 419
Alimin, 541
All Burma Student Movement, 522
All Burma Youth League, 521
Alliance Party of Malaya, 598
Almeida, Francisco de, 173
al-Uballah, sack of, 67
Amangkurat I of Mataram, 220
Amangkurat II, 220
Amarapura, 289, 293, 296
  British Residency at, 382
Amaravati, Pallavan capital of, 34
Amboina, 180, 206
  Christianity in, 369, 567
  massacre of, 207
American Baptist Mission in Burma,
  302, 387
American Clipper Ships, role of, 303,
  311, 312
American Dairy Association, Philip-
  pines policy of, 481
American domination of Philippines
  economy, 473
American High Commissioner McNutt,
  484
American "interlopers" in India trade,
  315
American Protestant missionaries in
  Siam, 339
American record in Philippines, 484
American Revolution, Dutch involve-
  ment in, 231
American support of Vietnamese re-
  fused, 582
American trade in opium, 314
American treaty with Rama III, 339
Amoy, trade of, 25
Amsterdam Company, 207
Amsterdam Trading Society, 374
An Pass, 112, 113

Ananda temple at Pagan, 123, 126
Anaukpetlun, King, 195
Anda, Governor de, at Manila, 256
Andaman Islands, 5, 12, 28, 71
Andhra state of Telegus, 33
Andrade, Fernando de, 186
Andrade, Simon de, 187
Ang Chan of Cambodia, 148, 192
Ang Duong of Cambodia, 337, 347
Angkor, Indian culture at, 46
   Portuguese monks at, 197
Angkor (Borei), 88
Angkor Thom, 99, 100
   building of, 94
Angkor Wat, character of, 97
   historical significance of, 99
   repair of, 148
Anglo-Burman War of 1824–1826, 322,
   410
Anglo-Dutch War, of 1652–1654, 214
   of 1781, 368, 440
Anglo-French rivalry, 427
Anglo-French War with China, 388
Angrok, replacement of, 137
Anh Eng of Cambodia, 325
Animist survivals in Malaya, 593
Aniruddha (Anawrahta), 114, 116, 117
Annam Campaign of 1859, Spanish par-
   ticipation in, 416
Anon (Amangkurat II), 220
Anti-Fascist Peoples' Freedom League
   (AFPFL), 578, 579, 599
Antioch merchants, trade, 26, 27
Anuradapura, Ceylon port of, 26
Arab traders, 67, 80, 82
   to Ceylon, 26
   to India, 23
   to Indonesia, 361
   to Malacca, 160
Arahan, 127
Arakan, 18, 23, 193
   British rule over, 381, 383
   independence of, 189
   slave trade in, 189
Arakan-Chittagong border troubles, 295
Arakan pagoda at Amarapura, 293
Arakan and Pyu languages, 18
Arakan Yoma, 4

Arakanese, 288
Arana forest dwellers, 120
Argun, Ilkhan of Persia, 138
Arjuna, allegory of saint, 136
Armenians at Malacca, 161
Arthasastra, political treatise of, 35, 45
Aru Palakka, 219
Asia, Dutch trade in, 222
"Asia for the Asiatics," 505, 563, 568
Asoka, Emperor, 33, 47, 48
Assam, 285
   Burmese claims to, 381
   Mongoloid peoples in, 4
   Thai migration to, 20
Association of Burmese Medical Prac-
   titioners, 592
Association of Professional and Business
   Men in Burma, 514
Ateneo de Manila, Jesuit, 463, 471
Attlee, Clement, 579
Atwinwuns, 287, 296
Augustinians in Philippines, 249, 252
Augustus, Emperor, 26
Aung San, Thakin, 522, 527, 566
   and Japanese, 575
   and Mountbatten, 579
Austrian Succession, War of, 309
Austroasiatic civilization, North Indian,
   16
Austroasiatic Khmers, migration of, 4
Austroasiatic Mons, migration of, 4
Ava, 286, 296
   attack by Manchus on, 263
Ayuthia, Anglo-Dutch rivalry over, 213
   Burmese capture of, in 1569, 148, 191,
    192
   Burmese destruction of, in 1767, 261,
    267, 281
   versus Chiengmai, 147
   Dutch factory at, 279
   English factory closed at, 262
   English Mission to, 273
   founding of, 110, 146
   French Company at, 271
   Japanese at, 261
   Louis XIV's Mission to, 275
   Missions Étrangères at, 279
   in 1720, 278
Azevedo, Father d', 196

Ba Maw, Dr., 506, 518, 526
  and "Freedom Bloc" program, 526
  government, fall of, 524
  Minister for Education, 522
  and Premier Tojo, 576
  Prime Minister, 523
  puppet government of, 575
  and Saya San trial, 516
  war role of, 576
Ba Pe, U, 522, 523, 527
Baghdad, caliphate, 66
Baguio, Japanese at, 480
Bagyidaw, reign of, 322, 382
Baho regime, 575
Bahrayn pirates, 67
*Bako,* 90, 91, 100
Balambangan Island, British occupation of, 309, 439
Balanini pirates, 439
Balaputra, 74, 80
Balestier, Joseph, at Bangkok, 340
Bali, 169
  Kertanagara's suzerainty over, 368
Banda islanders, 180, 189, 210
Bandon, Bay of, 9, 28, 30
Bandula's army, defeat of, 323
Bandung Study Club, 541
Banjermasin, pirate base of, 210
Banka Island, 5, 137, 219
  Dutch sovereignty over, 356
Bantam, 167, 182
  Dutch conquest of, 220
  Islamization of, 180
  pepper port at, 205, 208
Banteay Srei, 92, 97
Bao Dai, Emperor, 559
  abdication of, 582, 593
Barnaby, George, 271, 272
Barros, João de, 179, 199
Basco, Governor Don José, 256, 257
Basilan, French gesture at, 413, 438, 461
Basma (Pasai), 139
Bassac, Khmer center at, 30, 51, 89
Bataan peninsula, 567
Batavia, Dutch port of, 209, 212, 216
  free trade at, 311
Batavia government in 1900s, 362
Batavia Hollander, 229
Batavian Republic, 310

Battambang, 325
  and Siemreap, Siam's surrender of, 428
  Thailand's recovery of, 420, 564
Batu Khan, 133
Batu Pahat inscriptions, 60
Bayinnaung, King, 191, 192, 285
Bayon temple, 94, 99, 100
Beau, Governor Paul, 558
Behaine, Pigneau de, 281–283, 406, 411
  treaty of, 416
Belgium, secession of, 359, 362
Bendahara at Malacca, 157
Benedictines in Philippines, 249, 250
Bengal-Burma relations, 295
Bengali ships at Malacca, 160, 1656
Bengali silk, 226
Benkulen, 221, 231, 305
  Raffles' fiasco at, 320
Bernard, Commissioner, 392, 393, 400
Berythe, Bishop of, 268
Bhadravarman of Champa, 59
*Bhagavad Gita,* heroes of, 37
Bhamo, 125
  British steamers to, 389
  Chinese freebooters at, 391
  Chinese trade via, 299
Bhavapura, Land Chenla capital at, 88
Bhavavarman of Chenla, 54, 86
Billiton Island, 5, 219, 366
Binnya Dala, 289
Binnya U of Martaban, 149
Blundell, Commissioner, 383
Bo Myogo ("Colonel Thunderbolt"), 568
Bocarro, Antonio, 199
Bodawpaya, King, 292, 293, 325
  death of, 296
Bodhisattva principle, 40, 48, 77, 89, 293
Boer War, second, 390
Bohal, rebellion in, 255
Boleta tickets at Manila, 246
Bombay-Burma Trading Corporation, fine of, 391
Bonifacio, Andrés, 464, 467
Bordeaux trader, 409
Borel, Auguste, 409, 410
Borel, Eduard, 409

Borneo, American Trading Company of, 441
Borobudur, 62, 74–76, 78
Borodin, in China, 453
and Nguyen Ai-Quoc, 560
Boromoraja II, 147, 192, 243
Bosch, Governor Johannes van den, 359, 362
Bose, Rash Behari, 574
Bose, Subhas Chandra, 574, 577
Bowring, Sir John, at Hongkong, 344, 345
Bowring-Parkes treaty with Siam, 345, 350
Bradley, Dr. Dan, 340
Brahma principle in Hinduism, 36
Brahman priests at courts, 40, 42
Brazil, coffee production of, 365
British advisers in Siam, 350, 491, 492
British Burma, Mindon's friction with, 389
British hegemony, 304, 307
British-Indian rule in Burma, 380
British Malaya, problems of, 454
British North Borneo, 461
British traders licensed from India, 230
British treaty of 1925 with Siam, 500
Brito, Philip de, 193–195
Broglie, Duc de, 421
Brooke, Charles, 440, 441
Brooke, James, at Bangkok, 340
as Brunei consul-general, 439, 440
knighting of, 440
of Sarawak, 368, 439, 440
Brunei, 179
James Brooke at, 439, 440
Brunei Sultan, bribing of, 441
Bruno, capture of, 290
Bryan, William Jennings, 466
Bucas Grande rebellion, 480
Buddha tooth of Ceylon, 118, 188
Buddhism, principles of, 39
Buddhist lay school movement, 404
Buddhist missionary influence in Gupta times, 34
Buddhist *Sangha* in Burma, 301
Budi Otomo, 377, 543
Buginese, 70, 180

Buginese, Hindu influence on, 45
royal symbolism of, 14
Buginese pirates, 307, 438
Buginese traders, 6, 12
Bugis at Malacca, 159
Bugis "gypsies," 162
Buitenzorg, agricultural station at, 374, 538
Burma, agricultural expansion in, 398
antiseparationists in, 518
*athi* element in population, 122
Constitution, of 1922, 511
of 1935, 519
Cooperative Bank, 400
crimes of violence, 402
dyarchy reform scheme, 511
front-line military position of, 575
Legislative Council, 400, 508, 519
national schools system, 510
oil industry, 399
palace rebellion of 1866, 389
parliamentary government, 523
seventeenth-century trade, 214
and Siam, comparison of, 496
spirit propitiation in, 115
village-committee report on, 525
Burma Chamber of Commerce, 396
"Burma Free State," proposal of, 514
Burma government in exile, 575
Burma National Army, 577, 578
Burma Railways, 399
Burma Research Society, 404
Burma Road, 527, 565
Burma Roundtable Conference of 1931, 517
Burman cultural contact via Manipur, 116
Burman rebellion, 393
Burman school funds, 403
Burman-Tartar relations, 128
Burmans, early home of, 18
Burmese, relations with China, 596
Burmese civil service, 397
Burmese society, 300
Burney as British Resident, 382
Burney mission to Siam, 326, 334, 335
Burney treaty of 1826, 336
Butler, Sir Spencer Harcourt, 508, 511

Caciquism in Philippines, 237
Cairo, University of, 377, 540
Calcutta, opium auctions in, 313
  and Tenasserim, 336
  trade at, 312
Calicut, 173, 174
Cambay, Bay of, 161, 173, 174, 179, 211
Cambay cloth, 162
Cambodia, Central Consultative
    Assembly, 550
  decline of, 109
  French impact on, 432, 550, 557
  French suzerainty over, 420
  westernization of, 343
Cambodians, displacement in Cochin-
    China, 556
Campocam, 166
Campot, conference at, 347
Camranh Bay, 52
  Cham control of, 85
Canning, Captain, 295
Cansu I (Alaungsitha), 119, 123, 127
Cansu II (Narapatsithu), 124, 125, 127
Cansu IV (Narathihapate), 128
Canton, early use of, 23, 24
  Japanese capture of, 564
Canton trade, 279
Cao-bang, Trinh capture of, 266
Cao Dai of Cochin-China, 562, 591
Cape of Good Hope, British annexation
    of, 308
  founding of, 216
Cape St. Jacques, 419
Cape Town, Dutch surrender of, 317
Capellan, Governor van der, 358
Cardoman Mountains, 5
Caroline Islands, 246
"Cassayer" (Manipuri) cavalry, 289
Caswell, Rev. Jesse, 339
Catholic chaplains in Burma, 288
Catholic Church in Malacca, 180
Catholic faith in Vietnam, 408
Catholic missionary program, 339
Catholic revival in Europe, 411
Catholics in Siam, 195
Cayeyro, João, 190, 191
Cebu, Spanish settlement in, 235
Cebu straits, use of, 246
Cecille, French Admiral, 413, 414

Celebes, mountains of, 6
Ceylon, British control of, 308
  Dutch conquest of, 217, 218
  early entrepôt in, 26
  Mon contacts with, 113
  Mon trade with, 30
Ceylon-Burma quarrel, 123
Chaigneau, Eugène, 408, 409
Chaigneau, Jean-Baptiste, 283
  departure of, 410
  in Paris, 409
Chaigneau, Michel, 409
Chaise, Père de la, 269
Chakravartin (universal monarch), 89,
    117, 119
Chakri dynasty, founding of, 292, 325
  government of, 326
Cham art standards, 96
Cham capture of Vijaya, 104
Cham refugees to Malacca, 168
Cham state, origin of, 17
Cham traders, 108
Cham Yasoharapura, destruction of, 94
Champa, 59, 66, 75, 108
  character of, 106
  coast of, 28
  fall of, 105, 168
  Funan alliance with, 53
  Indianization of, 33, 42, 107
  longevity of, 60, 108
Champa-Vietnam feud, 103, 105
Champassak, French, 426, 428
Chams, in Annam, 5
  cultural borrowings of, 13
  economic development of, 6
  Javan contact with, 13
  local genius of, 46
  maritime activities of, 107
  role of, 60
Chandra Gupta II, 34, 47
Ch'ang-an, Nan Chao mission to, 18
Chantaban, 89
Chapata, 95, 124
Chapelle, Archbishop P. L., 469
Charles III of Spain, reforms of, 232,
    256
Charles V of Spain, 235
Charles X of France, 412
Charner, Admiral, 418

Chasseloup-Laubat, Admiral, 418, 421
Chau, Phan Boi, 559
Chau Ju Kua report, 78, 82, 110, 233
Chauk-Yenangyaung oil deposits, 6
Chaumont, Chevalier de, 275
    and Narai, 275
Cheng-ho, hero spirit of, 453
    and Majapahit, 155
    and Malacca Straits, 155
    naval expeditions of, 150
Chenla, Khmer state of, 51, 54
Chenla (of the Land), 87
Chenla (of the Water), 87
Chenla Khmers, relations with Mons, 58
Chen-li-fu, 94
Chennault, General Claire, 567
Chettyar moneylenders, in Burma, 398
    in Malaya, 159, 183
Chettyar titles to land, 399
Chettyars of Madras, 188
Chiao-chi, Annamese port of, 23, 28
Chieh-ch'a (Kedah), 68, 71
Chiengmai, 191, 193, 325
    Bayinnaung at, 191
    Burman rule over, 263, 285, 291
    capture by Narai, 264
    rebellion of, 146
    Siam's suzerain rights over, 193
    and Trailok, 147
Ch'ih-t'u, 86
Chin Hills border, 382
Chin tribes, 395
China, "country" vessel trade with, 305
    French war with, 1885, 423
    market for opium in, 315
    Siamese tributary missions to, 331
China's suzerainty tradition, 596
Chindwin River, 282
Chindwin Valley trade, 18
Chinese, at Batavia, 210
    in Cambodia and Laos, 549
    in Cochin-China, 549
    in Indonesia, 361
    Indonesian-born, status of, 539
    at Malacca, 156
    Malay dependence on, 452
    in Malaya, 446
    overseas, 597

Chinese, in Siam, 328
    at Singapore, 442, 443
Chinese Commission on Overseas Affairs, 597
Chinese culture in Annam, 16
Chinese customs' inspectorate, 82
Chinese disabilities in Siam, 503
Chinese factions at Bangkok, 349
Chinese Ming exiles, 266
Chinese population, of Indies, 366
    outside of Java, 533
Chinese rebellion of 1741 in Java, 230
Chinese role in Java, 534
Chinese secret societies, 448
Chinese tea, demand for, 226
Chinese trade at Bangkok, 331, 332
Chinese workers, recruitment of, 448
Chittagong, 285, 292
    border problems, 294
    coast, 189
    Indians from, 4
Chola Empire of Tamils, 35, 81
Chola raids on Śrivijaya, 58, 93
Cholas, conquest of Ceylon by, 36
Cholon, 419, 552
Chou Ta-kuan, 84, 99
    report on Angkor, 101
Christian Karens, 387
Christian missionaries, role of, 590
Christian missionary activity of Dutch, 369
Christian population at Malacca, 177
Christians, in Cochin-China and Tong-king, 409
    in Japan, persecution of, 241
Chudha-mani, Prince, 342, 343
Chulalongkorn, King, 325, 348, 427, 487
    accession, 351
    coronation, 351
    nostalgic memories of, 505
    reforms of, 488
    status of, 489
Churchill, Randolph, in 1885, 391
Clarke, Governor Andrew, selection of, 444
Clive, Robert, role of, 285, 304
Cochin-China, 66, 407
    Chinese Chamber of Commerce, 430

Cochin-China, Christians in, 409
  colony of, 432
  French capital, 555
  French protectorate over, 419
  rice cultivation, 547
  Trotskyite party, 561
Cocks, Richard, 241
Code of Manu, Mon digest of, 129
Coen, Governor-General Jan Pieter-
  zoon, 207, 209
  threefold policy of, 215
Coffee trade, 226
Coffee-tribute system, 228
Co-hong system at Canton, 460
Colombo, 188, 218
Colonial Office, Malayan policy of, 452,
  455
Colonializing process, effects of, 587
Colorum movement, 462, 464
Communist rising in Indonesia, Novem-
  ber, 1926, 541
Compocam, 158
Confucianism, triumph in Annam, 104
Congress Party in India, 506
Conseil Supérieur des Colonies, 431
Conto, Diogo de, 199
Conway, Governor, 283
Cooper Act (Organic Act) for Philip-
  pines, 468
Cornish, Admiral, at Manila, 255
Cornwall sea dogs, 204
Coromandel Coast, 68
  Mon trade with, 15, 30
Coromandel weavers and Dutch, 226
Correa, Anthony, 177
Corregidor Island, defense of, 567
Cort, Edwin C., 493
Council of State, Wood's abolition of,
  in Philippines, 478
Council of Trent, decisions of, 250
Councils of Notables in Indochina, 552,
  553
Court procedure in Burma, 396
Courteen, William, 214
Cowie rebellion at Sandahan Bay, 441
Cox, Hiram, 295
Craddock, Sir Charles, 508
Crawfurd, John, 315, 323, 381
  at Bangkok, 332, 410

Crawfurd, John, on characterization of
  Siamese, 332
  on Chinese emigration, 442
  at Hué, 410
Cromwell's defeat of Dutch, 207, 217
Crosthwaite, Sir Charles, 395
Cruz, Jão da, 265
Ctesiphon, 66
Cultivation system in Java, 363


Daendels, Marshal Herman Willen, 316,
  317
Dalhousie, Governor, 384
Damrong, Prince, 491, 492
Danish drillmasters in Siam, 490
Darul Islam, 572
Dasmariñas, Governor, 196, 241
  murder of, 239
Dasmariñas, son of ex-Governor, 243
Davao, Japanese settlers at, 564
Dayot, Admiral, 284
De Jonge, Dutch Governor-General, 542
Dekker, Douwes, 365
  relative of, 378
Demak, 178, 180
Demographic pressures on Southeast
  Asia, 595
Dent Brothers in North Borneo, 441
Depression, Great, 450
  of 1921–1922, 450
Desa, Javanese, 360
Desfarges, Marshal, Siam mission of,
  276, 277
Deshima Island, Dutch trade at, 222,
  229
Deutero-Malays, coastal settlements, 12
Devaraja cult, 44, 45, 88–91, 94, 119
  in Burma, 117
  in Cambodia, 88, 89, 100
  in Funan, 87
Devawongse, Prince, 492
Dewey, Admiral, 466, 485
  and Aguinaldo, 467
Dewey hats and cocktails, 466
Dharmashastras, 45, 47
Dharmavamsa, King, 81
Dianga Island, 189
Diard, 410

Diem, Ngo Dinh, 559
Diemen, Governor van, 216
Disraeli's Suez canal coup of 1875, 446
District Councils, operation of, 513
Diu, 174
Dobama Asiayone Party, 514, 521
Dominican missionaries, 240
Dominicans in Tongking, 240
Dong Minh Hoi, 561, 562, 581, 582
Dongs'on bronze culture, 13, 17, 22
Dooley, Dr., 591
Dorman-Smith, Governor, at Simla, 575
  opposition to AFL, 578
Doumer, Governor-General Paul, 425
  reforms of, 428, 430
  trading proposal, 548
Drake, Francis, 186, 204
Draper, General, at Manila, 255
Duarte, Fernandes, at Ayuthia, 175, 177
Dufferin, Viceroy Lord, 393
Dupius, Jean, 422
Dupré, Admiral, of Saigon, 422
Dutch, access to Lisbon denied, 204
  administrative reform proposals, 529,
    530
  British control of properties of, 310
  cultural contributions of, 537
  defiance of Japan by, 565
  education program in Indonesia, 537
  ethical policy of, 369–371, 373
  government after 1820, 356
  monopoly policy, 213
  naval victory in 1602, 206
  plantation system, effects of, 534, 535
  press censorship, 531
  religious policy of, 221
  resistance to Japan by, 566
  trade in India, end of, 307
Dutch-Acheh War of 1873, 368
Dutch Communist Sneevliet, 540
Dutch East India Company, 205
  collapse of, 228, 231
  powers of governors of, 215
Dutch Indies, new products of, 366
  after World War I, 529
Dutch population of Indies, 366
Dutch-Sinhalese victory, 1656, 218
Dvaravati, Chinese intercourse via, 32

Dvaravati, Indian influence in, 42, 59
  Mon state of, 15, 58, 59
Dvaravati (Tun-sun), 86

East India Company's monopoly, can-
  cellation of, 322
École Française de l'Éxtrême Orient,
  432
Economic Society of Friends of the
  Country, 257
Einshemin of Burma, 298
Ekat'otsarot, King, 261
El Filibusterismo, 464
Elephant, white, 119
Elizabeth I, Queen, 204
English East India Company, formation
  of, 205
  trade in Surat cloth, 224
  trade patterns of, 313
Ethical policy, contradictions in, 377
  of Dutch, 369–371, 373
  replacement of, 528
Europeans in Siam, 349

Fa-Hsien, in Ceylon, 31
  journey of, 31–33
  report on Buddhism by, 34
Fa Hsun, 51
Fa Ngum of Lan Ch'ang, 148
Faifo, 410
  mission to, 265
Fan Chan, usurper, 51
Fan Shih-man, founder of Funan Em-
  pire, 51
Fansur, 139
Federated Malay States, 445
Fenton, Captain, 204
Ferlec (Perlak), 139
Ferry, Jules, 392, 423
Filipinization process, 474
Filipino Commission, membership of,
  476
Filipino Council of State, 477
Filipino opposition to Wood, 479
Filipino unrest, 461
Filipinos at Malacca, 164
Fitch, Robert, journey of, 204

Flores Sea, islands of, 6
Flying Tiger Corps, 567
Forbes, Cameron, as Governor-General, 478
Force, 136, 579
Forestry Department of Burma, 386
Franciscans in Philippines, 249
Franco-Prussian War, 390
Free Thai movement, 580
Freedom Bloc in Burma, 526, 527, 574
Freil, Captain, 280
French, colonial service of, 432
  commercial relations in seventeenth century, 271
  cultural influence, measure of, 415
  economic policy of, 550
  mercantilist trading system, 547
  missionary activity in Vietnam, 412
  naturalization requirements of, 433
  naval action of, at Saigon, 417
French African Troops, 419
French clergy, liberal elements of, 412
French Cochin-China, capital of, 554
French East India Company, 280
French Indochina, administration of, 549
  Chambers of Agriculture in, 430
  Chambers of Commerce in, 430
  colonists, 548
  investments, 554
  railways, 551
French Messageries Maritimes, 446
French Ministry of Colonies, departments of, 431
French rule, mercantilist character of, 546
  Vietnamese opposition to, 433
French treaties with Siam, 348, 499
French treaty with Phnom Penh, 419
Friar lands agreement, 469
Fukien, vessels from, 233
Fullerton, Governor, of Penang, 334–337
Funan, destruction of, 15
Furnivall, John S., 404, 510

*Gaingyoks,* Burmese, 297
Gaja Mada era, 141–143

Galle, port of, 217
  cinnamon lands behind, 217, 218
Galleon trade of Manila, 246–248
Gallinato in Cambodia, 242
Gandhi, visit to Burma, 513
Gandhian boycott tactics, 509
Gandhian movement, influence of, 404
Ganges-Brahmaputra delta, 189
Garnier, Francis, 421
  death of, 422
  at Hanoi, 390
  report by, 421
Garuda bird legend, 107, 142
"Gatherings" in Java, 372, 405
Gautama, 76, 119
  Mahayana interpretation of, 40
  message of, 38
  personality of, 38
Gawdawpalin temple, 125, 127
GCBA, 512, 513, 518, 521
General Council of Buddhist Associations, 404
General Council of Burmese Associations, 507–510
George Washington, Prince of Siam, 343
German advisers in Siam, 490
German Norddeutscher Lloyd, 446, 447
Gia Lon, 325, 406, 408
  death of, 409
Gisignies, De Bus de, 359
Gladstone, Prime Minister, 1886, 393
Glasgow East Indian Association, 322
Go Oc Eo, Funan's port of, 28, 52
Goa, 173, 187
  Manila's trade with, 244
Goan relations with Ceylon, 188
Goens, Governor Rijklof van, 218, 220
Golconda, 273
Gold Coast of Africa, British acquisition of, 368
Grandière, Governor de la, 419, 421
  at Saigon, 420
Great Lake basin development, 6, 52
"Greater East Asia Co-Prosperity Sphere," 505, 566, 568
Greater East Asia Ministry of Japan, 568, 576
Greek Bactria, 33

Greek trade to Ceylon, 26
Grisee, port of, 178, 180
Guards in Honor of Mary, 465
Guizot, Prime Minister, 412, 414
Gujerat, Muslim, 154
Gujerati, merchants, 67, 153
  at Muslim Malacca, 161
  and Portuguese, 175, 179
  spice trade of, 162
Gupta art patterns, 68
Gupta Empire, 25
  Mon relations with, 58
  supremacy of, 34
Gutzlaff, Carl, 339
Guzman, Francisco Tello de, 243


Haas, French consul, 391, 392
The Hague, reform proposals for, 529
Hainan faction in Malaya, 453
Hainan Island, 66
  Japanese capture of, 564
Haiphong, port of, 552
Haji, Sultan of Bantam, 220
Hakka Chinese faction in Malaya, 453
Halingyi, destruction of, 18, 114
  Pyu capital of, 113
  as vassal of Nan Chao, 114
Halmahera, 180
Han China, 16, 24
  annexation of Vietnam by, 22
  fall of, 17
  overland trade, 22
  sea trade, 23
  weakening of, 59
Hanoi, attempted coup at, 422
  coal site near, 423
  incident of 1873, 390
  Nan Chao attack on, 19, 143
  Portuguese adventurers at, 242
  Tay-son capture of, 282
  Thai attack on, 17
  Trinh capital of, 265
Hanuman, king of the monkeys, 142
Hare-Hawes-Cutting Act, 482
Harihara cult, 87, 89
Hariharalaya cult, 88
Haripunjaya, 59, 93, 94, 117

Haripunjaya, Mon state of, 58, 59
  refugees from, 117
Harris, Townsend, at Bangkok, 345, 346
Harrison, Governor-General Francis
  Burton, 476
Harsha, King, 34, 68
Hassan Udin, Sultan, 219
Hastings, Warren, 308, 321
Ha-tien, 281
Hatta Mohammed, ascendancy of, 571
  and Japanese, 545, 570
Hayam Wuruk, 141, 143
Haye, Admiral de la, 270
Heliopolis, Bishop of, 268
Henry the Navigator, 173
Heutz, Governor von, 369
Hideyoshi, General, 241, 261
High Commissioner, Malayan, powers
  of, 483
Hillside cultivation, 10
Hinayana Buddhism, of Ceylon, 36
  Mon transmission of, 46
Hindu cosmology, 330
Hindu influences in Muslim Malaya,
  171, 593
Hindu practices in Funan, 54
Hinduism, influences in Southeast Asia,
  36
  strength and weakness of, 40
Hinduizing process, 42
Hirado, galleon ships at, 241
Hitler's attack on Russia, 565
Hlutdaw Council, 123, 287, 296
  discarding of, 395
  effectiveness of, 297
  origin of, 125
Ho Chi Minh, 561, 581
Hoa-hao sect, 562
Hogendorp, 316
Home Rule Party, 512
Hon-gay, coal site at, 423, 431
Hongkong port, 436
Hoover veto of Hare-Hawes-Cutting
  Act, 482
*Hotar* chaplaincy at Angkor, 91
Hova peoples of Madagascar, 13
Hsinbyushin, King, 291
Huang Ch'ao, rebel, 67

Huè, 408
  Dutch access to, 214
  Imperial Court at, 550
Hukbalahap movement, 473, 480, 583
Hulegu Khan, 133
Hunter at Bangkok, 340
Hurgronje, Snouck, 369–371, 375

I-Ching, 18, 58, 68, 71, 104
  sea journey of, 35
  in Śrivijaya, 44
  writings of, 39, 70–73
Ilokano rebellion against Spain, 255
Imphal, defense of, 578
INA (Indian National Army), Japan's
  planned use of, 574
Independence Preparatory Committee
  for Burma, 576
Independent Party in Burma, 512
India, Burma's awareness of develop-
  ments in, 507
  Burmese aggression against, 295
  "country vessels" based on, 303
  end of Dutch operations, 307
  French threats to, 310
India Congress Party, 451, 525
India Roundtable Conference of 1930–
  1931, 516
Indian dock workers, Burman riot be-
  tween, 515
Indian Emigration Act of 1923, 450
Indian Immigration Ordinance, 448
Indian Independence League of
  Malaya, 574
Indian laborers in Burma, 380, 398
Indian National Army (INA), 574
Indianization, process of, 41
Indies, post-Napoleonic, 356
Indies Club in Holland, 373
Indochina, colonial administration in,
  431
  Colonial Council, 432
  Councils of Notables, 552, 553
  French naval interest in, 419
  depression of 1929–1930 in, 555
  hill peoples of, 14

Indochina, mining development in, 547
  postwar economic development of,
  554
  Resident-Generals, 424
Indonesia, depression in, 535
  modernization of, 534
  Nationalist Party, 536
  non-Muslim ethnic groups, 221
  after World War I, 533
  during World War I, 373
Indonesian Communist Party (PKI),
  541
Indonesian Nationalist Party (PNI),
  541
Indonesian parties, multiplicity of, 600
Indonesian Political Concentration, 544
Indra, avatar of, 40, 47
  storm god, 37
Indragiri, 158, 166
Indrapura, 88
Indravarman I, 89, 90
Indravarman III, 109
Inle Lake, 8
Innes, Sir Charles, 516
Inspection Générale du Travail of
  1927, 556
Intaw Syan, King, 124
Intrencherado, Florencio, 480
Irrawaddy, steamboats on, 386
Irrawaddy Flotilla Company, 386, 399
Isabella II of Spain, exiling of, 462
Isanavarman of Chenla, 86
Iskander Shah, Megat, 156
Islam, House of (*darul*), 539
  in Mindanao, 233
  in Palawan, 233
  in Philippines, 232
Islamic Federation or Council of Java,
  569
Islamic revival in Indonesia, 377
Islamization, Bali's escape from, 142
  of Bantam, 167
  of Java, 167
  of Malaya, 166
Islam's appeal, 170
Isthmian portages, early use of, 5, 9, 28
Isthmian trade after Funan, 57
Italian adviser in Siam, 491

Jacatra, 209
Jaffna, 218
    Buddha tooth at, 192
Jahangir, Mongol Emperor, 206
Jambi, 162
    port call at, 60
Jambi Sultan and Dutch, 219
Jambudvipa, 37
James I, accession of, 203
    and peace with Spain, 206
James II, 273
Janssens, Jan, 317
Japan, access of missionaries to, 252
    Burmese opinion of, 526
    Dutch trade with, 222, 224
    as "leader, protector and light of
        Asia," 566, 568
    Manila's relations with, 240
    Philippines threat from, 480
    Thailand's alignment with, 505
Japan (Okinawa), 67
Japanese, "arbitration" of Siam's claims
        by, 505
    at Manila, 241
    military preparations, 564
    Muslim propaganda of, 569
    Siam's orientation toward, 504
    use of Javan MIAI by, 570
    wartime propaganda by, 568
Japanese ambitions in Southeast Asia,
        565
Japanese brutality in Malaya, 572
Japanese conquest of Burma, 567
Japanese intrusion, effects of, 590
Japanese Islamic Association, prewar,
        569
Japanese language, study of, 568
Japanese rule, ordeal of, 584
Japara, 178, 180
Jaquemyns, Belgian adviser in Siam,
        492
Java, Chinese naval expedition to, 139
    civil war of 1820s, 359
    Councils, 532
    Dutch conquest of, 210
    Dutch cultivation operations, 227
    Japanese Peoples Loyalty Organiza-
        tion, 570
    Peta army, 570

Java, population increase in, 364
    Putera in, 570
    rainfall in, 7
    Regency Councils, 532
    soils, 9
Java coffee, 226
Java sea, Dutch control of, 210
Javan Mataram, reemergence of, 167
Javanese art forms, 64
Javanese Islam, 170
Javanese literati or prijaji, disintegra-
        tion of, 536
Javanese religion, traditional, 13
Javanese traders at Malacca, 177
Jay treaty, 312
Jayakatwang, 139, 140
Jayanagara, 141
Jayavarman I, 54, 60, 87
Jayavarman II of Cambodia, 74, 84, 88,
        89
Jayavarman III, 89
Jayavarman V, 92, 101
Jayavarman VII, 94, 99
    death of, 144
    as ruler of Champa, 105
    victory over Champa, 94
Jayavarman VIII, 109
Jayaviravarman, 93
Jenghiz Khan, 133
Jesuit Society, expulsion of, 256
    publications of, 252
    reconstitution of, 258
Jesuits in Philippines, 249, 250
Jogjakarta, 530, 532
    sultanate of, 372
Johore, 279
Jolo, Spanish capture of, 461
Jones Act of 1916, 473, 476
    shortcomings of, 477
Jonkers, Captain, 220
Jourdain, John, 207
    death of, 213
Judson, Adoniram, arrival of, 302
Junk Ceylon, 279, 325
    trade of, 314

Kabaw Valley, Burma's loss of, 286
Kabul, Russian threat at, 391

Kachin raiders in 1884, 391
Kachin tribes of Burma, 4, 14, 398
*Kala* coolies from India, 403
Kalah-bar, 66
Kali, wife of Śiva, 37
Kalidesa, poetry of, 34
Kalinga coast, 22, 164
Kalinga traders at Malacca, 160, 165, 177
Kampar, 158
Kanchi, Pallavan emigrants from, 34
Kandian army, 270
Kandian government, 217, 219
K'ang Hsi, Emperor, 266
K'ang Yu-wei, 552
Kangany recruiting system, 449
Kantu peoples, 125
Karen National Union, 395
Karen-Palaung, attack on Pyu by, 113, 114
Karenni, 393
Karens, of Burma, 4
  conquest of, 18
  intrusion into Minbu and Magwe by, 18
  kinds of, 15
Katipunan plot, 464
Kaundinya I, 52, 85
Kaundinya II, 53
Kedah, 279
  Hindu remains at, 33
  Mount, 30, 32
  Sultan of, 325, 333
Kedah-to-Patani portage trade, 28, 164
Kediri state, 137, 169
Kedu plain of Java, 75
Kelantan under Siam, 337
Kempeitai, brutality of, 571, 573, 576
Kengtung state, 395
Kertanagara, 138, 141
  assassination of, 139
  heirs of, 140
  and Mongols, 137
  rise of, 137
Kertarajasa (Vijaya), 140, 141
Kha tribesmen of Laos, 551
Khmer Chenla, rise of, 15
Klacwa (Kyazwa), 125, 128
Kohima, Allied defense of, 578

Ko-lo (Tavoy), 86
Kolofeng, chief of Nan Chao, 18
Konbaung dynasty, capitals of, 296
  emergence of, 260, 281, 292
  humiliation of, 383
Koranic law, interpretation of, 152
Korat plateau, 4, 85, 325
  Khmer occupation of, 15
  Mon trade with, 30
  savannah soil of, 8
Korea, 67
Kosma of the Mons, 14, 112
Krishna, 37, 98
Krom, 537
Kuala Lumpur, policy of, 455
Kuala Merbok, estuary of, 30
Kublai Khan, 105, 133
  capture of Hanoi by, 134
  seaborne trade of, 137
Kubo Valley, Burma's recovery of, 382
Kuomintang, 582
  advent of, 500
  influence of, 539
Kyaukse, 299
  granary of, 9, 15, 114, 129
  irrigated area, 18, 112, 117
  Shan princes' control of, 134
Kyawza (Klacwa), deposition of, 128


Labuan Island, British annexation of, 440
Ladang cultivation in Java, 11
Lagrée, Daudart, death of, 421
  and Norodam, 420
Lagrée-Garnier expedition, 389, 413, 421
Laksamana at Malacca, 157
Lakshmi, wife of Vishnu, 37
Lambri, 139
Lamph'un, Haripunjaya capital at, 59, 93, 144
Lan Ch'ang, 148
  breakup of, 425
Land Purchase Bill of Ba Maw, 524
Land Records Department of Burma, 396
Land Revenue Act of 1876, 398
Laneau, 268

Lanessan, Commissioner de, 425, 430

Lankasuka, 9, 86
  commercial importance of, 57
  extent of, 56
  Indianization of, 57
  trading activity of, 58

Laos, 191
  annexation by Siam, 426
  in 1859, 350
  French coup in, 426, 427
  French rule over, 428, 550

Laotian peoples, location of, 426

Larut war, 444

Laurel, José, 569, 583

Lavo, 15, 93

Law, John, 279

Lazarist Society, reestablishment of, 411

Lê dynasty, 103, 104
  decline of, 105, 264
  partisans of, 414

League of Eastern Asia, 559

Lefebvre, Bishop, 414

Legaspi, Admiral, 235, 236, 244

Legislative Council, Burma's, 513

Leicester, Earl of, 204

Leonowens, Anna, 330, 548

Liang Court of China, 54
  annals of, 57

Liberal Party, Dutch, 365

Libois, Father, 415

Light, Francis, 309

Ligor, 9, 28, 69, 75, 279, 327
  Bangkok ties with, 337
  Raja of, 335
  in Śrivijaya, 92

Ligor (Tambralinga), 81

Lin-i (Champa), 53, 63

Linschoten's *Itinerario*, 204

Lisbon, *patronato* monopoly of, 198

Liuchiu islanders, 188, 197

Liuchiu traders at Malacca, 163

Liuchiuans at Phnom Penh, 243

Liverpool-Glasgow traders, 315

Lodge, Senator Henry Cabot, 466

Lokesvara, Mahayana, Buddhist cult of, 54

Long, Governor-General, 552

Lonthor, 210

Lopburi (Lavo), 144
  Mon center of, 15

Lopez, Gregory, 269, 270

Louis XIV, 268, 269, 271, 274

Louis XVIII, 409, 411

Louis Napoleon (Napoleon III), 310, 316, 406, 416
  attitude toward Vietnam, 415, 421
  missionary pressure on, 415

Louis Philippe, policy of, 412

Louvois, 269

Lovek, Cambodian capital of, 147, 196
  Siamese capture of, 193

Lower Burma, British organization of, 385
  devastation of, 287

Lu T'ai, 146

Luang Prabang, 144, 193, 426
  in 1859–1860, 350
  French consulate at, 426
  king of, 550
  under Lan Ch'ang, 148
  under Rama Khamheng, 144
  under Siam, 337

Luzon, friar-owned lands, 459
  irrigation development in, 9
  Malacca trade with, 168
  rebellion of 1896, 464
  Tagalog rivermen in, 233

Macao, under Philip II, 240
  Portuguese occupation, 187, 197
  trade of, 197, 265

MacArthur, Field Marshal Douglas, 484, 567

Macassar, Dutch capture of, 219

MacDonald, Prime Minister, 517

MacFarland, Rev. S. G., 349

McKean, James W., 493

McLane, Robert, 345

McNutt, Paul V. (American High Commissioner), 484

Madagascar, Malay contacts with, 13

Madura Island, 180, 209, 539
  under Kertanagara, 137

Madurese islanders, 79

Maetsuycker, Governor-General, 218, 220, 227

Magellan, voyage of, 235
Magsaysay, President, 583
Maha Bandula, 322
*Mahabharata,* 44, 87
*Mahadanwun* of Burma, 297
Mahakam River in Borneo, 60
Mahammadijah modernists, 540
Mahammed Hatta, 542
Mahamuni Buddha, 293
Mahan, Captain, 466
Mahayana Buddhism, 40
Mahazedi pagoda, 192
Mahendra, Mount (Phnom Kulen), 89
Mahendravarman, 86
Mahesvara, Śaivite cult of, 54
Mahmud, Sultan, 159, 181, 175
  escape of, 176
Ma-i (Luzon), 164, 233, 234
Maingy, British Commissioner, 383
Maintenon, Madame de, 269
Majapahit empire, 140
  fall of, 169
  and Nusantara, 156
  palace of, 142
  rise of, 140
  Tumasik as vassal of, 154
Makuta (Manuha), King, 116–118
Malabar, 68
  Indians of, 165
  Mediterranean trade of, 25
  Muslims of, 154
Malacanan palace evacuation, 483
Malacca, Christian population, 177
  commercial attractions, 161
  Dutch capture of, 197, 211
  Dutch control of, 212
  Filipinos at, 164
  founding of, 154
  Javanese attack on, 178
  Manila's trade with, 244
  Portuguese capture of, 172
  Portuguese surrender of, 211
  trade in 1515 under Portuguese, 178,
    183
Malacca Straits, Mongol intervention
  in, 135
Malay Chinese, and Japanese, 569
  strength of, 452
Malay Communist Party, 453

Malay Federation, High Commissioner
  of, 445
Malay Kuomintang, 453
Malay language, spread of, 13
Malay Peoples Anti-Japanese Army
  (MPAJA), 573
Malay Planters Association, 449
Malay states, surrender of Siam's
  suzerain control of, 445
Malay Sultanates, British Residents in,
  444
Malaya, Labor Code of, 449
  plural society, 455
  rubber plantations, 448
  tin mining, 443, 447
Malayan Islam, 170
Malayu (Jambi), 67–69, 71, 82
  independence of, 138
Malwa, opium of, 314
Man Lulan (Sawlu), 118
Manar, island of, 188, 218
*Mancharya* (teacher of the king), 120
Manchu regime, downfall of, 558
Mandalay, French influence at, 391
Mandarin status in Vietnam, 408
Mangu Khan, 133, 134
"Manifest destiny," American, in 1898,
  466
Manila, appearance of, 248
  Bishop of, 238, 460
  British conquest of, 309
  Cambodian adventure of, 243
  Chinese at, 238, 239
  Dutch attack on, 237
  after 1815, 257
  in 1820, 258
  galleon trade, 237, 258
  Koxinga's threat to, 239
  obras pias at, 246
  Parián quarter of, 250
  in 1763, 255
  Space Allocation Board at, 246
  trade of, 460
Manila Bay, battle of, 466
Manipur, 285
  Burmese claims to, 381
  Mongoloid peoples in, 4
  trade route via, 18

Manipuri, Brahmans of, 296
  raids from, 289
Manipuris, 286, 288
Manoel, King, 174
Mansur Shah, 158
Manu, Code of, 35, 45, 47, 286
  in Siam, 146
Marco Polo's description of Southeast
  Asia, 138, 139, 166
Margary expedition, 390
Marine and Colonies, French Depart-
  ment of, 425
Marshall Islands, 246
Martaban, 25
  Gulf of, 4
  Mon port of, 30
  Tun-sun trade with, 28
Marx, Karl, 521
Marxism, attractions of, 601
Marxist dogma, Philippine refutation
  of, 486
Marxist principles, applicability to
  Burma, 526
Masjumi Party, 540, 570–572
Masonic Order, Rizal and, 463
Masulipatam, port of, 272
Mataram, 62, 74, 78
  attack on Batavia by, 209
  hostility of Srivijaya toward, 58
Mauritius Island, 287
  British control of, 308
Mauryan Empire, extent of, 33
Maw Shans of Burma border, 150
*Max Havelaar*, 355, 364, 365
Mecca, opium from, 161
  pilgrimages to, 171, 533, 570
Meklong Valley trade route, 23, 31
Mekong River boundary of Siam, 395
Melanesian peoples, 11
Mello, Diogo Soares de, 191
Menadonese Christians, 537
Mendoza, Admiral, 205
Mendut temple, 75, 76
Meo hillside cultivations, 557
Mercantilism, French policy of, 430
Mergui, 31, 279, 325
  Barnaby and White at, 273
  early use of, 28
  portage trade via, 194

Meru, Mount (*see* Mount Meru symbolism)
Mexico, French fiasco in, 421
  transferred system of, 236
MIAI in Java, 571
Miche, Father, 347, 420
Middleton, Henry, 206
Minahasa, 539
Minangkabau peoples, 9, 377, 537
  immigrants to Malaya, 154, 159
  and Islam, 169
  reforms of, 539
  trade at Malacca of, 166
Minbin, King, of Arakan, 189
Minbu-Magwe granary, 9, 18, 113, 114,
  191, 299
Mindanao, 167
  cinnamon from, 235
  jungles of, 6
  pirates of, 253
Mindon, King, 298, 301, 341
  accession of, 385
  daily routine of, 388
  and Mongkut compared, 385, 387
  reform efforts of, 388
Ming China, mission to, 143
Ming Chinese, fleets of, 105, 155
  occupation of Annam by, 105
Ming Yung-li, 286
Mingalazedi pagoda, 46, 125
Mingun pagoda, 293
Minh Mang, 406
  death of, 412
  French relations with, 409, 411
  Peking's investiture of, 409
Mining development in Indochina, 547
Minto, Lord, 316
*Mission civilisatrice* of France, 422
MJAPA sabotage, 573
Mocha, coffee culture at, 226
Modernist and traditionalist views, po-
  larization of, 594
Modernization, impulse toward, 586, 588
Mogaung, founding of, 144
Mohnyin Shans, 151, 190
Moi tribesmen, 281, 556
Moksobo (Shwebo), myothugyi of, 285
Moksobomyo, 289

Molucca islanders, Dutch control of, 210
Moluccas, 7, 69
Mon Confederacy of Ramanyadesa, 93, 108, 117
Mon-Karen rebellion of 1826, 381
Mon Pegu, 111, 117
Mon role as teachers, 109
Monastic schools, decline of, 403
Mongkut, King, 301, 324, 330, 334, 341, 487
  accession of, 341, 342
  death of, 351
  international policy of, 349
  letters to Louis Napoleon, 342
  modernization efforts of, 348
  as monk-scholar, 340, 341
Mongnai, 294
Mongol expansion, effects of, 133
Mongol horde, Kublai as leader of, 134
Mongol-Thai intrusion, 96
Mongols, attacks on Annam, 135
  capture of Hanoi, 105
  conquest, of Nan Chao, 19, 109, 135
    of Pagan Burma, 109, 128
  withdrawal from Burma, 129
Mons, of Burma, 18
  exodus to Siam, 291
  in Menam Valley, 15
Monsoon winds, 7
Montagu, Secretary, in 1917–1918, 508
Montigny, at Bangkok, 346, 347, 446
  at Hué Court, 348
Moraes, Fernando de, 190
Morgas, *Sucesos de las Filipinas,* 463
Moro population, 233, 236
  conquest of, 467
Motte, Lambert de la, 268, 270
Moulmein, English Company rule at, 384
Mount Meru symbolism, 37, 38, 47, 89, 91
  in Funan, 52
  replica of, 45
Mountbatten, Lord Louis, 577, 579
Mrohaung, 189, 295
Muda Hassim of Brunei, 439
Muhammadijah, 377, 536, 537, 569

Mulavarman of Borneo, 60
Mun Valley, 30, 85
Munich agreement, effects of, 564
Münster, treaty of, 237
Muntinghe as Raffles' aide, 316, 318
Muong Nai, founding of, 144
Murunda, 52
Muslim Arabs, trade of, to Kedah, 30
Muslim Champa, 167
Muslim faith in Java, 170
Muslim Malays, aversions of, 451
Muslim Perlak, 166
Muzaffar Shah, rule of, 155, 157, 158
Myazedi inscription, 119
Myitkyina, capture by American-Chinese forces, 578
Myitnge River, 129, 296
Myooks, 385, 386
Myosade, Burman practice of, 14, 115
Myosas in Burma, 122, 297
Myothugyi, 115, 385

Naga snake earth god, in Burma, 119
  royalty symbol, 38, 47, 52, 100
Nagari alphabet, 92
Nagore, 165
Nahdatul, Ulama, 536, 540, 569, 572
Nai Khuang Aphaiwong as Premier, 580
Nalanda, 68
  Buddhist center at, 39, 71
  hostelry at, 43
  University of, 35, 73, 92
Nam Viet, in Han China, 16
  rise of, 103, 104
Namdinh, 423
Nan Chao, 87, 143
  Burman relations with, 125
  capture of Hanoi by, 17, 18, 114
  fall of, to Mongols, 144
  founding of, 19
  Indian writing system, 25
  Mongol destruction of, 134, 140
  political organization, 11
  Pyu musicians from, 18
  T'ang Chinese attack on, 25
Nanda Bayin, 192, 193

Nanking, Treaty of, 258
Nanyang Chinese, Red China's relations with, 597
  in Siam, 500
Napoleon Bonaparte, three-foot puppet of, 333
Napoleon III (*see* Louis Napoleon)
Narai, King, 260, 286
  accession of, 263
  and Dutch, 263
  flirtation with foreign adventurers, 278
  and French, 269
  and Macassars, 263
  war with Burma, 263
Naresuen, King, 193, 242
Nat spirits of Burma, 13, 115
National Congress Party, 574
National Schools in Java, 373
Nationalist (the Twenty-one) Party, 512
  election victory, 474
Natonmya (Nandaungmya), 125
Nederburgh, 316
Negapatam, Buddhist hostelry at, 43, 137
  Dutch port of, 307
  labor assembly depot at, 448
Negombo, 217, 218
Negrais massacre, 290
Negrito peoples, 12
Nehru, Pandit, 595
Nerini, Bishop, 288
Netherlands under Napoleon, 355
Netherlands Constitution, of 1848, 364
  of 1922, 532
Netherlands Indies, world depression in, 542
Netherlands States General after 1867, 365
Netherlands Trading Society, 364, 368
New Caledonia, Vietnamese labor in, 556
New Hebrides, Vietnamese labor in, 556
Ngo Dinh Diem, regime of, 599
Nguyen Ai-Quoc, and Borodin, 560
  at Moscow in 1922, 560
  prewar career of, 561
  return to Moscow by, 561
(*See also* Ho Chi Minh)

Nguyen Anh, 261, 281, 282
  French aid to, 283
Nguyen Canh, Prince, 282
Nguyen dynasty, Trinh feud of, 264, 406
Nguyen Truong To, visit to France, 420
Nguyen Van Tranh (*see* Nguyen Ai-Quoc)
Nicobar Islands, 5, 12, 28, 30, 71
Ningpo, 187
*Noli me Tangere,* 463, 464
Norodom, 420
North Borneo, American named Moses in, 441
North German Lloyd, 493
North Vietnam, Trinh rulers of, 280
Noumea, indentured Vietnamese laborers in, 556
Nu, Premier U, 594
Nu, Thakin, 522, 526
Nusantara, imperialist dream of, 143
Nyaungyan, prince of, 390

Ogotai, Khan, 133
Okinawans, 187
Opium, price of, 314
  traffic in, 305, 313
  Turkish and Persian, 314
Opolinario de la Cruz, Father, 461, 462
Ord, Harry, at Singapore, 444
Organic Act of 1902, 468, 469, 474
Orissa, Mon contacts with, 113
Orleanist monarchy, 412
Ormuz, trade of, 162, 174
Osias, 482
Osmeña, Sergio, 482
  evacuation of, 567
  provisional government of, 583
  as speaker, 475
  as Vice-President, 484
Ostend Company ships in Burma, 289
Ottama, U, 506, 510
Outer Islands, development of, 366, 537
  Dutch control of, 367
Overseas Chinese Banking Corporation of Singapore, 454
Overstraten, 316

Pagan Burma, 6
  borrowings of, 46
  destruction of, 129
Pagan Empire, founding of, 19, 116
Pagan Min, 382
Pahang, and Majapahit, 141
  and Malacca, 167
Paknam, dry dock at, 489
  governor of, 333
Pala state, 68, 80
  art and script of, 74
  impact on Java, 77
  University of, 68
Palakka's Buginese forces, 220
Palaungs, 18
Palembang, 60, 63, 162
  Chinese brigands at, 139, 155
  Dutch trade with, 219
  port of, 42
  river estuary at, 62
Pallavan state, 33
  art patterns of, 68
  decline of, 34
  Śaivite influence of, 56
Pallegoix, Father, and Mongkut, 340,
    342
  in Siam, 339, 346, 347
Pallu, Monsignor, 268–270
Palmerston, Lord, 322
P'an P'an, Chinese description of, 57
  isthmian state of, 34, 56, 57, 86
Panay rebellion of 1663, 252
Pancapana, 74, 75
Pandit Nehru, 47
Pan-Pacific trade union, 541
Pan-Thai movement, 504
Parameswara, 154–156
Parián Chinese quarter, 238, 239, 255
Paris, Minh Mang's effort to negotiate
    at, 412
Paris Geographical Society, 421
Paris Missionary Society, reestablish-
    ment of, 411
Paris treaty of 1763, 255
Parkes, Harry, at Bangkok, 345
Parliamentary Concentration coalition
    in Java, 544
Parsees, 165
  at Malacca, 160, 161

Parvati, bust of, 96
  wife of Śiva, 37
Pasai, Muslim, 154, 178
  and Perlak, Malacca's loss of, 158
Pasquier, Governor-General, 553
Patani, 23, 28, 179, 279
  Indian trade use of, 30
  Indianization of, 56
  rebellion of, 262
Patna, Gupta capital at, 34
  Mauryan center of power at, 33
  opium production, 306
Pavie, Auguste, 426, 427
Pearl Harbor, 544, 563
Pechabun, proposed Thai capital at,
    580
Pedir, Chinese trade in pepper at, 161
Pedir port in 1505, 164
Pegu, capture in 1757, 290
  Mon capital of, 14, 112, 151
  Siamese attack on, 193
Pegu Yoma, 4
Peguan Mons, at Malacca, 165, 168
  Portuguese trade with, 190
Peking, political objectives of, 596
  and Portuguese, 180
Pelaez, Father, 461
Pellerin, Monsignor, 416, 417
Penal Code, revision in Siam, 492
Penang Island, British title to, 333
  Chinese emigrants from, 383
  lease of, 304, 309
Peninsular and Oriental Steam Naviga-
    tion Company, 446
Peoples' Anti-Japanese Army of Luzon,
    583
Peoples' Liberation Army, 583
People's Party in Siam, Pridi's, 502
Pepper trade, decline of, 225
Perak, 334, 444
Pereira, Diogo, 191
Perlak, Muslim, 154
Permissio at Manila, 245
Persian Gulf sheikdoms, 380
Persian traders, 66, 67, 80
  at Malacca, 160
  in Malaya, 26, 30
  silk trade of, 226
Peta army in Java, 570, 571

P'etraja, 278
Phaulkon, Constantine, 270–272
  death of, 277
  French aid to, 274, 275
  knighting of, 276
Phaya Bahol, 503
Phayre, Arthur, 388
Philip II, and Catholic revival, 234
  King of Spain, 203
  ruler of Portugal, 182, 197, 204
Philippine League of Rizal, 464
Philippine Legislature control of land
  disposal, 470
Philippine productivity to 1930, 473
Philippines, Christianization of, 237
  Commonwealth of, 484, 545
  Constitution of 1935, 483
  education in, 471
  exports to United States, 473
  independence promise to, 460
  Indian cultural effect on, 6, 233
  missionary work in, 234, 251
  nationalism in, 472
  native rebellions in, 255
  religion in, 234
Philippines Assembly, 468, 474
Philippines Commission, 468, 470
Philippines Legislature, powers of, 473
Phimeanakas palace, 94, 97
Phnom Bakeng, 92, 97
Phnom Penh, approaches to, 552
  founding of, 147
  French treaty with, 419
  Liuchiuans at, 243
  Portuguese in, 197
  Thai capture of, 281
Pho-hien, Dutch factory at, 214
Piaster, franc ratio with, 555
Pibun Songgram, Luang, 503, 504
  fall of, in 1944, 580
  imperialist plans of, 505
  nonaggression treaties, 564
  westernizing fads of, 504
Pierce, President, 346
Pilar, Marcelo H. del, 463
Pi-lo-ko of Nan Chao, 19
Pindale, King, 286
Pindar, Paul, 214
Pinto's Peregrinations, 181

Pinya of Sagaing, 149
Piracy, British suppression of, 437
  Dutch suppression of, 438
Pires, Tomé, account of, 156, 160, 178,
  186
  in China, 186
PKI (Indonesian Communist Party),
  541
Planters Association of Malaya, 451
Poivre, Pierre, 280, 282
Pondicherry, 270, 279
Pongyi kyaungs, 301
Poor Man's (Sinyetha) Party, 522
Popa, Mount, 115
Population of Burma, athi element in,
  122
Portuguese, alienation of peoples by,
  198
  at Canton in 1522, 187
  in Ceylon, 189
  missionary effort of, 181
  in Moluccas, 183, 186
  in Phnom Penh, 197
  policies of, 179
Portuguese adventurers, 181
  in Burma, 190
Portuguese Goa, 174
Portuguese language, use of, 199
Portuguese Malacca, 176
  Indonesian opposition to, 172
Portuguese Timor, 221, 539
Po-ssŭ ships in trade to China, 24, 26,
  66, 71
Potts, 272, 273
Pra Naret of Siam (King Naresuen),
  192, 193, 242
Pra P'etraja, General, 277
Prachothipok, King, 497
Prapanca, poet of Java, 142
Prasat T'ong, King, 262
Pre-Islamic rites in Malaya, 593
Preparatory Committee for Javan inde-
  pendence, 571
Pridi Phanamyong, 501–504
  and Free Thai, 502, 580
Prjaji aristocracy of Java, 372
  second level of, 536
Propagation of the Faith, agency for,
  411

Proto-Malays in Sunda islands, 12
Province Wellesley, 304, 309
Pu, Premier U, 525, 526
Pulicat, 165
Pulo Condore Island, 66, 280, 282
*Puranas,* influence of, 34, 44, 87
Purim, 166
Purnavarman, 63
Purohita official, 89, 91, 100
Putte, Isaac Fransen van de, 365
Puymandel, 284
P'ya Taksin, 281, 292
Pyanchi of Toungoo, 149, 150
Pye, King, 286
Pyu, ancient, 4, 17
  Buddhist connections of, 34
  downfall of, 113
Pyu capital of Śrikshetra, 38, 112, 113
Pyu script, 113
Pyu soldiers in Nan Chao armies, 114
Pyu state, extinction of, 18

Quang-nam, Cham control at, 59
Quebec Conference, 577
Quelong, Formosa, Spanish fort at, 240
Quezon, Manuel, 467
  death of, 583
  evacuation of, 567
  opposition to Hare-Hawes-Cutting
    Act, 482
  as President, 484
  as Senate President, 475
Quirino regime, 598
Quoc-Dan Dang or Nationalist Party of
  Vietnam, 559

Raffles, Thomas Stamford, 315
  at Benkulen, 320
  Javan reforms of, 318
  and Palembang Sultan, 319
  personality of, 317
  and Riau Sultan, 320, 321
  as scholar, 318
  at Singapore, 356
Raja Sinha, 218
Rajaguru (teacher of the king), 120
Rajendravarman II of Cambodia, 89, 92
Rama I, 292, 325

Rama II, 325
Rama III, 324, 334, 335, 339
  and Burney, 335
  death of, 341
  and Malaya, 337
Rama VI, 496
Rama VII, 497, 502
Rama Khamheng of Sukhotai, 37, 98,
    129, 135
  death of, 110
  in Malaya, 138
  reign of, 109, 144, 145
Ramadhipati, 146, 149
*Ramayana* epic, 37, 44, 78, 87
Rangoon, University of, opening of, 509
    Student Union, 520, 521
Rangoon Trades Association, 396
Razadarit of Pegu, 150
Razagri, King of Arakan, 189
Recollects order, 250
Red River delta, 5
Red Sea–Nile River canal, 27
Red Sea traders, 25
Reforms Committee investigation in
    Burma, 509
Regents, role of, in Java, 361
Religious fanatics, influence of, 588
Republican Party Mandate, 478
Rhodes, Alexander of, 265, 267
Rhuynansyan (Kyawza), 128
Riau Archipelago, Dutch control over,
    321, 356
  Dutch policy in, 438
Rigault de Genouilly, Captain, 414, 416
Riot Inquiry Committee report, 524
River delta areas, development of, 7
Rizal-Mercado y Alonso, José, 463–465,
    480
  execution of, 464
  novels of, 459, 465
Roberts, Edmund, at Hué, 339, 411
Rohan, 166
Roman trade to India, 25, 26
Rome missions to Cathay, 27
Roosevelt, President Franklin, 483
  Indochina policy of, 582
Roosevelt, Theodore, 466, 485
Ross, Dutch Governor at Chinsura, 306
Roxas, 482

Royal Code Commission of Siam, 499
Rubber Growers Association, 449, 451
Rudravarman of Funan, 54, 86
Rudravarman III of Champa, 104
Ruiz, Blas, 196, 242
Run, island of, 210
Rupot, 166
Russo-German pact of 1939, 564

Sabeans, 26*n*.
Sagaing, 289
    Chinese at, 289, 299
Saigon, 410
    annexation by France, 418
    docks at, 552
    Franco-Spanish garrison at, 418
Śailendra dynasty, 62, 74
Sakyamuni (Buddha), 77
Salisbury, policy of, in 1885, 391
Salween River gorge, 4
Samara (Samudra), 139
San-fo-ch'i, 63
*Sangha,* assembly of monks, 120
Sanjaya, 74
San Juan de Letun, College of, 250
Sankharach monastic community, 330
Sanskrit literature of Cambodia, 100
*Santiparvan* from the *Mahabharata,* 35
Santo Tomas, University of, 250, 463,
    471
*Santri* faction in Java, 536, 537
Sarawak, Brooke's coup in, 439–441
Sarekat Islam, 537
    and Communists, 540, 541
    legal status of, 375, 376
    organization of, 374, 375
    after World War I, 540
    during World War I, 375
Sarraut, Albert, as Governor, 431, 433
    as Minister of Colonies, 552
Sartono, Dr., 541, 542
Sassanid Persians, 27, 66
Satha, King of Cambodia, 148, 196, 241
    death of, 242, 243
Saw, U, 520
    newspaper of, 527
    in 1938, 524
    as Premier, domestic policy, 527

Saw, U, as Premier, visit to London, 575
    wartime detention, 575
    tactics of, 520
Sawah cultivation in Java, 9
Saya San, trial of, 516
Saya San rebellion, 512, 515–517
Sayre, Francis B., as Siam's Foreign Of-
    fice adviser, 484, 492, 499
Selangor, 334
Seleucid traders, 25
Semaoen, 541
*Senabodi* council, 327
Senghasari, 169
    as capital of Java, 137
    leadership of, 139
    spice trade, role of, 137, 154
Seni Promoj, Prince, 502
    and Free Thai, 580
    as Premier, 580
Sepauk inscriptions, 60
Sepoy Rebellion, 388
Sequeira, Diogo Lopez, at Malacca, 174,
    175
Serrao, Francisco, 177
Service orders in Burma, *ahmudan,* 122
Seven Years' War, 290
Shah Jahan, 189
*Shahbandars,* 68
    role at Malacca, 157
Shan brothers, three, 128
Shan peoples, 19
Shan plateau, 4
    British control of, 393
Shan Sawbwa princes, 294, 299
Shanghai port, 436
Shin Arahan, 118
Shwe Dagon pagoda, elevation of, 151
Shwebo, 191, 296, 299
Shwebo granary, 9
*Shwedaik,* 297
Shwezigon pagoda, 46, 118, 120, 125
Siak, 158, 166
Siam, British treaty of 1925 with, 500
    Burma's boundary with, 395
    comparison between Burma and, 496
    Constitution of 1932, 502
    Crawfurd on, 330
    economic expansion, 493, 494
    escape from legal disabilities by, 498

Siam, extraterritorial rights, 350, 498
  French threat to, 427
  French treaty of 1925 with, 499
  nationalism, 504
  patron system, 328
  program of modernization, 489
  reform program, barriers to, 49
  religion, 332
  revolution of 1932, 501
  slavery, 328
  social status, 327
  traditional foreign policy, 594
  treaties, 348
  in World War I, 487
Siam crisis of 1893, British view toward, 427
Siamese, commercial activities of, 339
Siemreap, 325
  recovery by Thailand, 564
  to Siam, 420
Silliman University, founding of, 471
Simmons Tariff Act of 1913, 473
Simon Commission report, 513, 514, 516
Sindok, King, 78
Singapore, Britain's achievement at, 454
  development of, 435
  founding of, 321
  free port entrepôt, 436, 437, 447
  High Commissioner, 455
  surrender of, 566
Singapore passage, 66
Singh, Captain Mahan, 574
Singora, 28, 327
  rebellion of, 262
Singu, King, 292
Sinhalese Buddhism, 36
Sinyetha Party, 522
Sita, wife of Rama, 37
*Sitke*, 298
Sittang River, 4
Śiva, avatar of, 40, 47
  worship of, 37
Śiva cult, influence of, 34
Śiva worship, eventual decline of, 41
Sjahrir, Sultan, 542, 545
Slave trade, West African, 224
Slavery, in Burma, 121
  Dutch abolition of, 364
Smith, Adam, 315

Smoot-Hawley Tariff Act, 482
Sneevliet, Hendrik, 378, 540
*Société des Missions Étrangères*, 268
Soe, Thakin, 566
Songt'am the Just, King, 262
Southeast Asia, British hegemony in, 231
  demographic pressures on, 595
  Marco Polo's description, 138, 139, 166
  soils of, 8
Southeast Asia Treaty Organization (SEATO), 602
Souza, Salvador Ribeiro de, 194, 195
Spain, Anglo-Dutch alliance against, 207
Spanish at Tourane, 417
Spanish America and Philippines system, 237
Spanish clergy, replacement of, 475
Speelman, Cornelius Janszoon, Governor-General, 218, 219
Spice Islands, Spanish role in, 235, 236, 244
Spice trade, Dutch, decline of, 437
Spices, Dutch monopoly of, 225
Spirit propitiation cults, persistence of, 592
Śri Indradit of Sukhotai, 144
Śri Maharaja, 56
Śri Varnarendra, 63
Śrikshetra, Pyu capital of, 18, 112, 113
Śrivijaya, conquest by, 63
  entrepôt of, 69
  longevity of, 70
Śrivijayan Empire, 63
Stilwell, General Joseph, 567, 577
  retreat of, 567
Stimson, Henry L., as Governor-General of Philippines, 479, 481
  as Secretary of State, 481
Strachey's *Theory and Practice of Socialism*, 521
Straits authorities and Malay sultans, 436
Straits pirates, 437
Straits Settlements, Chinese role in, 442
  Colonial Office control of, 436
  creation of, 436
  Indians in, 442

Student strike at Burma, of 1920, 509
of February, 1936, 522
Subardjo-Tan Malaka Communists, 572
Suez Canal, opening of, 386, 436, 446,
462
Sufi mysticism, influence of, 153
Sugar cultivation, Dutch introduction
of, 225
Sujita, conquest of Lavo by, 93, 109,
117
Sukarno, 538, 541, 571
government problems, 599
"guided democracy," 600
internment of, 542
Japanese relations with, 545, 570
religious policy, 594
Sukhotai, emergence of, 95, 109, 134
fortress of, 145
Siam's rule over, 146
Small Thai capture of, 144
as vassal to Ayuthia, 146
Sulamani temple at Pagan, 125
Sulu, Sultan of, 441
Sulu Archipelago, Spain's sovereignty
over, 441, 443
Sulu Islands, 461
*Suma Oriental,* 186
Sun Yat-sen, 453, 521, 552, 559
Sunda, Gaja Mada's war with, 141
Sunda Straits, 6, 68
Dutch use of, 167
Hindu remains in, 33
possible use by Fa Hsien, 31
Sung China, and Luzon, 234
trade of, 93, 95
Sung dynasty, 80
Sungai Ujong, British measures in, 444
Surabaya, 180
sultanate of, 372
Surakarta, 530, 532
Surat, 161, 162
Bengali trade at, 304
French Company factory at, 270
Surat cloth, 211
Suryavarman I, 93, 117
Suryavarman II, 94, 97
wars on Vietnam by, 104
Suzuki in Burma, 568
Swarajist Party in Burma, 511, 512

Swasawke of Ava, 149
Swatow, German passenger service from,
447
Symes, Michael, missions of, 310
1795, 294, 295
1802, 295
Syriam, French dockyard at, 287
port of, 287
refinery, 400

Tabinshweti, assassination of, 191
conquest of Pegu by, 190
Tachard, Father, 274, 276, 277
Taft, Wiliam Howard, as Chief Commissioner, 468
as Chief Justice, 481
concern for Filipinization, 474
as President, 468
as Secretary of War, 468
Tagalog hostility to Chinese, 255
*Taikthugyis,* 297, 385, 386
Taiping rebellion, 416
Takeo temple, 94, 97
Takkola (Trang), port of, 23
Takuapa, 81
portage to Chaiya from, 28, 31
Tali, Lake of, 19
Mongol capture of, 134
Tambralinga, 9, 69, 80, 84, 86, 92, 93
conquest of Lavo by, 59
emergence of, 58
independence of, 144
relations with Śrivijaya, 58
Tamerlane (Timur) in Central Asia,
155
Tamil Immigration Fund Ordinance,
449
Tamil laborers, recruitment of, 448, 451
Tamils, Burma relations with, 124
Chola Empire, 36
T'ammaraja, King, 192
Tamon Siwa Schools in Java, 542
Tamralipti, Bengal port of, 27, 31, 71
Tan Malaka, 541
T'ang China, 86
decline of, 17
defiance of, 19
overseas trade of, 24

T'ang dynasty, 62, 63, 80
  government of, 67
  pilgrim from, 65
  prior to, 24
  reunification of China by, 25
Tantric cult practices, 45, 46, 77, 116
Taoist convent in P'an P'an, 56
Taruma (Yeh-po-ti), port of, 60, 63
Tattooing for invulnerability, 401
Tavoy, 31, 325
  Burman raiders from, 293
  Mon port of, 30
  Tun-sun trade route from, 28
Tay-son rebellion, 281, 325, 558
  carryover from, 411
  defeat of, 284
Telingana, 22
  Mon contacts with, 15, 58, 113
Temenggong at Malacca, 157
Tenancy Act of 1939, 523, 524
Tenasserim, 84
  British rule in, 336, 383
  Burma's loss of, 381
  Cambodian attack via, 117
  Mon ports of, 30
  Siam's desire for, 336
Tensions between traditional and modern, 591, 592
Ternate, 177, 184
  Spanish ouster from, 206
  Sultan of, 186
Textiles, Dutch trade in Surat, 225
Thai peoples, 19
  southward movement of, 95, 143
Thai raiders in isthmus, 144
Thai state of Nan Chao, 143
Thailand, gains at Japan's hands for, 564, 573, 580
  Japanese supply requisitions from, 568
  official name of, 504
  postwar problems in, 598
  royal prestige in, 597
Thakin (*Dobama*) Party, 520
*Thakins*, 506, 526
Thalun, King, 286
Than Tun, Communist, 574
Thanh-Nien, or Association of Revolutionary Annamite Youth, 560

Thap, Prince (Rama III), 334
Tharrawaddy, Prince, as Einshemin, 382
*Thathameda* land tax, 388
Thathanabaing, 297
  end of, 401
Thaton, Mon capital of, 30, 58, 59, 112
Thatpinnyu at Pagan, 123, 127
Thein Maung, Dr., 526
Thein Pe, Communist, 578
*Theras* (teachers), 120
Theravada Buddhism, 40, 48, 119, 125
Thibaw, King, 298
  accession of, 390
  exile of, 392
Thieu Tri, death of, 414
  hostility toward French, 414
Thihatthura, King of Ava, 149
Thiluin Man (Kyanzittha), 118, 123, 127
Thinhkaba of Toungoo, 149, 150
Thirty Years' War, 208
Three Pagodas Pass, early use of, 23, 30
Tibão, Gonsalves, 189
Tibetan threat, 19
Tibeto-Burman tribes, entry of, 19, 114
Tidore, 184
  abandonment by Spain, 208, 245
Tidore Sultan, Speelman's defeat of, 219
Timor, Portuguese, 221, 539
Timur Khan, 135
Tin mining in Malaya, 443, 447
Tiyuma, 66
Tjipto, 541
Tjokro, 375, 376
Tojo, Prime Minister, and India's independence, 574
Tojo government, collapse of, 571
Tokugawa, Ieyasu, 241, 261
Tongking, 53
  Christians in, 409
  early settlement of, 16
  nationalism in, 558
  population density in, 556
  Spanish Dominicans in, 280
  unpopularity in France, 424
  Viet Minh League in, 582
  Wu Ti's conquest of, 16
Tonle Sap, 4, 51, 52
Torre, Governor de la, 256

Toungoo dynasty, 148
Toungoo state, 151
  Burman revival in, 147
  expansion of, 190
  rise of, 130
Tourane, 410
  French expedition to, 416
  harbor of, 282
    evil health conditions at, 416
Trailok of Siam, 147
Trajan, Emperor, canal built by, 27
Tran Van-Giau, 581
Trang (Takkola), food resources of, 30
  portage route from, 28, 31
Trengganu, port of, 279
  Siamese control of, 337
Trent, Council of, 234
Tribhuvana, Queen, 141
Trincomalee, French fleet at, 270
Trinh, Phan Chou, 558
Trinh-Nguyen feud, 264
Trinh rulers of Vietnam, 280
Trotskyite Party in Cochin China, 561
Trunojoyo, 220
Tu Duc, 422
  derision of French by, 416
  rebellion against, 414
Tuban, 180, 209
Tumasik (Singapore), 141, 154
Tun Ali, 158
Tun Mutahir, 158, 175
Tun Perak, 158, 166, 175
Tun-sun (Dvaravati), Mon state of, 15,
    23, 28, 31, 51
Turkish guns at Malacca, 182
Turkish mercenary soldiers, 175
Turkish Muslims in India, 152
Turuc, Luis, 583
Twenty-one Party, 510
Tydings, Senator, 482
Tydings-McDuffie Act, 460, 483


Udong, 343
Ultramontane enthusiasm after 1815,
    258
Unfederated Malay States, 445
United States role after World War II,
    595

University of Hanoi, 443
University Act (Burma) of 1920, 509
  amendment in 1939, 522
Uparat or vice-king, 147, 278, 327
Upper Burma, annexation to India, 392
  granary areas of, 299
Uthon as founder of Ayuthia, 59
Uxumites or Ethiopians, 26n.


Vachet, Father, 275
Vaderlandsche Club, 538
Van Goens of Ceylon, 270
Van Leur's theory of Indianization, 42,
    43
Vannier, 284, 409
  departure of, 410
Varenne, Governor-General, 553
Vasco da Gama, 173
Veddoid peoples, 12
Veloso, Diogo, 195, 196, 242
  Naresuen's capture of, 196
Versailles Peace Conference, 499
Vespasian, Emperor, prohibition of bul-
    lion export, 27
Vicars apostolic, 267
Vichy regime, treaty with, 565
Vientiane, 191
  Burmese attack on, 291
  French control of, 428
  under Lan Ch'ang prince, 426
  Resident Superieur at, 550
  under Siam, 337
Viet Minh, 561
  Congress of 1945, 582
  League of, 581
Vietnam, description of, in 1820, 407
  schooling in, 433
Vietnamese, 5, 16
  anti-Cham feud of, 103, 105
  fear of China, 596
  Javan contact with, 13
  participation in World War I, 552,
    558
  southward migration of, 546, 555
Vietnamese nationalist sentiment, 552,
    558
Vietnamese soldiers in World War I,
    558

Vijaya, Prince, 139, 140
Village Regulating Act of 1906, 371, 372
Village *thugyi* (headman), 396
Visayas, Jesuit mission in, 240
Vishnu, avatar of, 40, 47
  cult of, 34, 37
Vishnu tradition, 98
Vishnu worship, eventual decline of, 41
Volksraad, 528
  approval of, 376
  character of, 530, 531
  reform proposal by, 544
Vyadhapura (city of the hunters), 52

Wachirawut, 496
Wang Ching-wei, regime of, 572
Wang Mang, 23
War in Far East, 527
Wareru of Martaban, 135
  accession of, 129
  death of, 149
  as Sukhotai vassal, 145
Wat Pra Kian, 490
Water Chenla, 88
We Burmans Association, 521
Wedana officials, 360, 361
Weldten, Captain, at Mergui, 274
Wellesley, Governor-General, 308
Western influence, in Burma, 404
  scope of, 590
White, George, 272
White, Samuel, 272
White Huns of Central Asia, 35
"White man's burden," in different form, 587, 588
"Wild Tiger Corps" of Bangkok, 496
William, King of Netherlands, 358
William and Mary, 213
Wilson, President, 468, 476, 499
  advocacy of self-determination, 529

*Winhmus,* 296
*Wiratham,* code of honor, 505
Wisara, U, 513
Wood, General Leonard, quarrel of Filipino nationalists with, 478, 479
Workers of the Orient, University of, 560
Wu Ti, Emperor, 19
*Wundauk* (support or prop), 287
*Wungyis,* 123, 287, 296
*Wutmyewun* official, 297

Xavier, Francis, 180, 184, 188
Xieng Khouang, French, 428
Ximenes, Father, 242, 243

Yamada at Ayuthia, 261, 262
Yandabo, Treaty of, 323, 335, 381
Yasoharapura, 92
Yasovarman I, 84, 89, 92
Yavadvipa, 63
Yeh-po-ti, 32
  Buddhism at, 33
Yemen, Persian conquest of, 66
Yin Ching, Admiral, 155
Yoga practices, 77
Young Men's Buddhist Association of Burma, 403, 404, 506, 507
Young Muslim League, 377
Young Pioneer Corps, 571
Young Pongyi's Association, anti-Muslim rioting by, 524
Yung Ch'ang, Chinese prefecture of, 23
Yunnan River gorges, 17
Yunnanfu, French railway to, 551
Yusuf Adil Shah of Goa, 174
*Yuvaraja,* 90

Zaibatsu combines role in Burma, 576
Zamboanga, Spanish at, 236, 245, 413